The **Rough Guide** to

The Bahamas

written and researched by

Natalie Folster and Gaylord Dold

ROUGH
GUIDES

NEW YORK · LONDON · DELHI

www.roughguides.com

Contents

Bahamas beach culture colour section following p.160

Underwater Bahamas colour section following p.272

◄◄ Cape Santa Maria Beach, Long Island ◄ Sailing at the George Town Cruising Regatta

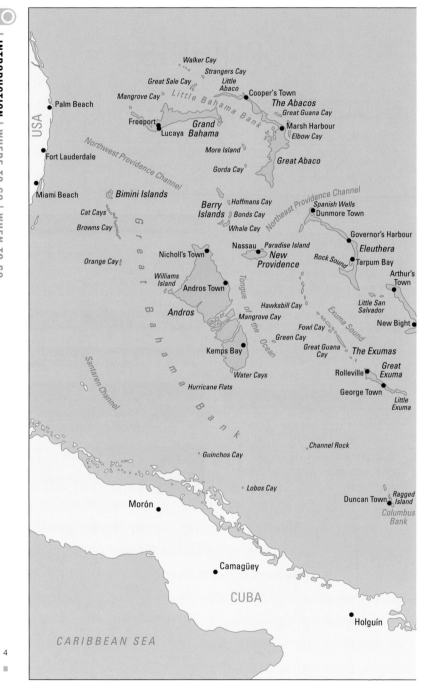

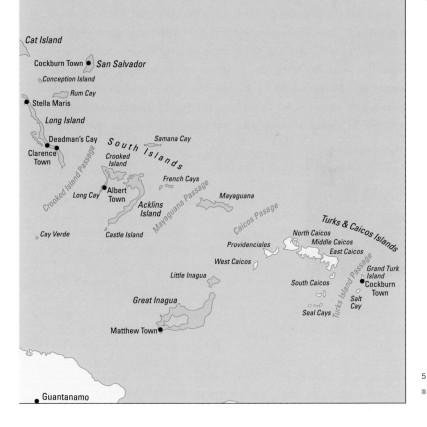

0   100 miles

N

ATLANTIC OCEAN

Cat Island

Cockburn Town ● San Salvador

Conception Island

Rum Cay

● Stella Maris

Long Island

● Deadman's Cay   Samana Cay

Clarence   South   Islands
Town   Crooked
         Island
                          French Cays

Long Cay ● Albert   Mayaguana
          Town
          Acklins
          Island

Cay Verde   Castle Island   Caicos Passage

                                              Turks & Caicos Islands
                              North Caicos
               Providenciales   Middle Caicos
                                   East Caicos
            West Caicos

         Little Inagua   Grand Turk
                                  South Caicos   Island
                                              ● Cockburn
                                                  Town
       Great Inagua   Salt
                                               Cay
                              Seal Cays

● Matthew Town

Crooked Island Passage

Mayaguana Passage

Turks Island Passage

● Guantanamo

5

Introduction to

The Bahamas

Graced with beautiful beaches, turquoise seas, reliable sunshine, an admirably relaxed lifestyle and countless opportunities for diving, snorkelling, boating and fishing, the Bahamas are well established as one of the world's top draws for both sun-seeking vacationers and adventurous explorers. Indeed, more than three million people visit the country yearly, the majority here for outdoor sports and sun worship. Despite the volume of visitors, it is easy to avoid the hordes and find your own quiet patch of paradise when you crave it or to get a feel for Bahamian culture – there is some history and authenticity behind the gloss.

An archipelago beginning a mere 55 miles east of Miami, the Bahamas include around seven hundred islands, no more than forty of which are inhabited, as well as scores of smaller cays (pronounced "keys"). Unlike some of its Caribbean neighbours, the islands offer an array of accommodation that ranges from plush high-end resorts to rustic lodges, appealing to travellers of all tastes and budgets.

Though visiting all of the major islands on the Bahamian archipelago in one trip would involve some complicated logistics and a thick wallet, it is well worth soaking up more of the region's culture by exploring several islands. While they share a similar geography and culture, each island has its own distinct character and unique charms. The quickest way to hop around is by plane, though if time permits a trip on a government mailboat, fast ferry or chartered yacht is both more relaxing and memorable. Most island-hopping adventures entail spending time in either New Providence or Grand Bahama, the two most cosmopolitan destinations and the target of innumerable package holidays.

> **Most islands are encircled by shallow, crystalline water that reflects a light turquoise hue during the day and glows with purple luminescence at night**

However, forays into the Out Islands reward visitors with a slice of genuine fishing-village culture and a glimpse of Bahamian life outside of the pre-packaged tour circuit.

Wherever you happen to land, it is possible to immerse yourself in the Bahamas' intriguing mix of colonial and African traditions. This fusion is perhaps most apparent during Nassau's annual Junkanoo celebrations, when the exuberant street party propelled by African drumming and outlandish costumes marches past the capital's impressive colonial edifices. Other islands come to life for numerous sailing regattas, featuring beachside fish fries and the sounds of rake 'n' scrape, a distinctly Bahamian style of music.

The ocean, though, is still the main draw. Although deeper oceanic troughs surround some of the islands, most are encircled by shallow, crystalline water that reflects a light turquoise hue during the day and glows with purple luminescence at night. This

▲ Grand Bahamas Island schoolgirls

Fact file

- The name Bahamas comes from the Spanish *baja mar*, meaning "shallow sea".

- The population of the Bahamas is approximately 321,000, of whom more than two-thirds live on the island of New Providence. Eighty-five percent of the populace is black, about twelve percent is white and the remainder is largely Asian or Hispanic.

- While the Bahamas achieved independence from Britain on July 10, 1973, the head of state is Queen Elizabeth II, who is represented in Nassau by a governor general. The Bahamas are governed by a Prime Minister, and the legislature is a bicameral body that is constituted by a sixteen-member Senate and a forty-member House of Assembly.

- The average per capita income in the Bahamas is a relatively high $16,000; tourism accounts for around sixty percent of the national income.

- The Yellow Elder is the national flower of the Bahamas, and the national tree is the lignum vitae, or tree of life.

Bahamian seafood

With the Bahamas' reputation as a fisherman's paradise, the wide array of **seafood** available is unsurprising. Ubiquitous on menus throughout the islands and a firm local favourite, **conch** (pronounced "konk") is a snail-like mollusc that can be broiled, grilled, steamed, stewed, served raw or presented "cracked" with its tenderized meat deep-fried in batter. Deep-fat-fried balls called conch fritters are a top side dish, while one of the islands' culinary delights is conch chowder; we've included a recipe below, though it undoubtedly tastes best when eaten beachside. The grouper, a light, fleshy white fish, is another staple of the Bahamian diet and, like much Bahamian fish, is most often served deep-fried in batter. Bahamian lobster can be eaten freshly grilled or broiled, steamed and curried, while crab is generally baked and served in the shell.

Perhaps the freshest – and certainly the cheapest – places to sample these dishes are the seafood shacks that are pervasive on all islands. From Arawak Cay (see p.82) in busy Nassau Harbour to those in rustic Out Island fishing hamlets, these low-key restaurants and grills should not be missed, both for the freshness of the food and the congenial atmosphere.

Conch chowder Bahamian-style

3 or 4 ground conch	1 bay leaf
2 medium diced onions	1/2 cup sugar
1 cup chopped celery	1 teaspoon oregano
1 medium green pepper, chopped	2 teaspoons lime juice
1/2 teaspoon thyme	1 large can of tomatoes
1 clove garlic	

Fry the onions, green pepper, celery, garlic and all the spices in a small amount of fat. When onions are transparent, add tomatoes and simmer for thirty minutes. Add conch and simmer for another thirty to forty-five minutes. Add lime juice and some sherry to taste after cooking and serve piping hot. If you'd like to eat it as the locals do, liberally add hot pepper sauce from time to time while the chowder is cooking

combination of shallow and deep water makes for superb diving and snorkelling, with numerous reefs, wrecks and blue holes waiting to be explored just beyond the islands' shores.

These waters also boast some of the best fishing in the Caribbean. Schools of silvery bonefish swim directly offshore and anglers of all levels stand waist-deep in the warm water awaiting the chance to pull in these elusive fish. Those who prefer sport fishing can ride the waves stalking sailfish, tuna, marlin and even sharks in the improbably deep Tongue of the Ocean. And if you are in search of a less taxing activity, there is always the beach – and plenty of it.

Where to go

The most popular Bahamas destination is **New Providence** – site of the bustling capital **Nassau**. With its resort areas in **Cable Beach** and **Paradise Island**, the island offers glamorous accommodation, enticing nightlife and casinos, fine restaurants and shopping and, of course, great beaches; Nassau Harbour is also a fixture on the Caribbean cruise circuit. Nearly everyone who visits the Bahamas will pass through the capital, the hub of intra-island travel, and those killing time before journeying on to another island will enjoy a jitney ride through **Old Nassau** and its stirring British colonial architecture, or even a tour of the **Atlantis** resort's 34-acre waterscape on Paradise Island.

Almost as popular as New Providence, **Grand Bahama** has been drawing tourists since the 1950s, when the resort town of **Freeport/Lucaya** sprung up expressly for that purpose. While the hurricane-damaged town of Freeport itself is a bit depressing and of little interest to visitors, its seaside suburb Lucaya features several postcard-grade beaches and some of the best resort hotels in the country, minus the traffic snarl that surrounds Nassau.

▼ Getting ready to dive a blue hole

9

Rake 'n' scrape music

Throughout the islands, **rake 'n' scrape** music resounds in nightclubs and during most local celebrations. The most popular authentic Bahamian music form, it harks back to the days before most of the islands had electricity and makes use of a variety of handmade instruments, notably a saw, which is played by bending it and scraping it with a screwdriver to produce a rhythmic sound. The saw is generally joined by accordions, guitars, drums or maracas, devised from the pods of poinciana trees. Often the music is in three-four time, evocative of the waltzes and polkas from which rake 'n' scrape is derived.

Many travellers prefer the quiet, remote charms of the **Out Islands** – essentially all of the Bahamian islands save for New Providence and Grand Bahama. Here the accommodation is often on a smaller scale and more rustic – although the number of bijou luxury resorts is on the rise. Better yet, the beaches and reefs within the laid-back Out Islands are typically deserted. **Andros**, the largest island in the Bahamas, is fringed by the **Androsian barrier reef**, which presents wonderful snorkelling opportunities. Besides the reef – the third longest in the world – the island is celebrated for its **blue holes** and abundance of **bonefish**. Those who enjoy **sport fishing** will prefer the deep waters off the even calmer **Bimini and Berry islands** located due north, whose fishing was immortalized by Ernest Hemingway.

While there is certainly no shortage of **beaches** on the Bahamas, **Eleuthera** contains some of the softest and most unspoilt of the lot, including the fabled Pink Sands Beach. The most populous of the Out Islands, Eleuthera is still relatively untouched by tourism, though **Dunmore Town**, on Harbour Island just off its northern tip, boasts some of the Out Islands' more cosmopolitan restaurants and finer hotels.

The most northerly of the Bahamian islands, the **Abacos** are also the most Americanized, home to a large expatriate community and a popular destination for boaters and other vacationers. The

▲ Colourful street corner, Eleuthera

▲ Iguana

clapboard houses, neat lawns and picket fences on the **Loyalist Cays** are remnants of the first wave of American immigration to the Abacos after the American Revolution, when small bands from New England and the Carolinas still loyal to the Crown fled the new republic. Besides sunshine, beaches and relaxation, the Abacos have excellent bonefishing. Further south and less touristed, the **Exumas** consist of some 365 cays and islets, fifteen of which comprise the **Exuma Land and Sea Park**, where sea kayaking the shallow protected waters among the islands is unparalleled.

The rest of the Out Islands feel light years away from New Providence and Grand Bahama. Much of interiors of isolated **Cat Island** and **San Salvador** are dense and impenetrable, though the latter – believed by many to be the site of Columbus's first landfall in the New World – offers great **birdwatching**. **Long Island** affords visitors the luxury of a few fine resorts in the midst of its rustic fishing settlements and untrammelled beaches, while **Great Inagua** is home to the 127-square-mile **Inagua National Park** and the West Indian flamingos it was established to conserve.

When to go

The southern Atlantic high-pressure system and constant trade winds make Bahamian **weather** consistent throughout the year, with temperatures in the mid-70s°F (23°C) during the dry winter season from December to May, and ranging between the high 70s°F (25°C) and the low 90s°F (32°C) degrees over the summer rainy season (June through November). Just as a steady cooling breeze moderates the hottest hours of the day, nights in the Bahamas are temperate and, in the northern islands, even cool. Late summer and fall comprise **hurricane season**, delivering the occasional menacing tempest as well as less destructive tropical storms. Luckily, the Bahamas are rarely in the direct paths of hurricanes, which usually bypass the islands to the south before hitting mainland North America directly. The major storms which hit the northern islands in 2004 and 2005 – Hurricanes Frances, Jeanne and Wilma – were the first big whacks in decades, and relative anomalies.

▼ Aerial view of the Glass Window, Eleuthera

Predictably, **winter travel** is a major draw, with December-to-May prices as much as 25 percent higher than during the rest of the year. **Late spring** and **early summer travel** are popular with bargain hunters, divers and anglers and sailors drawn by the summer round of fishing tournaments and regattas. Travelling during the Christmas **holiday season** can be bustling and wearisome, with tourists thick on the ground and many locals taking trips to the North American mainland. Likewise, college students often crowd the major resorts during Spring Break in February and March, while other travellers escape to the Bahamas during **late summer** and **autumn** to enjoy a respite in that relatively tranquil period, the odd hurricane notwithstanding.

Average monthly temperatures and rainfall on New Providence

	Jan	Feb	Mar	Apr	May	Jun	Jul	Aug	Sep	Oct	Nov	Dec
Nassau												
max. temp. (°F)	87	87	89	90	90	90	93	95	93	90	89	87
max. temp. (°C)	30	30	32	33	33	33	34	35	34	33	32	30
min. temp. (°F)	65	66	66	71	76	78	79	79	78	73	71	66
min. temp. (°C)	18	19	19	22	24	25	26	26	25	23	22	19
rainfall (inches)	1.8	1.7	1.6	2.7	5.2	7.0	6.0	6.6	7.1	6.6	2.8	1.7
rainfall (mm)	46	44	40	70	130	178	152	170	180	170	73	44

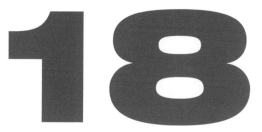

18

things not to miss

It would be a major undertaking to see everything that the Bahamas have to offer in one trip – and we don't suggest you try. What follows is a selective and subjective taste of the islands' highlights: from their lush blue waters to their quaint colonial towns. They're arranged in five colour-coded categories to help you find the very best things to see, do, eat and experience. All highlights have a page reference to take you straight into the guide, where you can find out more.

01 **Sea kayaking in the Exuma Cays** Page **267** • Spend an exhilarating day or week paddling through a long string of mainly uninhabited islands set in a turquoise sea.

02 Out Island bar life

Page **34** • In the small hamlets and settlements of the Out Island, tourists and locals congregate to practice the fine art of "liming" – relaxing and solving the world's problems over a rum cocktail.

03 Dunmore Town, Harbour Island Page 233 •

The settlement's Loyalist heritage is carefully preserved in the daintily painted wooden cottages and picket fences lining the narrow lanes of this picture-perfect resort village.

04 Eleuthera's beaches

Page **216** • Sample a different powdery strand each day of the week, starting with the chic Pink Sands Beach on Harbour Island and working your way down to the scoured white sand at Lighthouse Point on Eleuthera's southern tip.

05 Pompey Museum Page 74 •

An informative history of slavery in the Bahamas is revealed in this Nassau museum, located on the site of a former slave auction house.

06 Saturday at the souse house

Page **86** • Definitely an acquired taste but with many devotees, souse (stew) made with pig's feet, sheep's tongue or chicken bits is a Saturday tradition in the Out Islands. In Nassau, get it at the *Bahamian Kitchen*.

07 The Out Island Regatta Page 259 •

Crews and spectators from all over the Bahamas converge on George Town every April for three days of races and celebrations, with lots of food and music to keep things going.

09 Mount Alvernia Hermitage, Cat Island
Page **288** • The highest point in the Bahamas at 206ft above sea level, this lonesome hilltop was once home to a hermit priest and is now a prime spot to watch the sun rise or set.

08 Junkanoo Page **76** • In the small hours of the night of December 26 and again on New Year's Day, the streets of Nassau and communities in the Out Islands come alive with cowbells, drums and costumed revellers.

10 Long Island Page **306** • Slow down to Out Island time, meandering past whitewashed churches, tidy fishing villages and secluded coves edged with sugary sand and blue holes.

11 Inagua National Park
Page **323** • An unearthly and utterly silent landscape of salt pans and shallow water populated by flocks of West Indian pink flamingos, pelicans, Bahamian parrots and a couple of hundred other species of birds.

12 Swim with dolphins
Page **111** • A face-to-face encounter with these playful animals is one of the highlights of a visit to Grand Bahama.

13 Island hopping Page **23** • Life in the Bahamas is focused on the sea and boat travel is part of everyday existence. Go with the flow and do some island hopping, either by mailboat or aboard your own vessel.

14 Bonefishing Page **176** • The Bahamas are fabled fishing grounds and almost every island in the archipelago boasts fine bonefishing flats.

15 The Aquarium at Atlantis, Paradise Island Page **94** • An impressive display of Bahamian marine life in its varied forms, including the shark-infested Predator Lagoon, built to thrill the ten year-old boys of the world.

16 Underwater Andros Page **175** • The spectacularly vibrant Androsian barrier reef draws divers and snorkellers from all over, and makes the perfect training ground for novices who want to take the plunge.

17 The great lizard cuckoo Page **178** • Birdwatchers can tick off plenty of boxes on their Life List, including the Smooth-billed Ani, the Bahamian Parrot, the Yellow-crowned Night Heron, the Magnificent Frigate Bird and the great lizard cuckoo, pictured here.

18 Thunderball Grotto Page **271** • Snorkel past stalactites and stalagmites in the undersea cavern in the Exuma Cays, and see the colourful corals and fish – just as 007 did in *Thunderball*.

Basics

Basics

Getting there

The Bahamas are well connected to the outside world, with daily flights to and from numerous American cities and several flights per week to and from Canada and the UK. Unsurprisingly, the archipelago is also accessible by sea, with cruise ships calling in at Nassau and Freeport every week. The Bahamas are prime cruising grounds for private yachts as well, and there are dozens of marinas sprinkled throughout the islands.

When travelling to the Bahamas, it's almost invariably cheaper to buy a **package deal** covering transportation and accommodation from a tour operator, travel agent or discount travel website than it is to buy your ticket and accommodation separately. However, if you're looking to live by your own schedule, head off the beaten track away from the resorts, and maybe do some island hopping; you will have to book your bed and your transportation separately.

Airfares depend on the season. Although the Bahamas are blessed with beautiful sunny weather and relatively constant temperatures year-round, **high season** for travel runs from mid-December to mid-April, when folks in the northern hemisphere are most eager to escape chilly temperatures. Fares drop May through to November, with especially good deals available throughout the **hurricane season** (July–October), when you are still more likely to experience brilliant sunshine than fierce storms. Prices are highest over Christmas and New Year, and American college spring-breakers head for Nassau and Freeport mid-February to mid-April, filling up the larger hotels and budget motels. Many divers visit in the summer (May–August) when the water is especially clear and calm. Note that flying on weekends ordinarily adds a few dollars to the round trip fare.

In addition to the sun and sand beach holidays offered by the tour operators listed below, several companies specialize in diving and kayaking expeditions and eco-tours in the Bahamas. See "Sports and outdoor activities", pp.37-40 for information on these niche operators.

Flights from the US and Canada

One of the greatest attractions of the Bahamas for **North American** sunseekers is the ease of access. With direct flights from several American and Canadian cities, you can leave New York or Toronto on a dark snowy morning and be on the beach with a margarita in hand in time for a late lunch. In high season, a non-stop flight from New York to Nassau costs in the range of US$500–600, with flights to Freeport starting from around US$400–600. Flights from Fort Lauderdale or Miami to Nassau or Freeport should cost US$150–250 round-trip. Direct flights from Toronto to Nassau in high season can be had for around CAN$800–1000, provided you book far enough in advance. Under current pricing, a connecting flight from the Canadian hinterland to Toronto generally adds less that CAN$100 to this fare. The best deals generally require advance booking, and discounted seats can sell out several months in advance. Nassau and Freeport are the major ports of entry for international flights, though a number of airlines fly directly from Florida to the Abacos, Andros, Bimini, Cat Island, Eleuthera, the Exumas and San Salvador, as listed on p.21.

Flights from the UK and Ireland

Bahamas-bound travellers from the **UK** have two choices for a direct flight to Nassau: British Airways and Virgin Atlantic. Expect to pay anywhere between £450 and £800. You can also fly from the UK

Fly less – stay longer! Travel and climate change

Climate change is a serious threat to the ecosystems that humans rely upon, and air travel is among the fastest growing contributors to the problem. Rough Guides regard travel, overall, as a global benefit, and feel strongly that the advantages to developing economies are important, as is the opportunity of greater contact and awareness among peoples. But we all have a responsibility to limit our personal impact on global warming, and that means giving thought to how often we fly, and what we can do to redress the harm that our trips create.

Flying and climate change

Pretty much every form of motorized travel generates CO_2 – the main cause of human-induced climate change – but planes also generate climate-warming contrails and cirrus clouds and emit oxides of nitrogen, which create ozone (another greenhouse gas) at flight levels. Furthermore, flying simply allows us to travel much further than we otherwise would do. The figures are frightening: one person taking a return flight between Europe and California produces the equivalent impact of 2.5 tonnes of CO_2 – similar to the yearly output of the average UK car.

Fuel-cell and other less harmful types of plane may emerge eventually. But until then, there are really just two options for concerned travellers: to reduce the amount we travel by air (take fewer trips – stay for longer), and to make the trips we do take "climate neutral" via a carbon offset scheme.

Carbon offset schemes

Offset schemes run by ⓦwww.climatecare.org, ⓦwww.carbonneutral.com and others allow you to make up for some or all of the greenhouse gases that you are responsible for releasing. To do this, they provide "carbon calculators" for working out the global warming contribution of a specific flight (or even your entire existence), and then let you contribute an appropriate amount of money to fund offsetting measures. These include rainforest reforestation and initiatives to reduce future energy demand – often run in conjunction with sustainable development schemes. Rough Guides, together with Lonely Planet and other concerned partners in the travel industry, are supporting a **carbon offset scheme** run by climatecare.org. Please take the time to view our website and see how you can help to make your trip climate neutral.

ⓦwww.roughguides.com/climatechange

to the US or Canada and then to the Bahamas on one of the North American carriers that fly to the islands. A number of British **tour operators** also offer charter flights and package holidays in the Bahamas, as listed opposite.

Flights from Australia and New Zealand and South Africa

There are no direct flights from **Australia**, **New Zealand** or **South Africa** to the Bahamas. The cheapest and most convenient option for most travellers involves flying to North America for a connection to the Bahamas on one of the North American carriers listed opposite.

Flights from elsewhere in the Caribbean

It is also possible to fly into Nassau from other Caribbean islands. Bahamas Air and Cubana Airlines both fly the Nassau–Havana route several times a week (about $450 return). You can also travel to Nassau via the Turks and Caicos, the Cayman Islands and Jamaica, as detailed opposite.

Airlines, agents and operators

Online booking

ⓦwww.expedia.co.uk (in UK), ⓦwww.expedia .com (in US), ⓦwww.expedia.ca (in Canada)

ⓦ www.lastminute.com (in UK)
ⓦ www.opodo.co.uk (in UK)
ⓦ www.orbitz.com (in US)
ⓦ www.travelocity.co.uk (in UK), ⓦ www
.travelocity.com (in US), ⓦ www.travelocity
.ca (in Canada)
ⓦ www.zuji.com.au (in Australia), ⓦ www.zuji
.co.nz (in New Zealand)

Airlines

Air Canada ☎ 1/888-247-2262, UK ☎ 0871/220 1111, Republic of Ireland ☎ 01/679 3958, Australia ☎ 1300/655 767, New Zealand ☎ 0508/747 767, ⓦ www.aircanada.com. Flies directly to Nassau from Toronto and Montreal once or twice a week (depending on the season), with connecting flights from other Canadian cities.

Air Jamaica US ☎ 1-800/523-5585, Canada ☎ 416/229-6024, UK ☎ 020/8570 7999, ⓦ www .airjamaica.com. Flies between Montego Bay and Nassau.

Air Tran Airways ☎ 1-800-Air-Tran from the US or ☎ 678/254-7999 from elsewhere, ⓦ www .airtran.com. Direct service from Atlanta and Chicago to Freeport.

American Airlines US ☎ 1-800/433-7300, UK ☎ 0845/7789 789, Republic of Ireland ☎ 01/602 0550, Australia ☎ 1300/650 747, New Zealand ☎ 0800/887 997, ⓦ www.aa.com. Direct service from New York and Newark and several flights a day from Fort Lauderdale, Miami and Orlando to Nassau and Freeport on the American Eagle connector service, with daily flights from Miami to George Town, Marsh Harbour and Governor's Harbour.

Bahamasair US and Canada ☎ 242/377-5505 or 1-800/222-4262, ☎ 011 44 129 359 6638 in Europe, ⓦ www.bahamasair.com. Daily flights from Fort Lauderdale, Miami and Orlando to Nassau, Freeport and Marsh Harbour in the Abacos. Also flies to the Turks and Caicos and Havana.

British Airways US and Canada ☎ 1-800 /AIRWAYS, UK ☎ 0870/850 9850, Republic of Ireland ☎ 1890/626 747, Australia ☎ 1300/767 177, New Zealand ☎ 09/966 9777, ⓦ www.ba.com. BA flies from London (Heathrow) to Nassau, and from Nassau to Grand Cayman and Provinciales, Turks and Caicos.

Continental Airlines US and Canada ☎ 1-800-523-3273, UK ☎ 0845/607 6760, Republic of Ireland ☎ 1890/925 252, Australia ☎ 02/9244 2242, New Zealand ☎ 09/308 3350, International ☎ 1800/231 0856, ⓦ www.continental.com. Has daily service from Miami, Fort Lauderdale and West Palm Beach to Nassau, Andros Town, Freeport, Marsh Harbour and Treasure Cay, Eleuthera, George Town and Cat Island.

Cubana Canada ☎ 416/967-2822, UK ☎ 020/7537 7909, ⓦ www.cubana.co.cu. Runs several flights a week between Nassau and Havana.

Delta Air Lines US and Canada ☎ 1/800/221 -1212, UK ☎ 0845/600 0950, Republic of Ireland ☎ 1850/882 031 or 01/407 3165, Australia ☎ 1300/302 849, New Zealand ☎ 09/379 3370, ⓦ www.delta.com. Direct service to Nassau from New York/La Guardia, Boston and Atlanta several times a day.

Jet Blue US and Canada ☎ 1/800-JETBLUE, international ☎ 801/365-2525, ⓦ www.jetblue .com. Direct flights to Nassau from Boston and New York (JFK).

Lynx Air US and Canada ☎ 1/888-LYNXAIR, ⓦ www.lynxair.com. Direct flights from Fort Lauderdale to Treasure Cay, Abacos; South Andros; Bimini; Cat Island; Governor's Harbour and North Eleuthera; and Great Exuma.

Qantas Australia ☎ 13 13 13, New Zealand ☎ 09/661 901, ⓦ www.qantas.com.au. Can get you as far as Europe or North America.

Spirit Air US and Canada ☎ 1/800-772-7117 or 586/791-7300, ⓦ www.spiritair.com. Flies between Fort Lauderdale and Nassau, and once a week from Fort Lauderdale to San Salvador. Good fares on connecting flights to Fort Lauderdale from Chicago, Los Angeles, Providence and Washington DC.

Twin Air US and Canada ☎ 954/359-8266, ⓦ www.flytwinair.com. Offers regular flights from Fort Lauderdale to North Eleuthera; Governor's Harbour and Rock Sound on Eleuthera; and Treasure Cay and Marsh Harbour in the Abacos.

US Airways US and Canada ☎ 1/800-428-4322, UK ☎ 0845/600 3300, Ireland ☎ 1890/925 065, ⓦ www.usair.com. Has direct service to Nassau and Freeport from Charlotte, Philadelphia and New York. They also have a connecting service from Miami to Treasure Cay, Marsh Harbour, North Eleuthera and Governor's Harbour.

Virgin Atlantic US ☎ 1/800-821-5438, UK ☎ 0870/380 2007, Australia ☎ 1300/727 340, SA ☎ 11/340 3400, ⓦ www.virgin-atlantic.com. Flies from London to Nassau once a week.

Watermaker's Air US ☎ 954/467-8920, ⓦ www .watermakersair.com. Flies from Fort Lauderdale to Staniel Cay.

WestJet US and Canada ☎ 1/888-WEST-JET, UK and Ireland ☎ 0800/5381 5696, ⓦ www.westjet .com. Flies daily from Toronto to Nassau, November through April.

Agents and operators

Caribtours ☎ 020/7751 0660, ⓦ www.caribtours .co.uk. Long-established operator offering tailor-made breaks – including trips designed for families, spa-seekers, island hoppers and honeymooners.

ebookers UK ☎ 0800/082 3000, Republic of Ireland ☎ 01/488 3507, ⊛ www.ebookers.com. Low fares on an extensive selection of scheduled flights and package deals.

North South Travel UK ☎ 01245/608 291, ⊛ www.northsouthtravel.co.uk. Friendly, competitive travel agency, offering discounted fares worldwide. Profits are used to support projects in the developing world, especially the promotion of sustainable tourism.

Majestic Holidays Bahamas ☎ 1/242-323-1410, ⊛ www.majesticholidays.com. A Bahamas-based operator offering accommodation and transportation packages, including island-hopping holidays that allow you to experience two or three of the Out Islands in one go.

Trailfinders UK ☎ 0845/058 5858, Republic of Ireland ☎ 01/677 7888, Australia ☎ 1300/780 212, ⊛ www.trailfinders.com. One of the best-informed and most efficient agents for independent travellers.

STA Travel US ☎ 1/800-781-4040, Canada ☎ 1/888-427-5639, UK ☎ 0870/1630 026, Australia ☎ 1300/733 035, New Zealand ☎ 0508/782 872, SA ☎ 0861/781 781. Worldwide specialists in independent travel; also student IDs, travel insurance, car rental, rail passes and more. Good discounts for students and under-26s. ⊛ www.statravel.com.

Thomas Cook ☎ 0870/750-5711, ⊛ www.thomascook.co.uk. Long-established one-stop 24-hour travel agency for package holidays or scheduled flights, with bureau de change issuing Thomas Cook traveller's cheques, travel insurance and car rental.

Getting to the Bahamas by boat

Several **cruise ships** call at Nassau or Freeport offering tours through the Bahamas and the Caribbean lasting from three days to several weeks. Most of these cruise ships spend a day or two in port, with the opportunity to take a sightseeing tour, do some snorkelling or lie on the beach. A few of the large cruise lines own private beaches or entire small islands in the Bahamas, where they deposit their passengers for the day. These places are usually isolated from any settlement and are set up with handicraft kiosks, beach toys and snack bars.

The **Internet** is a good place to start your research. Websites such as ⊛ www.cruise.com and ⊛ www.cruisereviews.com

are helpful resources for deciding which cruise is the best fit, taking into account price range, size of boat and length of trip. Travelocity.com (⊛ www.travelocity.com) and Tripadvisor (⊛ www.tripadvisor.com) also provide useful reviews of the major cruise companies. While some companies offer cruises only, there are still many others that negotiate rates with major airlines allowing for fly/cruise options from most major airports in the US and the rest of the world. Most cruises depart from Florida, with a couple of exceptions, as noted below. Fares vary widely, beginning at about $300 for a three-day trip up to $4000 for a week-long luxury cruise through the islands.

You can also reach the Bahamas by **sea ferry** from Fort Lauderdale. The MSV *Discovery Sun* (☎ 305/597-0336 or 1-800/866 -8687, ⊛ www.discoverycruiseline.com) is a quadruple-decker passenger ferry/cruise ship sailing daily between Fort Lauderdale and Freeport. It departs from Florida at 8am, arriving in Freeport/Lucaya at 1pm, making the return journey at 4.45pm. Regular round trip tickets cost around $180.

The Bahamas are also popular cruising grounds for private yachts, and listings of **marinas** are found throughout the guide. More detailed information for sailors and nautical charts for the Bahamas are found in several cruising guides to the Bahamas, as listed on p.354.

If you want to explore the islands by boat but don't have your own, several companies based in Florida **charter** sailboats or motorized yachts for use in the Bahamas, either with crew or bareboat. The costs range from $5000–25,000 a week for a crewed sailboat sleeping six passengers, depending on how much polished wood, brass and other touches of luxury you want.

Cruise lines

Carnival Cruiselines ☎ 1-888/CARNIVAL, ⊛ www.carnival.com. A youthful cruise line with a big emphasis on fun, offering 3–5 day cruises from Miami, Orlando or Fort Lauderdale. Rates from as little as $300 per person.

Disney Cruise Line ☎ 1-800/951-3532, ⊛ www.disneycruise.com. Three-night cruises from Florida starting at $850, including a trip to Disney's own Bahamian island.

Holland America ☎1-877/932-4259, 🌐www
.hollandamerica.com. Family cruise line, with
hefty scheduled entertainment for both adults
and kids. Week-long cruises depart from Fort
Lauderdale.
Princess Cruises & Royal Caribbean ☎1-800
/PRINCESS, 🌐www.princesscruises.com. A variety
of 7–10 day luxury cruises (including spas and scuba
diving) departing from Fort Lauderdale.
Radisson Seven Seas ☎1-877/505-5370,
🌐www.rssc.com. Fifteen-day cruises from Florida to
LA via the Caribbean and South America.
Regal Cruises ☎1-800/270-7245, 🌐www
.regalcruises.com. A rare opportunity to cruise
straight from New York to the Bahamas.
Silversea ☎1-800/722-9955, 🌐www.silversea
.com. Top-notch cruises and fly/cruise options from
all over the world.

Boat charters

Atlantic Yacht Company ☎1-888/496-3287,
🌐www.yachtworld.com.
Bareboat.com ☎1-800/227-3262, 🌐www
.bareboat.com.
Cruzan Yacht Charters ☎1-800/628-0785,
🌐www.cruzan.com.
Florida Yacht Charters ☎ 1-800/537-0050,
🌐www.floridayacht.com.
Moorings ☎1-888/952-8420, 🌐www.moorings
.com.
Sailboat Charters of Miami ☎1-800/328-8838,
🌐www.sailboat-charters.com.
Sailing Paradise ☎1-800/864-7245, 🌐www
.sailingparadise.com.
Swift Yacht Charters ☎1-800/866-8340,
🌐www.swiftyachts.com.

Getting around

The Bahamas archipelago is spread out over a great chunk of the south Atlantic
ocean. Nassau is the nation's transportation hub, and all of the other settled
islands are connected to New Providence by regular and frequent flights, weekly
mailboat service and some inter-island ferries. Looking at a map of the Bahamas,
the close proximity of the islands to one another might lead you to think that
hopping from one to another should be quick and convenient. It is, if you have
your own plane or yacht. If not, island hopping can be both time-consuming and
expensive.

Whether travelling within the Bahamas by air
or by sea, you will almost invariably have to
return to Nassau to catch a flight or boat to
your final destination, even if it means back-
tracking a few hundred miles. This can eat
up a whole day of your holiday and in some
cases will require over-nighting in Nassau.
There are a few exceptions – some direct
flights from one Out Island to another – and
these are listed in the "Inter-island airlines"
section below and in the "Getting there"
section for each island.

   Once on your chosen island, getting
around is pretty straightforward. The "Getting
around" sections with each chapter have full
details on public transportation, taxis, rental
options and tours.

By air

Even among laidback Bahamians, complain-
ing about the inefficiencies of the national
airline **Bahamasair** is a favourite pastime
– "When you have time to spare, fly Bahamasair." Fortunately, there are a number of
reliable alternatives. Most of the Out Islands
are served by one or more smaller airlines,
and if there are two or more people in your
party it's often more cost-effective as well as
faster to **charter** a plane. Bahamasair and
its competitors charge similar fares, ranging
from $60 (one way) from Nassau to Andros
to $180 (one way) from Nassau to Inagua
at the southern end of the chain. A five- or
seven-seater costs $700–1000 an hour to

charter, and for most places in the Bahamas an hour's airtime is all that is needed.

Inter-island airlines

Abaco Air ☎367-2267, ⓦwww
.abacoaviationcentre.com. Based at Marsh Harbour Airport, Abaco Air has daily flights from Marsh Harbour to Nassau; from Marsh Harbour to North Eleuthera on Fri and Sun; and from Marsh Harbour to Moore's Island on Mon, Wed and Fri.

Bahamasair ☎377-5505 in Nassau, Out Islands 242/300-8359, US and Canada 1-800/222-4262, ⓦwww.bahamasair.com. Serves all of the Bahamas from its base in Nassau. The frequency of flights ranges from several flights daily to the more populous settlements to twice or three times a week to the out of the way corners of the country.

Cat Island Air ☎377-3318. Flies from Nassau to New Bight, Cat Island; Great Harbour Cay in the Berrys; and Sandy Point, Abaco.

Cherokee Air ☎367-3450, ⓦwww.cherokeeair .com. Based at Marsh Harbour Airport, Cherokee Air has flights to West Palm Beach, Florida as well as North Eleuthera.

Flamingo Air ☎377-0354, ⓦwww
.flamingoairbah.com. Serving some of the smaller, harder to reach islands in the Bahamas. Several flights a week from Freeport to Moore's Island, Walker's Cay, Great Harbour Cay in the Berrys and Sandy Point on Great Abaco. They also fly from Nassau to Staniel Cay and Blackpoint in the Exuma Cays every day but Saturday.

Major's Air Service ☎352-5778, ⓦwww
.thebahamasguide.com/majorair. Flights from Grand Bahama to Bimini; Treasure Cay and Marsh Harbour in the Abacos; Governor's Harbour and North Eleuthera; and all airports on Andros.

Pineapple Air ☎377-0140. Flights from Nassau to Arthur's Town, Cat Island; Chub Cay, Berry Islands; and Deadman's Cay, Long Island.

Sky Unlimited ☎337-8993. Several flights a day from Nassau to George Town.

Southern Air ☎323-6833/7217, ⓦwww
.southernaircharter.com. Flights from Nassau to Chub Cay Arthur's Town, Governor's Harbour, Marsh Harbour, Treasure Cay, and Deadman's Cay.

Western Air ☎377-2222, ⓦwww
.westernairbahamas.com. Several flights a day from Nassau to all airports on Andros, Bimini and Grand Bahama.

Charter airlines

Air Charter Bahamas ☎305/885-6665 or 1-866/359-4752, ⓦwww.aircharterbahamas .com. Flights to all of the islands of the Bahamas from

Nassau or South Florida, plus trips from Nassau to the Turks and Caicos, Cuba or Cayman Islands.

Air Sunshine ☎954/434-8900 or 1-800 /327-8900, ⓦwww.airsunshine.com. Offers charter flights on demand from Fort Lauderdale to Marsh Harbour and Treasure Cay on Great Abaco, George Town, Stella Maris, New Bight on Cat Island, Great Inagua and San Salvador.

Island Wings Charter ☎338-2022, ⓦwww
.islandwingscharter.com. Charter flights between Long Island's Stella Maris Airport and any of the other Bahamian islands in a five-seater plane. As an example, up to five passengers can fly to Long Island from George Town, Exuma (where direct flights from the US land) for a total of $360.

Yellow Air Taxi ☎1-888/935-5694, ⓦwww
.flyyellowairtaxi.com. Charter flights from Fort Lauderdale to Andros, Bimini, Freeport, North Eleuthera, Marsh Harbour and Treasure Cay.

By mailboat and ferry

Bahamian **mailboats** are holdovers from a long tradition of maritime service going back to 1832. These days, mailboats carry passengers along with cargo, and the official headquarters of the mailboat service is the **Dockmaster's Office** (☎393-1064) under the Paradise Island Bridge on Potter's Cay in New Providence. The mailboats depart once a week from here (see schedule p.26-27). The vessels come in various sizes, states of repair and levels of comfort, and they serve all of the inhabited Bahamian islands on journeys that take anywhere from four to 72 hours. On average, tickets range from $25 to $60, including a bunk and sometimes meals from the ship's galley (but don't count a hot meal on board; bring your own grub).

Beware that scheduled departures, especially on longer trips, are often delayed, and difficult weather or high seas can stretch a ten-hour journey into fifteen hours or more. Moreover, some passages are difficult anyway, especially those like the Crooked Island Passage, where crosscurrents toss the boat up and down.

If you take a mailboat, you'll be riding a high-sided rusty cargo freighter with a couple of rows of bench seats down the port and starboard gunwales, and on longer overnight journeys, an inside cabin with a few bunk beds. The deck may be piled with cases of liquor and soft drinks, mounds of coal or gravel, drums of industrial chemicals,

Fast Ferries schedule for inter-island service

All ferries depart from the Bahamas Fast Ferries Potter's Cay terminal in Nassau. Call or check the website for information on possible changes to schedule (ⓦ www.bahamasferries.com, ☎ 242/323 2166). Boarding time is one hour prior to departure. Reservations recommended.

Destination	Service Days	Departs	Arrives	Departs	Arrives	Duration (one way)	Fare (one way)
Spanish Wells and Harbour Island	Daily Mon–Sat	NASS 8am	SW 9.40am HI 10.15am	HI 3.55pm SW 4.35pm	NASS 6.15pm	1hr 40min to SW, 2hrs 15min to HI	$65
	Sun	NASS 8am	SW 9.40am HI 10.15am	HI 2pm SW 2.35pm	NASS 4.15pm		
Governor's Harbour, Eleuthera	Tues & Thurs Fri Sun	NASS 8am NASS 7pm NASS 4.45pm	GH noon GH 9.00pm GH 6.45pm	GH 2pm GH 9.15pm GH 7pm	NASS 6pm NASS 11.15pm NASS 9pm	4hrs	$35
Morgan's Bluff, Andros	Sat	NASS 8am	MB 10.35am	MB 12.30pm	NASS 3.05pm	2hrs 35mins	$35
Sandy Point, Abaco	Fri & Sun	NASS 1pm	SP 4.45pm	SP 5.30pm	NASS 9.15pm	3hrs 45mins	$50
Fresh Creek, Andros	Wed Fri Sun	NASS 9am NASS 7am NASS 8am	FC 11.35am FC 9.35am FC 10.35am	FC 1.30pm FC noon FC noon	NASS 3.35pm NASS 2.35pm NASS 2.35pm	2hrs 35mins	$35
Current, Eleuthera	Fri Sun	NASS 4.30pm NASS 4.30pm	CUR 6.35pm CUR 6.35pm	CUR 8pm CUR 7.30pm	NASS 10.35pm NASS 10.05pm	2hrs 45mins	$35
George Town, Exuma	Mon Tues Wed	NASS 5pm NASS 7.30pm NASS 9.30pm	GT 3.00am (Tues) GT 5.30am (Wed) GT 7.30am (Thurs)	GT 6am (Tues) GT 8am (Wed) GT noon (Thurs)	NASS 4pm (Tues) NASS 6pm (Wed) NASS 10pm (Thurs)	10–12hrs	$50

Bahamas Mailboat Schedule

All boats depart from Potter's Cay, Nassau. Call the Dockmaster ☎ 242 393 1064, ℻ 394-1240 for exact weekly departures times.

Destination	Vessel	Departure	Return	Duration	Fare (one way)
Abacos Marsh Harbour Green Turtle Cay Hope Town	Legacy (☎ 393-4371)	Tues 7pm	Fri 6am	12hrs	$50
Abaco Cays Sandy Point More's Island **Berry Islands** Bullock Harbour	Captain Gurth Dean	Tues 11pm	Fri 5am	7hrs	$40
Acklins and Crooked Islands Spring Point Colonel Hill Long Cay	K.C.T./United Star (☎ 341-3468)	Mon 10pm	Thurs 10pm	36hrs	$60
North Andros Nicholl's Town Morgan's Bluff **North**	Lady Rosalind (☎ 323-6888)	Wed 2.30pm Thurs 6pm	Tues 12.30pm Sun 1pm	6hrs	$30
Cat Island Arthur's Town Dumfries Orange Creek Bennett's Harbour				14hrs	$50
Central Andros Fresh Creek Stafford Creek Blanket Sound Behring Point	Lady 'D'	Thurs 10am	Sun 1pm	5hrs	$35
Mangrove Cay, Andros Moxey Town Lisbon Creek	Lady Katherina	Thurs 2am	Mon 5pm	6hrs	$45
South Andros Kemp's Bay The Bluff Long Bay Cays	Captain Moxey	Mon 11pm	Wed 11pm	7hrs	$35
Bimini Alice Town Cat Cay Chub Cay	Bimini Mack	Thurs 2am	Sun 8am	12hrs	$50
Cat Island Smith Bay	Lady Emerald (☎ 326-4426)	Tues 3pm	Sat 1pm	12hrs	$50

San Salvador **Rum Cay**					
South Eleuthera Rock Sound Governor's Harbour	Bahamas Daybreak III	Mon 5pm	Tues 5pm	5hrs	$30
North Eleuthera Harbour Island Spanish Wells	Bahamas Daybreak III	Wed 5pm	Sun 4pm	5hrs	$30
North Eleuthera Current Hatchet Bay The Bluff	Current Pride	Thurs 6am	Tues 11am	5hrs	$25
South Eleuthera Rock Sound Governor's Harbour	Eleuthera Express	Mon 5pm	Tues 8pm	5hrs	$25
North Eleuthera Harbour Island Spanish Wells		Thurs 6am	Sun 12.30pm	5hrs	$25
Exuma Cays **and Ragged** **Island** Ragged Island Staniel Cay Blackpoint Little Farmer's	Captain 'C'	Tues 4pm	Fri 8pm	14hrs	 $60 $40
Great Exuma Georgetown	Grand Master (☏393-1041)	Tues 2pm	Thurs 10am	14hrs	$45
Grand Bahama Freeport	Fiesta Mailboat (☏393-2628)	Mon 5pm Wed 5pm Fri 8am	Wed 2am Fri 10am Sun 3pm	8hrs kids $29	$57
N. Long Island Deadman's Cay Salt Pond Seymour's	Captain Emmett	Tues 2pm	Thurs 11am	8hrs	$50
Eleuthera Hatchet Bay			Sat 8am Fri 1pm	3hrs	$30
S. Long Island Clarence Town	Mia Dean	Tues noon	Thurs 8am	18hrs	$60
Mayaguana Abraham's Bay **Inagua** Matthew Town	Lady Mathilda (☏323-6888)	Tues 2pm	Sat 6am	36hrs	$90
San Salvador **Rum Cay**	Lady Francis	Tues 4pm	Fri 7am	18hrs	$50

even bunches of bananas. Nevertheless, for travellers with time, they can be an enjoyable experience, a chance to rub elbows with Bahamians from many walks of life. It is also a much cheaper way to travel than by air; see the "Getting there" sections in each chapter for more details.

In sharp contrast to the mailboat, privately operated **ferry services** are speedy and luxurious. The slick **Bahamas Fast Ferries** (☎323-2166, ⊛www.bahamasferries.com) operates out of Potter's Cay, connecting Nassau to Harbour Island, Spanish Wells, Eleuthera, Andros, Great Exuma and Great Abaco. A nicely appointed high-speed airboat catamaran with an enclosed cabin, upper observation deck and food service, it makes the trip to Harbour Island and Spanish Wells in under two hours, taking slightly longer to reach the other ports. Taking into account the time required to get to the airport, go through security and arrange ground transport at the other end, taking the ferry is often just as fast – or faster – than flying. Example prices include a $65 one-way fare to Harbour Island and Spanish Wells, $50 to George Town or Abaco and $35 to Governor's Harbour and Andros.

By car

Renting a car is a simple affair. For stays of three months or less, your homeland license is valid and no other license is needed. Beyond that, you'll need an international license, available from either AAA in the US or AA in the UK.

On both New Providence and Grand Bahama, the major international car rental agencies are all represented, each offering a wide selection of vehicles ranging from small compacts ($70 per day on average) to large 4wd SUVs (around $125 per day), with added fees for taxes and insurance. See p.69 and p.106 respectively for specific information.

On the Out Islands, conversely, rental cars are offered by small agencies operated by locals who often rent out their personal cars – sometimes clunkers are all that's on offer – at more expensive rates (daily rentals starting from $80). And with few rental cars available in Out Island settlements, they can be scarce as well.

Driving on the islands is usually a snap, though North Americans should remember that one must **drive on the left**. Driving in Nassau can be a bit nerve-wracking, with frequent traffic jams and slowdowns, as in any larger city. On the Out Islands, traffic is light, and it is almost impossible to get lost, as there is usually only one main road – usually called the King's or Queen's Highway. Side roads often cut through scrub brush where the going can get tough on muddy and rutted roads. On the Out Islands, these byways often offer the reward of an isolated beach. Side roads often become sandy or rocky by turns, making driving a chore for anything other than 4WD.

Car rental agencies

A number of agencies have international offices in Nassau and Grand Bahama where you can arrange a rental before your trip. For details of smaller firms on the other islands, see their respective chapters.

Avis US ☎1-800/230-4898, Canada ☎1-800/272 -5871, UK ☎0870/606 0100, Republic of Ireland ☎021/428 1111, Australia ☎13 63 33 or 02/9353 9000, New Zealand ☎09/526 2847 or 0800/655 111, ⊛www.avis.com.

Budget US ☎1-800-527-0700, Canada ☎1-800/268-8900, UK ☎0870/156 5656, Australia ☎1300/362 848, New Zealand ☎0800/283 438, ⊛www.budget.com.

Hertz US and Canada ☎1-800/654-3131, UK ☎020/7026 0077, Republic of Ireland ☎01/870 5777, New Zealand ☎0800/654 321, ⊛www.hertz.com.

National US ☎1-800/CAR-RENT, UK ☎0870/400 4581, Australia ☎0870/600 6666, New Zealand ☎03/366 5574, ⊛www.nationalcar.com.

Bicycles, motorcycles and motor scooters

Renting a **bicycle** can be a convenient and cheap way to see small areas surrounding a resort, or to ride to and from town for supplies. Most hotels and resorts rent bicycles for $7–20 per day, though you probably won't find fancy mountain bikes for rent, with most cycles being one-speed beach cruisers. The city centres of Nassau and Freeport aren't particularly suited to touring by bike, but resort areas on the Out Islands, where traffic is light, roads flat and distances short, are perfect.

Another good option for getting around are **motorcycles** and **motor scooters**. Many local agencies rent motorcycles for $30–50 per day plus insurance and tax. Motor scooters cost $20–40 per day, though many agencies offer an hourly rate as well. You must wear a helmet when operating a motor scooter or motorcycle and a deposit is always required. Beware that in the Bahamas, storms can come up fast and obscure vision and wet the roads, while near constant loose gravel can challenge your balance and potholes abound in places.

Taxis

Taxis are abundant in and around Nassau and Freeport, where they are licensed by the government and the fares are set by law. From the airports in Nassau and Freeport, established rates – clearly posted in the taxi and at the airport – are in operation for trips to various hotels and resorts and should be agreed upon before setting out. Rates are for two passengers and two bags. You will pay extra for more people and $2 for each additional bag. Some hotels and resorts have a taxi or limousine service to pick up guests at airports, a service that is usually included in the room price.

Most Out Island taxi drivers are locals who own their own cars and answer calls as needed. Contact details are listed in each island chapter. Taxis meet all incoming flights, and most Out Island resorts and hotels will make certain that guests are met by one.

Taxis are also authorized by the government to conduct **tours**, and while rates are supposedly set by regulation, most taxi drivers and travellers simply eyeball the situation and agree on a fee. Rates vary, but average at about $150 per day, more for minivans and extra persons. Almost every Out Island taxi driver who meets a plane will also offer to conduct visitors on a tour of the island. Many are quite good at their job, and if you wish to see an island without the hassle of renting a car, it can be a bargain.

Tipping ten percent is customary for cab rides.

By bus

While there are excellent bus services on New Providence and Grand Bahama, and a twice-daily service on Great Exuma, there is no organized bus service at all on the other islands. Called "jitneys", Nassau buses are actually minivans or large Mitsubishi buses that run regular routes around the city and to the western and eastern suburbs. On Grand Bahama, buses are an excellent means of travelling between Freeport and Lucaya and to the eastern and western ends of the island.

Accommodation

Although there are relatively few inexpensive places to stay in the Bahamas, the islands still offer a solid variety of accommodation options. Super-deluxe resorts, some all-inclusive properties, small budget motels, cozy inns and family-run guesthouses are available on most of the islands. Some resort and hotel properties are dedicated to diving, snorkelling and watersports, while others are geared to relaxation and fine dining. Many visitors, especially those with large families or those making extended stays, choose time-share condos, vacation homes or island cottages where self-catering is an option.

Those travelling on a semblance of budget should note that camping is rarely a legal option, youth hostels do not exist in the Bahamas, and student discount cards are not widely accepted.

Rates

Rates vary from $50 for a simple guesthouse room with shared bath to $1000 per night (and more) for a penthouse suite in a deluxe resort. During the low season, from mid-April through mid-December, rates average 25–40 percent less than during the corresponding high season, when many upscale resort hotels and all-inclusives are booked solid months in advance.

Save yourself a heart attack at checkout by always enquiring before booking an accommodation what **taxes**, if any, will be applied to the quoted rate. Hotels and resorts charge a standard 12 percent room tax, and many apply mandatory service fees ranging from $2–20 a day for a double room. On top of that, some establishments even charge levies for water and electricity ($4 a night). In some cases, these additional fees can add $40 to the advertised room rate, while in others they're pre-included in the rate. Smaller hotels (under ten rooms) generally have lower taxes (6 percent), while bed and breakfasts and vacation rentals generally do not charge any additional fees. The prices quoted in this guide include all applicable taxes and charges for two people sharing a double room.

You will often pay more for ocean-view rooms, or rooms around or near the pool. If you choose to stay at a hotel or inn on the windward side of an island, you can expect strong trade winds, access to Atlantic beaches, and cooler nights. Staying at a leeward resort expect shallow, snorkel-friendly waters, calm conditions and warmer nights. On most islands, getting from one coast to the other takes only a matter of minutes.

Hotels, motels and inns

Hundreds of **hotels** are dotted on or near a beach in the Bahamas, with something for every taste. There are sprawling four and five star beach resorts featuring multiple swimming pools, bars and restaurants,

Accommodation price codes

All accommodation reviewed in this guide has been graded according to the following **price codes** in Bahamian dollars. Unless noted otherwise, the prices refer to the least expensive double or twin room in high season, including all taxes and surcharges.

❶ Under $60	❹ $120–150	❼ $210–250
❷ $60–90	❺ $150–180	❽ $250–300
❸ $90-120	❻ $180–210	❾ $300 and over

spas, gyms, tennis and golf, though one can also find lovely small resorts with just five, ten or twenty rooms. Many of the latter are in the Out Islands, and again range from full-bore luxury (gourmet cuisine, high thread count sheets and anything else your heart desires) to relaxed seaside inns where you can kick off your shoes and pour yourself a drink at the bar. The price range is enormous – starting at $120 a night for a clean, comfortable standard motel room with air conditioning and television (which most have) to $700 on up.

All-inclusives

All-inclusive resorts are advertised as cash-free, self-contained getaways. In truth, some charge extra for alcoholic drinks, watersports and services like laundry and island excursions, so always ask before you book. Three major all-inclusive chains have a presence in the Bahamas – *Club Med*, *Sandals* and *Superclubs Breezes*. Their rates begin at about $225 per day per person, and include all three meals, entertainment and many excursions and watersports. *Club Med* charges extra for alcoholic drinks and has one property in the Bahamas, on San Salvador. Less secluded are the couples-only *Sandals*, which operates the *Royal Bahamian*, and the *Superclubs Breezes*, both of which are on Cable Beach in Nassau. Many additional resorts in the Bahamas offer all-inclusive packages as an option, generally covering meals and a selected programme of activities like daily golf or diving. For information and contact numbers, see the "Accommodation" sections in the relevant chapters.

Guesthouses and bed-and-breakfasts

There are a few **guesthouses** in the islands, generally catering to local business travellers. They typically offer basic accommodation with shared baths, a sitting room and cooking facilities. Almost every settlement in the Bahamas has at least one simple guesthouse where you can put up for the night in a pinch, but some are pretty dire and grubby. The guesthouses recommended in this guide range in price from $60 to $100 a night.

Bed and Breakfasts are a homely alternative to hotels and guesthouses. They generally comprise a guestroom or two in a private home, most with private bath. Generally less expensive than a hotel (around $100, including breakfast), they also give you the opportunity to talk to knowledgeable local residents. The B&B is just beginning to catch on in the Bahamas, but there are a few very charming establishments on the islands.

Camping

Camping is not a Bahamian pastime, and the Bahamian government has deliberately pursued a policy of attracting tourist dollars at the upper end of the market – meaning herding visitors into hotels and mega-resorts where they will spend more money. Rough camping is, in fact, illegal in the Bahamas. There are, however, a few places where you can legally pitch a tent. The isolated Exuma Land and Sea Park has dozens of deserted beaches you can call your own for a night or a week for $5 a night (see p.273). The *Sivananda Ashram Yoga Retreat* on Paradise Island rents tent space for $55 a night including meals (see p.93). There is also a rustic bunkhouse in Inagua National Park where you can stay for $25 a night (see p.323). Alternatively, a number of outfitters run camping and kayaking or sailing expeditions in the Exuma Cays (see p.267).

Vacation rentals: cottages, condos and villas

Renting a cottage, **condo** or a multi-bedroom **villa** is often a fantastic and economical option for families, groups and others wanting to hunker down in one spot for a week, do their own cooking and have a bit more privacy than a hotel or resort can offer. The Bahamas are liberally dotted with enticing rentals ranging from simple seaside shacks to modern condominium developments and grand villas with swimming pools, tennis courts, full-time chefs and butler service. Cottages, condos and villas generally rent by the week and range in price from $500 for a simple one-bedroom cottage to $10,000 for a villa with all the perks. If you go for this route, you may need to rent a car, as many cottages (though not all) are located on the beach outside of the main settlements.

Condo and cottage rental sources

ⓦ **www.4beachnuts.com** Tiny apartments to large villas across the whole island chain.

ⓦ **www.brilandrealestate.com** Island Real Estate handles dozens of rentals on Harbour Island.

ⓦ **www.going2travel.com** A decent amount of rentals, particularly strong on Eleuthera.

ⓦ **www.hopetown.com** Hope Town Hideaways acts as agent for several dozen cottages and villas on Elbow Cay, Abacos.

ⓦ **www.myharbourisland.com** Listings for Harbour Island.

ⓦ **www.vacationrentals.com** Worldwide broker with a few dozen Bahamian options.

ⓦ **www.vrbo.com** A long list of rental options directly through individual owners.

Eating and drinking

The eating and drinking habits of Bahamians have been influenced first and foremost by being surrounded by one of the most abundant marine life realms in the world, an environment where seafood of nearly every type is readily available. For the Lucayans, who inhabited the Bahamas before Columbus's arrival, fish and lobster were the central sources of protein, and today, seafood and basic vegetables like the potato are the backbone of Bahamian cuisine.

The second influence on Bahamian cuisine is the **African**, the result of slaves and freed blacks bringing their own indigenous cooking and ingredients with them from their homelands, including flavourings like nutmeg, ginger and chili pepper. These days, dishes like grits, peas and rice, and johnnycake are the result of African modifications of Bahamian/English dishes.

Another influence is the **English colonial cuisine**, which affected virtually every nuance of Bahamian diet. Today, meat pies, stews and breads all show a distinctly English influence. At a Bahamian restaurant, you can order smothered grouper with a distinctly African-style sauce, or an old-fashioned English shepherd's pie with a side of chips.

More and more, tourism demands have created an influx of **nouvelle cuisine**. Particularly in Nassau, Paradise Island and Freeport/Lucaya, restaurants abound that specialize in Continental, Asian and North American cuisine. Many fine chefs now make their homes at Bahamian resorts, blending cuisine from exotic cultures and faraway places with Bahamian seafood or vegetables. Expect to encounter the likes of blackened grouper, sweet-and-spicy mango sauces and "Pacific Rim" chutney with lobster broil. A further influence of tourism is that Bahamians are eating more **fast-food** pizzas, burgers and fried chicken or doughnuts from corporate-owned franchise outlets, so while tourists are finding their choices expanding, the daily eating habits of Bahamians are being gradually homogenized.

Ultimately, the menus at most Bahamian-style restaurants look pretty much the same, with a heavy emphasis on grouper, peas and rice, potatoes and heavy English-style desserts.

Seafood

No single marine organism contributes more to the Bahamian diet than the **conch** (pronounced "konk"), a snail-like mollusk encased in a beautifully curled, pinkish-coloured shell. Bahamians love conch because it's cheap and plentiful;

it reportedly also acts as an aphrodisiac. Conch-cracking contests are held on National Heroes Day, and locals demonstrate their dexterity by hitting the shell with a heavy implement at the correct spot, then "jewking" the meat by an appendage and pulling it from its shell.

The conch's delicate, whitish meat forms the basis of myriad dishes: it can be eaten fried, broiled, grilled, steamed, stewed or raw in **conch salad**, the meat diced and mixed with chopped onion, tomato, cucumber, and celery, then sprinkled with lime juice. Because the conch meat itself is both rubbery and somewhat slimy, it must be liberally tenderized by pounding, then rinsed in salt water or lime juice, and often marinated before it is ready to eat. **Cracked conch** is tenderized meat deep-fried in batter and usually served with french fries. **Conch fritters** are deep-fat-fried balls of conch covered with corn batter that has bits of sweet peppers, onions and tomato included. Conch is also made into a light chowder (for a recipe, see p.8).

Crawfish, locally referred to as a Bahamian lobster, is another popular seafood, and is caught fresh in the months between April and late August. Bahamian lobsters have no claws, and only the tail is eaten. They can be eaten freshly grilled or broiled, steamed and curried and are often served cold in salads with local ingredients including coconut and lime juice. The **land crab** is another mollusk that winds up on Bahamian tables, especially during summer's rainy season when they are plentiful near the beaches. The most common dish is the baked crab where the meat and eggs are combined with breadcrumbs and served in the shell.

The waters surrounding the Bahamas teem with grouper, shrimp, tuna, jack, snapper and whelk. A particular favourite, the **grouper**, is a light fleshy white fish, is most often served baked with a red tomato sauce accompanied by the ubiquitous peas and rice and French fries. Grouper is just as often eaten deep-fried in batter, or cut into "fingers" and fried. On the Out Islands in particular, baked bonefish in a creole sauce is popular, and in many places, especially the Exumas, turtle is still eaten, despite its status as an endangered species.

Another very common Bahamian dish is **boil fish**, sometimes referred to as "stew fish". Boil fish, a stew of grouper, salt pork, onions, potatoes, celery, tomatoes and spices, can be served for any meal, and many Bahamians start their day with boil fish and coffee.

Meats and vegetables

Bahamians depend on simple staples like imported rice, potatoes, peas, red beans, pigeon peas and lima beans, all of which they serve with seafood or stew. A generous pile of grits (ground corn), cornmeal mush, or potatoes, often forms the basis of a meal in the typical Bahamian home. You're unlikely to escape **peas and rice**, but there are as many ways to prepare the dish as cooks in the islands.

Souse is also a vitally important dish in the Bahamas. Basically a combination of very inexpensive cuts of meat (sheep tongue, chicken wing, conch, pig ears) boiled with salted water and spices, souse is usually flavoured with lime juice and pepper, then eaten with freshly cooked bread. English-influenced dishes like meatloaf, pasties, macaroni and cheese, and broiled or fried chicken are also popular.

Fruit

During the nineteenth century, many types of edible exotic **fruit** were imported to the Bahamas, some becoming the basis of once-thriving industries, like the sweet Eleutheran pineapple and the Androsian orange. These days, only small quantities of fruit are commercially produced and sold, though fresh fruit and vegetables are available everywhere in groceries, markets and roadside fruit stands. Check the box and very often the fruit will be from Florida or Mexico.

Nevertheless, visitors to the Bahamas can enjoy the luxury of buying fresh, tree-ripened papayas and mangoes, and in some markets the deliciously sweet sugar loaf or Spanish scarlet variety of pineapple. Open-air markets and roadside food stands often feature fruit that are unknown in many parts of the world. The dark green **soursop** looks like a pinecone and weighs from one to five pounds. Its fibrous white pulp is both slightly sweet and tart at the same time, and although children eat it as a treat, it is mostly used in puddings, ice cream or drinks. The **sugar apple** is related to the soursop, though a lighter green, and is about the size of a tennis ball. You eat it by splitting open the fruit and spooning out the smooth white flesh. It is filled with black seeds, however, so you need patience to get a good mouthful. Oval and brown, the smallish **sapodilla** has a tan-coloured flesh that tastes something like pear. Other distinctly exotic fruit available in the Bahamas include the **jujube**, the yellow flesh of which is used to flavour the gumdrops of the same name, the leathery dark purple **star apple**, and the delicious **ugli fruit**, a roundish fruit with a green skin and a sweet, ready-to-eat pulp.

Bahamians often use their exotic fruit to flavour many kinds of jams, jellies, ice cream, puddings and punch. The **guava** is blended into puddings called "duffs", a favourite Bahamian dessert. A duff is essentially a boiled pudding filled with any kind of fruit. It has a cake-like consistency and is typically covered by a special sauce.

Drinking

While **tap water** throughout the Bahamas is drinkable, it's often highly saline due to its surface source, making it brackish at best. Anything made with tap water, including coffee and tea, is likely to take on a brackish flavour as well, so most people choose bottled water, which usually costs $1 per litre, though grocery stores and markets sell larger, bargain one-gallon containers. On some Out Islands, rainwater is a major source of drinking water and every house has a cistern to catch and store it. It's never a good idea to drink cistern-stored rainwater, and bottled water in these areas is a must. Resorts tend to double-filter their water, and add extra chlorine.

Most North American soft drinks are available in the Bahamas, and locally produced soft drinks like the favourite **Goombay Punch** are very much sweeter than their North American counterparts. Fresh-fruit drinks tend to take the edge off hot days

and many visitors enjoy lime coolers, orange juice and pineapple juice with shaved ice.

The alcoholic drink of choice in the Bahamas is the very fine **Kalik beer**, a lager brewed on New Providence. Its premium brand, Kalik Gold, is slightly stronger, with a deeper texture and colour. Many Bahamians drink locally brewed Heineken, or imported beers like Amstel Light, Guinness, or commonly available American and Canadian beers. Many pubs in Nassau offer English ales on tap.

Unlike many of their Caribbean neighbours, the Bahamas never had an active sugar plantation culture, and therefore never had a large-scale **rum** culture. Some rum is distilled in the Bahamas, and many poor Bahamians choose to drink stiff shots of high-octane white rum on hot days. Brands include Bacardi, Ron Matusalem and Todd Hunter. Many of the fancier rum drinks are concocted to serve to tourists at resort bars and restaurants. The famous **Bahama Mama** (rum, bitters, creme de cassis, grenadine, nutmeg, citrus juice), **Goombay Smash** (see the last page of the *Bahamas beach culture* colour section) and the **Yellow Bird** (rum, creme de banana, Galliano, apricot brandy, pineapple or orange juice) were all created strictly for the tourist trade. A very popular liqueur is the rum-based **Nassau Royale**, which comes in several flavours, including coconut, banana and pineapple, and can be mixed in cocktails, or splashed over ice and drunk straight.

Wines were never particularly popular in the Bahamas because of importation costs and the ready availability of beer and rum. These days, many restaurants in better hotels have exhaustive wine lists to cater to international tastes.

A bottle of Kalik at most bars costs $1, though at fancier places the price will be at least twice that. Rum-based drinks usually go for $5–6, though in some discos and dance palaces in Nassau or Paradise Island that cater to a late-night crowd, the price of drinks skyrockets.

The media

The Bahamas have an independent if somewhat unsophisticated press that exercises its freedom to criticize the government without recrimination. You'll get most of your on-island information from just a few key sources.

Newspapers and magazines

Two daily **newspapers**, the *Nassau Guardian* (Ⓦwww.thenassauguardian.com) and the *Tribune*, are available in New Providence, on Grand Bahama and in some of the larger settlements in the Out Islands. In addition, Grand Bahama has its own daily, the *Freeport News* (Ⓦfreeport.nassauguardian.net). All cover local, national and international news, while the *Nassau Guardian* also publishes free monthly newspapers devoted to local news and events on several of the Out Islands. The *Bahamas Journal* is a national weekly published out of Nassau and available mainly in the larger centres. Foreign newspapers and magazines can be bought at newsstands in Freeport, Nassau and some of the more heavily touristed settlements in the Out Islands.

Radio and television

The government-owned Bahamas Broadcasting Corporation **radio** station (ZNS-1) broadcasts on AM 1540 and FM 107.1 throughout the islands. It is devoted to national and local news, talk shows focused on political issues and some music. There are also several commercial radio stations that play music of various genres. To find information on the world service frequencies, check out BBC (Ⓦwww.bbc.co.uk/worldservice), Radio Canada (Ⓦwww.rcinet.ca) or the Voice of America (Ⓦwww.voa.gov).

ZNS is also the major source of national news on **television**. ZNS Channel 13 broadcasts the national news 7pm nightly at 7pm. Most hotels have satellite or cable TV beaming in American and other foreign programming.

Festivals

While the Bahamas are host to a variety of special events throughout the year, none is as big as Nassau's Junkanoo celebration, a citywide carnival on Boxing Day (December 26) that is repeated on New Year's Day. Each year, the capital is engulfed in the music of this raucous street extravaganza, which is repeated on a smaller scale on several of the islands.

Few Bahamian festivities are as intimate as the annual **Homecoming** festivities on the Out Islands. These occur when prodigal sons and daughters return for a visit from Nassau and Freeport, where they are forced to seek their fortunes. Locals whoop it up for a few days with events that include street fairs, concerts, games, lots of food and often sailing races, and visitors are welcome to attend.

As a big-time sailing nation, with a long tradition in wooden boat building, the annual **regattas** held throughout the island chain are well worth attending. They are generally accompanied by music, food and other festivities on land. Some of the larger events

35

are listed below, while others are listed throughout the guide.

For detailed **information** on upcoming events, including regattas, Homecomings and special events, and for precise dates – which can change from year to year – contact the Ministry of Tourism (☎356-4231, ⓦwww.bahamas.com) or the Bahamas Out Islands Promotion Board (☎1-800/688-4752, ⓦwww.boipb.com). Detailed calendars of upcoming events are also found at ⓦwww .whatsonbahamas.com.

Special events

January
Junkanoo Parade, New Year's Day. Beginning at 1am in Nassau, with prizes for best floats awarded at 8am; see p.35 for more information. Several settlements throughout the Out Islands also hold Junkanoo festivities, notably in Staniel Cay in the Exumas.

February
Farmer's Cay Festival, first Friday of the month.
Combination Homecoming and regatta in the Exumas. Overnight boat excursions from Nassau are available. Contact Terry Bain (☎355-4006 or 2093) for details.

March
George Town Cruising Regatta, first Friday of the month.
A week-long party in the Exumas, drawing yachters from all over the world.

April
Out Island Regatta, late April. George Town's biggest regatta and the most exciting in all the Out Islands; see p.259 for full details.

June
Andros Crab Fest, Fresh Creek, Andros. In early June, the forest paths and streets on Andros are crawling with land crabs, a local delicacy. This three-day festival celebrates the hunt, with crab cooked in every way, music and a regatta. Call the Andros Tourism Office in Fresh Creek for details (☎368-2286).
Cat Island rake 'n' scrape Music Festival, late June.
New Bight comes alive for this

annual event. Contact Eris Moncur (☎342-3030).
Pineapple Festival, early June. Three-day extravaganza in Gregory Town, Eleuthera, featuring pineapple-eating contest, music, games and a pineathelon – a combined swim, run and bike race.

July
Goombay Festival, Fridays through July and August.
Festival throughout Andros featuring rake 'n' scrape bands, dances and lots of native cuisine. Contact Doris Adderley (☎368-2117) or Andros Tourism (☎368-2286) for details.

August
Rolleville Sailing Regatta, Emancipation Day weekend.
Great Exuma. Contact Kermit Rolle (☎345-0002).
Annual Cat Island Regatta, early August. Every August this race draws hundreds of yachters to New Bight for Cat Island's biggest event of the year. Call Philip McPhee for details (☎368-2286).

December
Festivale Noelle, the first week of the month.
Freeport's Rand Nature Centre hosts this festival, featuring live music, wine tasting, arts and crafts. Call ☎352-5438.
Plymouth Historical Weekend, mid-December. The Abacos' Green Turtle Cay hosts this event, a celebration of the settlement's Loyalist heritage with musical concerts, art exhibitions, drama and picnics.

Sports and outdoor activities

With great weather year-round, warm waters, miles of pristine beaches, and rich, teeming coral reefs surrounding the islands, the Bahamas offer endless amusement for outdoor enthusiasts, especially for divers and snorkellers.

Watersports

The Caribbean's vast, clear waters make the region a veritable playground for watersports. The quality of **diving** and **snorkelling** in many places is superb, thanks to the sheer abundance of marine life, and there are excellent opportunities for **sport fishing, kayaking, glass-bottomed boat trips, sailing, water-skiing, windsurfing, parasailing** and **jet-skiing**, most of which are usually offered by the major resorts. Resort areas are also packed with operators offering dive trips and snorkelling excursions; the most reputable are listed throughout the guide.

Diving and snorkelling

The Bahamas are a **diving** and **snorkelling** idyll. The crystal-clear waters surrounding the islands are filled with luxurious multicoloured coral reefs and spires, sea gardens, underwater mountains, canyons and valleys carpeted with sponges and corals, home to a multitude of tropical fish and other sea creatures. The Bahamas are also renowned for their **blue-hole** diving, especially in Andros or Long Island. In many places, notably Grand Bahama, dive operators offer several speciality excursions, including diving with dolphins or sharks, or around one of dozens of offshore wrecks. Most islands – with the exception of the undeveloped southernmost Bahamas – have at least one dive operator, and these are listed in the "Diving and watersports" sections of each chapter.

The most popular destinations for divers are Andros, the Exumas, Grand Bahama, Long Island and San Salvador. Operators charge around $70 for a two-tank dive and many offer all-inclusive packages in conjunction with a resort. Diving and snorkelling are great year-round in the Bahamas, but at their best in the summer months when the water is generally flat and still, although the heat topside can be intense.

If you wish to spend your entire time on or in the water, there are also a number of operators who offer **live aboard dive excursions**, on vessels ranging from purely functional to luxury yachts serving gourmet meals. You live at sea for a few days, a week or more, travelling from dive site to dive site. These trips range $900–1600 per person for a week all-inclusive, and many can be chartered by a group.

If you have never dived before, the Bahamas make for a fine location to learn and several dive operators offer complete PADI or NAUI **certification courses** for around $500 for three to five days of instruction, as noted in the chapters on each island. One of the most popular and well-established places to do this is at UNEXSO, the Underwater Explorers Society (☎373-1244 or ☎1-800/992-3483, ⓦwww.unexso.com), on Grand Bahama. Another top-notch instructional and recreational diving outfit based in the Out Islands is *Small Hope Bay Lodge* on Andros (☎368-2014 or 1-800/223-6961, ⓦwww.smallhope.com). Many other resorts have dive masters on staff and offer diving trips and certification, as listed in each chapter. Note that if you want to get certified, some operators require you to complete some coursework using materials sent in advance of your trip. If you just want a taste of the underwater world, you can take a **resort course**, which gives you some basic instruction and a shallow-water dive with an instructor for around $90. A number of dive operators also offer advanced certification courses for experienced divers.

Anybody that can swim can **snorkel**, and most dive operators rent snorkelling gear for $7–10 a day and offer guided excursions for around $30 for a half-day trip. It is amazing what you can see by just wading into the water and floating over a promising dark clump of coral, let alone the magic that awaits in the magnificent reefs and sea gardens in the shallow waters surrounding the islands. Don't miss the chance.

Useful contacts for divers

Bahamas Diving Association ⓦwww .bahamasdiving.com. This website contains listings of dive operators in the Bahamas, plus descriptions of some prime dive sites, including wrecks certified for recreational use.
NAUI ☎813/628-6284 or 1-800/553-6284, ⓦwww.naui.org. The National Association of Underwater Instructors is geared mainly to professional divers, with information on courses and certification.
PADI ☎949/858-7234 or 1-800/729-7234, ⓦwww.padi.org. The Professional Association of Diving Instructors presents basic information on diving, courses and certification as well as a dive-trip booking service. They also sell medical insurance for divers, who are often not covered under basic travel insurance policies.

Full-service diving trips

Blackbeard's Cruises ☎305/888-1226 or 1-800/327-9600, ⓦwww.blackbeard-cruises.com. Blackbeard's runs live-aboard scuba-diving trips on three 65ft sailboats with room for 22 passengers; on the sailboat *Cat Ppalu*, which sleeps twelve, and on the 102ft motorized catamaran the *AquaCat* with room for thirty. Details of dive sites, including the Exuma Land and Sea Park, are posted on the website. Seven-day/six-night all-inclusive trips departing from Miami, Nassau and Freeport cost US$900–1700 a week per person including tax, depending on the vessel. Longer and shorter expeditions and group charters available.
Bottom Time Adventures ☎1-800/234-8474, ⓦwww.bottomtimeadventures.net. Features diving with wild dolphins and humpback whales, with accommodation aboard a luxury motorized catamaran sleeping fourteen divers. Departures from Fort Lauderdale and the Bahamas. $1600 a week per person.
Nekton Diving Cruises ☎954/463-9324 or 1-800/899-6753, ⓦwww.nektoncruises.com. Offers dive trips on the *Nekton Pilot*, a catamaran like a small floating hotel, with en-suite cabins and a Jacuzzi on board. Departures from Fort Lauderdale and George Town, Exuma. $1800 a week.

Sea Dragon ☎954/522-0161 in port, ☎242/359-2058 on boat mid-May through August, ⓦwww .seadragonbahamas.com. A 65ft research vessel that can accommodate eight in four double cabins. The *Sea Dragon* can be chartered for $10,200 a week meals included, or $1275 plus 4 percent tax per person on scheduled diving excursions. Trips in the Exuma Cays.

Fishing

Fishing is a way of life as well as a pastime in the Bahamas, and the islands are a fabled destination for sport fishers, particularly for bonefishing on shallow sapphire and white sand flats, reef fishing for snapper and grouper, and for deep-sea fishing for big-game fish. There are dedicated fishing lodges catering to serious fishers with guides, boats and equipment for hire in the Biminis, Exumas, Andros, Grand Bahama and Long Island. There are also fishing guides, lodges and charter outfits on many islands, as listed throughout the guide. You must have a **permit** to fish in the Bahamas if on your own ($25 per trip, $150 yearly), obtainable at the Customs Office at your Port of Entry or from the Department of Fisheries, PO Box N-3028, Nassau (☎393-1777). The *Bahamas Flyfishing Guide* (ⓦwww .bahamasflyfishingguide.com) website and guidebook written by Stephen and Kim Vletas (Lyons Press) is a great source of information for sportsfishers, including listings of independent guides and tips on where to fish and what gear to use.

Sea kayaking

Sea kayaking is an increasingly popular way to explore the Bahamas, and outfitters offer day-trips and overnight paddling and camping excursions in the Abacos, on Grand Bahama and in the Exumas. These trips explore the coastline, mangrove-fringed tidal creeks or hop between sandy beaches on the cays that surround the larger islands. In addition, many seaside resorts have recreational – as opposed to excursion – kayaks for guests to paddle about for a few hours.

The prime destination for sea kayakers is the **Exuma Cays,** a forty-mile-long string of small, mainly uninhabited islands set in shallow turquoise waters. In the middle of this island chain is the serenely beautiful Exuma Land and Sea Park, a wilderness area encompassing 176 square miles of pristine water and twenty-odd islets rimmed with fine white sand for camping. Several outfitters offer guided kayaking excursions in the Exuma Cays and elsewhere in the Bahamas, as listed below.

Kayaking outfitters

Abaco Outback ⊛ www.abacooutback.com. Based in Marsh Harbour, Abaco, this outfitter offers day trips exploring tidal creeks in the Abacos.
Ibis Tours PO Box 208, Pelham, NY 10803 ☎ 914/409-5961, ⊛ www.ibistours.com. Runs guided expeditions through the Exuma Land and Sea Park.
Kayak Nature Tours ☎ 373-2485 or 1-866/440 -4542, ⊛ www.gbntours.com. Runs paddling excursions on Grand Bahama, offers both day trips and overnight camping expeditions.
North Carolina Outward Bound 2582 Riceville Rd, Asheville, NC 28805 ☎ 828/299-3366, ⊛ www .ncobs.org. Offers an eight-day sea-kayaking course in the southern Exuma Cays.
Starfish George Town ☎ 1-877/398-6222, ⊛ www.kayakbahamas.com. Starfish offers kayaking day-trips and multi-day camping and paddling expeditions through the southern Exuma Cays (see p.275).

Sailing

Sailing is an integral part of Bahamian culture, and the annual calendar of sailing regattas in the islands is quite full (the more major annual regattas are listed under "Festivals" on p.36). Everybody is welcome to come and watch and partake in the music, eating, drinking and other festivities that accompany the races. Some race events are open to visiting yachts.

The Bahamas, especially the Abacos and the Exumas, are favoured destinations for yacht cruisers and the harbours and anchorages in the islands are filled with visiting pleasure craft throughout the winter season. If the idea appeals to you, but you don't have your own vessel or a clue how to pilot one if you had it, see 'Getting there', pp.22–23 for a list of companies chartering yachts for excursions through the Bahamas.

Many of the larger resorts have small sailboats, sunfish or hobiecats available for guest use, and there are boat rental agencies in several communities, as listed in the chapters on each island.

Other outdoor activities

While the sea is definitely the star attraction in the Bahamas, there are plenty of activities on dry land to add some variety to your days.

The Bahamas attract serious **golfers** with several championship-grade courses. There are two courses on New Providence and three on Grand Bahama, plus one on Treasure Cay in the Abacos. Greens fees for eighteen holes range from $70 to $225 including cart and you can rent clubs for $20–50 a day. All of the Bahamas' major golf courses are part of resorts, which offer all-inclusive golfing packages; please see individual resort reviews for details.

Horseback riding is also available for an hour or two on Grand Bahama, New Providence and Harbour Island. Stables offering trail rides through forests and along the beach are listed in the "Outdoor activities" sections of these chapters.

The Bahamas are pretty flat and not known as a **hiking** destination. Mount Alvernia on Cat Island is the tallest peak in the archipelago, at 206ft high. Despite that, there are walking trails ranging from a few hundred yards to three or four miles in length on several of the islands as well as miles of empty beach to walk. Good destinations for day hikes are Warderick Wells Cay in the **Exuma Land and Sea Park**, where there are seven miles of walking trails crisscrossing the island; nearby Compass Cay; **Abaco National Park** with trails along the shore and through the forest; the **Mount Alvernia Hermitage** on Cat Island; and the short walking paths through **Lucayan National Park** on Grand Bahama.

Sunny weather and a generally flat topography make for easy **cycling** in the Bahamas. As spectacular as the ocean views are, however, island roads often cut through long, monotonous expanses of scrubby bush. If you want to do a lot of cycling, head for Long Island or Eleuthera, where there is little traffic and particularly beautiful and varied scenery along the Queen's Highway. Many resorts have single-gear bicycles for

National parks

The Bahamas has 25 national parks and conservation areas, all under the stewardship of the Bahamas National Trust (☎393-1317, ⍟www.thebahamasnationaltrust.org), which has its headquarters at The Retreat on Village Road in Nassau. These wildlife preserves range in size from the eleven-acre forested enclave at the Retreat in Nassau (see p.84) to the 287 square-mile **Inagua National Park** (see p.323), encompassing the remote breeding grounds of the west Indian flamingo and hundreds of other species of birds. All of the parks are open to visitors, although some are easier to get to than others and often there are no facilities for tourists.

Along with the Inagua National Park, the 176 square-mile **Exuma Land and Sea Park** is the spectacular centrepiece of the park system, drawing sailors, sea kayakers and divers to its pristine protected waters and uninhabited islands. Other natural refuges worth making an effort to see are the **Lucayan National Park** on Grand Bahama, a forty-acre chunk of tall pine forest, tidal creeks and white sand beach (see p.127), and **Peterson Cay National Park**, a tiny smidge of white sand popular with day-trippers (see p.126). Both Abaco and Andros have large tracts of undeveloped bush set aside as national parks, where bird nerds can see their fill. Hardcore nature enthusiasts can hire a boat to **Conception Island** (see p.301), the whole of which is designated a migratory bird sanctuary.

guest use, but if you have serious peddling in mind, bring your own bike as well as a tyre patch kit and spare inner tubes.

Eco-tour vacations

The Bahamas offer several unique **eco-tour** style holidays, ranging from assisting marine biologists conducting scientific research to learning about Bahamian culture in its ancient or modern forms. There are also a few eco-resorts in the islands, most notable being the gorgeous *Tiamo Resort* on South Andros, which manages to offer seamless casual elegance while using as much electricity in five years to power their ten guest bungalows as the average North American household uses in three days. See p.189 for details.

Dolphin Research ☎1-800/326-7491, ⍟www.oceanic-society.org. Since 1984, the Oceanic Society, a non-profit-making marine research organization based in San Francisco, California has sponsored field research on dolphin behaviour in the waters off Grand Bahama.

Earthwatch Institute 3 Clock Tower Place, Suite 100, Box 75, Maynard, MA ☎978/461-0081 or 44(0) 1865 318838 in the UK and ☎03/9682 6828

in Australia ⍟www.earthwatch.org. Earthwatch accepts volunteers to assist scientists on several ongoing research projects in the Bahamas. Current projects include the Bahamian Reef Survey which is examining the impact of coral bleaching in the waters around San Salvador Island; the coastal ecology of southern Eleuthera; and long-term research on dolphins and whales near Sandy Point in the Abacos. Trips are offered several times throughout the year and cost from $1350 per week.

Exuma Land and Sea Park ☎359-1821, ⍟www.thebahamasnationaltrust.org. In the remote Exuma Cays, the park runs a volunteer programme for those with an interest in environmental conservation. See p.272 for details.

Ocean Explorer ☎561/288-4262 or 1-800/338-9383, ⍟www.oceanexplorerinc.com. The *Ocean Explorer* is a 55ft dive boat with room for up to four passengers to accompany researchers on expeditions to explore blue holes, wrecks and reefs as well as to observe and interact with wild dolphins; $2000 per person per week. The dive boat is also available for charter.

People to People ☎356-0435. The Ministry of Tourism co-ordinates this programme, which connects visitors interested in learning more about life in the Bahamas with local volunteers on several islands for a meal or a community get-together.

Culture and etiquette

Bahamians are in general a mobile population, travelling frequently to the United States and beyond, while millions of people from all over the world visit the islands every year and the expatriate American, Canadian and European community numbers in the thousands. Considering all this, it's unlikely you will be able to faze local residents with your strange foreign tastes and behaviour. However, Bahamian culture is generally conservative, particularly outside Nassau. The churches are well-attended and drinking is for the most part left to tourists.

Smoking is socially acceptable, but not inside restaurants or indoor public areas. Many hotels have designated non-smoking guestrooms. Public **toilets** are few and far between. The best place to find a restroom is in a hotel or restaurant.

As for **dress codes**, local women dress quite modestly, although shorts, sleeveless tops, and form-fitting trousers are perfectly acceptable. Bikinis are fine at the pool or the beach, but not out and about in town. Bathing topless or nude in public is socially unacceptable. Most restaurants and resorts are pretty casual, but upscale eateries generally expect you to dress for dinner – long trousers

and collared shirts for men; trousers, skirts or dresses for women. Establishments with a definite dress code are flagged in the guide.

Bahamians in general treat each other and visitors with courtesy and respect. It is a warm, outgoing and friendly culture. If you meet a stranger on an empty street, it is customary to say hello. Bahamians do not, as a rule, shout at each other or demand service in a loud voice. Visitors often become frustrated at the sometimes glacial speed at which things (restaurant orders, line-ups, delayed flights) move in the islands. There is little you can do about it, and the best antidote is to relax and have a cool drink.

Shopping

Duty-free is the most popular form of shopping in the Bahamas. Offering savings of up to 50 percent below international retail prices, duty-free shopping is a good way to find bargains for luxury goods like jewellery, perfume, watches, china, crystal and liquor, with the tourist zones of Nassau and Freeport providing particularly fine buying opportunities.

Nassau's Bay Street is famous for its **Straw Market**, offering a wide array of mats, baskets, hats, dresses, T-shirts, and handcrafted items at bargain prices. While many items at the market are cheap imports, others may be genuine, so a close inspection of the merchandise is usually worthwhile. There are also large straw markets in Freeport

and Port Lucaya on Grand Bahama Island selling a mix of locally made straw work and cheap manufactured knockoffs. While straw market purchases are subject to negotiation, **bargaining** is not a typical Bahamian custom. In small shops in many settlements in the Out Islands, you can buy handmade straw work directly from local artisans.

The Bahamas are also known for their **Androsian batik** fabrics made by a small operation in Andros Town on Andros. Although a visit to the factory is an interesting side-trip, batik items are available at many outlets in Nassau, Freeport and major Out Islands like the Abacos and Eleuthera.

Cuban cigars and local **art** are often worthwhile purchases as well, with Bahamian painters, water colourists, wood carvers and jewellers creating original works for sale **in galleries and giftshops** in Nassau and Freeport and throughout the Out Islands, as noted in the chapters on the various islands.

Travelling with children

While many people see the Bahamas as an adult-oriented, honeymoon and cruise-ship destination, the islands can be a great destination for family vacations. Nassau, Paradise Island and Grand Bahama offer a wide array of suitable day trips for kids and adults, ranging from swimming with dolphins to snorkelling boat excursions to offshore cays. Many of the larger resorts (notably Atlantis on Paradise Island and Our Lucaya on Grand Bahama) run day camps and special activities for kids.

If muom and dad prefer something more low key and perhaps less costly, the Out Islands offer miles and miles of **beaches** for running, picnics, sandcastle building and swimming. Eleuthera, Great Exuma and Long Island are probably the best options for families as they have a good range of things to see and do to go with some lovely small resorts and appealing cottage rentals. Be sure to check with your accommodation about bringing children as some hotels cater to adults or couples only. The combination of ten sets of kissy-face newlyweds and one tired, hungry five-year-old faced with a plate of unrecognizable gourmet food might ruin everyone's holiday.

Diapers, baby food and other **supplies** are readily available on the larger islands, though on the less-developed Out Islands, you should bring all you need. There are medical clinics on all of the islands, as noted in each chapter.

Travel essentials

Costs

The **Bahamian dollar** is pegged to the US dollar, and both currencies are accepted throughout the country. Despite the relatively cheap air transportation to and from the islands themselves (particularly from the US), the Bahamas are ultimately an expensive destination. Budget accommodation options are few and far between, and almost everything Bahamians use on a daily basis is imported, some of it subject to high duties and tariffs. Travellers should budget their money as though they were travelling to a major US city, although some of the money-saving options found in other countries – like campgrounds and public transport – are almost completely non-existent in the Bahamas.

If you stay at a basic guesthouse, do without a rental car, eat simply, and make your own fun, you could get by on about $120–140 a day (per person; sharing a room will lower costs per person by $30–40). The **average room rate** for a decent tourist hotel is $120–440 per night for double occupancy. Nassau and Freeport have budget options that go for as little as $60 per night, but these properties are often small, noisy motel-style lodgings in the town centre. Conditions are no different on the Out Islands, where there are typically a few budget-option motels, but where most hotels are rather expensive. Renting a cottage is often more economical; see p.32 for listings of vacation rentals.

> It is customary to **tip** for service in the Bahamas: generally $1–2 a bag for porters; 10 percent for taxis; $2 a day for housekeeping where mandatory service fees are not applied; 15 percent for bar and restaurant service where gratuities are not automatically added to your bill; 10 percent for tour guides; and between $40–50 a day for bonefishing guides.

Other than seafood, some fruit and a few vegetables, all **foodstuffs** in the Bahamas are imported. An average breakfast costs about $6, lunch $10, and dinner $10–20. Of course, you can find roadside food stalls and fruit stands, and there are take-away joints on almost every street corner, but the food in budget joints is almost always deep-fried and difficult to stomach day after day. Groceries often stock expensive canned goods, dairy products and sweets that have been imported from the US and UK.

Unless you are prepared to stay put in one place, **ground transportation** can eat up a good chunk of your travel funds. Taxis have a monopoly on transportation from the airports, which on most islands will cost between $20–40 to get you to your hotel. New Providence and Grand Bahama have inexpensive public bus systems, with $1 fares within the city limits, and Great Exuma has a limited bus service; elsewhere, you will have to walk, bicycle ($20 a day) or rent a car ($70–80 a day). **Inter-island travel** varies in cost from ferries and mailboats to puddle-jumping commercial flights and more expensive charter flights. Commercial flights can cost as little as $60 (Nassau to Andros), but island-hopping is typically costly because in almost all cases, travelling from one of the Out Islands to another requires first returning to Nassau to catch a flight to the second island. **Tours** and day excursions (snorkelling, diving, kayaking, island hopping) start at about $45 a day and run up to $180.

Every traveller departing the Bahamas must pay an **airport departure tax** of $20 ($22 if you are leaving from Freeport). Some airlines include this in the cost of your ticket. Otherwise, you pay the tax at the departure desk.

Crime and personal safety

The **crime rate** in the Bahamas as a whole is extremely low, and in resort areas, crime is rare. On the Out Islands, crime rates in general are so low that few people even lock their cars or houses.

Nevertheless, the city of **Nassau** has a growing problem and you should exercise caution when travelling in and around the downtown core. Most misdeeds occur in the Fox Hill and Grant's Town neighbourhoods "Over-the-Hill", and these areas are not safe to roam on your own, especially after dark. If you are out and about in Nassau after dark, take a taxi.

Cable Beach and **Paradise Island** are safe for the most part, but you should exercise the same caution you would in visiting any large city. The only significant dangers in tourist areas are from petty crime like pickpocketing and theft, or from involvement in drugs. Always lock the doors of a rental car, and never leave valuables in plain view. If you must take valuables along, lock them in your trunk and never leave them unprotected in a hotel room. Most hotels provide a safety deposit box in their lobbies or a safe in the room. Use it.

Drugs are an absolute no-no in the Bahamas. The penalties for possession and use of illegal drugs are severe. It will make no difference that you are a foreign citizen, and prison sentences can be long.

The Bahamas are a relatively safe and hassle-free destination for **women travelers**. Bahamians in general treat each other and visitors with kindness and respect, and while a woman travelling alone may attract some unsolicited male attention, a polite "no thanks" is usually sufficient to reclaim your privacy. Other tourists, of course, come in all stripes and degrees of offensiveness. Incidents of sexual assault are comparable to Europe and North America. It is wise to stick to the common-sense rules of not walking alone at night or accepting rides from strangers, especially in the cities of Nassau and Freeport. There is a Women's Crisis Centre (☎328-0922) located on Shirley Street in Nassau.

The Bahamian **police** are both professional and helpful. A police station is located in every settlement, usually near the commissioner's office or other government buildings. See the "Listings" section in each chapter for police station locations.

Electricity

Bahamian current is 120volt/60cycle, compatible with all US appliances. Electrical outlets are the two- or three-pronged outlets common in the US and Canada.

Entry requirements

As of January 2007, all visitors to the Bahamas require a **passport** to enter the country and it must be valid for at least six months beyond your planned departure from the islands. All citizens also require a return ticket and evidence of sufficient funds to support themselves while in the country. Citizens of US, British Commonwealth, Japan and EU countries do not require a visa to enter. Americans, Brits, Canadians, Australians and visitors from some EU countries (Belgium, Greece, Italy, Luxembourg and the Netherlands) may stay for up to eight months without a visa. Other EU nationals and citizens of Japan can enter for three months without a visa. All other nationals require a visa, obtainable from Bahamian embassies overseas. Visitors to the Bahamas are required to fill out standard immigration cards upon disembarkation that should be kept with other travel documents. The immigration card must be surrendered to Bahamian immigration authorities upon departure. Travel within the Bahamas is unrestricted, and no travel permits are required.

Bahamian embassies abroad

Canada High Commission for the Commonwealth of the Bahamas, 50 O'Connor St, Suite 1313, Ottawa, ON K1P 6L2 ☎613/232-1724, ✉ottawa-mission@bahighco.com.
UK and Ireland Bahamas High Commission, 10 Chesterfield St, London W1X 8AH ☎020/7408 4488.
US The Embassy of the Commonwealth of the Bahamas, 2220 Massachusetts Ave NW, Washington DC 20008 ☎202/319-2660.

Embassies and consulates in the Bahamas

Canada Canadian Consulate, Shirley Street Plaza, Nassau ☎393-2123.
UK and Ireland British Consulate, East Street, Nassau ☎325-7471.
US US Embassy, Queen Street, Nassau ☎322-1181.

Gay and lesbian travellers

Gay and lesbian travellers are unlikely to encounter overt discrimination in the Bahamas, where citizens generally subscribe to a "live and let live" philosophy of life. However, Bahamian society is generally very conservative and open displays of affection by same-sex couples are apt to draw attention and occasionally hostility. While the couples-only resort *Sandals* has been forced by international public pressure to drop their heterosexuals-only policy, the tourism industry in general does not go out of its way to welcome homosexual visitors. On several occasions in recent years fundamentalist Christian preachers have led demonstrations against gay cruise ships visiting Nassau and in 2006, the Bahamas Plays and Films Control Board banned the screening of the cowboy love story *Brokeback Mountain* in the Bahamas. The prime minister has made speeches denouncing homophobia in Bahamian society, but there remains no legal protection from discrimination in Bahamian law. Same-sex sexual activity between consenting adults in private is legal. However, sexual activity in a public place is an offence punishable by up to twenty years in prison. For further information, contact the Rainbow Alliance of the Bahamas (☏328-1816 and ☏380-1696, Ⓦwww.bahamianglad.tripod.com).

Health

The Bahamas present few major **health** issues for visitors. The quality of healthcare facilities is on par with those in the US, Canada and UK, and there are several private and government-funded hospitals and clinics in Nassau and Freeport. There are also private and government-run health clinics in the major settlements on each of the Out Islands, which have the capacity to transport patients to hospitals in Nassau or Freeport by air ambulance in the event of an emergency. Medical treatment can be very expensive, and it is strongly advised that you purchase traveller's health insurance (see p.46). Addresses and telephone numbers for medical clinics and hospitals are found throughout the Guide.

There are **pharmacies** in Freeport, Nassau and in the larger settlements on the Out Islands, but it is recommended that you carry sufficient supplies of any prescription medication and contact lens cleaning solutions for the duration of your trip. Be sure to bring a spare set of spectacles or contact lenses if you wear them.

There are no **vaccinations** required to enter the Bahamas unless you are coming from an area infected with yellow fever, in which case you need to have an International Health Certificate indicating that you have had immunization against yellow fever sometime in the past ten years.

Most Bahamians drink bottled water, which is relatively inexpensive and easily available throughout the islands. You don't need to fear ice cubes or water in bars and restaurants as everyone uses bottled water or a reverse osmosis purification system. The most serious health concerns for visitors to the Bahamas are overexposure to the powerful rays of the sun, which can cause sunburn and/or heat stroke; and insect bites, which are less debilitating, but nevertheless irritating.

Heat stroke

Heat stroke is a serious and sometimes fatal condition that can result from long periods of exposure to high temperatures. The tropical sun is intense and can fry unprotected skin to a crisp in short order. The wisest approach is to use a sunscreen with a high SPF (35 or over), not forgetting your lips, ears, eyelids, feet and around your nostrils, which can suffer a nasty burn from light reflected off the water. Wearing a wide-brimmed hat, sunglasses and covering exposed flesh with a long-sleeve shirt if you are spending a lot of time outdoors is also recommended. Above all, the best prevention is stay out of the sun as much as possible, and drink lots of water. Symptoms of heat stroke include nausea and general discomfort, fatigue, a high body temperature, severe headache, disorientation and/or little or no perspiration despite the heat. Eventually, the sufferer can become delirious and fall into convulsions, and rapid medical treatment is essential. First aid is to seek shade, remove the victim's clothing, wrap them in a cool, wet sheet or towels and fan the air around them.

Bites and stings

Insect **bites** from mosquitoes and sand fleas are not life-threatening – there is no malaria in the Bahamas – but can spoil an otherwise perfect night outside under the stars. Fortunately, they are easily dealt with by using insect repellent, covering up with light-coloured trousers and a long-sleeved shirt, and avoiding scented soaps, shampoos and perfumes, which bugs find very enticing. While they are generally not a problem in urban and resort areas, in less developed parts of the islands they are most vicious at dawn and dusk, so you might also just yield the battlefield to them at these times.

Though there are no poisonous snakes in the Bahamas, there are scorpions that can sting but are not life-threatening. If you go tramping around in the bush, you should also be wary of brushing against the **poisonwood tree**, the sap of which causes the skin to blister, swell and itch, much like poison ivy. It grows mainly in coastal areas, has shiny green leaves and a reddish, scaly bark, and is well known to local inhabitants, who can point it out to you.

Medical resources for travellers

US and Canada

CDC ☎1-877-394-8747, ⓦwww.cdc.gov/travel. Official US government travel health site.
International Society for Travel Medicine ☎1-770-736-7060, ⓦwww.istm.org. Has a full list of travel health clinics.
Canadian Society for International Health ⓦwww.csih.org. Extensive list of travel health centres.

Australia, New Zealand and South Africa

Travellers' medical and Vaccination Centre ⓦwww.tmvc.com.au, ☎1300/658 844. Lists travel clinics in Australia, New Zealand and South Africa.

UK and Ireland

British Airways Travel Clinics ☎0845/600 2236, ⓦwww.britishairways.com/travel /healthclinintro/public/en_gb for nearest clinic.
Hospital for Tropical Diseases Travel Clinic ☎0845/155 5000 or ☎020/7387 4411, ⓦwww.thehtd.org.

MASTA (Medical Advisory Service for Travellers Abroad) ⓦwww.masta.org or ☎0113/238 7575 for the nearest clinic.
Travel Medicine Services ☎028/9031 5220.
Tropical Medical Bureau Republic of Ireland ☎1850/487 674, ⓦwww.tmb.ie.

Insurance

You should always have **travel insurance** that covers you against theft, loss, illness and injury. Before paying for a new policy, however, it's worth checking whether you are already covered: some all-risks home insurance policies may cover your possessions when overseas, and many private medical schemes include cover when abroad. If you need to make a **claim**, you should keep receipts for medicines and medical treatment, and in the event you have anything stolen, you must obtain an official statement from the police confirming this.

If your existing policy does not cover your possessions and medical treatment, you might want to contact a specialist travel insurance company, or consider the travel insurance deal we offer. A typical travel insurance policy usually provides cover for the loss of baggage, tickets and – up to a certain limit – cash or cheques, as well as cancellation or curtailment of your journey. Most of them exclude so-called dangerous sports unless an extra premium is paid: in the Bahamas this can mean snorkelling, scuba diving and windsurfing, though probably not kayaking or jeep safaris. Rough Guides has teamed up with Columbus Direct to offer you **travel insurance** that can be tailored to suit your needs. Products include a low-cost **backpacker** option for long stays; a **short break** option for city getaways; a typical **holiday package** option; and others. There are also annual **multi-trip** policies for those who travel regularly. Different sports and activities (trekking, skiing, etc) can usually be covered if required.

For eligibility and purchasing options see our website (ⓦwww.roughguidesinsurance .com). Alternatively, UK residents should call ☎0870/033 9988; Australians should call ☎1300/669 999 and New Zealanders should call ☎0800/55 9911. All other nationalities should call ☎+44 870/890 2843.

Internet

Most of the larger hotels and resorts provide **Internet** access to their guests, either at a terminal in the lobby or by high-speed connection in guestrooms. Almost all of the Out Islands have at least one "Internet café" (maybe just a laptop propped up on the bar) and some BaTel Co offices have terminals for public use. However, getting online can be expensive, with rates typically ranging $5–10 for fifteen minutes. Listings for each island in the Guide contain addresses for local Internet access points.

Laundry

Most hotels and resorts provide a **laundry service** for guests, and listings for laundries are found in each chapter. Otherwise, marinas are a good bet to find a washing machine and dryer. Costs typically are about $1.50–2 per load in the washer or dryer.

Living in the Bahamas

Due to high levels of unemployment, it is not easy to obtain a **work permit** for the Bahamas. However, there are a few options if you want to really sink your teeth into the culture and stay a while. There is, for example, a shortage of qualified teachers in the country and you can contact schools directly about employment opportunities. A prospective employer in any field must demonstrate that they have conducted an exhaustive but unsuccessful search for a qualified Bahamian candidate and post a bond to cover the costs of shipping you home if you become incapacitated. Few are willing to go through the process.

Alternatively, a variety of marine **conservation organizations** offer paid, un-paid or you-pay internships for periods lasting a week to several months; see p.47. There is also a large **expatriate resident** community in the Bahamas. If you buy a residential property and have a big enough chunk of change to invest in the local economy ($500,000), you too can move here and set up a business or just lie on the sand. Specific questions about immigration can be addressed to the Bahamas Immigration Department (☎377-7032 or 377-6337).

Mail

In general, **post offices** are open Monday–Friday 8.30am–5.30pm. Larger post offices are full-service operations that sometimes offer telegraph and fax services. Assistance is generally friendly and efficient, though delivery can be somewhat slow. It is always a good idea to mail letters and parcels by airmail, for surface delivery is more unreliable.

Postcards to the US, UK, Canada, Europe and Australia cost 55¢, though don't be surprised if you make it home before your postcards do. In general, postcards take ten days to arrive in North America or Europe from Nassau, somewhat longer from Out Islands. Airmail letters cost 65¢ per half-ounce to those same destinations. All airmail parcels should be securely wrapped.

UPS, DHL and Federal Express have offices in Nassau and Freeport, and each has some agents on larger Out Islands. UPS offers 24-hour delivery and customs clearance to North America on parcels sent from Nassau.

Stamps are available from many hotel desks and gift shops, as well as from bookstores. Many of these souvenir shops will mail your postcards as well. Public mailboxes are very rare, and you should always hunt out the post office to mail your most important items. Bahamian postal rates for in-country service are 15¢ per half-ounce, 25¢ for each half-ounce thereafter. Remember that airmail packages and letters mailed from overseas to any Out Island probably go by airmail to Nassau, and then by boat to the specific destination, so mailing letters and parcels to Out Island destinations can be desperately slow.

Nassau's main post office on East Hill Street offers a **Post Restante** service. Letters may be addressed to you in Nassau in care of this general delivery service, and they will be held for three weeks. Letters should be marked "to be collected from the General Delivery desk". To receive a parcel in the Bahamas, you must collect it from Customs. Mail and telegrams can be received through American Express Travel Service in Nassau and Freeport by prior arrangement (☎1-800/221-7282).

Maps

Free and easy to follow **tourist maps** are widely available on the more developed islands. Most of the Out Islands have just a single main road, making it relatively easy to get around without getting lost. The best maps available for the islands are **nautical charts** for the Bahamian archipelago, which include not only info for boaters but detailed maps of the islands, including road systems, topography and landmarks. *Explorer Chartbook* (☎410/213-2725, ⓦwww .explorercharts.com) covers the Bahamas with three sets of detailed charts: Near Bahamas (northern islands); the Exumas; and the Far Bahamas (southern islands). Each set costs $50 and they are available at marinas and bookstores in the Bahamas or by direct order from the publisher.

Measurements

Bahamian **measurements** are made in the Imperial system, which uses inches, feet and miles, along with ounces, pounds and tons. Road maps show distances in miles and speed limits are denominated in miles per hour. All liquid measurements are in standard pints, quarts and gallons, which includes measurements at the petrol pump and pub.

Money

The **Bahamian dollar** is pegged to the US dollar, and both currencies are accepted throughout the country. Because all hotels and tourist facilities freely exchange both currencies, there is little need to formally change US dollars before travelling here. Plan on spending all of the Bahamian currency you receive as change before leaving the island, however, as you will have a hard time exchanging it outside the country. **Traveller's cheques** are widely accepted, although on islands where there is no bank (like Staniel Cay or Cat Island), the corner store may not be keen on taking a traveller's cheque that must be flown to another island to exchange. Major **credit cards** are accepted readily at most hotels, resorts, restaurants and shops on New Providence, Grand Bahama, the Abacos and Eleuthera. On some Out Islands, credit cards are not accepted or accepted with a surcharge,

and you should check with your destination hotel for information on card use. With only a couple of exceptions (noted in the guide to each island), ATMs dispensing American and Bahamian currency are widely available throughout the islands and connected to the Cirrus and Plus networks. If you plan on using your debit card or credit card at an ATM, make sure you have a personal identification number (PIN) that's designed to work overseas. In addition, most islands have one or more **banks** generally open 9.30am–3.00pm Mon–Thurs and 9.30am–4pm on Friday. In the Out Islands, some banks are only open one or two days a week; specific bank details are listed throughout the Guide.

Wiring money

Having **money wired** from home using one of the companies listed below is never convenient or cheap, and should be considered a last resort. It's also possible to have money wired directly from a bank in your home country to a bank in the Bahamas, although this is somewhat less reliable because it involves two separate institutions. If you go this route, your home bank will need the address of the branch bank where you want to pick up the money and the address and telex number of the Nassau head office, which will act as the clearing house; money wired this way normally takes two working days to arrive, and costs around $40 per transaction.

American Express Moneygram
US and Canada ☎1-800/926-9400, Australia ☎1800/230 100, New Zealand ☎09/379 8243 or 0800/262 263, UK and Republic of Ireland ☎0800/6663 9472, ⓦwww.moneygram.com.
Thomas Cook US ☎1-800/287-7362, Canada ☎1-888/823-4732, UK ☎01733/318 922 (Northern Ireland ☎028/9055 0030) Republic of Ireland ☎01/677 1721, ⓦwww.us.thomascook.com.
Western Union US and Canada ☎1-800/325-6000, Australia ☎1800/649 565, New Zealand ☎09/270 0050, UK ☎0800/833 833, Republic of Ireland ☎1800/395 395, ⓦwww.westernunion.com.

Opening hours and public holidays

Regular **business hours** at government and private offices are Mon–Fri 9am–5pm. Regular **banking hours** are Mon–Thurs

9.30am–3pm and Friday 9.30am–5pm, although there are some exceptions to this rule in smaller branches on the Out Islands as noted throughout the guide. Shops are generally open from 9am or 10am to 5.30pm or 6pm, Monday to Saturday. In most communities, at least one grocery store and petrol station will open for business early Sunday morning – 7.30 or 8am to 10.30am – and then close for the rest of the day. **Restaurants** are generally open seven days a week, although some are closed one day a week and/or close for a couple of hours in the late afternoon.

Public holidays

The following are **public holidays** in the Bahamas, and government offices, banks, schools and shops are generally closed. Note that holidays that fall on a Saturday or Sunday are usually observed on the previous Friday or following Monday.

New Year's Day January 1
Good Friday the Friday before Easter
Easter Monday the Monday after Easter
Whit Monday seven weeks after Easter
Labour Day first Friday in June
Independence Day July 10
Emancipation Day first Monday in August
National Heroes Day (formerly Discovery Day) October 12
Christmas December 25
Boxing Day December 26

Phones

Telephone and **email** service in the Bahamas has grown by leaps and bounds in the last decade. Most hotels have reliable phone service along with email capability, now direct-dial long distance between North America and Nassau, Grand Bahama, the Abacos, Andros, Berry and Bimini Islands, Eleuthera, Harbour Island, Spanish Wells, Exumas and Long Island is available. On the other hand, some of the more remote islands and cays still have limited phone service, often a single antiquated phone at the best hotel or lodge in the area. Much communication on these isolated cays is accomplished by radio.

Telephone services in the Bahamas are a monopoly of the government-owned Bahamas Telecommunications Corporation or **BaTelCo** (☎323-4911), with its national headquarters on John F. Kennedy Drive in Nassau. The centralized branch of BaTelCo is in downtown Nassau on East Street off Bay, and you'll find a local BaTelCo office in almost every town and settlement throughout the islands. Local and inter-island calls can be made from any hotel or BaTelCo office, as well as from a phone booth. There are many phone booths through out the Bahamas, even in the most remote settlement on the Out Islands. Those phone booths that are operational – and there are many which aren't – often accept Bahamian 25¢ pieces to make local calls or to reach the international assistance operator. Old booths operate by first dialling the number and then, when a tone appears, putting in the coin. Many newer phone booths are geared to accept **calling cards** – purchased from any BaTelCo office – issued by BaTelCo in the denominations of \$5,10, 20 and 50.

Making calls

Making within the Bahamas couldn't be simpler as the entire nation shares a **countrywide area code** (☎242). For local calls, simply dial the seven-digit phone number to be connected. For calls from one island to another, dial the countrywide area code plus 1 – ☎1-242 – and the seven-digit number. You'll need a BaTelCo calling card to make inter-island calls.

International calls may be made from many phone booths, from hotels, or from any BaTelCo office. Direct-dial international calls are offered by some phone booths, especially with calling cards, and from some hotels. In general, calls to the US are \$1 for the first minute, 80¢ thereafter. Calling Canada costs \$1.25/1.15, while rates to Europe average \$2.75/2. Costs to call Asia and Australia are considerably higher. Operator-assisted calls from hotels are expensive, and you can save money by calling home from abroad with a telephone charge card. Also keep in mind that most toll-free (800/866/877) numbers cannot be accessed from the Bahamas. Numbers with 1-880 prefixes cost about \$1 per minute to use.

Calling the Bahamas **from overseas** is also a breeze as the same rules apply as when calling the US. From the US or

Canada, simply dial 1 plus the area code, ☏242, and the seven-digit local number. From all other countries, dial 001-242, plus the seven-digit number.

If you bring a **cellphone** into the Bahamas you may be charged a temporary customs fee, refunded on exit. However, your cellphone will not send or receive in the Bahamas without first registering it for use on a roaming cellular line through BaTelCo. You can get a roaming cell number in advance from Cable and Wireless Caribbean Cellular (☏1-800/262-8366 in the US; ☏1-800/567-8366 in Canada; ☏268/480-2628 elsewhere). Cable and Wireless also arranges for cellular service from yachts and other vessels. You can establish a system for billing your cellular service to your credit card. It is also possible to rent a cellphone on some islands; see "Listings" for each island.

Calling cards

One of the most convenient ways of phoning home from abroad is via telephone **charge card** from your phone company back home. Using a PIN number, you can make calls from most hotel, public and private phones that will be charged to your account. Since most major charge cards are free to obtain, it's certainly worth getting one at least for emergencies; enquire first, though, whether your destination is covered, and bear in mind that rates aren't necessarily cheaper than calling from a public phone.

In the US and Canada, AT&T, MCI, Sprint, Canada Direct and other North American long-distance companies all enable their customers to make credit card calls while overseas, billed to your home number. Call

Calling home from abroad

US and Canada international access code + 1 + area code.
Australia international access code + 61 + city code.
New Zealand international access code + 64 + city code.
UK international access code + 44 + city code.
Republic of Ireland international access code + 353 + city code.
South Africa international access code + 27 + city code.

Note that the initial zero is omitted from the area code when dialing the UK, Ireland, Australia and New Zealand from abroad.

your company's customer service line to find out if they provide service from Bahamas and, if so, what the toll-free access code is.

In the UK and Ireland, British Telecom (☏0800/345 144, ✆www.chargecard.bt.com) will issue free to all BT customers the BT Charge Card, which can be used in 116 countries. NTL (☏0500/100 505) issues its own Global Calling Card, which can be used in more than sixty countries abroad, though the fees cannot be charged to a normal phone bill.

To call Australia and New Zealand from overseas, phone charge cards such as Telstra Telecard or Optus Calling Card in Australia, and Telecom NZ's Calling Card can be used to make calls abroad, which are charged back to a domestic account or credit card. Apply to Telstra (☏1800/038 000), Optus (☏1300/300 937), or Telecom NZ (☏04/801 9000).

Useful Bahamian phone numbers

Operator, International Calls ☏0
Countrywide area code ☏242
Weather Hotline ☏915
Directory Assistance ☏916
Time ☏917
Emergencies/Police/Fire ☏919 (Nassau), ☏911 (Freeport/Lucaya)

Photography

Film and memory cards are widely available in Nassau and Freeport and the larger Out Islands like Harbour Island and Great Exuma, although prices are generally higher than in the US and Europe. Basic photo **etiquette** applies to taking pictures of people in the Bahamas; always ask politely first, and you will rarely get turned down.

Bahamas Ministry of Tourism offices

US

Atlanta 2957 Clairmont Rd, NO. 150, Atlanta, GA 30345 ☏770/270-1500

Boston PO Box 1039, Boston, MA 02117 ☏617/485-0572

Charlotte 11133 Leaden Hall LN. Charlotte, NC 28213 ☏704/543-0091

Chicago 8600 W. Bryn Mawr Ave, Suite 820, Chicago, IL 60631 ☏773/693-1500

Dallas World Trade Center, 2050 Stemmons Freeway, Suite 116, Dallas, TX 75258 ☏214/742-1886

Fort Lauderdale 1100 Lee Wagener Blvd, Suite 204

Fort Lauderdale, FL 33315 ☏1-800/BAHAMAS or 1-800/224-3681, 954-359-8099

Los Angeles 3450 Wilshire Blvd, Suite 208, Los Angeles, CA 90010 ☏1-800/439-6993

Miami 1 Turnberry Place, 19495 Biscayne Blvd 809, Aventura, FL, 33180 ☏305/932-0051

New York 150 E 52nd St, NY 10022 ☏212/758-2777

Canada

Toronto 121 Bloor St E, Suite 1101, Toronto ON M4W 3M5 ☏416/968-2999 or toll-free 1-800/667-3777.

UK

London 10 Chesterfield St

London, W1J 5JL 020-7355-0800 020-7493-9031,ⓦwww.bahamas.co.uk

Surrey The Billings, Walnut Tree Close, Guildford, Surrey GU1 4UL ☏01483/448900

Time

The Bahamas is in North America's Eastern Standard Time Zone (the same as New York and Miami) and five hours behind Greenwich Mean Time (GMT).

Tourist information

Maps, hotel directories, slick colour brochures and additional **information** on the Bahamas is readily available from the official Bahamas Tourist Offices (see box, above). No tourist office acts as a reservation centre, though there is a Bahamas reservation office in North America (☏1-800/700-4752).

In addition to the Ministry of Tourism's information offices, the islands of New Providence and Grand Bahama have their own individual promotion boards. For New Providence information, contact the Nassau/Paradise Island Promotion Board (☏322-8383 or 1-800/327-9019, ⓦwww .nassauparadiseisland.com). Grand Bahama is represented by the Grand Bahama Island Promotion Board at the International Bazaar, PO Box F-40252, Freeport, Grand Bahama (☏352-8044 or 1-800/448-3386, ⓦwww .grand-bahama.com). Travellers interested in visiting the Out Islands should contact the Bahamas Out Islands Promotion Board (☏954-475-8315 or 1-800/OUT-ISLANDS; ⓦwww.boipb.com).

For exact locations and details on specific tourist information offices in the Bahamas, see the "Information" sections within the Guide.

Useful websites

An impressive array of **websites** can guide visitors through a wealth of information on airfares, accommodation, eco-tours, cultural events, excursions and more. The list below highlights a few of the best.

ⓦ**www.bahamas.com** The Bahamas Ministry of Tourism site, covering everything from travel info, watersports and accommodation to local cuisine.

ⓦ**www.bahamasnet.com** Comprehensive website with details on accommodation, activities and restaurants, and a calendar of events.

ⓦ **www.bahamas-on-line.com** Directory of restaurants, accommodation, dive shops and more.
ⓦ **www.caribbeanaviation.com** Very up-to-date and comprehensive website detailing charter and scheduled airlines serving the Caribbean.
ⓦ **www.cruisecritic.com** Detailed reviews of cruise ships serving the Caribbean.
ⓦ **www.interknowledge.com/bahamas** A site that includes a clickable map for virtual island hopping.
ⓦ **www.roughguides.com** Post any of your pre-trip questions – or post-trip suggestions – in Travel Talk, our online forum for travellers.

Travellers with disabilities

The Bahamas are gradually upgrading public facilities to meet international standards of access for people with physical **disabilities**, but travelling in the islands can still pose some (not insurmountable) challenges. Public transport is not adapted to accommodate wheelchairs, and broken pavement or non-existent sidewalks can make getting around somewhat difficult. Few older multi-storey buildings are wheel-chair-accessible, though the newer resorts in Nassau and Freeport are equipped with ramps and elevators with braille signage and bells, and many hotels have handi-capped-accessible rooms.

The following two organizations can offer advice and information on the facilities of hotels and cruise lines in the Bahamas.
Bahamas Council for the Handicapped ☎ 322- 4260.
Bahamas Association for the Physically Disabled ☎ 322-2393, ℻ 322-7984. Provides a minibus service for disabled visitors and offers guided tours of Nassau and New Providence.

Guide

Guide

1

New Providence and Paradise Island

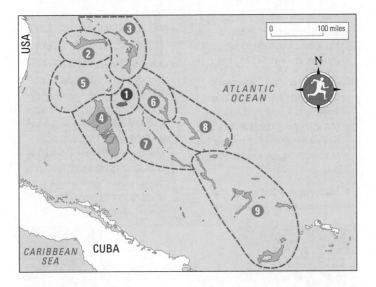

CHAPTER 1 # Highlights

✳ **Pompey Museum of Slavery and Emancipation** This fine museum documents in pictures, artefacts and their own words the bleak history of the thousands of people who lived and died as slaves in the Bahamas. See p.74

✳ **The Straw Market** Rummage through handcrafted baskets, shell jewellery, carved mahogany dolphins and Chinese-made trinkets at Nassau's huge open-air craft market. See p.74

✳ **Junkanoo** Join the crowds on Boxing Day (Dec 26) or New Year's Day and see the marching bands, dancers and the whole colourful pageant of Nassau's biggest celebration. See p.76

✳ **National Art Gallery of the Bahamas** Once the British governor's mansion, the National Gallery has been beautifully restored as a showcase for Bahamian visual artists, and offers an interesting programme of lectures and discussions on the island's art scene. See p.81

✳ **Arawak Cay** On weekends, the waterside seafood shacks here, just west of downtown Nassau, jump with local music and lots of fresh fish and conch salad. See p.82

✳ **Atlantis Resort** The highlights of this jaw-droppingly decadent resort – seemingly shipped straight from Vegas – are its marvellous Aquarium and Predator Lagoon, a massive manmade pool filled with sharks and reef fish complete with a transparent underwater observation tunnel. See p.93

△ The Aquarium, Atlantis Resort

New Providence and Paradise Island

NEW PROVIDENCE is the thumping heart of the Bahamian archipelago. Despite its tiny size – just 21 miles long and seven miles wide – the island holds more than two-thirds of the country's population as well as its capital, **Nassau**, a thriving city of around 190,000 residents. Initially settled in the seventeenth century for its sheltered harbour and strategic location on the shipping route between the New World and Europe, the island has variously served as a refuge for pirates and privateers, a base for smuggling African slaves, illegal booze and drugs, and a haven for fishermen, and is now a buzzing centre of offshore banking and tourism. Nearly two million holiday-makers arrive annually to soak up the sun at New Providence's resort enclaves at Cable Beach and Paradise Island, a small cay situated just offshore, and billions of dollars flow through Nassau's financial institutions, as evidenced in the shiny yachts and palatial villas that line the island's shores.

Situated on the northeastern side of the island, the high-rises of downtown Nassau spread over a gentle slope climbing up from the harbour. Tourist action is focused around **Prince George Wharf** and along **Bay Street**, a block inland from the water. Duty-free shopping hits fever pitch here when the hulking cruise ships are in port, looming above the rooftops of the waterfront market and shops. The grand edifices of Nassau's colonial period surround **Rawson Square** and look down on the harbour from hillside perches. The modern city spreads up and over the hill, covering the whole eastern half of the island in featureless suburban sprawl. East and west of the city centre, crumbling colonial fortifications stand sentinel on sun-baked ridge tops.

Two long toll bridges a mile east of downtown Nassau connect the city centre to **PARADISE ISLAND**, a glitzy tourist enclave centred on the mega-resort *Atlantis*. Paradise Island's main natural attractions are **Cabbage Beach** and **Paradise Beach**, covering most of the north coast and offering soothing vistas of deep blue water and gentle trade winds that cool even the hottest of afternoons.

West of Nassau, lovely **Cable Beach**, with its powdery white sand, lies completely surrounded by high-rise hotels, exclusive resorts, private estates, condominiums and time shares. This area has a permanent holiday atmosphere, offering those in search of fun and relaxation the comforts of poolside bar service, fine dining, a wide array of water sports and nightly entertainment.

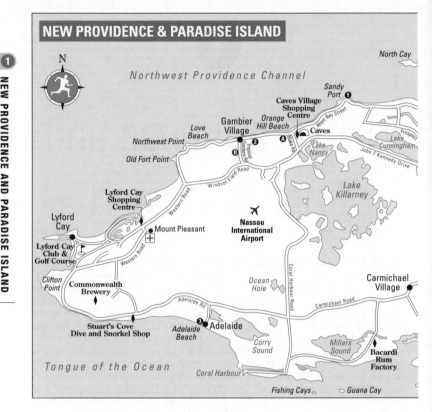

West of Cable Beach, the shore opens up. The coastal road passes through a couple of luxury residential developments en route to semi-wild **Orange Hill Beach**, a particularly appealing spot. On the western tip of the island is exclusive **Lyford Cay**, where celebrities and the moneyed class live in hermetically sealed luxury. New Providence's **south shore** has a few unkempt beaches and isolated settlements. Its main attractions lie offshore, along lush, vibrantly coloured reefs and precipitous underwater walls that draw large numbers of divers. Although the **central interior** of New Providence is mainly marshy scrub, adventurous nature aficionados can bushwhack the area around **Lake Killarney** in pursuit of rare birds, or join organized nature and cycling tours.

The blowsy, party-hearty persona of modern New Providence can sometimes obscure its genuinely courteous Bahamian character and natural beauty. As a visitor, you have three choices: embrace it and enjoy the casinos, limbo contests, duty-free shopping and plush high-rise hotels; block out the tinny goombay music and tacky souvenir stands and immerse yourself instead in Nassau's fascinating cultural heritage, the wealth of outdoor excursions on offer, the opportunities for fine dining and the quiet stretches of beach that lie outside the city centre; or admit defeat and hop on a plane to the Out Islands, where ordinary life is easier to find.

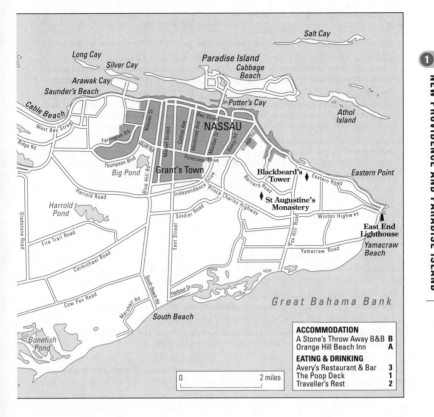

ACCOMMODATION
A Stone's Throw Away B&B **B**
Orange Hill Beach Inn **A**

EATING & DRINKING
Avery's Restaurant & Bar **3**
The Poop Deck **1**
Traveller's Rest **2**

Some history

Long after the Spaniards had abducted and enslaved the indigenous Arawaks from the Bahamian islands but years before the first package tour, the first foreign visitor to New Providence was Bermudian **William Sayle**, who, armed with permission from the English crown, arrived in 1648 and attached his own name to the island before moving on to Eleuthera to found his doomed colony. Sayle's Island possessed a fine anchorage, protected by a string of offshore cays and reefs. Here, on a piece of flat ground facing the sea, **Charles Town** – modern-day Nassau – was established in 1666, named in honour of the reigning English king. By 1670, the population numbered three hundred English settlers who scrounged a living from the sea gathering ambergris, salt and wreck goods and denuding the island's once dense forests for timber.

The winds of war that swept across Europe in the seventeenth and eighteenth centuries were keenly felt in Charles Town, which was simultaneously claimed by England and Spain. With England, Spain and France almost constantly at war with one another, the seas were awash with pirates and privateers, who overran the nascent colony and made the town a "stinking hole" of dirt streets, brothels and taverns. The first governor of the island, appointed by the Six Lord Proprietors of Carolina (a private trading company established with the authority of the British crown;) in 1670 to oversee their commercial interests there,

Salvagers in New Providence

Since 1648, when the Eleutheran Adventurers (see p.215) first came to Bahamian shores, Bahamians have been **salvaging ships** and their cargoes wrecked on the rocks and reefs of the shallow seas that surround the islands. One of the first acts of the Eleutherans was to establish *Articles and Orders* governing the wrecking industry. As trade increased in the islands, and between North America and England, Nassau's wrecking industry took off, and, circa 1815, many in town had wrecking as their second calling. At the call of "Wrack Ashore", farmers dropped their hoes, fishermen their nets and carpenters their hammers to board a wrecking vessel.

By 1856, 302 ships out of Nassau were licensed to engage in salvage, and nearly ten percent of the population held individual salvage licences. The bulk of salvage went through Nassau's Vendue House, with the proceeds at auction divided among the government, warehousemen, agents, wreckers and, finally, if lucky, the owners.

reported with disgust that the residents lived "a lewd, licentious sort of life". When he tried to set them right, they marched him aboard a ship and sent him off to Jamaica. In 1684, Spaniards attacked Charles Town and plundered it in retribution for constant attacks launched by pirates against their shipping. The settlement – newly christened Nassau in honour of William of Orange-Nassau who ascended the English throne in 1695 – was sacked again in 1703 by a combined French and Spanish fleet.

The first British royal governor, **Governor Woodes-Rogers**, was a tough former privateer who had once rescued sailor Alexander Selkirk – the inspiration for Daniel Defoe's novel *Robinson Crusoe* – from the deserted island where he had been stranded for four years. Arriving in Nassau in 1718, he found the place in a shambles and immediately set the residents to work cleaning up and ridding it of pirates and filth. Edward "Blackbeard" Teach and many of his murderous peers who had found Nassau a congenial base were hunted down and killed. Sensing a change in the atmosphere, others saw the error of their ways and transformed themselves into upstanding citizens. Unfortunately for Woodes-Rogers, his efforts left him personally bankrupt and earned him a stay in a London debtor's prison and an early death from ill health.

One of Woodes-Rogers' successors, **Governor William Shirley**, was responsible for laying out a grid of streets, draining swamps and organizing agricultural plantations in the 1760s. The American Revolution further boosted the city's fortunes as former pirates and privateers turned to running the English blockade to trade with the Americans. At the same time, many **Loyalists** from America fled to Nassau, bringing with them new energy and a new architectural style, visible in the grand limestone houses lining the leafy residential streets climbing the hill. Additional streets were laid out, docks were built, a new jail and workhouse constructed and a city market established.

Arriving with the Loyalists was the dissolute **Earl of Dunmore** (see box, p.236), who in 1787 became royal governor. Dunmore surrounded himself in Nassau with thieves and hangers-on, and promptly went on a spending spree that nearly bankrupted the treasury. His legacy includes forts Fincastle and Charlotte. Nassau settled into its existence as a provincial backwater where Loyalist planters lived languid lives, amassing small fortunes from the sweat of **African slaves**. Whilst not on the scale of the sugar- and cocoa-producing Caribbean islands (due more to the Bahamas' poor soil rather than an enlightened populace), slavery was nonetheless the foundation of the Loyalist economy in Nassau, and at least 4000 slaves inhabited New Providence in the late eighteenth century.

Most of them were brought over from sub-Saharan West Africa, particularly from modern Nigeria, Dahomey, Togo and Ghana. In 1804, the last slave sales were recorded in Nassau, and in 1833 parliament passed the Abolition Statute. Slavery formally ended in the Bahamas in September 1834.

During the nineteenth century, Nassau's economic fortunes rose and fell in accordance with events in the United States. Construction in Nassau boomed during the American Civil War as local entrepreneurs were only too happy to supply the rebellious American South with arms and stores. The first wealthy tourists arrived in Nassau during the heyday of the **Royal Victorian Hotel** in the 1870s, which was filled to capacity every winter. In 1900, tycoon Henry Flagler, having made millions in real estate and railroad construction in Florida, turned his attention to Nassau and built the magnificent **British Colonial Hotel**, which set the resort standard here until it burned in 1922. Less than eight months later, the **New Colonial Hotel** rose in its place, built, some say, with revenues from rum running and smuggling during **Prohibition**. Thanks in part to Prohibition, the mid-1920s witnessed a land boom in Nassau, with many of the large estates to the west of the city built during this period. It was the development of the mass tourist industry and congenial banking regulations that kicked Nassau's economy into high gear. Air service was established between Nassau and Florida in 1929 – just in time for the Great Depression, although World War II quickly revived Nassau's fortunes. Far from the battlefields, Nassau was a glamorous destination for the upper classes during the war, with the Duke and Duchess of Windsor installed at the governor's mansion.

The post-war Bahamian-born Minister of Finance, **Sir Stafford Sands**, has been credited with laying the groundwork for Nassau's modern tourist industry, aided by the invention of air conditioning. The construction of new hotels began in the mid 1950s, coupled with the laying out of Nassau's **International Airport** in 1957 and, finally, the dredging of a deepwater harbour during the 1960s. In 1964, the first casinos opened, and *Life* magazine reported that gambling "has proved a bigger tourist attraction than all the sun and sea and French perfume and duty-free liquor put together". Sands liked to predict that Nassau would host one million tourists by 1970, a number that was reached two years ahead of schedule. A decade later, after the construction of the **Paradise Island Bridge** and the development of the **Cable Beach** hotel strip, the city was receiving twice that number. One wonders what Blackbeard would think of his ramshackle town now.

Arrival

Nassau International Airport (☎ 377-7281) is the hub of international and Bahamian air transport and is located in the west-central part of New Providence, a fifteen-minute taxi ride from downtown Nassau and ten minutes from Cable Beach. While there are no buses from the airport, there are plenty of **taxis**, with the fare for two people to Orange Hill Beach $9, Cable Beach $15, downtown Nassau $22 and Paradise Island $27 (plus the $2 bridge toll). Current rates are posted on a billboard at the taxi stand at the airport. The **Paradise Island Airport** serves small private and charter aircraft, with short runways and limited facilities.

Cruise ships arriving in Nassau dock at Prince George Wharf at the foot of Rawson Square in downtown Nassau, within walking distance of all the

Marinas

Nassau Harbour is ringed by eight full-service **marinas**, all of which are official ports of entry. Dockage rates are in the range of $2 to $7 per foot per day. All monitor VHF 16.

Atlantis Marina Paradise Island ☎363-6068, ⓦwww.atlantis.com. Room for boats up to 220ft long, but don't bother if your tub is less than 40ft – it only takes big and showy.

Bayshore Marina Nassau ☎393-7873. Twelve slips, fuel, power, water; minimum draw 6ft.

East Bay Marina between the two Paradise Island Bridges, East Bay Street, Nassau ☎394-1816. Twenty-five slips, water, ice, electricity and showers.

Harbour Central Marina Nassau ☎323-2172. Dinghy tie-up, fuel and water.

Hurricane Hole Marina Paradise Island ☎363-3600, ⓦwww.hurricaneholemarina .com. Ninety slips and on-site *Green Parrot Bar and Grill*; near shops and hotels.

Lyford Cay Harbour Lyford Cay ☎362-4131. At the west end of New Providence with water, fuel, electricity and shops nearby; non-members are welcome to stay up to four days.

Nassau Harbour Club and Marina ☎393-0771, ⓦwww.nassauharborclub.com. Sixty-five slips with fifty hotel rooms harbourside.

Nassau Yacht Haven East Bay Street ☎393-8173, ⓦwww.nassauyachthaven.com. One hundred slips accommodating vessels up to 150ft with a draw of 18ft; *Poop Deck Restaurant* and *Bahama Divers* dive shop on site.

sights and shopping in Historic Nassau. **Bahamas Fast Ferries** from Exuma, Eleuthera, Andros and Abaco dock at the west end of **Potter's Cay**, a mile east of the downtown; the **mailboats** coming and going from all of the Out Islands dock at the east end of Potter's Cay. From here you can catch a taxi into town or hop on a bus ($1) heading downtown from a stop on Shirley Street.

Information

The Ministry of Tourism (☎302-2000 or 1–800/Bahamas, ⓦwww .bahamas.com) operates **information booths** at the airport (Mon–Fri 9am–5pm; ☎377-6806) and in downtown Nassau at Festival Place (Mon–Fri 9am–5pm, also Sat & Sun same hours when cruise ships are in port; ☎323-3182). The Nassau-Paradise Island Tourism Board (☎322-8381, ⓦwww.nassauparadiseisland.com) maintains a website and dispenses information by telephone.

For entertainment listings and discount coupons, look for the ubiquitous, free, tourist-oriented magazines and tabloids such as *Where to Dine*, *Where to Shop* and *What's On*; this last has an infrequently updated website, ⓦwww .whatsonbahamas.com. Free **maps** are widely available in hotel lobbies and shops; the most detailed is the *Trailblazer* map published by Etienne Dupuch Ltd (ⓦwww.bahamasnet.com). The Island Shoppe on Bay Street (☎322-4183) has a well-stocked second-floor bookstore carrying books by Bahamian authors and about the Bahamas as well as a selection of international bestsellers. Check out local news in the daily *Nassau Guardian* newspaper (ⓦwww.thenassauguardian.com).

Sports and outdoor activities

Surrounded on all sides by coral reefs and set in a glittering sapphire ocean, New Providence and Paradise Island give water-lovers plenty of room to play. Experienced **divers** gravitate to New Providence's South Beach area for its deep water walls, wrecks and reefs, while **snorkellers** find lots to see along the shallow water reefs ringing the northwest coast and the smaller cays nearby, accessible by boat excursions offered by a number of operators. **Anglers** also

Beaches on New Providence and Paradise Island

New Providence and Paradise Island have a variety of beaches for swimmers and sunbathers to sample. Most stretches of the sugary white sand that rims the island have been heavily developed, although there are a few half-wild strands left. The more heavily populated patches fronting the high-rise hotels of Cable Beach and Paradise Island offer the compensation of bar service and sunloungers.

The city beach for Nassau is the **Western Esplanade**, extending roughly from the *British Colonial Hilton* in the east all the way to Arawak Cay in the west. While sometimes roughed up with garbage and litter and subject to noise on busy West Bay Street which runs alongside, the beach itself is OK, and provides nearby hotel guests with a patch of sand

Just past the Western Esplanade, **Saunders Beach** stretches for half a mile beneath casuarina trees. It's a popular weekend hangout for locals, who set up barbecue rigs and drink beer, but is still less crowded than Cable Beach and those on Paradise Island.

Further west sits silky-soft **Cable Beach**, perhaps the most famous of the New Providence beaches. The four-mile-long strip is backed by massive resort hotels and condo developments and permanently littered with sunbathers, parasailers and jetskis.

Just west of the Caves Village Shopping Centre and the airport turn-off, **Orange Hill Beach** begins, with parking on the side of the road. This lovely undeveloped white-sand beach stretches for about half a mile from the *Orange Hill Beach Inn* to the *Traveller's Rest* restaurant and is never crowded, making it a nice spot for a swim, picnic and stroll in the surf. To get there, just hop on a westbound #10 bus ($1) anywhere along West Bay Street.

More isolated and harder to get to without a car, private **Old Fort Beach** lies a fifteen-minute drive west of the airport, near the fashionable enclave of Lyford Cay. Though windy and cool in the winter, the beach is a paradise in summer. Even more remote is breezy **Adelaide Beach**, which runs on both sides of Adelaide village on the south shore and offers good white sand to the few who venture in this direction (the infrequent #12 bus travels from downtown Nassau to Adelaide). **South Beach** is Nassau's beach of choice for the Over-the-Hill gang and is reached directly from that Nassau neighbourhood via Fox Hill Road. On weekends it is wall-to-wall with people, while on weekdays it is nearly deserted.

Over on smaller Paradise Island, blush-coloured **Cabbage Beach** runs for three miles along the northeast coast. At its western end sits the hulking *Atlantis Resort*; at the eastern tip, the exclusive *One and Only Ocean Club* – a luxury resort, golf course and gated community. In between is an expanse of public beach, accessible from Casino Drive by a short path through the trees. A more appealing, less heavily trampled stretch of sand is **Paradise Beach**, accessible from the northside of the Atlantis Sports Centre, although you may have to pick your way through a construction site as *Atlantis* continues its expansion eastward. Not to be forgotten, the beaches of pretty **Rose Island** are a popular day-trip destination for snorkelling and picnicking (see p.64 for excursions).

have a wealth of options to chose from. Sadly, the heavy industrial development of New Providence over the past fifty years has taken its toll on the surrounding marine life, and nature's vibrant colours have dulled somewhat. Land-based diversions include **golf**, **tennis**, off-road **cycling** tours and **birdwatching** in the interior of the island.

Boat excursions

The Bahamas are all about the sea, and the best way to experience it is aboard a **boat**. In addition to the excursions listed below and with the exception of Bahamas Fast Ferries, all of the companies listed here also offer crewed boat charters (sailboat or powerboat) for groups, weddings and other special occasions. Think in the region of $2000 a day. Most boat trips leave from either the Paradise Island ferry terminal or one of the Nassau marinas, but most also provide transportation from your hotel to the dock.

Bahamas Fast Ferries Potter's Cay ☎ 323-2166, ⓦ www.bahamasferries.com. Day trips to historic Dunmore Town on Harbour Island, off Eleuthera, including a walking tour, lunch, and cabana facilities on lovely Pink Sand Beach. $169.

Barefoot Sailing Adventures Nassau ☎ 393-0820, ⓦ www.barefootsailingcruises.com. A real sailing excursion (ie no engine noise) with a small group, to Rose Island and nearby cays, for snorkelling and a beach BBQ. Half-day outings $55, full day with picnic $89, sunset champagne cruises on Wed and Fri $49.

Flying Cloud Catamaran Cruises Paradise Island Ferry Terminal ☎ 363-4430, ⓦ www.bahamasnet .com/flyingcloud. The *Flying Cloud* makes half-day sailing and snorkelling excursions to Rose Island ($60, departures 9.30am and 2pm daily except Mon morning and Sun), plus evening cruises ($60, departure 6pm), and a five-hour Sunday outing to Rose Island including snorkelling and a BBQ lunch on the beach ($75, departure 10am).

Island World Adventures Paradise Island Ferry Terminal ☎ 363-3333 or (after 6pm) 357-7782, ⓦ www.islandworldadventures.com. Zoom by powerboat to uninhabited Saddle Cay in the northern Exumas, where you spend the day swimming, snorkelling and eating. $190.

Majestic Tours tour desks at most major hotels in Nassau, Cable Beach and Paradise Island ☎ 322-2606, ⓦ www.majesticholidays.com. A long menu of daily excursions around Nassau, including a popular "Robinson Crusoe" cruise to nearby Rose Island (Wed, Fri & Sat; $50) featuring snorkelling, beach lounging and island exploration fuelled by a boozy picnic lunch. Also offers a three-hour double-decker motorized catamaran cruise with food, drink and live calypso music ($25; does not include transfer from your hotel); and the *Majestic Lady* Dinner Cruise (Tues & Fri evenings; $55).

Powerboat Adventures based at Nassau Harbour Club ☎ 363-1466, ⓦ www .powerboatadventures.com. Exhilarating day trips to Allen's Cay and Ship Channel Cay in the northern Exumas by high-speed powerboat, with time for snorkelling, a visit to the resident iguanas, an elaborate picnic lunch on the beach, a nature walk and relaxation. Recommended. $190.

Sea Island Adventures ☎ 325-3910, ⓦ www .seaislandadventures.com. Full-day excursions to Rose Island, including snorkelling, use of kayaks, beach volleyball and other games, and picnic lunch. $70.

Diving and snorkelling

Long reefs and deep drop-off walls line the south coast of New Providence, shallow reefs fringe the western side, and a few hundred-year-old wrecks are scattered here and there, making Nassau an interesting destination for **divers**. Along the South Wall where the Tongue of the Ocean eats away at the Great Bahama Bank, the ocean floor abruptly drops off from 50ft to 6500 ft, creating a rich and challenging venue for divers, clothed in hard and soft corals and populated by colourful schools of grunts and parrotfish, stingrays and reef sharks. Popular shallow-water dive sites include the Elkhorn Gardens off Lyford Cay, where photogenic copses of lacy elkhorn, star and brain coral provide a backdrop for passing stingrays and nurse sharks. Underwater scenes in several movies have been filmed here, including *20,000 Leagues Under the Sea*, *Splash* and *Cocoon*. Another magical place is the Fish Hotel, a flat circular reef of waving seawhips and seafans at depths of ten to 35 feet that is home to yellow and blue-striped grunts and silvery Bermuda chub. One of the more unusual dive sites surrounding the island is the **Lost Blue Hole**, a shallow crater in the ocean floor ringed by colourful clumps of sponges and coral frequented by sergeant majors, angel fish, giant southern stingrays, eels and sharks. Two of the most popular and well-established operators are listed below. Both provide transportation from your hotel to the dock.

Bahama Divers Nassau Yacht Haven, East Bay St ☎393-5644 or (in the US and Canada) 1-800/398-DIVE, ⓦwww.bahamadivers.com. A reputable outfit, established thirty years, offering a diverse range of reef, wreck, wall and blue hole dives as well as certification courses, with multi-day packages available. Two-tank dives each morning ($89) and one-tank in the afternoon ($55). Open-water referrals $249 and complete PADI certification $499. Half-day snorkelling outings $39. Prices include hotel pick-up.

Stuart's Cove Dive Bahamas Coral Harbour ☎362-4171 or (in the US and Canada)

1-800 /879-9832, ⓦwww.stuartcove.com. The island's largest operator, with 26 years' experience, running an extensive menu of snorkelling and diving excursions and certification courses, with hotel pick-up. In addition, it offers underwater field trips on one-person submarines that look like a cross between a motor scooter and a space suit ($99). Two-tank dives $99; full-day excursions to dive the Andros Barrier Reef $185; PADI certification course $425; and a range of speciality dives including night dives and diving with sharks. Packages are available. Half-day snorkelling excursions by boat $55.

Fishing

For many visitors, the lure of **sport fishing** off New Providence is irresistible, although those coming to the Bahamas with a steady diet of fishing in mind usually head for the Out Islands. New Providence's inshore waters attract grouper and snapper, while the deep waters of the Tongue of the Ocean southwest of Nassau provide a terrific habitat for tuna, bonito, blue marlin and more. You can also troll for wahoo and dorado, cast the shallows for snapper, grouper, amberjack and yellowtail, bottom fish by anchor and even fly-fish for the odd bonefish here and there. The drawback is that deep-sea angling is expensive. Parties of two to six can expect to pay at least $450 to $700 for half-day and upwards of $900 for full-day charters with the customary tip for the guide on top. Almost all the big hotels will make arrangements for guests to go fishing. All of the charter fishing outfits listed below also do sightseeing and snorkelling tours for around the same rates. The vessels used carry five ($700 half-day) to twenty people ($1400 half-day) for sightseeing.

Born Free Charters ☎393 4144, ⓦwww .bornfreefishing.com.
Brown's Charters ☎324-2061, ⓦwww .brownscharter.com.
Chubasco Fishing Charters ☎324 3474, ⓦwww.chubascocharters.com.

Hunter's Charters ☎364-1546, ⓦwww .huntercharters.com.
Paradise Island Charters Hurricane Hole Marina ☎363-4458, ⓦwww.paradise-island-charters.com.
Sterling's Fishing Guide ☎333-3418 or cell 464-0340.

Golf and tennis

Visitors to Nassau have two **golf** courses to choose from. The *Cable Beach Golf Course* (daily 7am–5.15pm; ☎327-1741, ⓦwww.cablebeachresorts.com) is open to the public for $135 and upwards, with reduced rates for guests at the

Radisson Hotel; club rental is $30 a day. On Paradise Island, the *Ocean Club Golf Course* (☎363-6682) is for guests of *Atlantis* and the *Ocean Club* exclusively; its many sandtraps include one billed as the world's largest. The *South Ocean* course, in the southwest corner of the island at the defunct *South Ocean Golf and Beach Resort*, is currently closed.

If your hotel doesn't have a **tennis court**, you can get in a game at the Nassau Beach Hotel Tennis Centre (daily 9am–10pm; $7 an hour per court; ☎327-7111) in Cable Beach, which has three courts lit for night play.

Nature tours

While its shoreline is heavily developed, New Providence's interior is spotted with shallow lakes and scrub that appeal to several dozen species of indigenous and migratory birds, including the loggerhead kingbird and the La Sangra flycatcher, among others. The **Bahamas National Trust Retreat** (see p.84) offers an oasis of natural beauty in the city where you can take a self-guided tour of Bahamian flora and fauna. The Trust also organizes monthly bird-watching outings; call ☎393-1317 for details. In addition, **Bahamas Outdoors** (☎362-1574, ⓦwww.bahamasoutdoors.com) runs birdwatching tours, nature hikes and cycling day trips in New Providence's little visited interior, with group size limited to six people. A half-day guided tour is $59 per person, full-day outings are $99. If you can't drum up any more nature enthusiasts, a personal tour is $100/$150 a half-/full day. The tours cover local plantlife and traditional bush medicine, as well as butterflies and birds.

Dolphins and horses

One of the most popular activities is run by **Dolphin Encounters** (☎363-1003, ⓦ www.dolphinencounters.com), which runs four trips a day to visit and swim with the dolphins at Blue Lagoon Island, leaving Paradise Island ferry terminal. Trips are priced according to proximity to a dolphin – observation is $20, "close encounter" (giving the dolphin a pat on the back while standing next to it in the water) is $85, while swimming with it $165.

For **horseriding**, head to Happy Trails Stables at Coral Harbour (☎362-1820, ⓦwww.windsorequestriancentre.com; $110 including hotel pick-up; reservations required), which offers ninety-minute rides through the woods and onto the beach. Children must be 12 years or older.

Nassau

Prosperous and compact, the easily negotiable city of **NASSAU** is an effervescent blend of British colonial architecture and modern convenience. Though its population of about 200,000 – including suburban sprawl – occupies most of the eastern half of the island, the Nassau most visitors see is a mere square mile of shops, government buildings, offices, parks, restaurants and museums. This part of town, **Historic Nassau**, which comprises the core of downtown Nassau, extends for perhaps ten or twelve blocks on flat

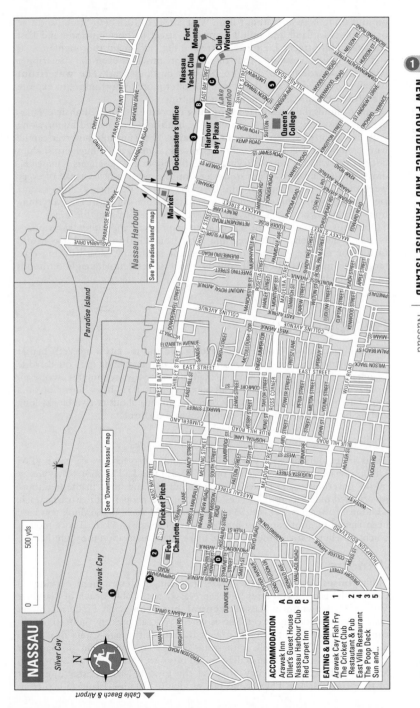

NASSAU

Silver Cay

Arawak Cay

Paradise Island

Nassau Harbour

Casuarina Drive

Paradise Beach Drive

Casino

Paradise Island Drive

Harbour Road

Bayview Drive

Drive

See 'Paradise Island' map

Market

Dockmaster's Office

Harbour Bay Plaza

Nassau Yacht Club

Fort Montagu

Club Waterloo

Lake Waterloo

Queen's College

See 'Downtown Nassau' map

Cricket Pitch

Fort Charlotte

N

500 yds

▲ Cable Beach & Airport

ACCOMMODATION
Arawak Inn — A
Dillet's Guest House — D
Nassau Harbour Club — B
Red Carpet Inn — C

EATING & DRINKING
Arawak Cay Fish Fry — 1
The Cricket Club Restaurant & Pub — 2
East Villa Restaurant — 3
The Poop Deck — 4
Sun and... — 5

ground along Nassau Harbour from West Street to Elizabeth Street, and five or six blocks inland and uphill from Bay Street to Fort Fincastle and East and West Hill Streets. Taking Bay Street – the city's main thoroughfare – as a starting point, a walking tour of the sights provides even the day tripper with an opportunity to dig into Nassau's bustling heart. The **waterfront districts** east and west of the city centre offer more opportunities to explore the island's history and contemporary culture.

Nassau affords the most varied **shopping** opportunities in the Bahamas, ranging from jewellery and art to straw goods, hand-rolled cigars and liquor, along with the country's widest range of **restaurants**. These pursuits, however, can be hampered by the fact that, several times a week, as many as six huge cruise ships dock at the wharf – some carrying up to five thousand passengers – expelling droves of sun-and-fun seekers to descend on the city. For at least half of every week then, Nassau is jammed with bermuda-shorted passengers taking advantage of the town's limited facilities, meaning queues can form for everything from sitting down to eat to buying a postcard to even crossing the street.

Oblivious to most of the cruise-ship passengers and other vacationers, Nassau is also a city with a real life away from tourism, a workaday world focused on finance and banking, government and family. Most working-class locals live in **Over-the-Hill**, and in the vast residential neighbourhoods east of the city.

Getting around

The compactness of Nassau makes **getting around** the city a breeze. Whether one is staying in downtown Nassau, out at Cable Beach, or over on Paradise Island, no major destination is more than fifteen or twenty minutes away, even in heavy traffic, and the city is easily negotiated by taxi, jitney, surrey or on a tour. The historic centre of Nassau occupies an area about twelve blocks long and six blocks deep, and can be easily explored **on foot**.

Taxis

Taxis are ubiquitous, with almost all hotels and resorts having taxi stands (Taxi Union dispatchers can be reached on ☎322-5111 and 323-4555). Rates are set by the government and posted outside the airport and listed in the free tourist-oriented publications. The rates are set for two people with two bags each; additional passengers will cost $3 and extra bags $1 each. If you think you have been ripped off (not common practice, but it happens), call the Taxi Union. If you're travelling early in the morning, make a taxi reservation the night before.

Jitneys

Public **buses**, known as jitneys, are frequent and convenient, serving all parts of the island, with fares between Nassau and Cable Beach or Gambier Village $1. Downtown Nassau's **central bus stop** is on Frederick Street near the corner of Bay Street. This is where you can pick up the #10, which runs **west** from downtown along West Bay Street through Cable Beach and Sandyport to Orange Hill, with some drivers continuing on to Gambier Village (ask when you board). Eastbound buses to Potter's Cay (#24 or #30) and beyond depart from Bay Street at the foot of Market Street, just east of the Straw Market. There is no bus service to Paradise Island (a taxi from downtown Nassau to Paradise Island costs $10, but the water taxi – see below – is cheaper and faster). Bus stops are signposted along the main routes, but you can usually flag a bus down between designated stops. When you want to get off, yell "Bus stop!" and pay the driver as you leave. Note that the buses stop running around 6pm.

Car, bicycle and scooter rentals

If you are planning to explore the rest of the island outside of Nassau, **renting a car** is more economical than hiring a taxi and more convenient than waiting for sporadic buses in outlying villages. Rates range from $49 to $119 for 24 hours, with the average around $80 plus $15 a day insurance. All agencies will deliver to your hotel and to the airport. If you are travelling in high season (mid-December to April), it is advisable to book in advance. See "Listings" on p.90 for reliable operators.

Some hotels offer **bike** rental, but cycling on the traffic-clogged, shoulderless roads of New Providence is neither pleasant nor safe. Off-road cycling day trips of the interior are offered by Bahamas Outdoors (see p.66). You can rent a **scooter** at Knowles Scooter Rental, outside the *British Colonial Hilton* (T 356-0741; $50 full day or $40 half day, including helmet and insurance).

Water taxis

Water taxis offer frequent service between Prince George Wharf in Nassau and the ferry terminal below the outbound bridge on Paradise Island for $3 each way, running between 8.30am and 6pm.

Guided tours

If you would rather leave the logistics and the driving to someone else, several operators offer guided tours of the city and the island. **Majestic Tours** (T 322-2606, W www.majesticholidays.com) has agents in most hotels, and handles bookings for an extensive menu of excursions, including bus tours of Nassau and boat trips to the Out Islands and nearby cays. Its twice-daily, two-hour bus tour of Historical Nassau costs $40 per person; adding the Ardastra Gardens makes it a $50 tour; a combined tour of Nassau, Paradise Island and the Ardastra Gardens is $60. Interesting and informative ninety-minute **walking tours** of Historic Nassau, offered by Nassau Walking Tours (Mon–Sat 10am & 2pm; $10; T 325 8687) and given by a personable local guide, depart twice-daily from the tourist information desk in Festival Place. Finally, **horse-drawn surrey rides** cost $15 for about an hour, leaving from Prince George's Wharf. The drive takes in the major historical sights in downtown Nassau, although the amount of information you will glean from the tour depends on the knowledge and enthusiasm of the driver, which varies greatly.

For **boat tours**, which generally combine sightseeing with snorkelling and swimming, see p. 64.

Accommodation

Lodging in Nassau ranges from expensive to breathtakingly expensive, with just a couple of budget options in the $55–100 a night range. During high season and especially at Christmas and New Year, hotels are often fully booked well in advance; prices go down and availability up during the summer months.

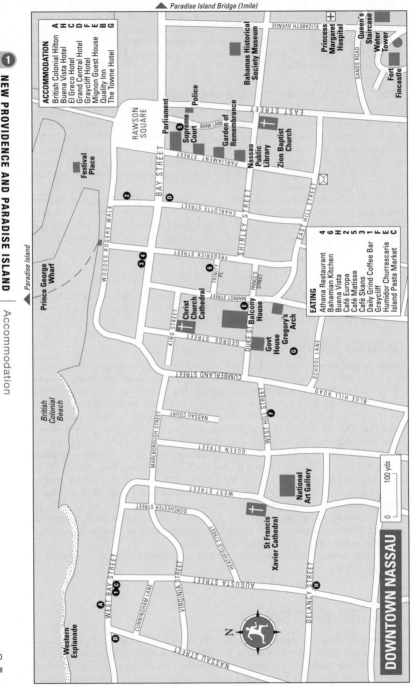

DOWNTOWN NASSAU

ACCOMMODATION
British Colonial Hilton   A
Buena Vista Hotel   H
El Greco Hotel   C
Grand Central Hotel   D
Graycliff Hotel   F
Mignon Guest House   E
Quality Inn   B
The Towne Hotel   G

EATING
Athena Restaurant   4
Bahamian Kitchen   6
Buena Vista   H
Café Europa   2
Café Matisse   5
Café Skans   3
Daily Grind Coffee Bar   1
Graycliff   F
Humidor Churrascaria   E
Island Pasta Market   C

Paradise Island Bridge (1mile)

Paradise Island

Prince George Wharf

Western Esplanade

British Colonial Beach

Festival Place

WOODES ROGERS WALK

BAY STREET

WEST BAY STREET

MARLBOROUGH STREET

CUMBERLAND STREET

KING STREET

GEORGE STREET

MARKET STREET

DUKE ST

PRINCE'S STREET

FREDERICK STREET

CHARLOTTE STREET

PARLIAMENT STREET

SHIRLEY STREET

EAST STREET

EAST HILL STREET

BLUE HILL ROAD

SCHOOL LANE

TRINITY PL

QUEEN STREET

WEST STREET

DORCHESTER STREET

NASSAU COURT

WEST HILL STREET

NASSAU STREET

CUNNINGHAM LANE

VIRGINIA STREET

AUGUSTA STREET

DELANCY STREET

BANK LANE

SANDS ROAD

ELIZABETH AVENUE

RAWSON SQUARE

Parliament
Police
Supreme Court
Garden of Remembrance
Nassau Public Library
Zion Baptist Church
Bahamas Historical Society Museum
Princess Margaret Hospital
Queen's Staircase
Water Tower
Fort Fincastle
Christ Church Cathedral
Balcony House
Govt House
Gregory's Arch
St Francis Xavier Cathedral
National Art Gallery

N

0   100 yds

Standards of comfort and service vary considerably, even in the poshest of resorts. Choosing to stay in or near **downtown Nassau** means putting up with a substantial level of urban clatter – though it also puts you near the action.

The **Cable Beach** hotel strip is in the midst of a wholescale multi-million dollar redevelopment that will continue for several years. It involves the *Nassau Beach Hotel*, the *Radisson*, and the *Wyndham*, which have all been bought by Starwood Resorts (which owns *Our Lucaya* on Grand Bahama) and will be razed or redesigned to create one massive beachfront resort completed by 2010. West of this zone are several very nice, secluded self-catering options that are economical for families or groups. The big draw in this area is the beach and easy access to downtown, which is a ten-minute bus or taxi ride away.

An appealing alternative is to stay well outside the city in the **Arawak Cay** area, or on the more secluded and scenic **Orange Hill Beach** (see p.96), which, just five minutes from the airport, is also a good choice for those en route to or from the Out Islands.

Downtown Nassau

British Colonial Hilton Nassau 1 Bay St ☎322-3311 or 1-800/742-4276, ⊛www.nassau .hilton.com. Built in 1922 and once the epitome of elegance in colonial Nassau, the *Hilton* still offers plush, upscale accommodation after a $70 million refurbishment in 2004, but sits sandwiched between banks and shops on the main street in downtown Nassau. The 305 rooms have opulent gold and claret decor, Internet access, cd players, and cable TV, and the ocean-facing rooms have a spectacular view, but there are no balconies. There is a formal dining room, a small swath of beach and a pool bar with a view of the cruise-ship dock and Paradise Island. ❽

Buena Vista Hotel Delancy St at Augusta St ☎322-2811, ⊛ww.buenavista-restaurant.com. A slightly shabby but still grand old-fashioned hotel set back from the road on a sloping lawn overlooking the city. Built in 1788 and enlarged in the nineteenth century, the hotel posed as the Liberian Embassy in the 2006 James Bond flick *Casino Royale*. The hotel is for sale, so renovations are on hold, but the five guest rooms – although dated circa 1980 – are clean and comfortable. ❸

El Greco Hotel West Bay St at Augusta St ☎325-1121/3, ⊛www.bahamasnet.com /elgrecohotel. A centrally-located small hotel across from the water, with an inviting Spanish-style decor and small courtyard pool. The rooms are motel standard, but spacious and comfortable with TV, a/c and a coffee maker. Ask for a room at the back of the hotel, if possible. You may be offered a poolside room, which sounds nice but can be noisy after swimmers knock back a few daiquiris. ❸

Grand Central Hotel Charlotte St ☎322-8356, ⊛www.grand-central-hotel.com. One of several basic commercial hotels in central Nassau. The

very plain and rundown rooms have TV and a/c and not much else, but it's a back-up if you are stranded in town late at night. ❷

Graycliff 8–12 West Hill St ☎322-2796, ⊛www .graycliff.com. Perched on a hill above Nassau, *Graycliff* is a glamorous British colonial pile with secluded "garden rooms" and private cottages where Churchill once slept, done up in rich woods and luxurious fabrics and set around a lushly planted courtyard. The main house was built by John Howard Graysmith, a pirate who pillaged Spanish shipping as commander of the *Graywolf*. Amenities include an inviting pool – in which the Beatles once swam – a hot tub, health club and one of the finest restaurants in town. Rates start at $375. ❾

Mignon Guest House 12 Market St ☎322-4771. The best budget choice in town. Six simple but scrupulously clean, bright and homey rooms with a/c and shared baths. There is also a fridge, microwave and dining nook for guest use. Rooms cost $56. ❶

Nassau Palm Resort West Bay St ☎356-0000 or 1-877/229-6322, ⊛www.nassau-hotel.com. Standard hotel rooms with a patchy reputation for cleanliness and guest service, located right on the main thoroughfare, with no grounds or greenery, three blocks from downtown Nassau. There is a scruffy public beach across the road, a heated pool in a cement courtyard with a view of the street, and several restaurants nearby. ❹

Quality Inn West Bay St at Nassau St ☎322-1515, ⊛www.choicehotels.com. Small but neat doubles, with a small pool and café on site. ❸

The Towne Hotel 40 George St ☎322-8450, ⊛www.townehotel.com. One of the oldest hotels in Nassau, *The Towne* has certainly seen better days, but is a serviceable option. The 46 modest rooms of varying sizes all have TVs and overlook a small central courtyard and pool. ❷

West of downtown

Arawak Inn West Bay St ☎ & ⊕ 322-2638, ⓦ www.bahamas-treasures.com/arawakinn. This guesthouse has six simple but comfortable en-suite rooms with kitchenettes grouped around a garden patio. Situated on the main bus route with a couple of restaurants within easy walking distance. No credit cards. ❷

Dillet's Guest House Dunmore Ave at Strachan St, Chippingham ☎ 325-1133, ⓦ www.islandeaze .com. A gem of a place set in an acre of gardens, in a residential west Nassau neighbourhood near Arawak Cay, within walking distance of the #10 bus route. Weekly and monthly rentals only for $800/$1400 respectively for spacious one-bedroom suites with full kitchen and private bath. Breakfast and 4pm tea served in the inviting and imaginatively decorated sitting room.

East of downtown

Nassau Harbour Club East Bay St ☎ 393-0771, ⓦ ww.nassauharborclub.com. A popular hangout for yachties, the *Harbour Club* rents out fifty recently renovated rooms with TV, a/c and mini fridge with a nice pool patio and bar overlooking the marina. Situated on busy Bay St, it can get a bit loud at times, especially during Spring Break. However, it offers good lower-priced accommodation with shopping and dining nearby. ❸

Red Carpet Inn East Bay St ☎ 393-7981, ⓦ www .redcarpetinnbahamas.com. Even though this forty-room motel-style lodge is located on Nassau's busiest street, high surrounding walls ensure a sense of tranquillity. Popular with divers due to its proximity to the harbour, the rooms here are clean and comfortable. The rooms have TV, a/c, mini fridge or kitchenette, and there's a pool and laundry on site. A decent budget option. ❸

Cable Beach

Casuarinas of Cable Beach West Bay St ☎ 327-7921, ⊕ 327-8153. A less expensive alternative to the large resorts on the strip, this small hotel offers clean, simple guestrooms with TV and a/c grouped around a quiet courtyard and pool. There is a restaurant on site, access to the beach directly across the street, and restaurants and shops nearby. ❹

Guanahani Village West Bay St ☎ 327-7568 or 1-866/854-3322, ⓦ www.guanahanivillage .com. Very private, well-maintained and attractive three-bed/two-bath units, each with a patio enclosed by a tall fence, TV, a/c, washer and dryer, a full kitchen, a spacious sitting room and dining area. Some units are ocean-front, some are set further back in the nicely landscaped grounds. There are tennis courts, a snack bar and a palm-shaded pool backed by a break-water beyond which is a small scrap of beach. The property has just been sold, so things may change. Rates begin at $300 per night, $2100 per week including taxes for two people; $20 more a night per each extra person.

Land Shark Hotel West Bay St ☎ 327-6364, ⓦ www.landsharkdivers.com. Pretty rough-looking with small, dark rooms with TV situated around a permanently shady covered patio bar and grill. Cramped, but friendly and fine if all you want is a place to lay your head, but there are cheaper, nicer options. ❷

Nassau Beach Hotel West Bay St ☎ 327-7711 or 1-888/627-7282, ⓦ www.cablebeachresorts.com. A venerable Nassau institution, this low-rise hotel has an intimate feel, built in a U-shape enclosing an attractive ocean-facing pool. The 403 balconied, carpeted rooms are nicely if unimaginatively furnished; ask for one high up facing the water. However, some of the bathrooms are a decade overdue for renovation and maintenance is spotty in areas – upgrading seems to be on hold pending a complete redevelopment of the property over the next few years. For now, there's a nice beach, a state-of-the-art fitness centre, pleasant staff and one of the best casual restaurants in Nassau – *Café Johnny Canoe*, with live music several nights a week. ❻

Radisson Cable Beach Resort West Bay St ☎ 327-6000 or 1-800/333-3333, ⓦ www .radisson-cablebeach.com. This 700-room high-rise hotel draws the multitudes with its fine beach and golf course, but also boasts eighteen tennis courts, a health club, several restaurants, three pools and abundant water sports. Plush, nicely decorated common areas, lushly landscaped grounds and comfortable guest rooms with the standard amenities; half with ocean views. Set for a revamp in the near future as part of the Cable Beach Resorts' redevelopment. $360 a night. ❾

Sandals Royal Bahamian Resort and Spa ☎ 327-6400 or 1-800/726-3257, ⓦ www .sandals.com. This pseudo Roman spa-style resort is a fifteen acre all-inclusive enclave on the beach ensconced behind high walls. It's billed as an intimate couples retreat, with about 400 deluxe rooms and suites, eight restaurants, seven bars, seven pools, a dive shop, spa and private offshore cay. There is a minimum three-night stay; a week costs $3500–$4500 per couple in high season.

Sun Fun Resort West Bay St ☎327-8827, ⓦwww.sunfunresort.com. A drab but cheap and serviceable alternative to the big boys lining the shore. The guest rooms are equipped with a/c, TV and telephone and there is a small pool as well as a bare-bones restaurant, but the draw is the price and easy access to the beach, a short walk away. ❸

Superclubs Breezes West Bay St ☎327-5356 or 1-800/859-7873, ⓦwww.superclubs.com. A huge all-inclusive package hotel (part of the *Superclubs* chain) serving up countless activities and party games to endless busloads of holidaymakers. The common areas are bright and cheerful; the stand-ard-grade hotel rooms are housed in four-storey blocks set around a landscaped courtyard with a large pool, climbing wall and rows of lounging chairs. Guests must be 17 or over. ❽

Wyndham Nassau Resort West Bay St ☎327-6200 or 1-800/222-7466, ⓦwww .wyndhamnassauresort.com. Bringing a touch of Las Vegas to the Bahamas, this monster resort has some 800 rooms and suites, attractively done-up with all the usual amenities, housed in a cluster of high-rise towers fronting a nice stretch of beach. The common areas are tarted up in tired and garish shades of 1980s mauve and peach with brass accents, but the whole place is slated for an over-haul in the near future as part of the Cable Beach redevelopment. There are five restaurants, five bars, full water-sports facilities, a miniature golf course and a large pool with a crude man-made island and waterfall, as well as the 800-seat *Rainforest Theatre* and the *Crystal Palace Casino*. ❻

West Wind I West Bay St ☎327-7680, ⓦwww .westwind1.com. A quiet and secluded refuge for those looking for a comfortable home from home. Twenty-four bright and appealing duplex bungalow units are set in attractively landscaped grounds, each with plenty of privacy, as well as a full kitchen, two bedrooms (a king and a loft with twin beds), one bath and a patio fitted out with a barbeque. There is an inviting ocean-front swim-ming pool and a snack bar open for lunch. ❼

West Wind II West Bay St ☎327-7211 or 1-866/369-5921, ⓦwww.westwind2.com. An attractive self-catering option, with two clusters of two-bed/two-bath condo units, each set around a swimming pool, some with an ocean view. Other attractions include tennis courts, a bar and a piece of Cable Beach. It's a good option for a group of four or a family. ❼

Downtown Nassau

Downtown Nassau's narrow, bustling streets are clogged with cars and buses but lined with sidewalks, and the city centre is small enough to explore on foot. Most of the city's historical buildings and sites are located in this compact downtown core, hence its sobriquet "Historic Nassau". Allow at least half a day to take in all the sights and slather on the sunscreen before you head out. The graceful palms and citrus trees shown shading the town's sandy hillside lanes in early-twentieth-century photographs have for the most part given way to tarmac.

An appropriate place to begin a tour is in front of the **British Colonial Hilton Hotel** on Marlborough Street. From here, you can make a loop through the historic downtown area, proceeding east along Bay Street, heading uphill and south at Parliament Square, strolling west on Hill Street along the top of the ridge, then heading back down the gentle slope to the *British Colonial Hilton* via West and Queen streets, with a few optional detours along the way.

The waterfront from the British Colonial Hilton Hotel to Rawson Square

Bay Street is New Providence's main drag, running the length of the north coast through the centre of Nassau, interrupted for a short distance on downtown's western edge where the imposing butter-yellow **British Colonial Hilton Hotel** occupies several city blocks on the waterfront. The hotel, with its main entrance on Marlborough Street, is built on the site of **Fort Nassau**, constructed by a ragtag English militia in 1697 and the site of one of the most dramatic

Slavery in the Bahamas

After the expulsion of the pirates, an influx of Loyalist settlers from the American colonies drove the growth in plantation agriculture on New Providence and in the Out Islands. About 20,000 **West Africans** were transported to the Bahamas to work as domestic and agricultural **slaves** and on arduous public works projects like road construction and fortifications. The majority of the Bahamas' present-day populace is descended from these people. Shackled and stacked head to foot on shelves with not enough room even to sit up, about twenty percent of those abducted from Africa did not survive the voyage across the ocean, succumbing to disease or despair. Those who did endured meagre lives used up in this outpost of the Empire. The British slave trade was abolished in 1807, but Emancipation did not come until 1834.

and pivotal events in Bahamian history. On December 12, 1718 nine pirates captured in Governor Woodes-Rogers' campaign to rid Nassau of cutthroats and marauders (see p.60) were hung from the battlements as townsfolk looked on. On the gallows, one of the condemned called for a glass of wine and toasted the governor, wishing him success in his efforts. After this show of might, the pirate stranglehold on Nassau gradually loosened. Fort Nassau was abandoned in 1800 when new gunposts were built in more protected positions above the harbour. A hotel was built on the site in 1900 to accommodate visitors arriving on the weekly steamers from New York. It burned down in 1922, and the vaguely Art Deco structure now presiding over the harbour opened the following year. Remnants of the fort's stone walls and cannons are still scattered around the hotel grounds, and a statue of Woodes-Rogers in the forecourt commemorates its historical significance.

Nearby, at the corner of King and George Streets, kids especially will have fun at the small but well-executed **Pirates of Nassau Museum** (Mon–Sat 9am–6pm; $15, children $6; ☎356-3759), complete with a life-size replica of a stretch of Nassau's seedy eighteenth-century waterfront, with creepy sounds and interactive displays.

Heading towards the water along George Street to its junction with Bay Street brings you to the **Pompey Museum of Slavery and Emancipation** (Mon–Wed & Fri–Sat 9.30am–4.30pm, closed Thurs & Sun; $3; ☎356-0495), which occupies Vendue House, constructed in 1763 and where throughout the eighteenth and early nineteenth centuries slaves were auctioned from the front step. Named after the leader of an almost triumphant slave rebellion on Exuma in the 1830s (see p.249), the museum traces the rise of the African slave trade in the seventeenth century to its abolition in 1807 and the emancipation of slaves in British colonies, including the Bahamas, in 1834, using photographs, artefacts and personal accounts. The appalling reality of a life of slavery is made concrete in the display cases of neck and foot shackles used to bind captives on the long Middle Passage, tarnished buttons from slaves' clothes imprinted with the name of their owners, and the crude branding irons similarly used to identify slaves as someone's property. In stark contrast, the tasteful gift shop sells a good selection of books about the Bahamas, attractive handmade jewellery, straw goods, framed prints, cards, jams and jellies.

Next door to the Pompey Museum, and filling much of a square block, is Nassau's vast **Straw Market**, a covered warren of upwards of 150 vendors who congregate each morning to peddle everything from cheap bric-a-brac to exquisitely beautiful artworks. Piled high are stacks of t-shirts, sundresses, bags and baskets, dolls, beads, slippers, wall hangings, polished pink conch shells,

△ Straw Market

sunglasses, wood carvings and the occasional oil painting. Among the more unusual items on offer are shark-tooth necklaces, charms and hexes, and batik fabrics from Andros (see p.184). Hand-carved wood and shell pieces tend to fetch the highest prices, but inexpensive wooden bead necklaces are popular souvenirs. While many visitors bargain with vendors, haggling is not a cultural rite with Bahamians, and stiff competition means that most goods are already fairly priced.

Continuing east along Bay Street brings you to the heart of the **shopping district**, generally thronged with browsers and bargain hunters. In 1992, in an effort to promote economic growth on its largely infertile islands, the Bahamas removed import duties on eleven categories of goods, mainly luxury items. Duty-free shopping is a big draw for tourists, and Bay Street is lined with shops hawking gem stones and jewellery, crystal, liquor, Cuban cigars, fine linens and all manner of fancy goods.

Junkanoo

Junkanoo is the Bahamas' most important and spectacular party – two all-night street parades held over the Christmas season: the first on December 26, the second on New Year's Day. A sensory blast of organized pandemonium, Junkanoo floods the streets of Nassau with floats, stilt-dancers, clowns, acrobats, go-go girls, goatskin-drum players, and conch and cowbell ringers, all blaring out their tunes in a wild celebration of life. The parade is also known as a "rush-out", as competing groups or "crews" rush out to meet the dawn, traditionally moving toward one another from all directions rather than following one another in the semi-organized fashion of the modern parade. Reminiscent of New Orleans' "Mardi Gras" and Rio's "Carnival", with its roots in traditional music and dance brought by transported slaves from Africa, Junkanoo is distinctively Bahamian. There's no other festival like it – not in the Caribbean, not anywhere.

History

A celebration of emancipation from slavery, Junkanoo began in the late sixteenth and early seventeenth centuries, during plantation times, when the slave owners in Jamaica, the Bahamas, and southern states of the US traditionally gave their chattels three days off at Christmas to see family and friends and generally let off steam, mainly as a way of preparing them for another year of hard work.

The word "Junkanoo" is thought to have derived from the French phrase *gens inconnus* ("unknown people"), an appropriate term for the anonymous slaves who first donned grotesque masks and paraded on stilts during these holidays. An alternative explanation is that the term Junkanoo derives from the name "John Canoe" or John Cannu, who depending on historical interpretation was either a real-life West African slave trader responsible for selling many of his compatriots into bondage, a slave revered for rebelling against his master, or a sort of a mythical West African "Everyman" who encapsulated the slave experience as a Christian movement grew to suppress the festival as dangerous and pagan.

Following the abolition of slavery, the festival survived only in the Bahamas, and even there colonial authorities attempted to put an end to it on many occasions – during World War II, the British authorities, aghast at the 1942 Burma Road riots which saw Bahamian construction workers working on the new Nassau airport demonstrate for wages on par with Americans brought in to work on the project – banned it altogether. Since then, however, Junkanoo has made a comeback, and is now more popular than ever – both as a joyous Christmas and New Year's celebration, and a political expression of independence and freedom.

Just up from the waterfront, at the junction of Bay and Parliament streets **Rawson Square** is a cobblestone pedestrian mall bordered on all sides by pastel-painted colonial-style buildings, the majority built between 1785 and 1815. On its south side is the unobtrusive **Churchill Building**, where the Bahamian Cabinet meets on Tuesday mornings, its sessions evidenced by a string of shiny black cars and chauffeurs at the entrance. From the centre of the square, you get a fine view uphill along Parliament Street toward the capital's daintily painted government buildings. A relatively peaceful oasis in the midst of the city – save during the raucous Junkanoo celebrations (see below) – Rawson Square is shaded by tall palms, dotted with benches where office workers meet for lunch, and adorned with public sculptures. One is a bronze bust of **Sir Milo Butler**, the first black Bahamian-born governor-general of the newly independent Bahamas (1973-79). A successful Nassau merchant, Sir Milo was elected to Parliament in 1937

The parades
The first parade takes place in the small hours of December 26, starting off from the *British Colonial Hilton Hotel* at around 2am, when upwards of forty thousand people assemble on Nassau's historic Bay Street to witness the first Junkanoo crew pass by. The distant beats of goombay drums indicate that the performers are shifting into formation, and spectators start jockeying for the best views, climbing trees and spilling onto balconies and the verandas of storefronts, hotels and houses. Under the Christmas lights, the crowds reach a frenzy of anticipation. The first cowbells are heard soon after, everyone swigs from bottles of rum, and fireworks crackle in the sky. Behind, in Nassau harbour, the looming cruise ships form an almost surreal counterpoint to the crowds, who are now stamping and clamouring in time to the drumbeats. Then, as if from everywhere and nowhere, Junkanoo crews – some numbering a thousand costumed revellers – burst onto the streets in a swirling, kaleidoscopic mass of singing and dancing. They keep on coming for hours, but if anything, the crowds grow larger and louder than ever, chanting, cheering and stamping their feet. Standing in the throng, it's hard to imagine that barely one week later another, even larger and more elaborate Junkanoo parade will attract more than sixty thousand islanders – over half Nassau's population – who will jam the city's main shopping street in a pitch of excitement and fervour.

Doing Junkanoo
You can attend one of the smaller Junkanoo celebrations on the islands of Eleuthera, Grand Bahama, Bimini, or Green Turtle Cay in the Abacos, but Junkanoo in Nassau is the granddaddy of them all, a truly once-in-a-lifetime celebration. On each side of Bay Street in downtown Nassau, around Rawson Square, bleacher-type seating is constructed, but it's much more fun to whoop it up with the rest of the revellers on the street. Tickets cost between $5 and $100 depending on location and are available through the Junkanoo ticket agency (☎324-1714 or 1-877/THE-RUSH, ⊛www.junkanoo.com) or the Ministry of Tourism in Nassau (☎302-2000 or 1-800/BAHAMAS in North America).

For an overview of the history of Junkanoo and a close-up look at some of the elaborate costumes made for the celebrations in years past, head to **Educulture**, 31 West St N at Delancy Street (Mon–Fri 9am–5pm, Sat & Sun by appointment; $5; ☎328-3786, ⊜educulture@coralwave.com). This community organization operates a small museum devoted to Junkanoo and workshops on the history of the festival – including a hands-on session in costume construction. It also can also arrange Junkanoo workshops ($25 per person) for groups of two or more if you call in advance.

and served almost continuously until 1973, holding several ministerial portfolios; a man with a lot to say, he responded to the 1956 introduction of a twelve-minute limit on speeches from the floor of the House of Assembly by pitching the Speaker's hourglass out of the window. Nearby is a modern sculpture of a woman and child, commissioned to mark the birth of the independent nation in 1973 and honour the role of women in Bahamian society.

Along the northern side of Rawson Square, the valiant efforts of Woodes-Rogers in ridding Nassau of pirates have been commemorated in a quayside passage – **Woodes-Rogers Walk** – lined with tacky souvenir stalls, food kiosks and the cruise-ship terminal. Skip the stands and walk along **Prince George Wharf**, which offers great views of the buzzing harbour, where water taxis, huge cruise vessels and tour boats all crowd the blue water. You can pick up a water taxi to Paradise Island from here (see p.69).

The cruise-ship terminal is labelled **Festival Place**, and features a tourist information desk and a collection of gift shops. The first port of call for many cruise-ship visitors is the **Hairbraider's Centre** located in a kiosk in front of Festival Place on its inland side. Here, Bahamian women braid hair for around $1 a strand. Elaborate dos with twisting phantasmagorias of braids go for as much as $100 and can take several hours. Also in front of Festival Place on Woodes-Rogers Walk is the depot for **horse-drawn surrey rides** around town (see p.66).

Parliament Square

Crossing Bay Street on the south side of Rawson Square, you leave the crowds behind and enter **PARLIAMENT SQUARE**, the centre of Bahamian government. Facing Rawson Square are the peppermint-pink **Houses of Parliament**, built between 1805 and 1813. The centre block houses the Senate, or upper house of sixteen appointed members. The Bahamian coat of arms hangs above the door: a blazing sun rising above the Santa Maria, one of the ships aboard which Christopher Columbus "discovered" the Bahamas. It is flanked by a blue marlin and a pink flamingo and crowned with a pink conch. The national motto, "Forward, Upward, Onward, Together", was chosen in a competition for Bahamian schoolchildren at Independence in 1973. The east block is occupied by the Magistrate's Court and the office of the Speaker of the House. The west block is where the forty-member elected House of Assembly meets each Wednesday. The Bahamian House of Assembly is one of the world's longest standing elected governments, having been in continuous existence since 1729, its first meetings held in private homes. Visitors are welcome in the public gallery when the House is in session; obtain a free pass from the Office of the Clerk of the House on the ground floor (☎322-7500). All three buildings are superb examples of the Georgian style of architecture that was so popular in the early 1800s at the height of the Napoleonic Wars, featuring smooth limestone facades, Neoclassical pillars and pilasters and broad staircases. A statue of **Queen Victoria**, erected in 1905, looks sternly down from a throne in front of the Senate.

Behind the Senate is a pleasant patch of green space and a few grand public buildings connected by walking paths. The **Supreme Court** is an imposing 1920 neo-Georgian edifice where all of the criminal cases in the Bahamas are tried, with the exception of those on Grand Bahama, which has its own court. Juries of twelve are selected for three-month terms and may hear several cases during their period of duty. Further up the gentle slope beyond the courthouse is the **Garden of Remembrance**, where a cenotaph recalls the Bahamian dead of the World Wars.

Continuing uphill, the distinctive **Nassau Public Library and Museum** (Mon–Thurs 10am–8pm, Fri 10am–5pm, Sat 10am–4pm; free; ☎322-4907), on the corner of Parliament and Shirley Streets, occupies the octagonal former city jail built in 1798. Converted into a library in 1879, the structure is cramped and rather mysterious, with piles of mouldering books – rotting away in the humid Bahamian climate – lining what were once jail cells, and stacks of newspapers placed here and there in no apparent order. On the second floor, reached by a rickety metal staircase, is a motley collection of historical artefacts, maps, photos, shells, botanical drawings and horrifically and without explanation, four human skulls. The third-floor gallery once housed a bell used to call the members of the House of Assembly into session and now affords the non-vertiginous a fine view of Parliament Square.

The Historical Society Museum, the Queen's Staircase and Fort Fincastle

Two blocks east of the library along Shirley Street at Elizabeth Avenue stands the **Bahamas Historical Society Museum** (Mon–Tues & Thurs–Fri 10am–4pm, Sat 10am–noon; $1; ☎ 322-4231). With a modest but entertaining collection of anthropological materials and artefacts, this museum is devoted to life in the Bahamas before European settlement and during the early colonial period, with exhibits devoted to the Lucayan era, Columbus, bush medicine, wrecking and political history. A chief attraction is the collection of prints and lithographs featuring high-seas adventures, items collected from shipwrecks around the Bahamas and a gorgeous, structurally perfect model of the Spanish galleon *Santa Luceno*. Built in 1570, the ship sank off the north coast of New Providence, loaded with treasure and yet to be recovered.

From here, those with wind in their sails can make the steep trek up Elizabeth Avenue to the **Queen's Staircase**. A deep limestone gorge near where Elizabeth Avenue crosses Sands Road presented slaves in the 1790s with the "opportunity" of cutting a long, steep stone staircase into the hillside to provide access to Fort Fincastle. Later named in honour of Queen Victoria, today the stairs are mainly frequented by tourists, with a gaggle of unofficial guides at each end ready to regale you with stories they've been rehashing for years. A mini-tropical garden has been planted to add a bit of life to the spot.

Topping a bluff with a commanding prospect of the harbour, **Fort Fincastle** (free admission) was built in 1793 under the rule of Lord Dunmore, the royal governor of the Bahamas and the Viscount of Fincastle. Its cannons were trained on the harbour and the battery on Hog Island (now Paradise Island), in anticipation of intruders and marauders who never came. Dunmore emptied the treasury to fortify Nassau between 1789–93, but the settlement was never attacked again after a Spanish raid in 1782. During the nineteenth century, the fort was pressed into service as a lighthouse. The adjacent 126-foot-high **water tower** was built in 1928 and is still used to store some of the 30,000 gallons of water brought daily by barge from Andros to quench dry New Providence. It also has a fine panoramic view of the city, but the observation deck is currently closed for repairs.

Royal Victoria Garden

Back down the hill on Parliament Street just uphill from Shirley Street, a small patch of grass and trees and a commodious parking lot forms the **Royal Victoria Garden** (open to the public; free). The garden occupies the site of the former *Royal Victoria Hotel*, which opened at the onset of the American Civil War in 1861 and became the unofficial headquarters for a colourful collection of Confederate officers, gunrunners, spies and officials in town doing business with Nassau's smugglers and blockade runners. It closed in 1971 and burned to the ground in 1991. A great photograph of the three-storey balconied hotel in its nineteenth-century heyday is on display in the National Art Gallery of the Bahamas (see p.81), along with the crystal punch bowl from its elegant dining room.

East Hill, Duke and West Hill streets

Nestled behind a wrought iron fence on the northwest corner of Parliament and East Hill Streets is **Jacaranda House**, a private home built by Nassau's Chief Justice in the 1840s using a load of ballast stone he bought off a ship arriving from Georgia. The house is a fine example of the architecture of the period, with jalousied verandahs, detailed wooden latticework and stone quoins (cross-laid cornerstones) painted white in contrast to the pink limestone walls. The house was occupied for a time by the Duke and Duchess of Windsor after the Duke was sent abroad as governor of the Bahamas during World War II. Before the arrival of the Windsors, the House of Assembly had approved £1500 to modernize the governor's official residence for them. The Duchess called in a fashionable decorator from New York and spent £5000 of public money on new draperies and modern furnishings. This did not endear her to ordinary Bahamians, although invitations to her glamorous cocktail parties were highly prized. She was said to have viewed the Duke's sojourn in Nassau as an exile, referring to New Providence as "Elba". The Duke perhaps had more to occupy his mind, as the role of governor was not a ceremonial position. He chaired a committee on economic development promoting measures to improve agricultural production, built an infant care clinic and, during a fire that threatened to flatten the whole of downtown in 1942, was part of a chain of citizens emptying the shelves of the Island Shoppe of stock before it burned.

Around the corner on East Hill Street is the green-painted **East Hill Club**, another stately home built between 1840 and 1860 and one-time winter residence of Lord Beaverbrook, the Canadian-born newspaper baron who owned the *London Evening Standard* and *Daily Express* and smoked cigars with the likes of Winston Churchill in the cocktail lounges of fashionable Nassau. It is now a private club. The similarly grand pink-and-white confection at the corner of East Hill and Glinton streets houses the **Ministry of Foreign Affairs**.

East Hill continues towards Market Street, where the intersection is marked by **Gregory's Arch**. Named for John Gregory, royal governor from 1849 to 1854, this stone passage was built in 1852 as a decorative flourish marking the boundary between Nassau and the settlement of freed slaves "over the hill" in **Grant's Town**, itself named for Lewis Grant, governor from 1821 to 1829. Early visitors to Nassau often treated Grant's Town as a pleasure dome, slipping away to its pubs and bawdy houses, though these days, the suburb is a residential working-class neighbourhood.

East Hill Street meets West Hill Street at Mount Fitzwilliam, crowned by **Government House**, the official residence of the governor-general, the ceremonial head of state. Built in the mid-1730s as the home of royal governor Fitzwilliam, it was extensively rebuilt in 1806 and again in 1932 after a hurricane destroyed the old structure. Presided over by a statue of Christopher Columbus, the pink mansion, with its graceful columns, broad driveways, quoins and louvered windows, is the quintessence of British-Bahamian colonial style. The house is not open to visitors, but you can stroll the pleasant grounds to get a close-up view as well as attend the **Changing of the Guards** every other Saturday morning at 10am, an event modelled upon the Buckingham Palace ceremony. The guards are headed by the Royal Bahamian Police Force, who wear red tunics, white pith helmets and march to the beat of drummers dressed in leopard-skin. In a less martial vein, the governor-general's consort hosts an hour-long "People to People" tea party on the lawn at 4pm on the last Friday of each month except December. Visitors are welcome to sip Bahamian bush tea and chat with friendly local volunteers about life in the Bahamas.

Among the more prominent buildings on West Hill Street is **Graycliff**, built in 1720 and adorned with turrets, verandahs and cornices galore. Now an intimate luxury hotel, it adjoins the **Graycliff Cigar Factory** (Mon–Fri 9am–5pm; free tours; ☏322-2796), which operates in a wing of an old Victorian pile next to the *Graycliff* hotel. Overseen by Avalino Lara, the factory produces fine hand-rolled cigars made from Cuban tobacco.

At the junction of West Hill and West streets, **Dunmore House** is a beautifully restored three-storey mansion built by Governor Lord Dunmore in 1787 as his private residence. Today, it's home to the **National Art Gallery of the Bahamas** (Tues–Thurs 10am–4pm, closed public holidays; $3; ☎328-5800, ⓦ www.nagb.org .bs), with a permanent collection which traces the development of Bahamian visual art from its original domination by nineteenth-century "tourist artists" like American Winslow Homer to the work of modern Bahamian painters like Eddie Minnis and Nicole Minnis-Ferguson and French immigrant Thierry Lamare, who all paint in a

△ Guard at the Government House

romantic realist tradition. The paintings and photographs from the nineteenth and early twentieth centuries are particularly interesting for their depiction of Bahamian daily life at that time. The gallery runs an evening lecture series and screens art-house films; check the website for a calendar of events.

Just across from the gallery at the end of West Hill Street is the weathered stone **St Francis Xavier Roman Catholic Church**, the first Roman Catholic church in the Bahamas, constructed during 1885–86. The bell-tower of the church is something of a landmark, its light calmly piercing the tropical night.

Queen and George streets

Heading downhill and back to the *British Colonial Hilton* via Queen Street takes you past a few finely preserved colonial residences. If your appetite for architecture is still keen, saunter over to Cumberland Street, where Nassau's oldest house, built in 1710, is located. Acquired by the Anglican Church in 1800 and known as the **Deanery**, the two-storey house has wraparound verandahs and still has its slave quarters and the original kitchen with its brick oven; it is not open to the public, but you can take a peek through the gate. Two blocks east on Market Street, the eighteenth-century **Balcony House** is identified by its sloping second floor balcony, supported by aged wooden braces. Formerly open to the public as a museum, it is currently closed. For a town settled by wreckers, rum runners and pirates, Nassau built a lot of churches in its early days, most of which are well attended in modern times. Admirers of ecclesiastic architecture might peek inside **St Andrew's Presbyterian Kirk** (constructed

1810–64) on Market Street and the massive **Christ Church Anglican Cathedral** on the corner of George and King streets, built in 1840 on ground originally consecrated in 1670.

West of downtown

Two blocks west of the *British Colonial Hilton Hotel*, Marlborough Street becomes **West Bay Street**, a busy, shaded two-lane road that runs along the waterfront on its way to Cable Beach. Here, on the western outskirts of Nassau, the waterfront is heavily developed, the busy seaside thoroughfare backed by residential suburbs. Between the road and the water is a narrow strip of grass and trees shading a couple of decent public beaches. Local Bahamians often park their cars on the sand to snooze, have lunch or drink a beer amid the rusting cannons along the beachside, which is most popular on Sundays and holidays. The ruins of historic **Fort Charlotte** look down on the beach, and there are a couple of city parks adding splashes of green to the landscape, venues for soccer and cricket matches on weekends. A lively collection of seafood shacks draw local crowds to the **Arawak Cay Fish Fry** in the evenings and on weekends. A sidewalk runs intermittently alongside the road en route to Cable Beach, but for most of the distance, West Bay is narrow, shoulder-less and busy with fast moving traffic. It is tricky to navigate on foot, and should be avoided by bicyclists altogether. The easiest way to get around the area is by hopping on a #10 bus in front of the *British Colonial Hotel* or downtown on Frederick Street or flagging one down anywhere along West Bay Street.

Fort Charlotte and Clifford Park

About half a mile west of the city centre, the ruins of **Fort Charlotte** (daily 9am–4.30pm; free) top a low ridge with a magnificent prospect of the sea. Construction was begun in 1787 by Lord Dunmore, who managed to complete the building in 1790 – at an enormous cost to the English treasury – in the hope of protecting the colony from possible French invasion. Chiselled from solid limestone, the walls are buttressed by cedar, and there's a surrounding moat, a warren of dungeons and supply rooms, as well as a keep and cannonades. At the end of the regular fifteen-minute **tour**, be sure to give a donation to the guide – who may or may not be dressed in period costume – of $2 to $3 per person. Deep inside the fort is a wax museum of tortures consisting of racks, thumbscrews and stocks.

Below the fort sits **Clifford Park** and the **Haynes Oval**, where the Bahamian Cricket Association holds games every Sunday around 1pm. Entrance is free, though the best seats are in the pitch-side pub and restaurant, where basic Bahamian and British fare is served along with cold beer. A breezy balcony provides great views of the field and the ocean nearby.

Arawak Cay

Directly opposite Fort Charlotte across West Bay Street is man-made **Arawak Cay**. Built originally as a harbour entrepôt, the now-abandoned cay is now home to dozens of colourfully painted seafood shacks – a popular hangout that shouldn't be missed by anyone interested in local culture. An army of cooks prepare cracked conch, conch salad, and fried conch, along with smothered grouper and other seafood treats at good prices. On weekends, the grounds are rocking with Bahamians who come to play loud music and drink gin with coconut milk.

The Ardastra Gardens and Zoo

Off West Bay Street on Chippingham Road (and clearly signposted), the six-acre **Ardastra Gardens and Zoo** (daily 9am–5pm; $12, children $6; ☎323-5806) houses about fifty species from around the world, including some from the African savannah. There are a few examples of rare Bahamian animals, like the nearly extinct agoutis and hutias, tiny rodent-like nocturnal mammals that are hunted out in the wild. A welter of pathways connected by bridges wind around the grounds, where one can spot caged parrots and a large boa constrictor that can be handled with permission from caretakers. Flamingos are paraded out for a show three times a day at 10.30am, 2.10pm and 4.10pm, though not on Sunday.

Cable Beach and around

With its hotels, restaurants and sport facilities, easy-going **CABLE BEACH** offers tourists a functioning, rather affordable self-contained base. The major hotels here (see "Accommodation", p.69) – which in terms of style and aesthetics very much resemble the ocean-going vessels that dock at Prince George Wharf – are well endowed with a variety of bars, pools, shops and water-side activities. The **beach** itself is four miles in length, its sand broader and cleaner than any of Nassau's public beaches. Non-guests of the seaside resorts can enjoy the sandy stretch, though some short portions are claimed as private, reserved for hotel guests.

Five miles west of downtown Nassau, Cable Beach is an easy taxi ride from either the city or the airport, and is also served by a steady stream of jitneys (route #10) and shuttles. On the Nassau side, along West Bay Street, lies **Saunders Beach**, lined with whispering casuarinas and very popular on

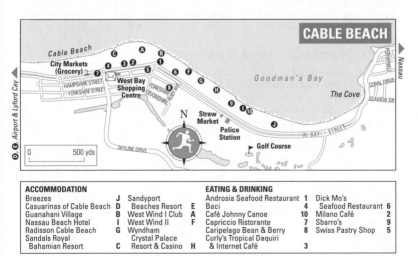

ACCOMMODATION			EATING & DRINKING			
Breezes	J	Sandyport	Androsia Seafood Restaurant	1	Dick Mo's	
Casuarinas of Cable Beach	D	Beaches Resort E	Baci	4	Seafood Restaurant	6
Guanahani Village	B	West Wind I Club A	Café Johnny Canoe	10	Milano Café	2
Nassau Beach Hotel	I	West Wind II F	Capriccio Ristorante	7	Sbarro's	9
Radisson Cable Beach	G	Wyndham	Caripelago Bean & Berry	8	Swiss Pastry Shop	5
Sandals Royal		Crystal Palace	Curly's Tropical Daquiri			
Bahamian Resort	C	Resort & Casino H	& Internet Café	3		

weekends with locals. The area around Saunders Beach used to be a massive sissal grove developed by English interests, but is now the exclusive **Highland Park** residential area. Just west is a dangerous curve in the road that marks **Brown's Point**, a small isthmus that marks the leading or windward edge of **Goodman's Bay**, which swings down toward Cable Beach itself. Locals call the road turn "Go-Slow Bend", though many ignore the injunction at their peril. After about half a mile, the big hotels loom up out of the casuarinas, and for the next two miles or so the roadway divides into two avenues split by a wide central median used by walkers and joggers from the hotels.

East of downtown

It is almost impossible to walk the length of **East Bay Street**. The majority of the strip is a jumble of commercial enterprises, fast-food joints, construction projects and smaller government buildings, along with hotels used mostly by Bahamian salesmen and Out Islanders here on short stays. One pleasant exception is **Potter's Cay**, a mile from Rawson Square but still a major component of Nassau's central core. To travel out this way, catch a #24 or #30 eastbound bus in front of the Straw Market.

Potter's Cay

In the shadow of the Paradise Island Bridge, which spans Nassau Harbour and leads to Paradise Island (see p.91), **Potter's Cay** is home to a bustling market where locals peddle fish, vegetables and hardware. A colourful slice of island life, the cay is a place where fishing boats and sloops from all parts of the northern Bahamas haul in their fresh catch, including grouper, mackerel, snapper, turtle and the ubiquitous conch. Stalls open around 9am every morning, at which point fresh herbs, vegetables and fruit – especially paw-paw (papaya), pineapple, bananas, Eleutheran tomatoes and avocados – are sold. Potter's Cay is the departure point for the fast ferries to the Abacos, Andros, Eleuthera and Exuma (p.25). The slower but more colourful mailboats servicing the far-flung Out Islands also pick up and discharge their cargo and passengers here. The remains of an eighteenth-century gun battery are still visible at the east end of the cay.

Fort Montagu and beyond

Around a mile past Potter's Cay, the main road becomes Eastern Road and passes old **Fort Montagu**, built in 1741 and now an abandoned and neglected ruin. Though it was intended to protect the eastern approaches to Nassau's harbour, the Americans in 1776, Spanish in 1782 and British Loyalists in 1783 captured the fort without firing a shot by landing soldiers on the eastern edge of New Providence, then overrunning the fort at night. Due to these inadequacies, the fort saw little further action and was left to decay. What remains are a few crumbling walls which face a broad public beach that stretches for about a mile in front of the fort, and look out to Montagu Bay, where many yacht regattas and sloop races are held.

One mile south of the fort, on Village Road, is **The Retreat** (Mon–Fri 10am–4pm; $2; ⓦ www.thebahamasnationaltrust.org), an eleven-acre botanical garden nicely maintained by the Bahamas National Trust, which is headquartered here. This peaceful oasis on the edge of the city is mainly devoted to the palm, of which there are 200 species in evidence. Scattered among the palms

△ Cruise ship docked near Bay Street

are examples of many orchid species, ferns and hardwoods now rare on the islands due to over-harvesting. The gardens also have many arbours on which bougainvillea and orchids grow, stone arches which act as passageways and even a Buddha statue.

Two miles due south of Fort Montagu, along the major Yamacraw Road, is a ruin known locally as **Blackbeard's Tower**. A pile of tile-like stones that rises to a height of fifteen feet, the tower is free and open to the public. According to legend, it was built by the pirate Edward "Blackbeard" Teach as a lookout against officials hunting his fellow freebooters. In truth, the structure was built in the late 1700s, well after Teach died. Windswept and eerie, it offers fine views of the island, and the stretches of ocean off to the east. Finding the tower, though, can be tricky. To do so, head south on Fox Hill Road, a major road off Eastern Road, to a house called Tower Leigh on Yamacraw Road. The path to the tower is unmarked, but you'll see it in the distance.

Continuing south on Fox Hill Road leads to the suburb of **FOX HILL**, established in the mid-1700s as a settlement for freed slaves. By far the best time to visit the suburban neighbourhood is during its **Emancipation Day celebrations**, held on the second Tuesday in August, when bands play all day and craft exhibits, especially quilts and straw work, and copious food stalls are in evidence. Call the Ministry of Tourism (☎302-2000) for more information. During the rest of the year, the neighbourhood's highlight is the Romanesque **St Augustine's Monastery** (☎364-1331), on Barnard Road, a working monastery and small college where Latin is still taught to the local boys who attend. Begun in 1946 under the guidance of Benedictine monk Father Jerome (see p.288), the structure of blocky sandstone stands on a nearby outcrop and is surrounded by neatly tended gardens. Call ahead and the friendly monks will conduct a tour of the place for a small donation.

Back up at the coastal Montagu Fort, Eastern Road continues east past **Montagu Foreshore**, an area of palatial homes perched on shaded cliffs above a beach. The road here is narrow and winding, and there is no access to the beach, though you can get down to the water at Montagu Ramp, a boat launch and market where locals bring conch to sell. Further along Eastern Road sits the **East End Lighthouse**, an automated signal not open to the public that constitutes the farthest eastern point on New Providence Island.

Over-the-Hill

True to its name, **Over-the-Hill** sits on the inland side of Nassau's Prospect Ridge, the largest hill in Nassau. It's a relatively poor residential area where descendants of former slaves built compact wooden houses and painted them in rainbow colours. Though there are some points of cultural interest here – shops selling local crafts and hards-crabble bars featuring rake 'n' scrape bands – it's not really a place to wander on your own, and can be dangerous, especially at night.

Eating

To feed the heavy influx of tourists from all over the world, Nassau's **restaurants** have mastered seemingly every style of cooking, at prices ranging from moderate to ludicrously expensive. On top of the kaleidoscopic array of international cuisine, though, the city offers great opportunities to feast on strictly Bahamian fare and to grab a cheap but delicious bite at a bakery or café. There are also a number of **take-out** places in town useful for eating on the quick. The best of the bunch is the *Imperial Take-Away*, across from the *British Colonial Hotel*.

On **Cable Beach**, one is never far from food or drink. Dining here, though, presents few budget options, with most prices ranging from moderate to very expensive. Most of the hotel restaurants – with the exception noted below – are nothing to write home about. The all-inclusive hotels on the strip – *Sandals* and *Breezes* – are not open to non-guests. There are, however, a few nice spots for a drink or a meal within walking distance of all hotels. Not to be overlooked is the *Traveller's Rest* a couple of miles west of Cable Beach, one of the island's nicest casual restaurants (reviewed on p.97).

Downtown Nassau

Athena Restaurant Bay St at Charlotte St ☎ 326-1296. A busy spot attracting large numbers of hungry cruise-ship day-trippers with tasty but overpriced Greek food on a pleasant second-storey verandah. Modestly sized appetizers $12, salads $10–25, main dishes $20–25. Open Mon–Sat 9am–6.30pm, Sun 9am–4pm.

Bahamian Kitchen Trinity Place off Market St ☎ 325-0702. Authentic Bahamian home cooking served in clean, spartan surroundings, with wonderful grouper, snapper and conch dishes for under $10. Smartly dressed office workers stop in for take-away tuna and grits or Johnny cake and chicken souse ($2). Open Mon–Sat 11.30am–10pm & Sun 1–8pm.

Buena Vista *Buena Vista Hotel*, Delancy St ☎ 322-2811/2, ⓦ www.buenavista-restaurant.com. Located in an eighteenth-century manor house, this elegant chintz and white-linen French restaurant has a fine reputation for its outstanding caesar salads, smoked salmon, duck pate, jumbo shrimp and a fabulous wine list. Entrees from $30. Open for dinner only from 7pm; reservations required.

Café Europa Charlotte St between Bay St and Woodes-Rogers Walk ☎ 328-4360. A bright, modern, trendy coffee bar serving coffees of all kinds as well as breakfast, healthy salads, sandwiches (included Norwegian smoked salmon and cream cheese), German dishes like schnitzel and bratwurst and sweets like chocolate coconut rum cake and tiramisu. Dishes range from $7 to $15. There's a happy hour on Fridays (6–9pm) with special drinks and live music/DJ. Open Mon–Thurs 7am–6pm, Fri 7am–10pm, Sat 8.30am–6pm.

Cafe Matisse Bank Lane off Parliament Square ☎ 356-7012, ⓦ www.cafe-matisse.com. Popular with locals and visitors alike, this sophisticated but relaxed bistro is the nicest place for a meal out in Nassau, with great service and a constantly refreshed menu that includes the likes of stone crab with a mustard dill sauce, freshly made spinach gnocchi with gorgonzola and walnut sauce, grilled lobster tail in a light champagne sauce and a smoked mozzarella, asparagus and sundried tomato pizza; with pink-grapefruit sorbet with vodka or crème brulee for dessert. Dishes are $18–32. The atmosphere is delightful – a whimsical mix of polished wood, hot pink, velvet and gilt inside, and a lovely courtyard shaded by leafy trees for dining al fresco. Occasional Thursday or Sunday night jazz. Reservations recommended for dinner. Open Tues–Sat noon–3pm & 6–10pm.

Café Skans West Bay St at Frederick St ☎ 322-2486. A popular greasy spoon, catering to both tourists and locals who crowd inside for bacon and eggs or stewed fish with Johnny cake for breakfast ($5–8) and conch fritters, chowder, sandwiches, salads and barbeque chicken and ribs later on ($8–12). Open Mon–Sat 8am–6pm, Sun 9am–4pm.

Chez Willie West Bay St ☎ 322-5364/6, ⊛ www .chezwillierestaurant.com. A cordial French restaurant with an old-fashioned chintz and heavy wood decor, serving excellent mussels in wine and a delicious steak tenderloin, with choice wines on a lengthy list. There's a good brunch on Sundays. Dishes from $30. Open nightly from 6.30pm, plus Mon–Fri noon–3pm & Sun 11.30am–4pm.

Daily Grind Coffee Bar West Bay St next to the *El Greco Hotel*. A bright, pleasant corner café facing the water on the edge of town. Fry-up breakfasts ($5) as well as coffee, sandwiches, quiche, salads and pastries. Lunch $6–8. Open daily 7am–7pm

Graycliff *Graycliff Hotel*, 8–12 West Hill St ☎ 322-2796 or 1/800-552-2839, ⊛ www.graycliff.com. *Graycliff's* main restaurant has four indoor dining rooms dripping in lace, crystal, silver, art and antiques, and a beautiful outdoor dining terrace; a perfect setting for a memorable evening, with cocktails served in the lounge before dinner. The five-star, predominantly French menu features the likes of stone crab, caviar, duckling with calvados and apples, and rack of lamb ($30–70). Wine-tasting luncheons hosted by *Graycliff's* sommelier include a tour of the famous 250,000-bottle wine cellar and a three-course meal paired with appropriate wines. Reservations are required, as are jacket and tie at dinner. Open nightly 6.30–10pm, plus Mon–Fri noon–3pm.

Humidor Churrascaria *Graycliff*, 8–12 West Hill St ☎ 322-2796 or 1/800-552-2839, ⊛ www.graycliff .com. Attached to the hotel's cigar factory and smoking lounge, this Brazilian-style steakhouse offers thick, juicy steaks and lots of other meat dishes accompanied by a salad bar ($30–70). Open Mon–Sat noon–3pm & 6.30–10pm.

Island Pasta Market *El Greco Hotel*, West Bay St ☎ 322-1188. Good food, nice atmosphere and moderately priced Italian food, including a seafood pizza fresh from the brick oven. Some tables overlook the harbour. Reservations recommended. Open nightly 6–10pm.

Lum's Iguana Café Prince George Plaza, Bay St ☎ 322-3119. Situated upstairs with a good view of the crowds on Bay St, this casual chrome and vinyl restaurant serves American and Bahamian breakfasts ($8), burgers, sandwiches, pasta and seafood dishes ($10–25). Open Mon–Sat 9am–7pm.

Sbarro Island Shoppe Building, Bay St ☎ 356-0800. A busy, narrow cafeteria with a good range of options for a quick meal. Lunch and dinner offerings include pizza, pasta and Bahamian curried or fried chicken; breakfast on bacon and eggs, chicken souse or a breakfast burrito. Dishes $8–12. Open Mon–Thurs 7am–8pm, Fri & Sat 7am–9pm, Sun 7am–6pm.

Toto Manila Restaurant 20 Parliament St ☎ 325-4554. A simple but appealing patio café offering inexpensive Filipino, Thai and Indonesian food ($7). Open Mon–Sat 11.30am–10pm, Sun 10.30am–4pm.

West of downtown

Arawak Cay Fish Fry West Bay St, Arawak Cay. This collection of more or less permanent wooden seafood shacks situated in a large paved area is a weekend hotspot with locals and tourists alike, though you can get a cheap seafood lunch or dinner with traditional sides of plantain, coleslaw and macaroni and cheese here during the week as well. Perennial favourites are *Twin Brothers* (closed Mon), *Seafood Haven* (closed Wed) and *Goldie's* (closed Mon), but there are a dozen or more establishments to choose from, with indoor and outdoor seating. Easily reached by the #10 bus, with taxis waiting to take you home.

The Cricket Club Restaurant and Pub Haynes Oval, West Bay St ☎ 326-4720 ⊛ www .bahamascricket.com. The menu is a mix of Bahamian-style seafood and English standards like bangers and mash and roast beef with Yorkshire pudding. Wednesday is darts night. Mains $10–15. Open daily for breakfast, lunch and dinner.

East of downtown

East Villa Restaurant East Bay St ☎ 393-3377. Moderately-priced Chinese and Continental cuisine in an elegant formal dining room, considered the best restaurant on the island by some residents. Reservations suggested and "proper attire" requested. Dinner mains average $25. Open

Mon–Fri noon–3pm & 6pm–midnight, Sat 6pm–midnight, Sun 12.30–3pm & 6–10pm.

Gaylord's Dowdeswell St near Victoria St ☏ 356-3004. Upscale Indian restaurant housed in an 1870s colonial mansion, serving delicious tandoori and curries, including a large selection of vegetarian dishes and curried conch. Mains average $20–25. Open Mon–Fri noon–3pm & nightly 6.30–11pm.

The Poop Deck Nassau Yacht Haven, East Bay St ☏ 393-8175, ⓦ www.thepoopdeckrestaurants .com. The original *Poop Deck* is a popular seafood restaurant just east of the Paradise Island Bridge. The elaborate menu features fresh seafood, grilled meats and salads, an extensive wine list, and a justly famous guava duff for dessert. Lunch $10–20, dinner $20–35. Open daily noon–10.30pm. There's another branch six miles or so out of town (see p.97).

Sun and. . . Lakeview Rd off Shirley St E ☏ 393-1205, ⓦ www.sun-and.com. This dinner-only establishment is considered one of Nassau's culinary highlights, offering elegant, formal dining in a slightly snobbish atmosphere with a menu of imaginative, beautifully presented French cuisine ($35–45). Reservations recommended, jackets required. Open Tues–Sun 6.30–10pm; closed Aug–Sept.

Cable Beach

Cafe Johnny Canoe *Nassau Beach Hotel*, West Bay St ☏ 327-3373. A colourful, popular spot for good food and people-watching; recommended dishes include the Bahamian fried chicken, meat loaf and macaroni and cheese, as well as the luscious desserts and filling breakfasts. Dining inside at comfy casual booths or outside on a covered terrace. The bar's a good place to oil up

an appetite too, with live music on Friday nights. Breakfast $8; dinner plates of more than you can eat $12–25. Open Mon–Thurs & Sun 7.30am–11pm, Fri & Sat 7.30am–midnight.

Capriccio Ristorante West Bay St at Cable Beach, across from *Sandals* ☏ 327-8547. A nice little Italian eatery, with four tables inside and a few more on a covered terrace. Dishes $15–25. Open Mon–Sat 11am–10pm, Sun 5–10pm.

Dickie Mo's West Bay St ☏ 327-7854. This popular roadside spot sports a nautical look and serves seafood, burgers and Bahamian specialities like conch, stone crab, grouper, snapper and guava duff. Most of the dining is outside, though there is a covered bar where soca and calypso are played some nights. Average dishes are priced $15–25. Open Mon, Tues, Thurs, Sat & Sun 5pm–midnight, Fri 5pm–2am.

Milano Café West Bay St ☏ 327-5456. A sidewalk café adding a touch of European sophistication to the Cable Beach strip, serving quiche ($4–5) and sandwiches on panini bread ($7–8) along with coffee, pastries and more elaborate Italian desserts. Open Mon–Sat 7am–7pm.

Nettie's Place at *Casuarina's of Cable Beach Hotel*, West Bay St ☏ 327-7921. *The* place to head in Cable Beach for a home-style Bahamian meal; popular with locals celebrating special occasions. Mains around $20. Daily 8am–10pm.

Sbarro next to the *Nassau Beach Hotel* ☏ 327-3076. Good for a quick bite or take-away – fast food pizza, pasta and fried chicken for under $10. Open daily for lunch and dinner.

Swiss Pastry Shop West Bay St, across from *Sandals* ☏ 327-7601. Divine cream shells and various *kugels* are the reason for dropping into this roadside bakery, which also specializes in fancy wedding cakes. Open Mon–Sat 9am–6.30pm.

Nightlife: bars, clubs and shows

To a very large extent, Nassau's **nightlife** is tourist nightlife. Nassauvians store up their party fever for the two annual dusk-to-dawn Junkanoo blow-outs (see p.76) – the rest of the year, downtown Nassau is deserted by 6pm most evenings, and on Sunday night, it looks like a plague has struck. Visiting vacationers, however, party every night of the week, with most of the action centred on the Cable Beach and Paradise Island resort strips (see p.95). All hotels have their own watering holes, ranging from **casual sports bars** to **chic piano jazz lounges**. If you want to escape the resort enclave, there are a few bars and **dance clubs** scattered around town. Another option is a **sunset boat cruise** with dinner and/or drinks (see p.64). To immerse yourself completely in the local after-hours culture, you have to head to a local bar in the residential districts "Over-the-Hill", but roaming around on your own after dark isn't recommended given Nassau's increasing violent crime rate. There is a good reason why most Bahamians stay in after dark.

Gambling at the **casino** (there are two – one at Cable Beach, the other on Paradise Island, see p.93) is strictly a tourist activity; Bahamians themselves are prohibited by law from indulging in this pastime. More high-brow **cultural performances** occur occasionally throughout the year at Nassau's performing arts venue.

Note that Nassau bars and nightclubs seem to open and fold in a hurry; your best bet for up-to-the-minute night-time entertainment options is to check the free tabloid *What's On* (available in hotel lobbies) or ask a hotel concierge.

Cafe Johnny Canoe West Bay St, Cable Beach ☎327-3373. The outdoor bar is a fun place for a drink and a bite anytime; you can catch a mini Junkanoo (live calypso music and a small band of costumed dancers) on Friday nights from 8pm.

Club Waterloo East Bay St, one mile east of Paradise Island Bridge ☎393-7324. This splashy, crowded disco features five bars and dancing, with a four-hour happy hour beginning at 4pm and free buffet eats on Fridays. Cover $20 on weekends. Open Mon–Thurs 4pm–midnight, Fri & Sat 4pm–4am, closed Sun.

Crystal Palace Casino *Wyndham Nassau Resort*, Cable Beach; ☎327-6000. No fewer than 760 slot machines and fifty gaming tables open 24 hours a day, seven days a week.

Dundas Centre for the Performing Arts Mackey St ☎393-3728. This lovely white stucco theatre presents home-grown drama, choral music, occasional dance and readings by both local and international artists, mainly between January and April. The *Sunday Nassau* newspaper carries listings of its performances or call the box office during the week.

Fluid Lounge Bay St between Frederick and Market streets ☎356-4691, ⓦwww .clubfluidbahamas.com. A dance club geared to the 25-and-over set. Cover $5. Open nightly 10pm–4am.

Graycliff 8–12 West Hill St ☎302-9150. For a tipple in a sophisticated setting, meander uphill to this fabled eighteenth-century mansion, where you can sample one of the 250,000 bottles in *Graycliff*'s celebrated wine cellar, or finish off the evening with a hand-rolled cigar in the smoking lounge. Open nightly 6.30–10pm.

Hammerheads Bar and Grill East Bay St, just west of the Paradise Island Bridge ☎393-5625. A small beer bar with a few booths and a jukebox, popular with holiday-makers. Open daily 11am–2am, with a happy hour 4–7pm.

Rainforest Theater at the *Crystal Palace Casino, Wyndham Nassau Resort*, Cable Beach ☎327-6200, ext 6758, ⓦwww.cablebeachresorts .com. At 8.30pm (Tues–Sat) this 800-seat venue presents a Las Vegas-style spectacular replete with bosomy dancers, show tunes, magicians and/or female impersonators. Once a month or so, the regular show is replaced by a performance by entertainers like the Pointer Sisters, Boyz II Men and Rich Little. Advance reservations are almost always necessary. Regular show $25–35, special events $60–80.

Shopping

For many, duty-free **shopping** is the activity of choice during their stay in Nassau. On any day of the week, Bay Street is jammed with shoppers perusing the aisles of a bewildering array of stores. As far as duty-free items are concerned, the best deals can be had on **jewellery** and **watches** (including great deals on Colombian emeralds), and **liquor** – a fine bottle of Bahamian or Haitian rum costs about $8. **Cigars** can also be a good buy, and are best found at either *Graycliff Cigar Factory* (see p.80) or the "Pipe of Peace", at the corner of Bay and Charlotte streets (☎325-2022). Bay Street is also home to the Bahamas' best bookstore, the Island Shoppe, good for picking up a Bahamian cookbook, local history or a novel for the beach. Regular shopping hours are Monday to Saturday 9am to 5.30pm; some gift shops open on Sunday mornings.

Nearly everybody who comes to Nassau winds up at the **Straw Market** (see p.74) on the western end of Bay Street, only a couple of blocks from Rawson Square and a good place to search out locally-crafted items or a "Made in China" trinket. Serious shoppers should obtain a copy of the glossy tourist mag *What to Do: Where to Shop*, available at hotels and in all information booths.

Listings

Airlines Air Canada ☎1-888/247-2262; Air Jamaica ☎1-800/523-5585; American Airlines ☎1-800/433-7300; Bahamasair ☎377-5505; British Airways ☎1-800/247-9297; Continental ☎1-800/231-0856; Continental Connection ☎377-4314; Cubana Airlines ☎377-7141; Delta/Comair ☎1-800/221-1212; JetBlue ☎377-1174; Spirit Airways ☎377-0152; US Airways ☎1-800/622-1015; Virgin Atlantic ☎377-1220. For charter airlines flying between Nassau, Florida and the Out Islands see p.21.

Banking Scotiabank has branches in downtown Nassau next to the *British Colonial Hilton* (☎322-7401), on Rawson Square (☎356-1400), on West Bay Street in Cable Beach (☎327-7380) and on Casino Drive, Paradise Island (☎363-2591). First Caribbean (☎356-8000) has branches around the island, including one on Bay Street just west of Rawson Square. The Royal Bank of Canada has a branch at the airport (☎377-7179), in Cable Beach Shopping Centre (☎327-6077), downtown at 323 Bay St (☎322-8700), and on Paradise Island at 1 Marine Drive (☎363-6760). Banking hours are generally Mon–Thurs 9.30am–3pm, Fri 9.30am–5pm. Most banks have ATMs dispensing either US or Bahamian dollars and additional ATMs are easily found throughout Nassau, mainly in the hotels, shopping centres and casinos. American Express is represented by Destinations (☎322-2931) at 303 Shirley St (between Charlotte and Parliament streets). The Western Union (ⓦwww.westernunion.com) has offices downtown at 51 Frederick St (☎356-7764) and on West Bay St in Cable Beach (☎327-5170).

Car rental Orange Creek Car Rentals on West Bay Street in Cable Beach (☎323-4967, ⓦwww.orangecreek.com) is the cheapest, with decent "pre-owned" compacts starting at $39 plus insurance. Otherwise, the big internationals have the following branches: Avis Cumberland St across from the *British Colonial Hilton* ☎5326-6380, Paradise Island Shopping Centre ☎363-2061, Cable Beach ☎322-2889, the airport ☎377-7121 (ⓦwww.avis.com); Budget the airport ☎377-9000, Paradise Island ☎363-3095 (ⓦwww.budget.com); Dollar downtown Nassau (☎325-3716) the airport (☎377-7301 (ⓦwww.dollar.com); Hertz the airport ☎377-8684 (ⓦwww.hertz.com); National/Alamo the airport ☎377-0355 (ⓦwww.alamo.com).

Dentist Princess Margaret Hospital, downtown at Elizabeth Ave at Sands Rd (☎322-2861) has a dental care unit.

Emergencies Police and fire dial ☎911. There are police stations in every district of Nassau, painted green, with officers out front in most cases. The main department is on Parliament Square. Bahamas Air-Sea Rescue can be reached on ☎325-8864 or 322-3877.

Eyeglasses The Optique Shoppe, 22 Parliament St ☎322-3910 (Mon–Fri 9am–5pm, Sat 9am–noon).

Groceries City Markets, West Bay Street, Cable Beach; Gourmet Market, Caves Shopping Plaza, West Bay Street; Lyford Cay Shopping Center, West Bay Street; Paradise Supermarket and Deli, Hurricane Hole Shopping Plaza, Paradise Island.

Internet access Most hotels provide Internet access for guests. If yours doesn't, there are branches of Cybercafe upstairs in the Prince George Plaza on Bay St (Mon–Sat 9am–6pm, Sun 9am–4pm) and at the Paradise Island Shopping Centre (Mon–Sat 9am–6pm); Café Europa is on Charlotte St (Mon–Thurs 7am–6pm, Fri 7am–10pm, Sat 8.30am–6pm; $5 for 20min). In Cable Beach, the business centre at the *Radisson* (Mon–Fri 9am–5pm; $7 for 15min) charges usurious rates, but provides the connection.

Laundry Superwash on Nassau St at Boyd Rd (☎323-4018) has coin-operated machines and is open 24 hours a day, seven days a week. In the same building is Oriental Dry Cleaner (☎323-7249). Many hotels offer laundry and dry-cleaning service, and most of the marinas have laundry facilities.

Library The main library is the Nassau Public Library on Shirley St (Mon–Thurs 10am–8pm, Fri 10am–5pm, Sat 10am–4pm; ☎322-4907).

Medical Attention Princess Margaret Hospital, Elizabeth Ave at Sands Rd ☎322-2861; Cable Beach Medical Centre, West Bay St, Cable Beach ☎327-2886; Doctor's Hospital, Shirley St at Collins Ave, ☎302-4600.

Pharmacy People's Pharmacy is downtown on Bay St at Elizabeth Ave (Mon–Sat 9am–5.30pm; ☎356-9806). Alternatively, try Lowes Pharmacy at the Harbour Bay Shopping Centre on East Bay St east of the city centre (Mon–Sat 8am–8.30pm, Sun 9am–5pm; ☎393-4813).

Post office The main post office is on East Hill St at Parliament St (Mon–Thurs 8.30am–5.30pm, Fri 8.30am–12.30pm; ☎322-3025).

Telephone There's a BaTelCo storefront on East St off Bay St (daily 7am–10pm; ☎323-6414), with booths for international calls. Many shops sell pre-paid phone cards.

Paradise Island

A monument to the reckless buildup of mass tourism, **PARADISE ISLAND** consists of 686 acres of hard-pack coral and wind-blown sand lying just offshore from New Providence and connected to it by a two-pronged, mile-long bridge. Visitors on package tours come in droves for a week or a weekend at the island's high-priced resorts and the place is overbuilt almost to the point of lunacy, chock-a-block with hotels, restaurants, shops and holiday-makers. The gargantuan **Atlantis Resort** towers over everything and continues to buy up and build up large chunks of property on the island. There is no real town or settlement here, just acres of tourist facilities. Nevertheless, Paradise Island still has a marvellous north coast where pink sand meets mellow turquoise water, explaining why commercialism found the isle in the first place.

After its early brief settlement in the seventeenth century by itinerant fishermen, Paradise Island was given over to the raising of pigs, which gave the cay its original name of Hog Island. Nassauvians took up the habit of rowing over to the cay to spend a leisurely day on its deserted beaches and thus its tourist industry began. During the late eighteenth century, an ornate Banquet House

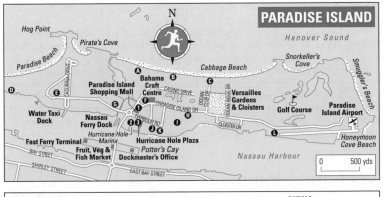

ACCOMMODATION				EATING	
Atlantis Paradise Island	A	Holiday Inn Sunspree Resort	K	Sheraton Grand B	Anthony's Caribbean Grill	1
Bay View Village	I	Ocean Club	C	Sivananda Ashram	Blue Marlin	G
Club Land'or Resort	G	Paradise Harbour		Yoga Retreat D	Dune	C
Club Med, Paradise Island	E	Club & Marina	L	Sunshine	Green Parrot Bar and Grill	2
Comfort Suites	F	Paradise Island Fun Club	J	Paradise Suites H	News Café	3

was built on the island (since demolished) and local Bahamians offered boat rides to the island, provided changing rooms for bathers and began to sell fresh fruit, especially the succulent oranges that were cultivated there.

As Nassau nurtured a nascent hospitality industry catering to wealthy winter visitors in the early twentieth century, so Hog Island began its transformation from sun-bleached scab of land to highly sought-after million-dollar real estate. Its undeniably fine beaches and cheap, undeveloped tracts of bush drew the attention of Swedish industrialist Axel Wenner-Gren (of Electrolux vacuum-cleaner fame), who arrived in Nassau in 1939, dredged a brackish sump-hole, renamed it Paradise Lake and built a grand villa. Blacklisted by the American government amid rumours of Nazi connections, Wenner-Gren sold his estate to Huntington Hartford (the American A&P supermarket mogul), who renamed the island **Paradise**, and was soon busy building the posh **Ocean Club**, a 59-room Georgian-style charmer.

In 1967, a new owner, Resorts International, built the arching **Paradise Island Bridge** linking the island with Nassau and added a casino to the amusements on offer. In 1994, Resorts cashed out its considerable investment, paving the way for billionaire Sol Kerzner's Sun International – specializing in mega-developments – which now owns seventy percent of the island (and increasing), including the *Ocean Club* and the *Atlantis Resort and Casino* complex. In December 1998, a second bridge spanning Nassau Harbour was completed to accommodate the steady flow of traffic and goods that keep the hotels humming.

Whether or not you will enjoy your visit to Paradise depends on your definition of "getting away from it all". If your tropical daydreams involve lounging by the pool, people-watching, gambling at the casino, waterslides and paragliding, you will have a good time here. If not, you might find the Paradise Island carnival overwhelming. Still, there's always the marvellous north coast, its soft pink beaches lapped by the clear, turquoise waters of the Atlantic.

Getting around

If you are staying on Paradise Island, don't bother renting a car unless you plan to tour New Providence; see p.69 for a list of agents. The *Casino Express*, a shuttle bus making the rounds of the major hotels for a $1 fare, is based at the *Atlantis* hotel. If you set out to explore Paradise Island on foot, keep in mind that distances are greater than they appear on the tourist maps and much of the island is private property protected by security. For longer trips or when it is hot, taxis circulate on the main roads and carry passengers across the Paradise Island Bridge for shopping in Nassau ($10). The easiest way to get to Nassau is by water taxi or ferry ($3), which leave the Paradise Island ferry dock every half-hour between 8.30am and 6pm. Water taxis also ply the waters between Hurricane Hole Marina and the Nassau waterfront.

Accommodation

Paradise Island is dominated by the sprawling and obscenely expensive **Atlantis Resort**, which continues to gobble up real estate on the island and build row upon row of candy-coloured condos and tourist shops. However, there are alternatives to *Atlantis*, ranging from exclusive luxury resorts to a couple of secluded and relatively inexpensive but very charming guesthouses. Be warned that almost nothing is cheap here.

NEW PROVIDENCE AND PARADISE ISLAND | Accommodation

Atlantis Casino Drive ☎ 363-3000 or 1-800/321 -3000, Ⓦ www.atlantis.com. A huge, package-tourist hotel with 2239 rooms, 230 suites, seventeen eateries, eighteen bars, eleven swimming pools and three spectacular aquariums housing 250 species of marine life and 50,000 fish (tours available for non-guests), with every kind of recreational facility – a casino, water sports, a putting course and a golf course, fitness centre, tennis courts, library, children's day camp, concerts by big-name performers, a comedy club, a shopping arcade stocked with designer gear and trinkets and a movie theatre. The whole complex has been developed on the theme of the mythical civilization of Atlantis, and there is little here to suggest that you are in the Bahamas. If you just want to relax by the pool with a cool drink and are in the mood for glitz, decadence and lots of company, you'll love it. If not, you might go mad. From $350. ❾

Best Western Bay View Suites Bay View Drive ☎ 363-2555 or 1-800/757-1357, Ⓦ www.bwbayviewsuites.com. Relatively secluded in a residential area, this four-acre resort is a thirty-unit condo-style expanse with a few villas. The suites (either one- or two-bedroom units) and three-bedroom villas are all spacious, stylish and clean with a/c, TV and kitchen. The property, a 10-min walk from Cabbage Beach, also boasts three swimming pools and a laundry room. ❼

Chaplin House ☎ 363-2918. Located on the peaceful and secluded western tip of Paradise Island (call from the Paradise Island ferry dock for pick-up by water taxi), it is hard to imagine a greater contrast with Atlantis. Three homey, casually elegant sunbleached white clapboard cottages set in a green tree-shaded garden, each with a deep wooden verandah appointed with white wicker chairs. Some rooms are directly on the beach, others just a few feet away, and all have a view of the water. On one side is Nassau harbour, on the other, a gorgeous, private stretch of Paradise Beach you can follow for a mile to Atlantis. No TV or telephone (telephone and Internet available on request in the main house), but this doesn't seem to put off the many contented return guests. ❸–❺

Club Land'Or Resort Paradise Beach Drive ☎ 363-2400 or 1-800/552-2839, Ⓦ www .clublandor.com. Overlooking the marina, this three-storey timeshare/hotel has 72 attractive one-bedroom suites with kitchens and balconies surrounding a quiet, green courtyard where breakfast and lunch are served by the pool. Guests have access to the beach at Atlantis a 5 min walk away. There is formal dining room, a laundry on site, and a shuttle bus to the grocery store every Friday and Saturday. $450. ❾

Comfort Suites Casino Drive ☎ 363-2234 or 1-800/451-6078, Ⓦ www.comfortsuites.com. This three-storey pink hotel holds 320 junior suites and nicely furnished doubles with king-size beds, sofa, cable TV and a big bathroom. There is a pool and hot tub, and Cabbage Beach is nearby. Rates include continental breakfast. ❽

One and Only Ocean Club Casuarina Drive ☎ 363-2501 or 1-800/321-3000, Ⓦ www .oceanclub.com. Originally a private residence and now an exclusive getaway with fifty luxurious rooms along with a few suites and villas. Located at the quiet end of Cabbage Beach, the Ocean Club encompasses lush vegetation and transplanted stone ruins along with a great gourmet restaurant, a pool, golf course and tennis courts. For the basic $700 a night, you get 35 acres of luxury and quiet.

Paradise Harbour Club and Marina Harbour Drive ☎ 363-2992 or 1-800/742-4276, Ⓦ www .phc-bahamas.com. A small collection of accommodations ranging from king-size hotel rooms to two-bedroom apartments with kitchens and views of the harbour. There is a pool, an exercise room, free transportation to the beach and into Nassau, and a laundry room. Some units have kitchens and the relaxed and inviting Columbus Tavern Restaurant is here too. ❺

Riu Resort next door to Atlantis ☎ 1-866/845 -3765, Ⓦ www.riui.com. Formerly the Sheraton and recently refurbished, this is an ornate, very grand beachfront hotel with a European feel. Its 379 pink and floral rooms are all nicely furnished and have balconies, with the best views oceanside on the seventh storey and higher. Five restaurants, including the blue-and-white-tiled breakfast room, a Japanese glass pagoda on the beach, and white linen and silver service in a formal dining room. All-inclusive; call for current rates, which fluctuate.

Sivananda Ashram Yoga Retreat West island ☎ 363-2902 or 1-800/441-2096, Ⓦ www .sivananda.org. Located on the secluded western tip of the island on four acres of private beach, shaded by palms and accessible only by water taxi (any water taxi will drop you there, or call for pick up). A lovely, peaceful retreat established for yoga practice and training, with accommodation in basic, comfortable cabins or camping (tent site $55). Daily classes and vegetarian meals included. ❷

Exploring the island

Only four miles long and half a mile wide, Paradise Island is vaguely teardrop-shaped, tapering to a point at its western end where there is a small lighthouse (inaccessible by land). The best beaches are on the north side facing the Atlantic Ocean, while the south shore is edged with marinas, a couple of hotels and private homes. At the foot of the Nassau-bound prong of the Paradise Island Bridge sits a roundabout, the northern axis of which leads to the **Atlantis Resort**, **Casino** and **Marina Village**, with its dozens of shops and restaurants. The resort envelopes the western end of **Cabbage Beach**, two miles of fabulous blush-coloured sand. Well worth the trip alone is the fantastic **Atlantis Aquarium** (guided tours several times daily between 9am and 5pm; $29; ☎363-3000), home to 50,000 sea creatures representing 250 species. Even the most jaded adult will marvel at the graceful, rainbow-hued natural wonders drifting past the floor-to-ceiling windows in the winding underground pathway through the tanks. A highlight is the thirty-yard underwater Plexiglass tunnel running through the **Predator Lagoon and Reef**, with sharks, spotted and eagle rays, and reef fish soaring overhead. A suspension bridge hangs above the lagoon for viewing the daily feeding (times vary).

East and west of Atlantis, palatial private villas are interspersed with a clutch of hotels. On the grounds of the *Ocean Club*, the 35-acre **Versailles Gardens** are a cool refuge from the beach, given an ancient feel by the Grecian-style statuary tucked into shady bowers. On the grounds are the **Cloisters**, the stone ruins of a fourteenth-century Augustinian monastery transported from France to the USA by William Randolph Hearst, who couldn't find room for them at his fairytale castle in California and sold them to Huntington Hartford for his Bahamian hotel. The photogenic archways are popular backdrops for weddings, fashion shoots and movies.

On the western side of the island, the intrepid can bushwhack from the north side of the Atlantis Sports Centre to **Paradise Beach** west of the *Atlantis Resort*, a long curved strand dotted with more million-dollar villas, but otherwise undeveloped.

Eating and drinking

Only a handful of restaurants on **Paradise Island** are unconnected to hotels or resorts, and eating here can be a rather expensive pastime. Still, there are a few culinary highlights and a couple of appealing eateries with some character outside the fortress of Atlantis. A couple of casual bars and grills outside *Atlantis* provide a change of pace and the opportunity to sample Bahamian cooking.

Anthony's Caribbean Grill Paradise Shopping Plaza ☎363-3152. A colourful, family-friendly eatery serving good pizza, lobster and chicken and burgers for around $10 a plate. Open daily 11.30am–11pm.

Atlantis Resort ☎363-3000, ⓦww.atlantis.com. The gargantuan *Atlantis Resort* seems to have a place to chow down around every corner – seventeen restaurants in the main resort and five more in the adjacent *Atlantis Marina Village*. Among those open to outside guests, the elegant *Ville d'Este*

has freshly made pasta, the *Bahamian Club* offers steaks and grilled seafood and *Fathoms Seafood Restaurant* has expansive glass walls affording diners a blue-lit view of the exotic creatures in the Aquarium. At the other end of the price range, *Murray's Deli* is a 1950s-style burger diner and the *Clock Tower* serves pizza and salads. All five restaurants at the *Marina Village* are open to the public (ranging from quasi-Caribbean beach grub at *Bimini Road* to French cuisine at the upscale *Café Martinique*). Dining at *Atlantis* is uniformly expensive: think $40–60 for gourmet dishes and $15 for a burger.

Blue Marlin Hurricane Hole Shopping Plaza ☎ 363-2660. A lively spot dishing up Bahamian seafood, ribs, chicken and sides. Live calypso steel band and limbo dancing nightly except Mondays. Specials $15, with a two-course seafood dinner preceding the floor show for $16; other mains $15–30. Open nightly for dinner from 5pm; the show begins at 8.30pm.

Columbus Tavern *Paradise Harbour Club* ☎ 363-5923, ⓦ www.columbustavernbahamas .com. Creative Bahamian and international dishes served on an inviting breezy verandah overlooking Nassau Harbour, with an emphasis on seafood. Mains average $20–25. Open daily 7am–midnight; happy hour with free conch fritters 5–7pm; live music Fri and Sat nights.

Dune at the *One and Only Ocean Club* ☎ 363-2501. Pricey food-as-art cuisine in a spare, glass-walled dining room with wrapround views of the ocean.

🏃 **Green Parrot Bar and Grill** at the *Hurricane Hole Marina* ☎ 363-3633, ⓦ www .greenparrotbar.com. A pleasant open-air retreat from the hustle and bustle, serving moderately priced light snacks as well as more substantial meals and drinks, with a recommended chicken caesar wrap. Burgers, salads and sandwiches $7–12, curried chicken and steak around $17. Occasionally has live music on weekends. Open daily noon–midnight.

The News Café at the Hurricane Hole Shopping Plaza ☎ 363-4684. A cheerful nook serving inexpensive breakfasts, sandwiches and salads ($7) on an outside patio with a view of the road. Open daily 7.30am–10.30pm.

Nightlife

As in Nassau, nightlife on Paradise Island is focused on the resorts, and mainly revolves around hotel bars and the casino at *Atlantis*, with a few off-site bars like the *Blue Marlin* and the *Green Parrot* providing additional diversions and a change of atmosphere.

Atlantis Casino *Atlantis Resort* ☎ 363-2400. Some 800 slot machines and 78 gaming tables running 24hr a day.

Dragons Lounge and Dance Club *Atlantis Resort* ☎ 363-2400. Jam-packed with sunburned flesh every night of the week. Entry free for *Atlantis* guests; others $30 cover. Open nightly from 9pm until the small hours.

Joker's Wild Comedy Club *Atlantis Resort* ☎ 363-2000, ext. 64002. Shtick from local and

international acts. Ticket price varies with the performer's level of celebrity, but average $20. Open nightly Tues–Sun.

Oasis Lounge at *Club Land d'Or* ☎ 363-2400. A cocktail lounge with a more subdued atmosphere, featuring live music and dancing on Saturday nights and open for cocktails the rest of the week; popular with the over-50 crowd.

The rest of New Providence

The western and southern quarters of New Providence are little visited and can be taken in on a loop of the island in a half-day or so. To be frank, there is little of real interest to detain you out this way, though a few choice stretches of empty beach, a good accommodation option and an enticing waterside restaurant are well worth the trip out of town and may urge you to linger.

To the west of Nassau, undeveloped **Orange Hill Beach** is both pretty and quiet, offering swimmers and picnickers the perfect getaway from the crowds. The coastal road passes through the residential community of Gambier Village en route to **Lyford Cay**, where millionaires live in gated splendour. At the southwest corner of New Providence lies **Clifton Point**, a windy, industrialized wedge of land jutting into an ocean bristling with dive and snorkel sites. The coastal road along the south shore leads toward **Coral Harbour**, a retirement housing development with a **rum distillery** on its doorstep. Just inland from the sea, the quiet village of **Adelaide** has the air of small-town Bahamian life in years gone by and as it continues today in the Out Islands.

Getting around

The best way to see the western and southern portions of New Providence is by car, taking West Bay Street all way around to the south shore, returning by Adelaide and Carmichael Road into Nassau. Many visitors also rent **motorbikes** and make the run to Gambier Village and points south. Nassau **taxis** can be seen as far west as Gambier, but as the evening progresses they become fewer and fewer. A taxi from downtown to Orange Hill or Gambier costs about $15.

By far the cheapest mode of transportation is the public **buses**. To go west out of Nassau toward Gambier/Compass Point, simply catch a #10 anywhere downtown or in Cable Beach. For $1, these buses go only as far as Compass Point. To go directly to the south shore from downtown Nassau, catch a #6 bus which runs to Carmichael Road, then along Adelaide Road.

West to Gambier Village

Six miles west of downtown Nassau, steadily narrowing West Bay Street becomes a tricky two-lane highway loaded with numerous curves and blind turn-offs. The views of the sea are magnificent, as are the colours at sunset, but much of the beach along here is private, including sizable chunks fronting the luxury condo developments at *Sandyport* and *Caves Village*, both of which have shopping and dining opportunities for passers-by (see below). Shortly past *Sandyport* are **The Caves**, a couple of hollowed-out rock cavities sitting roadside. In truth, there is little to them save for a small inscribed plinth commemorating the arrival of Prince Albert, Duke of Edinburgh (the consort of Queen Victoria) on December 3, 1861, the first member of the royal family to visit the Bahamas. *Caves Village* is located at the turn-off to the airport along Blake Road. At this spot, US President Kennedy, Canadian Prime Minister Diefenbaker and British Prime Minister Harold Macmillan met in a Cold-War summit conference during 1962. Bahamians still call the spot **Conference Corner**.

Just beyond the turn-off is Orange Hill, so called because of a huge orange grove that once stood here as part of a large estate. Both the grove and estate are long gone, but the *Orange Hill Beach Inn* is here, while below it is **Orange Hill Beach**, a long band of white sand backed by low dunes, running along the shore for half a mile. It's a fine spot for bathing and picnics and popular with kite flyers and windsurfers. The *Traveller's Rest Restaurant* (see opposite) sits roadside a short distance beyond the western end of the beach.

The increasingly rocky coastline approaches **GAMBIER VILLAGE** about a mile beyond Orange Hill. The village is a scattered settlement of wood-frame and concrete houses originally inhabited by liberated African slaves from a vessel captured on the seas by Britain's Royal Navy during and after 1807. Another group of residents came from the slave ship *Creole*, whose slaves revolted in 1840 near the Abacos.

Practicalities

This stretch of New Providence is relatively rich in facilities. There's good **accommodation** above the beach at Orange Hill at the 🌴 *Orange Hill Beach Inn* (☎327-7157, 🌐www.orangehill.com; ❹), a relaxed, seaside hotel topping a low knoll above Orange Hill Beach, away from the noise and bustle of the city centre, but with frequent and easy transportation downtown on the #10 bus ($1) in about fifteen minutes. The 32 airy doubles, studios and villas are finished with light, natural wood and tasteful florals; each has a balcony or patio, kitchenette, TV and air conditioning, and some have ocean views. Other facilities include an inviting pool deck, an honesty bar furnished with games and books, a laundry and a daily grocery run to Cable Beach. The inn is five minutes away from the airport, making it an even more appealing choice for those on a stop over to or from the Out Islands. There's a casual **restaurant** on site, serving hearty breakfasts (daily) and dinner (nightly except Wed & Sat), with basic Bahamian dishes for under $20. Otherwise, a short distance beyond the western end of the beach, the roadside 🌴 *Traveller's Rest* restaurant (daily 11am–11pm; lunch from $8, dinner around $14; ☎327-7633) is great, with shaded patio seating overlooking the beach, hearty Bahamian cooking and killer banana daquairis. Service can be almost comically slow, so be prepared to relax with a drink.

At *Sandyport*, the waterfront *Poop Deck West* (Tues–Sun noon–10.30pm; ☎327-DECK, 🌐www.thepoopdeckrestaurants.com) is a popular outpost of the Nassau original (see p.88), big on seafood and sundowners, with main dishes priced $15 to $30. At *Caves Village*, *Ristorante Villaggio* (Mon–Sat 5.30–10pm; ☎327-0965, 🌐www.villagiorestaurant.com) is an expensively stylish Italian dining room with an attached cocktail and wine bar; dishes cost $30 to $40.

Lyford Cay

From Gambier, West Bay Street continues westward past upscale residential developments en route to **LYFORD CAY** at the western tip of the island. Not really an island, but separated from the rest of New Providence by a guarded security barrier, this gated community is the swankiest address on New Providence. Named for the Loyalist William Lyford, it is home to showbiz celebrities like Sean Connery and well-heeled business types who moor their gigantic yachts at the foot of their manicured lawns. Just outside the gates is **Lyford Cay Centre**, a small shopping centre with boutiques, dry-cleaners, petrol station, a pharmacy, the *August Moon Café* (☎362-6631) and a small art gallery. Nearby, Bahamians live in **Mount Pleasant**, a tract of modest homes with a few shops for locals, and commute to work in Lyford or elsewhere on the coast.

Clifton Point and Adelaide

Winding south past Lyford Cay, Western Road soon reaches **CLIFTON POINT**, the westernmost point on New Providence. In the early 1800s, William Wylly ran a large plantation near the point, and his Great House lies there in ruins, as do the slave quarters. Clifton Point is now heavily industrialized, being the site of Bahamas Electricity Corporation's main plant, a gasoline storage depot – you can watch tankers off-load – and the Commonwealth Brewery where Kalik is brewed.

As the road turns back east and south, it passes the boarded-up *South Ocean Golf and Beach Resort*. Stuart's Cove dive operation (see p.65) is located on the shore here, close to the prime dive sites off the southwest coast. Continuing along the coastal road for a couple of miles brings you to the signposted turn-off to the unassuming village of **ADELAIDE** at Southwest Bay. The village was founded in 1831 when Governor Sir James Carmichael Smyth settled 157 Africans, liberated from a Portuguese slave ship named *Rosa*, on this south-shore site, providing them with basic supplies and land. The Africans established a school and church, then commenced lives as fishermen and subsistence farmers, living for the most part in thatched huts, a few of which could be seen even into the 1960s. Today, some modern trappings have settled in – electricity, phones, decent roads – though not enough to upset the laid-back, ramshackle character of the place. Its quiet lanes of small cottages are shaded by ancient trees, there's a tranquil stretch of beach used mainly by fishermen, and *Avery's Bar and Restaurant* (☎362-1547; closed Mon) offers simple **refreshments** – you can even order a daiquiri by ringing the gong at a hole in the wall along the access road.

Coral Harbour and north

Back on the main west coast road (Adelaide Road), continuing eastward brings you to a roundabout, from which you can head south to **Coral Harbour**, a residential marina-style district with man-made canals and a yacht harbour; cut north across the scrubby interior of the island to the west coast; or continue straight on the main road, which changes its name to Carmichael Road. Carmichael leads to the turn-off to the **Bacardi Distillery** (Mon–Thurs 10am–3pm; free; ☎362-1412), where the famous rum is made. Bacardi moved much of its business to the Bahamas after the Cuban revolution in 1959. Visitors are welcome for the half-hour tours for groups of eight or more, best of course for the complimentary samples of rum provided. Call in advance if you would like to make up the numbers on an already scheduled tour. Also in the Coral Harbour area is Happy Trails Stables (see p.66).

Carmichael Road winds gradually back into the southern sprawl of Nassau, passing by the old Carmichael Bible Church, a clapboard relic of bygone days, and a half-mile further on the site of an abandoned village known as Headquarters, one of the earliest residences of liberated African slaves. All that is left are a few barely observable foundations.

Grand Bahama

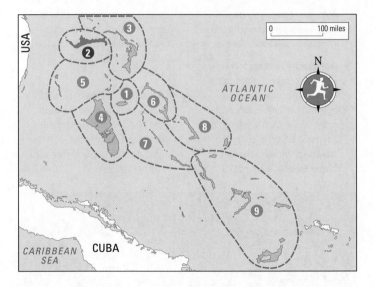

CHAPTER 2 # Highlights

* **Kayaking in Lucayan National Park** The paddling excursions include a lazy float along a mangrove creek, a nature walk and a picnic lunch on spectacular Gold Rock Beach. See p.111

* **Swimming with dolphins** Sanctuary Bay, twenty minutes east from Port Lucaya, is home to a pod of semi-wild dolphins. Here, you can swim with, feed, and observe these intriguing creatures. See p.111

* **Our Lucaya Resort** The sprawling resort dominates the waterfront in Lucaya, but does it with class and calm. More than a match for anything on offer on more crowded Paradise Island or Cable Beach. See p.123

* **Smith's Point Community Fish Fry** Every Wednesday night, the place to be is Taino Beach at Smith's Point, the scene of a beach party featuring lots of Bahamian-style food, cool drinks, music and conversation. See p.125

* **Gold Rock Beach** A world away from the bustle of Freeport/Lucaya, at low tide this swathe of sugary sand is the ideal setting for a secluded picnic and long walk. See p.128

* **Deadman's Reef** The snorkelling from shore is great, the sand is soft, and there's a relaxed beach bar – all the makings for a great day out. See p.130

△ Kayaking in Lucayan National Park

Grand Bahama

GRAND BAHAMA boasts gorgeous sugary white beaches, a sapphire sea and a colourful profusion of lush coral reefs and marine gardens lying beneath the water's surface, yet its greatest attraction is probably its accessibility. Just 55 miles east of Miami – with daily ferry service as well as direct flights from several major American cities – the 96-mile-long island exists almost solely as a big offshore playground for vacationers.

Most of the approximately half-million annual visitors who come to Grand Bahama do not stray far beyond the urban conglomeration of **Freeport** – three miles inland from the south coast – and its seaside suburb **Lucaya**, which, together, are home to most of the island's 47,000 residents. Unique among the islands of the Bahamas, most of which were settled in the seventeenth and eighteenth centuries, Grand Bahama had only a few hundred residents until the 1950s, when Freeport/Lucaya sprang up almost overnight as a deliberately designed tourist "destination" rather than an organic Bahamian community. Its hotels and casinos enjoyed a bright period of glamour in the 1960s, but in the 1970s and 1980s, Grand Bahama's novelty began to fade, leaving Freeport and Lucaya the target of continuous waves of Spring Break college students and cruise-ship day-trippers coming to play the slots and purchase items duty-free. It came to be regarded as a cut-rate package holiday destination passed over by more discerning travellers in favour of Nassau and Paradise Island.

Damage caused by the hurricanes of 2004 and 2005 and the closure of the *Royal Oasis Hotel* have more or less shuttered the tourism industry in the inland city of Freeport. However, its pretty seaside suburb Lucaya continues to hum with a holiday vibe, enjoying an economic rejuvenation fuelled by five-star resort developments – led by *Our Lucaya* – that have helped the island shake its image as Nassau's poorer, unsophisticated cousin. In fact, for sun-seeking vacationers, the charms of Grand Bahama are more than a match for anything on offer in Nassau, without the traffic, crowds and overdevelopment of the capital city. Among Lucaya's attractions are two championship golf courses, a casino, a good range of restaurants and several inviting beaches within easy reach, especially the mile-long **Lucayan** strand and the less developed **Taino Beach**. During the daylight hours there's an almost endless variety of well-organized day-trips and outdoor activities, including world-class watersports and swimming with dolphins, while nightly entertainment – manufactured solely for the pleasure of vacationers – ranges from live music to sunset dinner cruises.

If rounds of miniature golf or the presence of other sun-seekers wrecks your vacation karma, it's possible to leave the tourist gridlock behind without actually leaving the island. To the **east of Freeport** are the unspoilt and generally empty sands of **Barbary**, **High Rock** and **Gold Rock** beaches and

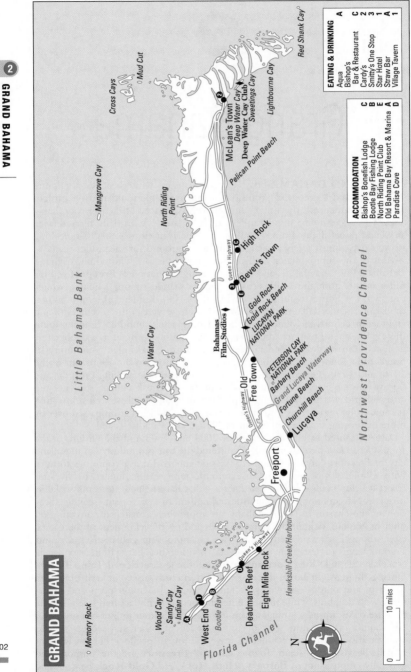

GRAND BAHAMA

ACCOMMODATION

Bishop's Bonefish Lodge	C
Bootle Bay Fishing Lodge	B
North Riding Point Club	E
Old Bahama Bay Resort & Marina	A
Paradise Cove	D

EATING & DRINKING

Aqua	A
Bishop's Bar & Restaurant	C
Cardy's	2
Smitty's One Stop	3
Star Hotel	1
Straw Bar	A
Village Tavern	1

Little Bahama Bank

Memory Rock

Wood Cay
Sandy Cay
Indian Cay

West End

Bootle Bay

Deadman's Reef

Eight Mile Rock

Florida Channel

Water Cay

Mangrove Cay

Cross Cays

Mud Cut

Red Shank Cay

North Riding Point

McLean's Town
Deep Water Cay
Deep Water Cay Club
Sweetings Cay

Pelican Point Beach

Lightbourne Cay

Queen's Highway

High Rock

Beven's Town

Gold Rock

Gold Rock Beach

LUCAYAN NATIONAL PARK

Bahamas Film Studios

Queen's Highway

Old
Freeport

Free Town

PETERSON CAY NATIONAL PARK

Barbary Beach

Grand Lucaya Waterway

Fortune Beach

Churchill Beach

Lucaya

Hawksbill Creek/Harbour

Queen's Highway

Northwest Providence Channel

N

0   10 miles

the nature reserve of **Lucayan National Park**, which encompasses walking trails, limestone caves and mangrove creeks that can be explored by kayak. Also here, only an hour out from Freeport, are two small fishing villages, **McLean's Town** and **Sweeting's Cay**, offering a glimpse of what life on Grand Bahama was like before the invention of package holidays for the masses.

The sights **west of Freeport** are fewer, but still worth the drive out of town. **Deadman's Reef** is the site of several Lucayan archeological excavations, around which are excellent and easily accessible snorkelling grounds from a long strand of sandy beach. At the island's western tip, the scruffy settlement of **West End** has a wildly romantic history of pirates, sunken treasure and rum-runners. Though it isn't much to look at these days, the expanding *Old Bahama Bay* luxury resort nearby has helped begin turning things around.

The mainly uninhabited north shore of Grand Bahama is dominated by a swash of mangroves and choice fishing grounds that draw **bonefishing** fanatics from around the globe. For those who really want to get off the beaten track, the tiny settlement on **Water Cay** off the north coast can be visited by powerboat or on a kayaking expedition.

Some history

Archeologists have made some of their most exciting discoveries of **Lucayan artefacts** on Grand Bahama, particularly at Deadman's Reef in the west and in the caverns that are now part of Lucayan National Park to the east. Traces of Lucayan culture have been few and far between in the Bahamas, thanks to Spanish Conquistadors, who had exterminated nearly all the natives by the end of the fifteenth century. Though Ponce de León stopped here briefly in 1513 to take on water on his quest for the Fountain of Youth, most vessels traversing the waters of the Bahamas over the next couple of centuries passed Grand Bahama by and the island remained virtually uninhabited.

Throughout the seventeenth and eighteenth centuries, about the only group who set foot here were the bands of pirates and privateers camped out around the West End, ambushing treasure-laden ships as they sailed through the Florida Channel headed for Europe. Many a Spanish galleon and British man-of-war wrecked on the reefs that encircle the island, and some of these wrecks have only recently been discovered. Although thousands of **Loyalists** – and their slaves – from the southern states flooded the Bahamas after the end of the American Revolution, none settled on Grand Bahama, most likely because of its poor soil and lack of a natural harbour. The island's first recorded settlement – also at West End – was not established until 1806, and it took the Emancipation of slaves in 1834 for any form of significant growth to occur.

The island experienced a spate of attention during the **American Civil War**, when the West End became a staging ground for Confederate blockade runners smuggling guns and supplies into the southern states (much as it was to become a base for rum-runners during Prohibition in the 1920s). Despite this nefarious economic activity, there were still less than 700 people living on the island by 1888, the majority getting by on fishing, turtling, sponging and minimal cultivation. Over half a century later, American businessman **Wallace Groves** acquired the rights to harvest timber on Grand Bahama. Looking out over acres and acres of bush and swamp, he envisioned a thriving new city and a winter playground for the rich and famous, and set about building it. The 1955 Hawksbill Agreement and subsequent amendments between the Bahamian government and Groves' company, **Grand Bahama Port Authority Ltd**, earned the company the rights to develop and administer

150,000 acres of land – where Freeport and Lucaya now stand – for a period of 99 years. Freeport/Lucaya was declared a tax-free zone, and the Port Authority was granted control over immigration into the city and the licensing of businesses to operate there. Development of Lucaya as an ocean-front resort area began in the 1960s. The Grand Lucayan Waterway, which bisects the island east of Freeport/Lucaya, as well as the other man-made channels and canals in Lucaya, were built to increase the value of real estate by creating more waterfront property.

While not all of Groves' dreams were realized – the bush around Freeport is crisscrossed with a grid of roads built to serve residential neighbourhoods that were never built – tourism has become the backbone of the local economy, supplemented by an active port and oil bunkering facility.

Getting there

As the site of the island's airport, cruise-ship dock and three of its four official ports of entry **marinas** (see box opposite), Freeport/Lucaya is the island's obvious point of entry. The **Grand Bahama International Airport** (☎352-6020), located on the northern outskirts of the city, is only a half-hour flight from Florida, and a bit over two hours from New York, with direct flights from several other US cities. Air Trans, American, Continental Connection/Gulfstream, Delta and US Airways run flights into Freeport every day and Bahamasair flies several times a day from both Nassau (the major transportation hub in the Bahamas, with connections to the Out Islands and international destinations) and directly from Florida (cutting the time-consuming transit through Nassau for visitors without direct flights to Freeport). You can fly daily from Freeport to **Marsh Harbour** in the Abacos on Major's Air Service (☎352-5778) and from Freeport to **Great Harbour Cay** in the Berry Islands on Fri and Sun with Flamingo Air (☎351-4963).

Cruise ships come ashore at Freeport Harbour, five miles west of Freeport proper. In addition to Caribbean island-hopping cruise ships, the *MSV Discovery Sun*, a quadruple-decker passenger ferry, makes a daily five hour crossing between Fort Lauderdale, Florida, and Freeport (US$179 round trip; ☎1-800/937-4477 in Florida, ☎1-800/866-8687 in the US and Canada, ☎305/597-0336 elsewhere, ⓦwww.discoverycruiseline.com). On board there's a casino, swimming pool, buffet meals and a floorshow to amuse passengers en route, and the ticketing office in Freeport is located at the Tanja Maritime Centre (☎352-2328), on Queen's Highway near the Port Facility. As with the airport, there is no public transport from the dock, but both taxis and tour buses can take you into town for around $10.

The more plebeian government M/V *Marcella III* **mailboat** departs from **Nassau** on Wednesdays at 4pm, arriving in Freeport twelve hours later, heading back to Nassau on Fridays at 5pm (tickets $50 one-way); call the dock-master's office in Nassau (☎393-1064) or Freeport Harbour (☎352-9651) to confirm. You'll have to take a taxi ($10 to Freeport; $12 to Lucaya) to get between the mailboat dock and town. Access to Grand Bahama by sea is also available twice daily from the Abacos via Pinder's Ferry Service (☎365-2356; $90 round trip) crossing between Crown Haven in Little Abaco and McLean's Town, sixty miles east of Freeport. There is an infrequent public bus from McLean's Town to Freeport, departing about 12:30pm and 3pm ($8), although it may also be possible to take a shared taxi at similar rates.

Marinas

There are four full-service **marinas** in Freeport/Lucaya – three of which are official ports of entry to the Bahamas – and one marina located at *Old Bahama Bay* at the west end of the island, 25 miles from Freeport. Dockage rates range $1.40–1.90 per foot/per day and all have electricity and freshwater hookups, as well as showers, bathrooms and laundry facilities. All marinas monitor VHF Ch 16.

In Freeport/Lucaya

Grand Bahama Yacht Club at Lucayan Marina Village (℡373-8888, ⓦwww .grandbahamayachtclub.com) can accommodate vessels up to 175ft long in 150 deepwater slips (entrance through Bell Channel). It is an official port of entry with 24-hour customs and immigration services, a fuelling dock, waste pump-out and phone and cable TV hookups. A one-minute water shuttle departs every half-hour to Port Lucaya, where there are provisions stores, hotels, restaurants and other tourist amenities.

Ocean Reef Yacht Club (℡373-4661/2, ⓦwww.oryc.com) lies on an inland waterway carved out just west of Silver Point Beach. The 55 slips here have a depth of 6ft at low tide and can accommodate boats up to 140ft, with phone and satellite TV hookups, hotel accommodations on site and a shuttle service to the shopping district of Lucaya. Not an official port of entry.

Port Lucaya Marina (℡373-9090, ⓦwww.portlucaya.com) is an official port of entry in the centre of Lucaya (entrance through Bell Channel) and can accommodate vessels up to 175ft in 106 slips, some in front of hotel rooms in the contiguous *Port Lucaya Resort and Yacht Club* (See p.117). All amenities are close at hand.

Xanadu Beach and Marina Resort (℡352-6782, ⓦwww.xanadubeachhotel.com) can accommodate 77 boats, and its office sells fuel and marine supplies. While an official port of entry, the attached hotel is pretty dreary and the marina is somewhat isolated (beyond walking distance of shops and restaurants).

West of Freeport/Lucaya

The Marina at Old Bahama Bay (℡346-6500, ⓦwww.oldbahamabay.com) is the only official port of entry on Grand Bahama not in Freeport/Lucaya. Twenty-five miles outside of Freeport, the marina has 72 boat slips for vessels up to 120ft; the entrance channel is 13ft deep and the inner basin is 8ft deep. Customs and immigration open 8am–5pm.

Given the costs and time involved (Crown Haven is also an isolated community a long taxi ride from a major settlement), it's certainly easier to fly from Freeport to Abaco.

Information and maps

The **Grand Bahama Island Tourism Board** (PO Box F 40251, Freeport, Grand Bahama Island, Bahamas; ℡352-8044 or 1-800/448-3386, ⓦwww .grand-bahama.com) has information booths at the airport, the cruise-ship dock, in the Port Lucaya Marketplace and a main office in Freeport's International Bazaar. Along with dispensing maps and general advice, the knowledgeable officers coordinate the 'People to People' cultural exchange programme connecting visitors interested in learning more about Bahamian culture with friendly local volunteers, for a conversation over a cup of coffee or a community event. The newsgroup on the board's website is also a great place to pick up advice and information from recent visitors and island residents.

While free **maps** covering Grand Bahama can be picked up just about anywhere, the *Bahamas Trailblazer Map of Grand Bahama Island, Freeport and Lucaya* published by Etienne Dupuch (Ⓦ www.bahamasnet.com) is the most detailed of the bunch. Visitors seeking a map of diving sites should purchase *A Grand Bahama Island Snorkelling Map* ($10), designed by local diving legend Ben Rose and sold at the UNEXSO dive shop in Lucaya. For current events, look out for the *Freeport News*, published daily except Sunday, or the free *Happenings Around Town* monthly community newspaper. More tourist-oriented publications include *What's On*, a self-explanatory free newspaper, and the gratis and pocketsize *Grand Bahama Island* magazine, containing good maps and a dining guide.

Getting around

You can give the whole of Grand Bahama a quick once-over in a day, although **exploring** its many secluded beaches could easily absorb a week or more. Most visitors never feel the need to venture beyond Freeport/Lucaya, where the major attractions can easily be reached on foot, bicycle, motor scooter or bus. Most hotels also run complimentary shuttle buses to local beaches and the town centres of Freeport and Lucaya, and many of the restaurants located on the outskirts of town will pick you up for dinner and drive you home again. For those who want to roam further afield, a variety of modes of transport are available; however, with a sizable urban conglomeration and the attendant petty crime that comes with it, hitchhiking on Grand Bahama is not recommended.

Buses

Freeport/Lucaya and the communities to the east and west of the city are well connected by a fleet of privately owned **buses**, though note that most don't run on Sundays. To get between Freeport and Lucaya, it's easiest to catch a bus at the stop in front of the International Bazaar in Freeport or on the corner of Seahorse Road and Royal Palm Way in Lucaya. The buses leave when full and cost $1 anywhere within the city limits. Buses to settlements east and west of Freeport/Lucaya leave from the pink **main bus stand** in the parking lot of the Winn Dixie Plaza in downtown Freeport. The #16 bus departs for West End ($4) on the hour between 6am and 6pm, while rides to the eastern end of the island are less frequent – the #10 bus to McLean's Town ($8) leaves from near the main bus stand at 11.30am and 2pm. A last bus departs from here at 5.30pm, going only as far as High Rock.

Taxis and car rentals

Taxis meet every arriving flight and cruise ship and any hotel will call one for you. Flat rates for frequently travelled routes are set by the government, and the fare from the airport to hotels in Freeport or Lucaya is around $11/$20–25 respectively. To order a taxi, try Freeport Taxi (☎ 352-6666) or the Grand Bahama Taxi Union (☎ 352-7101).

Car rentals on the island start from about $80 a day, including strongly recommended liability and collision insurance. Most rental agencies prohibit the use of their cars on dirt roads, meaning if you want to explore the bush tracks and side roads that crisscross the island a jeep or truck is necessary. The following companies can deliver a car to the airport or have desks at the airport and will also deliver a car to your hotel: Avis has two locations (airport ☎352-7666; Port Lucaya ☎373-1102); Brad's (☎352-7930); Dollar-Rent-a-Car (☎352-9325); Econo Car Rental (☎351-6700); Hertz (☎352-3297); M&K Car Rental (☎351-3830); Thrifty (☎352-9308); and Zulu (☎351-5230).

Scooters and bicycles

Motor **scooters** are a fun way to explore the quiet (until you get there) residential streets of Lucaya and the beaches east of town. West of Freeport, however, the heavy truck traffic from the port and local cement plant make it a less attractive option. Scooters with a top speed of about 30mph can be rented for $50 a day in the parking lot across the street from the *Sheraton* in Port Lucaya, from Lucayan Watersports (☎373-6375) in the A-Frame building across from the *Westin at Our Lucaya* and at the *Island Palm Resort* (☎352-6648) in Freeport.

The flat terrain of Grand Bahama makes for easy **biking**, but the traffic in Freeport/Lucaya and the vast stretches of unbroken bush along the Queen's Highway beyond the city limits dampen the appeal. However, there are numerous (unmapped) dirt logging-roads through the island's tall pine forests that can be explored by the adventurous. Well-maintained beach cruisers with one gear are rented by the hour, day or week in Lucaya at Lucayan Watersports (see above) for about $30 a day. If you are planning to put in some heavy mileage, consider bringing your own bike. For information on guided cycling tours, see p. 112 .

Ferries

A public passenger **ferry** runs between Port Lucaya and the *Flamingo Bay Hotel* on Taino Beach every hour 8am–11pm ($5 round trip). It leaves the dock beside the *Pelican Bay Hotel* in Port Lucaya (on the east side of UNEXSO) at ten minutes past the hour for the ten-minute trip to Taino Beach, and returns from Taino Beach on the hour. Because the ferry is not licensed to carry luggage, only daypacks and handbags are permitted.

Watersports and outdoor activities

One of the most attractive features of a vacation on Grand Bahama is the huge array of organized **watersports** on offer in and around Freeport/Lucaya. **Snorkelling** and **diving** are arguably the most popular options, but there's plenty more to do including **kayaking**, **fishing** and even **swimming with dolphins**. For those looking to maximize their beach time, there are plenty of **water toys** available for an hour or more. Operating out of Port Lucaya, Reef Tours (☎373-5880) runs parasailing trips for $60 a trip; they also rent jet skis ($60 for 30min) and offer banana boat rides – an inflated tube pulled behind a powerboat – for $15. On the beach at *Our Lucaya*, Ocean Motion Watersports (☎373-2139) can also set you up for a parasail, along with water-skiing, banana boat rides or a round on their water trampoline at similar rates. They also rent jet skis, sailboats, sit-aboard kayaks and windsurfers. At *Island Seas Resort*, Paradise Watersports (☎373-4002) offers much the same.

Organized tours of Grand Bahama

For those needing a little more action than simple sun-soaking on the beach, there's a long list of **land and sea tours** on Grand Bahamas. Many hotels also offer tour booking services for their guests and most tour operators will pick you up at your hotel in the morning and deposit you back there again in time for cocktails at no extra cost. The downside of this efficiency is that tour groups in many – though not all – cases can be large, and the experiences on offer are manufactured solely for the entertainment of tourists.

Bus and jeep tours

East End Adventures (☎373-6662, ⊛www.bahamasecotours.com). An excellent all-day jeep and boating safari to the unspoiled eastern tip of the island, with a guaranteed group size of ten or less. Along the way, you visit fishing villages, bump along bush trails and sample wild fruits before zipping along by boat to Sweeting's Cay for a conch-cracking demonstration. Then it's on to the pristine powdery beaches of Lightbourne Cay for a picnic lunch, some lolling in the sun, followed by snorkelling ($120). East End Adventures also offers a 4.5 hours jeep convoy excursion to Lucayan National Park and points east ($90), as well as a 3.5 hour bus tour of the same sights ($60), both outings including lunch.

Executive Tours (☎373-7863, ⊛www.executivetoursbahamas.com). Three-hour bus tours of Freeport/Lucaya and the surrounding area, including a drive by the palatial vacation homes lining "Millionaire's Row", a trip to Freeport's open-air fruit market and some time for browsing the cheap souvenirs and luxury goods at the depressingly rundown International Bazaar or the much more lively Port Lucaya marketplace ($30 adults, children $18). They also run guided half-day tours of Lucayan National Park ($43).

Grand Bahama Nature Tours (☎373-2485, ⊛www.grandbahamanaturetours. com). One of the island's more adventurous tour options lets you join a convoy of jeeps on a 4.5 hour off-road excursion through Grand Bahama's tall pine forest and along sandy tracks running beside the ocean. A guide offers historical anecdotes along the way and then prepares a Bahamian picnic lunch on the beach while you go for a swim ($100).

H. Forbes Charter and Tours (☎352-9311, ⊛www.forbescharter.com). Three-hour bus tour that includes similar stops as Executive Tours above as well as visits to the port facility and the local brewery ($35 adults, children $25, including hotel pick-up). Forbes also offers tours of Lucayan National Park ($50/35 per adult/child, including lunch) and a four-hour historical tour to West End ($40/30 per adult/child).

Pat's Adventures (☎559-2921, ⊛www.smilingpat.com). Several different outings around the island aboard a 29-seater bus, including beach-hopping, shopping, an all-day excursion to an uninhabited island off West End for some snorkelling and a lunch of fresh fish on the beach ($120) or a visit to the village of West End

On *terra firma*, **golf** is one of the more popular outdoor activities, with a trio of fine courses on the island. Other possible pursuits include **tennis**, **cycling**, **horseback rides** and even **bird-watching**.

Diving

Among divers, Grand Bahama is known for its variety of targets, including underwater caves, reefs, wrecks and shark dives. It is therefore a good destination for experienced divers, though beginners looking to give it a try for an afternoon or take a full certification course in the warm, clear waters surrounding the island are also catered to.

($35). Pat's also offers transportation to the Wednesday night Fish Fry at Smith's Point ($10), along with a guided Friday night pub crawl through Port Lucaya's water holes ($45).

Boat tours

Exotic Adventures (☎374-2278 or 375-7885, ⊛www.exoticadventuresbahamas .com.). The best choice for those looking for a smaller group or private cruise experience. Most popular are the full ($140) and half-day ($100) cruise to Peterson's Cay National Park, with snorkelling, a barbecue lunch and games. They also offer romantic strandings for couples, involving being left alone together on a deserted island for the day ($100–300 a couple; $450 for dinner) in addition to customized day-trips to neighbouring islands.

Fantasia Tours (☎373-8681, ⊛www.snorkelingbahamas.com). From their booth at the *Port Lucaya Hotel*, Fantasia Tours organizes daily boat excursions aboard a motorized, double-decker catamaran sporting a climbing wall, waterslide, food, cash bar and lots of fellow fun-seekers. Outings include a half-day trip to Peterson Cay National Park for some snorkelling and a picnic lunch (daily 10:30am; adult/child $75/$45), and a two-hour snorkel tour (daily 10:30am and 2pm; adult/child $40/$20). They also offer a sunset dinner cruise featuring unlimited rum punch, loud music and limbo dancing (departs 6pm on Tues, Fri and Sat; $75 with dinner, $45 without).

Reef Tours (☎373-5880, ⊛www.bahamasvg.com/reeftours). Embarking from Port Lucaya Marketplace, this operator offers several daily excursions. A 1.5 hour tour in a glass-bottomed boat allows you to view the wonders of the sea without getting wet (several departures daily, but mornings only Mon and Fri; adults $25, children $15). Short sailing cruises aboard a catamaran are also offered in the morning ($30/$16 adult/child), as are a highly recommended 2.5-hour sailing-and-snorkel excursion each afternoon ($45/$25 adult/child, including snorkel gear) and a more serene two-hour wine and cheese sunset sail ($40).

Superior Watersports (☎373-7863, ⊛www.superiorwatersports.com). Leaving from Port Lucaya, Superior Watersports takes the glass-bottomed boat experience one step further, offering two-hour snorkelling and sightseeing excursions aboard the *Seaworld Explorer*, a semi-submarine vessel with seating for all 34 passengers in a submerged hull fitted out with large glass windows for viewing schools of tropical fish herded past the customers by divers swimming alongside ($40/$25 adult/child). Other options include a "booze cruise" on the *Bahama Mama*, billed as "Freeport's #1 Party Boat" (Mon , Wed, Fri and Sat 6pm, $75 with dinner/$45 without), and a daily Robinson Crusoe Beach Party – a five-hour floating party with snorkelling, beach volleyball, lunch and lounging (departing late morning, $60/$40 adult/child).

Sunn Odyssey Divers located near *Island Seas Resort* on Beachway Drive ☎373-4014, ⊛www .sunnodysseydivers.com. A reputable dive outfit guaranteeing maximum group sizes of ten and offering a range of reef, wreck and cave dives. Two-tank dives start at $80 including tanks and weight belt (plus other equipment for $26 if you need it), with six and ten dive packages for $190 and $290. Night dives start at $60, and a progressive series of introductory dives for novices costs $90 for the first session and $40 for the next two dives; full PADI certification courses cost $375 plus textbooks ($450 if you decide to do the course in three stages). Transportation to and from your hotel offered, and considering limits on group size it pays to book upwards of three weeks in advance. Underwater Explorer's Society (UNEXSO) Port Lucaya ☎373-1244 or 1-800/992-3483, ⊛www .unexso.com. This well-established operation runs a variety of daily dives. The most highly adventurous and experienced will want to look into either a long dive into Ben's Cave (see p.128) or a shark dive, during which a decoy dressed in chainmail feeds the sharks to keep them occupied while you observe them from a few feet away. Example rates include a one-tank reef dive for $35, two-tank $70, shark dive $90, dolphin dive $160 and wreck dive $70 – all including equipment rental. UNEXSO also offers a range of courses for everyone from beginners to experienced divers. The former can test the waters with an introductory session in the pool ($25), progressing to a shallow reef dive under the watchful eye of a dive master ($60 for the first shallow dive and $80 for the next one in deeper water). Full PADI/NAUI certification costs $450.

Xanadu Undersea Adventures Xanadu Beach ☎ 352-3811, ⓦ www.xanadudive.com. Dive shop offering a range of guided excursions and certification courses, including shark, night, reef, wreck and cave dives and day-long excursions to sites at the east and west ends of the island. One dive costs $40, two $70; a ten-dive package is $280. A night dive is $60 and a swim with the sharks at Shark Alley $80. Note that these rates do not include equipment rental, which is about $24 per dive or $48 for a full day. A three-hour resort course for novices is $100. A PADI open water certification course costs $450 and the open water referral completion $250, plus equipment rental.

Snorkelling

Many hotels and watersports outfitters rent out **snorkelling** gear and there are a few spots around the island where you can do some interesting snorkelling swimming out from shore – notably Gold Rock Beach to the east of Lucaya, and Deadman's Reef and Old Bahama Bay to the west. However, an organized boat trip (gear included) is the best way to see the prettiest undersea gardens and their colourful inhabitants.

East End Adventures ☎ 373-6662, ⓦ www .bahamasecotours.com. A good outfitter offering a six-hour Blue Hole Snorkelling Safari that explores the vibrant profusion of marine life in a series of blue holes off the eastern end of Grand Bahama. The tour is followed by a picnic lunch on a deserted cay. $85, including hotel pick-up.

Nautical Adventures ☎ 373-7180. Affordable one-hour snorkelling cruises aboard the double-decker *Coral Princess* departing from the Port Lucaya Marketplace three times daily. $30 adult, children and non-snorkellers $16.

Paradise Cove Deadman's Reef ☎ 349-2677, ⓦ www.deadmansreef.com. A great day out twenty minutes west of Freeport on a secluded beach, where you can snorkel from shore over a lush reef, float in a glass-bottomed kayak or simply relax on the sand. $35 adult, children $23, including transportation to hotel and lunch at the beachside snack bar.

Reef Tours Port Lucaya, ☎ 373-5880, ⓦ www .bahamasvg.com/reeftours. Snorkelling trips on both motorized and wind-powered catamarans. The daily combined snorkel and sail on the catamaran *Fantasea* is especially recommended for a relaxed afternoon cruise with a smaller group of passengers, $45/$25 per adult/child; reservations required.

Superior Watersports ☎ 373-7863, ⓦ www .superiorwatersports.com. The 5hr Robinson Crusoe Beach Party incluces 1.5 hours of snorkelling followed by a buffet lunch on a deserted beach, volleyball and plenty of time to chill out. Free rum punches and soft drinks served all day. Includes pick-up and return to your hotel. $60 adult, children $40. Ninety-minute snorkelling-only trips to Treasure Reef also depart three times daily, with snacks and equipment included, for $35/$25 adult/child.

Fishing

Grand Bahama has a healthy sport fishery and is a popular retreat for anglers. Fine **bonefishing** can be found along its east shore around McLean's Town and around the offshore cays and in the mangroves along the north shore, particularly around North Riding Point. You can also try your luck with the big game fish like tuna on a **deep-sea** expedition off the south coast, or go **bottom fishing** for the likes of snappers and grunts closer to shore. In addition to the outfitters listed below, there are a couple of dedicated fishing resorts located east of Freeport (see "Accommodation", p.115) and most hotels can arrange a trip for you.

Up close with the dolphins

Getting face to face with a highly sociable dolphin is one of the most popular tourist activities on Grand Bahama. Run by UNEXSO, **The Dolphin Experience** (☏373-1244 or 1-800/992-3483, ⊛www.unexso.com) departs from their dock at Port Lucaya, heading out on a twenty-minute boat ride to Sanctuary Bay, where the semi-wild dolphins come and go freely from a quiet cove donated by a local philanthropist. Three dolphin experiences are offered:

The Close Encounter As you sit with your feet dangling in the water, the dolphins swim around a small pool and perform synchronized tricks in response to their trainers. Stand waist-deep in the water, while an accommodating dolphin swims alongside to be petted. $75 for adults, $35 for children age 4–12, free for children under 4.

Swim with the Dolphins After the animal-care staff dispense their guidelines for interacting with the dolphins, take to the water in Sanctuary Bay and swim with them for 25 minutes. $170; all participants must be at least 55 inches tall.

Open Ocean Dolphin Experience Spend the whole day observing the dolphins, participating in their feeding and training sessions in Sanctuary Bay and out on the open water. $200; must be at least 55 inches tall.

Dolphin research

For those who want a more in-depth educational encounter with dolphins, the Oceanic Society, a non-profit marine research organization based in San Francisco (☏1-800/326-7491, ⊛www.oceanic-society.org), sponsors **field research** on dolphin behaviour in the waters off Grand Bahama. Living aboard the 68-foot vessel *Hanky Panky* for a week at a time, participants can assist scientists in identifying individual animals and collecting data on their movements and behaviour. You must know how to swim and snorkel, but no other special skills or experience is required. The maximum group size is eight and trips generally depart from Lucaya in July and August. The cost averages $1650 a week (in double-occupancy cabins with shared bath).

Captain Perry Demeritte McLean's Town ☏353-3301, ⊛www.captinperry.com Based near the prime bonefishing flats at the eastern end of the island, Capt. Perry leads angler bonefishing for $400/$250 full/half day.

Captain Phil and Mel's Bonefishing Guide Services McLean's Town ☏353-3023, ⊛www.bahamasvg.com/p&mbonefishing. Captains Phil and Mel offer guide services for $350 a day ($250 half-day) to fish bones and other wily local fish like permit, shark and tarpon, plus packages with accommodation at a waterfront cottage on Sweeting's Cay near McLean's Town ($2055 a week per person double occupancy) .

Exotic Adventures Lucaya ☏374-2278 or 375-7885. Deep-sea fishing trips up to twenty miles off shore for tuna and dolphin for $950/$650 for a full or half-day for up to six people. They will take groups fishing for dolphin, tuna and wahoo two to four miles offshore for half a day ($440 for up to four people), and bottom fishing for $50 per person (with a minimum of $200 for the boatload).

Reef Tours Port Lucaya ☏373-5880, ⊛www.bahamasvg.com/reeftours. Three hour deep-sea and bottom-fishing excursions are led twice daily for $100 and $50 respectively. You can also charter a boat and crew for the whole day.

Kayaking

🛶 Kayak Nature Tours (☏373-2485 or 1-866/440-4542, ⊛www.grandbahamanaturetours.com) runs a variety of enjoyable and well-organized **paddling excursions** that explore the varied geography and ecology of Grand Bahama. The naturalist guides, who are well versed in local history, give six-hour excursions to Lucayan National Park that include a leisurely 1.5

hour paddle through a mangrove creek, a nature walk and a picnic lunch on spectacular Gold Rock Beach, twelve miles east of Freeport/Lucaya. They also offer a five-hour snorkelling tour to **Peterson Cay National Park** featuring a thirty-minute paddle to the cay followed by snorkelling and a picnic on its powder white beach. Both tours are offered daily for $80 and are suitable for children and beginners. Those seeking a more intense wilderness experience might enjoy the moderately strenuous day-trip to the tiny remote settlement of Water Cay (see p.129) or a three-day camping expedition on the same cay on request. Both trips include several hours of paddling, nature walks, birdwatching and fishing.

Golf and tennis

There are three **golf** courses on the island (two others, the Ruby and Emerald at the former *Royal Oasis Resort*, are currently closed pending the sale of the boarded-up hotel, with no plans to reopen in the near future). The challenging Reef Course at *Our Lucaya* (☎373-2002) is known for its numerous water hazards, with 13 of 18 holes offering the opportunity to splash your ball in the deep. The links of the Lucayan Course – also at *Our Lucaya* (☎373-1067) – host the Caribbean Open in December and are home to the Jim McLean School of Golf (☎374-2604 or 1-800/723-6725, ⓦwww.jimmclean.com), which offers instruction ranging from hour-long private lessons to multi-day clinics. Green fees at both courses are $140, with limited discounts for guests; after 3.30pm, you can play for $50. The nine-hole course at Fortune Hills (☎373-4500; $57; closed Mon) is less glamorous, but it provides some variety for insatiable golfers.

A few of the island's hotels have **tennis** courts for guest use, as listed in the accommodations section. Unsurprisingly, the island's best courts are at *Our Lucaya* (☎373-1333) and they are open to non-guests and lit for night use. The different playing surfaces of the four Grand Slam tournaments are available and rates range $25–100 per hour.

Horseback riding, cycling and bird watching

The Pinetree Stables, Beachway Drive in Freeport (☎373-3600, ⓦwww .pinetree-stables.com; closed Mon), offer pleasant two-hour guided **trail rides** (9am and 11:30am; $75) on well-cared-for horses that start by weaving through a sun-dappled pine forest and end with a ride into the surf à la *The Black Stallion*. There is a rider weight limit of 200lbs and a minimum age of 8. Trikk Pony Adventures (☎374-4449, ⓦwww.trikkpony.com) lead a daily 1.5 hour ride along Barbary Beach east of Lucaya ($80), as well as a sunset ride on Saturdays ($90), including free transportation from your hotel.

If you'd rather ride under your own steam, Kayak Nature Tours (☎373-2485 or 1-866/440-4542, ⓦwww.grandbahamanaturetours.com) run guided 12- or 20-mile **cycling** day-trips ($80, including cycle rental) on scenic bush tracks and byways along the shore, with a stop for a snack and a swim at a seaside restaurant. To rent your own bike for around $30 per day, stop in at Lucayan Watersports (see p.107).

Kayak Nature Tours also lead guided **bird watching** expeditions on request (call for rates), while the Bahamas National Trust Rand Nature Centre near Freeport (Mon–Fri 9am–4:30pm; ☎352-5438, ⓦwww.thebahamasnationaltrust .org; $5) has a bird-watching tour in their 100-acre nature reserve at 8am on the first Saturday of each month. Good spots to do some solo spotting of the island's 200 varieties of indigenous and migratory birds include Lucayan National Park and Peterson Cay National Park, both covered in detail later on in the chapter.

Freeport/Lucaya

The only inland town of note in the Bahamas, **FREEPORT** is a commercial and industrial centre deliberately built in the interior of Grand Bahama to preserve the ocean-front property of **LUCAYA** for tourist development. The master plan for the city was drawn up by urban planning students at Cornell University in 1960, and envisioning an urban centre with an eventual population of 200,000, the class laid out a broad grid of streets and roads, extending from Freeport Harbour on Hawksbill Creek west of the main commercial district, to the man-made Grand Lucayan Waterway, fifteen miles to the east. A map of Freeport/Lucaya, with its intricate web of dozens of avenues, drives and crescents, might give the impression of a large, densely populated metropolis. In reality, the city only has about 40,000 residents, and many of these roads lead nowhere, through undeveloped bush and grandly-named but deserted subdivisions still waiting for people to come. Here and there are what Bahamians call "pocket houses" – husks of concrete in various stages of construction or disrepair. It is difficult for many Bahamians to get a mortgage, so many build their homes out of their own pocket bit by bit over several years.

A utilitarian town with no organic centre or street life – everyone lives in the suburbs – Freeport is not a city for strolling or sightseeing, although it is easy enough to get around on foot to do your shopping, go out to eat or to see a movie. The brutal **hurricanes** of 2004 and 2005 have set back the city terribly as well, leading to the closure of the large **Royal Oasis Resort**, including its golf courses and casino, that has long been the town's tourism anchor. The resort stands deserted, waiting for a buyer, and the deadening effect of the resort's demise has been felt at the nearby **International Bazaar**, which is generally deserted and half boarded up.

Running along the ocean-front three miles south of Freeport, Lucaya has managed to rebuild and bounce back from nature's tantrums with all evidence of hurricane damage sopped up and repainted. The seaside resort maintains a festive atmosphere, centred around the **Port Lucaya Marketplace** and the busy **Port Lucaya Marina**. Dominating the scene is the grand **Our Lucaya Resort**, which is surrounded by smaller hotels, restaurants, tour operators and several quiet residential blocks. A steady influx of holidaymakers, including daily arrivals from mammoth cruise ships and weekending Americans, contributes to Lucaya's party atmosphere, but it's still easy to escape the crowds. Within Freeport's city limits is the **Rand Nature Centre**, a forest preserve offering a peaceful respite from the daily grind of lying on the **beach**. With respect to beaches, there are a half-dozen in the immediate area, split between the typically bustling Lucayan, Xanadu and South Seas strands to the more secluded Taino, Churchill and Fortune beaches.

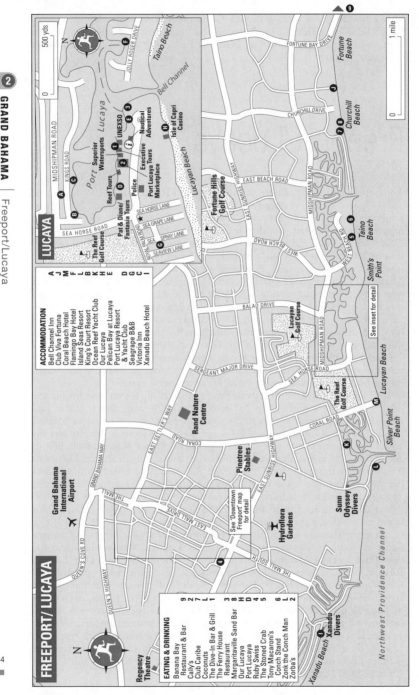

FREEPORT/LUCAYA

LUCAYA

N

0 — 500 yds

MIDSHIPMAN ROAD
KINGS ROAD
JOLLY ROGER DRIVE
Taino Beach
Bell Channel
Port Superior Watersports
Lucaya
UNEXSO
Nautical Adventures
Isle of Capri Casino
Executive
Port Lucaya Tours
Marketplace
Police
Reef Tours
Pat & Diane/ Fantasia Tours
The Reef Golf Course
SEA HORSE ROAD
SEA HORSE LANE
SEA GRAPE LANE
SPRAY LANE
SEAVIEW LANE
ROYAL PALM WAY
ROYAL SEA
Lucayan Beach

ACCOMMODATION

Bell Channel Inn	A
Club Viva Fortuna	J
Coral Beach Hotel	M
Flamingo Bay Hotel	F
Island Seas Resort	L
King's Court Resort	B
Ocean Reef Yacht Club	K
Our Lucaya	H
Pelican Bay at Lucaya	E
Port Lucaya Resort & Yacht Club	D
Seagrape B&B	G
Victoria Inn	C
Xanadu Beach Hotel	I

Grand Bahama International Airport

QUEEN'S COVE RD
QUEEN'S HIGHWAY
GRAND BAHAMA WAY
THE MALL
EAST MALL DRIVE
EAST SETTLER'S WAY
SERGEANT MAJOR DRIVE
BALAO DRIVE
CORAL ROAD
EAST SUNRISE HIGHWAY
MIDSHIPMAN ROAD
SEA HORSE ROAD
WEST BEACH RD
EAST BEACH ROAD
FORTUNE BAY DRIVE
CHURCHILL DRIVE
THE MALL SOUTH

Regency Theatre

Rand Nature Centre

Pinetree Stables

Hydroflora Gardens

See Downtown Freeport map for detail

Sunn Odyssey Divers

The Reef Golf Course

Lucayan Golf Course

Fortune Hills Golf Course

Xanadu Beach
Xanadu Divers

Silver Point Beach
Lucayan Beach
Taino Beach
Smith's Point
Churchill Beach
Fortune Beach

Northwest Providence Channel

See inset for detail

N

0 — 1 mile

EATING & DRINKING

Banana Bay Restaurant & Bar	9
Cally's	7
Club Caribe	2
Coconuts	L
The Dive-In Bar & Grill	3
The Ferry House	
Margaritaville Sand Bar	8
Our Lucaya	H
Port Lucaya	D
Ruby Swiss	4
The Stoned Crab	5
Tony Macaroni's Conch Stand	6
Zonk the Conch Man	L
Zorba's	2

Accommodation

Accommodation in Freeport/Lucaya ranges from the luxurious and secluded to no-frills motels. Though there is little available for the real budget traveller, you can often snag a discounted rate on a package deal by keeping a vigilant eye on resort and tour operator websites, discount travel websites or by calling hotels directly. If staying in Freeport, frequent complimentary shuttle buses head to the beach at Xanadu or Lucaya (five- or ten-minute drives away, respectively), also easily accessed by frequent public buses between Freeport and Lucaya. By far the largest resort on the island is *Our Lucaya* (see box p.123), encompassing 372 acres, including two championship golf courses and seven acres of gorgeous white sandy beach.

Note also that it seems as if most of the hoteliers in Freeport made a pact to confuse prospective travellers by using the words "royal", "palm" and/or "island" in naming their establishments – a curious fetish given that royal palms are not indigenous to the island. Hotels east and west of Freeport/Lucaya are covered within those sections later on in this chapter.

Freeport

Best Western Castaways Resort East Mall Drive ☎ 352-6682 or 1-800-WESTERN in the US and Canada, ⓦ www.castaways-resort.com. With 118 clean and attractively furnished rooms and suites overlooking the pool or the street, this refurbished resort within short walking distance of several restaurants and the International Bazaar is an excellent lower cost option. Amenities include a nicely landscaped pool area, a bar and pleasant restaurant, laundry facilities, a/c, cable TV and a complimentary shuttle service to the beach at the *Island Seas Resort*. Like the *Island Palm* below, it's a comfortable place to lay your head at night after a day out and about, rather than a holiday destination in itself. ❺

Island Palm Resort East Mall Drive ☎ 352-6648, ⓔ ispalm@batelnet.bs. Another decent budget choice located several blocks north of the *Best Western Castaways* and a notch or two lower in comfort, but still within walking distance of the International Bazaar and other tourist amenities. Bright and cheerful, the comfortable air-conditioned, TV-equipped rooms surround a paved courtyard and a small pool. The pool bar serves breakfast and an all-day lunch menu al fresco, while a recently renovated restaurant is open for

average dinners. A complimentary shuttle bus runs several times a day to the pleasant beach at the *Island Seas Resort*. Some wheelchair accessible rooms and one room with kitchenette available, as well as motor scooter rentals ($40 a day). Double ❸, efficiency ❹

Royal Islander Hotel East Mall Drive ☎ 351-6000, ⓦ www.royalislanderhotel.com. Once a gem of a small hotel, the *Royal Islander* has fallen on hard times. Its lush courtyard garden was lost to recent hurricanes, and the rooms, while serviceable (TV, a/c), are overdue for a refurbishment. The now paved over grounds feature a pool and hot tub, and there's an adequate if uninspired restaurant inside. Free transportation to Xanadu Beach. ❸

Royal Palm Resort East Mall/Settler's Way ☎ 352-3462, ⓦ www.royalpalmresort.com. At the far end of East Mall Drive, the bright salmon pink *Royal Palm* is looking spruce and appealing following a recent renovation. Catering primarily to business travellers, each of the 50 rooms are equipped with a kitchenette with a microwave, TV, a/c and Internet access, and amenities include tennis courts, a swimming pool and the nondescript *Red Snapper* restaurant (daily 7am–3pm). Free transportation to Xanadu Beach twice a day. ❻

Lucaya and the adjacent beaches

Bell Channel Inn King's Road ☎ 373-1053, ⓦ www.bellchannelinn.com. A hot pink, two-story motel located on the south side of Bell Channel Bay opposite Port Lucaya, with clean and spacious if dated rooms, each with a balcony. There is a

small dipping pool set in an attractive wooden deck overlooking the channel. Amenities include TV, a/c and a fridge in each room, a utilitarian bar and restaurant and an on-site dive operator (Caribbean Divers; ☎ 373-9111). ❸

Club Viva Fortuna Fortune Beach ☎305/266
-6465 or 1-800/898-9968, ⓦwww.vivaresorts
.com. Bright yellow and green with music blaring
out of seemingly every door, this is an all-inclusive summer camp for adults on their own or with
kids with a family-oriented rather than honeymoon atmosphere, attracting a predominantly
Italian clientele. Located a couple of miles east
of Lucaya on a stretch of lovely Fortune Beach,
the resort has nearly 300 rooms spread across
twenty-odd buildings on 26 acres of landscaped
grounds. Besides a large swimming pool next
to the beach, amenities include two restaurants,
two discos, tennis courts, a gym and children's
day camp. Organized activities include diving and
snorkelling, day-trips around the island, dance
classes and live entertainment nightly. ❻

Coral Beach Hotel Royal Palm Way/Coral Road
☎373-2468, ⓦwww.cbbahamas.com. At the
opposite end of the noise and activity spectrum
from *Club Viva* is this quiet, secluded high-rise
condominium complex on Lucayan Beach, about
a 15min walk from the Port Lucaya Marketplace.
Most of the units are time shares occupied by
American retirees, but there are ten guestrooms
rented on a daily or weekly basis: four with kitchenettes, six with just a coffeepot and refrigerator,
all with a/c and TV. Clean and comfortable, with
red carpets, white walls and floral bedspreads, the
rooms do not face the ocean, but the beach and
swimming pool are only a few steps away. Has the
feel of a slightly shabby apartment building rather
than a hotel. Not recommended for families with
small children. ❸

Flamingo Bay Yacht Club and Marina Hotel
Taino Beach ☎373-4677 or 1-800/824-6623,
ⓦwww.flamingobayhotel.com. On the edge of
the waterway connecting Taino Beach to Port
Lucaya, the three-storey, 68-unit *Flamingo Bay* is
located a three-minute walk across the grounds
of the Ritz Beach condominium complex to the
fine white-sand beach. Renovated with style, the
nicely landscaped exterior is painted a vibrant
lilac with redwood trim, while the interior features
crisp cool colours and natural wood furnishings;
each room comes with TV, a/c and a kitchenette
(microwave, sink and mini fridge). The palm-
shaded pool (across the drive at Ritz Beach) with
its waterfall, man-made beach and grotto bar is a
delight. Though it has a reputation for slow service,
the *Taino By the Sea Restaurant* is open daily for
breakfast and lunch, and Sat, Sun and Wed for
dinner, with nice open air seating overlooking the
beach. ❹

Island Seas Resort Silver Point Drive ☎373
-1271, ⓦwww.islandseas.com. A combined

beachfront hotel and time-share complex with a
relaxed atmosphere. The one- and two-bedroom
suites come with fully equipped kitchens and living
quarters furnished with rattan, floral fabrics, tiled
floors, a/c and cable TV. The blocks of rooms are
situated in a quadrangle around a large swimming pool with a rock garden and waterfall, a
swim-up bar, hot tub and the attractive open-air
Coconuts Bar and Grill (see p.124). Several recently
constructed blocks sit across the road with no
view, so ask for a sea view when you book. On
the pretty curve of soft golden sand in front of the
hotel, *Zonk the Conch Man* cooks up the Bahamian
delicacy eleven different ways, while thatched
umbrellas provide shade for sunbathers. Watersports, bicycle rentals and a free shuttle bus to
the International Bazaar are offered. A bit isolated
– taxis required to eat out or go sightseeing – but a
pleasant enough place to be stranded. ❻

Kings Court Resort 4 King's Rd ☎373-7133,
ⓦwww.kingscourtbahamas.com. Modest but
clean and roomy apartments situated a short walk
from Port Lucaya Marketplace. Kitchenettes, TV,
laundry facilities and a small dipping pool; some
units with two doubles or a king bed, some with
an extra sofa bed. The one-bedroom units are also
available for $570 a week. ❸

Ocean Reef Yacht Club and Resort Bahama
Reef Boulevard ☎373-4662, ⓦwww.oryc.com.
Built on a quiet canal in a residential area near
Silver Point Beach west of Lucaya, this resort
caters primarily to boaters. Captain or not, though,
it's worth looking into as the grounds are well
maintained and the suites nicely fitted out with
ubiquitous rattan furniture, floral print fabrics and
polished tile floors, with boat slips in front of each
unit. Amenities include two small swimming pools,
an outdoor hot tub, two-person in-room whirlpools,
laundry facilities, car and bicycle rentals and a
cozy pool bar serving light meals. Complimentary
shuttle service; larger apartments and weekly rates
available. Boat slips an additional $40 a day for
vessels under 50ft long, plus electricity. ❼

Pelican Bay at Lucaya Seahorse Road
☎373-9550, ⓦwww.pelicanbayhotel.com. Across
the street from *Our Lucaya*, this lovely hotel is
built on a far more intimate scale around a quiet,
landscaped courtyard with a swimming pool, hot
tub and open-air bar serving light meals. Providing
an oasis of calm in the midst of busy Port Lucaya,
the comfortable double rooms are done up in cool
colours and tile floors, each with TV, refrigerator,
a/c and a deep balcony furnished with Adirondack
chairs facing the courtyard and the marina. The
adjoining block of luxury one-bedroom suites are
stylishly and artistically furnished with canopied

wrought iron bedsteads, overstuffed sofas and chairs, natural wood shelves stocked with beach reading, an espresso maker and microwave. Doubles from ④; one-bedroom suites ⑧

Port Lucaya Resort and Yacht Club Seahorse Road ☎ 373-6618, ⓦ www.portlucaya.com /resort. Well-maintained and conveniently located next door to the Port Lucaya Marketplace and Marina, this hotel sits across the street from Lucayan Beach with boat slips just outside the rooms. The 150-plus guestrooms are housed in a multicoloured two-storey building encircling a large swimming pool and hot tub set in a broad expanse of lawn. The spacious rooms have polished terracotta tile floors, bright floral print textiles and white rattan furniture; extras include a microwave, coffee maker, mini fridge, TV and either a patio or balcony overlooking the marina or pool. ⑤

🏃 **Seagrape Bed and Breakfast** 40 Sea Spray Lane ☎ 373-1769, ⓦ www .seagrapehouse.com. On a leafy residential street within easy walking distance to Port Lucaya, this B&B offers two attractive en suite doubles accessed by a private entrance. The rooms boast

a homey yellow and white décor with a/c, fan, TV and mini fridge, and one room has an extra twin bed. Continental breakfast served each morning in courtyard shaded by mature trees or in the garden – all open to guests for lounging. Lucayan Beach is two minutes walk away at the end of the lane. ③

Victoria Inn King's Road ☎ 373-3040, ⓕ 373-3874. Perfectly serviceable budget motel-style rooms, freshly painted and clean, if a little worn. Situated on the south side of Bell Channel Bay, a ten-minute walk to Port Lucaya Marketplace. ②

Xanadu Beach Resort and Marina Sunken Treasure Drive ☎ 352-6782, ⓦ www .xanadubeachhotel.com. Pity the poor newlyweds who get sucked in by the glossy brochure and find themselves spending their honeymoon at this desolate, shabby, peeling monument to 1980s kitsch, with its litter-strewn patch of beach. In 2005, Hurricane Wilma added further insult and left the hotel with only 38 habitable rooms. Renovations are planned, but not yet completed. Notable only as the last permanent residence of reclusive billionaire Howard Hughes (see box, p.121), it is ridiculously overpriced and not recommended. ⑤

Downtown Freeport and around

The main commercial district, **DOWNTOWN FREEPORT**, is centred along **The Mall**, the main thoroughfare that runs between Ranfurly Circus and Churchill Square, about ten blocks to the north. Just north of Ranfurly Circus, The Mall divides to surround the city centre, which is bound on one side by West Mall Drive, and on the other by **East Mall Drive**, where most of the hotels and restaurants are located. In truth, the twenty square blocks that make up downtown Freeport offer little in terms of worthwhile exploration, being home to little beyond banks, the main bus stand, a post office, a few office buildings and large apartment complexes – colonial-style confections in pink, blue and yellow – separated by blocks of pine forest that threaten to swallow the city back up.

Churchill Square itself is just a tiny patch of littered earth sandwiched between strip malls and parking lots surrounding **Winn Dixie Plaza**, where a small bust of Winston Churchill stands. This end of town is generally back to normal, with little evidence of recent hurricane damage. Likewise, most of the hotels lining East Mall Drive sport a fresh coat of paint and new furnishings thanks to Wilma. Less well off is the former tourist centre around **Ranfurly Circus** (named for the British governor of the Bahamas who supported the development of Freeport in the 1950s), which sits at the south end of East Mall Drive. Here, the **International Bazaar**, marked by red Japanese-style gates, preserves a faded warren of tacky shops and cafés. The bazaar was created by a Hollywood set designer hired to build a tourist attraction with a cosmopolitan feel, and its roots show in the flimsy plaster archways and garish paintwork meant to mimic Chinese, Middle Eastern, South American and Parisian architecture. In addition to a couple of uninspired restaurants, a straw market and shoddy souvenir stands, there's a collection of average

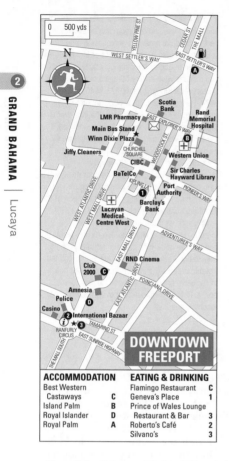

ACCOMMODATION		EATING & DRINKING	
Best Western		Flamingo Restaurant	C
Castaways	C	Geneva's Place	1
Island Palm	B	Prince of Wales Lounge	
Royal Islander	D	Restaurant & Bar	3
Royal Palm	A	Roberto's Café	2
		Silvano's	3

duty-free shops selling jewellery, perfume, Cuban cigars and the like. The Bazaar was pretty depressing before the storms, but the closing of the nearby *Royal Oasis Resort* and the ministrations of the triple whammy of recent hurricanes have resulted in the boarding up of many of the shops and restaurants.

Rand Nature Centre and the Hydroflora Gardens

Northeast of the city centre, with its entrance on East Settler's Way just east of Coral Road about a mile east of Ranfurly Circus, is the **Rand Nature Centre** (Mon–Fri 9am–4.30pm, Sat 9am–1pm; $5/$3 adult/child; ☎352-5438, ⓦ www.thebahamasnationaltrust .org). Named for its benefactor James Rand, the inventor of the telephone dialing system who lived on his yacht in Freeport in the 1960s, this peaceful wooded retreat covers a hundred acres. Besides an assortment of easy-going nature trails and a pond that's home to a small flock of West Indian flamingos, exhibits explore the natural history of the island, from marine life and bush medicine to Lucayan artefacts recovered at Deadman's Reef. The local office of the Bahamas National Trust is here as well, where you can find a good selection of books on the Bahamas.

While the Rand Nature Centre offers a natural slice of Grand Bahama's flora and fauna, the **Hydroflora Gardens** (Mon–Fri 9am–5pm, Sat 9am–4pm, closed daily for lunch 1–2pm; $5; ☎352-6052) present a carefully cultivated representation. Located a short distance south of Ranfurly Circus, on East Beach Drive off the East Sunrise Highway, the garden's three-acre plot is a riot of colour, laced with all manner of tropical and subtropical plants and fruit trees. When in season, the garden's fresh tropical fruits – including jackfruit, akee and starfruit – are available for tastings. Also on site is a small chapel surrounded by flora mentioned in the Bible.

Lucaya

Heading off Ranfurly Circus on Sunrise Highway then south on Seahorse Road takes you two miles to **Port Lucaya** and the beachfront hotels of **LUCAYA**.

△ Port Lucaya Marketplace

Unsurprisingly, this resort area has a more cheerful, holiday atmosphere than downtown Freeport, with carefully tended gardens and tidy, candy-coloured shops and houses. Lucaya itself is dominated by the **Our Lucaya Resort**, which leads on to Lucayan Beach. Across the street stands the **Port Lucaya Marketplace** (shops open Mon–Sat 10am–6pm), a bustling, pedestrian-only outdoor market overlooking the boats at Port Lucaya Marina on Bell Channel. Open-air stalls display straw work, jewellery and other souvenirs, and several lively restaurants and bars full of vacationers surround the harbour-facing **Count Basie Square**, the market's performance space named for the jazz musician who lived in Freeport for several years. Live entertainment is organized here nightly, ranging from fire-eaters and dance troupes to calypso music or Sinatra standards.

The market area is flanked on both sides by canals and the quiet residential neighbourhoods where Lucaya's predominantly expatriate and seasonal population lives. If you'd like a glimpse of how the tax-fleeing upper crust lives, head east on **Spanish Main Drive** to check out the multimillion-dollar beachfront properties that line the street. In the same direction, **Sanctuary Bay**, an inland waterway east of the Lucayan and Taino beaches, is likewise surrounded by sumptuous winter villas. It's also home to a pod of sixteen semi-wild **dolphins**, donated by Hollywood producer Merv Griffin in 1987 to the Underwater Explorer's Society (UNEXSO), which moved the dolphins several years ago from Port Lucaya because of water pollution. They have since been joined by other dolphins, some of which came in from the sea of their own accord, and others of which were born at Sanctuary Bay. Free to come and go as they wish, the dolphins are not held in pens and are sociable animals that seem to like human company. The Dolphin Experience, operated by UNEXSO from Port Lucaya, runs several tours out to Sanctuary Bay daily; see p.111 for details.

The beaches

Of the half-dozen public beaches within the limits of Freeport/Lucaya, **Xanadu Beach**, just two miles south of Ranfurly Circus, is the closest to downtown Freeport. Unsurprisingly given such proximity, this charmless broad swath of coarse brown sand is heavily used and backed by faded souvenir kiosks. Truncated by a wire fence demarcating the boundary between the *Xanadu Hotel* (see box opposite) and the Princess Isles gated community, Xanadu Beach is where some of the hotels in Freeport deposit their guests for the day. About the only good reason to visit is to sign up for one of the dive or snorkel trips run by Xanadu Undersea Adventures (see p.110), who keep an office here.

About a mile east of Xanadu Beach, separated from it by two water channels, is **Island Seas Beach**, a far prettier and more relaxing curve of golden sand in front of the *Island Seas Resort*. Thatched umbrellas are available for shade here, as are refreshments at the *Coconuts Bar and Grill* (see p.124), as well as from *Zonk the Conch Man's* kiosk in front of the bar. One man-made channel to the east is the little-used **Silver Point Beach** (accessible from the southern terminus of Coral Road or by walking west down the beach from *Our Lucaya*), a white sandy strand that merges into the adjoining **Lucayan Beach**. Justifiably popular, the Lucayan Beach runs for about a mile in front of *Our Lucaya*, with several beach bars and restaurants to choose from along with the Ocean Motion Watersports outfitter (see p.107). Both the Lucayan and the adjoining Silver Point beaches are within walking distance of all of the hotels in Lucaya.

On the east side of Bell Channel and accessible by a five-minute ferry ride, **Taino Beach**'s soft white sand fringed by palms and pines makes for a pleasant outing from Port Lucaya. The *Ritz Beach Resort* condominium complex fronts the beach, but you can usually find a secluded patch of sand to spread your blanket by walking east. Consider bringing your own lunch as the resort's snack bar is mediocre at best, though also look out for *Tony Macaroni's Conch Stand*, a mobile kiosk often found on the beach during high season – the proprietor serves island-famous grilled conch and conch salad.

A mile or so further east, on the far side of Sanctuary Bay, are two more equally pleasant and relatively empty beaches with cool drinks and snacks close

Howard Hughes and the Xanadu Hotel

For those with an interest in the weird and wonderful, the highlight of Freeport might well be the **Xanadu Beach Resort and Marina,** a pastel painted tower on the edge of the ocean two miles south of the International Bazaar. Now just a peeling shadow of its former glamour, the *Xanadu* opened in 1969 with luminaries like Frank Sinatra and Sammy Davis Jr on hand. It is most famous, however, as the final residence of reclusive billionaire **Howard Hughes,** who arrived in December 1973 on his private jet, and ensconced himself on the twelfth and thirteenth floors of the hotel, which he subsequently bought. Intensely paranoid and agoraphobic, he stayed in his blacked-out rooms for more than two years, running his empire in pyjamas and partaking in such bizarre pursuits as collecting his toenail clippings and urine in jars. Hughes left the Xanadu just a few weeks before his death in 1976.

at hand. **Churchill Beach** is pretty, but little used and perhaps for that reason, the patio furniture, oil cans and other marine refuse that washes up on shore all over the Bahamas stay here a longer time before they are removed by local volunteers. **Fortune Beach,** named after a treasure-loaded shipwreck found here by a group of scuba divers in 1965, adjoins Churchill to the east and is itself about five miles from Port Lucaya. The powdery stretch of sand here is lovely, long and often deserted, with the all-inclusive *Club Viva Fortuna* resort located in the middle.

Eating

Fresh seafood features prominently on local menus, although **restaurant** offerings run the gamut from Greek and Chinese to Italian and traditional Bahamian cooking. Absolutely everything but the seafood has to be imported, and eating in Freeport/Lucaya tends to be expensive, although there are a few places where you can grab a cheap bite. As residents prefer take-away – either traditional dishes or fast food – to dining in, the most pleasant surroundings and the best food are generally found in **hotel restaurants**. Many of the best are within *Our Lucaya,* home to fourteen restaurants and cafés ranging from a couple of casual and inexpensive grills to formal, polished-wood and marble dining rooms. While not the place to seek out a down-home Bahamian meal, the restaurants here are of uniformly high quality, and we've listed the most noteworthy below. On the beaches just east of Freeport/Lucaya are some cheerful and relaxed **beach bars and restaurants** that make a good change of pace. Note that the restaurants on Taino Beach, Churchill Beach and Fortune Beach listed below are not within walking distance of the ferry dock at the *Flamingo Bay Hotel* – try calling ahead if you don't have a car as some establishments offer complimentary transportation.

Freeport

Flamingo Restaurant *Best Western Hotel,* East Mall Drive. A family-style dining room with comfy banquettes, serving hearty if un-fussy Bahamian and North American meals. Expect to pay $6–8 for a breakfast of bacon and eggs or tuna and grits; at lunch time, sandwiches cost $5 – while dinner entrees like baked chicken or steak with potatoes and veg average $14. Daily 7.30am–10pm.
Geneva's Place East Mall Drive at Kipling Lane ☎ 352-5085. Popular and lively local restaurant dressed up in bright yellow and white, serving Bahamian and American food at reasonable

prices (breakfast $4–7; lunch around $10; dinner $14–26) including Bahamian favourites such as steamed grouper, minced turbot, chicken and lobster with guava duff and key lime pie for dessert. Open from 7am until everyone goes home.

Prince of Wales *Pub on the Mall*, East Mall Drive ⊤ 352-5110. Dark, psuedo-English style pub with wood-panelled walls, red velvet and brass, serving standard pub fare with a seafood slant. Meals average around $10. Open Mon–Sat for lunch noon–2pm and for dinner 5.30–10.30pm; free transportation to and from your hotel with dinner reservations.

Roberto's Café Ranfurly Circus. Cheerful café popular with both locals and tourists, serving inexpensive breakfasts and lunch at a few tables inside and outside. Simple but satisfying fare, including an egg and bacon muffin for breakfast and sandwiches for lunch. Daily 8am–11pm.

The Ruby Swiss West Sunrise Highway and Atlantic Drive ⊤ 352-8507. Popular with the Freeport business crowd during lunch and dinner hours, the *Ruby Swiss* gets its second breath late at night when a younger clubbing crowd takes over. The filling if uninspired seafood and meat-heavy menu contains an extensive selection of American and European (entrees range $14–25), served in a high-ceilinged dining room. Open daily from 11am until late; dinner served from 6pm.

Silvano's *Pub on the Mall*, East Mall Drive ⊤ 352-5111. Italian cuisine served in a small, sophisticated and romantically lit Mediterranean-styled dining room, with a rough stone floor and sunny yellow walls. Entrees run $15–30. Mon–Sat for lunch noon–3pm, dinner 5.30–11pm. Free transportation with dinner reservations.

Lucaya

Andy's Ice Cream Port Lucaya Marketplace. A tiny shop with a couple of outside tables serving Bahamian-made ice cream (including coconut), pastries and traditional Bahamian breakfasts of boiled fish and grits. Mon–Sat 8.30am–late, Sun 10am–9pm.

Cally's Bar and Grill Port Lucaya Marketplace ⊤ 352-5932. *Cally's* serves tasty and inexpensive to moderately-priced Greek and Bahamian dishes, including fresh Greek salad, savoury grilled vegetable wrap and octopus with oregano for the more adventurous. Despite the slow service, the overall atmosphere is cheerful with both indoor and outdoor seating on the wooden verandah. Daily 7am–11pm; breakfast served until 2pm.

The Dive-In Bar and Grill UNEXSO, Port Lucaya ⊤ 373-1244. Pleasant, casual poolside grill overlooking the marina serving American-style eggs, pancakes and cooked meats or Bahamian tuna and grits for breakfast ($4–6). Burgers, sandwiches, pizza, salads, conch chowder and fritters take over the rest of the day ($4–10). Daily 8am–5pm.

Dolce Vita Port Lucaya Marketplace ⊤ 373-8652. Recommended Italian fare served in a modern decor of mirrored walls and an open kitchen, with seating inside and outside overlooking the marina. Entrees run $22–33. Daily 5–11pm.

The Ferry House Port Lucaya waterfront ⊤ 373-1595, Ⓦ www.ferryhousebahamas .com. One of the island's culinary highlights, the *Ferry House* offers imaginative dishes like grouper braised in Nassau Royale sauce, shrimp with ginger glace, and sesame-crusted yellow fin tuna,

created with flair by the Scandinavian chef and served in an elegant waterside dining room done up with gauzy white linen and pale wicker and wood with modern folk-art flourishes. Sunny and inviting at lunch, the mood turns romantic in the evening with lit candles and views of the harbour lights. Tied up at the dock alongside the restaurant, the floating Martini Bar with its deep sofas is a cosy setting for a quiet nightcap. Lunch runs $20–25, while dinner mains cost $35–40. Open for lunch Mon–Fri noon–2.30pm, and dinner Tues–Sun 6pm–9.30pm (last seating). Reservations recommended for dinner.

H & L Bookstore and Café Port Lucaya Marketplace. A quiet nook serving muffins, coffee and cool drinks with seating at a small lunch counter. Mon–Sat 9am–6pm.

The Harbour Room Port Lucaya Marketplace ⊤ 374-4466, Ⓦ www.harbourroom.com. An upscale option for dinner, with tables on a waterfront patio or wood-panelled interior, featuring a well-stocked bar and an elaborate menu of seafood, meats and pasta dishes (entrees $15–35). Especially notable for its decadent Sunday brunch buffet (11am–4.30pm; $32) including a conch chowder, smoked salmon, duck pate, rack of lamb and the usual waffles and omelettes, along with a table full of desserts. Dinner Wed–Sun 5–10pm. Reservations required.

Le Med Port Lucaya, ⊤ 374-2804. A cosy eatery with indoor/outdoor seating situated at the quiet edge of the marketplace, *Le Med* receives positive reviews for its Mediterranean-based dishes including sweet and savory crepes, gazpacho and conch chowder followed by pasta, fish and grilled meats. Most mains cost $18–23. Open for breakfast, lunch and dinner.

Luciano's Port Lucaya. On a second floor verandah overlooking the marina, this eatery with pink linen and rattan furniture dishes out French cuisine and enjoys a reputation as one of Grand Bahama's premier fine-dining establishments. Start with an appetizer of thin slices of smoked duck breast over cantaloupe or the lobster bisque ($10–15), then move on to one of the main dishes featuring local and imported fish, including seared yellow fin tuna served with a cabernet sauvignon sauce ($25–45). For dessert, try the banana flambéed with Caribbean rum. Reservations recommended. Dinner only, with an early bird special ($27) 5.30–7pm.

The Pub at Port Lucaya Port Lucaya ☎ 373-8450. One of the better Marketplace choices, with a good view of the marina and Count Basie Square from its busy, outdoor patio. Selections off the international menu include crab claws, lobster bisque, and several salads for starters, and entrees ($8–22) of seafood, burgers, traditional English pot pies and chicken done several ways (including spicy jerk chicken served Bahamian-style with plantains and macaroni). This is also one of the few places on the island where vegetarian choices extend beyond grilled cheese and fries. The entertaining drinks menu includes such colourful selections as Nelson's Blood, named for British Vice-Admiral Horatio Nelson who legend says was returned to England in a cask of rum after being killed in the Battle of Trafalgar; his rum-soaked sailors reputedly tapped into the cask on the way home. Daily 11am–midnight.

Zorba's Port Lucaya Marketplace ☎ 373-6137. *Zorba's* does a booming business thanks to a menu filled with tasty and inexpensive Greek favourites like souvlaki, pitta wraps and salads loaded with feta cheese. Seating inside or outside on a pleasant shaded wooden verandah; take-away also available. Daily 7am–11:45pm.

Our Lucaya Resort

China Beach ☎ 373-1333. On the water in front of the Westin, *China Beach* is one of the few spots on the island that can satisfy an Asian cuisine fix. Decorated in rich red tones and black lacquered wood with moody lighting, the pan-Asian menu includes the likes of Pad Thai chicken with grilled papaya, dim sum samplings, and even make-it-yourself sushi. Both the pan-seared tuna and conch stir fry are recommended. Mains range $19–30,

the dress code is smart casual. Dinner only 6–11pm; closed Wed and Thurs.

China Grill ☎ 373-1333. One of the less expensive *Our Lucaya* options, this outdoor grill overlooking the serpentine pool at the Westin serves burgers and snacks with Asian touches like peanut sauce and sushi. Open daily for lunch.

Churchill's Chophouse ☎ 373-1333. Located in the Manor House at the *Westin* (the reception building), this elegant and expensive glass-walled dining room with attached piano bar serves the likes of grilled steaks or lobster to go with a selection of vintage wines. Appetizers ($6–14) include spicy crab and lobster cakes. Reservations recommended, and trousers (no jeans) and collared shirts required for men. Dinner only 7–11pm; closed Sun, Mon and Wed.

Iries ☎ 373-1333. Pricey Caribbean fusion cuisine served in several rooms of a two-story Colonial-style timber house. Start with crab fritters or conch chowder with roasted plantain and okra ($13) and move on to the grilled Bahamian lobster tail topped with sour orange butter ($50). Delicious desserts include traditional guava duff ($10). Dinner only; closed Sun.

Portobello's ☎ 373-1333. At *Lighthouse Pointe* overlooking the ocean, *Portobello's* specializes in family-style Italian served in a dining room with stone floors, heavy wooden furniture and an outdoor terrace. The menu features fresh-baked breads, pasta dishes including a lobster penne, a mushroom and asparagus risotto and wood-fired pizzas. Entrees $22–34. Dinner only from 6pm.

The Prop Club ☎ 373-1333. Located on the beach in front of *Breaker's Cay*, this casual sports bar, decked out like a weather-beaten aeroplane hanger, is the place to head if on a tight budget but still looking for holiday atmosphere and a view of the ocean. The menu features a flavourful margarita pizza, fried chicken, rum-soaked bbq ribs, a blacked grouper burger with tamarind mayo, vegetable wraps and lots of fruity drinks dressed up with mini-umbrellas. Expect to pay $12–28 for a main. For entertainment, there's a pool table, televised sports on five screens, happy hour twice a day (4–7pm and 10pm to close) and dancing every night.

Sugar Mill Bar and Grill ☎ 373-1333. Open-air snack bar on the beach in front of the *Sheraton*, offering moderately-priced burgers, sandwiches, salads and cool drinks for lunch and dinner. The least expensive place for a bite at *Our Lucaya* and particularly handy when lounging on the beach.

Willy Broadleaf ☎ 373-1333. Overlooking the beach on the ground floor of *Breaker's Cay*, *Willy*

Broadleaf offers a heaping breakfast buffet of fresh fruits, omelettes, cooked meats, coconut French toast and plenty more for $23. The decor is a delightful romp around the globe, with Middle Eastern, Mexican, African and Mediterranean touches. Daily for breakfast only.

The Nearby Beaches

Banana Bay Beach Bar and Restaurant Fortune Beach ☎ 373-2960. A delightful spot for breakfast or lunch, either in the brightly painted café with its tropical fish tank and murals or on the broad wooden deck overlooking a lovely stretch of beach. Imaginatively presented lunch plates include conch burgers, cheese quesadillas, crab cakes and mouthwatering desserts. Caters primarily to day-trippers off cruise ships, but worth the short drive out from Freeport. Daily 9am–5pm.

Club Caribe Churchill Beach, at Mather Town off Midshipman Road at Doubloon Drive ☎ 373-6866. Sadly closed at press time, plans were afoot to reopen the inexpensive and unpretentious *Club Caribe*, with umbrella-shaded picnic tables within view of the sea that make for a near-perfect spot to down drinks or munch on simple pub-grub-style lunch or early dinner. Call ahead to check on status, and note that transportation from Freeport or Lucaya is available. Closed Mon.

Coconuts *Island Seas Resort*, Beachways Drive ☎ 373-1271. A relaxed atmosphere surrounds this thatch-roofed poolside bar and grill, where the moderately-priced American favourites, think burgers and fries, are best chased with a frozen tropical cocktail.

Margaritaville Sand Bar Churchill Beach off Midshipman Road at Doubloon Drive, Mather Town ☎ 373-4525. The interior of this small candy-striped bar next to *Club Caribe* is cool and dark, with a sand floor and coloured lights. You can have burgers, sandwiches, conch fritters and occasionally wild boar at picnic tables under a thatch roof overlooking the beach – and then play some volleyball afterwards. Transportation from Freeport/Lucaya available; closed Mon.

The Stoned Crab Taino Beach ☎ 373-1442. Notable for its distinctive double pyramid roof, this upscale seafood restaurant serves fresh crab claws, lobster and seafood platters, along with some meat and pasta dishes, in a tastefully designed dining room overlooking the beach. Mains $22–45. Reservations recommended; daily 5–10pm.

Drinking and nightlife

For a daytime **drink**, you're best off hitting up any of the myriad poolside bars located in nearly every resort. In the evening, the liveliest spot is Count Basie Square in the Port Lucaya Marketplace, patronized primarily by holidaymakers and yacht cruisers; the square plays host to live music nightly (7–9pm). There are also a few elegant jazz lounges and cigar bars to choose from at *Our Lucaya Resort* and nearby hotels. For a novel night out, hop aboard a **booze cruise** or take a **sunset sail**, or if you prefer dry land try one of the various **fish fries** held on the beach (see box opposite).

For a more sedate evening, the Galleria Cinemas on East Mall Drive in Freeport (☎ 351-9190/2) has three daily **movie** showings during the weeks and four come the weekend. Two local **amateur dramatic** societies, the Freeport Player's Guild (☎ 352-5533) and the Grand Bahama Players (☎ 373-2299), stage Bahamian and international plays between September and June at the Regency Theatre on Regency Boulevard in Freeport.

Churchill Bar *Our Lucaya* ☎ 373-1333. A polished piano bar on the ground floor of the *Westin's* reception building with live jazz Thurs–Sun. Upstairs, the deep comfy chairs on the verandah are an ideal place to toast the sunset.
Coconuts *Island Seas Resort* ☎ 373-1271. Has live entertainment under the stars some nights.
Havana Cay Cigar Bar *Our Lucaya* ☎ 373-1333. Connoisseurs of fine wines and cigars should pay this bar a visit, an elegant stop for a nightcap while puffing on a Cuban on the front porch. Daily 6pm–2am.
Rum Runner's Bar Count Basie Square ☎ 373-7233. A popular Port Lucaya Marketplace bar with views of the marina and the bandstand, where there is live entertainment every night. Don't leave without sampling one of their potent coconut and rum-based concoctions.

Pub crawls, fish fries and more

Though undoubtedly touristy, taking part in one of the many pre-packaged nights out organized (mainly) by local hotels and restaurants around Freeport/Lucaya can also be a great night out. What follows is just a sample of what's on offer; check the listings in the *Freeport News* and in *Happenings Around Town* for more options.

Monday: Smiling Pat's Adventures (☎373-6395) offers a four-hour bar-hopping safari starting at 7pm ($45). Stops range from a locals' bar in William's Town to drunken limbo dancing at Port Lucaya's *Rum Runners*.

Tuesday: Churchill Beach's *Margueritaville Sand Bar* (☎373-4525) hosts a beach party with a bonfire, food and party games, and free transportation from area hotels.

Wednesday: Residents host a community fish fry at Smith's Point on Taino Beach that has become a popular local institution. You can buy drinks and fresh fish cooked Bahamian-style at open-air kiosks on the beach. There are plenty of tables set up on wooden decks and live music to entertain all.

Thursday: *Rocker's Cay Restaurant and Bar* (☎346-6080) in the settlement of West End (25 miles west of Freeport) hosts the West End Fish Fry, serving up fried fish, conch done several ways, jerk chicken, grilled lobster and Bahamian side dishes of coconut and rice and potato bread washed down with Irish Moss (seaweed) juice, if you like.

Shenanigan's Irish Pub Port Lucaya Marketplace ☎373-4734. Friendly pub that's home to a selection of beers from around the world, including arguably the finest pint of Guinness in the Bahamas. Open from 5pm until late.

Listings

Banking Banks are open Mon–Thurs 9.30am–3pm, Fri 9.30am–5pm. There are branches of the Bank of the Bahamas (☎352-7483), Barclays (☎352-8391), British American Bank (☎352-6676), First Caribbean International Bank (☎352-6651), Royal Bank of Canada (☎352-6631) and Scotiabank (☎352-6774) in Freeport and a Royal Bank of Canada (☎373-8628) at Port Lucaya Marketplace. All have ATMs. Scotiabank ATMs dispensing American currency are located in the casino at *Our Lucaya* and at the *Westin* in the Manor House. There's a Western Union (☎352-6676; Mon–Fri 9am–4pm) at the British American Bank on East Mall Drive.

Books and Magazines In the Lucaya Marketplace, both the Oasis pharmacy (Mon–Sat 9am–6pm, Sun 9am–5pm) and H&L Bookstore (closed Sun) stock a small collection of books, including some by Bahamian authors, and Oasis carries magazines.

Dentist Bain Dental Office, Pioneer's Way, Freeport (☎352-8492).

Groceries In Freeport, Winn Dixie supermarkets (Mon–Sat 7.30am–9pm, Sun 7–10am) are located at Lucayan Shopping Centre on Seahorse Road

(☎373-5500) and in downtown Freeport at Winn Dixie Plaza (☎352-7901). They offer free delivery to visiting yachts on orders over $100. The open-air fruit and seafood wholesale market across the street from Winn Dixie Plaza is open Mon–Sat 7am–7pm (closed Sun). Butler's Specialty Foods (☎373-2050) in Port Lucaya Marketplace has a selection of gourmet foods, including deli meats and cheeses.

Internet access Head for the *Chat and Chill Cyber Cafe*, in the Port Lucaya Marketplace (Mon–Sat 8.30am–10pm, Sun 10am–10pm; $5 for 15min).

Laundry Jiffy Cleaners and Laundromat (☎352-7079), corner of West Mall Drive and Pioneer's Way. Most hotels offer a laundry service or have a laundry on site.

Library The Charles Hayward Public Library (☎352-7048) is on East Mall Drive near Pioneer's Way.

Medical services In an emergency, dial ☎911. For an ambulance, call ☎352-2689. The Rand Memorial Hospital (☎352-6735) is located on East Mall Drive near Pioneer's Way in Freeport. The Lucaya Medical Centre/West (☎352-7288)

is on Adventurer's Way in Freeport. The Lucaya Medical Centre/East (☎373-7400) on East Sunrise Highway at Seahorse Road is the closest clinic to Lucaya. New Sunrise Medical Centre and Hospital (☎373-3333), also on East Sunrise Drive, has out-patient services 8.30am–5.30pm and a walk-in clinic until 10.30pm.

Petrol There are petrol stations on the corner of East Sunrise Highway and Coral Road (nearest to Lucaya) and on the corner of East Settler's Way and East Mall Drive in Freeport, and a few more around town.

Pharmacy A pharmacist is on duty daily (8am–3pm) at LMR Drugs, 1 West Mall Drive (☎352-9075). For non-prescription drugs and toiletries, try the Oasis pharmacies, located at Port Lucaya Marketplace and at the airport.

Police In an emergency, dial ☎91. There are police detachments at the *International Bazaar* in Freeport (☎352-4156) and on Seahorse Drive in Lucaya (☎373-1112).

Post office The main post office (Mon–Fri 9am–5.30pm; ☎352-9371) is located on Explorer's Way in the commercial district of Freeport. Stamps can be purchased at the Oasis pharmacies.

Telephone Payphones can be found in hotel lobbies and shopping centres. You can purchase prepaid BaTelCo debit cards at the phone company (☎352-9352) on Pioneer's Way in Freeport or BaTelCo and other brands of phonecards at the Oasis pharmacy in Port Lucaya Marketplace. Cellphones from the US can be connected for local use for $75 at BaTelCo; calls cost 40/20¢ a minute during the day/night.

East of Freeport

Escape from Freeport/Lucaya's crowded resorts lies east of the city, and the Queen's Highway, which extends for sixty miles out to **McLean's Town**, can spirit you away. Leaving the city, the road cuts a straight line through tall pine forest with an understory of emerald-green thatch palm. Less than half an hour out, the road passes by the unspoilt and usually empty **Barbary** and **Gold Rock beaches**, as well as **Lucayan National Park**, encompassing a varied landscape of blue holes, mangrove creeks, coastal forests and beach traversed by several hiking trails. McLean's Town itself is a small fishing village with little to see or do, but from the docks there you can visit a handful of small **cays** sitting a short distance offshore. If counting on public transport to **get around**, the #10 **bus** runs from downtown Freeport to McLean's Town twice a day (8am and 2pm; $8), with an additional shorter trip going only as far as High Rock (5.30pm).

Barbary Beach and Old Freetown

Fifteen miles east of Freeport, **Barbary Beach** is a long, empty stretch of white sand backed by casuarina trees. Initially, the students of Cornell who designed the master plan for Freeport in 1960 envisioned a university town here, but the founding fathers of Freeport didn't buy into the idea and it remains an undeveloped piece of coastline. You are likely to have it all to yourself, and a mile offshore is tiny **Peterson Cay National Park**, a conservation area for sea birds with an inviting beach and good snorkelling. Several outfitters run day–trips to the island (see p.112 for details).

A few miles further east, just off the main highway, are the ruins of **Old Freetown**, one of the first settlements of freed slaves on the island; there isn't much left to see except the remnants of a few stone foundations. Continuing further eastward, keep an eye out on the left-hand side of the highway for the huge **sound stage** in the woods, built by Bahamian favourite son Sidney Poitier and other investors in 1968 in hopes of sparking a local movie industry. Much more recently, portions of the *Pirates of the Caribbean* swashbucklers were filmed at the Grand Bahama Film Studios, newly constructed on the nearby and decommissioned American naval base at Gold Rock Creek (closed to visitors).

Lucayan National Park and Gold Rock Beach

Straddling the Queen's Highway less than thirty miles east of Freeport is **Lucayan National Park** (daily 9am–4pm; $3, tickets available at the Rand Nature Centre in Freeport or at Smitty's One Stop petrol station in Beven's Town; ☎352-5438). The park encompasses forty acres of mixed forest, limestone caverns and sinkholes, mangrove creeks, a spectacular beach and several marked nature trails all less than a mile long. One of these leads from the parking lot on the north side of the highway to Ben's Cave and the Burial

△ Going for a stroll at Gold Rock Beach

Mound Cave, which are part of a six-mile-long **underwater cave system**, one of the world's longest. In one of nature's mysteries, a lens of fresh water rests atop the salt water that fills the underground caverns. Certified divers may explore the underwater stalactites and stalagmites of the tunnels with a permit obtainable from the park and UNEXSO (see p.109) offers guided expeditions as well. The opening of Ben's Cave, accessible by a steep staircase, is home to a large colony of buffy flower bats and is closed to visitors in the summer months when they nurse their young. Nearby, Burial Mound Cave, another limestone sinkhole, was named after divers discovered the skeletons of four indigenous Lucayans inside.

Perhaps the Lucayans who lived hereabouts were attracted to the spot by the stunning vista of **Gold Rock Beach**, accessible by a trail on the south side of the highway across from the parking lot. At high tide, it's just another pretty strand of powdery white sand edged with feathery casuarina trees. But when the tide heads out to sea, a pristine, sweeping expanse of beautiful rippling patterns carved into the sand by the retreating waves is revealed – the ideal setting for a picnic and a long walk in the surf. Half a mile offshore lies the minute cay of Gold Rock itself, and behind it is the ocean outlet of the underwater cavern system that connects to Burial Mound Cave and Ben's Cave.

A few miles further east on the Queen's Highway, beach lovers should make a beeline for **High Rock Beach**, a long ribbon of white sand with a gentle surf, accessible at the village of High Rock and extending for several miles in either direction. A further ten miles or so east, the highway runs alongside another pearly white beach fringed with coconut palms at the sleepy hamlet of **Pelican Point**.

Practicalities

The best **tours** of Lucayan National Park are run by Kayak Nature Tours (see p.111 for details), whose trips include plenty of paddling along with short hikes and lunch. Note that as a national park, fishing and the removal of any material from the park are not permitted. If thinking about **spending the night** in the area, *Bishop's Bonefishing Resort* in High Rock (℡353-4515, Ⓕ353-4417; ❸) offers half a dozen large and modern motel-style rooms steps from the beach. Guided fishing packages are available, and meals are served in a friendly, simple bar and dining room next door. A bit closer to Freeport but no less secluded is the all-inclusive *North Riding Point Club* (℡353-4250, Ⓦwww.northridingpointclub.com; $3225–3800 per person based on double occupancy for a week of guided bonefishing, with discounts for non-fishing companions), an elegant hideaway catering exclusively to fishermen. The club offers accommodation for up to fourteen guests in charming wooden cottages, shaded by mature trees and fronting the beautiful, private white-sand beach. The rooms, each with two double beds, are simple but tastefully furnished and each cottage sports a deep, screened-in porch facing the water.

Eating options in the area are pretty basic. There are a couple of basic road-side bars along the Queen's Highway and Smitty's One Stop petrol station (Daily 8am–8pm) at Beven's Town five miles east of the park has a convenience store and a small café serving Bahamian staples like conch fritters and fried chicken. In Pelican Point village, *Breezes Bar and Restaurant* – overlooking the beach and open on weekends only – dishes out standard Bahamian cuisine. Off the highway at High Rock, *Bishop's Bar and Restaurant* (℡353-4515) serves similar basic but satisfying fare within sight of High Rock Beach.

> ## Water Cay
>
> Though nowadays development on Grand Bahama is focused solely on its southern shore, in the nineteenth century a hardy band of settlers chose to create an outpost on the small and rocky **Water Cay** off the island's north shore. From their isolated spot off the island's midpoint, the settlers fished and farmed sisal for export. Today, just a handful of residents remain, along with a picturesque little church and plenty of birdlife. If you'd like to take a look, a rough road east of Freeport leads to Dover Sound, where you might find a fisherman willing to boat you over to Water Cay. Alternatively, Kayak Nature Tours offers both an all-day paddling excursion to the cay and a three-day camping trip (see p.111 for details).

McLean's Town and the east-end cays

Marking the eastern terminus of the Queen's Highway, **McLEAN'S TOWN**, a small fishing village of a dozen or so modern bungalows, was originally a base for harvesting sponges. There are no real sights to speak of in town, though if you're around on National Heroes Day (October 12), be sure to call in for the annual **conch-cracking contest**. There are several separate cracking and eating events – including a division for tourists who've never conked a conch before – along with a Junkanoo parade, three-legged races, greasy-pole climbing and music from the local police force band.

The rest of the year, the majority of visitors out to McLean's Town are here to catch the ferry to Crown Haven (see p.151) or to visit one of the nearby cays curving off the frayed southeastern end of Grand Bahama. The bonefishing around them is superb, and anglers looking to head out should contact one of the local guides listed earlier in this chapter. The closest of the cays is **Deep Water Cay**, site of a private bonefishing club. Three miles further south and accessible by boat only is the tiny fishing settlement on **Sweeting's Cay**, home to a few cottages, a primary school and a huge pile of empty conch shells near the wharf. Having only recently received electricity, the cay offers a delightful glimpse of Out Island life. Uninhabited **Lightbourne Cay**, separated from Sweeting's Cay by a narrow channel, boasts a long, broad swath of brilliant white sand lapped by shallow, clear waters frequented by graceful eagle rays and schools of bonefish.

Practicalities

The best **tours** around McLean's Town and the nearby cays are run by East End Adventures, who offer excellent snorkelling and sightseeing excursions that include visits to Sweeting's Cay and a picnic on Lightbourne Cay; see the tour and snorkel operator listings earlier in the chapter for information. It's also possible to hire a water taxi on the wharf in McLean's Town, though be prepared to haggle for a fair fee. **Accommodation** is limited to the three-storey green and pink house on your left as you enter McLean's Town; the owners rent out very basic rooms, mainly to people arriving or departing on the ferry to Abaco (☎353-3440; $50, ❶). The main hub of activity in town is *Cardy's* **restaurant** (☎353-3150), serving down-home Bahamian specialities like cracked conch and sheep-tongue souse, as well as burgers and sandwiches. The proprietors, Cardinal and Ginny Higgs, also organize a **fish fry** every afternoon at nearby Crabbing Bay Beach (noon–4pm; $55), an outing that includes transportation to and from your hotel in Freeport/Lucaya, a picnic lunch, conch-cracking demonstration and games. They host a Pig Roast on Sunday afternoons (3–7pm), with live rake 'n scrape music. They also rent kayaks, paddle boats, snorkelling gear and will take you fishing, sightseeing or snorkelling through the cays and blue holes off the east end. On Sweeting Cay, the *Seaside Fig Tree* is a pleasant lavender-painted restaurant with a verandah lapped by the turquoise water that's great for a cool drink or a meal of basic Bahamian and deep-fried fare served all day.

West of Freeport

Unless you're staying at the luxury *Inn at Old Bahama Bay* resort, there are really only two reasons to head **west of Freeport**. The first is the stunning, wild beach around the *Paradise Cove* resort – a picturesque strip of sand made even finer by **Deadman's Reef** just offshore. The second reason, and one that's only attractive to history buffs, is the storied settlement of **West End**, a once bustling rum-running centre. To reach West End without a car, the #16 bus leaves daily from downtown Freeport on the hour between 6am and 6pm ($4).

Paradise Cove and Deadman's Reef

Leaving Freeport, the Queen's Highway skirts an industrial landscape surrounding Freeport Harbour, including the oil bunkering facility and a massive container port. It's ironic that while settlers and trading vessels over the centuries passed Grand Bahama by because of its lack of a natural harbour, today Freeport is one of the busiest ports in the Caribbean. Ten miles west of Freeport, the road enters **Eight Mile Rock**, a string of high-density, low-income settlements spread out along eight miles of rocky shore.

A couple of miles further on, a sign on the left marks the turnoff to *Paradise Cove* (☎349-2677, ⓦ www.deadmansreef.com; ❻). This family-run beach bar and grill caters primarily to sea and sand day-trippers from Freeport/Lucaya hotels, but also has a pair of homely, well-maintained two-bedroom cottages right on the beach, a beautiful stretch of white sand backed by tall grass and bush. Best of all, there is great snorkelling from the shore over a lush sea garden protected by the exposed dark coral hump of **Deadman's Reef**, which runs parallel about fifty yards offshore. The resort owners run a friendly and relaxed snack bar here, rent snorkelling gear and glass-bottomed kayaks, and offer day excursions to Paradise Cove from Freeport/Lucaya, which include a day of swimming and snorkelling as well as lunch at the snack bar. Sample rates are $35 for a day of snorkelling including equipment and lunch, kayak rentals for $30 an hour for a glass-bottom option or $20 for a regular one, and $35 for a bonfire on the beach including supper; all rates include transportation from your hotel.

Several hundred yards long, Deadman's Reef is the site of an important archeological find. The remains of a Lucayan settlement from the twelfth or thirteenth century was discovered here in 1996, and since then over 60,000 artefacts have been uncovered by researchers and volunteers, including shell beads, tools, pottery and animal bones. The site itself is on private land.

West End and the Inn at Old Bahama Bay

A village of less than a hundred residents located a couple of miles west of Deadman's Reef, **WEST END** was the scene of much wild intrigue as a hideout for pirates in the days of Blackbeard. Things heated up again during US Prohibition, when rum-running drew bootleggers and thrill-seekers here as well. Warehouses, bars and flophouses sprang up along the waterfront, and up to thirty flights a day took off from the airstrip cut out of the bush where the *Inn at Old Bahama Bay* stands today. With Miami so close, dozens of boats a week left the wharves at West End loaded with contraband. Ingeniously, they often left towing their cargo in aluminum tubes that could hold up to 400 cases of liquor – if the Coast Guard appeared, the lines were cut and retrieved from the sea only after the Coast Guard left empty-handed. The fun and easy money ended with the repeal of Prohibition in 1933, and the town's been on a decline ever since.

The West End of days gone by was just the kind of place that would appeal to the macho Ernest Hemingway, who reputedly stayed at the now near-derelict **Star Hotel, Restaurant and Bar** (☎346-6207), built in 1946. The hotel is closed, and the closure in 1982 of the *Jack Tar Village*, another large all-inclusive resort built on the site where the *Inn at Old Bahama Bay* stands today, put many locals out of work, an economic blow from which West End has never recovered. You can have a drink for old times' sake at the *Star*, whose friendly and knowledgeable proprietor Robert Grant can fill you in on local lore. The *Star* also hosts a street party every weekend, with music and fresh conch salad and other foods grilled on the waterfront; call for details. Another **dining** option in town is *The Village Tavern* (☎346-6102), located in a tidy, bright-yellow building on a side street in West End; inside you can order Bahamian food like souse, fried chicken and boiled fish breakfasts.

The Inn at Old Bahama Bay

Following the road out of West End about two miles leads you to the **Inn at Old Bahama Bay** (☎346-6500, ⓦ www.oldbahamabay.com; suites from $600; ❾), a development encompassing 228 secluded wooded acres on the tip of the island, crisscrossed with peaceful walking trails. A full-service marina has been up and running since 2001 and the inn recently opened nearly fifty, one- and 2-bedroom ocean-front suites. Construction is still under way on the water's edge, where lots are being sold for luxury vacation homes, part of a long-term plan to develop a resort community for wealthy snowbirds. The sumptuous guestrooms – featuring dark-wood accents, rich fabrics and luxurious touches like feather duvets and leather steamer trunks – are housed in pastel gabled cottages with private verandahs overlooking a palm-fringed curve of white sand. The point is surrounded by rich, teeming sea gardens and reefs, and seven different snorkelling trails have been mapped out, accessible either from the shore or by boat. There are bicycles for guest use, as well as a fitness centre and spa services.

The inn is also home to *Bonefish Folley's Bar and Grille* (☎346-6500; daily 7am–10pm), a cheerful **bistro** with open-air seating and a view of the marina that's named for a local bonefishing legend. Try the warm cinnamon buns at breakfast and the spicy conch fritters or herbed crab cakes for lunch ($10). More substantial meals include mahi mahi served with a coconut lemon sauce ($17). Fine dining is available at **Aqua**, done up in white linen and crystal (☎346-6500; daily for dinner 7pm–10pm, reservations and collared shirts required; Sun brunch 11am–3.30pm). The cuisine is billed as 'Bahamian fusion' with home-made sorbet served between courses of gazpacho and seafood dishes like lobster stuffed with mushrooms, almonds, sweet peppers and corn bread. The chic, thatch-roofed *Straw Bar* (☎346-6500) sits on a lovely strip of white sand beach and serves cocktails and light snacks all day, along with occasional live music and bonfires on the beach.

The Abacos

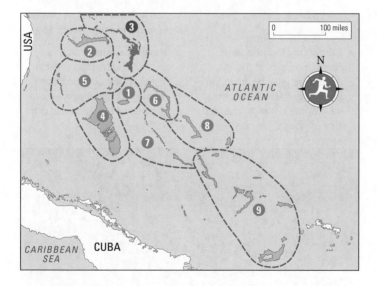

CHAPTER 3 # Highlights

✳ **Pelican Cays Land and Sea Park** The spectacular snorkelling here features coral tunnels, spires and caves that make for intriguing underwater vistas. See p.144

✳ **Hole-in-the-Wall** Located along the cliff-bound seashore of South Abaco, sea birds abound and trails lead through lush stands of wild orchids and sea grass. See p.147

✳ **Elbow Cay Lighthouse** Climb the stairs at the lighthouse in Hope Town for an unforgettable 360-degree view of the Loyalist Cays and Sea of Abaco. See p.154

✳ **Cap'n Jack's** After wandering the quaint streets of Hope Town, refresh yourself with a scrumptious conch burger at this celebrated local restaurant. See p.157

✳ **Joe Albury's Studio** The Bahamian craft of wooden sailboat building is on display at this studio on remote Man O' War Cay, filled with authentic sailboats as well as wooden models. See p.159

✳ **New Plymouth** A picture perfect and historic seaside village in the Loyalist Cays offering a carefully preserved glimpse of the Bahamas circa 1800. See p.163

△ Elbow Cay Lighthouse, Hope Town

The Abacos

The northernmost of the Bahamian islands, the **Abacos** – 200 miles east of Miami and 75 north of Nassau – are the most accessible of all the Bahamian Out Islands, and, consequently, the most developed, visited and affluent. Each year the Abacos, whose population hovers around 10,000, receive more than 120,000 visitors, a good portion of whom arrive on yachts and other sailing vessels, taking advantage of fine marinas and excellent shallow-water cruising amid the many cays and islands.

The Abacos' two main islands, **Little Abaco** and **Great Abaco**, form a narrow boomerang bowing to the east. Running parallel to them is a stunning chain of approximately 25 cays that form a 200-mile-long barrier and reef system off the Abacos' Atlantic coast. Two more reef systems oceanward of the cays provide additional protection for the mainland against the waves and occasional storms of the cool Atlantic Ocean. **Marsh Harbour**, located at the midpoint of Great Abaco, is the administrative, accommodation and yachting centre of the Abacos. With a population of nearly 4000, the town attracts visitors in all seasons and serves as the gateway for activities in the **Loyalist Cays**, home to the enchanting towns of **New Plymouth** and **Hope Town** on Green Turtle and Elbow cays respectively. **Treasure Cay**, north of Marsh Harbour and actually a peninsula not a cay, also has excellent marina facilities and year-round tourist accommodation.

Despite the influx of tourists, the Abacos are far from overrun and naturalists are well served here as well. Because of the heavy forestation of Great Abaco, there are good opportunities for **bird-watching**: warblers, West Indian woodpeckers, yellowthroats, flycatchers, swallows and Cuban emeralds all call the Abacos home. And in the **Abaco National Park** in southern Great Abaco, 2500 acres have been set aside as a reserve to protect the endangered **Bahamian parrot**, colourful birds that have been referred to as "rainbows in the sky". Everything from wild horses and boars to several varieties of bats inhabit the islands as well, but it's along and in the water that you'll want to do most of your explorations. Southeast of Marsh Harbour, the Abacos' only underwater preserve is the **Pelican Cays Land and Sea Park**, a 1200-acre area consisting of shallow reefs and mangroves. Harbouring a vast array of marine life, including the endangered green turtle, it's understandably popular with snorkellers and divers. The western seaboard of northern Great Abaco, called the **Marls**, is one vast wetland, an important nursery for many reef fishes and invertebrate populations.

The **weather** of the Abacos is markedly different from the other Bahamian islands due to its northern latitude. The climate falls between temperate and subtropical, with an average rainfall of 50–60in per year,

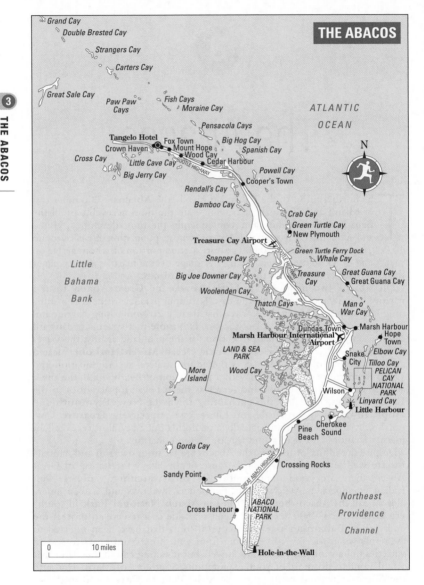

THE ABACOS

encouraging the many citrus farms on the island. Winter is a long, dry period, when **forest fires** often flare, some started by farmers to clear land or drive away the endemic wild hogs. Fire-cleared land makes way for a blooming of pines, orchids and the typical **fresh grass** (*Andropogon glomeratus*) of the Abacos. Soon after a fire, you can catch sight of tiny pine seedlings peeping up through the soil of Great Abaco, a pulse of green against the red-grey land.

The Marls

The least explored part of Great Abaco is the nearly uncharted **Marls** of the west coast, a great pattern of small cays, rocks and inlets. At high tide, water depth in creeks on the Marls' shoreward side might be only three feet, a perfect depth for kayaks. Paddling in the Marls one can see red mangroves, which pioneer the making of new land by rooting directly in the mud under shallow water, then sending out a system of stilt roots that catch creek silt, thus providing a home for reef fish, nurse sharks and stingrays. Black mangroves are abundant as well, though they have no stilts, sending up breathing tubes from their roots as sources of oxygen. The Marls, thick with marine life, are also loaded with birdlife similar to the Florida Everglades to the west, including beautiful greenback herons, little blue herons, turkey vultures and great white egrets. The rock islands throughout support pines, bromeliads and orchids and the quiet lagoons dotted about are good for snorkelling.

The few visitors venturing out to the Marls are mainly bonefishers travelling with local guides. *Abaco Island Tours* (☎367-2936 or 375-8718, located in *Sapodilly's* restaurant) can also arrange day-trips of Abaco's wilderness areas, including historical and nature tours of the cays and south Abaco, picnics on the beach, bird-watching, kayaking, snorkelling and diving.

Some history

Though the original Lucayans disappeared about fifty years after Columbus sailed through the Bahamas in 1492, the Spanish, who moved on once their slave raids had decimated the population, kept the Lucayan name, **Habacoa**, for the islands. No remains of an early French attempt at colonization in 1625 have been found, and the main wave of settlement here came in 1783, when immigrants from New York, the Carolinas and Florida came to stay at the end of the American Revolutionary War.

Most of the **original inhabitants** of the Abacos were these Loyalist settlers. Some of them were freed black slaves who arrived near present-day **Treasure Cay** aboard the *Nautilus* and *William*, founding the village of Carleton, naming it for Sir Guy Carleton, commander of British forces in North America. Most of the early Carleton Loyalists went their separate ways after disputes over lands that had been granted them by the Crown, with splinter groups settling on the **Loyalist Cays**.

The Loyalist settlers eventually dwindled from 2000 to about 400 hardy souls, most of whom made a living through fishing, trade and crafts, though a healthy minority also engaged in wrecking. From their American homes they brought with them a dour **Calvinist Protestantism**, much of which lives on today in the spiritual life of the Loyalist Cays. They also patterned their villages on the New England mould – clapboard houses with steeply pitched roofs, tiny lawns surrounded by picket fences, and a narrow complex web of streets with the church at its centre of life. Unlike the New England model, though, the Abaco style features bright paint and a profusion of flowers like oleander, hibiscus and bougainvillea decorating each lawn.

Self-reliant, church-going and serious yet friendly, today's residents of the Abacos are among the most industrious in the Bahamas. Many still fish for conch and spiny Bahamian lobster, and continue to make money from boat building and maintenance, repair and storage, as well as charter businesses. People in the Abacos are increasingly employed in the tourist industry, while the islands have drawn large numbers of wealthy North Americans and a growing number of retirees, who have built luxury homes in and around Marsh Harbour.

Getting there

The main entry point for most visitors to the Abacos is **Marsh Harbour International Airport**, located at the midpoint of Great Abaco, receiving direct flights from Florida, Nassau and other Bahamian islands. There is also an airport located near **Treasure Cay** to the north primarily serving guests staying at the resort there or those heading to Green Turtle Cay. Alternatively, two government **mailboats** service the Abacos weekly from Nassau and there is a twice-weekly **ferry service** from Nassau and a daily ferry from Grand Bahama.

Arriving by air

Several **airlines** service the tiny terminal at Marsh Harbour. Bahamasair (T 377-5505 or 1-800/222-4262, W www.bahamasair.com) has daily flights from Nassau, West Palm Beach and Miami, with many continuing on to Treasure Cay; American Eagle (T 954/367-2231 or 1-800/433-7300, W www.aa.com) and US Airways (T 1/800-428-4322, W www.usair.com) also run trips from Miami. Fort Lauderdale flights are offered by Continental (T 1-800-523-3273, W www.continental.com) and Yellow Air Taxi (T 1-888/935-5694, W www.flyyellowairtaxi.com), while Southern Air (T 323-6833, W www.southernaircharter.com) shuttles between Nassau and Marsh Harbour.

It's also possible to reach the Abacos by air from some of the smaller Bahamian islands. Abaco Air (T 367-2267, W www.abacoaviationcentre.com) has daily flights to Nassau, along with less frequent hops to North Eleuthera and Moore's Island. Flamingo Air (T 377-0354, W www.flamingoairbah.com) has trips from Freeport to out of the way Walker's Cay and the airstrip at Sandy Point on the south tip of Great Abaco, and Major's Air Service (T 352-5778) flies from Freeport to Marsh Harbour.

It's a short **cab** ride ($10–12) from the Marsh Harbour International Airport into town or on to the ferry dock to catch a ferry to Hope Town, Guana Cay, or Man O'War Cay. If heading to any of the offshore cays without ferry service, a taxi will take you to a boat rental outlet.

Arriving by sea

The Abacos are the Bahamas' most popular destination for **yacht cruisers**. With an estimated 1000 boat slips in twenty marinas scattered through the Abacos, there are more boat slips than hotel rooms, and specific marina details are listed throughout the chapter. If you don't have your own vessel, but want to sample the sailing life, see the list of charter companies (bareboat and crewed) on p.23.

As for regular boat services, Nassau has the most connections. The **mailboat** *Legacy* ($50) departs from Nassau on Tuesdays at 7pm for the twelve-hour crossing, calling at Green Turtle Cay, Hope Town and Marsh Harbour. The mailboat *Captain Gurth Dean* departs from Nassau around 11pm on Tuesdays, taking seven hours to reach tiny Moore's Island off Abaco's west coast and continuing on the Sandy Point, Great Abaco. Call the Dockmaster at Potter's Cay, Nassau for the latest exact departure times (T 393-1064). Bahamas Fast Ferries (T 323-2166, W www.bahamasferries.com; $50 one-way) has **ferry service** on Friday and Sunday between Nassau and Sandy Point, at the southern tip of Abaco. Keep in mind that as Sandy Point is 50 miles from Marsh Harbour, it's an expensive taxi ride to town ($135), although the Islander Express **bus** (T 366-4444) occasionally runs a connection service.

Ferry access is also available from Grand Bahama via Pinder's Ferry Service (☎365-2356; $45 one-way), crossing twice a day between Crown Haven on Little Abaco and McLean's Town, sixty miles east of Freeport. To reach Crown Haven from Marsh Harbour, the Great Abaco Express bus service (☎367-2165) leaves Marsh Harbour at 5am and 12.30pm; return trips are run at 9.30am and 5.30pm.

Marsh Harbour

Founded in 1784 by Loyalists, **MARSH HARBOUR** started life as a logging, sponging and "wrecking" town, with boatbuilding as a secondary industry. While the town had only a single paved road until relatively late into the twentieth century, **tourism** is now the town's major source of income, its marinas filled with yachts and surrounded by swank vacation villas.

With a population of 4000, Marsh Harbour is the third-largest settlement in the Bahamas, and is the commercial and tourism centre for the Abacos.

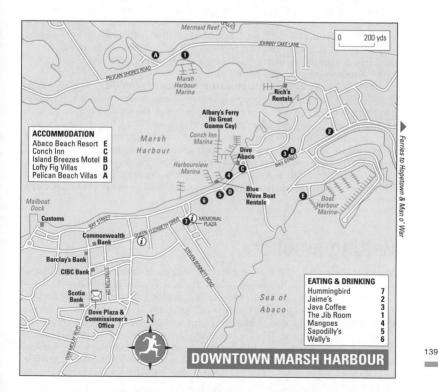

DOWNTOWN MARSH HARBOUR

ACCOMMODATION
Abaco Beach Resort   E
Conch Inn   C
Island Breezes Motel   B
Lofty Fig Villas   D
Pelican Beach Villas   A

EATING & DRINKING
Hummingbird   7
Jaime's   2
Java Coffee   3
The Jib Room   1
Mangoes   4
Sapodilly's   5
Wally's   6

Located on a peninsula just off the main **Great Abaco Highway,** a smooth paved road that runs down the spine of Great Abaco, the town is also the jumping-off point for travel to and from the Loyalist Cays and around both Little and Great Abaco. Tidy and functional rather than picturesque, the town has a pleasant holiday atmosphere and offers most of the services you might require, including a post office, bookstore, grocery stores, gift and clothing stores, several marinas, and tour operators for diving, fishing and kayaking. There are also several waterfront bars and restaurants offering live music a few nights a week. With the exception of the swathe of beach in front of the *Abaco Beach Resort,* there is no local **beach**, but white sand and turquoise water are in abundant supply nearby.

Arrival and information

Marsh Harbour lies three miles northeast of its eponymous international **airport**, through which most visitors to the Abacos will pass. **Taxi** rates from the airport to downtown or the marinas on Bay Street average $10, a few dollars more to Albury's Ferry Dock. For those arriving by boat, there are four **marinas** in town; all offer hookups, groceries, laundry, electricity and water, with dockage rates in the range of $1–1.75 a foot. Harbourview Marina (☎367-3910, ⓦwww.harbourviewmarina.com) can accommodate vessels up to 100ft in length and boasts cable TV, wireless Internet and telephones at each slip, a pool, showers and *Snappa's* bar. Boat Harbour Marina (☎367-2736 or 1-800/468-4799, ⓦwww.abacoresort.com) has 165 slips for yachts up to 150ft, and the Conch Inn Marina (☎367-4000, ⓦwww.go-abacos.com/conchinn), also called The Moorings, has 75 slips. On the north side of the harbour and the smallest of the bunch, the Marsh Harbour Marina (☎367-2700, ⓦwww.jibroom.com) has 68 slips.

There is a **tourist information office** (Mon–Fri 9am–5.30pm; ☎367-3067/8) in a small shopping centre in the heart of town on Queen Elizabeth Drive. The glossy periodical *Abaco Life* (ⓦwww.abacolife.com) is widely available and publishes regular features on island history and events. *The Abaconian* (ⓦwww.abaconian.com), a weekly newspaper, is a good source for local news and up-to-date listings on restaurants, emergency services and ferry schedules. For yachting knowledge, grab a copy of *The Cruising Guide to the Abacos* by Steve Dodge (ⓦwww.wspress.com). The Abacos also has its own **radio station** – Radio Abaco (93.5FM) – where you can catch local news and music.

Getting around

Marsh Harbour is small enough to make walking a favoured mode of transportation; it's only a half-mile jaunt from the town centre to the ferry dock for boats going to Elbow and Man Of War cays, with those to Guana Cay departing from the Union Jack dock in the village. Only if you plan on exploring the rest of Great Abaco or Little Abaco, or to take the ferry to Green Turtle Cay, will **renting a car** become necessary. There are several rental agencies in Marsh Harbour, but demand frequently exceeds supply and reservations should be made well in advance. Centrally located *Rental Wheels* (☎367-4643, ⓦwww.rentalwheels.com) offers excellent service and well-maintained cars and vans from $65 a day as well as motor scooters and bicycles for $45 and $10 a day, respectively. Similar rates can be had via *A&P Auto Rentals* on Don McKay Boulevard (T367-2655), H&L Rentals at the downtown Shell petrol station (T367-2840), or *Sea Star Car Rentals* within the Marsh Harbour International Airport (T367-4887).

Boats and ferries

The Sea of Abaco fills a shallow basin between Great Abaco and the many cays scattered along the main island's northeast flank. These protected waters are generally calm and the coastline and cays beckon to be explored by watercraft. Several companies in Marsh Harbour rent putt-about **motorboats**, with prices starting at $80 a day for an 18ft boat with discounts for rentals by the week. The demand often exceeds supply, and you should reserve a boat weeks or preferably months in advance of your trip. Some of the finer Marsh Harbour boat rentals are available from Blue Wave Boat Rentals (T367-3910, W www.bluewaverentals.com), Island Marine (T336-0282, W www.islandmarine.com), Rainbow Rentals (T367-4602, W www.rainbowrentals.com) and Rich's Rentals (T367-2742, W www.richsrentals.com).

If you'd rather have someone else do the piloting, there are regular **ferries** to the more populated cays. *Albury's Ferry Service* (T367-3147 or 365-6010, W www.oii.net/alburysferry) operates trips several times a day from Marsh Harbour to Elbow Cay, Man O' War Cay, Guana Cay and private Scotland Cay, and specific details are included with each cay later in the chapter. The ferries to Elbow Cay and Man O' War leave from Albury's Ferry Dock at the north edge of town, while those to Guana Cay and Scotland Cay leave from the Union Jack Dock in the centre of town. Taxis from the airport can drop you at either dock for $10–12. The cays are visible from Marsh Harbour and it takes about 20 minutes to reach any of them by boat or ferry. Green Turtle Cay Ferry services to New Plymouth leave from the Airport Ferry Dock near Treasure Cay (see p.148).

Accommodation

Marsh Harbour was hit hard by hurricanes in the autumn of 2004, but reconstruction and renovations have been intensive, and local businesses are for the most part back in operation. **Accommodations** are mainly small establishments clustered around the marinas in the town centre, with a couple of beachfront options. The fact that the Abacos is one of the most expensive destinations in the Bahamas is reflected in hotel rates.

Abaco Beach Resort and Boat Harbour Marina T367-2158 or 1-800/468-4799, W www.abacobeachresort.com. A sprawling, peach coloured stucco complex with eighty comfortably appointed if overpriced oceanfront rooms. There are also a half-dozen two-bedroom cottages and a large marina, and amenities include a pool with swim-up bar, casual restaurant, tennis courts, beach volleyball, kayaks and organized snorkelling and diving trips. On a strip of beach a short walk from the town centre. **8**

Conch Inn and Marina Bay Street T367-4000 or 1-800/688-4752. In the centre of town facing the harbour, the nine rooms here were completely renovated and refurnished following a thorough beating from Hurricanes Jeanne and Frances in 2004. Each room contains a small fridge, coffee maker, TV and a/c. There is a pool, plain restaurant and a pleasant outdoor bar serving light food and heavy drinks. The hotel's marina also has an excellent dive shop. **5**

Island Breezes Motel East Bay Street T367-3776. This is one of Marsh Harbour's top budget options, with eight simple but adequate air conditioned rooms on the western side of town, within easy walking distance of the shops, restaurants and ferry docks. ❷

Lofty Fig Villas East Bay Street ☎367 2681, ✉loftyfig@mymailstation.com. Centrally located, the six charming, quiet and very well kept one-bedroom efficiency units here are grouped around a small kidney-shaped swimming pool. The grounds are pleasantly dotted with trees and flow-ers, and each villa has its own screened-in porch, kitchen and television, with a shared barbecue out by the pool. ❸

Pelican Beach Villas Pelican Shores Road ☎367-3600 or 1-877/326-3180, Ⓦwww .pelicanbeachvillas.com. On a secluded peninsula a couple of miles from the centre of town, the six cute, cotton candy-coloured two-bedroom cottages here front a small scallop of beach facing the open sea. Each cottage has a kitchen, TV and rattan furniture, with docking for boats, a small swimming pool, showers and laundry facilities. While the winds often whip up, the location remains serene. Costly for two, but an economical alternative for four people sharing, with the two-room cottage renting for $350 a night. ❽

The town and around

From the airport, the Great Abaco Highway turns slightly east and becomes **Don McKay Boulevard** once in Marsh Harbour. At the town's only stoplight, the boulevard intersects **Queen Elizabeth Drive**, home to many shops and stores, before ending at **Bay Street**, which runs east along the harbour itself until it ends at the exclusive **Eastern Shores** housing development and the **Albury Ferry Dock**.

As there's not a whole lot to see or do in town, a top diversion for visitors is a bike ride or long walk east out of town to gawk at the substantial vacation and retirement homes on Eastern Shores. From here, you can also look south to **Sugar Loaf Cay**, home to more huge mansions rising from the scrub. For a look at the opposite side of the economic scale, head instead west along **Bay Street** out of town to **Dundas Town**, a flat area of shanties inhabited mostly by Baha-mians of African descent. Many Haitians also call Marsh Harbour home, living in hovels and shacks in The Mud and Pigeon Pea quarters near Dundas Town.

Eating and drinking

Marsh Harbour **eateries** are for the most part casual but still a bit pricey, catering primarily to tourists with menus heavy on seafood and tropical cocktails. Bahamian home-style cooking can be found at several reasonably priced restaurants drawing a predominantly local crowd. Most hotels and restaurants are situated within easy walking distance of one another along Bay Street running along the waterfront.

The **nightlife** in Marsh Harbour rotates around a handful of bars hosting the occasional live band and dancing, along with pool tables, TV and lots of relaxed yachtie camaraderie over the bar. *Sappodilly's* bar is a cosy spot for a sundowner, with live music on Friday nights, while *The Jib Room* at the Marsh Harbour Marina has live music and dancing on Saturday nights. The waterside *Conch Out Bar* at the *Conch Inn* has live music several nights a week and a full range of libations all afternoon and into the small hours.

The Conch Crawl Restaurant *Conch Inn*, Bay Street ☎367-4000. This laid-back, waterside eatery is justifiably popular for its jumbo Fresh toasts, breakfasts and tasty dinners of calypso

grouper, stuffed jalapeños, and fine gumbos and stews. Open daily.

Hummingbird Restaurant Memorial Plaza on Queen Elizabeth ☎367-2922. An inexpensive, dark and cool refuge from the heat, recommended for delicious Bahamian home cooking including a grouper burger marinated in jalapeño pepper sauce and olive oil. Inexpensive. Open daily for breakfast and lunch, with dinner only on weekends from 5pm.

Jamie's Bay Street ☎367-2880. A popular cash-only restaurant offering home-cooked favourites for under $10 and good ice cream. The fried chicken is highly recommended. Closed Sundays.

Java Coffee ☎367-5523. Located on the main road heading toward the Hope Town/Man-O-War Cay ferry dock, this café is a great place to start your day with fresh coffee and pastries, comfy sofas and a patio where you can watch everyone else heading to work. Mon–Fri 8am–5pm, Sat 9am–noon.

The Jib Room Marsh Harbour Marina ☎367-2700. Basic seafood dishes, burgers, "drunken chicken" and salads served at picnic tables both indoors and outside facing the marina. You can eat well for $10–20. Lunch Wed–Sat 11.30am–2.30pm, and BBQ dinners Wed, Thurs and Sat, with music and dancing on Sat.

Mangoes Bay Street ☎367-2366. White linen service on the waterfront in downtown Marsh Harbour. Entrees ($15–22) include the likes of pork tenderloin with mango sauce, grilled chicken with garlic and ginger, cracked conch and ribs. Save space for the home-made desserts such as coconut tart and pineapple sorbet. Dinner daily 7–10pm.

Sapodilly's Lookout and Bar Bay Street ☎367-3498. A local hotspot, with tables on a rainbow painted wooden deck, comfy wicker chairs and an open air bar. The menu features sandwiches and burgers served with classic side dishes like peas and rice, coleslaw and plantains, as well as salads and seafood dishes. Live music Friday nights.

Snappa's Harbourview Marina ☎367-3910. A popular waterside open air bar and grill serving casual meals and cool drinks. Open daily for lunch and dinner.

Wally's Bay Street ☎367-2074. One of Marsh Harbour's most elegant options, housed in a two-story pink colonial house facing the water; ask for a table on the pleasant covered patio furnished with white wicker furniture. Lunch items include burgers and conch salad, with fancier dinner choices including grilled lamb chops (entrees $12–25). Lunch Mon–Sat, dinner Fri and Sat only.

Diving and watersports

While the **diving** along the Abacos' two outer reefs is not as spectacular as at Cat Island or San Salvador for example, a number of wrecks, caverns and towering coral formations keep things interesting, and three sites near Walker's Cay in the far north are known for shark sightings. Dives out of Marsh Harbour concentrate on sites north and west of town near Green Turtle Cay and Great Guana Cay, usually taking no more than half an hour to reach good spots on the outer reefs. Run out of the *Conch Inn,* Dive Abaco (☎367-2787 or 1-800-247-5338, ⓦwww.diveabaco.com) offers a full slate of **snorkelling** and diving trips to two dozen sites; one and two-tank dives cost $65 and $85 respectively, with full PADI certification costing $450. Their snorkelling trips start at $50. There are also plenty of excellent **bonefishing** grounds accessible from town. Reputable guides in the area include Jay Sawyer (☎367-2089), Justin Sands (☎367-3526) and O'Donald MacIntosh (☎365-0126). Costs run about $350 a day for two, plus tip ($40).

Listings

Banking Teller hours are generally Mon–Thurs 9.30am–3pm and Fri 9.30am–4.30pm, and all banks in town have ATMs. The Commonwealth Bank (☎367-2370) is on Queen Elizabeth Drive, while the First Caribbean International Bank (☎367-2166), Royal Bank of Canada (☎367-2420) and Scotiabank (☎367-2142) are all on Don McKay Boulevard on the west side of town.

Emergency ☎919, ☎911

Groceries For picnic provisions and self-catering, head to *Da Best Bakery* in Marsh Harbour, locally renowned for their oatmeal raisin cookies. *Solomon's* in the big blue building in the centre of town is a well-stocked grocery store, and *Bahamas Family Markets* (open seven days a week, but closed during church hours on Sunday) near the traffic light offers fresh produce and baked goods.

Internet Available at *Bahamas Family Markets* as well as *Out Island Inter.net* (Mon–Fri 9am–5pm) on Queen Elizabeth Drive.

Laundry The Harbour View Marina, Conch Inn Marina and the Marsh Harbour Marina all have laundry facilities.

Medical The Family Medical Centre (☎367-2295 or 359-6569 after hours; Mon–Fri 9am–5pm) is on Don McKay Boulevard.

Pharmacy Love's Pharmacy (☎367-3292) on Don McKay Boulevard (Mon–Fri 8.30am–5pm).

Police The station is on Dundas Town Road (☎367-3500).

Telephone BaTelCo, situated on the west side of town just off Queen Elizabeth Drive, has phone cards and service. There are also phone booths in the centre of town.

South of Marsh Harbour

The highway heading south from Marsh Harbour is a straight shot that barrels through a stretch of clear cut pine forest and scrub until you reach the turn off to **Cherokee Sound** and **Little Harbour**, 13.5 miles south of Marsh Harbour. While occasional paved or dirt roads head off towards the Atlantic coast, where limestone cliffs enclose tiny beaches, this part of the Abacos is not known for its swimming because of the predomination of cliffs, rocky shores and muddy creeks.

Abaco Farm Road, five miles south of the hamlet of Spring City, is a rough track leading east to the Atlantic and **Pelican Cays Land and Sea Park**, though most people who visit the park do so as part of package tours, or on their own yachts, sailboats and rental motor boats. Lying eight miles north of Cherokee Sound, and just south of Tilloo Cay, the park encloses 2100 acres of shallow reefs and tiny cays. Numerous marine species swim about in the protected area, including turtles and eagle rays, and the reefs are known for their maze-like canyons, gullies and byways. Here and there deep in the reefs are caverns that divers explore.

Back on the main highway and five miles further south, a clearly marked turn-off onto a dirt road leads to **Cherokee Sound** and **Little Harbour**. The former is a small, rather forlorn Loyalist fishing village that stands at the point of a peninsula jutting out from Great Abaco like an anchor. The northern spike of the anchor leads to Little Harbour, set on a semi-circular bay of great beauty and charm overlooked by an old lighthouse and lots of bougainvillea and hibiscus. Encompassing the southeastern tip of Great Abaco, **Abaco National Park** was established to preserve the habitat of the endangered Bahamian parrot, which lives here amid casuarinas and towering Caribbean pines. Continuing south to the highway's end brings you to **Sandy Point**, a somnolent fishing village that's home to an airstrip, mailboat dock, marine research station as well as a clinic and several bonefish lodges.

Getting around

Taxi tours of south Great Abaco out of Marsh Harbour are tremendously expensive: a simple one-way journey to Cherokee Sound – only half-way down

Birding guides in South Abaco

The Abacos are blessed with an abundance of **birds**, and there's nowhere better on the island to go birding than southern Great Abaco. From its pine forests, which harbour such lovely species as the West Indian red-bellied woodpecker and the Bahama parrot, to the Sandy Point creeks, where you're likely to spot roseate spoonbills, grey kingbirds, and a host of shorebirds like terns and herons, this area is truly a birder's dream. To help facilitate your search, think about hiring a local **guide**. In Sandy Point try Patrick Roberts (☎366-4286), Paul Pinder (☎366-4061) or Lensworth Bain (☎366-4280). In Marsh Harbour contact Reggie Patterson (☎366-2749).

Great Abaco – can cost as much as $80 for two people. A better bet is to rent a **car** or a **boat** for the day from outlets in Marsh Harbour (see p.139). The Islander Express (☎366-4444 and cell 457-9958) offers occasional **bus service** between Marsh Harbour and Sandy Point, generally timed to meet incoming ferries and mailboats. It is too long a trip for rental **bicycles**, but enthusiastic bicyclists who bring their own racing bikes will find the journey south a good flat ground work out.

Little Harbour and around

Little Harbour is reached by taking the Great Abaco Highway 13.5 miles south of Marsh Harbour, turning west at the signpost onto the hard-pack road for Cherokee Sound and Little Harbour. Eight miles in, another well-marked turnoff points to Little Harbour, which follows a very rough track (passable in a car) for a further two miles. The end of this trail isn't so much a village as a collection of cottages. The bay itself is quite scenic, with its limestone cliffs backing a crescent bay and beach, its myriad of flowers and its artist-colony feel. The windswept cliffs and bay are protected by the Bahamas National Trust, meaning stiff penalties for anyone disturbing turtle eggs, or any animal or plant. A number of small uninhabited cays nearby are perfect for kayaking, snorkelling and birding.

Little Harbour's main claim to fame is the **Johnston Bronze Art Foundry** and its associated gallery, founded by the Canadian artist Randolph Johnston who came to Great Abaco in 1952 with his wife, the ceramist Margot Broxton. Johnston raised three sons on the island and established an electric generating plant to power his foundry and a furnace to cast huge pieces. His *Monument to Bahamian Women*, *Sir Milo Butler* and many others are well known, with the former prominent in Rawson Square in Nassau. Although Johnston died in 1992, his son Peter runs the foundry and gallery (foundry Mon–Sat 10am–noon & 2–4pm; gallery Mon–Sat 11am–4pm; ☎366-2250). The latter not only features works by Johnston, but many elegant pieces by other local jewellers, sculptors and painters. Peter Johnston also runs ⚓ *Pete's Pub* (☎366-3503; daily for lunch and dinner from 11am until whenever;), a funky **bar** near the beach adorned by T-shirts and pennants of all kind. The menu includes burgers, barbecue and fish cooked on an open grill ($8–11), and they also have a vacation cottage for rent ($1400 a week), but you'd be pretty isolated here without a car or boat. Most overnight visitors are on boats anchored in the harbour.

Cherokee Sound

Five miles south of Little Harbour, but reached by the same turn-off from the main highway, **Cherokee Sound** is a working fishing village that until recently was approachable only by boat and had no electricity, save for genera-tors running on gasoline. To reach it by car, continue past the turn-off to Little Harbour for a couple of miles. This takes you past the exclusive *Abaco Club* gated vacation community and into the village itself. Composed mainly of well-maintained clapboard and cement houses raised on pillars and painted in pastel colours, Cherokee Sound sports a BaTelCo office, a post office, several churches and a large shallow sound fringed by mangroves. There is not much doing in these parts for a visitor, but its still worth seeking out for a cool drink and lunch at the spectacularly situated *Sand Bar* (☎366-3503), which sits on stilts in the water at the end of a 200 yard-long pier. To reach the bar, look out for the sign one mile before you reach the village and follow the narrow road ending at a locked gate. Park here, and walk to the *Sand Bar*. At the time of writing, the bar was up for sale, so ask around in Marsh Harbour before you head down for updates.

Casuarina Point

Back on the Great Abaco Highway south of the turn-off to Little Harbour is another side road leading to the small village of **Casaurina Point.** Hunched along a quiet waterfront lane, a few bungalows front an absolutely spectacular curve of white sand beach and turquoise water that runs uninterrupted all the way back to Cherokee Sound. This is prime bonefish territory where you can wade in from the shore and wile away the day hunting the grey ghosts. There are no restaurants, but there are a couple of private vacation rentals in the area; see p.153 for online rental listings.

Abaco National Park and around

Ten miles south of the ramshackle roadside settlement of Crossing Rocks on the Great Abaco Highway is the turn-off for **Abaco National Park** and the **Hole-in-the-Wall Lighthouse**. If you wish to drive to the lighthouse, be aware that the seriously potholed road traverses fifteen miles of tightly packed pine scrub and palmetto bush before reaching another dirt track for the final five miles to the lighthouse. Note that taking a rental car on these rough tracks is often prohibited unless you get a 4wd.

Abaco National Park is 32 square miles of Caribbean pine and hardwood forest laced with nature trails boasting wild Atlantic coastal scenery. A walk down any of the unmarked trails will reveal all manner of birdlife: rare egrets, herons, spoonbills, hummingbirds and the **Bahamian parrot**, which is best seen around dawn. An endangered species, found only on Great Abaco and Great Inagua far to the south, the population of Bahama parrots in 1989 was estimated between 850 and 1150. The campaign to establish its habitat as a national park in 1994 has been a conservation success, and today it's estimated that the parrot population exceeds 1500. Also visible are plenty of bromeliads and orchids and mangrove swamps – even wild boars. Check at the tourist information centre in Marsh Harbour for trail maps, or with the staff at the lighthouse (see opposite).

△ Bahamian Parrot at Abaco National Park

Hole-in-the-Wall Lighthouse

Hardy souls who make it all the way to **Hole-in-the-Wall Lighthouse** will be repaid with a spectacular view of windswept Atlantic headlands and rocky outcrops. The area around the lighthouse is known as the Hole-in-the-Wall at Lands End, so named because of a 30ft diameter hole that appears in a natural shelf of limestone that extends into the wild Atlantic Ocean off the southern shore. Offshore, **whale and dolphin sightings** aren't uncommon, especially in winter, when humpbacks pass by on their pilgrimage to more southerly waters to calve. On calm days, Hole-in-the-Wall offers good beachcombing and secluded swimming, though the water has a reputation for sharks. A half-hour walk south of the lighthouse brings one to **Alexandria**, a mysterious abandoned settlement of limestone and cement that looks to date back to the early 1800s.

Sandy Point

Fifty miles south of Marsh Harbour and west of Abaco National Park, the road ends at **Sandy Point**, a quiet fishing settlement most often visited for it's bonefishing opportunities. Just offshore is Disney Island, formerly Gorda Cay, where cruise ship passengers are let out to play. Near the wharf, *Nancy's Seaside Inn* (☎366-4120) is a good spot for a cool drink; call ahead to arrange lunch or dinner as the kitchen opens only when business warrants. Local lodgings cater primarily to fishermen, often with all-inclusive packages covering simple but comfortable lodgings, hearty Bahamian meals and expert guides. If that's your bag, call *Rickmon's Bonefish Lodge and Motel* (☎366-4477; ❷), with ten seaside rooms, or *Pete and Gay's Guest House* (☎366-4119; ❷), with fourteen double rooms. Both offer weekly all-inclusive fishing packages as well as rooms only.

North of Marsh Harbour

The resort community of **Treasure Cay**, 17 miles from Marsh Harbour, is the first major settlement reached travelling north on the Bootle Highway. Otherwise, the main reason for heading north of March Harbour is to access Green Turtle Cay (see p.162) or the unspoiled **Northern Cays**, which are known for their sport fishing. The largest town in the area is **Cooper's Town**, from where it's possible to head over via water taxi to a high-end resort on **Spanish Cay**. North of Cooper's Town, the highway crosses a narrow causeway to Little Abaco. There isn't much to the island, and the settlements are small and poor, with most of the population making its living off fishing and lobstering. Little Abaco narrows to a needle thin point at the tiny settlement of **Crown Haven**, with spitting distance (and daily ferry service) of Grand Bahama.

Treasure Cay

Actually not a cay but a slender peninsula, **Treasure Cay** is a self-contained community formed around a large 150-slip marina and resort. In the 1950s, the first tourist hotel on the Abacos was built on Treasure Cay, ushering in a period of development, and the area now supports a variety of villas, condos, time-share unit – even a golf course. North Americans currently make up the bulk of the residents, maintaining more than 150 expensive vacation and retirement homes. Its **beach**, which stretches in a mild semi-circle for four miles along the Sea of Abaco, isn't the most spectacular looking, but it's perfectly fine for swimming and sunning; the water is shallow and rather tame most of the time. Between the beach and the outer island of **Whale Cay** are shallow banks that shimmer with turquoise and green colours, and are especially lovely during sunrises and sunsets.

Treasure Cay started life in 1783 as **Carleton Point**, a Loyalist settlement of about 600 who hoped to develop a major commercial and agricultural centre at the northern end of what was known then as Sand Banks Cay. Owing to civil strife, land disputes and a devastating hurricane, the settlers soon abandoned the town, and it wasn't until 1979 that the eighteenth-century site was located with the discovery of several artefacts including anchors and various pieces of glass – now preserved in the Albert Lowe Museum on New Plymouth to the east (see p.163). For those hardy souls wishing to make the trek to the bronze historical **plaque** placed at Carleton Point near the original settlement, it's located two miles down the beach from the *Treasure Cay Beach Hotel*.

Arrival and getting around

Treasure Cay Airport is located fifteen miles north of the resort community, and a taxi ride in costs $15. Yachters arrive at the **Treasure Cay Marina** (☎365-8250 or 1-800/327-1584), where there is a full range of dock services. Most visitors here get around using **golf carts**, which should be reserved well in advance through Cash's Resort Carts (☎365-8771) or Blue Marlin Resort Carts (☎355-8687); daily rates average $45.

To rent a **car** for sightseeing up and down the islands, reserve early with Triple J (☎367-2163), Cornish (☎365-8761) or Bodie's (☎359-6681); daily rates for cars average $80. Touring along the coast by boat is even more enjoyable, and JIC Boat Rentals (☎365-8582, ⓦwww.jicboatrentals.com) have 21–26ft boats from $140 a day, with discounts for weekly rentals and guided boat tours on request. Alternatively, Abaco Adventures (☎365-2356) offers **ferry service** ($25 round-trip) from Treasure Cay to Guana Cay on Sundays at noon, returning at 4.45pm. They also run trips from Treasure Cay to Hope Town and Man-O-War Cay on Wednesdays at 9.30am, returning at 4.30pm ($35 round trip), and do occasional sunset cruises to Guana Cay ($25).

Accommodation

The centre of activity hereabouts is the **Treasure Cay Hotel** (☎365-88801 or 1-800/327-1584, ⓦwww.treasurecay.com; ❻), with golf, tennis and dive packages available), usually thronged with fun-seekers and spring breakers. The resort sprawls over several flat, wooded acres running alongside the Sea of Abaco and a long stretch of white sand beach. The uninspired accommodations are spread across several hundred tightly set and slightly shabby rooms, suites, condos and small, self-catering villas. On the grounds are a handful of restaurants and bars and a shopping centre with a grocery store, pharmacy and branch of the Royal Bank of Canada (Mon, Tues & Thurs 9.30am–2pm). The resort also is home to the island's sole **golf** course (☎365-8045; $85), a long 72-par affair with several holes right on the water, along with a handful of **tennis courts** ($20 an hour for guests and non-guests). If looking for privacy, the resort is probably not a good choice as it's almost impossible to find an unpopulated nook.

Eating and drinking

Food choices are limited and nightlife sparse on Treasure Cay. North of the resort on the Bootle Highway is the best Bahamian **restaurant**, *Touch of Class* (☎365-8195; dinner only), serving grouper and delightful desserts. In the shopping plaza in Treasure Cay not far from the marina office, *Cafe La Florence* (☎367-2570; daily 7am–6pm) is essentially a bakery, but serves good quiche and cinnamon rolls; there is an ice cream parlour next door. At the hotel marina, *The Spinnaker* (☎365-8489; reservations required for dinner) serves wonderful johnnycakes for breakfast, specializes in conch salad for lunch and catch-of-the-day for dinner, with an outside deck to enjoy them on. Other resort options include the open air *Coco Bar and Grill* on the beach and the *Tipsy Seagull Bar*, which serves drinks all day, and pizzas on Thursday nights. The *Tipsy Seagull* is also the night-time hotspot, with live music and dancing on weekends.

Diving and watersports

All the major watersports are represented at Treasure Cay. Run out of the marina, Treasure Divers (☎365-8465, ⓦwww.treasure-divers.com) rents **snorkel** and **scuba** equipment and offers a number of dive packages and classes (PADI certification $500). Dives cost $60/80 for one/two tanks, and snorkellers are welcome on boats for $35. The most popular sites for do-it-yourself snorkelling are around No Name Cay and Whale Cay, an area just offshore from Treasure Cay that's home to the wreck of the *San Jacinto* and where you can find rays and moray eels. Both **bonefishing** and deep-sea charters can also be organized through the marina (☎365-8250); local guides average f$375/$500 a half/full-day for two people going big game fishing or $350 for a day on the flats. Alternatively, you can also call the independent bonefishing guides working out of March Harbour (see p.143). Near the hotel, concessionaires rent out tiny sailboats, kayaks and banana boat rides as well.

Cooper's Town and around

Ever since the Bootle Highway was paved, more and more travellers have been heading north of Treasure Cay to see what's up in north Great Abaco. Smooth ride or not, the answer is not too much. Essentially, the thirty-mile stretch between the airport and the lower tip of Little Abaco holds little more than a couple of motels, restaurants bars and nightclubs.

The scenery in north Great Abaco is much the same as the rest of the island – low ridgelands, rocky outcroppings and dense pine forests, while the few beaches here are bound by rocks and shallows, and are not particularly good for swimming. A number of beautiful islands lie off the coast, though, including **Powell Cay**, a favourite stopover spot for yachters on day-trips, and the exclusive Spanish Cay. The largest village in north Great Abaco is **COOPER'S TOWN**, fifteen miles north of Treasure Cay, with a population of nearly 2000. A sleepy, rather down-at-heel place, Cooper's Town has a few shops and bars and little else. The best overnight option is *M&M Guest House* (☎365-0142; ❷), located at the south end of town with exceedingly basic en-suite rooms. There's also a restaurant on site serving lobster, big burgers and hearty breakfasts, while Wright Seaside Grocery and Bakery (☎365-0057) on the waterfront sells both fresh-baked bread and crawfish. For a drink, try the *Conch Crawl* (☎365-0423), a lively bar decorated in fishnets with a porch suspended over the water. Open until midnight, the bar also servers cracked conch, grouper and fried chicken.

Spanish Cay

Spanish Cay's well-heeled visitors are lured by the luxurious rooms, suites and homes of *The Spanish Cay Resort* (☎365-0083, Ⓦwww.spanishcay .com; ❾). A privately owned 200-acre island three miles off the northern tip of Great Abaco, the cay is named for galleons that sank off the coast during the seventeenth century. Uninhabited for many years, the island is rocky and windswept but its five beaches and seven miles of shoreline are gorgeous. Like Walker's Cay far to the northwest, Spanish Cay was bought by former Dallas Cowboys owner Clint Murchison in the early 1960s, who after sealing the deal planted hundreds of palms that continue to thrive in the sandy-coral soil.

Most visitors **arrive** either by air charter or private plane at the 5000ft airstrip or come by yacht to the 81-slip marina at the resort, which also houses a PADI-certified dive shop. If staying overnight, the resort will arrange for a ferry for guests from Cooper's Town. **Accommodation** ranges from double rooms to one-or two-bedroom apartments or villa suites, both with private garden, double beds and refrigerator. The apartments have a full kitchen, living room, dining room and deck overlooking the marina. The resort also leases private homes, though if you have to ask for the rate you probably can't afford them. Two waterfront **restaurants** at the resort, *Point House* and *Wrecker's Raw Bar*, serve Bahamian, Continental and American food, with fresh fish predominating at dinner.

Little Abaco

Past Cooper's Town, the Bootle Highway traverses a short bridge that hooks Great Abaco to Little Abaco. Shaded by pines and casuarinas, the Bootle Highway through **Little Abaco** passes a number of quiet beaches, though there's very little in the way of notable sights on your way to the Northern Cays. **Cedar Harbour**, 22 miles from Treasure Cay, is the largest settlement on the island, where you'll find *Nettie's Snack Bar*, a pleasant place for conch and fried fish. In **Fox Town**, another seven miles down the road, local Gladys Saunders operates the *Tangelo Hotel* (☎365-2222; ❷), which has sixteen plainly furnished and basic rooms with a/c and TT. Call ahead and the owners will send a car to Treasure Cay Airport or Crown Haven Ferry Dock for you. The small restaurant serves basic fish dishes for $8. The end of the line is tiny **Crown Haven**, a quiet tumbledown village with a wooden wharf and a struggling lobster business; it's most notable for Pinder's Ferry Service, with daily trips to Grand Bahama (see p.139).

The Northern Cays

The remote and exclusive **Northern Cays** sit some fifty miles north of Little Abaco, and are worth considering only for their sport fishing or for getting well off the beaten path. A small coral outcrop that forms the northernmost limit of the Little Bahamas Bank, **WALKER'S CAY** is the largest of the bunch. Ringed entirely by a fantastic shallow reef and surrounded by deep water outside the reef (the water drops off 1000ft at some points), the cay itself covers only 100 acres, most of it scrub and rock inhabited only by lizards and terns, who play among the ficus, cactus and palmetto. Sport fishing, diving and yachting account for the island's allure: barracuda, bonefish, grouper, sailfish, as well as the great blue marlin are in abundance. The diving north of Walker's Cay is punctuated by such alluring spots as **Spiral Cavern**, a spectacular shark dive, **Barracuda Alley**, where the large fish lurk amid the gullies and reef canyons, and **Pirate's Cathedral**, a coral canyon famous for its mazes of coral teeming with reef fish. In addition to diving, visitors often enjoy yachting to nearby cays like **Tom Brown's Cay**, **Seal Cay** and **Sit Down Cay** for an entire day of isolated snorkelling and swimming. Unfortunately, at the time of writing visiting the cay has been put on hold as the sole resort, *Walker's Cay Hotel and Marina* (☎1-800/925-5377, ⓦwww.walkerscay.com; ❺), had closed pending sale to a new owner.

A few miles to the east of Walker's Cay sits **GRAND CAY**. For a quirky experience, visitors can head here for the day by private boat. On the cay's west side is the unforgettable **Well's Bay**, two miles of super-secluded white beach. Several locals guide bonefishermen in the area as well.

The Loyalist Cays

A half-moon chain of teardrop islands jutting off the eastern side of Great Abaco, the **Loyalist Cays**, originally settled by fleeing Englishmen and their slaves after the American Revolution, run southeast to northwest of Marsh Harbour. The settled islands, **Elbow Cay, Man o' War Cay** and **Great Guana Cay** are each accessible by a 20 minute ferry ride from Marsh Harbour. Further north, **Green Turtle Cay** is accessible by a 10 minute ferry from Cooper's Town. Each of these tiny islands is topped by a two hundred year old settlement, with quiet shady lanes lined with well-preserved wooden cottages and fenced gardens overflowing with colourful blooms; ocean views and long strands of white sand are abundant. Each cay still has its own unique atmosphere, and sampling them all makes for a series of enjoyable day-trips by ferry or rental boat. Green Turtle Cay is most popular because of picturesque **New Plymouth**, the tiny colonial-style town with New England-style clapboard houses. Elbow Cay, with its **Hope Town Lighthouse** and enchanting harbour, is popular as well. A dozen other cays are clustered alongside the settled Loyalist Cays, waiting to be explored by private boat. Among these, **Lubber's Quarters Cay** near Elbow Cay is notable as a quiet refuge with a holiday vibe, a few grand vacation homes and attractive rental cottages and a casual beach bar and grill.

Elbow Cay

Just six miles southeast of Marsh Harbour, **Elbow Cay** is home to 600 residents, many of whom have family histories here going back centuries. Most live in **Hope Town**, the only real settlement and the arrival point of most visitors, which is located at the northern end of the isle. The five-mile-long cay is crossed by two narrow lanes called Back Street and Bay Street (also called "Up Along" and "Down Along" by locals). No cars are allowed in Hope Town, and most people get around by golf cart, though these too are banned from Hope Town's narrow lanes.

Founded in 1785 by Loyalists from South Carolina, Elbow Cay had relatively humble beginnings, though boat building, wrecking and some pineapple agriculture did bring cash into the economy during the nineteenth century. During the 1920s, the town boomed with sponging and shipbuilding at its core – the harbour often home to as many as 200 schooners – and the cay thrived on the export of rare turtle shell, oranges and sisal. Hope Town builders created a famous style of wooden dinghy and sailboat building, carried on today by artisans who continue to build them by hand.

Arrival, information and getting around

Albury's Ferry Service (☎367-3147 or 365-6010, ⊛www.oii.net/alburysferry) operates regular **ferries** seven times a day from Marsh Harbour to Elbow Cay (same day roundtrip $20; one way $15). The ride takes twenty minutes and the ferry lays over long enough to take on passengers before returning to Great Abaco. Other arrival options include a **water taxi** ($7 one-way) from Man O' War Cay to Hope Town's Albury Ferry Dock every morning at 7.30am, returning at 4.30pm, and the **mailboat** *Legacy*, which departs from Nassau on Tuesdays (see p.138).

Yachts can call in at a number of good **marinas** on Elbow Cay, most located in Hope Town's harbour. Hope Town Marina (☎366-0003) on the west side of the harbour has dockage, water and ice and is also the site of the *Club Soleil* restaurant. At the harbour entrance, the Lighthouse Marina (☎366-0154) provides not only dockage but fuel as well, along with ice, rigged bait, repairs and caulking, and the Hope Town Hideaways Marina (☎366-0224) accommodates boats up to 70ft, specializing in visitors to its villas.

The **visitor's information bureau** is located in a turquoise municipal building at Hope Town's government dock, but don't expect anything beyond an unmanned booth with some pamphlets. Look for the nearby bulletin board where you'll find more information on local events, restaurant menus and the like. The BaTelCo office is at the south end of Hope Town just off the Queen's Highway near the *Harbour Lodge*. The post office is in the historic waterfront building at the main public dock (Mon–Fri 9am–1.30pm & 2.30–5pm).

Visitors staying in Hope Town get around by foot or bicycle. If staying south of town at one of the resorts, you may wish to rent a **golf cart** or **boat**. Island Cart Rentals (☎366-0448, ⓦwww.islandcartrentals.com) and T&N Cart Hire (☎366-0199) both rent golf carts for $45/$270 a day/week. Island Marine Boat Rentals (☎366-0282, ⓦwww.islandmarine.com), and Seahorse Boat Rentals (☎367-2513, ⓦwww.seahorserentals.com) rent outboard motorboats, with rates starting from $100 a day. Cruise Abaco (☎375-8313, ⓦwww.cruiseabaco.com) based on nearby Lubber's Quarters Cay offers **sailing cruises** through the Abacos and lessons aboard a 37ft vessel that sleeps up to four; day-trips are $350 and a one week captained charter runs $2650.

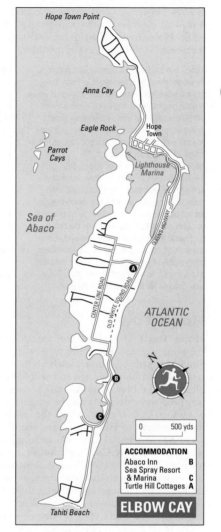

Accommodation

There are several appealing **lodgings** on Elbow Cay, but the *Hope Town Harbour Lodge* is the only hotel in the village. Most of the wooden clapboard **cottages** lining the narrow lanes of the settlement are vacation rentals, however, and for those seeking more privacy there are a few small beachfront cottage resorts on the south end of the island. Hope Town Hideaways (☎366-0224,

@www.hopetown.com) manages dozens of lovely cottage and beach house rentals all over the island starting at $1000 a week for a one-bedroom cottage, while Hope Town Villas (☎366-0030, @www.hopetownvillas.com) has units starting at $1600 for a one-bedroom villa.

Abaco Inn ☎366-0133, @www.abacoinn.com. On White Sound, two miles south of Hope Town, this attractive lodge sits on a bluff with great views. The inn has 14 rooms and 8 one-bedroom villas with kitchenettes, as well as a pool, an elegant dining room and a beach nearby. If you stay here, you will probably want to rent a golf cart, as it is a couple of miles from the village. ❺
Hope Town Harbour Lodge ☎366-0095 or 1-800/316-7844, @www.hopetownlodge.com. At the upper road with both harbour and town views, the only in-town hotel has twenty tightly set but cosy rooms that overlook the harbour and cottages that tumble down towards the beach – all gorgeously furnished and decorated with twin or queen beds, private bath and a pool. *Hope Town* offers plenty of watersports, excellent breakfasts and dinners, and lively and friendly staff. Ocean-view doubles ❺, one-bedroom cottages ❾.

Sea Spray Resort and Marina ☎366-0065, @www.seasprayresort.com. At the southern tip of White Sound, Sea Spray lies three miles from Hope Town. On the six-acre property sit brightly painted one-bedroom villas perched on a bluff overlooking the sea, each with kitchen, a/c, satellite television and broad wooden verandahs complete with hammocks, as well as a good dockside restaurant, a seafront pool, the Garbonzo Reef Bar and access to watersports. The resort also offers a free shuttle service into the village. ❻
Turtle Hill Cottages ☎366-0557 or 1-800/339-2124 @www.turtlehill.com. Close to the village but still private and away from the crowds, *Turtle Hill Cottages* has a clutch of 2- and 3-bedroom, light-wood panelled villas near the Atlantic beach; from $400 a night with discounts for weekly rentals. ❾

Hope Town

Hope Town, located on the eastern side of a nearly enclosed harbour of the same name, is hopelessly picturesque, its hundred or so clapboard houses huddled together on dunes, each home surrounded by a picket fence and clusters of colourful orange, red and yellow hibiscus, purple bougainvillea and pink oleander. The New England-style houses are mostly painted white with pastel trim, and these days many serve as rental cottages for the island's growing rank of visitors. Despite these crowds, the lack of motorized activity brings a refreshing naturalness to Hope Town, and the place exudes a real charm.

The town's tranquil harbour is usually jammed with sailboats anchored by the red-striped **Elbow Cay Lighthouse**, on the west shore directly opposite the town itself. Built in 1863, it is kerosene-powered and keepers still use a system of weights to wind it daily. At sunset, its mirrors magnify the mantle's beam and are brilliantly illuminated, and after dark the light is visible for twenty miles. If you can, hitch a ride on a local boat across the narrow harbour and climb the 100 steps for a spectacular 360-degree view of the outer cays.

The town itself lies north to south on a hook-shape of land that is around a thousand yards wide at its north end, narrowing to no more than one hundred yards at the south end. Narrow **Bay Street** runs the length of town along the waterfront, past several private docks, and most of Hope Town's eateries and shops towards its northern end. At the south end of town is the **Government Dock**, where the mailboats and ferry let off their passengers and goods. Just behind the dock stand the main public buildings, the post office, library, clinic and tiny information booth.

South of government dock is the delightful **Byrle Patterson Memorial Garden**, which exudes peace and quiet with its pines, gazebo and bronze dolphin sculptures and makes for a great spot to relax with a packed lunch purchased at one of the town's groceries or cafés. One hundred yards south

△ Elbow Cay Lighthouse

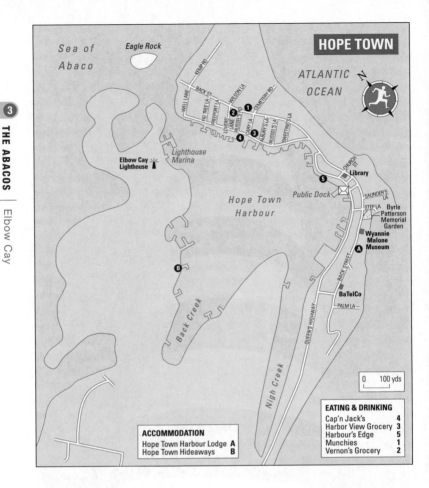

ACCOMMODATION

Hope Town Harbour Lodge A
Hope Town Hideaways   B

EATING & DRINKING

Cap'n Jack's   4
Harbor View Grocery 3
Harbour's Edge   5
Munchies   1
Vernon's Grocery   2

of the gardens, on quiet Back Street, is the **Cetacean Museum**, open all day with free admission, a bare-bones affair with a dusty collection of whale bones, charts and some old maps. Just steps away to the south is the more worthwhile **Wyannie Malone Museum** (Mon–Sat 10am–3pm; $3; ☎ 366-0033 to request a tour), which presents an eclectic collection of local photographs, artefacts and dusty exhibits, all in a house maintained in Loyalist style, complete with the original outhouse.

The northern section of Hope Town provides the most excitement in this distinctly quiet town. The couple of restaurants here are often jammed with day-trippers. East of Bay Street lies the narrower Back Street, which accesses the glum but fascinating **Cholera Cemetery**, just off Cemetery Road. The graves are those of the one-third of Hope Town's residents who perished in the great epidemic of 1850. Just north, at the end of town off Wilson Lane, is the **Old Cemetery**, two acres of grave sites of the original Loyalists, with a church at the top of the hill and a magnificent view of the Atlantic Ocean to the west. A small wooden staircase leads down to the beach here, though access to the

Atlantic beaches is readily available all up and down Hope Town's length via numerous paths and lanes that run to the east from Back Street. **Hope Town Beach**, which lines the eastern shore, is a rugged patch full of wild dunes, heavy surf, and high winds.

Around Hope Town

Outside of Hope Town, Elbow Cay is basically a big sand dune covered by windswept sea grape and palmetto scrub. To the north, the Queen's Highway soon becomes a dirt lane, running to Cook's Cove and ending at **Hope Town Point**. This northern end is especially good for **snorkelling**, with a reef loaded with fine stands of elkhorn, staghorn and brain coral close enough to swim to.

South of Hope Town, the Queen's Highway turns inland slightly and becomes Centre Line Road, which leads past a nude beach on the leeward side, and **Garbanzo Beach**, excellent for swimming and sunning, directly opposite White Sound about two miles south of Hope Town. Further south, a dirt road leads to **Aunt Pat's Bay**, a pretty little curve of beach that fronts a wild Atlantic shore. At the furthest south part of Elbow Cay is the fantastic **Tahiti Beach**, backed by palm groves and home to many marine turtles. It is idyllic, but before coming to it you'll encounter what appears to be a private estate barring the way. The road is public, so proceed ahead ignoring all signs saying otherwise.

Eating, drinking and nightlife

If looking for fancy **dining**, the resorts are undoubtedly your best bet; they all have decent restaurants and pool bars, but there are a couple of very popular casual eateries in the village as well. Vernon's Grocery sells freshly baked bread, cakes and pies – including a tasty Key Lime – in the town centre. Elbow Cay's **nightlife** is very low key; about the best one can do is watch satellite TV at *Cap'n Jack's* or *Munchies* or listen to one of the few bands playing at either on Wednesday or Friday night.

Abaco Inn ☏ 366-0133. This inn serves all three meals; reservations suggested at dinner. Open-air terrace dining with a menu including blackened fish, lobster and Bahamian-style seafood like smothered grouper.

Boat House Restaurant *Sea Spray Resort* ☏ 366-0065. Located 3.5 miles south of Hope Town on White Sound, this restaurant is open for breakfast, lunch and dinner. Breakfasts ($4) are substantial, lunches include a mixed green salad with fresh fish and dinners cover the gamut from steaks to seafood ($17). Reservations required for dinner.

Cap'n Jack's ☏ 366-0247. Wanders around Hope Town and at some point you'll find yourself at *Cap'n Jack's* overlooking the harbour. Specialities include the superb conch burger and grilled grouper with macaroni and cheese. *Jack's* has live music on Wednesday and Friday, and there's usually a crowd on the outdoor dance floor. Breakfast is $10, while lunches and dinner range as high as $40.

Harbour's Edge ☏ 366-0087. Recently renovated following a visit from Hurricanes Frances and Jeanne, the *Harbour's Edge* is a popular spot for a drink and a bite. Located close to the main government dock and post office, it offers crawfish salad, burgers and Saturday night pizza. The patio outside has covered seating with picnic tables, while there is air conditioning inside. Closed Tues.

Hope Town Harbour Lodge ☏ 366-0095. Very popular for breakfast on the verandah when huge omelettes and tasty French toast is featured. The lodge serves lunch by the ocean-front pool, happy hour is 4–5pm, and dinner is served until 9pm.

Munchies ☏ 366-0423. Essentially a take-away, *Munchies*, in the town centre, is known for fried fish and Bahamian fast food like their special hot chicken wings and conch burgers.

Exploring the Adirondack and Deborah K II wrecks

Thanks to countless miles of treacherous reefs, rocks and sandbars, the Bahamas is a great spot for exploring wrecks. No more than a thirty-minute boat ride from Elbow Cay are two wrecks of particular note. On the inner reef just off Man O' War Cay is the hulk of the wooden screw sloop **Adirondack**, launched in June 1862. A British gun-ship 207ft long and weighing 1240 tons, she ran aground en route from Port Royal to Nassau and quickly broke up in heavy surf before she could be salvaged. Now in 10–25ft of water, two of her larger cannons can be clearly seen, and plenty of reef fish like sergeant majors and damselfish make the wreck their home. On the outer reef between Fowl Cay and Man O'War Cay lies the wreck of the scuttled coastal freighter **Deborak K II**, once used to carry supplies around the Abacos; 165ft long, she sits upright and intact, covered by algae that attracts wrasse and damselfish.

Diving and watersports

Diving and snorkelling, as well as deep-sea, reef, and bonefishing, are all excellent around Elbow Cay. Froggies Out Island Adventures (☏366-0431, ⓦwww.froggiesabaco.com) conduct half-day and full-day scuba and snorkelling trips, including trips to the Pelican Cays Land and Sea Park (see p.144). A full day trip taking in snorkelling at Sandy Cay in the park and a visit to *Pete's Pub* in Little Harbour on South Abaco costs $55. A one-tank dive is $7, plus equipment rental if necessary. Fishing trips can be arranged through the *Seaspray Resort and Marina*, which also specializes in windsurfing.

Lubber's Quarters Cay

Just off the southwest side of Elbow Cay, **LUBBER'S QUARTER'S CAY** is dotted with holiday homes and rental cottages. There is no actual settlement, but the tiny dollop of sand and vegetation less than two mile long and a half-mile across is a wonderfully peaceful refuge for vacationers. The cay is a ten-minute boat ride from Hope Town or fifteen minutes from Marsh Harbour, but there is no ferry service and you'll need to rent a boat for the day in both places. *Sea Level Cottages* (☏366-3121, ⓦwww.sealevelcottages.com) has nine one- and two-bedroom cottages renting for $1650 and $2200 a week respectively; each comes with a 20ft motor boat for zipping around the cays and use of sea kayaks at no extra cost. Alternatively, Abaco Seaside Vacation Rental Cottages (ⓦwww.abacoseaside.com) has a scattering of one- to four-bedroom cottages and villas available around the island, starting at $950 a week. There are docking facilities for boaters at *Cracker P's Bar and Grill* (☏366-3139 or VHF 16; closed Tue and Wed, reservations required) where you can get fish and chips or fried chicken for lunch and dinner. The *Sunshine Bakery* (☏366-3141) makes pizzas and pies to order.

Man O' War Cay

While Elbow Cay bustles with tourism, quiet **Man O'War Cay,** slightly more than three miles north and a thirty-minute ferry ride from Marsh Harbour, is little touched by visitors. The island is prim, almost placid, and its residents

The Alburys

On Man O' War Cay, the name **Albury** is ubiquitous. The original Albury family of Benjamin and Eleanor Albury – part of the Loyalist migration – had thirteen children, most of whom also had large families; in no time, Man O' War Cay was overrun with Alburys. These days the family is still involved in shipbuilding, the oldest traditional craft on the island, with Joe Albury's Studio and Emporium (☎365-6082) on the Lower Road displaying wooden models. Joe Albury's long-ago ancestor Billie Bo is renowned for building the first sailboat in the Abacos, and Lewis Albury created the distinctive hourglass shape for ships.

maintain a strict code against the sale of alcohol on the island, although they don't mind if visitors bring their own, so long as they're reasonable about its use. The tiny main settlement is scattered along the east shore of North Harbour, almost smack in the middle of the cay itself. Most of the homes are modern breeze-block or stucco constructions, though there are a handful of gingerbread classics mixed in along with three churches, all faithfully attended, a one-room schoolhouse, and a small number of shops, groceries, bakeries and restaurants, none of which opens early, or at all on Sundays.

The cay is five miles long, at most six hundred yards wide near the settlement, and is home to no more than 300 residents, descendants of Loyalists who initially inhabited other cays, then migrated in the 1820s to farm its modestly productive soil and build handcrafted boats by traditional methods. In the village, you can see a veritable beehive of shipwright activity, with boats of all sizes and shapes bobbing in the narrow and protected harbour, set off from the Sea of Abaco by narrow Dickens Cay.

There are two main roads on the island, the **Lower Road**, or Sea Road, which runs north to south along the waterfront, and the island-long **Queen's Highway** that, in town, is also called the **Upper Road**, which holds the shops, churches, schoolhouse, post office and most of the homes. Follow the Queen's Highway from the centre of town south to the Church of God, take a left, and you'll find Man O' War's in-town **beach**. Man O' War's other beaches are along the Atlantic coast, accessible by footpath. North of the village, Upper Road becomes a dirt path winding through scrub, occasional pinewoods and mangrove, where secluded private homes are set behind gates and fences; it's a couple of hours there and back.

Practicalities

Albury's Ferry Service ($12 round-trip, children $6; ☎367-3147) at Crossing Beach has five scheduled crossings to Man O' War from Marsh Harbour each day except Sunday, the last one leaving at 3.15pm. A **water-taxi** service operates between Great Guana Cay and Man O' War at 7.30am and 3.30pm on Fridays, while another service operates between Elbow Cay and Man O' War at 7.30am and 4.30pm, also on Friday only. For those with their own boats, the full-service Man O' War Marina (☎365-6008, ✉albury@batelnet.bs) has sixty slips and a small dive shop (☎365-6013) renting some equipment, including snorkelling gear for $8/day; organized dives are not offered.

Along the Upper Road in town is a **BaTelCo** (☎366-6001), located next to the post office and library. There are two **banks** as well: a First Caribbean (Thurs 10am–2pm; ☎365-6098) at the Man O' War Marina on Lower Road, and a Royal Bank of Canada branch (Fri 10am–1pm; ☎365-6323). There are no hotels on Man O' War, but for condo and cottage rentals check with Island Treasure Gift Shop (☎365-6072 or 367-4469), through whom you can also rent golf carts. Alternatively, *Schooner's Landing* (☎365-6072, ⓦwww .schoonerslanding.com; ◗) offers two-bedroom condo rentals on the beach at the edge of the settlement. As for **eating**, the *Hibiscus Café* (☎365-6380; lunch Mon–Sat, dinner Thurs and Sat) up the slope from the dock serves coconut fried fish-burgers, conch cooked up several ways, lobster, salads and sandwiches. There's also an open-air bar with typical pub-grub at the Man O' War Cay Marina, and the village has a couple of shops where you can buy provisions and souvenirs. Jody Albury (☎367-5119 or 375-8068) is a local bonefishing guide, and David Albury (☎365 6502) has boats for rent for $120 a day/$675 a week should you want to explore neighbouring cays.

Great Guana Cay

The least built-up of all the Loyalist Cays, **Great Guana Cay** is nevertheless becoming increasingly developed as more and more vacation mansions are thrown up. The cay, which lies five miles northwest of Marsh Harbour, is the permanent home to no more than 150 residents, many of whom make their living by lobstering or subsistence farming. Some work in the burgeoning construction and tourist trades in the **Guana Harbour Settlement** on the developed southern part of the seven-mile-long island. There are no automobiles allowed on the island, and most visitors walk in the village, which takes about ten minutes to circumnavigate on foot, though some prefer to rent golf carts or bicycles.

Great Guana Cay's singular gift is the fringing reef that circles it about fifty yards from shore, making the island ideal for **snorkelling** and **diving**. Most divers are day-trippers from Marsh Harbour, who come on organized trips with Dive Abaco (see p.143), but enthusiasts should note that Dive Guana (☎365-5178, ⓦwww.diveguana.com) on the island offers full and half-day diving and snorkelling excursions as well as open water certification. One-tank/two-tank dives are $80/$95, the full PADI certification course is $550, and snorkelling trips start at $45. Only a five-minute boat ride north and east on the first barrier reef from the cay lies a superb cave dive known as **The Cathedral**, well suited to beginners as it's located in shallow water and has a roomy entrance and large chambers cut by sunlight. Thereabouts the reefhead is teeming with damselfish, red-lipped blennies, bluehead wrasse and striped parrotfish. The cavern itself is covered with fragile spiky coral forms, as well as white and cream sponges.

Back on the mainland, the Guana Harbour Settlement residents go about their business rather quietly, and some seem to resent intruders, though they make much of their income from cottage and cart rental or at the three nearby resorts. The settlement has a liquor store, grocery store, a variety store and several gift shops. Behind the two dozen houses in the village, and up a slight sandy rise, lies a graveyard dating from Loyalist times, an Anglican church, and a one-room schoolhouse that hosts no more than twenty students at a time.

South of the settlement, a 215-acre real estate development is gaining steam, and looks set to become home to more and more rich North Americans. Even now, over fifty vacation homes are scattered throughout the island, most hidden behind high gates. Because of this isolation, which at times can be almost intimidating, many visitors make their way around the island by

Bahamas beach culture

Bahamian beaches are the stars of many wistful mid-winter daydreams. Sun-soaked blankets of soft white sand washed by translucent turquoise water, they truly are some of the most spectacular strands in the Caribbean. Here and there, the sand is tinged with a delicate pink hue or dotted with inviting beach bars, while others are splendidly empty and wild. Vacationers tend to flock to the surf to soak in the sun, swim, snorkel and snooze. Locals, on the other hand, hold their biggest celebrations on the waterfront, with a continuous round of regattas, island homecomings and community fish fries, to which outside visitors are warmly welcomed.

▲ Fernandez Bay, Cat Island

Picking your spot

You could spend a year in the Bahamas sinking your toes into a different **beach** every day and still not run out of fresh options. Every island in the chain has been daubed with at least one inviting swath of sand, but the most generously endowed are those in the middle of the archipelago: **Eleuthera** and nearby **Harbour Island**; the **Exumas**; and **Long Island**. Liberally sprinkled with secluded beaches, these islands are made for exploring on your own, with a beach blanket and picnic lunch in tow. An added bonus on each of these slender islands is that you can sit in the sand and watch the sun come up over the Atlantic Ocean, then amble the couple of miles across the island to the western shore and watch a spectacular Bahamian sunset from a cosy beachfront bar. The most populous and visited, Eleuthera and Harbour Island boast a couple of delicately pink-tinged sand beaches, created by the mixing

The best beaches

Ideal beach atmosphere is a matter of personal taste – some crave a long empty vista, while for others the perfect beach day involves music, drinks and people-watching. What follows is a subjective list of the **best beaches** in the Bahamas, plucked from the literally hundreds on offer.

- **Coco Plum Beach, Great Exuma** Breathtakingly beautiful – a shallow, intensely turquoise cove rimmed with brilliant white sand, with a stellar beach bar and grill just steps from the surf.
- **Pink Sands Beach, Harbour Island** So very chic and equally gorgeous, the sand here is pink or blush-coloured depending on the light. A gentle surf and top-notch amenities nearby add to the attraction.
- **Club Med Beach, Eleuthera** Long and narrow Eleuthera has more than its share of fine beaches, and Club Med Beach is one the loveliest – rosy-hued, long and blissfully empty.
- **Greenwood Beach, Cat Island** Eight miles of undeveloped, blush-coloured beach boasting both a crashing surf and a relaxed dive-friendly resort.
- **Lucayan Beach, Grand Bahama** One of the best choices in the Bahamas for beach-lounger bar service and people-watching, plus there's a full range of watersports.
- **Guana Cay Beach, Abacos** Hit *Nipper's*, the cay's storied beachfront bar for its Sunday pig roast, then walk off the piña coladas on seven miles of white powder dotted with good snorkelling spots.
- **Gold Rock Beach, Grand Bahama** Gold Rock shows off its beauty best at low tide, when the receding waves reveal intricate patterns carved in the sand.
- **Cape Santa Maria Beach, Long Island** A pristine, secluded expanse of fine white sand offering good swimming and snorkelling.
- **Cabbage Beach, Paradise Island** The blanket of soft, white sand that anchors otherwise overbuilt Paradise Island's claim as a sun and surf destination.

▼ Harbour Island's Pink Sands Beach

of crushed tiny red skeletons of sea creatures with white coral powder. Little-visited **Cat Island** has a slightly more modest bounty of beach, but there are several gorgeous powder-lined coves and pieces of coastline to explore, most of which are conveniently set up with excellent small inns.

Perhaps surprisingly, the most touristed island – **New Providence** – has a rather meagre selection of beaches. Nevertheless, for a quick southern getaway, the white-sand charms of Cable Beach, Cabbage Beach and Orange Hill Beach are enticing enough for those who want to mix swimming with shopping, gambling and eating out. The best place to combine resort hotel comforts with a wide array of watersports like snorkelling safaris is **Grand Bahama**. Lightly populated **Andros** has some small hidden gems beach-wise, but the big draw here is spectacular diving and world-class bonefishing. Likewise, the narrow and neglected patches of beach in the **Biminis** and the more enticing strands in the **Abacos** play runners-up to fishing and boating. Serious beach junkies should probably give **Inagua** a pass. The island has its own unique and compelling charms, but towel space is limited along its mainly rocky shores. The same could be said of **San Salvador**, outside of the Club Med compound there.

Community fish fries, homecomings and regattas

Community celebrations are a key component to Bahamian life, and the local beach is often the party venue. Many settlements throughout the island chain have daily or weekly **community fish fries** on the waterfront, where visitors and locals get together for fresh conch salad and barbequed fish cooked at open air kiosks, with music and cool drinks to ease conversation. These informal events, held mainly in small settlements, have developed as an opportunity for locals to generate some income from the tourist trade. The atmosphere is friendly and the food is genuine Bahamian fare.

The otherwise tranquil village life and undeveloped coastlines of the Out Islands make them great places to visit, but not always to live as employment opportunities are limited. Many Out Islanders must head to Nassau or beyond to find work. Acting as giant reunions, annual **homecoming celebrations** are held on all of the Out Islands, giving sons and daughters a time to come back for a visit. The public festivities combine waterfront fairs and games for kids, heaps of home-style food, traditional music, and plenty of time spent visiting friends and family. As an example, the Long Island Homecoming, held in Glinton's over a weekend in early July, gets rolling with a church service and an early morning 5km "health walk," followed by a "muttonfest" on the village green, featuring live music, cultural performances, dominos and bingo tournaments, and a model boat race.

As wooden boatbuilding has such a storied tradition in the Bahamas, almost all of the islands have an annual **regatta**, if not a series of them, as well. These draw weekend sailors from throughout the archipelago and elsewhere for a weekend of races and carousing. The biggest of them all is the Out Island Regatta (also known as the Family Island Regatta), held over four days in late April in George Town, Great Exuma. Bahamian-designed and built sailboats crewed by local teams from all of the islands in the chain race for glory in front of throngs of spectators.

▼ Out Island Regatta, George Town

▲ Bar life by the beach

Great beach bars

Even if you're not around during one of the colourful regattas or homecomings, there is no shortage of fun and flip-flop-friendly watering holes to help you acclimatize to the beach lifestyle.

- **Tippy's, Eleuthera** A justly popular bar and bistro perched above a spectacular five-mile strand of Atlantic beach. See p.224
- **Cocoplum Beach Club, Great Exuma** A gorgeous white sand cove is made all the more enjoyable by the truly superb food – think blackened grouper with pineapple salsa. See p.265
- **Paradise Cove, Grand Bahama** A snack bar with a fine selection of après-lunch activities: great snorkelling from shore, kayaking, snoozing and swimming. See p.110
- **Staniel Cay Yacht Club, Staniel Cay** The beach here may be lacking, but this fine waterfront hangout is imbued with an easy-going nautical vibe. See p.272
- **Traveller's Rest, New Providence** A few steps west of Orange Hill Beach, Nassau's best shot at a casual, Out Island beach bar hits the mark. See p.97
- **Blue Bar, Pink Sands Hotel, Harbour Island** Very blue – from the blue walls and floor to the blue ocean vista – and equally trendy, but worth the plod up the pink sand beach for an up-to-the minute soundtrack and tasty meals. See p.237
- **Pete's Pub, Great Abaco** Sooner or later, everyone washes up at Pete's driftwood cabana bar for an immobilizing cocktail, barbeque lunch, and stress-free conversation. See p.145
- **The Chat 'n Chill, Stocking Island, Great Exuma** The epitome of Bahamian beach-bar cool, with hammocks strung in the trees surrounding a beach volleyball court. See p.264

▼ The Goombay Smash

The perfect beach cocktail

The **Goombay Smash** is a Bahamian institution, invented by Miss Emily at the *Blue Bee Bar* on Green Turtle Cay, Abacos, to quench the thirst of passing boaters. You can still get it at the source, but in the meantime, here is a fair approximation of her secret recipe:

1 oz. dark rum	¾ oz. coconut rum
3 oz. pineapple juice	¼ oz. lime juice
½ oz. Cointreau	

Shake all ingredients with ice and strain into a tall glass with crushed ice. Garnish with a slice of lime or pineapple and a little paper umbrella. Bon voyage!

rented boat, exploring the ethereally beautiful **Atlantic beach**, a five-mile stretch of white sand, reachable by several dirt tracks, that makes up almost the entire windward coast of Guana. The leeward coast is rugged, rocky, and beset with coves and shallow bays perfect for bonefishing, but accessible by boat only. In July, Great Guana is host to the **Regatta Week**, during which time the place is besieged with yachts.

Arrival, information and getting around

Albury's Ferry Service (☎367-3147 or 365-6010, ⓦwww.oii.net/alburysferry) operates regular **ferries** several times a day between Marsh Harbour and Guana Cay ($20 round-trip) departing from the Union Jack Dock in the centre of Marsh Harbour. Abaco Adventures (☎365-2356; $25 round trip) offers ferry service from Treasure Cay to Guana Cay on Sundays at noon, returning at 4.45pm. Because *Guana Seaside Village* is located up the coast from Guana Cay's only settlement, you should request to be let off there if that's your destination. There is a public payphone on the waterfront at Kidd's Cove, but there no bank on the island. Donna's Golf Cart Rentals (☎365-5196) rents carts for $40 a day. *Dive Guana* (☎365-5178, ⓦwww.diveguana.com) rents kayaks and bicycles for $12 an hour and 21ft power boats from $145 a day.

Accommodation

While Guana Cay is most popular as a daytrip destination from Marsh Harbour and Elbow Cay, there are several beachfront choices if you want to hunker down for a while.

Dolphin Beach Resort ☎365-5137 or 1-800/222-2646, ⓦwww.dolphinbeachresort .com. An upscale B&B-style inn with pool fashioned from Abaco pine. The two-storey main building has four rooms painted in Junkanoo colours, while its three cottages are individually furnished, including a kitchen, and have room for at least six. The staff arrange for bonefishing, kayaking, snorkelling, bikes and island-hopping trips. The *Blue Water Grill* and *Red Sky Lounge* offer food and drink on-site and the popular *Nipper's* restaurant is a five-minute walk away. ❼

Guana Beach Resort ☎365-5133, ⓦwww .guanabeachresort.com. With eight hotel rooms and seven suites, this elegant resort is set in a coconut palm grove just west of the settlement. The guest rooms are a stylish mix of tropical wood and colourful textiles, each with a kitchenette (microwave, toaster and fridge). There are a full range of watersports on tap and dockage for boats up to 150ft, as well as bayside anchorage.

Guana Seaside Village ☎365-5106 or 1-877/681-3091. Two miles north of the settlement on an isolated beachfront, this new resort features eight rooms and seven two-bed/two-bath cottages steps from the beach. There is a small restaurant, pool, bar, grill and a dock for boaters who drop in. The resort offers boat rentals, bonefishing, complimentary use of kayaks, snorkelling gear and paddle boats, and lots of peace and quiet. Closed mid-Sept to Oct. ❹

Ocean Frontier Hideaway ☎1-888/541-1616, ⓦwww.oceanfrontier.com. A handful of log cabins closely grouped around a small pool, each equipped with a microwave, coffee maker and a mini fridge. Discounts available for stays of a week or more. ❼.

Sea Shore Villas, Harbour View Haven and Sunrise Cottage ☎365 5028, ⓦwww .guanacayvillas.com. A collection of one- and two-bedroom villas, each with a kitchen, screened in verandah, satellite TV, and a/c. Guests at *Sea Shore Villas* share use of a small swimming pool. ❺

Eating

Most Guana Cay visitors end up sitting down for a bite at *Nipper's* (☎365-5143; daily for lunch and dinner), a colourful beach bar and grill on a broad wooden deck overlooking the ocean. Along with tropical cocktails and cold beer, you can dine on an expected array of bar food as well as a regular Sunday Pig Roast. At the *Dolphin Beach Resort*, the *Blue Water Grill* is open for lunch and dinner by reservation (☎365-5230; closed Tuesdays). The wooden deck is an inviting spot for a leisurely lunch, while the mood in the soft-lit dining rooms goes romantic in the evenings, with floor to ceiling windows framing the sea; Thursday night is pizza night, with mainly Bahamian dishes on Fridays. **Groceries** are available at Guana Harbour Grocery (Mon–Thurs 8am–5.30pm, Sat 8am–6.30pm; ☎365-5067), located on the waterfront near the public dock. The grocery also has some non-prescription drugs and sundries.

Green Turtle Cay

Eight miles due north of Treasure Cay and eighteen miles northwest of Marsh Harbour, **GREEN TURTLE CAY**, with its pretty bays, inlets and amazingly well-preserved New England-style village, **New Plymouth**, is the most popular of all the Loyalist Cays. Not only does the cay have a varied leeward shore – including three large enclosed sounds, an area of bluffs and cliffs on the White Sound peninsula, and mangroves in the north – but its Atlantic coast is replete with stunning beaches and rimmed by a reef tailor-made for snorkelling and diving. Because New Plymouth, on the southwest tip of the island, is only a ten-minute ferry ride from the Treasure Cay Airport Dock (see p.148), the town often teems with day-trippers crowding its narrow streets and winding wind-blown lanes.

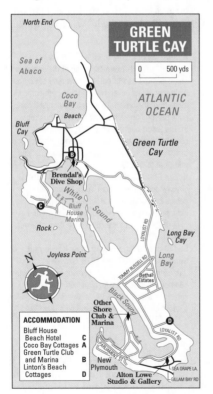

Arrival and getting around

The Green Turtle Ferry ($7 one-way; ☎365-4166) operates out of the Treasure Cay airport dock on the Abaco mainland. The **ferry** makes eight scheduled trips a day from Abaco, with the first leaving at 8am and a final trip at 4.30pm; the last ride from Green Turtle Cay back to the mainland departs at 5pm. Rates to New Plymouth are $7 one-way, $11 round trip, and ride takes about fifteen minutes, though intermittent stops around the island often can double that time. Charters can be arranged with advance notice, with a minimum charge of $35 for the run to New Plymouth, with higher rates for White and Black Sounds. The **mailboat** *Legacy*, which departs from Nassau on Tuesdays (see p.138), also calls in at Green Turtle Cay. **Marinas** are located at the Green Turtle Club (☎365-4271, ⓦwww.greenturtleclub.com) on White Sound, with 35 full-service slips, fuel, showers and laundry, and the Bluff House (☎365-4247, ⓦwww.bluffhouse.com) on other side of White Sound with 45 slips and similar amenities. Dockage rates at both are $1.75 a foot.

The most popular forms of transit are **golf carts**, **motor scooters** and **bicycles**. D&P Rentals (☎365-4655) at the Green Turtle Club Marina rents golf carts and scooters for $45 and $50 a day. Alternatively, try Bay Street Golf Cart Rentals in New Plymouth (☎365-4414) or Kool Kart Rentals (☎364-4176, ⓦwww.koolkartrentals.com) who charge similar rates. Carts should be reserved well in advance as they are a hot commodity on the island. Brendal's Dive Center (☎365-4411, ⓦwww.brendal.com) at the Green Turtle Club Marina rents bicycles for $12 and ocean kayaks for $10 an hour. To explore the surrounding cays by **boat**, check with Reef Rentals (☎365-4145) in New Plymouth or Donny's Boat Rentals (☎365-4119) in Black Sound, both with options for $65–100 a day.

Accommodation

The major **resorts** on Green Turtle are located either around White Sound, or in a cluster from New Plymouth to Gilliam Bay. For those wishing to avoid resorts and hotels, Green Turtle has an impressive variety of **cottages**, **villas**, and **apartments** for rent, usually by the week. Local agents Ocean Blue Properties (☎365-4636, ⓦwww.oceanblueproperties.com), Island Property Management (☎365-4047, ⓦwww.abacoislandrentals.com) and Robert's Cottages (☎365-4105) manage dozens of options. Prices begin about $950 a week for a one-bedroom unit.

Bluff House Beach Hotel and Marina ☎365-4247 or 1-800/745-4911, ⓦwww.bluffhouse.com. Sitting on a hill eighty feet above White Sound, this upscale resort has great views of the village and overall island. It is composed of hotel rooms, town-house suites and three-bedroom villas, including a "treehouse" with kitchenette and stove. There are two miles of beaches here, as well as a tennis court, boat rental, gift shop, bar lounge and a marina. ❼ **Coco Bay Cottages** ☎365-5464 or 1-800/752-0166, ⓦwww.cocobaycottages.com. Five one, two and three-bedroom cottages located on a secluded five-acre estate running down to the beach. The cottages are tastefully decorated and have full kitchens, decks, ceiling fans and phone. From $1700 a week.

Green Turtle Club and Marina ☎365-4271 or 1-800/688-4752, ⓦwww.greenturtleclub.com. At the north end of White Sound, the *Green Turtle Club* has 32 poolside rooms and eight villas. The deluxe suites are decorated with period mahogany furniture and hardwood floors have rugs. The standard rooms are less elegant, but still offer all the modern conveniences and comforts. The full-service marina has 35 slips accommodating yachts up to 150 ft. ❽ **Linton's Beach and Harbour Cottages** ☎365-4003 or 615/269-5682. On the Atlantic side at Long Bay Beach, just northeast of New Plymouth, *Linton's* has five cottages with full kitchens dotted across 22 acres, each with two bedrooms, patio, ceiling fans and bicycles for guests. ❹

New Plymouth

Compactly laid out on a peninsula formed by Black Sound and Settlement Creek, **NEW PLYMOUTH** is a joy, if rather a quiet one. Visitors come year-round to gawk at its gingerbread-trimmed houses painted in lively pastel colours, as well as its often noisy gospel churches or the picturesque schoolhouse perched on a hill overlooking the settlement. For a good view of it all, head behind the village where a slight rise reveals clear vistas of the waterfront and harbour.

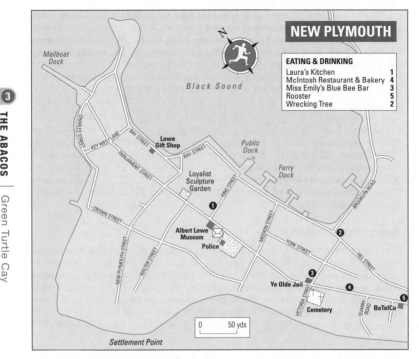

NEW PLYMOUTH

EATING & DRINKING

Laura's Kitchen	1
McIntosh Restaurant & Bakery	4
Miss Emily's Blue Bee Bar	3
Rooster	5
Wrecking Tree	2

Like other cay settlements in the Abacos, New Plymouth began with Loyalists fleeing America in 1783. Among them were 500 Irish New Yorkers, Protestants whose property was taken by American rebels, who soon established the town as one of the busiest in the islands. At one point, New Plymouth was the second largest city in the Bahamas, and a centre for banking, smuggling and even rum-running during Prohibition. Things are quieter now, and though you may notice a stiff reserve in some of the residents who aren't particularly fond of outsiders, tourism is the prime source of income, with lobstering important as well.

To many, the highlight of New Plymouth's year is the annual **Junkanoo** festivities, which begin on Boxing Day, and are held again on New Year's Day. On each of those two nights, the streets are thronged with dancers and musicians, all decked out in colourful Junkanoo costumes. The most popular sight in town the rest of the year is the **Albert Lowe Museum** on Parliament Street (Mon–Sat 9–noon & 1–4pm; $6; ☎365-4094), housed in a 200-year-old colonial house refurbished in 1976. The collection consists of old photos, model ships, paintings and memorabilia from the Abacos' past, and works by James Martin, a local sculptor. The museum is the work of Alton Lowe, whose father Albert was a much noted mariner, inventor, musician, artist and historian. **Schooner's Gallery** in the basement of the museum displays paintings by Alton himself. More of Lowe's paintings can be seen in the **Alton Lowe Studio** about half a mile outside New Plymouth in a handsome pastel house on a hill; any local can give you directions.

On Parliament Street, the **Loyalist Memorial Sculpture Garden** is free to the public. Laid out in a Union Jack pattern as conceived by Alton Lowe, the garden memorializes Loyalists and slaves with 25 bronze busts, with plaques to detail their accomplishments. One plaque commemorates Jeanne I. Thompson, a Bahamian playwright and the nation's second woman lawyer, whose roots go back to Loyalist times. Another worthwhile place to stroll is the **New Plymouth Cemetery** located at the southeast end about 250yd down Parliament Street, whose graves date back to the late eighteenth century. Across from the cemetery is **Ye Olde Jail**, unused for several generations and housed in a building damaged by the 1936 hurricane.

East of New Plymouth, a ten-minute walk from town down Gilliam Bay Road, lies beautiful **Gilliam Bay Beach**, a gently curving slice of white sand that is perfect for swimming. The Atlantic coast, reachable by Loyalist Road, also has good beaches, particularly the secluded beach at **Long Bay** that stretches for nearly a mile.

Eating, drinking and nightlife

Beside the resort **restaurants,** dining options in New Plymouth are represented by several small cafés and a couple of bars. When it comes to **drinking**, Green Turtle Cay is on the teetotal side, as are most of the Loyalist Cays, but there are a few places worth visiting. **Theatre** enthusiasts should check out the offerings at the Garden Theater on Black Sound, out by the Alton Lowe Studio; you can find flyers and playbills in town.

Beachside Bar *Bluff House Beach Hotel*, White Sound ☎365-4247. A quiet bar overlooking the sound that often plays host to live bands Thurs–Sat nights. The *Beachside* is also open for lunches of burgers, seafood platters and the like.

The Green Turtle Club ☎365-4271. *The Green Turtle Club* accepts reservations – which must be made by 5pm – for dinner at its exclusive restaurant. Evening specialties include veal and huge slabs of prime rib, and you can have breakfast or lunch on the patio as well.

Laura's Kitchen King Street ☎365-4287. This simple two-room Bahamian-style eatery serves a mean conch burger and will fetch you from your hotel if you call ahead. $10 will buy you lunch, with dinner plates ranging from $13–25. Mon–Sat 11am–3pm and 6–9pm. Closed Sept.

McIntosh Restaurant and Bakery Across from the cemetery ☎365-4625. Best for breakfast and lunch, the *McIntosh* has especially wonderful baked bread, homemade ice cream, and decent Bahamian dinners until 9pm every day but Sunday.

Miss Emily's Blue Bee Bar ☎365-4181. For sheer ambience and history, nothing on Green Turtle Cay surpasses *Miss Emily's*, truly a local institution. Founded by Miss Emily, the originator of the Goombay Smash, this bar is a wooden structure tattooed with business cards, with underwear on the ceiling and a rowdy mood. Open 9am until late, and things can get quite raucous.

Rooster's Rest Pub and Restaurant Gilliam's Bay Road ☎365-4066. A lively roadhouse on the edge of town, serving up fresh fish with traditional Bahamian sides for $10–20. On weekends, you'll often be able to hear authentic rake 'n' scrape by local musicians the Gulley Roosters. Open Mon–Sat 11.30am–9.30pm.

Wrecking Tree Bay Street ☎365-4263. A favourite with passing boaters, the *Wrecking Tree* is the best place for breakfast and lunch and serves dinner until 9.30pm. Its specialty is fried chicken. Closed Sunday.

Diving and watersports

The centre of **diving activity** on the island is Brendal's Dive Shop (☎365-4411, Ⓦwww.brendal.com) on White Sound. Operated in conjunction with the *Green Turtle Club and Marina*, Brendal's offers everything from basic scuba instruction to wreck, cavern and catacomb dives. All-day snorkelling tours and picnic can also be arranged, as can the rare opportunity to snorkel with wild dolphins (both $75) They also do glass-bottom-boat trips and sailboat cruises and rentals. The main resorts can arrange **sport-fishing** packages, but you should be able to negotiate a better rate by contacting guides directly. Ronnie Sawyer (☎365-4070; April–July only) is the premier bonefishing guide on Green Turtle. Ricky Sawyer (☎365-4261) leads drift fishing, reef and bonefishing trips, while Joe Sawyer (☎365-4173) has a well-equipped boat for either reef or bottom fishing. For bigger excursions, Lincoln Jones (☎365-4223) operates full day-trips for fishing, snorkelling and sightseeing to nearby cays, including a beach picnic day where he cooks up the catch and serves it with conch salad and drinks. The highlight of the fishing season is the annual **billfish tournament** in May, hosted by the *Green Turtle Club*. Regatta Week is also a big deal on Green Turtle in July, when dozens of races and festivities are in swing.

Andros

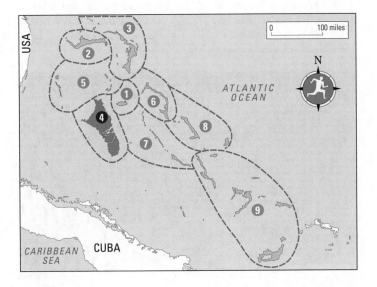

CHAPTER 4 | # Highlights

✳ **Diving and snorkelling** along the Andros Barrier Reef. Snorkel over huge stands of elkhorn, staghorn and brain coral hosting an astonishing variety of marine life in 12–20ft of clear water, or dive deeper along the edge of the abyss. See p.174

✳ **Cycling on Mangrove Cay** Sleepy Mangrove Cay is perfect for unwinding. A leisurely pedal around the island takes you through coconut groves, a couple of small settlements and along a lovely seashore. See p.174

✳ **Tiamo Resort** A seamless blend of luxury and ecologically sound design on South Andros. This high-end resort treads lightly on the land without sacrificing any of the perks. See p.175

✳ **Bonefishing the flats** Enjoy some of the finest bonefishing in the world, followed by a barbeque dinner at one of the island's rustic lodges. See p.177

△ Andros Island

4

Andros

Often called the "Big Yard" of the Bahamas, **ANDROS**, located midway down the archipelago, is the largest island of the entire chain – one hundred-plus miles north to south and forty miles east to west. A dense, largely impenetrable tract of pine forests, mud flats and mangroves, it is bisected by all manner of tidal creeks, large brackish bights and rivers running east to west, cutting off whole chunks of land. At high tide, the water covers much of that land with a shallow film of saltwater, and when the tide wanes, the mud reappears and glistens under a sun that always seems to shine.

It is not surprising, then, that what lies offshore is of more interest than what is on the island. Visitors come for the **diving**, **snorkelling** and **bonefishing**, each of which ranks among the best of its kind in the world. In addition, the magnificent **Andros barrier reef**, running the length of the island's east coast and then some, is reportedly the third longest in the world after Australia's Great Barrier Reef and the barrier reef off the eastern coast of Central America. Home to many species of marine life, including southern stingrays and grouper, it is composed of a massive inner barrier of elkhorn coral, which protects Andros from the brunt of bad weather, tides and hurricane surges.

Andros proper is divided into three chunks of flat, pine-covered land divided by wide bights of turquoise water. **North Andros** is the largest piece, containing the island's most substantial towns, Nicholl's Town and Fresh Creek, and much of its population – only some 8000 all told. It is separated by an islet-strewn passage from **Mangrove Cay**, which offers lovely beaches, lagoons, coconut trees and caves. Across the southern bight from Mangrove Cay, **South Andros** is very lightly populated, and has little commercial development apart from a couple of lovely small resorts and bonefish lodges, and, consequently, is a great place to escape the cares of civilization. In fact, some parts of central and South Andros have seen electricity only in the last twenty years, and the road system is limited, lending a charmingly isolated aspect to the region – augmented by the lack of any real industry, save for fishing and family farming plots.

Some history

Following the landfall of Columbus on San Salvador in 1492, Andros was passed over by other Spanish expeditions to the southern oceans until around 1550, when one such expedition arrived seeking slaves. After twenty years of enslavement, suicide and disease, any **natives had completely disappeared** from the island. Virtually bereft of an agricultural base because of a lack of soil, and totally unsuited to colonial-style plantation exploitation, Andros became a backwater in the Spanish empire. The original Spanish name for the island, **La Isla del Espiritu Santo**, alludes to Andros' seemingly providential supply of freshwater

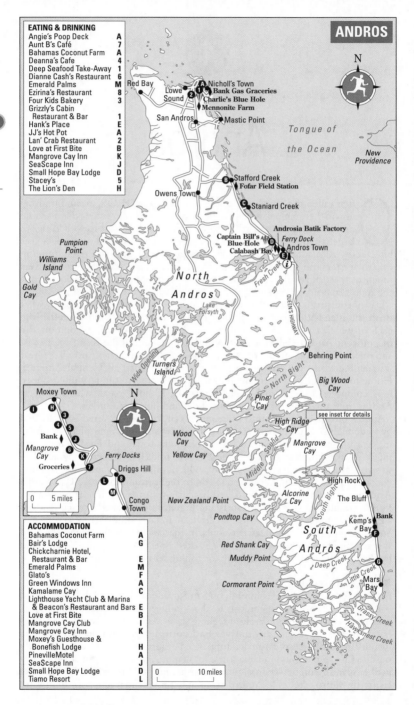

EATING & DRINKING

Angie's Poop Deck	**A**
Aunt B's Café	**7**
Bahamas Coconut Farm	**A**
Deanna's Cafe	**4**
Deep Seafood Take-Away	**1**
Dianne Cash's Restaurant	**6**
Emerald Palms	**M**
Ezirina's Restaurant	**8**
Four Kids Bakery	**3**
Grizzly's Cabin	
Restaurant & Bar	**1**
Hank's Place	**E**
JJ's Hot Pot	**A**
Lan' Crab Restaurant	**2**
Love at First Bite	**K**
Mangrove Cay Inn	**J**
SeaScape Inn	**D**
Small Hope Bay Lodge	**5**
Stacey's	**H**
The Lion's Den	

ANDROS

Red Bay
Lowe
Sound
San Andros
Nicholl's Town
Bank Gas Graceries
Charlie's Blue Hole
Mennonite Farm
Mastic Point

Tongue of
the Ocean

New
Providence

Stafford Creek
B Fofar Field Station
Owens Town
Staniard Creek **C**

Androsia Batik Factory
Captain Bill's
Blue Hole **D** Ferry Dock
Calabash Bay Andros Town
E
i

North
Andros
Lake
Forsyth

Fresh Creek

QUEEN'S HIGHWAY

Pumpion
Point
Williams
Island

Gold
Cay

Turners
Island

Behring Point

Wide Opening

North Bight

Big Wood
Cay

Pine
Cay

see inset for details

High Ridge
Cay

Wood
Cay
Mangrove
Cay
Yellow Cay

Middle Bight

High Rock
Alcorine
Cay
The Bluff

South Bight
Bank

New Zealand Point
Kemp's
Bay
F

Pondtop Cay

South
Andros

Red Shank Cay

Muddy Point

Cormorant Point

G

Mars
Bay

Grassy Creek

Little Creek

Deep Creek

Hawksnest Creek

Moxey Town
I **H** **3**
4 **5**
Bank
J
Mangrove
Cay
6 **K**
Groceries
7
Ferry Docks
Driggs Hill
L
8
M
Congo
Town

0   5 miles

ACCOMMODATION

Bahamas Coconut Farm	**A**
Bair's Lodge	**G**
Chickcharnie Hotel,	
Restaurant & Bar	**E**
Emerald Palms	**M**
Glato's	**F**
Green Windows Inn	**A**
Kamalame Cay	**C**
Lighthouse Yacht Club & Marina	
& Beacon's Restaurant and Bars	**E**
Love at First Bite	**B**
Mangrove Cay Club	**I**
Mangrove Cay Inn	**K**
Moxey's Guesthouse &	
Bonefish Lodge	**H**
PinevilleMotel	**A**
SeaScape Inn	**J**
Small Hope Bay Lodge	**D**
Tiamo Resort	**L**

0   10 miles

for sailors in an area that was sorely lacking it. Even today, Nassau relies completely on Andros for its potable water supply; six million gallons are shipped out daily by barge.

Sitting astride the Great Bahama Bank on one side of the Florida Straits, Andros soon became an ideal perch for pirates, who preyed on Spanish shipping circling back to Spain. Because of the island's abundant supply of freshwater and its vast stands of mahogany and pine, the infamous **Sir Henry Morgan** made northern Andros his special base during the middle of the eighteenth century, raiding Spanish shipping on a regular basis. By the nineteenth century, Andros was primarily home to **freed or runaway slaves** who fished and farmed in small settlements up and down the east coast, having found protection from the weather and tides behind the barrier reef. These tiny settlements were isolated from the rest of the Bahamas, and their residents made a small subsistence living raising corn, plantains, yams, potatoes and peas, supplementing this meagre living with fishing. During the 1830s and 1840s, many **Seminole Indians** fled Florida, took up residence in Red Bay, intermarried with descendants of freed slaves and continue to this day a culture noted for its straw-weaving and fishing in their isolated hamlet.

When, in 1841, a shipwrecked Frenchman noticed that Androsian **sponges** were of higher quality than those found in the Greek isles, the Androsian sponge industry took off. Soon hundreds of Greek schooners and thousands of spongers made Andros their centre of operations, and by 1917, as much as one and a half million pounds of sponges from the forty-mile-wide shoal off the west coast had been harvested. Over-harvesting weakened the remaining beds, which led to the harvesting of juvenile members of the species. During the late nineteenth century, the English attempted to cultivate crops like cotton and sisal for export. It took only two crops of cotton before the thin soil of Andros stopped producing. Indeed, Sir Neville Chamberlain, later Prime Minister of Great Britain, started a sisal plantation on north Andros during the 1890s; its subsequent failure was blamed by the local population on mythical elfin creatures known as chickcharnies.

In 1938, blight struck the sponge beds, killing most commercial activity. Today, while some Androsians still sponge as a sideline, and sponges can be purchased in roadside shops and certain gift shops in hotels, the activity is largely a memory and a cautionary tale about ecological irresponsibility. The modern economy is sustained by a modest fishery and small-scale tourism, built mainly around spectacular bonefishing and diving.

Getting there

Getting to Andros is easy, but you must make sure to land on the correct section of the island as it's surprisingly difficult to get across the bights that divide the island without your own boat; if you book a flight to North Andros, but your hotel is on South Andros, your only option will be to hire a fisherman to get you across. There is a twice-daily ferry between South Andros and Mangrove Cay, but no transportation links between North Andros and Mangrove Cay, or between North Andros and South Andros.

By air

Andros is an hour direct flight from Fort Lauderdale and only fifteen-minute hop from Nassau. From the latter, reliable Western Air (T377-2222,

Ⓦ www.westernairbahamas.com; $120 round-trip) has two flights per day to each of the four airports on Andros: Congo Town on South Andros (Ⓣ 369-2222); Moxey Town on Mangrove Cay (Ⓣ 369-0003); and Andros Town (also known as Fresh Creek, Ⓣ 368-2759) and San Andros Airport (Ⓣ 329-4000), both on North Andros. Major's Air Service (Ⓣ 352-5778, Ⓦ www .thebahamasguide.com/majorair; $300 round-trip) flies from Grand Bahama's Freeport International to all four airports on Fridays and Sundays. From Fort Lauderdale, Lynx Air (Ⓣ 1-888/596-9247, Ⓦ www.lynxair.com; $240 round-trip) flies direct to Congo Town, South Andros on Saturdays and Wednesdays. Continental Connection, operated by Gulfstream International (Ⓣ 1-800/525-0280 US, 1-800/231-0856 Bahamas, Ⓦ www.continental .com), flies from Fort Lauderdale to Andros Town on North Andros four days a week at similar rates.

By boat

A fleet of four government **mailboats** serve the settlements of Andros from Potter's Cay on Nassau once a week, and all take passengers for the five to seven hour journey. The Lady Rosalind (Ⓣ 323-6888; $30) leaves Nassau on Wednesday afternoon for Morgan's Bluff and Nicholl's Town on North Andros, continuing on to northern Cat Island. The Lady 'D' ($35) departs on Tuesdays at 10.30am, heading for Fresh Creek, Stafford Creek, Blanket Sound and Behring Point, then back to Nassau on Sunday. The Lady Katherina ($45) sails to Moxey Town and Lisbon Creek on Mangrove Cay on Thursdays at 2am, departing for Nassau on Monday at 5pm. And the Captain Moxey ($35) serves South Andros, leaving Nassau Monday at 11pm, calling at Kemp's Bay, The Bluff and Long Bay Cays before turning back to Nassau at 11pm on Wednesday. Schedules are subject to change by a few hours or even days, so always call the dockmaster (Ⓣ 393-1064) at Potter's Cay for the current schedule.

A more comfortable option, **Bahamas Fast Ferries** (Ⓣ 323-2166, Ⓦ www .bahamasferries.com; $35 one-way) makes the 2.5-hour trip from Potter's Cay in Nassau to Andros four days a week. Boats travel to Fresh Creek on Wednesday, Friday and Sunday mornings, and to Morgan's Bluff on Saturday mornings. Boarding time is one hour prior to departure, and reservations are strongly recommended.

Yachters have two **marinas** to tie up at on Andros. The eighteen-slip Lighthouse Yacht Club and Marina (Ⓣ 368-2305) is in Andros Town–Fresh Creek, while Kamalame Cay (Ⓣ 368-6281) in Staniard Creek offers eight guest slips. Docking facilities are also available at the public wharves in Morgan's Bluff, Lisbon Creek, Driggs Hill and Fresh Creek. Rates at all average $1.30 a foot, plus water and electricity.

Getting around

Getting around Andros is straightforward. There is only one main road, the Queen's Highway, a narrow strip of tarmac that runs along the east coast of North Andros, Mangrove Cay and South Andros, in sight of the sea for most of its length. The major settlements are widely spaced along the highway, with traffic ranging from light to non-existent. There is no public transport on Andros, but a small fleet of taxis, rental cars, bicycles and a passenger ferry service make it quite easy to get around. Surprisingly for an island so permeated

Tourist information

There is a **Ministry of Tourism information office** in Fresh Creek on North Andros (☎368-2286; Mon–Fri 9am–5pm). There is also a sporadically open office in Congo Town on South Andros (☎369-1688, ⊛www.so-andros.com). Ragan Turnquest (☎369-0331) serves as a contact person for tourist information on Mangrove Cay.

with creeks and bights, there is no motorboat rental business, although several of the resort hotels have sit-on-top kayaks for guest use, a great way to explore the shallow inland waterways and the shoreline.

Taxis

Taxis meet all incoming flights, mailboats and ferries from Nassau and Fort Lauderdale. If taking ferry between Mangrove Cay and South Andros, it pays to make arrangements ahead of time. Most taxi drivers also offer expensive island tours ($300 per day for two people), though you might try negotiating for a cheaper rate. Many hotels and resorts include a taxi ride from the airport to the lodge as part of the first day's service. Taxis are owned by individuals and come in all shapes, sizes and states of repair. Approximate taxi fares from Andros' four airports to the respective nearest settlements range $10–25, with Congo Town Airport to The Bluff (4 miles) being the cheapest and San Andros to Nicholl's Town (10 miles) the most expensive. For a taxi in the San Andros/Nicholl's Town end of North Andros, call ☎329-2273 or ☎329-2140. Around Andros Town (Fresh Creek) on North Andros, call ☎368-2333, ☎357-2998 or ☎357-2149. On Mangrove Cay, call Harry Saunders at ☎382-0312, and on South Andros try ☎369-4548, ☎369-5505, or ☎369-1702.

Car rental

Renting a car for a day will give you plenty of time to explore the quiet charms of North or South Andros. Mangrove Cay is so small that you can get around by bicycle or taxi. The highway is in generally good repair and runs through small roadside villages connected by stretches of tall pine forest or long strands of white sandy beach. The main sights to see along the way are a few secluded coves and inland blue holes, with a handful of down-home restaurants in each settlement at which to soak up some of the local culture. Rental rates range between $70–85 for a car and $120 for a van. There are at least a dozen agencies on North Andros, with GJ's Car Rental (☎329-2005) and A&H Car Rental (☎329-2685) both working out of Nicholls's Town. Other worthwhile options include R&S Enterprise (Mastic Point; ☎329-3305), Shorr's Car Rental (Blanket Sound; ☎368-6140), Adderley's Car Rental (Fresh Creek; ☎357-2149), D&E Car Rental (Love Hill; ☎368-2010) and Thomas Mackey Car Rental (Bowen Sound; ☎369-4136). Options are more limited on South Andros, including NASCOV Car Rental (Deep Creek; ☎369-5001), Lenglo Car Rental (Congo Town; ☎369-1702), Melony Car Rental (Congo Town; ☎369-3593) and Rahming Car Rental (Kemps Bay; ☎369-1608).

Ferry

A **passenger ferry** runs between Lisbon Creek, Mangrove Cay and Driggs Hill on South Andros, making it possible to take a day-trip over to one or the other, with a bicycle in tow if you'd like. The ferry is free and runs twice a day,

The hole story

The Bahamas contain the largest number of **blue holes** in the world, none as spectacular as those on the eastern portion of Andros. During the Ice Age, when water levels were significantly lower, large circular pits were carved in the limestone owing to erosion from rainwater and carbon dioxide. The blue holes of Andros are now underwater entrances to those holes, entrances that reveal a spider web of caverns covering many square miles in length. They range from around thirty to several hundred feet deep. Tidal action, currents and surf well below the surface cause strong updrafts of water that are known as blowing, or **boiling holes**.

These boiling holes are probably the source of the myth of the **Lusca**, creatures that purportedly inhabit blue holes and kill intruders. Androsians claim these gigantic lobsters will feed on any human silly enough to swim or dive into their domain. But the hazard of blue holes is no myth: boiling effects and strong currents can make subterranean passage exploration treacherous – particularly at the reef's edge, where tides and sulphur eruptions complicate matters – unless you are properly qualified and proceed with extreme caution. These holes are best visited in the company of very experienced divers. For more information, visit the website of Rob Palmer's Blue Holes Foundation (ⓦ www.blueholes.org), a non-profit organization dedicated to research on blue holes in the Bahamas.

departing from South Andros at 8am and 4pm and returning from Mangrove Cay at 8.30am and 4.30pm. If you are unable to make the scheduled departure, the operator will almost always make the trip for a fee.

Bicycles

A few of the guest lodges have bicycles for their guests to use, as detailed in the accommodation listings throughout the chapter. On South Andros, you can also **rent bicycles** from Len-Glo Transit Service (ⓣ 369-1702 or cell ⓣ 357-2531). The Queen's Highway is narrow, with almost no shoulder, but the limited traffic (especially on Mangrove Cay and South Andros) ensures this is not a major problem. Mangrove Cay is an especially enjoyable place to ride, with frequent views of the sea and tall graceful palms shading the road in places. Cycling short distances in and around Fresh Creek on North Andros is fun, but as you head north past Stafford Creek, the highway moves inland into a long unbroken tract of tall pines, pleasant enough in a car, but making for tedious cycling. Avoid biking at night, as there are no streetlights.

Diving and watersports

Divers from all over the world come to Andros to explore the outer wall of the barrier reef – third largest in the world – that runs the length of Andros, located between a half-mile and a mile offshore along the east coast. On the ocean side of the reef Andros Wall, the begins at depths of 70–90ft, plunging spectacularly 6000ft straight down to the bottom of the Tongue of the Ocean in a slope riven with canyons, caves, blue holes and sand chutes. At 90ft, divers can explore caverns and tunnels along the edge of the wall. At depths of 15–70ft are lush gardens and valleys filled with rainbow-coloured fish and towering coral heads harbouring improbable sea creatures. There is also good **snorkelling** from shore, especially in the many creeks that traverse the island.

Recommended diving spots and dive operators

While there are hundreds of deep and shallow dives along the 140 miles of reef front off the east coast of Andros, several **diving spots** stand out along with Ocean Blue Hole mentioned on p.176.

Central Park, offshore from Fresh Creek. An expansive coral garden that's lush with soft corals, particularly gorgonians, at a comfortable depth of 30ft and less.

Conch Sound Blue Hole, just south along the beach at Nicholl's Town. Located only a dozen feet offshore in a bed of eelgrass, this blue hole is a speciality dive offered by *Small Hope Bay Lodge* and should be attempted only by experienced divers with a guide as the variable tidal flow in the hole makes it dangerous.

Diana's Dungeons, due east of Love Bay on the outer wall about a mile and a half southeast of Staniard Creek. Drops off at about 60ft into passageways and canyons that lead through coral caverns, sand chutes and gullies. The reef throbs with colourful sponges and parrotfish.

Hole in the Wall, northeast of Staniard Creek on the outer wall. Accessible only by boat, this spot is a speciality dive of *Small Hope Bay Lodge* and consists of a wall, tunnel and trough. Considered one of the most spectacular dives on Andros, it's a one-on-one speciality dive for experienced divers and a guide.

Shark Buoy, northeast of Fresh Creek, 20min by boat. For this ocean dive, a submarine tracking device produces vibrations, which attract pelagic fish, and in turn, pelagic silky sharks. Some New Providence dive-shops offer this dive as an option.

Local dive operators

Kamalame Cay Staniard Creek, North Andros ☎368-6281, ⓦwww.kamalame.com. This luxury resort offers guests guided diving and snorkelling trips and PADI certification courses. One and two-tank dives are $145 and $200 respectively; a two or four day full PADI certification course is $600 or $850. Guided snorkelling trips are $75 for the first hour and $50 for each hour thereafter.

Seascape Inn Moxey Town, beachfront on Mangrove Cay ☎369-0342, ⓦwww .seascapeinn.com. The lodge's full-service dive-shop offers dive and snorkel trips along the Great Andros Barrier Reef, as well as diving instruction. Cosy seaside accommodations is combined with small group sizes. Snorkelling boat trips are $35 per person with a minimum sign-up of two people. A two-tank morning dive is $85, and an introductory, one-tank Discover Scuba session is $95.

🏃 **Small Hope Bay Lodge** Three miles north of Fresh Creek, North Andros ☎368-2013, ⓦwww.smallhope.com. This complete, full-service dive centre and lodge has been in operation for nearly fifty years and has a deserved reputation for its attention to safety, professional staff and knowledge of the surrounding areas. An excellent place to learn to dive, with free introductory sessions as well as full certification courses on offer. Experienced divers are also catered for with a wide variety of dive sites and advanced training courses. The sixty-odd dive sites they use range from 15ft shallow reef dives to 90ft wall or cavern dives, with numerous blue holes and wrecks to explore in the vicinity. Costs are $60 for a one-tank dive, $80 for two-tanks, $70 for a night dive, $85 for the shark observation outing ($45 for snorkellers) and $120 for a full day of diving. Speciality dives run $140 per person or $100 each for two or more. A free two-hour introduction to scuba diving session is available to all beginners. Full PADI/NAUI Open Water Certification courses are $250, with the Open Water referral portion only available for $150 (if you've done your classroom coursework at home). Snorkel trips by boat are $45/$25 adult/child with free use of the equipment from shore. All-inclusive food/accommodation/dive packages give you a discounted rate.

Tiamo Resort South Andros ☎357-2489, ⓦwww.tiamoresorts.com. This exquisite eco-resort runs a dive-shop for its guests, with one-tank and two-tank dives for $100 and $145 respectively.

Bonefishing clubs

If you want to fish everyday, any of the hotels on the island can fix you up, and several have fishing guides on staff. However, if you want to *completely* immerse yourself in the fishing fraternity without the soft distractions offered by a resort, look into one of Andros' well-established **bonefishing clubs**. Most of the lodges are rustic, with a minimum of amenities and devoted almost solely to the pursuit of bonefish. They offer packages for one or two fishermen that include lodging, food, guide and boat, and usually there's little entertainment beyond a small bar.

Andros Island Bonefishing Club Cargill Creek ☏368-5167, ⓦwww .androsbonefishing.com. Twelve cabins (some wood, some breeze-block) with two double beds, private bath, fridge and fans. There's a restaurant on site with a bar with TV. Three to eight day all-inclusive fishing packages available, with seven nights/six days at $3145 per person based on double occupancy.

Bair's Lodge Little Creek, South Andros ☏369-5060, ☏1-877/637-8420 US, ⓦwww.bairslodge.com. A favourite with the fishing classes, with a few more creature comforts than the norm. Recently bought and renovated by an Argentinean angling outfit, *Bair's* offers luxurious accommodation for ten guests in four twin and two queen rooms, each with private bath, a/c and a light, modern decor. The location gives anglers easy access to the prime fishing grounds in Deep Creek, Little Creek and the island's wild west side. There is a lovely patch of beach out front, gourmet meals, a comfortable lounge equipped with a bar, satellite TV and a fly-tying table, plus a tackle shop on site. Rates $4000/$6000 double/single occupancy in high season (March–June), with a thirty percent discount for non-fishing companions.

Glato's Bonefish Club Kemp's Bay, South Andros ☏369-4669 or 1-800/824-1255 US, ⓦwww.glatosbonefishing.com. Twelve simple a/c rooms, with Bahamian-cooked meals served in the common dining room, and satellite TV and liquid refreshment to wile away the evening. A week package is $2150/$2350 double/single occupancy.

Mangrove Cay Club Mangrove Cay ☏369-0731 or 1-800/772-7479 US, ⓦwww .mangrovecayclub.com. Overlooking the Middle Bight with room for sixteen anglers in eight suites, each equipped with two queen beds, private bath and a separate sitting room in which to sort your tackle. The menu is varied, incorporating lots of fresh fish and vegetables, and the showers have lots of hot water, but everything takes a backseat to the fishing. A week of fishing $3700/$4575 double/single occupancy.

Nottage's Cottages Behring Point ☏368-4293. Owned and run by sought-after fishing guide Charlie Neymour and his wife, *Nottage's* has ten basic rooms with an additional five two-bedroom cottages for self-catering. There is also a good restaurant and bar where the speciality of the house is seafood and Bahamian fixings like macaroni and cheese and mashed potatoes. Rates $2680 a week based on double occupancy, with single occupancy available at a surcharge.

Tranquillity Hill Lodge Behring Point, North Andros ☏368-4132, ⓦwww .tranquilityhill.com. Eleven attractive rooms, with an equally pleasing setting overlooking North Bight. Rates around $2800 a week per person, based on double occupancy, with shorter four day packages available.

Andros also offers the highest concentration of blue holes anywhere in the Bahamas. The most famous of these is the Ocean Blue Hole, a vast circular cavern entrance about a mile off the coast of North Andros and exactly opposite the lodge operation on Small Hope Bay. The cavern's entrance gives onto a vast system of lateral and vertical caverns underwater, and snorkellers who accompany the divers are able to see the 100ft-diameter circular rim of the crater, and watch while divers descend into the sulphurous depths.

Fishing

While **reef fishing** and **deep-sea fishing** are good off the coasts of Andros, perhaps nowhere else in the world do **bonefish** grow to such a large size as on Andros. They are abundant too – enough so that even a novice can often hook one. Any hotel should be able to arrange a good bonefish guide for you, and there are also several dedicated bonefish lodges on Andros (see box opposite). The standard package for a day of bonefishing is $400 per day for two fishermen, with boat and lunch provided, or $250–275 per half-day. A week of fishing with

△ Diving with grunts

everything included save for flight and gratuities runs $2700–3600. Deep-sea fishing packages usually start at $500 per day for two to four people. Anglers out for bonefish may use either spinning or fly equipment, and if staying at one of the more established and elaborate hotels or lodges, gear is often supplied. Otherwise, you should plan to come to Andros with a complete supply of equipment, tackle, flies and line, as there are no real shops in which to stock up.

There are plenty of options if looking to hire a guide independently. On North Andros, start by contacting any of the famous "fishin' Neymours": highly recommended guide Charlie Neymour (☎368-4293) operates out of Behring Point, where he runs *Nottage's Cottages* (see, box p.176); other Neymour's to try include Barry (☎368-4132), Deon (☎368-5125), or Frankie and Dwayne (☎368-4485). Alternatively you could try to hook up with Andy Smith (☎368-4261) or Benry Smith (☎368-2204), Brent Mackey (☎368-4318) in Bowen Sound, or Ricardo Mackey (☎368-5237) in Behring Point. On South Andros, Jolly Boy Enterprises (☎369-2727) arranges boats and guides for bonefishing, reef fishing, or deep-sea fishing, or give Nathaniel Adams (☎369-4659) a ring. On Mangrove Cay, Eddie Bannister guides for bonefish (☎369-0025).

Kayaking

Escorted or self-guided **kayaking** expeditions are a unique way to get a close look at the island's ecosystems. Most tours parallel the white beaches, explore the creeks and mangroves, or paddle toward uninhabited cays offshore. Use of kayaks are available free to guests at the Seascape Inn on Mangrove Cay; the Kamalame Cay resort in Staniard Creek, North Andros; the Small Hope Bay Lodge on Small Hope Bay, North Andros; and at Tiamo Resort and Emerald Palms on South Andros. Small Hope Bay Lodge also offers a half-day boat safari by kayak up Fresh Creek for $45/$25 per adult/child, on which you can sometimes catch sight of turtles, ospreys and dolphins. Kamalame Cay resort offers guided kayaking trips in the waters of Staniard Creek and around at $75 for the first hour and $50 for each hour thereafter. Tiamo Resort includes free guided outings in their daily rates.

Other outdoor activities

If you've had your fill of watersports, **nature walks** can be arranged through several hotels on Andros, particularly Small Hope Bay Lodge on North Andros and Tiamo Resort on South Andros who both have naturalists on staff to lead guests on walks through the inland forests and along the coast. The tourist office on South Andros (☎369-1688, ⊛www.so-andros.com) also has some information on walks and can arrange a guide for you. Alternatively, trained nature guide Barbara Moore (☎369-2525 or 369-2922) leads informative 2-hour tours that loop through the tall, dense forest behind Congo Town ($45 per person). The walk takes in three rock-rimmed inland blue holes along the way, overhung with flowering vines.

Andros' vast, undeveloped interior is home to huge numbers of **native and migratory birds**. The most prized of sights for birders are the Cuban emerald, Bahama woodstar, the great lizard cuckoo and the easier to spot but thrillingly exotic-looking yellow-crowned night heron. Andros is also prime hunting ground for white-crowned pigeons in October, and there have been reported sightings of flamingos in the far southwestern corner of South Andros. Be advised that many woodland trails are actually old logging roads or rough, unmarked paths. Most don't see much use and can be overgrown over in spots and some (particularly on South Andros) are hard to follow on your own.

North Andros

The biggest chunk of land in the agglomeration of cays, creeks and bights making up the island of Andros is **NORTH ANDROS**. This is where you'll find the larger settlements (though none is what you'd call large), the bulk of population, a good percentage of the bonefishing lodges, as well as one of the finest dive operations in the country, all overlooking the Andros Barrier Reef. Though every creek, flat, bight and river sports large numbers of hungry bonefish, many of the unique bonefishing sites are located around Cargill Creek and Behring Point on North Bight, about thirty miles from Andros Town Airport, at the southern tip of North Andros. At the other end of the island, Nicholl's Town is a good base for exploring northern North Andros, situated within easy distance of the twee fishing villages of Lowe Sound and Red Bay, as well as Charlie's and Benjamin's inland blue holes.

Diving on North Andros centres around the first-class resort at Small Hope Bay. Continuing south along the east coast brings you to the small settlement at Fresh Creek, just south of San Andros Airport and the last major settlement on North Andros before the road runs out at Behring Point, facing uninhabited Big Wood Cay across the water.

Nicholl's Town and around

While there isn't much to see in the coastal village of **NICHOLL'S TOWN**, it is the centre of activity in North Andros. The town is a base for trips north to Lowe Sound for bonefishing, west to historic Red Bay, and south to Charlie's Blue Hole and Benjamin's Blue Hole. Nicholl's Town itself has about 600 permanent residents, including a few retired expatriates, who live in breeze-block and tin-roofed homes as well as scattered wooden shacks. Just as interesting to gaze at is the Administrator's Office, attractively Georgian in style, and facing the curiously named "International Square"; elsewhere, you'll find a post office (Mon–Fri 9am–5.30pm), supermarket and several bars and restaurants serving simple Bahamian fare. Fringed by tall palms, the beach is marked by a wharf at its east end that hosts a melange of fishing boats used in the busy conch and grouper trade.

Lowe Sound and Morgan's Bluff

Two miles west of Nicholl's Town lies the pleasant fishing village of **LOWE SOUND**, which doesn't have much more than a few bar-restaurants and some bonefishing guides, notably Arthur Russell (☎329-7372), who can lead you to excellent fishing in the nearby creeks and marshes. Most locals make their living from conch, sponging or fishing, with a few doing small-scale vegetable farming in the surrounding triangle of countryside – there really isn't much to do here but relax and watch the water.

If you turn right, or north, at the crossroads outside of town, you'll find yourself at **Morgan's Bluff**, which looms two miles ahead where the road ends at the beach. It is said to be where Henry Morgan secured his headquarters during the eighteenth century, and visitors have spent countless hours searching in vain for the pirate's buried loot. Coming here is also largely a fruitless exercise, for outside of a nice stretch of white sand, good views of the Atlantic Ocean breakers, and a few tidal-action limestone caves – one of which is the garbage- and graffiti-strewn Henry Morgan's Cave – there's little doing here.

The biggest deal in the area is July's annual All Andros and Berry Islands Independence Regatta, for which people come to the small harbour to celebrate the holidays and watch the colourful boat races that take place. Food stalls, craft displays and music highlight the onshore festivities, while locals participate in darts, dominoes and bonefishing competitions.

Red Bay

RED BAY, the only settlement that can really claim to cling to Andros' swampy, bug-infested west coast, can be reached by a bumpy, unpaved road leading west from just north of the San Andros Airport, and rocking along for fifteen hard miles. The population is largely descended from Seminole Indians who fled Florida during the 1840s or who joined with black slaves fleeing Florida, taking canoes all the way to Andros where they set up a small fishing village and intermarried with locals. These days, Red Bay is a rather weather-beaten village with a cultural heritage known for straw-basket weaving. Ovoid and watertight, these baskets derive from the Seminole tradition, which is significantly different from palm and raffia weaving styles used by other Out Island Bahamians. Local resident Gertrude Gibson (T 329-7739) crafts beautiful vessels out of silver palm and sells her wares from her home and at resorts around the island. Some locals still sponge for a small living, and a couple of small bars serve snacks, but there are no hotels or other services at all.

Uncle Charlie's and Benjamin's blue holes

Take the Queen's Highway one mile south of Nicholl's Town and, just before you get to San Andros, you'll see a battered sign to the east of the highway. A rugged track (passable in a car) leads half a mile into the bush, where you'll see **Uncle Charlie's Blue Hole**. This spectacular limestone cavern is filled with deep blue-green water and is locally famous for its rapid "boiling", the signal that water is rushing in and out of the hole during tides. **Benjamin's Blue Hole** is half a mile inland toward Conch Sound from Charlie's. On a dirt track that is largely overgrown, you'll probably need local guidance to find it, yet the stalagmites and stalactites for which it is celebrated are well worth the effort.

Practicalities

While the holiday action on North Andros is focused further south, there are a few if good places to stay at the north end of the island. On the beach in Nicholl's Town, the *Bahama Coconut Farm* (T 329-2827, W www .bahamacoconutfarm.com) has a couple of charming, colourful cottages (one-bedroom ❾; two-bedroom ❽) facing a stretch of white-sand beach in a stand of tall coconut palms. Each cottage is equipped with satellite TV, a/c and either a kitchenette with a barbeque or a full kitchen. All are furnished with books and games, and there are bikes and kayaks for guest use. There is a restaurant on site, fishing trips can be arranged along with wild boar hunting ($200 for two people) and island tours. Two other Nicholl's Town choices are: the *Pineville Motel* (T 329-2788, W www.pinevillemotel.com; ❷), situated just off the highway on the south edge town and a kitschy but clean and friendly budget inn with 16 rooms is set in a small shady garden landscaped with a man-made waterfall and a reconstruction of a Seminole Indian village; and the *Green*

Windows Inn (☎329-2833/2207; ❷, with all-inclusive bonefishing packages available), which was undergoing an extensive renovation at the time of writing. The new rooms are bright and fresh, with a/c, TVs, wood-laminate floors, TV, a/c and a full bath, and there is a restaurant on site for guests only.

People travel from all over the island to eat at the *Lan' Crab Restaurant*, on the Queen's Highway just south of Nicholl's Town (☎329-4172/3; Mon–Sat 11am–9pm). Housed in a light, airy hexagon, the restaurant doles out chicken, conch and lamb done with flare, served with absolutely delicious sides of potato salad and coleslaw; mains average $10–15. *JJ's Hot Pot* (☎329-2270; Mon–Thurs 10am–11pm, Fri and Sat 9am–midnight, Sun 9am–2pm) is a colourful and inexpensive seafood shack on the waterfront near the wharf in Nicholl's Town that is at its busiest on weekend evenings. The specialities of the house are – not surprisingly – conch, souse and fresh lobster. West of the wharf, the thatched beachside cabana bar and restaurant at the *Bahama Coconut Farm Inn* (☎329-2829; daily 8am–10pm) serves cool drinks all day. Breakfast is done both Bahamian and American-style; lunch is sandwiches and conch fritters, and the dinner menu ($10) features cracked conch and fried fish with sides of peas and rice. Also recommended in these parts is *Big Josh's Seafood Restaurant* (☎329-7517) in Lowe Sound. Serving breakfast, lunch and dinner, Big Josh's specializes in seafood, though good steaks, pork chops and fried chicken are also available for around $10. The bar/restaurant stays open late to the throb of satellite TV, but the best nightlife spots are *JJ's Hot Pot* or the *Sly Fox* next door, both popular local spots for unwinding at the end of the day.

Listings

Banking Nicholl's Town has a Scotiabank (☎329-2700; 9am–3pm Mon–Fri, 24-hour ATM).
Government offices Nicholl's Town ☎329-2278
Groceries There are a couple of small shops in Nicholl's Town selling a limited selection of non-perishable foodstuffs.

Medical clinic Nicholl's Town ☎329-2055
Police and fire ☎919; Nicholl's Town ☎329-2353/2103
Telephone BaTelCo (☎329-2171; Mon–Fri 9am–4pm)

The east coast towards Fresh Creek

The Queen's Highway hurtles south from Nicholl's Town through thick pine forest and the stretch is riddled with deep potholes. Just past abandoned Owen's Town, the road turns due east towards the ocean, skirts a creek, and winds up at nondescript **Stafford Creek**, which hunkers down on the north side of its eponymous creek. One mile south on the highway, the Fofar Field Station caters to North American students of marine biology, geology and ornithology.

Further south along the highway, **Staniard Creek** is a wonderland of flowering plants, including wild orchid, hibiscus and wild lilies, though the dispersed settlement itself is scruffy at best. People come mainly for the mile or so of stirring white beach, which runs from the mouth of the creek at Blanket Sound until just north of Small Hope Bay and is often deserted, while those who can afford it stay at the expensive *Kamalame Cay* resort (see "Practicalities" p.182). Further south near Love Hill, a turn-off leads to *Captain Bill's Blue Hole*, a popular swimming and picnicking spot. The deep, rock-rimmed crater is 440 feet in diameter and surrounded by tall pines. The 2.7 mile drive in on a little-used lumber road is well marked from the highway, immediately south of the

Department of Environmental Health Building. About a mile offshore opposite Captain Bill's is the **Hole in the Wall** (see p.175), one of the most astonishing dives in the Bahamas.

South of Love Hill, the highway opens to views of **Small Hope Bay** – sometimes called Calabash Bay – a lovely stretch of coastal settlement, white-sand beach and casuarina trees about three miles north of Andros Town itself. Herea-bouts the pines of North Andros give way to vast seas of coconut palms, and the coastal beaches are both wide and empty. The bay here is wide, shallow and subject to great tidal movements, superb for snorkelling, diving and swimming.

Practicalities

While there is little accommodation between Nicholl's Town and Fresh Creek, two expensive and superb resorts stand out. *Kamalame Cay* (☎368-6281 or 1-800/688-4752, ⓦwwww.kamalame.com; ⑨) is a private luxury resort (rates start at $900 per day for two) located on a white-sand fringed island reached by boat launch from Staniard Creek. The rooms and cottages are the epitome of tropical glamour, with acres of ceramic tiled floors, creamy linens, soaring ceilings and deep private verandahs, but no phones or TVs to enhance the air of seclusion. A motorboat is available for guests, and the dining room features steaks as well as local seafood prepared Bahamian-style. The main house can sleep up to ten people, and all bedrooms have mosquito nets and king-size beds, while the separate villas and guesthouses have kitch-enettes. Outside, hammocks hang between palm trees, and there is a small pool and private beach. Snorkelling and eco-tours are included in the package, with diving trips also on offer.

Cheaper but still at the higher end of the price range is the all-inclusive 🌂 *Small Hope Bay Lodge* (☎368-2013 or 1-800/223-6961 US, ⓦwww .smallhope.com; ⑧). Built in 1960 out of native limestone and pine, the lodge is one of the finest resorts in the Bahamas. Most guests come for the excellent diving and snorkelling (see the box on p.176), but other activities and amenities include a hot tub and yoga classes on the beach, hammocks strung between palm trees, the use of kayaks and bicycles, along with nature walks and guided fishing trips of all sorts. A total of 21 guestrooms are nestled along the shore beneath tall coconut palms, each a spacious double with its own bath, stone walls and wood furnishings accented with bright Androsia fabrics. One wall is almost entirely taken up by a huge picture window framing the sea and the sunrise. Breakfast is served in the main lodge, where there is a reading room, stone fireplace and a corner bar made out of a dory. Lunch and dinner are served under thatch umbrellas waterside, ringed by tiki torches at night. Children are welcome, though those under nine years old dine early (6pm) in the games room with staff supervision. Drinks, meals, airport transfers and taxes are included in the price of the stay, with diving, snorkelling and fishing packages available at discounted rates.

Even if not staying at the *Small Hope Bay Lodge*, it remains the best dining option in the area. The first-rate menu features the likes of local lobster cooked on the outdoor open-air charcoal grill to Indian-style lamb chops served with mango chutney. Desserts like melt-in-the-mouth carrot cake and guava duff round out every meal in style. For those not staying, breakfast is $12, a lunch buffet $15 and the dinner buffet $30, including table wine. Also recommended is dinner at the *Love at First Sight* (☎368-6082), a restaurant located roadside on the north side of the bridge at Stafford Creek. Reservations are recommended.

Fresh Creek and around

Two miles south of Small Hope Bay, the big – for Andros – settlement of **FRESH CREEK** encompasses Coakley Town to the north of the creek and, connected by a lovely single-lane bridge, a small collection of buildings to the south that has come to be called Andros Town. The creek itself gradually widens heading inland for about ten miles, becoming a wide bight with uncounted interruptions by mud flats, islands and small creeks. Closer to shore, the tidal estuary supports lovely stands of bougainvillea, pine, palm and palmetto. For isolated swimming, visitors can go south of town to Somerset Beach at low tide, which is long and wide and quite handsome.

Near Fresh Creek, the US operates a naval base for submarine testing and evaluation known as AUTEC (Atlantic Undersea Testing and Evaluation Center), which employs a few locals but is off limits to visitors. A frequent sight at the Andros Town Airport is squads of enlisted men and officers of the US Navy, anxiously waiting their charter or scheduled flights to Miami for their R and R.

Swedish industrialist Axel Wenner-Gren (see p.92), who developed Paradise Island, also had a hand in the initial development of the marina at Fresh Creek in the 1940s. Refurbished and largely rebuilt on the same spot, the new marina, the only full-service one on Andros, now boasts eighteen slips and can accommodate vessels up to 150ft.

Accommodation

If your budget doesn't stretch to cover a stay at one of the beachside lodges north of Fresh Creek, there are a couple of comfortable accommodation options in the village that provide a good base for exploring the surrounding area by bicycle or rental car. If fishing is your passion, a few of the dedicated bonefishing lodges found south of Fresh Creek are listed in the box on p.175.

Andros Lighthouse Yacht Club and Marina Fresh Creek ☎ 368-2305, ⓦ www .androslighthouse.com, VHF Ch 16. With a patio overlooking Fresh Creek and an eighteen-slip marina, the club offers twelve comfortable if uninspired rooms with king-size beds and eight with two double beds, all featuring private baths, a/c, mini-fridge and cable TV. There is a restaurant on site serving three meals a day. Although many yachties call in here, it is also good for bonefishing and island tours. ❺

Chickcharnie Hotel Fresh Creek ☎ 368-2025/6, ⓦ www.chickcharnie.com. Centrally located in the village on Fresh Creek in Coakley Town, *Chickcharnie* has eleven simple but clean rooms with a/c, TV and private bath, as well as five sharing a central bath. There is a patio for guest use overlooking the water as well as a restaurant and grocery shop downstairs. The staff can arrange bonefishing for $350–400 a day (for two). The hotel has a few slips for modest yachts. Shared bath ❷; private bath ❸

Coakley Town and Andros Town

A quiet place, **COAKLEY TOWN** was named for Coakley House, a fabulous villa built by Wenner-Gren that's now a private home. The town is a not unpleasant collection of breezeblock and concrete homes, a few shops, restaurants, bars and a sixty-foot-tall white limestone lighthouse at the point, from which the views look down over cliffs to the blue sea. Hardly a town at all, **ANDROS TOWN**, across the bridge from Coakley Town, has a very small tourist office (Mon–Fri 9am–5pm; ☎ 368-2286) and a lovely little park with some disused tennis courts, all in the same shady hundred-yard square, but is only marginally of more interest than its neighbour.

Across the street from the tourist office and down an unpaved lane stands the **Androsia Batik Factory** (Mon–Sat 8am–4pm; free; ☏368-2020/2080, ⓦwww.androsia.com), which constitutes about the only commercial enterprise on Andros besides truck farming and tourism. Operated by the Birch family, which also owns Small Hope Bay Lodge, the factory produces colourful batiks, which make fashionable dresses, blouses, pants, T-shirts and scarves, as well as excellent wall hangings. The batik-making process, which visitors can view, begins with plain white fabrics on which wax-dipped sponge cut-outs of patterns are impressed, and then the whole is dipped in dye. The wax is melted in hot water and the fabrics, with attendant patterns, are sun-dried.

The factory itself employs some forty to fifty islanders and on most days production is in full, if somnolent, swing. You will see the distinctive, brightly coloured fabrics patterned with motifs like seashells and dolphins all over the Bahamas. Tours of the factory, including a batik-making session, can be arranged through the *Small Hope Bay Lodge* (☏368-2013). There is a gift shop on site stocked with batik fabric on the bolt, as well as clothing made with the textiles produced on site and a few handcrafts made around the island.

South of Fresh Creek

The Queen's Highway **south of Fresh Creek** runs through bush and pine scrub, and while there are no real settlements to speak of driving the road is pleasant enough provided you watch out for the big potholes. Ten miles south of Fresh Creek, Little Cargill Creek and its sister hamlet, Behring Point, are in the midst of prime bonefishing country, the most prominent tourist activity in this part of North Andros. Both towns have a few rustic, but delightful, fishing lodges, some small restaurants and bars serving Bahamian fare, and little else. The Queen's Highway potholes on for another mile beyond Behring Point, then stops at the bight. Twenty-five miles south leads you to the Bight of Andros, a wide estuary and swamp across which lies Mangrove Cay.

Eating and drinking

The **eateries** below all sit alongside the creek, with fine views of the water and seafood-heavy menus. If you still have something in the tank after a day exploring the reefs, *Donnie's Sweet Sugar Lounge* (☏368-2080) in Fresh Creek features an odd facade of conch shells, a dim low-ceilinged bar and a decrepit dance floor that is often crammed with locals on weekends. In Cargill Creek, *Leadon's Creekside Lounge and Disco* (☏368-4167) often hosts local bands, with a once-monthly performance by big names in Bahamian music.

Beacon's Restaurant and Bar at the Lighthouse Club and Marina Fresh Creek ☏368-2305. This bright dining room and lounge overlooking the marina manages to be cheerful by day and elegant at night. Omelettes, pancakes and stewed fish for breakfast ($7–11), and conch fritters, salads and burgers (fish, conch and beef) for lunch ($6–12). Dinner begins with conch chowder or fritters, followed by a choice of salads, with steamed snapper and stuffed chicken breast among the best mains on the menu ($16 and up). Daily for breakfast 7–11am, lunch noon–4pm, and dinner 6–9.30pm.

Chickcharnie Hotel Restaurant and Bar Fresh Creek ☏368-2025. Overlooking the water, the hotel's dining room rivals *Hank's Place* in popularity. Breakfast is the usual mix of Bahamian favourites like stewed fish with Johnnycake; lunch specials include veggie and regular hamburgers, conch steak and sandwiches. For dinner, steamed conch and crawfish are especially good. Basic dinner entrees run $8–15, with lobster $20. Daily for breakfast 8am–10.30am, lunch noon–3pm, and dinner 6–9.30pm.

Hank's Place Fresh Creek ☏368-2447. Easy to spot right near the water in the centre of the village, *Hank's* is an airy place with a deck hanging out over the water. The food is inexpensive and good, with standards such as fried chicken dishes, buffalo wings, ribs, grouper and conch. A dozen conch fritters costs $3, with dinners $9–18. Dinner only 5–9.30pm; closed Sunday.

Listings

Banks There is a Royal Bank of Canada just north of Fresh Creek (☏368-2071; Mon–Thurs 9.30am–3pm, Fri 9.30am–4.30pm; 24-hour ATM).

Government offices Island Administrator, Fresh Creek ☏368-2010; Bahamas Customs, Andros Town ☏368-2030.

Groceries There are two easy to find groceries in Fresh Creek, *Chickarnie Food Store* and *Adderley's*

Bargain Mart, both of which stock a good selection of goods. There are also small shops in Love Hill, Staniard Creek, Blanket Sound, Bowen Sound and Cargill Creek.

Laundry Adderley's Bargain Mart (☏368-2020) in Fresh Creek and Marshall's (☏368-6255) in Staniard Creek.

Medical clinic Fresh Creek ☏368-2038

Police and fire ☏919; Fresh Creek ☏368-2626

Mangrove Cay

Most visitors come to eighteen-mile-long **MANGROVE CAY** for its serenity and isolation. This peaceful, rural island has just a couple of hundred residents, long, empty stretches of white-sand beach shaded by tall coconut palms, and acres of dense bush. The reef offshore is near enough that snorkellers can easily swim out, spending time diving underwater to enjoy excellent views of Caribbean spiny lobster and natural sponges, which are particularly abundant on this part of the coast. There is also a dive operation at the excellent Seascape Inn – the island's best reason to visit – if you want to take the plunge.

While there is no ferry from the north, a twice-daily passenger ferry visits Mangrove Cay from Driggs Hill on South Andros. Otherwise, the easiest way to visit is by air on a 15-minute hop from Nassau's airport, or aboard the weekly mailboat from Potter's Cay, Nassau. If flying into the Mangrove Cay Airport, you'll find a couple of local taxis ready to transport you into Moxey Town, which has a few small hotels, south towards Lisbon Creek, a modestly scenic settlement known for its boat building. Every hotel or restaurant can phone one of the two or three taxis on the cay should you need to get around.

Accommodation

Most of the **inns** on Mangrove Cay are located either right on the beach or a few yards from it. The cay's narrow, recently re-paved version of the Queen's Highway runs from the far north at Moxey Town to Bastin Point and Lisbon Creek in the south. The interior is dense scrub palmetto and mangrove swamp, but the beach running along most of the length of the east coast is quiet and lovely, lined by tall coconut palms.

Helen's Motel Complex Mangrove Cay ☎369-0033 or 1-800/688-4752, ⓔhelensmotel @bahamas.net.bs. One mile south of Moxey Town, this modern motel-style place has ten rooms with bath and both a/c and fan. It's basic but clean, and popular with locals. ❷

Mangrove Cay Inn Grant's ☎369-0069. The twelve air-conditioned rooms here are on the dark side, but nicely furnished and carpeted. The grounds are the best part of the inn, lush with orchids, while the beach is a few minutes walk away. Amenities include bicycle rentals, nearby walking trails and a laundry. There's also a good on-site restaurant with an eclectic menu including conch, lobster, pasta and hoagies. ❸

Moxey's Guesthouse and Bonefish Lodge Moxey Town ☎369-0023. On the edge of the Middle Bight, a stretch of water that separates Mangrove Cay from Big Wood Cay to the north, this little village inn has a half-dozen rooms with

mud flats bonefishing close by. The popular restaurant features Bahamian and American dishes, and affords a good view of the water. Rates ❷

🚶 **Seascape Inn** Moxey Town ☎369-0342, ⓦwww.seascapeinn.com. A delightful spot on the beach south of Moxey Town, the *Seascape* has five adorable, spotlessly clean beachfront cabins done up with just the right touch – crisp white linens and walls, handcrafted wooden furniture, original art and a selection of paperbacks. Each cottage faces the sea with a private wooden deck. An atmospheric bar and restaurant in the elevated timber lodge serves three meals a day, and activities include snorkelling trips, diving excursions, nature walks, guided bonefishing and free use of kayaks, snorkel gear, bicycles and the hammocks strung between coconut palms. ❸, including breakfast.

The island

The main settlement on Mangrove Cay, **Little Harbour** rests at the northern tip of the island and is generally referred to by the name of its northern section, **Moxey Town**, in honour of its founding family. The town has a beach and a tiny dock where local catches are hauled in and where the mailboat calls, plus a couple of restaurants and bars for those passing through. Otherwise, there's little to waylay you here except a pharmacy, from which you'll doubtless want to pick up some mosquito repellant. The only other actual settlements on Mangrove Cay, Burnt Rock and Grant's, are quite tiny, almost specks on the roadway. At Lisbon Creek, the southernmost point on Mangrove Cay, the road ends, and one can catch a ferry for Driggs Hill on South Andros. The best Androsian sloops were built at Lisbon Creek, though the art has fallen into desuetude of late. The biggest social-sporting events come in August, when there are two separate regattas in Lisbon Creek.

Mangrove Cay activities

The main activity for visitors to Mangrove Cay is relaxation, from **napping in a hammock** by the sea to **diving**, **snorkelling** and **kayaking** or cycling the coastal road. The centre of diving life is the *Seascape Inn* (see above and p.175). Snorkelling trips are $35 per person, with a two-tank morning dive for $85; the introductory Discover Scuba session is $95 for a bit of dry-land instruction and a one-tank dive. There are more than twenty blue holes located inland on Mangrove Cay, most of them buried deep in the interior and reachable only by scrubbed-over logging roads and trails. In order to dive a blue hole, you'll need to contact the dive master at the *Seascape Inn*. Bonefishing guide Eddie Bannister (☎369-0025) best knows the flats above the cay. Many fishermen skiff over from Moxey Town to Bigwood Cay Flat, a fifteen-minute putt-putt away, where **fishing flats** stretch for miles in an utterly isolated environment.

Eating and drinking

Most of the inns and guesthouses on Mangrove Cay have pleasant enough **bar-restaurants** where tourists and locals pass the hours in conversation, playing dominoes or throwing darts. There are also several casual **local restaurants** that serve wonderful Bahamian fare. Because Mangrove Cay is such a small place, it is best to call ahead and let the owners know you are coming for dinner. Note that while the *Mangrove Cay Inn* and *Seascape Inn* take credit cards, most other businesses on the island do not. As for the relaxed nightlife scene, the cosy driftwood bar at the *Seascape Inn* is a fine place for an early drink and a friendly chat. Roadside in Grant's, *The New Happy Tree Soca Club* is a weekend hangout for music, dancing and a game of pool. The same amusements are on offer at *Club Dusk to Dawn* up the road and just south of Moxey Town.

Aunt B's Café Grant's, just south of the *Mangrove Cay Inn* ☎369-0162. A neat and inexpensive roadside café specializing in native dishes, with a few tables inside and one outside under a shady coconut tree. Lunch and dinner typically served, but call ahead just in case.

Dianne Cash's Restaurant Moxey Town ☎369-0430. Run out of the white house just south of the Medical Clinic (there's no sign), *Dianne Cash's* is truly informal dining. The owner has put together four simple tables made of rattan, and offers great pork chops, conch salad or stuffed baked crabs – a real speciality. If nothing on the menu ($5–20) looks appealing, Dianne will try to fix whatever you want, provided she has the ingredients. Call ahead for breakfast, lunch or dinner.

Four Kids Bakery Moxey Town, on the south edge of the settlement ☎369-0366. A friendly family bakery with a small, tidy dining room serving meals made to order. Open for three meals a day, but call ahead for lunch and dinner. Sun–Fri 8am–8pm, closed Sat.

The Lion's Den Moxey Town ☎369-0735. A red wooden shack on the water's edge, where the specialities of the house are seafood and souse. Inexpensive and popular with the local lunch crowd. Mon–Sat 7am–11pm, closed Sun.

Seascape Inn Two miles south of Moxey Town ☎369-0342. The timbered restaurant and bar of this fine resort sits on stilts and features large breakfasts, burger and conch lunches, and Continental and Bahamian-style seafood, meat and pasta dinners with warm fresh bread and vegetable side dishes that run from $12 to $20. Reservations required.

Stacey's Restaurant 1.5 miles south of Moxey Town ☎369-0161. A top spot for wonderful home-style Bahamian meals. The menu includes steamed conch and fried chicken with heaping sides of peas and rice, fried plantains and a delicious spicy coleslaw. You can eat very well for under $10. Open Mon–Fri 7am–11pm, but it's best to call ahead.

Listings

Bank A branch of the Bank of Bahamas (☎369-0502; Mon–Fri 10am–2pm) is located two miles south of Moxey Town. No ATM.

Government offices Island Administrator, Mangrove Cay (☎369-033).

Groceries Best selection at Bullmack's Convenience in Victoria Point, just over a mile north of Lisbon Creek (Mon–Sat 7.30am–8pm, Sun 1–8pm).

Laundry At the Twin Shop Rite in Pinder's, a mile south of Moxey Town (Mon–Sat 7am–8pm, Sun 7–10am).

Medical clinic Swains ☎369-0089.

Police and fire ☎919; local station ☎368-0083.

Telephone The BaTelCo office is located immediately south of the Medical Clinic (Mon–Fri 9am–4pm), with a payphone out front.

South Andros

If Mangrove Cay seems isolated, **SOUTH ANDROS**, composed mostly of mangrove and bush, mud flats and tidal swamps, feels like the absolute end of the world, and you will soon forget you are only about 175 miles from the tip of southern Florida. Until recently, South Andros received few tourists apart from diehard anglers, but the opening of the Tiamo Resort, a secluded and luxurious eco-lodge, has given beachgoers a very good reason to make this corner of the Andros a final destination.

From Driggs Hill – where the ferry from Mangrove Cay disembarks – the Queen's Highways heads south for about 25 miles to the southern tip of South Andros at Mars Bay. Along the way, the road presents several pleasant vistas, and it's easy to spend a full-day sightseeing along the drive. In fact, the coast of South Andros is one long white beach, perfect for snorkelling and swimming, though facilities are sparse. Offshore lies a fringing reef, while the interior is premier birding and nature hiking territory. If you are not taking the ferry, you will alight at Congo Town Airport, where there are typically a couple of taxis waiting to take you to Driggs Hill, three miles north, or to nearby Congo Town itself. There are no public marinas in South Andros.

Driggs Hill and around

While quiet **DRIGGS HILL**, the northernmost point on South Andros, isn't much to look at, it does have a pretty enough collection of pastel-coloured houses, a small church and a grocery store. The point where the ferry from Lisbon Creek disembarks, the town offers little to detain visitors, and you may only stop long enough to arrange a seat on the informal minibus operated by one of the locals that goes up and down the coast. Also at the ferry dock, a boat launch meets guests bound for Tiamo Resort, tucked away out of sight a short distance up the South Bight and accessible only by water.

Congo Town, two miles south of the airport and Driggs Hill, is largely known for the Emerald Palms by the Sea Hotel, a popular honeymoon destination. The town features an ocean-side walk through coconut palms and a historical cemetery in the town centre where many of the island's founding families are buried. Everything to the west of Congo Town is dense bush, and guided nature walks here reveal a little-explored side of the Bahamas. The highlight of the area lies right on the beach three miles south of Congo Town, where The Bluff, a hillock that gives the surrounding settlement its name, offers a wonderful view of the many cays and islands lying offshore. This panorama is particularly lovely when the light is soft at night, or in the early morning when the sunrise tints the sky a spectacular mix of pink and coral colours.

Practicalities

Visitors have two very nice choices to stay at this end of South Andros, with the stylish sleek cocktail bar and restaurant at *Emerald Palms* (☎369-2713) also supplying the best place to eat. Breakfast features huge portions of johnnycake, French toast, fluffy omelettes and eggs Benedict, while dinner choices include a number of grilled seafood dishes, and the house speciality of crab-stuffed chicken breast (mains $22–28). For inexpensive Bahamian fare, first choice should be *Ezrina's Restaurant* (☎369-2586) in Driggs Hill. The nearby *Bluebird Club* sports a bar, TV and a pool table, with occasionally blaring music on the weekends. The king of bonefishing guides hereabouts is Stanley Forbes, who runs Jolly Boy Enterprises (☎369-2767) and guides trips for $350 per day.

Accommodation

Emerald Palms Resort ☎357-2873 or 1-800/504-1794 US, ⦿www.emerald-palms.com. This resort sits on an alluring strip of white-sand beach, dotted with palms, between Driggs Hill and Congo Town. The twenty double rooms are decorated with a crisp, sophisticated flair, as are the half dozen over-the-top luxury villas with vast expanses of polished marble, sunken tubs, nooks strewn with silk-covered throw cushions, kitchenettes and spacious private verandahs. There is a restaurant and an ocean-front pool, with activities including diving, snorkelling, bonefishing, hiking and kayaking tours, and blue-hole swimming can all be arranged here. ❻

Tiamo Resort ☎357-2489, ⦿www .tiamoresorts.com. Situated on a thick swathe of palm-fringed white sand on South Bight, this one-of a kind all-inclusive resort is accessible only by boat. The ten one-room guest bungalows are tucked in among the trees a few steps from the water, each boasting a private wrap-around screened in porch. The fine meals are served in the cosy main lodge, which also has a library, comfy reading and lounging nooks and a polished, soft-lit bar, while activities include bonefishing with an expert guide, diving, daily snorkelling trips and kayaking and/or nature hikes with the staff naturalist. Adding to the allure is the fact that the award-winning *Tiamo Resort* has been designed to minimize its impact on the natural environment. Amongst other practices, all the electricity used is solar powered, the food is mainly organic, and bath water is sun-heated. According to the owners, the ten cottages together have used less energy in the past five years than the average American household uses in three days. An extensive recycling programme is also in place, and the resort runs environmental education programmes for local school kids. Truly a special place for a once-in-a lifetime holiday. $350 per person, per day. ❾

Kemp's Bay and around

Small, but reasonably lively, with a grocery and a fishing camp, **KEMP'S BAY**, about ten miles south of Congo Town, is only worth stopping for to see its photogenic Conch Shell House, whose limestone walls are covered by hundreds of pink shells. Grouper school offshore in Kemp's Bay, and the fish are manhandled aboard skiffs, cleaned, then shipped off to Nassau to be devoured by tourists. Deep Creek and Little Creek, both tiny fishing villages, look over ocean blue holes. Deep Creek is particularly known for the conch and crab lurking in its waters. Beyond it, a small bridge over the creek leads to Little Creek and Bair's Lodge, a bonefishing lodge overlooking miles of tidal swamp.

South of Deep Creek is the largely nondescript Pleasant Bay, notable for its "Slavery Wall", made of limestone and conch about 5ft high. Constructed by slaves in the eighteenth century, it is probably a surviving section of a plantation wall and is currently home to hordes of giant white crabs that make quite a spectacle during mating season.

Practicalities

Accommodation down this way are all bonefish lodges, ranging from barebones to deluxe; see the box on p.176 for some of the best. *Big J's on the Bay* (☎369-1954) is the most popular **place to eat** in Kemp's Bay, with standards like smothered grouper and peas and rice. Both the *Cabana Beach*

Bar and *Lewis' Bar* are grungy local hangouts, where you can get a beer and watch locals play dominoes. **Nathaniel Adams** (no phone) located in Deep Creek at the foot of the bridge is recommended for home-cooked meals of grouper, lobster and conch.

Mars Bay

With the pastel colours of its stone houses, miles of ocean views, a beached schooner offshore and spreading sapodilla trees, picturesque **MARS BAY** near the southern end of the line has an air of permanence and spiritual ease. Bonefishing is the name of the game here, but birders come for the tidal flats and offshore cays, as do divers on the run from more mundane experiences. Relax in the square by the large sapodilla tree, or head down to the town dock to watch the locals cleaning and shelling grouper and conch; either is a pleasant way to while away a few hours.

A mile past Mars Bay is the end of the road, where, standing on a dock, you can get a good view of the massive surrounding tidal flats dotted with feeding birds. Some people, mainly birders, make the trip by private hired boat (in Mars Bay) over to Grassy Creek Cays, a nine-mile journey southeast of the bay. Others ride over to Big Green Cay, where one of the world's largest colonies of white-crowned pigeons makes its home twenty miles east of Kemp's Bay. At one time, the cay was home to 20,000 of these pigeons, though the size of the colony has shrunk in recent years as birds have relocated to other cays. The island is currently protected under the Bahamian Wild Birds Act.

Practicalities

Places to **stay** in Mars Bay are limited. *Bair Bahamas Guest House* in Little Creek (☎369-5060; ●) is a three-bedroom inn where you can take meals. The inn also has two boats and guides for bonefishing. The best place to eat in Mars Bay is the *Fisherman's Paradise*, a local Bahamian eatery, where basic meals of grouper and souse cost about $10.

Listings

Banks There is a Bank of the Bahamas (☎369-1787) in Kemps Bay.
Government offices Island Administrator, Kemps Bay ☎369-4569.
Groceries There are small shops in Congo Town, The Bluff and Kemps Bay.

Medical clinic Kemps Bay ☎369-4849/4620
Police and fire ☎919; The Bluff, South Andros ☎369-4733.

The Biminis and the Berry Islands

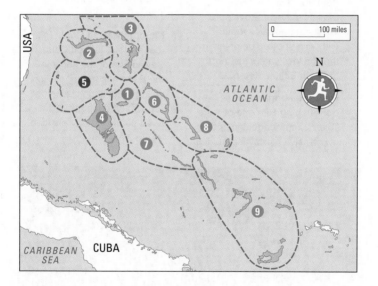

CHAPTER 5

Highlights

✳ **Hemingway's Haunts**. Papa Hemingway's bar stool at the *Compleat Angler Hotel* went up in smoke with the rest of that fabled establishment in 2006, but Alice Town is still steeped in the lore and memorabilia of its early glory years. See p.197

✳ **Swimming with wild dolphins** Join the folks at Bimini Undersea Adventure for an afternoon cavorting with wild spotted dolphins in the shallow waters just north of North Bimini. See p.201

✳ **Deep-sea angling and bonefishing** Hire one of Alice Town's knowledgeable and supremely entertaining guides and spend the day casting in the mangrove-lined shallows surrounding North Bimini or tracking monsters of the deep in the nearby Gulf Stream. See p.202

✳ **Sweet Bimini Bread** This deliciously original bread can be sampled at one of the delis or groceries along the Queen's Highway in Alice Town. See p.204

✳ **Mamma Rhoda Rock** This reef system, just off Chub Cay, is one of the finest in the Bahamas for snorkelling owing to its large size, close -proximity to land and sheltered southwesterly position. See p.210

△ Bimini bakery

The Biminis and the Berry Islands

racketing Andros like dual apostrophes, the **Biminis** and **Berry Islands** are tiny curving remnants of a huge paleo-island that once included all of the Great Bahama Bank, a vast U-shaped platform of limestone indented by the improbably deep Tongue of the Ocean sea-canyon.

Only fifty miles due east of Miami, the Biminis are the closest Bahamian cays to the United States – on a calm night it's possible to see the shimmering glow of Florida's biggest city. Composed of seventeen small, flat islands, the chain occupies a leeward position on the edge of the Great Bahama Bank, which helps explain why the entire eastern (or windward) shore of the two largest islands, **North** and **South Bimini**, are one long white-sand beach. Save perhaps during American college spring break, however, lazing about in the sand is not the main Biminis draw – it's the surrounding waters, and more specifically what's in them, that pulls in the lion's share of visitors. **Divers** and **snorkellers** are attracted to the clear, shallow waters, loaded with colourful reef fish, sunken wrecks and even a few mysterious structures claimed by some to

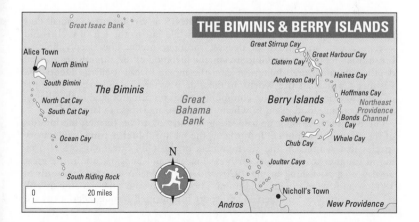

THE BIMINIS & BERRY ISLANDS

Great Isaac Bank

Alice Town
North Bimini
South Bimini
The Biminis
North Cat Cay
South Cat Cay

Ocean Cay

South Riding Rock

Great Bahama Bank

Great Stirrup Cay
Cistern Cay
Anderson Cay
Great Harbour Cay
Haines Cay
Hoffmans Cay
Berry Islands
Northeast
Providence
Sandy Cay
Bonds Channel
Cay
Chub Cay
Whale Cay

Joulter Cays

Nicholl's Town

Andros

New Providence

N

0   20 miles

The monk seal

An English traveller to the Bahamas in 1707 wrote "The Bahama Islands are filled with seals. Sometimes the fishers will catch a hundred in a night". The formerly abundant **monk seal** would cavort in masses of up to 500, passing its time basking in the sun, swimming and diving for food. Columbus had been the first European to describe monk seals, calling them *lobos del mar*, or sea wolves, and he calmly slaughtered eight of the harmless creatures off the coast of Hispaniola in 1494. Over the years, all of these beautiful seals were killed, the oil from their skins often sent off to Jamaica as lubrication for the sugar presses – a horrific situation in which a seal species went extinct in the service of human slavery. The last recorded sighting of a monk seal in Bahamian waters was in 1880, and today monk seals survive only in the Hawaiian Islands and in the Mediterranean Sea, though in very small numbers.

have come from the lost city of Atlantis. Just as alluring is the opportunity to reel in a record-breaking catch. A favourite casting place of Ernest Hemingway, both the **bonefishing** just off shore and the **deep-sea angling** in the nearby Gulf Stream are world-class, as evidenced by the mass of angling memorabilia hung in the hotels, restaurants and bars of North Bimini's **Alice Town**.

About 75 miles to the east, due north of Andros and less than forty miles northwest of Nassau, the Berry Islands consist of some fifty small cays and islands, some with rolling hills. Only two of these islands, **Great Harbour Cay** and **Chub Cay**, are inhabited, though, and are rarely visited, despite the exquisite white-sand beaches on most of the northern and eastern shores of each. Save for the South Islands (see Chapter 9), the Berry Islands are among the most difficult of all the Bahamian islands to reach – a fact that brings back the islands' few visitors time and time again.

The Biminis

One popular stylized print shows the **BIMINIS** as seventeen or so small dots against a huge blue background of ocean, while just to the left of each island sweeps a vast brushstroke of deepest turquoise-green. The deeply braided brushstroke represents the Gulf Stream, the lifeblood of the Biminis: its magical depths give these tiny dollops of sand the moxie to call itself the **Deep-Sea Fishing Capital of the World**. In these deep waters, much to the eternal joy of dedicated anglers, an entire community feeds on plankton and each other in a vast ascending food chain in which the largest predators are large indeed.

The Biminis have built up a sporting industry based on turning the hunters of the sea into the hunted. Top prize is the massive **bluefin tuna**, a migratory species that winters in the warm waters of the Gulf Stream before returning in summer to US waters off New England and Long Island. In the great heyday of sport fishing in the 1920s and 1930s, bluefin weighing upwards of 1800 pounds were caught off Bimini. Though large and small bluefin are still relatively common, commercial and sport fishing itself has markedly depleted the overall population, especially the intermediate sizes, those fish most likely to reproduce. Even larger than bluefins, the magnificent **blue marlin** and their relatives the **sailfish** both use their spear-like beaks to impale small fish and squid schooling in the open sea. Other notable Gulf Stream creatures include the **flying fish** – which evade predators by sailing through the air at speeds of up to 35mph – **wahoo**, **shark**, **barracuda** and floating schools of **Portuguese men-of-war**.

After fishing, **diving** is the most popular activity on the islands. Much of the diving here is done in shallow areas of reefs and cays, where an amazing abundance of reef fish are to be found, along with squadrons of reef sharks, lemon sharks, nurse sharks and barracuda. **Snorkelling**, often done among pods of wild spotted dolphins, is also popular.

On land, the main tourist centre in the island chain is **North Bimini**, a flat fishhook-shaped landmass whose slender spine runs nearly seven miles in length before curling back into a wider, marshier stretch dotted with mangrove swamps. Near its southern end sits **Alice Town**, easily the Biminis' largest settlement. Within shouting distance of the town, **South Bimini** is separated from its northern neighbour by a narrow 150-yard-wide ocean channel, and is home to few permanent residents, a tiny international airport amid palmetto-waste flats and a smattering of retirement homes. Busier **North Cat Cay** lies eight miles south of South Bimini. An exclusive resort for the rich and influential, North Cat Cay's other claim to fame occurs every spring in the shallow waters surrounding it, when upwards of 400,000 grouper gather to spawn. Bahamian fishermen follow, at which time a major catch comes about. The **other cays** in the chain are mainly all rocks fringed by sand – suitable to anchor nearby for a lazy day of uninhibited solitude, but not much else.

If it's solitude that you're after, avoid visiting in mid-March, when college students from across the US arrive to party hard during **spring break**. Late spring and summer are likewise busy, if calmer, due to the large number of fishing tournaments. At these times hotels are often jammed and reservations, if not made a year in advance, impossible to get. Winter, by contrast, is less crowded and more relaxed, though the weather is cool by Bahamian standards, and the water chilly. Temperatures in the water average 76 degrees, but can drop to 70 degrees in the winter when divers and snorkellers may be more comfortable in wet suits (rented by local outfitters).

Some history

During the Age of Discovery, the Biminis were of no particular importance to the Spaniards. **Juan Ponce de León** stumbled across the string of islands in 1513 before banging into Florida in his futile search for the Fountain of Youth (or gold, depending on how cynical you are), but never actually disembarked. Other nameless Spaniards stopped on the Biminis only long enough to enslave the native **Lucayans** living here, transporting them to the nascent gold and silver mines of Hispaniola and Cuba. Beyond these slave expeditions, the only notable visit during this period was made by **Sir Francis Drake**, who halted here in 1586 during one of his West Indian raiding sorties.

It didn't take long for Spanish slavers to strip the chain of Lucayans, and once they did the Biminis were basically forsaken. Since its lack of arable land and tiny freshwater supply created an extremely difficult life, for around two centuries the Biminis were visited only occasionally by wreckers and fishers. In 1835, however, a group of five families of freed slaves made the Biminis their home, a demonstration of both courage and desperation. Legend has it that before they could enter the narrow confines of the inner harbour of what is now **Alice**

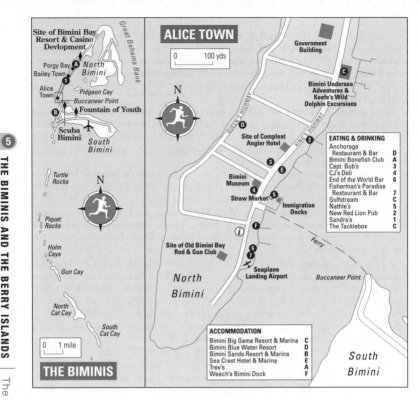

ALICE TOWN

Site of Bimini Bay
Resort & Casino
Devlopment

Great Bahama Bank

Porgy Bay
Bailey Town

North
Bimini

Alice
Town

Pidgeon Cay
Buccaneer Point
Fountain of Youth

Scuba
Bimini

South
Bimini

Turtle
Rocks

Piquet
Rocks

Holm
Cays

Gun Cay

North
Cat Cay

South
Cat Cay

0   1 mile

THE BIMINIS

Government
Building

Bimini Undersea
Adventures &
Keefe's Wild
Dolphin Excursions

0   100 yds

N

QUEEN'S HIGHWAY

KING'S HIGHWAY

Site of Compleat
Angler Hotel

Bimini
Museum

Straw Market

Immigration
Docks

Ferry

Site of Old Bimini Bay
Rod & Gun Club

North
Bimini

Seaplane
Landing Airport

Buccaneer Point

South
Bimini

EATING & DRINKING	
Anchorage	
Restaurant & Bar	D
Bimini Bonefish Club	A
Capt. Bob's	3
CJ's Deli	4
End of the World Bar	6
Fisherman's Paradise	
Restaurant & Bar	7
Gulfstream	C
Nathle's	5
New Red Lion Pub	2
Sandra's	1
The Tacklebox	C

ACCOMMODATION	
Bimini Big Game Resort & Marina	C
Bimini Blue Water Resort	D
Bimini Sands Resort & Marina	B
Sea Crest Hotel & Marina	E
Trev's	A
Weech's Bimini Dock	F

Town, they had to clear a gauntlet of damaged pirate refuse including cannon, ships' ballast stones, hulls and the like. Four of the salvaged cannon can today be seen on North Bimini, two on the grounds of the *Blue Water Resort* and two in front of *Blue Marlin Cottage*. The primary occupation of the original families was wrecking, though later sponging and fishing joined the list of acceptable ways of making a living.

Life on the Biminis hummed along at this low-key pace until the advent of American **Prohibition** at the beginning of the 1920s, an era that ushered in a boom of smuggling activities, enriching certain businessmen and turning Alice Town into a capital of illegal enterprise. In fact, Alice Town was the main southern jumping-off port – passing through Montréal was the main northern route – for illegal liquor shipments, which headed into the Florida Everglades. The Biminis' fame as a smuggler's den came to an end with the start of the Depression in 1932. It was this crisis that created the opportunity for a Bahamian named **Neville–Norton** to create the sport-fishing industry almost single-handedly. In the mid-1930s, Norton bought a Prohibition-era bar that had fallen on hard times with the repeal of the Volstead Act in 1933, transforming it into the now famous *Bimini Big Game Fishing Club*. Soon, the rich and famous were frequenting the islands, including Martin Luther King Jr and Adam Clayton Powell Jr, a charismatic US Congressman from Harlem, who made the *End of the World Bar* in Alice Town a haunt on his periodic visits to

Old man and the sea

In many ways, the Biminis' truest subtext is that of the legend of **Ernest "Papa" Hemingway**, the great novelist who was also one of America's largest braggarts and he-men. In the mid-1930s, the by now famous Hemingway was living life as the kept man of his second wife, Pauline, on Key West. Already having spent much time fishing in the Gulf Stream, he was well on his way towards building his reputation as a master sport fisherman and pursuer of blue marlin. Alice Town and its frontier spirit provided a perfect refuge for the heavy-drinking Hemingway, who would leave his wife and children at home for months at a time while he drank, wrote and fished his way around the Gulf Stream.

Stories abound, yet it is true that Hemingway stayed at the *Compleat Angler Hotel*, lived in the *Blue Marlin Cottage* and wrote bits of *To Have and Have Not* – a small, not particularly good novel about a tough-guy smuggler battling the odds – on Bimini. Hemingway also used Bimini as background for another of his lesser novels, *Islands in the Stream*, and he did manage a couple of fistfights on the docks while drunk. "Papa" caught some large marlin and posed for hundreds of photographs, many of which were on display in the bar of the *Compleat Angler* until the legendary hotel burnt to the ground in 2006. An interesting selection of rare fishing films featuring Hemingway and photographs from Bimini's glamorous sport-fishing past can be seen at the Bimini Museum (see p.200). With a reputation that is larger than life, Hemingway sticks to Alice Town like an overdose of perfume on Ethel Merman.

the mistress he kept on the island. The most lasting impression left by a famous visitor, though, is that of **Ernest Hemingway**. In 1957, an airport was built on South Bimini, opening the door for the tourist infrastructure that exists today.

North Bimini

Surprisingly enough, tiny **NORTH BIMINI** is, after New Providence, the most densely settled Bahamian island, its 1700 permanent residents crammed onto a narrow strip of land on the southern tip barely wide enough for two city blocks. For years, almost nothing has changed about North Bimini simply because there is little room for growth and because most of the native coppice has been long since chopped down. Things now, however, are bound to transform with the recent opening of the large *Bimini Bay Resort* condominium development and ongoing construction on its planned casino, hotel, marina and golf course. For now, sleepy **Alice Town** to the south is the hub of low-intensity activity and the island makes its living as a **fishing** and **diving** destination with a considerable – and deserved – reputation.

Arrival and orientation

Most visitors to the Biminis arrive at South Biminis' **airport**, where a well-coordinated combo of passengers' vans and water taxis will convey you the couple of miles to Alice Town ($5 one way) or to the resorts on South Bimini. *Western Air* has two flights a day to Bimini from Nassau (☎347-4100 in Bimini, ☎377-2222 in Nassau, ⊛www.westernairbahamas.com; $60 one way). *Bimini Island Air* (☎954/938-8991, ⊛www.flybia.com) offers regular charter service from Ft. Lauderdale, as does *Yellow Air Taxi* (☎954/359-0292 or 1-888/935-5694, ⊛www.flyyellowairtaxi.com).

The **mailboat** *Bimini Mack* (☎393-1064) serves Alice Town, Cat Cay and Chub Cay in the Berry Islands from Potter's Cay in Nassau ($50 one way). Be warned that the ride from Nassau takes a minimum of twelve hours – and often longer. It generally leaves Nassau Thursday at 2am, making the return trip on Sunday, but sails to a varying schedule, so call for an update, and be sure to bring along food and water.

The official port of entry to the Biminis by **private boat** is Alice Town, where yachts must pass customs and immigration. There are several **marinas** from which to choose here, the largest and best equipped being the *Bimini Big Game Resort and Marina* (☎347-3391 or 1-800/737-1007, ⓦwww .biminibiggame.com; VHF Ch 16). The marina has 74 slips and can handle yachts up to 120ft at $2.50 a foot plus electricity. Other marinas nearby include *Bimini Blue Water Resort* (☎347-3166; VHF Ch 16), which has 32 slips for 75¢ a foot plus $10+ a day for electricity, and the smaller *Weech's Bimini Dock* (☎347-3028, ⓦwww.weechsbiminidock.com; VHF Ch 18) has twenty slips at 60¢ a foot plus $7.50 for electrical hook-up.

Tourist Information (Mon–Fri 9am–5pm; ☎347-4110) is available at Alice Town's government tourist office located on the second floor above Burns House Ltd., just up from the water taxi dock. The only **bank** is a branch of the Royal Bank of Canada (Mon–Thurs 9.30am–3pm, Fri 9.30am–4.30pm; no ATM), located in the centre of Alice Town at the King's Highway and Parliament Street. The **post office** (Mon–Fri 9am–5.30pm) is in the pink Government Building on the north edge of town.

Getting around

Getting around North Bimini is simple in that you can dash across the width of the island in two minutes and walk nearly everywhere else. The King's Highway runs along the eastern shore for about three miles, dead-ending at the grand arch marking the entrance to the new *Bimini Bay Resort and Casino* enveloping the northern tip of the island.

There are no rental car agencies on the island, but you don't need one. **Golf carts** are available ($40–60 per day) from a number of vendors in Alice Town, including Capt Pat's Golf Cart Rental (☎347-3477) and nearby Bank and Dolphin Golf Cart Rentals (☎347-3407 or cell 464-5704). Sturdy single gear **bicycles** can be rented for $10/$15 a half-day/day at Bimini Undersea Adventure (☎347-3089), located at the *Bimini Big Game Resort*.

Two **water taxi** services (T.S.L. and P.H.K.) ply the few hundred yards separating North and South Bimini all day and you should never have more than a twenty-minute wait at either end ($5 including ground transport to the airport). The same firms run the bus service to the airport on South Bimini.

Accommodation

There are less than 100 **hotel** rooms on North Bimini, with few budget or self-catering options to choose from, and during the busiest periods – particularly spring, summer and around Christmas and New Year – it's likely you'll have a hard time finding a room, regardless of price. Things have become even tighter since the legendary *Compleat Angler Hotel* burned to the ground in early 2006, though the cotton candy-coloured condos stacking up at the construction site of the new *Bimini Bay Resort and Casino* (ⓦwww.biminibayresort.com) should ease the shortage even as the landscape changes. Some are now available for rent through their private owners; see p.31 for agencies and websites handling listings of vacation rentals in the Bahamas.

Bimini Big Game Resort and Marina
King's Highway, Alice Town ☎ 347-3391 or 1-800/737-1007, ⓦ www.biminibiggame.com. This rambling hotel is a locus of activity in town and perhaps the finest accommodation on the cay for those planning a trip around deep-sea fishing and diving. The excellent marina gives quick access to the sea, and the majority of guests are here doing one or the other, giving the place a sporty vibe. The rooms have a clean, stylish decor and either bay or garden views. There are forty-odd doubles and suites in the main lodge and twelve one-bedroom cottages nestled among the coconut palms. Amenities include a/c, TV, an assortment of lively bars and restaurants, tennis courts, a swimming pool and lots of watersports options. Doubles ❻, studio cottages ❼

Bimini Blue Water Resort King's Highway, Alice Town ☎ 347-3166 or 1-800/688-4752, ⓕ 347-3293. Straddling the island with buildings on both shores, the *Blue Water* is frequented mainly by anglers. Past guests include Hemingway and Mike Lerner, one of the Biminis' most famous fishermen (see p.200). Lerner's old home, now named the *Anchorage*, holds a dozen plainly decorated, but still comfortable rooms with balconies. Rooms in the newer extension are more like motel rooms and less desirable. The *Marlin Cottage*, a three-bedroom/three bath house where Hemingway bunked and described in his novel *Islands in the Stream* is also available for rent (❽). The on-site restaurant is excellent, as is the friendly bar. ❸

Katt's Cottage Queen's Highway, Alice Town ☎ 347-3131, ⓔ artsmart@batelnet.bs, ⓦ www .A1vacations.com. Tastefully done up in a soothing palette of green, white and grey, this cute one

bedroom cottage is a self-catering option in the centre of town. It sits a few steps from the beach and sleeps four at a pinch. $625 per week.

M&J Townhouses Alice Town ☎ 347-3184/3451, ⓕ 347-3488. Four two-bedroom split level units in the centre of town, each with three double beds, kitchenette and a small shaded courtyard equipped with a barbeque grill. ❻

Sea Crest Hotel and Marina King's Highway, Alice Town ☎ 347-3071, ⓦ www.seacrestbimini .com. Each room in this pale-yellow three-storey hotel features cable TV, a/c and a balcony with good views, especially in the high-ceilinged rooms on the third floor. Two and three-bedroom suites with kitchenettes also available. The digs are a bit austere – whitewashed walls, stone floors and a few sticks of furniture – but attractive nonetheless. No hotel restaurant or bar on-site, but several options nearby. Inland doubles ❸; dockside ❹; two-bedroom suites ❼; three-bedroom suites ❾

Trev's Inn Porgy Bay, North Bimini ☎ 347-2452, ⓦ www.trevinn.com. No frills, but a decent place to lay your head at night at the lower end of the price range. The half-dozen double rooms have bathrooms, a/c, cable TV and a kitchen shared by guests. Situated roadside about a mile north of Alice Town. ❷

Weech's Bimini Dock King's Highway, Alice Town ☎ 347-3028, ⓦ www.weechsbiminidock.com. The four walk-up rooms at *Weech's Bimini Dock* are big and clean, with a/c and a great view of the sunrise over the bay. Not a resort, but a welcome refuge for those looking for a soft bed and a hot shower on dry land, within a couple of minutes walk of all village amenities. ❹

Alice Town

Essentially two blocks wide, **ALICE TOWN** condenses the Bahamian experience – sun, fishing, food and music – into a diminutive yet dynamic area. The town's main drag, the narrow King's Highway, is home to most of the action, lined with hotels, bars and shops. Running parallel to the King's Highway two blocks to the west is the Queen's Highway, less a highway than a quiet, narrow street fronting a tranquil beach.

The settlement is steeped in its romantic history of big game sport-fishing and the wealthy Americans who played here in its glory days of the 1920–40s, as evidenced by the fishing nets and historical photographs of legendary catches and colourful characters found in most local watering holes. To get the full experience, start your wanderings at the charred wooden arch marking the entrance to the former site of Alice Town's most famous building, the **Compleat Angler Hotel,** right at the heart of the King's Highway. Built in the 1930s, the hotel was a frequent haunt of Hemingway but it unfortunately burnt down in January 2006, resulting in one death and the loss of a large collection of Hemingway memorabilia.

△ Alice Town Straw Market

A short walk from here is the **Bimini Museum** (open daily but unmanned; $2 donation), where visitors can wander in and gaze at the photos of most of the big-game sport fishermen who made Bimini famous, and some of their stuffed catch. There are some rare films of Hemingway himself cavorting on the docks and streets of Alice Town in the 1930s and an eclectic collection of photographs and other artifacts illustrating Bimini history, including President Nixon's golf tees from one of his several visits to the island, sponging gear and Martin Luther King's embarkation card from a visit in the 1960s. The museum also contains the Bimini Fishing Hall of Fame whose inductees include Skip Farrington, who recorded the first blue marlin catch off Bimini back in 1933, alongside other local angling legends like Mike Lerner and Neville Stuart, and guides Eric Sawyer, Manny Rolle, Bob Smith and Sammy Ellis.

At the far southern end of Alice Town are the remains of the old **Bimini Bay Rod and Gun Club**, a hundred room colonial-style hotel built in 1921 and blown into the sea by the 1926 hurricane that looms large in Bimini folklore. There isn't much left to look at, but the stone ruins and grand drive have a certain cachet considering this was a jazz-era hot spot. Also worth a look is Alice Town's small **straw market** across from the museum. There are a few stalls selling a mixture of handmade crafts and cheap imports, but the best buy is the fine home-baking; try Nathle's coconut rolls or a loaf of sweet bimini bread.

North of Alice Town

Towards Alice Town's north end, the King's and Queen's highways merge to run along the eastern waterfront through **Bailey Town** and **Porgy Bay.** In these two small villages live the majority of North Bimini's year-round residents, and though there are no real sights here, there are a few local restaurants and takeaways along the road. The highway follows the eastern shore, but cutting

The road to Atlantis?

Located not far off Paradise Point, opposite the *Bimini Bay Resort*, is the **Bimini Road**. The "road" consists of rows of limestone blocks constructed in a U shape some 20ft below the water's surface, standing on square pillars that allow the tide to flow underneath. Aerial surveys show that just a few hundred feet southwest of the site a level limestone bench has been "cleared" as well. Although New Agers enjoy claiming the "road" was built by the lost civilization of **Atlantis**, extensive surveys of the site have concluded that there is a link between the stonecutting techniques and those of the Mayan and Incan empires of Central and South America. This connection has led to speculation that the "road" was actually a dry-dock onto which ships were hauled for caulking and refitting.

Just north of Bimini, the **Moselle Shoal** presents another supposedly mysterious site for divers to investigate. The shoals are the site of underwater blocks of granite, which some theorists insist are the remnants of a lost civilization, perhaps again that of Atlantis. One explorer-author, Richard Wingate, has written *The Lost Outpost of Atlantis*, in which he describes evidence of human engineering in the blocks, like drill holes. Some less sanguine theorists have concluded that the granite blocks are ballast from galleons.

across island on side roads to the west shore lands you on secluded **Spook Hill Beach**, good for a picnic and a swim. Another two miles on the King's Highway, the road turns to dirt and runs north to **Paradise Point** where the sparkling white beach is excellent for picnicking and snorkelling. Offshore to the west lies the enigmatic Bimini Road (see box above). To the east, the **lagoon** formed by the hook of land at the top of the island is filled with mangrove shallows and swamps, the favourite haunts of bonefish, and the place where guides will lead fishermen for the elusive trophy fish. An incongruously elaborate arch and guardhouse marks the entrance to the site of the *Bimini Bay Resort and Casino*, still under construction. Check in at the guardhouse before proceeding to explore the property, where luxury condominiums are sprouting on patches of Bermuda grass, with a casino, hotel, marina, golf course and restaurants planned all for the future.

Diving and watersports

Easily the most popular outdoor activity on the Biminis is **fishing**, for which it is world-renowned; we've covered all the angling opportunities in detail on the box on p.202. **Diving** and **snorkelling**, though, are also justly popular reasons for visiting. Besides the slightly contrived trips out to the Bimini Road and Moselle Shoal (see box, above), much of the diving here is done in shallow waters, around the reefs and cays found in abundance just offshore. On almost every trip into the water, swirling schools of reef fish and a wide variety of coral formations can be spotted, along with nurse sharks and barracuda. There's also an array of wreck dives, including the *Sapona*, an old rum-running vessel that sank during the huge 1926 hurricane – it now provides a hulk visible from the surface (making it popular with snorkellers too), almost totally covered by coral, harbouring juvenile jacks. Biminis multi-purpose water sports operator is Alice Town's Bimini Undersea Adventure (☏347-3089 or 1-800/348-4644, ⓦwww .biminiundersea.com) run by Bill and Knowdla Keefe. The **dive shop** caters to everyone from dive masters to those looking to get PADI-certified. Their most intriguing trip is a deep-wall dive off the Gulf Stream that the staff claim is straight out of the movie *The Abyss*.

Fishing in the Biminis

There's a reason the Biminis are considered by many to be one of the world's top **sport-fishing destinations**. For starters, the mangrove flats on the eastern part of North Bimini are incredibly productive bonefishing areas. And, more often than not, anglers seeking tuna, wahoo, sailfish and marlin out in the deep Gulf Stream come back home with at least a decent-sized fish. And lest you think that Bimini fishing is more hype than fact, consider that more than fifty **world records** have been established by catches in the surrounding waters, including those in the categories of marlin, sailfish, bonito, wahoo, mackerel, tuna, barracuda, shark and grouper. The largest marlin caught was a 1060-pound specimen landed in 1979, and a massive 16-pound bonefish catch has been documented.

Because of the intense fishing pressure and overcrowded hotels during fishing **tournaments**, it's probably best to organize your fishing expedition around them. There are nearly a dozen big tournaments every year. The biggest of the bunch are the Annual Bacardi Billfish Tournament in March hosted by the Bimini Big Game Fishing Club, the Annual Midwinter Wahoo Tournament in February, the Bimini Open Angling Tournament in September, and the Bimini Festival of Champions in May. Anglers who do not have their own **gear** can rent it at several tackle shops or hotels, and every guide can provide tackle and gear for the cost of a day's charter.

Deep-sea fishing

Numerous charter boats are available for those who want to go out in the Gulf Stream and after the big pelagic specimens, sailfish, marlin, large wahoo and dolphinfish. We've listed some of the best guides below. The cost to charter with individual guides varies with the kind of expedition being mounted and the number of people tagging along, but count on paying at least $400/500 half/full day for the cost of boat, guide, gear and snacks. Sometimes, drinks are extra, but bait is always included. On full-day trips, guides usually provide a lunch of sandwiches. A tip is customary – generally around ten percent of cost.

In addition to the guides listed below (who have their own rigged-out boats and gear), the major **marinas** all charter vessels with a captain and mate with gear included. Bimini Big Game Fishing Club, Bimini Blue Water Marina, and Weech's Bimini Dock, will charter your trip for around $400–550 half-day, $750–900 full day. Weech's also rents some smaller Boston Whalers for around $135 a day/$75 half-

Bimini Undersea's **snorkelling trips** visit many of the same reefs the divers do ($30 for a 2–4hr trip). Even more exciting are the **wild spotted dolphin encounters** offered several times a week ($120/$80 adult/child). It takes about an hour to reach the dolphin grounds, and if the pod is encountered snorkellers then get to swim and play side by side with the curious creatures. Encounters with the wild pod are common, though not guaranteed, so if the thought of spending up to five hours circling about the ocean without any luck is overly vexatious, don't sign up. Dolphin-lovers can do a six-day wild dolphin adventure program that includes five daily excursions, a sunset cruise and five nights bed and breakfast accommodation at the *Bimini Big Game Resort* ($1065 per person double occupancy, $1370 single occupancy, plus taxes; reservations required).

Another outdoor option is skimming along in a **sea kayak**. *Bimini Undersea* offers day trips exploring the mangrove creeks and grassy flats of North Bimini ranging from one hour instructional sessions to full-day island tours ($50/$90 half/full-day trips). They also rent kayaks for $15/$25/$45 an hour/half-day/full-day.

day. On South Bimini the Bimini Sands Marina (☎347-3028, ⊛www.bimini.com) is a 35-slip marina where you can rent a 15ft whaler for $140 per day.

Frank Hinzey ☎347-3072
Bob Smith ☎347-2367
Edward Blinky Stuart ☎347-2328
Jerome Stuart ☎347-2081, ⊛www.biminifishing.com
Tony Stuart ☎347-2656

Bonefishing

While deep-sea fishing is a great draw because of its dramatic essence, **bonefishing** remains popular on North Bimini, and the island boasts a number of the Bahamas' best-known, most informative fishing guides. Known by their first names, these guides are available for angling throughout what are known as the "flats", and in general rates are about $250/400 half/full day, though there are some less experienced guides around who may charge less. Keep in mind that you'll need to bring tackle and that you should always negotiate a complete price before setting off, knowing in advance who is responsible for fuel, food, ice, beer and bait. Most skiffs hold two anglers and a guide, and part of the fun of going out with these guides is their patter, a stream of fishing information, lore and tall tale that is infectious. There are swarms of mosquitoes in eastern Bimini, so take plenty of repellant and wear long sleeves if necessary.

Ansil Saunders ☎347-2178 or cell 464-5113
Bonefish Ebbie ☎347-2053
Bonefish Ray ☎347-2269
Bonefish Rudy ☎347-2266
Bonefish Tommy ☎347-3234
Freddie Rolle ☎347-2248 or cell 464-5821.

Reef and bottom fishing

While bonefishing and deep-sea **fishing** are the "meat and potatoes" of Bimini lore, reef and bottom fishing on Bimini are just as productive and far less expensive. Fishing with bait for amberjack, grouper and snapper is a cheaper thrill than the big-time Gulf Stream experience, and you can hire a little 15ft whaler and a local guide, and have some fun for about $200, plus fuel and lunch. If lucky enough to catch some fish, you can take them back to your hotel and ask the cook to grill the fillets.

Eating

All of the major hotels, save for *Sea Crest*, have worthwhile **restaurants**, most featuring basic Bahamian fare, seafood and American specialties, though a few have slightly more eclectic European entrees. Those looking for a faster, cheaper meal have several options, with **takeaway** joints located throughout Alice Town, Bailey Town and Porgy Bay, including a classic *Burger Queen*, where you can get a "Little Whopper" without fear of violating trademark laws. If heading out for a dive or snorkel, note that most of the restaurants below will gladly put together a **packed lunch** at a reasonable rate.

Anchorage Dining Room *Bimini Blue Water Resort*, King's Highway, Alice Town ☎347-3122. Elegant panelled dining overlooking the entire harbour. Unpretentious main courses include conch, fried chicken, New York sirloin steak and a good spiny broiled lobster. It's good value (lunch is about $5–10; dinner $12–25) and a nice experience eating on the "hill". If you arrive early, enjoy a cocktail at the bar.

Bimini Bonefish Club Waterfront Bar King's Highway, Porgy Bay ☎347-2053 or 347-2283. A casual, seaside grill where the speciality of the house is garlic lobster with peas and rice, garden salad and fried plantain. Open for dinner and drinks.

🏃 **Captain Bob's** opposite the *Sea Crest Hotel*, King's Highway ☎347-3260. At times it can seem as if the entire cay has come here for the renowned early-bird breakfasts, including a delightful fish omelette and superb French toast made from sweet Bimini bread. Lunch is worth-while as well, featuring ribs, burgers and fresh fish. Try the deep-fried lobster if you dare. Open for breakfast (6.30am) and lunch only until 2pm. Closed Tues.

CJ's Deli Alice Town. A cubby-hole diner off the docks where you can plop on an orange stool at the bar and savour what's alleged to be the best conch salad on the island, along with a decent sausage and egg breakfast. Breakfast under $5, lunch for under $10. Mon–Sat 7am–10pm, Sun 7am–2pm.

Fisherman's Paradise Alice Town ☎347-3082. Simple restaurant located next to the old seaplane dock, which serves local-style soups and wonderful sandwiches without frills. It becomes a dance club on weekends, with live music from 7pm. Mon–Sat 7–11am, noon–3pm & 6–11pm; closed Sun.

The Gulfstream *Bimini Big Game Resort*, King's Highway, Alice Town ☎347-3391. The most expensive place in town to eat (entrees $25–30), and arguably the best, *The Gulfstream* is housed in a curved room that overlooks the hotel swimming pool, with bright murals decorating the walls. Freshly caught kingfish is a speciality, but there are a number of other good seafood dishes available, including a fine Bahamian gumbo, along with prime rib and lamb chops for those who've had their fill on fish. They will also cook your catch if you get it to them two hours before dinner. Open Wed–Sun 7pm–11pm; reservations recommended.

New Red Lion Pub King's Highway, Alice Town ☎347-3259. This dinner-only pub has a terrific ambience and equally good food. The stuffed Shrimp Delight is a must-try (large shrimp stuffed with conch and fish), but the barbecue ribs are wonderful too, cooked on a brick grill in the back. Tues–Sun 6–10.30pm; bar open 5pm–1am.

Sandra's Restaurant and Bar King's Highway, Bailey Town ☎347-2336. Located north of Alice Town, *Sandra's* is good for no-nonsense Bahamian meals and snacks, including fried grouper, snap-per and conch, peas and rice, corn on the cob, macaroni and cheese and simple desserts (mains $6–20). Open daily for lunch and dinner.

🏃 **The Tacklebox** *Bimini Big Game Resort*, Alice Town ☎737-1007. A breezy, timbered bar and grill upstairs overlooking the marina and festooned with fishing memorabilia. It serves a menu of American-style fried breakfasts ($3–7), sandwiches and deep-fried snacks ($6–10). Daily 7am–11pm. Live music Thurs–Sat 9pm–midnight.

Drinking and nightlife

Nightlife and **drinking** constitute a large part of the lifeblood of the Biminis, and sooner or later everybody passes everybody else doing the rounds of bars and barebones dance clubs up and down the King's Highway. The hotel bars at *Bimini Big Game Resort* and the *Bimini Blue Water Resort* are top gathering spots at day's end. The most notorious nightspot is the *End of the World Bar* near the Seaplane Landing (open until 3am; ☎347-2094), with its sand-covered floors, underwear-hung rafters and boisterous clientele. A combination bar and tourist sight, the *End of the World* comes most alive after midnight. If looking for a quieter drink, head to Alice Town's "mid-town" area and look out for the *Island House Bar* (11am–3am; ☎347-2439) across from the *New Red Lion Pub*, and *Bimini Breeze*, just down the street. **Bailey Town** sports a few hangouts popular with locals, including *Specialty Paris* near the Anglican church, which often has local rake 'n' scrape music. You can **dance** late on weekends at *Fisherman's Paradise* (see "Eating").

Shopping

The few **shops** on North Bimini are all clustered along the King's Highway in Alice Town. The best place to find authentic **folk art and crafts** is the **straw market**, located under the arch with the official welcome sign to Bimini in the middle of Alice Town, but beware that a lot of the goods are imported trinkets and t-shirts. Nevertheless, it's a fun place to hang out. One of the real buys in Bimini is **fresh bread**, which is justly famous.

South Bimini

SOUTH BIMINI lies within shouting distance or a five-minute water taxi from Alice Town. It is mainly blanketed in dense forest, with the diminutive Bimini International Airport and runway cut out of the bush in its midsection. The sights here are few – a sink hole in the woods that is a rather suspect contender for Ponce de Leon's Fountain of Youth along with a long stretch of beach. However, if sea and sand is all you're after, the island's only resort, *Bimini Sands*, has enough beach toys and cool drinks to fuel a holiday.

If arriving from Alice Town via the public water taxi, you'll be deposited at the ferry dock at **Buccaneer Point**, from which a road leads south down the western, more developed edge of the island. The road ultimately leads to **Port Royal**, a fancy name for a vacation community of homes owned mostly by wealthy Americans who jet or boat over for long weekend excursions. Running beside the road is the fine, white-sand **Tiki Hut Beach**; if looking for shade, head for the southern end where there's a tiny thatched hut.

Back at the water taxi dock, a second road heads east to the international airport two miles away, and, amazingly, runs through some of the best-preserved **native coppice** in all the Bahamas. About midway between the airport and the water-taxi dock is a "must see" (or at least that's what the sign on the road proclaims) – the **Fountain of Youth**. As the only sight on the island, it's pretty pathetic, a shallow mud hole with a couple of benches in the shade.

Activities

The majority of South Bimini visitors are here to **dive** or **fish**. You'll want to bring water toys along as the **snorkelling** opportunities off the west coast are very good. Near Buccaneer Point, the clear water is best at high tide, when huge numbers of fish, along with eel and octopus, congregate in the shallows. Further south, around the thatched hut, the water is about 15ft deep and crystal clear; expect to see dozens of different reef fish, along with spotted eagle rays and a few barracuda. Even further south is **Corner Reef**, whose flats are easy to snorkel, and often reveal rays, crabs, octopus and eels, along with starfish and echinoderms. The island is also surrounded by mangrove swamp, some of which can be explored by **kayak**, available for rent at the *Bimini Sands Resort* ($25/$35 single/double). Alternatively, rent one of their 18ft Boston Whaler boats to explore the coastline and nearby cays ($120 a day).

Practicalities

For information on **flights** to South Bimini, see "Arrival" in North Bimini. Shuttle vans wait for arriving flights and deliver guests to the *Bimini Sands Resort* or the water taxi to North Bimini for $5. The resort rents golf carts and bikes for about $70 and $15 a day respectively. Otherwise, you will have to hoof it; the island is roughly four miles long and a mile wide. **Boats** can dock at the *Bimini Sands*'s marina ($33 a day up to 30ft, plus $10 electricity; $1.10 each additional foot) where there is a store, laundry, customs and immigration and a bar and restaurant.

By the marina is the tiny island's sole **accommodation and dining** option, and it's on the expensive side. Sitting at the north end of Tiki Hut Beach, the *Bimini Sands Resort and Marina* (T 357-3500, W www.biminisands.com; ❾) rents one and two bedroom condo units facing either the marina or the ocean by the night or week. There is an attractive pool patio and bar, the *Petite Conch Restaurant* serving meals throughout the day, tennis courts, water sports gear for rent and a gorgeous beach on the doorstep. There is a water-taxi service to North Bimini for guests ($5). For self-catering, you can stock up on groceries at *Morgan's Grocery Store* and *Morgan's Liquor Store* near the water taxi dock at the north end of the island. The resort certainly is a bit isolated, catering mainly to boaters, but it has a little bit of all of the Bahamas' best holiday features – diving, fishing, a brilliant white sand beach and frozen cocktails.

Gun Cay and North Cat Cay

Some nine miles south of Bimini Harbour, which curves under South Bimini, is the uninhabited **GUN CAY**, an isolated rocklet known for its excellent fishing, and much visited by boaters. Gun Cay has no facilities, but there is an exquisite stretch of curved sand known as **Honeymooon Bay**. Yachters in the know often anchor off the bay to enjoy its isolation and excellent snorkelling. Those without their own vessels can get here by chartering a boat in Alice Town or visiting with fishing guide.

A mile southeast of Gun Cay is larger **NORTH CAT CAY**, a privately owned island purchased in 1931 by the late Louis Wasey as a secluded getaway for himself and his rich friends. Over the years, the club that they formed became the haunt of industrialists, politicians and Hollywood stars, and the cay basically remains the preserve of the **Cat Cay Yacht Club** (T 347-3565, W www.catcayclub.com). Only members and their guests can stay at the six-room hotel or at one of the more than seventy private villas perched on lush lots on the western and northeastern rims of the island, all surrounded by palms, hibiscus and bougainvillea. About the only way to visit North Cat Cay without being a guest of the club is to tie up at the Yacht Club's marina (T 347-3565, VHF Ch 16), a 108-slip facility that's home to the *Nauticat Restaurant* and *Bu's Bar*. The marina slips have cable TV hookups, water and electricity, and there's also a small grocery and liquor store (closed Sun) and a health clinic (daily 9-10am); dockage is $2.50 per foot per day ($4.50 on major holidays) and there is a two-day maximum stay. The marina is also a **port of entry** (daily 9–5pm). For what it's worth, the Nassau mailboat *Bimini Mack* does call at North Cat Cay on its way to Alice Town, so if you want a quick peak, you can get it by taking the mailboat from Nassau to North Bimini (see p.198 for details).

The Berry Islands

Wholly characteristic of the raised edges of the Great Bahama Bank, the fifty or so mostly uninhabited cays of the **BERRY ISLANDS** form a J-shaped archipelago stretching some 32 miles from north to south. Directly to the south of the Berry chain is the deep Tongue of the Ocean, while all of the territory west is part of the shallow Great Bahama Bank.

The Berrys share several characteristics with the Biminis, including secluded **beaches**, amazing **angling opportunities** and spectacular reefs tailor-made for **snorkelling** and **diving**. Still, the Berrys are less intensely developed and receive fewer tourists, probably because they are a bit harder to reach; indeed, though the southernmost point in the chain is located only 35 miles northeast of Nassau, the cays remain surprisingly isolated, populated primarily by vacationing millionaires.

Over half of the 800 or so permanent residents on the Berry Islands live on the largest island, **Great Harbour Cay**. Located at the northern end of the chain, it's only around ten miles long and no more than one mile wide, deeply indented by a number of salty inlets and lakes. Often referred to simply as "the settlement", the Berrys' largest town, **Bullock's Harbour**, sits on a self-contained cay off the leeward northern edge of Great Harbour Cay. Across the causeway joining Bullock's Harbour to Great Harbour Cay is the island's only accommodation, **Tropical Diversions Resort**. Nearly the entire eastern edge of Great Harbour Cay

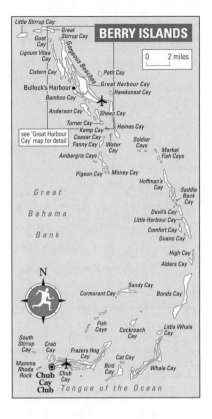

is one long sand beach – a practically deserted paradise for sunbathers and snorkellers – and the even quieter western shores of the cay are prime bonefishing territory.

The only other island that can boast anything near a steady trickle of visitors is swampy **Chub Cay**, dangling off the southern edge of the chain. On it sits the Berrys' only other tourist resort, **Chub Cay Club and Marina**, a semi-private resort that boasts the islands' best fishing possibilities. Several of the remaining cays are privately owned, including two small bumps north of Great Harbour known as the **Stirrup Cays** (Great and Little) – the private province of customers of the Norwegian and Royal Caribbean cruise lines. The rest are home to birds and not much else, and though the idea of sailing out to anchor by one may sound compelling, it's quite unnecessary – even on the Berrys' "populated" cays, solitude is easy to find.

Great Harbour Cay

GREAT HARBOUR CAY guards the northern end of the Berrys chain and is home to around 500 Berry islanders, most of whom live in the sole major settlement of **Bullock's Harbour**, located on its own island separated from

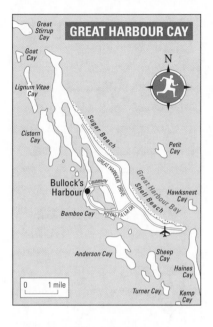

the rest of Great Harbour Cay by a thin causeway. The village is a rundown sort of place, sporting a couple of grocery stores and some small Bahamian restaurants, along with plenty of wandering chickens, bantam roosters and peacocks. Across the causeway to the south is the **Tropical Diversions Resort and the Great Harbour Cay Marina**, formerly the *Great Harbour Cay Yacht Club* and whose past guests include Brigitte Bardot and Cary Grant. Folks flock here today not for the star power but for the opportunity to land a load of fish and to play golf on the small attached nine-hole course.

Beyond here lies the best part of Great Harbour Cay, the **east shore**, made up of eight miles of nearly uninterrupted white beach. A long paved highway runs close to the entire length of the magnificently sandy shore, making searching around for that perfect spot simple indeed. To the north lies **Sugar Beach** and in the south, **Great Harbour Bay** holds two grand scallops of sand, all ideal for a day of sun-worshipping and splashing about.

Due to limited accommodation and infrequent flights, the majority of visitors to the Berrys arrive aboard their own boats. Bullock's Harbour Cay and the causeway joining it to Great Harbour Cay form the northern arm of a protected harbour known locally as the **Bay of Five Pirates**. The bay and the Great Harbour Cay Marina nestled in its sheltered inner reaches are accessed from the sea by a slender cut in the cliffs, making it one of the prettiest harbours in the Bahamas. The bay seems to change colour as the day progresses, from light blue to tranquil aquamarine, to a stunning green. On the southeastern side of the harbour's tranquil waters are a series of beautiful townhouse developments and the marina, typically hosting a wonderful array of vessels. Things are at their liveliest during the **Homecoming Regatta** at the end of August, when it's chock-full of colourful sailboats and yachts. An everyday pleasure is **Shell Beach**, reached by trekking east from the Marina up over the hill along Royal Palm Drive.

Diving and watersports

Though not as potentially memorable as the Gulf Stream angling off the Bimini chain, **deep-sea fishing** here is still top-notch, with possible catches including billfish, dolphinfish, king mackerel and wahoo. Reef fishing and light-tackle bottom fishing is also good with yellowtail, snapper, barracuda, triggerfish and grouper all present. And the bonefishing – particularly around Shark Creek, which separates the main body of Great Harbour Cay from its southern cays – is likewise superb. The centre for angling information is the **Great Harbour**

Cay Marina (☎367-8005, 🖷367-8115, VHF Ch 16 and 68), and guides here include Percy Darvill and Revis Anderson; both can be contacted at the marina on ☎367-8119 (expect to pay $350/500 for half/full-day trips). Also in the marina, Happy People Rentals (☎367-8117) hire out bonefishing skiffs, fishing rods and tackle, along with jeeps, bicycles, golf clubs and snorkelling gear. The dive shop at Great Harbour Cay Marina (☎367-8005) runs daily-dive trips and rents snorkel gear.

Practicalities

Getting to Great Harbour Cay requires some advance planning. Adventurous souls may try the **mailboat** route: the sea voyage aboard MV *Gurth Dean* leaves Potter's Cay (see p.198) on Tuesday evening at 11pm ($40), though this schedule is subject to change, so call the dock (☎393-1064) in Nassau for updates. Cat Island Air (☎361-8021 in Bullock Harbour, ☎377-3318 in Nassau) run **flights** from Nassau to Great Harbour Cay for approximately $50; return flights are much longer as they go by way of the Abacos. Flamingo Air flies in from Freeport (☎351-4963, 🌐www.flamingoairbah.com; $80 one way) on Fri and Sat at 1pm. Guests of *Tropical Diversions* often take Tropical Diversions Air (☎954/921-9084), who run puddle-jumper flights from Fort Lauderdale.

Getting around Great Harbour Cay is much simpler. A single well-paved road, Great Harbour Drive, runs north to south for four miles along the eastern shore. Happy People Rentals (☎367-8117) at the marina rents bicycles ($20), small Suzuki Jeeps ($65) and motor scooters ($50). Island Bus Service (☎477-6532) and Dean's Bus Service (☎367-8711) provide **taxi** service.

The only **accommodation** option is *Tropical Diversions* (☎367-8838 or 954/921-9084, 📧tdbahamas@aol.com; ❸), which acts as agent for a dozen or so privately owned beach villas along the eastern shore and two-bedroom townhouses on the marina, each with a private dock. Because they are private homes, the decor in each varies, but all have air conditioning and full kitchens.. The eighty-slip Great Harbour Cay Marina (☎367-8005) accommodates boats up to 150ft, with fuel dock, showers and laundry facilities. Dockage rates are in the range of $1 a foot.

Not surprisingly, the marina is the best place to **eat**. The *Wharf* (☎367-8762) is the place to go for breakfast and lunch, serving both American and Bahamian-style breakfasts ($4), and simple daily lunches including corned beef, burgers, soups and salads. The less exciting dinners include simple seafood dishes and pizza ($8–13). Also in the marina is the elegant *Tamboo Dinner Club* (Wed–Mon 6–10pm; ☎367-8203). The menu is Bahamian-style seafood and chicken, and during weekends local expatriates gather at the atmospheric bar to play backgammon or watch the huge TV. In Bullock's Harbour, the *Watergate* (☎367-8244) is the main sit-down restaurant, dishing out very good pork chops and macaroni and cheese, along with the ubiquitous peas and rice. Also popular is the *Beach Club* restaurant (☎367-8108) on Great Harbour Bay Beach. If you are looking for a quick snack, there are several take-away spots in town, including *Until Then* (☎367-8197) and *Cooly Mae's Take Away* (☎367-8730), as well as a dozen tiny general merchandise shops. The best **nightlife** option is *Roberts Disco and Lounge* at the north end of town, mainly frequented by locals.

There are no banks or information offices on Great Harbour Cay, though **travellers' cheques** can be cashed at *Tropical Diversions*. If you have pressing travel questions or concerns, the main **island administrative centre**

(☎367-8291) in Bullock's Harbour can sometimes supply answers on travel along with details on events like the Homecoming Regatta. Also in town are a **post office** (Mon–Fri 9am–5.30pm) and a **police station** (☎367-8344).

Chub Cay

Long uninhabited, tiny **CHUB CAY** began its development as an embryonic idea of a group of Texas-based anglers and investors who thought it would be fun to own a private fishing island in the Bahamas. Over the years they built makeshift dormitories, imported a permanent support staff and finally built a marina on the most prominent natural lagoon on the western edge of the island. When Hurricane Andrew struck in 1992, the island – along with the *Chub Cay Club* – was brutalized. After being completely rebuilt and refurbished, the *Club* opened again in 1994, and it was recently sold to Marinas International (🌐www.marinasinternational); at press time the club was closed for a major renovation.

Named for a fish that inhabits the shallow waters of the Great Bahama Bank, Chub Cay and its twin companion **Frazier's Hog Cay** are today visited mainly for the fine fishing and diving. At only four miles long, the two-island set doesn't invite much inland exploration, though there are two very good **beaches**, both with particularly marvellous shelling for collectors. Still, the **reefs** and rare corals just offshore, along with the deep, fish-filled **Tongue of the Ocean** due south, are the real stars here.

Diving and watersports

Clear visibility in the water – often up to a hundred feet – is a major reason for the high quality of both **snorkelling** and **diving** here, as is the frequent spotting of eagle rays, stingrays, abundant starfish and sea turtles. The best place to start snorkelling is **Mamma Rhoda Rock**, about marine park located a mile offshore southwest from the *Chub Cay Club* famed for its schools of grunt and yellow trumpetfish. Any day one can look across the straits and see Mamma Rhoda in the distance, where countless roosting birds like Sooty Terns and Brown Noddies make their home. A five-minute boat ride away, it's one of the best snorkelling reefs in the Bahamas thanks to its large size and sheltered southwestern position. Beyond here diving possibilities include deep-wall diving at **Chub Cay Wall**, known for its steep drop-off and huge tiger grouper fish congregations, and **Canyons and Caves**, a shallow reef which lies in only 20–40ft of water. For information on diving in the area, head to the small **dive shop** located at Great Harbour Marina on Great Harbour Cay (☎367-8005).

Practicalities

Though a majority of visitors arrive via private yacht, Chub Cay does have its own airport – basically a long concrete runway with enough space to land a 737; most **flights** are run by Island Express Airlines (☎954/359-0380) out of Fort Lauderdale. The *Bimini Mack* **mailboat service** from Nassau calls at Chub Cay once a week (☎393-1064). The cay's limited **accommodation** start and end with the laid-back *Chub Cay Club* (☎325-1490 or 1-800/662-8555, 🌐www.chubcay.com); though closed at the time of writing, check their website for the latest details on accommodation and restaurants. Nearby is the *Hilltop Bar*, where tired fishermen watch sunsets and talk about the one that got away.

Eleuthera

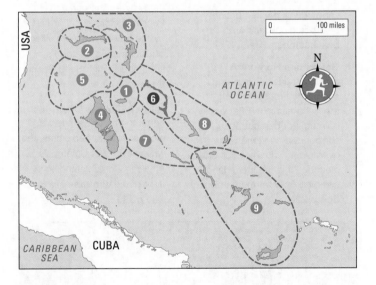

CHAPTER 6

Highlights

✳ **Club Med Beach** The resort is long gone, but this long curved expanse of powdery pink sand near Governor's Harbour remains, backed by a tall forest and protected by an offshore reef. See p.216

✳ **Surfer's Beach** A long, windswept stretch of Atlantic coast where sizeable rollers draw wave riders and the sandy dune-backed beach beckons picnickers and beachcombers. See p.217

✳ **Governor's Harbour** A gracious seaside town and site of the first settlement of the Bahamas in 1768. Daintily painted wooden cottages, surrounded by stone walls overflowing with hibiscus and oleander, line the steep lanes climbing up from the harbour. See p.220

✳ **The Glass Window** Towards Eleuthera's north end, the island dramatically narrows to a rocky sliver, bound on one side by the smooth, shallow waters of the Bight of Eleuthera and on the other by the deep, heaving Atlantic. See p.228

✳ **Harbour Island** A favourite getaway for the rich and trendy. Visitors are charmed by the tidy Loyalist-era village of Dunmore Town and its spectacular Pink Sand Beach. See p.230

✳ **Tarpum Bay** A fishing village home to one of Eleuthera's most photographed sights, the whitewashed St Columba's Anglican Church standing in front of the turquoise sea. See p.239

△ The Glass Window

Eleuthera

Meaning "freedom" in ancient Greek, the hopeful name of "**ELEUTHERA**" was giving to the island by a small band of European settlers who landed on its beaches in 1648, fleeing religious persecution in Bermuda. The original Lucayan inhabitants, long since gone, knew it as Cigatoo. Exceedingly long and thin, **Eleuthera** itself stretches over a hundred miles end to end and is less than two miles wide for most of its length. Congregating at the northern tip of Eleuthera are a cluster of small islands easily accessed from Eleuthera itself: these include tiny **Harbour Island**; **St George's Island**, which is more commonly known by the name of its only settlement **Spanish Wells**; and **Russell Island**, a hump of land that absorbs the population overflow from Spanish Wells. These three islands are in turn flanked by a handful of smaller uninhabited cays mainly frequented by recreational boaters and fishermen.

The most populous of the Out Islands, Eleuthera has 10,000 residents scattered in a dozen fishing villages spread up and down its long coastline, mainly along the western shore facing the Bight of Eleuthera, the curve of shallow water that fills the gentle bow in Eleuthera's coastline. In parts the landscape is rolling and green, farmed for citrus fruit, tomatoes and vegetables or clothed in tall grass punctuated by the occasional grove of pine or coconut trees. The Queen's Highway, which runs from north to south, also cuts through several stretches of low straggly bush and swamp, but travels mainly along the water's edge, offering long views of the turquoise sea, and occasionally of both coasts at once.

Smack in the middle of Eleuthera is the genteel community of **Governor's Harbour**, its capital and the earliest settlement in the Bahamas. To the north, **Gregory Town**, built on a steep hillside surrounding a deep horseshoe-shaped harbour, is the self-proclaimed pineapple capital of the Bahamas. South of Governor's Harbour, are the picturesque fishing villages of **Tarpum Bay** and **Rock Sound**.

Outside of a handful of comfortable resorts, there are few organized tourist facilities on the island, which is part of its appeal for many visitors. It's easy to fall into the slow-moving pace of life in its friendly villages, spending your days exploring the numerous side roads leading through tomato fields or palm groves to spectacular **empty beaches** fit for swimming, strolling, snorkelling and collecting shells. While the Bahamas are indeed awash with beaches, the Eleutheran chain offers some of the very finest and most unspoilt in the entire archipelago.

By comparison only, pretty Harbour Island – or Briland, as it is also known locally – bustles with activity. Its only settlement is the historic village of

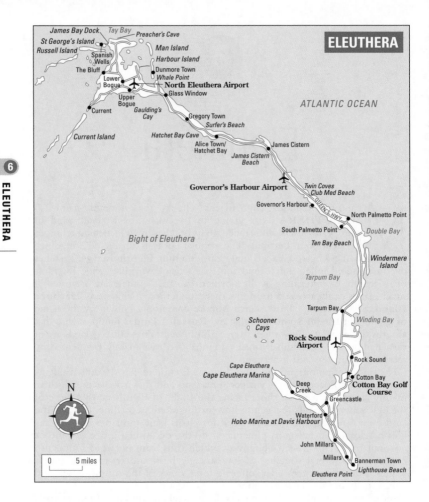

Dunmore Town, boasting several luxury resorts, trendy restaurants and bars, dive outfitters and the stunning, three-mile **Pink Sand Beach**. The contrast with nearby **Spanish Wells**, which occupies the whole of **St George's Island**, couldn't be more pronounced. With a population descended from the original group of Loyalist settlers, Spanish Wells is a working class settlement with a large fleet of fishing and lobster boats. It too has a long white sand beach, but a very modest tourist trade.

Some history

The **British** laid claim to the Bahamas in 1629, but failed to establish a permanent settlement in the islands for nearly twenty years. By 1647, the nation was in a state of upheaval: Oliver Cromwell's Roundheads were engaged in a bloody civil war against the crown, a conflict that reverberated in less violent forms in Britain's colonies overseas.

Bermuda, nominally independent during this period, was divided between Church of England royalists and republican reformers. Eager to escape the political instability and religious persecution engulfing the island, **William Sayle**, a former governor of the colony, obtained British approval to establish a new settlement in the uninhabited islands of the Bahamas. He advertised in the pubs and meeting houses of London for investors in the **Company of Eleutheran Adventurers**. For an outlay of 100 pounds, those who joined in were entitled to a large plot of land in the settlement, and agreed to adhere to its radical principles of liberty, religious tolerance and an elected government. Among the 26 investors Sayle signed on, most of whom never set foot on the island, were five men who later signed the death warrant of King Charles I.

Nevertheless, Sayle set forth from Bermuda in 1648 with seventy settlers bound for Eleuthera, coming ashore at **Governor's Harbour**. The historical record of the colony is murky, but it's known that there was an argument between Sayle and a Captain Butler, and Sayle set out for another part of the island – probably Harbour Island – taking most of the settlers with him. One of their ships was wrecked at sea, and they all had a rough first year. Were it not for the emergency supplies sent by the Puritan colonists of New England, the settlers would have starved to death on the beautiful white sand beaches. To repay the gift, the Eleutherans cut and sent a shipload of braziletto, a valuable dyewood, which was sold to help build Harvard College.

When Charles I was beheaded in 1649, republican sympathizers were expelled from Bermuda and a second batch of settlers headed for Eleuthera, joined from time to time by more Bermudians exiled for offenses such as adultery or inciting unrest among African slaves. Despite its lofty ideals, the Eleutheran colony failed to thrive. The inhabitants scraped a meager living harvesting wood and ambergris (an excretion of the sperm whale used to make perfume) and wrecking. By 1657, the few remaining settlers were living together in Sayle's house, and by 1659 when Cromwell directed the Governor of Jamaica to send a ship to rescue them and take them to Jamaica to be clothed and fed, most had already gone. Sayle himself returned to Bermuda to become Governor again, and the cannons found on Harbour Island are the only physical remnants of this period.

Seventy-five years later, the combined population of Eleuthera and Harbour Island had crept up to 390 (330 Europeans and 60 Africans) living the same hardscrabble life. The governor of the day decided to take the lawless Eleutherans and Brilanders in hand, and issued a directive that they were to abide by certain rules: regular attendance at Anglican Church services by everyone except for nine French and Swiss Calvinists who were specifically excused; swearing, drunkenness and "other scandalous actions" were to be met with severe punishment; all wrecks were to be registered with the government; and no one was to leave the islands without written permission from the governor. However, a short time later the governor was himself removed from office as a result of his wife's illegal activities in Nassau. An influx of Loyalist exiles and African slaves from the southern states at the end of the eighteenth century saw the establishment of large pineapple, cotton and citrus fruit plantations on Eleuthera and many of the quaint clapboard cottages in Governor's Harbour, Spanish Wells and Dunmore Town date from this period. Agriculture, fishing, wooden boat building, sponging and wrecking sustained the small settlements established up and down the coast by freed slaves for the next hundred odd years.

Eleuthera experienced a fleeting glamour in the 1940s and 1950s when the British royals were frequent visitors to **Windermere Island**, a spit of land lying a few metres off the Atlantic coast, and a number of wealthy expatriates built luxurious winter homes on Eleuthera and Harbour Island. Several resorts were established in southern Eleuthera, including the **Cotton Bay Club**, built by Pam Am Airlines President Juan Trippe and patronized by Sammy Davis Junior and other members of the rat pack; the **Islandia Resort** near Tarpum Bay; **Cape Eleuthera** on the very southern tip; and a **Club Med** built near Governor's Harbour in the 1980s. All have since closed, throwing a great many Eleutherans out of work, and forcing many young people to head to Nassau or elsewhere for jobs.

Today a loyal contingent of winter residents and travellers wandering off the beaten path make up most of the visitors occupying the island's many cottage rentals and small resorts, and they have miles of unspoiled beaches virtually to themselves. There are signs that Eleuthera is again capturing the imagination of the international leisure class, with the opening of new, hip resorts aimed at the high-end market. Whether or not this will translate into a boost for the local economy remains to be seen, but there's no question that Harbour Island, with its own pink sand beach, fine restaurants and several luxury resorts, is very back in with the "In crowd" once again.

Getting there

There are three **airports** on Eleuthera serving the whole archipelago. The busiest is Governor's Harbour International Airport (☎332-2321), eight miles north of the settlement. Rock Sound Airport (☎334-2177), two miles north of Rock

Eleuthera's beaches

Much of Eleuthera's long coastline is edged with fine sandy **beaches**, most of which you can have all to yourself on any given day. Listed from south to north, here are ten great destinations to whet your appetite:

Lighthouse Beach Six miles of scoured white sand on the very southern tip of the island, strewn with sand dollars and perfect for picnicking and walking, with good snorkelling on a calm day. Getting there is half the adventure (see p.243 for directions).

Nor'Side Beach A long Atlantic beach backed by high dunes, with a hypnotic surf, good snorkelling from shore and a great beach bar and restaurant on the bluff. From the centre of Rock Sound village, follow Fish Street for about a mile to a T-junction, then turn left. The *Nor'Side Resort* is about 500yd along this road on the right, with access up a steep sandy drive.

Ten Bay Beach A good swimming beach (suitable for small children) located on the sheltered Bight side, fringed by towering coconut palms. Heading north on the Queen's Highway, the turnoff is ten miles past Tarpum Bay. Keep an eye out for a Japanese-style building on your left, and take the dirt road that runs past it a few hundred yards into the parking area.

Club Med Beach Arguably the most beautiful beach on the island; a long expanse of powdery pink sand backed by a tall forest on the Atlantic side of Governor's Harbour. An offshore reef tempers the gentle surf. The *Club Med*, which closed a few years ago, is now just a cluster of overgrown buildings set back from sea, and the beach is often empty of visitors.

Twin Coves A secluded double scallop of white sand on the Atlantic side, with good swimming and snorkelling around a small cay a short swim offshore. Heading north from Governor's Harbour, take the paved road on your right just before you pass the *Worker's Hotel*. Follow it through one intersection, then take a right at the fork in the road, then right again on the road running along the beach (not always within sight).

Sound, handles the south, while North Eleuthera Airport (☏335-1700), on the main island, is only a ten-minute boat ride and five-minute drive from Harbour Island. Continental, Lynx Air, US Air and Twin Air all have regular **flights** from Fort Lauderdale to Governor's Harbour and North Eleuthera. Thrice daily air service from Nassau to all three airports is available on Bahamasair, and to Governor's Harbour and North Eleuthera on Southern Air. Flying time from Nassau is twenty minutes. Major's Air Service also has regular flights to Governor's Harbour and North Eleuthera **from Grand Bahama** on Fri and Sun. See p.21 in Basics for contact details of airlines serving Eleuthera.

There is also a fast **ferry** service from Nassau to Eleuthera. Bahamas Fast Ferries (☏323-2166, ⊛www.bahamasferries.com) makes the two-hour trip to Spanish Wells and Harbour Island daily ($65), and the four-hour cruise to Governor's Harbour twice a week ($35). Three weekly **mailboats** serve the communities on Eleuthera, Spanish Wells and Harbour Island, making the crossing from Nassau in five hours. Eleuthera also has a handful of small **marinas**, the details of which are listed throughout the chapter.

Information and maps

There are **Ministry of Tourism offices** in Governor's Harbour on the Queen's Highway in the centre of town (☏332-2142, ℻332-2480) and on

Just past a private home with large landscaped grounds, there is a short track on your left that leads to the beach.

James Cistern Beach A narrow rocky strand running along the Queen's Highway through the village of James Cistern, ten miles north of Governor's Harbour. Not a swimming beach, but one of the best places on the island for shell collecting.

Surfer's Beach Unlike any other place on the island, this long exposed piece of Atlantic coastline features exhilarating, wild crashing surf backed by high dunes. The turnoff is two miles south of Gregory Town on the Atlantic side.

Gaulding's Cay Beach A picturesque shallow curve of tree-backed beach on the bight side facing Gaulding's Cay, a lump of land about 50yd offshore that you can wade out to examine. Two miles north of the *Cove Resort*, take the dirt road on the bight/west side of the highway across from a yellow and white building, then turn left again at the fence strung with buoys. The way is signposted.

Tay Bay This secluded dollop of powdery white sand on the very northern tip of Eleuthera is of historical interest as the site of Preacher's Cave, where the Eleutheran Adventurers took refuge after one of their ships was wrecked on the Devil's Backbone reef in 1648. The turnoff is marked from the highway.

Pink Sand Beach The three-mile-long fine sandy strand that put Harbour Island on the map, with a rolling surf, several beach bars and small luxury resorts dotted along its length.

For hardcore sun- and sand-seekers, Geoff and Vicky Wells (⊛www.elusivebeaches .com; $25) – self-declared "beachologists" from the frozen north – have published *The Elusive Beaches of Eleuthera*, with detailed directions and ratings for privacy, swimming, shelling, snorkelling and diving prospects at a few dozen more sandy strands; available at *Pam's Island Made Gifts* in Gregory Town and in other shops around the island. The detailed Tarbox map of Eleuthera available at the *Rainbow Inn* (see p.219) also has several beaches and snorkelling spots marked on it.

Dunmore Street in Dunmore Town on Harbour Island (☎333-2621). Published in Nassau, the **Eleuthera Advocate** is a free monthly **newspaper** carrying local news, while the free monthly bulletin **Eleuthera Informer** (⊛www .eleutherainformer.com) contains advertisements for local businesses and tourist services and is available in hotels and island shops. A pocketsize yearly magazine, **Eleutheras** has feature articles on local attractions and businesses, along with restaurant and hotel listings. It is less widely available, but might be had from the tourism office. On the **web**, ⊛www.eleu.net has comprehensive listings of tourist services, cottage rentals and local sights. Another informative site, maintained by two long-time winter residents, is ⊛www.discover -eleuthera-bahamas.com, which has restaurant listings, an events calendar and in-depth coverage of things to see and do.

Tarbox Publications has produced an excellent and very detailed four-sheet **map** of Eleuthera, Harbour Island and Spanish Wells, including their numerous beaches and other local attractions. If you are going to spend any time exploring the island, it's a well-spent $10, available at some gift shops, or at the **Rainbow Inn**, whose owners commissioned it.

Getting around

There is no public transportation on Eleuthera, so to get around, you will need to hire a taxi or rent a car, both of which can be done at the airport upon your arrival. Be sure to book your ticket to the airport nearest to where you are staying as a taxi ride from one end of the island to the other will cost upwards of $160 and take two hours or more. Car rental agencies and taxi drivers serving the areas around Governor's Harbour, Rock Sound and North Eleuthera are listed in the sections on those regions. Car rental costs around $70/$350 a day/ week or $400 for a four-wheel-drive, useful if you want to explore the back roads. Lots of people hitchhike up and down the island and this is a reasonably safe and easy way to get around.

Central Eleuthera

Governor's Harbour, the genteel capital at the midpoint of Eleuthera, is a gracious seaside town and working fishing community of a few hundred residents with a distinctly colonial feel and a tangible expatriate presence. The Queen's Highway runs through the centre of town, which is spread out along the waterfront facing the broad, well-used harbour and Cupid's Cay. Quiet, tree-lined residential lanes climb the hillside behind the small commercial district, lined with freshly painted clapboard cottages. The streets lead you in a matter of minutes over the hill and down to the Atlantic coast and the gorgeous pink-sand **Club Med Beach**, about a mile from the town centre.

Well equipped with appealing accommodations and restaurants along with miles of gorgeous beaches close at hand, central Eleuthera makes a good base from which to explore the whole of the island. North from Governor's

Harbour, the Queen's Highway passes through the small fishing villages of **James Cistern**, **Alice Town** and **Hatchet Bay**. Along the way, side roads lead to blissful empty beaches on both the Caribbean and Atlantic coasts (see box p.216), while **Hatchet Bay Cave** makes a good destination on a rainy or sunburned day. South of the capital are more fine beaches and a few pleasant seaside bars and restaurants dotted along the Atlantic and Caribbean coasts en route to **Palmetto Point**, all good destinations for a leisurely day-trip.

Accommodation

Staying in Governor's Harbour gives you the option of foregoing a rental car. There are several restaurants and shops as well as a spectacular beach all within walking distance of the town centre. However, there are also some very appealing beachfront lodgings along the shores both north and south of town. These offer privacy and a gorgeous beach on your doorstep, but unless staying put for the duration of your stay, you will need to rent a car or bicycle (available at some resorts and rental cottages) to get around. **Holiday rentals** are available on the beaches around Palmetto Point and in Governor's Harbour in some of the lovely clapboard cottages that climb the hill overlooking Cupid's Cay. For listings of rental agents handling properties in Governor's Harbour and around, see p.31.

Governor's Harbour

The Duck Inn Queen's Highway ☎332-2608, ⓦ www.theduckinn.com. Centrally located on the waterfront, the wonderful *Duck Inn* has three charming early 1800s wooden cottages set in a verdant walled garden planted with a variety of orchids along with coconut, fig, starfruit and grapefruit trees. Cupid Cottage (❸) – which has an unimpeded view of the harbour – sleeps two, while the Honeypot Studio apartment sleeps up to four (❸) in homely rooms with hardwood floors and an unsurpassed view of the sunset and the sea from the private upstairs deck. The larger Loyalist Cottage sleeps up to eight in spare, airy rooms furnished with antiques and polished hardwood floors, plus there's a cosy colonial sitting room with overstuffed furniture and a verandah (❼).

Laughing Bird Apartments Birdie Lane ☎332-2012 or 1029, ⓦ www.vrbo.com/8969. Four neat, modern studio apartments in a quiet shady grove across the road from Arthur's Beach in Governor's Harbour, with hammocks hung in the trees for lolling. All the units have a/c, cable TV, fully equipped kitchens and an outdoor bbq, with a view of the harbour out front. ❸

Quality Inn Cigatoo Resort Haynes Ave ☎332-3060 or 1-800/467-7595, ⓦ www .choicehotels.com. On top of the hill in Governor's Harbour, this hotel has 24 clean, bright modern rooms – some with a view of the Atlantic, all with a/c and TV – painted a crisp white with attractive tropical accents and set in nicely landscaped grounds around a swimming pool. There are tennis courts, meeting room and an inviting bar and restaurant with additional tables on the courtyard terrace. Club Med Beach is a 15min walk away. ❸

North to Hatchet Bay

Cocodimama Six miles north of Governor's Harbour ☎332-3150, ⓦ www.cocodimama.com. A gem of a small beach resort with one of the finest restaurants on Eleuthera (see p.224). It is a relaxed and sophisticated retreat, with twelve spacious rooms in three two-storey chalets. The rooms are beautifully decorated with handsome wood furnishings and art pieces from Bali complimented by fine bed linens, clay tile floors and natural toiletries. Each room has a king or two doubles, and a private balcony with a hammock and a view of the sunset. The main house is a casual open area with a bar and a dining alcove, and amenities include Internet access, kayaks and snorkelling gear for guest use, with complimentary excursions around the island. Closed Sept–Nov. ❼

The Rainbow Inn Ten miles north of Governor's Harbour Airport, and 17 miles north of town itself ☎335-0294 or 1-800/688-0047, ⓦ www .rainbowinn.com. A small, relaxed resort with homely accommodation in hexagonal cottages built around a swimming pool overlooking the sea on the bight side. Facilities and amenities include a fine casual restaurant, tennis courts, free use of bicycles, kayaks and snorkel gear, and hammocks strung in the trees across the grounds. The various room options include a single or double with mini-kitchen (fridge, microwave, coffee maker; ❺); three-bedroom/three-bath cottage sleeping up to six with a full kitchen, living room and screened-in porch with a view of the sea (❼); and a two bedroom/one-bath cottage with living room, full kitchen and a sun deck facing the ocean (❼).

Seven Gables Estate Hatchet Bay ☎335-0070. *Seven Gables* has four little clapboard cottages for rent on a tidy seaside property. Simple and homely with satin appliqué bed quilts and original artwork by the owner, as well as a kitchenette, TV and small porches. A bit isolated and perhaps not a place where you'd want to hang around all day, but the nicest place to lay your head in these parts. $450 a week. ❷

South to Palmetto Point

Calypso Atlantic coast near North Palmetto Point ⓦwww.calypsocalypso.com. A superb location and an equally superb deal, *Calypso* has two one-bedroom seaside cottages set in a lush garden on a five-mile stretch of beach. The simple white washed cottages are done up in with crisp cottons and painted wood. There are bicycles and a two-person kayak for guest use, and a pond at the foot of the garden that attracts varied birdlife. The spacious Sea Star ($1000 a week) cottage is set back slightly from the shore on a low rise. Smaller but cosy, Morning Star ($500 a week) sits steps from the sand, with an outdoor shower. Weekly rentals only. ❷

La Tera Motel South Palmetto Point ☎332-1386, ⓦwww.eleutherainformer.com/mate_&_jennys.htm.

Spacious and modern one and two-bedroom apartments with kitchens, a/c and cable TV. They are situated just off the highway opposite *Mate and Jenny's Restaurant*. You will need a car to get to a beach. ❸

Pineapple Fields Banks Rd, between Governor's Harbour and North Palmetto Point ☎332-2221 or 1-877/677-9539, ⓦwww.pineapplefields .com. Across the street from the gorgeous beach that runs along the Atlantic most all the way from Governor's Harbour to North Palmetto Point, these one and two-bedroom condominiums are bright and airy with a spare, colourful decor. Each has a full kitchen, and *Tippy's Restaurant* is a short walk away. ❽

Tropical Dreams On a side road leading to the Atlantic shore north of North Palmetto Point ☎332-1632, ⓦwww.bahamasvg.com /Tropicaldream.html. *Tropical Dreams* rents large, clean, modern efficiency units and a couple of two-bedroom apartments. All units have a/c, cable TV, and full kitchens. The beach is a two-minute drive away. ❸

Unique Village Resort On the coast near North Palmetto Point ☎332-1830, ⓦwww.bahamasvg .com/uniquevil.html. The ten doubles and four one-and two-bedroom villas here are set on a nice piece of powdery beach. The villas have full kitchens, while all of the rooms are up to date and come with the requisite floral print bedcovers, rattan furniture and beige tiled floors. The perks include a coffee-maker, satellite TV, a/c and a casual dining room with an ocean view serving Bahamian and American cuisine. ❹

Governor's Harbour

The town centre of **GOVERNOR'S HARBOUR** is dominated by a large, ugly parking lot off the Queen's Highway, around which a grocery store, Shell station, First Caribbean Bank and several other shops are untidily grouped. Happily, the rest of the village is very picturesque. Daintily painted wooden cottages with gingerbread trim, surrounded by stone walls overflowing with hibiscus and oleander blooms, line the steep lanes climbing the hillside.

Shaded by coconut palms on the triangle of land connecting the village centre to Cupid's Cay, the pink and green wooden clapboard **Haynes Public Library** (Mon–Thurs 9am–6pm, Fri 9am–5pm, Sat 10am–4pm; ☎332-2877) was built in 1897 and lovingly restored by a local community group. There is public access to the Internet here ($5 for 15min, $20 a month), and small exhibits devoted to local history. Nearby stands the Gothic whitewashed **St Patrick's Church** and the hot pink colonial-style **Government Administration** building, where the post office is located.

△ St Patrick's Church

Dotted with fishing boats and pleasure craft, the harbour itself is enclosed by a curve of white sand joined to **Cupid's Cay** by a narrow causeway. A small hunk of flat rock, Cupid's Cay was the site of the first settlement on Eleuthera, by the Company of Eleutheran Adventurers in 1648 (although a big sign proudly declares it to have been 1646). A church, a few cottages and the ruins of nineteenth-century wooden houses remain. The mailboat and passenger ferries dock at the north end of the cay.

You will miss one of the highlights of Eleuthera if you pass through Governor's Harbour without a visit to **Club Med Beach**. Take Haynes Avenue up the hill from the Queen's Highway, past the **Quality Inn Cigatoo Resort** and down the other side, where you come to a T-junction. Park here and take the wooded path just to the right of the junction, which leads to the beach about 200yd in. A big billboard announces that this is the planned site for a new condominium development, but for the moment, you will probably have this broad curved swath of pink sand to yourself.

Back from the T-junction, a scenic, narrow paved road (Banks Road) follows the Atlantic coast south for eight miles between Governor's Harbour and Palmetto Point, past several ocean-front holiday estates, rental cottages and gorgeous strips of sandy beach (see opposite).

North to Hatchet Bay

North of Governor's Harbour, the Queen's Highway weaves inland and back along the shore to the fishing village of **James Cistern**, ten miles north. If you want to pause here for a quick meal, try **Lee's Café and Bakery** (see p.224). Three miles further on, Big Rock General Store has a good stock of groceries if you intend to take a picnic at Surfer's Beach.

Continuing north five miles, you come to **Hatchet Bay**, also known as **Alice Town**, a tidy, green settlement with a picturesque protected harbour. Though this sleepy little village does not receive many tourists, you may wish to break at the Gateway service station or at the general store on the highway about a quarter of a mile on where local boys gather to play dominoes under a tree.

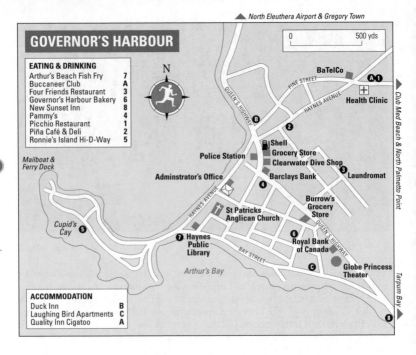

GOVERNOR'S HARBOUR

0   500 yds

EATING & DRINKING

Arthur's Beach Fish Fry	7
Buccaneer Club	A
Four Friends Restaurant	3
Governor's Harbour Bakery	6
New Sunset Inn	8
Pammy's	4
Picchio Restaurant	1
Piña Café & Deli	2
Ronnie's Island Hi-D-Way	5

N

BaTelCo

PINE STREET

HAYNES AVENUE

Health Clinic

Club Med Beach & North Palmetto Point

Mailboat & Ferry Dock

QUEEN'S HIGHWAY

Shell
Grocery Store

Police Station

Clearwater Dive Shop

Administrator's Office

Barclays Bank

Laundromat

HAYNES AVENUE

Burrow's
Grocery
Store

St Patricks
Anglican Church

Cupid's Cay

Haynes
Public
Library

BAY STREET

Royal Bank
of Canada

QUEEN'S HIGHWAY

Arthur's Bay

Globe Princess
Theater

Tarpum Bay

ACCOMMODATION

Duck Inn	B
Laughing Bird Apartments	C
Quality Inn Cigatoo	A

Two miles north of Hatchet Bay, a sign on your left – the Bight side – marks the turnoff to the **Hatchet Bay Cave**. This underground cavern of several chambers is filled with dramatic formations of stalactites and stalagmites that extend for a few hundred yards; its entrance is in the middle of a tomato field. The cave walls are adorned with the accumulated graffiti of several hundred years and you'll need sturdy shoes with a good tread and a flashlight for everyone in your party should you plan on entering. It's best to go with a local guide, which your hotel should be able to help arrange. Situated in the midst of a broad expanse of rolling fields dramatically punctuated by tall abandoned grain silos, the cave was once part of a large dairy and poultry farm established in 1937 by Austin Levy. An American textile tycoon, he paid wages above the Bahamian average, for which he was chided by the governor of the day, the Duke of Windsor. The farm went belly-up shortly after the government bought it in 1975.

South to Palmetto Point and around

Between Governor's Harbour and the community of Palmetto Point, the Queen's Highway cuts inland through bland bush. A scenic alternative route from Governor's Harbour to Palmetto Point is the old highway (Banks Road) running along the Atlantic coast and emerging in the jumbled settlement of **North Palmetto Point,** where you can rejoin the Queen's Highway. An agricultural community dating back a couple of hundred years, North Palmetto Point is comprised of a few dozen bungalows and a couple of tidy cafés and grocery stores. The village holds few scenic attractions, but the Atlantic coast here boasts a spectacular, faintly rose-coloured beach five miles long and dotted with rental villas, hotels and restaurants. Two miles south of Governor's Harbour on the Banks Road, **Tippy's Bar and Restaurant** offers gourmet refreshments and access to the beach. **South Palmetto Point** sits on the opposite shore, across the Queen's Highway facing the Bight of Eleuthera. Sustained by a modest fishery and gradually developing tourist trade, the village is just a few streets of modern bungalows and a couple of petrol stations.

South from Palmetto Point, the Queen's Highway again passes through several miles of straggly bush before it touches the coastline again a few miles north of Tarpum Bay (see p.239). About three miles south of Palmetto Point and ten miles north of Tarpum Bay, the ruins of a Japanese-style building and power lines mark the turn-off to **Ten Bay Beach** on the Bight side of the island (see box, p.216). A few miles further south, the highway passes through the settlement of **Savannah Sound**, and the turnoff to **Windermere Island**, site of the exclusive private beach club where Princess Diana was famously photographed several months pregnant in a bikini by paparazzi lurking in the bushes. Neither place is likely to offer much of interest to the common traveller: Savannah Sound comprises a few houses along the highway and the Atlantic shore, and the **Windermere Club**, which owns the whole of Windermere Island, is not open to the general public.

Eating and drinking

Governor's Harbour and environs boasts a range of good **restaurants** for both a casual night out and a gourmet meal, ranging from Bahamian favourites and fresh seafood to elaborate Italian cuisine served waterside. There are several decent restaurants in the town centre, but some of the nicest places are situated on the Atlantic and Bight side beaches within a few miles of the settlement. Nightlife in Governor's Harbour is low-key. **Ronnie's Island Hide-D-Way** (☎332-2307) on Cupid's Cay occasionally has live rake 'n' scrape or rock music by local bands, with dancing every weekend, and pool, drinking, and satellite TV every night. The Globe Princess Theatre (☎332-2735) on the south edge of town is the only **cinema** on the island, with shows at 8pm several nights a week.

Governor's Harbour

Arthur's Beach Fish Fry Haynes Avenue. On Friday and Saturday afternoons and through the evening, cheap, fresh seafood is cooked on an outside grill at this local kiosk on the beach.
Buccaneer's Haynes Avenue ☎332-2000. A bright cheery diner open for breakfast ($7–10) and lunch ($4–10). Mornings start with a hearty plate of eggs, bacon and toast, smoothies and yogurt and lunch is sandwiches, salads and conch chowder. 7am–3pm; closed Wed.
Four Friends Restaurant Governor's Harbour, above the Laundromat ☎332-3488. A casual restaurant recommended for its Bahamian cuisine. Mains $15–20. Mon–Sat 7am–10pm.
Governor's Harbour Bakery Behind the Royal Bank of Canada ☎332-2071. Popular with the

working crowd, the spot does a brisk business selling delicious fresh bread, pastries and pies (coconut and key lime), as well as breakfasts of grits and tuna ($3), chicken, beef and conch hot patties ($2). Daily specials include the likes of stew fish and chicken souse with johnnycake or potato bread. Mon–Fri 7am–5pm, Sat 7am–2pm.
Pammy's Queen's Highway in the centre of town ☎322-2843. A popular spot both with locals and winter visitors, *Pammy's* offers mouthwatering home-style Bahamian fried chicken, conch fritters, burgers and sandwiches, with traditional side-dishes like coleslaw, fried plantains, and peas and rice. You can eat in the casual diner or takeaway. More Bahamian favourites, including tuna and grits, are served for breakfast. Mon–Sat 8am–5pm; closed Sun.

Picchio Restaurant and Bar *Quality Inn Cigatoo Resort* ☏ 332 3060. *Picchio*'s menu includes plenty of seafood dishes like grouper with home-made fries on a bed of lettuce. The highlight, however, are two variations on conch – wrapped in puff pastry with soy vinegar, and conch risotto with fresh tomatoes and basil. The pleasant dining room has a view of the garden, white linen tablecloths and fresh flowers. Lunch $10–13, dinner entrees $22–26. Closed Sun and Mon.

Pina Café and Deli Haynes Avenue ☏ 332-3350. The inviting terracotta patio covered in climbing vines is a pleasant spot for breakfast or lunch, with ice cream, coffee and deli meats and cheeses for sale at the counter inside. The menu includes bagels with cream cheese for breakfast and soups, salads and sandwiches for lunch ($5–10). 8am–3pm; closed Sat and Sun.

North to Hatchet Bay

Alphenia's Takeaway James Cistern ☏ 335-6168. Grab some pizza, ice cream or fried chicken to eat on the beach. Tues is barbeque night. Open 7am–10pm.

Cocodimama Six miles north of Governor's Harbour ☏ 332-3150. On a wide terrace overlooking the white-sand beach, this is *the* place to watch the sunset with a glass of wine or a Goombay Smash in hand. The cuisine mixes Italian and Bahamian fare, featuring fresh seafood, locally grown vegetables and imported mozzarella. Top dishes include penne with anchovy fillets, raisins and pine nuts or a grouper in a white wine sauce. For dessert, try the vodka lemon sorbet. The restaurant boasts an extensive wine list with a good selection of Italian and Californian vintages. Mains $12–26. Closed Sept–Nov.

James Cistern Community Fish Fry James Cistern, on the waterfront. Every Friday and Saturday evening, village residents host a popular fish fry serving up fresh seafood and cool drinks. Everybody is welcome and it's a popular night out for visitors to mix with locals, and you can quell your hunger for about $10.

Rainbow Inn Ten miles north of Governor's Harbour Airport ☏ 335-0294. Among the nicest on the island, the restaurant has a cosy, inviting interior with a central backlit bar, polished wood tables situated with a view of the sea and the sunset, nautical paraphernalia and curios on the walls and a screened-in porch. The food is very good – fried chicken with fresh seafood options like grouper – and the home-made key lime pie is sublime. Live music with Dr Seabreeze on Friday nights. Open for dinner only from 6pm.

Closed Sun and Mon, when a cookout is put on for guests of the resort only. Closed Sept to mid-Nov.

Lee's Café and Bakery James Cistern, in the centre of the village ☏ 335-6444. Lip-smacking fish and chicken fried dinners; takeaway available. Open 7am–7pm.

South to Palmetto Point

Country Café North Palmetto Point ☏ 332-0100. A bright and welcoming village café with good pizza, jerk chicken, hot patties, burgers, ice cream and delicious home-made pies and cakes on the menu. Mon–Fri 11am–9pm, Sat 10am–10pm, Sun 3pm–9pm.

Dolce Vita Runaway Bay Marina, Shore Drive in South Palmetto Point ☏ 332-0220. A nice spot for an Italian lunch or dinner heavy on seafood, with pleasant seating on a verandah overlooking the Bight as well as a casual indoor dining room.

Island Farm Fresh Produce Queen's Highway, Palmetto Point. A godsend for self-catering cottage renters, this farm stand sells freshly picked salad greens, tomatoes and other vegetables and fruit. Also available are wonderful home-made salad dressings, pesto, chutney, pasta sauce, local honey, coconut relish, and smoked fish. Daily 10am–3pm.

Mate and Jenny's South Palmetto Point ☏ 332-1504. A beacon just off the highway, *Mate and Jenny's* has a dark and cosy interior featuring rafters strung with yachting pennants, a pool table and a jukebox stacked with Jimmy Buffett, Bob Marley and Frank Sinatra. On the food side, mains include delicious pizza ($20–24; try the conch-topped version), as well as bbq chicken ($20), steak ($23), sandwiches and immobilizing tropical cocktails. Popular and slightly overpriced, though all entrees are served with salad, potatoes and a vegetable. 11am–9pm; closed Tues.

New Sunset Inn One mile south of Governor's Harbour on the Queen's Highway ☏ 332-2487. Good and moderately-priced chicken, burgers and lobster are presented with friendly service in this bright if slightly barn-like dining room with a prime view of the sunset; order a drink and be prepared to wait a while for your meal. Cash and traveller's cheques only. Daily 9am–10pm.

Tippy's Banks Road, two miles south of Governor's Harbour ☏ 332-3331. A beachfront bistro boasting an energetic holiday atmosphere and some of the island's best meals. At lunch ($10–15), try the grouper burger or barbeque chicken sandwich with a side Caesar salad. Dinner offerings include the likes of a seafood chowder or avocado and feta cheese salad followed by seared tuna smothered in cilantro relish or a West Indian chicken and shrimp jambalaya (entrees average $28), with a selection of tempting desserts to finish. Daily noon–2.30pm and 6–9pm, though the bar is open all day with live music Fri and Sun nights. Reservations recommended.

Diving and watersports

The Clearwater Dive Shop (closed weekends; ☎332-2146) in the town centre near Barclays Bank rents and sells **snorkelling and diving equipment** and can give you the names of local guides who will take you out in their boats. Despite the name, they do not run diving trips. Gladstone Petty (☎332-2280) offers guided **fishing** expeditions. If you want to go diving or snorkelling with a regularly scheduled tour, head up to Harbour Island, where there are a couple of outfitters offering a full range of options (see p.238 for details).

Listings

Banking The First Caribbean Bank (☎332-2300), centre of town on the Queen's Highway, and the Royal Bank of Canada (☎332-2856), just south of the town centre on the highway. Both open Mon–Thurs 9.30am–3pm, Fri 9.30am–4pm; the First Caribbean Bank has an ATM.
Car Rental Stanton Cooper (☎332-1620 or cell 359-7007) and Arthur Nixon (☎332-1006 or cell 359-7879), both rent cars for $60 a day and will meet you at either Rock Sound or the Governor's Harbour Airport.
Groceries Burrows Grocery Store on the Queen's Highway on the south side of Governor's Harbour is well-stocked. The Shell station also has a small grocery and general store attached.
Laundry Sands Laundry and Cleaners (Mon–Sat 9am–5pm) is at the top of National Church Road, accessible by heading north on the Queen's Highway and taking the first right after the primary school as you enter town.
Medical There is a medical clinic at the top

of the hill on Haynes Avenue (daily 9am–5pm; ☎332-2774).
Petrol There is an Esso station on the Queen's Highway as you enter town from the south, and a Shell station in the centre of town on the highway near the First Caribbean Bank.
Police In emergencies, call ☎911. The local detachment (☎332-2111) is on the Queen's Highway in the centre of town across the street from the First Caribbean Bank.
Post office The local branch (9am–4.30pm; ☎332-2060) is in the pink Government Administration building.
Taxis For excellent taxi service and car rental call Clement Cooper (☎332-1726) in Palmetto Point, who rents cars for $300 a week and will meet you at the airport. Taxis also meet all flights.
Telephone There is a phone booth next to the police station, and a BaTelCo office where you can buy phonecards at the top of the hill near the clinic.

Northern Eleuthera and Spanish Wells

North of Hatchet Bay, the Queen's Highway runs for eight miles through rolling farm land and long stretches of dense bush to the hillside settlement of

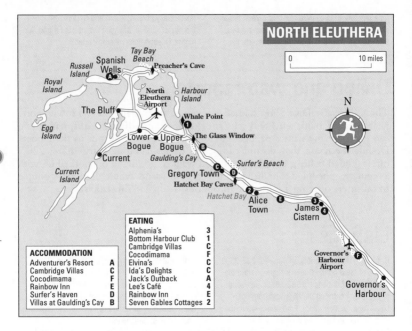

Gregory Town, once a major pineapple growing centre and now a destination for surfers, drawn to the rollers at the aptly named **Surfer's Beach** just south of town. Five miles north of Gregory Town you come upon the **Glass Window** – the rocky, wave doused moonscape where Eleuthera is barely a car width wide – is certainly a sight to behold. Beyond this thin neck of island are several down at heel settlements with little to detain a visitor, but you must come this way to catch a ferry to the resort community on Harbour Island (see p.230) or the working fishing settlement of **Spanish Wells**.

Gregory Town and around

Twenty-six miles north of Governor's Harbour, **GREGORY TOWN** is one of the largest settlements on Eleuthera, a colourful collection of semi-dilapidated wooden houses. The town is built into a steep hillside surrounding a narrow horseshoe harbour, which is flanked by high rocky cliffs on either side. During the nineteenth century, it became a major pineapple-growing area, with schooners leaving the harbour filled with fruit bound for London's Covent Garden. Although the pineapple is still celebrated here with a three-day festival in early June, the island and country on the whole has gradually been squeezed out of the pineapple market, and the young men of Gregory Town seem to spend a lot of time these days just hanging around the waterfront.

An interesting selection of locally made **crafts**, Bahamian straw work, clothing, jewellery, books and postcards may be found at Island Made Gifts on the Queen's Highway in the village centre and at Rebecca's Beach Shop next door. There isn't much else going on here, but musician Lenny Kravitz likes the relaxed atmosphere so much he is now a part-time resident.

Two miles south of Gregory Town, a side road on the Atlantic side leads to **Surfer's Beach**, a wild stretch of dune-backed coastline that draws wave-riders seeking a semi-wilderness experience; the dunes make for a fine picnic and surfer-gawking spot. To reach a more relaxed swimming beach, follow the Queen's Highway as it descends a steep hill and skirts green pastureland for four miles north of Gregory Town to the turnoff for **Gaulding's Cay Beach** (see box, p.216) on the left, opposite a white and yellow house. This sheltered secluded cove is a great place for a picnic and offers calm, shallow waters.

Practicalities

You can grab a quick decent fast **food** within Gregory Town at **Ida's Delights** (daily 11am–5pm), located on the Queen's Highway in the centre of town. Lined with comfortable booths, the restaurant at **Cambridge Villas** (daily 8am–9pm; ☎335-5080) serves up substantial Bahamian and American and you can eat quite well for under $8. For fine dining head for the hilltop restaurant at **The Cove Eleuthera** (☎335-5142; daily 8am–9pm, dinner reservations recommended), two miles north of town. While the attractive dining room is dressed up with white linen and rich polished wood, the tables to covet are on the poolside terrace, where a view of the turquoise sea surrounds you. The simpler lunch menu stretches from salads to jerk-shrimp kabobs, while more elaborate dinner offerings include coconut encrusted grouper served with red Thai curry sauce and roasted quail with proscuitto and black mission figs; dinner mains average $30. Back in town, **Thompson's Bakery**, behind the lime-green house at the top of the hill overlooking the harbour, sells bread and pineapple tarts. In the evenings, the local hotspot is **Elvina's Restaurant and Bar** (☎335-5032) on the Queen's Highway as you enter town from the south, especially for the Tuesday and Friday night jam sessions (musical instruments and karaoke machine available).

This part of Eleuthera feels somewhat isolated, although **staying** here puts you within easy distance (a twenty minute drive) of the delights of Harbour Island and (an hour's drive) of Governor's Harbour. The area's small motels and rental cottages attract mainly a surfing crowd, offering budget rates, free-flowing après-surf beverages and few other frills. The up-scale Cove caters primarily to those looking for a beach holiday away from the crowds.

Gregory Town accommodations

Cambridge Villas Queen's Highway on the north edge of Gregory Town ☎335-5080, ⓦwww .cambridgevillas.com. Best for budget-conscious travellers, *Cambridge Villas* has clean and basic double rooms equipped with a/c and a mini fridge. There's also a moderately-priced dining room, plus rental cars available. Downstairs rooms without TV ❷; upstairs with TV. ❸

The Cove Eleuthera Two miles north of Gregory Town ☎335-5142, ⓦwww.thecoveeleuthera.com. Recently renovated, *The Cove Eleuthera* aims at the high-end of the tourist trade. Set on 28 secluded acres, the resort boasts a sheltered cove with a small white-sand beach and good snorkelling from shore. The hilltop pool deck has spectacular sunset views and activities available free to guests include biking, snorkelling, tennis, a gym and a dramatic coastline ready to be explored by kayak. A handful of cottages house two dozen double rooms and suites done up in a cool mix of white rattan with green and orange accents, each equipped with a/c and an ipod. Some have a kitchenette and all have a private patio. The staff are friendly, but the management's desire to cultivate an air of exclusivity creates a somewhat uninviting atmosphere. Closed Sept. ❼

Gaulding's Cay Villas Four miles north of Gregory Town on the Queen's Highway ☎551-9900,

@www.gualdingcayvillas.com. On an isolated stretch of road but just a five-minute walk to Gaulding's Cay Beach, these new one and two-bedroom units are equipped with a/c, TV, mini fridge, microwave and coffee-maker. Rental cars are available, a necessity if staying here. ❷
Surfer's Haven Surfer's Beach ☏ 335-0349 or 333-3282, @www.bahamasadventures.com.

A rambling bright blue lodge perched high on a bluff overlooking spectacular Surfer's Beach. Geared to families and outdoorsy types, there are homely and tidy doubles with shared bath ($25) and a self-contained one-bedroom apartment with kitchen and bath ($75). The owners organize surfing safaris and kayaking and camping expeditions. ❶

❻ North to Spanish Wells

Beyond Gregory Town en route to **James Bay** and the water taxi docks serving Spanish Wells and Harbour Island, the landscape becomes more austere, with scrubby bush, exposed rock and stagnant saline ponds lining the road. Five miles north of town, the width of the island dwindles away to nothing at the **Glass Window**. In a rocky moonscape, beneath a narrow, constantly battered bridge, the turquoise plane of the Bight of Eleuthera meets the dark, heaving Atlantic in a dramatic cacophony of crashing waves. The arch of rock that gave the spot its name was smashed in a storm decades ago, and more recently, on a calm, sunny day in 1993, a huge freak wave known as a "rage" hit the bridge with such force that it shifted it 9ft towards the Bight. Maintaining the one-lane bridge in working condition keeps road crews busy, and, periodically, someone in a big hurry to get to one side or the other in bad weather gets washed into the sea.

On the north side of the Glass Window, an extremely rocky road to the east leads to the **Bottom Harbour Beach Club and Restaurant** at **Whale Point** one and a half miles away. Inside or on a pleasant wooden deck facing Harbour Island, a ten-minute boat ride away ($10 return by water taxi), you can dine on lobster salad, cracked conch, snapper and sandwiches. There is live rake 'n' scrape music here Friday and Sunday nights. Further north on the highway are the tatty settlements of **Upper** and **Lower Bogue**, where some residents have attempted to brighten the place up with colourful murals painted on the sides of their cement-block houses, but it's nothing worth stopping for.

At Lower Bogue, the road forks, and the road to the west continues for five miles until it reaches **Current**. A prosperous-looking fishing community with a long stretch of beach and few other amenities for visitors, it is home to Eddie Minnis, one of the Bahamas' best-known artists, renowned for his distinctive watercolour and oil portraits as well as his depictions of Out Island life.

James Bay and around

To continue northward from Lower Bogue to the tip of the island at **James Bay**, take a right when you come to a fork in the road and turn right again at the intersection a short distance further on. A Texaco station marks the turnoff to Harbour Island and the North Eleuthera Airport. Continuing northward on the highway, you come to a T-junction. The road on the right leads to the large **Preacher's Cave**, where the first settlers on Eleuthera found shelter and held church services after their ship wrecked on the **Devil's Backbone** reef in 1648. The cave is fronted by **Tay Bay Beach**, a small, private crescent of white sand that's perhaps the best reason to come this way (see box on p.216).

The road on the left from the T-junction leads to the wharf at James Bay, where you can catch the fifteen-minute water taxi (see below) to Spanish Wells, one mile away.

Spanish Wells

The settlement of **SPANISH WELLS** covers the eastern half of St George's Island, a flat, treeless slip of land two miles long and less than half a mile across. It is an insular but friendly community sustained by a prosperous lobster fishery. The approximately 800 residents are mostly descendants of a small band of Loyalist settlers of British extraction and speak English with a well-preserved Bostonian accent. A growing population of Haitian refugees has been established on nearby **Russell Island**, connected to St George's by a short bridge.

Spanish Wells' neat grid of paved streets is lined with tidy bungalows and clapboard cottages, some of which are over a hundred years old. Although the island boasts a spectacular **white-sand beach** running the length of its northern shore, the economy is not geared towards tourism and there are just a couple of simple restaurants, one motel and a small **museum** (Mon–Sat 10am–noon & 1–3pm; ☎333-4710) devoted to local history. The owner of the Islander Gift Shop next door will unlock the door for you. Daily life is pretty work-oriented here. Residents make their own fun, with well-attended weekly community softball games, church suppers and the like.

Practicalities

A government-operated **ferry** ($5 round-trip; no phone) leaves from James Bay on mainland Eleuthera and returns from Spanish Wells every half-hour, and private **water taxis** ($5 round-trip; ☎333-4291) wait for fares on the dock on both sides. These boats, along with the daily **Bo Hengy** ferry from Nassau (1.5 hours away), continuing on to Harbour Island ($65 one way; ☎323-2166, ⓦwww.bahamasferries.com) and the weekly mailboat all arrive at the main dock on the eastern tip of Spanish Wells.

Once on the island, you can rent a **golf cart** ($9 an hour or $45 a day) at Gemini Golf Carts (☎333-5188) in the little red clapboard house just up from the dock, though it is easy enough to get around on foot. If you choose to **stay** on the island, the **Adventurer's Resort** (☎333-4883, ⓦwww .bahamasvg.com/adventurers; ❸) is a well-maintained motel on the west side of town with nine double rooms and some one- and two-bedroom efficiency units, each with TV. Diving and fishing expeditions can be arranged and two-seater golf carts are available for $35 a day. Bahamas Vacation Homes Ltd (☎333-4080, ⓦwww.bahamasvacationhomes.com) handles holiday rentals for several quaint clapboard cottages in the village and along the beach.

When it's time to **eat**, try **Jack's Outback Restaurant** (☎333-4219), a popular spot serving filling simple meals in a retro black and yellow dining room right on the waterfront. The seafood-heavy menu features turtle and fries, lobster and various fish, along with steak or chicken dishes ($13–25); snacks come in the form of conch fritters and sandwiches ($5–7). The **Spanish Wells Yacht Haven** (☎333-4255) has a restaurant as well as 40 boat slips and a laundry. There are also a couple of grocery stores in town as well as a branch of the Royal Bank of Canada with an ATM.

While Manuel's Dive Station on the main street sells watersports equipment, it does not offer guided trips; local Chris Emery (☎333-4238) will take you **snorkelling**. Woody Perry (☎333-4433) is a recommended local bonefishing guide.

Harbour Island

Sitting two miles off the northeast coast of Eleuthera, **HARBOUR ISLAND** – also called 'Briland, a contraction of Harbour Island formed by dropping the "Har", "ou", and "s" – is the place to lounge with the rich and famous. Although a number of locals still fish and farm for a living, the atmosphere is decidedly upscale with a studied casualness. Tourism is king on this tiny green island, just three miles end to end and less than half a mile across, focused on the spectacular **Pink Sand Beach** running the length of the Atlantic side. The island's only settlement is the picture-perfect village of **Dunmore Town**, which climbs a low hill overlooking the harbour. It's perhaps a bit too precious, as charming little villages tend to become when being picturesque replaces all other forms of industry. A clutch of intimate and exclusive beach resorts cater to a wealthy clientele, and tucked in along the shore to the north and south of the village are sumptuous winter homes set in lush, carefully tended grounds.

The moneyed classes come here to let their expensively coiffed hair down and saunter in their designer-label beach togs. Movie stars go for a run on the beach without being accosted by starstruck fans, and when local homeowner Elle MacPherson drives her customized golf cart into town to pick up a few things at the market, people don't gawk. Meanwhile, the teenage set transported here by their stockbroker parents cruise the main drag – such as it is – in their golf carts, decked out in bikinis and sarongs with mobile phones in hand, looking for the action. For the average visitor, the action on Harbour Island is pretty low key, based around lounging on the beach, playing tennis and sipping piña coladas. There are also a couple of dive and snorkelling outfitters, and horseback rides through the surf and fishing charters can be arranged through all the hotels.

Arrival

The nearest **airport** to Harbour Island is the North Eleuthera Airport, a mile and a half from the docks on the eastern side of Eleuthera; see p.21 for flights information. If your Eleutheran destination is Harbour Island or Spanish Wells, book flights to this airport as taxis from Governor's Harbour are expensive ($60 or more). All flights are met by **taxis**, which shuttle to the wharf for about $4 per person. Water taxis depart regularly for the ten-minute ride to the government dock in Dunmore Town ($5 one way), which is within walking distance of the island's hotels, restaurants and Pink Sand Beach. If driving up from southern Eleuthera, there is a parking lot where you can leave your car (no charge).

The dock in Dunmore Town also gets a daily arrival from Nassau on the **Bo Hengy ferry**, named after a legendary Harbour Island boat builder. Run by Bahamas Fast Ferries ($65 one-way; ☎323-2166, ⊛www.bahamasferries.com), the boat leaves Potter's Cay in Nassau every morning at 8am, stops at Spanish Wells en route and arrives in Dunmore Town at 10.15am; it departs for Nassau again at 4pm except on Sundays, when it leaves for Nassau at 2pm. Two **mailboats** from New Providence also call at Harbour Island each week. **Bahamas Daybreak III** ($30 one-way; ☎335-1163) departs Nassau on Wednesdays at 5pm and the **Eleuthera Express** ($25 one-way; ☎333-4677) leaves Nassau for Harbour Island Thursdays at 6am. Call for the return-trip schedule.

To handle private yachts, there are two **marinas** on the island. Harbour Island Marina (☎333-2427 or 1-800/492-7909, ⊛www.harbourislandmarina.com, VHF Ch 16) has 32 slips with depths of 10ft or 12ft and the **Hammerhead's Bar and Grill** on site. Dockage fees are $1.75 per foot per day plus services. **Valentine's Resort and Marina** (☎333-2142 or 1-800/383-6480, ⊛www .valentinesresort.com,VHF Ch 16) has 39 berths for boats up to 160ft with 12ft draft and an open-air bar. **Valentine's Resort** is across the street, with hotel accommodation, a dive shop, pool and restaurant.

Getting around

Harbour Island is small and Dunmore Town itself is very compact and easy enough to get around on foot. **Taxi** drivers wait for fares on the dock, but most visitors buzz around on **golf carts**, which can be rented on the dock when you arrive, or arranged through your hotel. They are a fun and easy way to explore the far reaches of the island, but the narrow streets of Dunmore Town can be fairly clogged by golf cart traffic jams filled with those out to see and be seen, with a few pickup trucks and minivans mixed in for good measure. Ross's Garage (☎333-2064, ☎333-2585) rents well-maintained golf carts; a two/four/six-seater costs $35/$45/$65 per day or $210/$270/$310 per week. Ross's rents **minivans** for $75 a day and $450 a week as well. Minister's Taxi and Golf Cart Rentals (☎422-9269) offers golf cart rentals at similar rates along with a taxi service. Michael's Cycles (☎333-2384) on Colebrook Street rents **bicycles** for $30 a day. Robert Davis (☎333-2337) offers **historical tours** of Dunmore Town ($100 for a tour lasting an hour and a half for up to three people) as well as **horseback** riding on the beach ($30 for an hour, $20 for a half-hour).

Information

The Ministry of Tourism Bureau (Mon–Fri 9am–5pm; ☎333-2621) is on Dunmore Street. For pre-trip planning online, check out ⊛www .myharbourisland.com, an informative **website** maintained by Robert Arthur, lifelong resident of Harbour Island and proprietor of **Arthur's Bakery**, offering a virtual walking tour, map and a guide to local restaurants, accommodation, nightlife and local goings-on. Further information is available on ⊛www .briland.com, which has some local history and community news as well as tourist information. Colourful **maps** of Dunmore Town and Harbour Island as well as a selection of books about the Bahamas can be found at Dilly Dally on King Street.

Accommodation

Harbour Island has one of the most expensive, if not the priciest, **accommodation** scenes in the Bahamas. Spending $400 a night for a plush room is common, with some of the swankier bungalows going for twice that much. There are, however, a handful of moderately-priced motel options, and the tiny island also has a large selection of charming **cottage rentals** both in town and on secluded estates fronting the beach and the harbour. Island Real Estate (☎333-2377, ⓦwww.brilandrealestate.com) handles bookings for over eighty such properties. Generally rented by the week, they range in price from $700 to $7000 a week, with an average weekly rate of $1200–2000 for a one–or two–bedroom cottage.

🏃 **Bahama House Inn** corner of Dunmore and Hill streets ☎333-2201, ⓦwww.bahamahouseinn.com. This charming B&B is housed in a rambling late eighteenth-century mansion with a large garden and views of the harbour from the wraparound verandah. The seven guestrooms (one with a kitchen) evoke the colonial era with painted wood floors, high antique beds, polished mahogany wardrobes and colourful scatter rugs. The ground floor is a warm and inviting open space with an old-fashioned kitchen and solid wooden tables where breakfast is served. There are deep comfy sofas for chatting or watching TV and a cosy library nook. Closed Aug and Sept. ❻

Coral Sands Hotel On the beach ☎333-2350, ⓦwww.coralsands.com. The island's largest hotel, the beachfront *Coral Sands* has recently gone upscale with a sleek renovation. The sophisticated island decor blends polished dark hardwoods with white and cream textiles, bamboo ceiling fans and potted greenery. Most of the 39 guestrooms have a private balcony or patio with a view of the ocean or the extensive landscaped grounds, with the best housed in the Lucaya Block boasting spacious doubles and suites with floor-to-ceiling views of the ocean. On the grounds guest have access to tennis courts, a swimming pool, a romantic formal dining room and the breezy *Commander's Beach Bar* with steps down to the beach. From $365 a night. ❾

Dunmore Beach Club Facing the Pink Sands Beach ☎333-2200, ⓦwww.dunmorebeach.com. Seven guest cottages on eight acres tucked in among the flowering trees house fourteen double rooms and one-bedroom suites. They have an old-fashioned elegance with flowered chintz, honey-coloured wood and white wicker. Each room has a/c, ceiling fans, a large jetted tub, refrigerator and wet bar, and a private patio with an ocean view. From $600 a day for two, including meals. ❾

Eagle One Motel ☎333-2667. Simply furnished but very clean and spacious motel rooms on a quiet side street within earshot of the ocean and Pink Sands Beach. The one and two-bedroom units all have full kitchens and sitting rooms. ❸

The Landing On the waterfront overlooking the harbour ☎333-2707, ⓦwww.harbourislandlanding.com. An elegant inn tucked inside a walled garden with deep verandahs furnished with upholstered wicker chairs facing the water. The guestrooms are spare and airy, exquisitely restored to evoke the colonial period with four-poster beds and gauzy canopies, crisp white linens and walls, polished dark-wood floors, antique furnishings and dramatic original artwork. Some rooms have private balconies. The inn has one of the finest restaurants on the island, a cosy and popular bar, and a quiet upstairs sitting room for guests opening onto the verandah. From $320 a night. ❾

Pink Sands Hotel Pink Sand Beach ☎333-2030, ⓦwww.islandoutpost.com. Part of Island Records founder Chris Blackwell's collection of luxury boutique hotels, the *Pink Sands*' main building is an artfully-weathered pink stucco trimmed with queen conch shells and vaguely Moroccan and Balinese accents. Twenty-one one- and two-bedroom guest bungalows are nestled in secluded nooks around the sixteen-acre property, some boasting ocean views while others have private garden terraces. The interiors are bright and airy, with rough marble floors, walls painted in soft pastels and furnished with a mix of custom-made wood pieces and exotic accents like Indian tapestries and carved stone lanterns. Rates start at $900 per night including breakfast and dinner for two. ❾

Ramora Bay Club Colebrook Street ☎333-2325 or 1-800/688-0425, ⓦwww.romorabay.com. Cottages housing thirty guestrooms and suites are staggered down a gentle green slope facing a private dock with a view of Eleuthera across the water. A garish coat of pink and purple paint has tarnished the polish a bit, but there are still plenty of perks at this plush resort, including tennis courts, swimming pool, open-air bar and various watersports. From $375 a night, including breakfast. ❾

Red Apple Guesthouse Colebrook Street at Upalong Road ☎333-2750, Ⓦwww.redapplebb.com. Attractive one and two-bedroom apartments with a clean white and natural wood decor, a/c and TV. Golf cart rentals available. ❺

Rock House corner of Hill and Bay streets ☎333-2053, Ⓦwww.rockhousebahamas.com. This 1940's villa has been beautifully restored as a chic but not snobbish boutique hotel. The elegant dining room opens onto a view of the harbour and there is a poolside martini bar with plush red banquettes. Each room comes with its own poolside cabana, where you can have a private candlelit dinner should you choose. The artistic attention to detail is evident in the ten guestrooms, furnished with tropical woods, seagrass carpets, fresh orchids and a full range of artfully concealed modern electronics. $360, including continental breakfast. ❾

Royal Palm Hotel Clarence Street at Dunmore ☎333-2738; Ⓕ242-333-3177, Ⓦwww .royalpalmhotel.com. The cheapest lodgings on the island, the *Royal Palm* has clean and comfortable rooms done up in white with floral accents, located in the centre of the village. All rooms have a/c,

ceiling fans, TV, mini fridge and microwave. Golf cart rentals also available. ❷

Seashell Inn Nesbitt Street ☎333-2361, Ⓦwww .barettasseashellinn.com. Situated on a quiet corner on the western edge of the village, this small family-run inn has twelve large, airy double rooms, each equipped with TV and a/c and a couple with hot tubs. There is an attractive restaurant serving Bahamian dishes and golf cart rentals available, while the beach is a short stroll away up a sandy path. ❺

Tingum Village Hotel Colebrook Street ☎333-2161. Several rustic and homely self-catering cottages and apartment units set in a quiet grove of coconut palms and flowering bushes, with access to the beach a short distance away, The famous *Ma Ruby's* restaurant is only a few steps up a nearby path. ❸

Valentine's Resort and Marina On the waterfront on the harbour side of the island ☎333-2080 or 1-800/383 6480, Ⓦwww.valentinesresort.com. At the time of writing, *Valentine's* was in the midst of an extensive renovation, including the construction of new guestrooms and condominiums. Both the on-site dive shop and waterside *Boathouse Restaurant* have remained open through the re-building phase. While it was formerly one of the island's limited budget options, it looks like the owners are following the trend and going upscale.

Dunmore Town and around

With neat narrow streets lined with freshly painted clapboard cottages, flower boxes and white picket fences, **DUNMORE TOWN** – with a population of 1500 – evokes a small New England seaside town. It is a pleasant place to stroll around, with judiciously placed cafés and bars for refreshment along the way. When the sun goes down, people gather at one of Dunmore Town's several atmospheric bars and fine restaurants, and the more energetic stay up to catch some live music and dancing at one of the local clubs.

Just up from the government dock, directly across the street from the **Straw Market**, where local craftspeople sell handmade straw work and souvenir knick-knacks, stands the small **Higgs Sugar Mill**. Located on Bay Street, this white clapboard building currently houses a gift store and the tourism bureau, but was once owned and operated by a certain Hoppy Higgs in the early nineteenth century. One of three mills on the island at the time, sugar and syrup were made here from cane grown on the southern end of the island and then exported to the United States.

Running along the waterfront, **Bay Street** is lined with more well-kept cottages with verandahs and gabled windows facing the harbour. Walking north from the dock, you pass the clapboard and gingerbread-trimmed **Little Boarding House** (signposted), over 200 years old and now a private home. It was Dunmore Town's first lodging house, run by two sisters who held Catholic masses in their parlour before a church was built. A few doors down, the **Loyalist Cottage** (also marked) was built in 1797 as the home of a local sail maker.

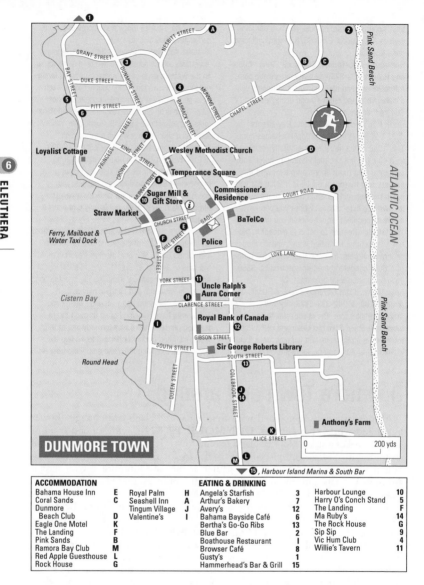

DUNMORE TOWN

Pink Sand Beach

ATLANTIC OCEAN

Pink Sand Beach

Loyalist Cottage

Wesley Methodist Church

Temperance Square

Commissioner's Residence

Sugar Mill & Gift Store

Straw Market

Ferry, Mailboat & Water Taxi Dock

BaTelCo

Police

Cistern Bay

Uncle Ralph's Aura Corner

Royal Bank of Canada

Sir George Roberts Library

Round Head

Anthony's Farm

0   200 yds

, Harbour Island Marina & South Bar

ACCOMMODATION				EATING & DRINKING			
Bahama House Inn	E	Royal Palm	H	Angela's Starfish	3	Harbour Lounge	10
Coral Sands	C	Seashell Inn	A	Arthur's Bakery	7	Harry O's Conch Stand	5
Dunmore		Tingum Village	J	Avery's	12	The Landing	F
Beach Club	D	Valentine's	I	Bahama Bayside Café	6	Ma Ruby's	14
Eagle One Motel	K			Bertha's Go-Go Ribs	13	The Rock House	G
The Landing	F			Blue Bar	2	Sip Sip	9
Pink Sands	B			Boathouse Restaurant	I	Vic Hum Club	4
Ramora Bay Club	M			Browser Café	8	Willie's Tavern	11
Red Apple Guesthouse	L			Gusty's	1		
Rock House	G			Hammerhead's Bar & Grill	15		

To reach the modest **commercial centre** of Dunmore Town, retrace your steps to the government dock and head straight up the hill on Church Street, then left onto Dunmore Street. **Temperance Square** is actually a small triangular park surrounded by a picket fence marking a memorial to Dr Thomas Johnson, who died in 1893 and was one of the first Harbour Islanders to qualify as a doctor. On the corner of Dunmore and Clarence streets nearby is **Uncle Ralph's Aura Corner**, a colourful collection of licence plates and

△ Dunmore Town

hand-painted signs offering words to live by like "When you are skating on thin ice, you might as well dance." Feel free to add your own piece of wisdom, and leave some change in the bucket. The originator, local resident Ralph Sawyer, donates all proceeds to the medical clinic. A block further south on Dunmore Street is the **Sir George Roberts Library**, built in 1969 and a rather grand edifice set back on a broad lawn. These days, the library amounts to a couple of shelves filled with old novels and textbooks, and the museum which used to be here is now closed. There are a few etchings and interesting old photographs of Dunmore Town on display.

From Dunmore Street, head down South Street towards Bay Street and the harbour. The south end of Bay Street is the area known as Roundheads, after the rebels who dethroned Charles I in England in 1649. Here, you will find the remnants of a battery of **cannon** mounted to protect the small settlement from pirate attacks.

The rest of Harbour Island

By far the biggest draw on the island is the undeniably lovely **Pink Sand Beach**, which can be reached by following either Chapel Street or Court Road over the dunes to the east and right onto the sand. The beach offers sweeping vistas, miles of walking, a gentle rolling surf and a sprinkling of beach bars where you can sit and decide for yourself if the faintly rosy hue of the sand really is pink.

If you continue south on the Queen's Highway from the Harbour Island Marina, you reach the gated residential community of **South Bar**, which encloses the treed southern end of the island. If you want to follow the dirt track – passable by golf cart – to the **ruins** of the seventeenth-century battlements at the far end, you must stop at the administrative office (☎333-2293) to ask for permission. The one

An unworthy namesake

Dunmore Town was named for the Scottish aristocrat **Lord Dunmore**, governor of the Bahamas (1787–96), who built a summer home in 1791 on the rise where the Commissioner's Residence (built in 1920) now stands. He laid out a neat grid of streets and divided the remainder of his estate into 190 lots, which he sold to prominent settlers. Using slaves, they farmed sugar cane on the south end of the island and built pineapple plantations over on north Eleuthera. Briland also became an important boat-building centre, turning out fishing smacks and the schooners that carried Bahamian sponges, pineapples, sugar and timber to Europe and America. The wooden buildings seen now were built mainly between 1800 and 1860.

Apart from being the original titleholder to the land on which it was built, Governor Dunmore did little to prove himself worthy of being lastingly honoured. Before arriving in the Bahamas, he had an undistinguished career as governor first of New York then of Virginia. When the American Revolution broke out, he abandoned his capital and fled to the safety of a warship anchored offshore, which he declared the seat of government, incurring the contempt of both Loyalists and republicans.

Upon being appointed to office in the Bahamas in 1787, Dunmore developed a mania for fort building and sleeping with other men's wives. He appointed his sons to lucrative offices and suspended the elected Assembly for over a year to prevent it from passing legislation he did not like. One of his contemporaries observed that he had "a capacity below mediocrity" and another charged that he was "obstinate and violent by nature". In 1796, a resident of Harbour Island testified that Dunmore had broken a stick over his head without provocation, and nine days later he was recalled to London, never returning to the pretty little village that bears his name.

cannon mounted here seems feeble protection from the pirate ships that cruised the channel for booty and periodically raided the settlement.

For a good walk or golf cart cruise in the opposite direction, follow Bay Street north into Nesbitt Street, and then left (or west) along a wooded trail, flanked by rather grand ocean-front estates. The track narrows to a small rocky point at the northern end of the island – about a mile and a half from the centre of the village – ending on a rocky shore with a view of Jacobs Island and the slightly larger Man Island beyond.

Eating

There are more **dining** spots on Harbour Island than anywhere else in the Eleutheran chain, and the variety of options is understandably greater here. You will find several **kiosks** on Bay Street along the waterfront selling fresh conch salad, hamburgers and chips, and wooden benches are situated with a fine view of the harbour. **Harry-O's** stand is a local favourite for its conch burgers and salads. Dinner reservations are recommended for all restaurants, and required if you would like to sample the fine gourmet fare at one of the hotels, where you are generally expected to dress smartly for dinner.

Angela's Starfish Barracks Hill ☎333-2253. A simple restaurant perched on top of Barracks Hill that receives rave reviews for its seafood dinners. The dining room is scrupulously clean, with a few tables in the courtyard outside. 8am–8.30pm.

Arthur's Bakery corner of Crown and Dunmore streets. Scrumptious cinnamon buns, rich chocolate brownies, freshly-baked pies, pastries and breads fill the display cases. The aroma of fresh baked goods and soft jazz music waft through the sunny café serving tasty breakfasts and lunches. Closed Sun.

Avery's Colebrook Street. A cheery bakery and café serving down home Bahamian grub. Open from 7am.

Bahama Bayside Café Bay Street ☎ 333-2174. A simple family restaurant serving inexpensive Bahamian favourites like fried chicken and steamed fish with traditional sides of plantain and coleslaw. Mon–Sat 8am–8pm, Sun 8am–2pm.

Bertha's Go Go Ribs Colebrook Street ☎ 333-3502. This takeaway with a few picnic tables beside it is the go-to spot for barbeque chicken and ribs. Daily 11am–9.30pm.

Blue Bar *Pink Sands Hotel* ☎ 333-2030. This open-air beach bar and grill painted a bright cobalt blue serves frosty drinks and fancy beach food like conch fritters with tossed organic lettuce, red pepper mayonnaise and fries (lunch $15–23). Open during the day for lunch, snacks and drinks.

Browser Café Murray Street ☎ 333-3069. An inviting, inexpensive courtyard café attached to the Briland Brush Strokes Art Gallery, with wood tables set on a shady flagstone patio and extra seating on an upstairs deck. Soft Latin music compliments the menu of elaborate bar food including a grouper sandwich with beer battered onion rings, soft shell tacos with a tequila and jalapeno aioli, and chicken satay with peanut dipping sauce. Lunch runs $7–12. Open Tues–Sun 11am–6pm.

Commander's Beach Bar *Coral Sands Hotel* ☎ 333-2350. Enjoy the sweeping view of the beach at this bar open for lunch and cocktails. The tasty lunch menu features a rock lobster salad sandwich, burgers (including a vegetarian option), seafood nibbles and tasty frozen drinks.

Dunmore Beach Club Facing the beach ☎ 333-2200. This small and formal white-wicker dining room with a view of Pink Sand Beach has a constantly changing menu that might include such creations as coconut milk soup with lemon grass and kafir, followed by seared tuna with green curry and seaweed or spaghetti squash, zucchini, apples and black-eyed peas with green curry. Dessert could be baked pineapple and vanilla coconut ice cream. Note that dinner reservations and choices from the menu must be made by noon of that day; three-course dinner about $65 per person.

Hammerheads Bar and Grill Harbour Island Marina ☎ 333-3240. On a deck overlooking the marina, this attractive lunch and dinner spot serves finger food, salads, sandwiches, jerk chicken, strip steak, veggie quesadillas and great drinks.

Harbour Lounge Bay Street, facing the government dock ☎ 333-2031. With tables on a wide verandah, this popular spot for people-watching features such specialities as spicy tequila shrimp, a grouper sandwich, pumpkin soup and other entrees from $10 to $35. Closed Mon, open for dinner only Sun.

The Landing Bay Street, south of the government dock ☎ 333-2707. An elegant and romantic candlelit dining room with dark hardwood floors and a gourmet menu that centres on fresh pasta, lobster, choice steaks and squid. Mains $35–42. Closed Wed.

Ma Ruby's at Tingum Village Colebrook Street ☎ 333-2161. Justly popular eatery famous for its hearty cheeseburger, *Ma Ruby's* also serves generous and tasty plates of grouper fingers, lobster, pasta and a scrumptious Key Lime pie, on a casual roofed patio surrounded by greenery.

Pink Sands Hotel Chapel Street, Pink Sands Beach ☎ 333-2030. An elegant bar and dining room with plenty of candlelight ambiance, opening onto a garden where tables are set for breakfast under the trees. The dinner menu changes daily, with delectable offerings like warm goat's cheese with asparagus and tomato in pastry as an appetizer, followed by grilled yellowfin tuna or a sautéed local grouper fillet, and mango cream pie or rum and coconut crème brûlée for afters. Pricey, but memorable, you can expect to pay $70 a person for dinner.

🏃 **The Rock House** corner of Hill and Bay streets ☎ 333-2053. The chef's table is set for a cosy candlelit dinner for fourteen under a sparkling chandelier, with a few more tables nestled into secluded nooks on the balcony overlooking the harbour. Start the evening with a cosmopolitan in the martini lounge, then sit down to gazpacho with lime-scented sour cream followed by yellow fin tuna steak with oranges, cucumber sesame salad and wasabi, with hokey pokey for dessert (home-made vanilla ice cream with honey comb chunks). If that's not enough, finish the meal off with a $30 glass of port. Entrees $38–60. Wed–Mon 6pm-11pm, reservations required for chef's table and recommended otherwise.

Sea Shell Inn Nesbitt Street ☎ 333-2361. A simple and casual peach-stucco bar and restaurant serving moderately-priced Bahamian and American dinners ($20–30) such as cracked conch, coconut chicken served with sweet potatoes and vegetables, pan-fried grouper, and sweet treats like guava duff. Live music Sunday nights.

🏃 **Sip Sip** Court Road, Pink Sand Beach ☎ 333-3316. Very popular, this casual beachfront bar and grill is done up in a combo of lime green, orange and blue that's hard to miss strolling down the beach. The menu has plenty of variety, with offerings like spicy conch chili, curried chicken salad with mango chutney, and salads made with organic greens as well as a $15 hotdog and $5 Bahamian style macaroni and cheese. Open 11.30am–4pm; closed Tues.

Drinking and nightlife

While you can sip a frosty cocktail at any of the appealing beach and waterfront **bars** and **restaurants** listed above, there are atmospheric watering holes at three of the nicest hotels in Dunmore Town. The cosy, warmly lit bar at **The Landing** (T333-2707) has overstuffed sofas, fine wines, whiskies and rum, evoking an earlier, more glamorous age; the bar at the casual chic **Pink Sands Hotel** (T333-2030) features live music Tuesday and Saturday nights; and the elegant polished bar at the **Coral Sands Hotel** (T333-2350) is a relaxing setting for a cocktail or a nightcap.

Gusty's on Coconut Grove Street at the north edge of the village (T333-2165; open at 10pm daily except Sun and Tues) has **live music** a couple of nights a week, while **Seagrapes** (T333-2439), a cavernous concrete block on Colebrook Street, sees a band play most weekends. The **Vic Hum Club** (T333-2161), on the corner of Munnings and Barrack streets, is a local institution. Home of what is supposedly the world's largest coconut – kept in a cardboard box near the bar – and a bartender with the unfortunate name of Hitler, it features all manner of entertainment, including a ping-pong table, a miniature basketball court that becomes a dance floor as the night wears on, and yellow and black striped walls plastered with old album covers and licence plates. Established in 1947, **Willie's Tavern** (T333-2021) on Dunmore Street is also a popular local hangout, with a pool table and live music on the weekends.

Diving and watersports

The premier local attraction for experienced divers is a high-speed drift dive through **Current Cut**, where you are swept along at speeds of up to ten knots through a narrow underwater canyon. The **Devil's Backbone**, a reef that extends for three miles along the northern edge of Eleuthera, has claimed many a ship over the centuries, including that of the Eleutheran Adventurers. While their vessel has not been found, the area is littered with wrecks, including a steam train locomotive that fell off a ship bound for Havana that's now a popular dive site. There are also plenty of other reefs and sea gardens to explore, although most must be reached by boat. Two dive shops in Dunmore Town can set you up for a day of diving or snorkelling and/or rent you a boat. If you'd rather catch fish than look at them, they can also arrange that.

Ocean Fox Dive Shop Harbour Island Marina T333-2323, W www.oceanfox.com. The Ocean Fox offers daily snorkelling excursions for $35, including equipment. Other diving options include a resort course for $95; a single-tank dive for $45; two-tank dive $75; and a night dive for $65. Equipment rental costs $15 for snorkelling gear, $35 for scuba. The owner, Jeff Fox, will also take you deep-sea fishing for $750 for a full day, $450 half-day, including all gear. Boat rentals are also available.

Valentine's Dive Center Valentine's Resort and Marina T333-2080, W www.valentinesdive.com. Snorkelling trips go for $45, including gear; $75 for a two-tank dive; $135 for a high-speed drift dive through Current Cut. They also do wall dives and night dives or you can charter the dive boat for the whole day for $725. The four-day PADI Open Water Certification costs $450 including video and textbook, dive equipment, pool sessions and four open-water dives. A number of other speciality courses including search and recover, underwater navigation and night diving also offered. Deep-sea fishing charters go for $750 for a full-day, $550 for a half-day, and kayak rentals are $45 for a full-day. **Lil' Shan's Watersports** With a booth on the waterfront near Valentine's Marina ☎333-3532, ⓦwww.lswatersports.com. Offers snorkel trips and gear rental, kayak, boat and jet-ski rental and waterskiing outings.

Listings

Banking The Royal Bank of Canada (Mon–Fri 9.30am–5pm; ☎333-2250) is located on Murray Street. There is a 24-hour ATM.

Groceries The Piggly Wiggly, King Street at Crown, and Johnson's Grocery, Dunmore Street near Munning, both have a good range of foodstuffs. Pineapple Fruit and Veg on Bay Street near Pitt sells produce.

Internet access Available at Arthur's Bakery on the corner of Dunmore and Crown streets and the *Red Apple Inn* on the corner of Colebrook Street and Upalong Road at $10 for 15 minutes.

Laundry Seaside Laundromat (☎333-2066) is on Bay Street.

Medical attention The Harbour Island Health

Clinic (☎333-2227) is the pink building on the corner of South and Colebrook streets.

Pharmacy A pharmacist is on duty at Bayside Drugstore (☎333-2174) on Bay Street.

Police Dial ☎911 in an emergency. The station is in the Government Administration Building on Gaol Street (☎333-2111).

Post office Located in the same building as the police and open 9am–5pm weekdays.

Taxis Taxis wait on the government wharf in Dunmore Town, or call Minister's taxi ☎422-9269.

Telephone BaTelCo (☎333-2375) is on the corner of Colebrook Street and Gaol Street and is open 8am to 5.30pm. There are pay phones, prepaid phonecards for sale and a fax service.

South Eleuthera

South Eleuthera, from Palmetto Point to Eleuthera Point, is the least developed part of the island. The largest settlement is sleepy **Rock Sound**, a prettily painted town with its "international" airport nearby. The picturesque fishing village of **Tarpum Bay** serves as another possible base. The remaining highlights are in the form of **stunning beaches**, including Winding Bay, Cotton Bay and Lighthouse Beach. There is not much to do in the region other than listen to the sound of the waves from the vantage point of any number of well-sited beachfront cottages, but that seems to be more than enough for the area's repeat visitors.

Tarpum Bay

Twenty miles south of Governor's Harbour the Queen's Highway runs through the centre of **TARPUM BAY**, a colourful fishing village nestled alongside a sweeping curve of turquoise water and white-sand beach, just five miles north of **Rock Sound International Airport**.

On the waterfront, the whitewashed **St Columba's Anglican Church** is one of Eleuthera's most photographed sites, a whitewashed steeple that pops

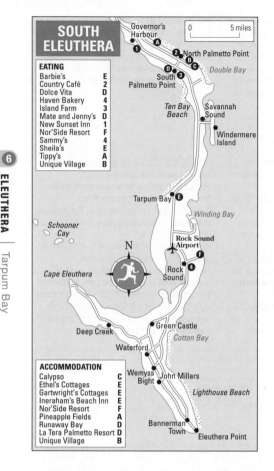

SOUTH ELEUTHERA

EATING

Barbie's	E
Country Café	2
Dolce Vita	D
Haven Bakery	4
Island Farm	3
Mate and Jenny's	D
New Sunset Inn	1
Nor'Side Resort	F
Sammy's	4
Sheila's	E
Tippy's	A
Unique Village	B

ACCOMMODATION

Calypso	C
Ethel's Cottages	E
Gartwright's Cottages	E
Ineraham's Beach Inn	E
Nor'Side Resort	F
Pineapple Fields	A
Runaway Bay	D
La Tera Palmetto Resort	D
Unique Village	B

0   5 miles

Governor's Harbour

North Palmetto Point

South Palmetto Point

Double Bay

Ten Bay Beach

Savannah Sound

Windermere Island

Tarpum Bay

Winding Bay

Schooner Cay

Rock Sound Airport

N

Cape Eleuthera

Rock Sound

Deep Creek

Green Castle

Cotton Bay

Waterford

Wemyss Bight

John Millars

Lighthouse Beach

Bannerman Town

Eleuthera Point

out brilliantly against the backdrop of the turquoise water. Originally settled by the descendants of freed slaves and now home to a small Haitian community, the village has several brightly painted wooden cottages and numerous examples of traditional Bahamian architecture in various states of repair lining its few narrow lanes. Surrounded by flowering trees and roaming chickens, they are picturesque in their decay, at least to a visitor. Roosters provide an early-morning wakeup call for the fishermen and women who sell their catch in the early afternoon on the wharf. Several nights a week the otherwise quiet side streets of the settlement ring with exhortations and hallelujahs from the pulpit of one of its many churches.

On the north side of town you can see the **castle** built by the self-titled Lord Macmillan Hughes, an oddball British artist who lived here for thirty years. The narrow sandy **beach** at Tarpum Bay extends two miles northward on the bight side, and there is another fine beach on the Atlantic side at **Winding Bay**, one mile south of town. A fun time to visit for the **Junkanoo** rush-out on either December 26 or New Year's Day, when colourful parade floats, traditional dancers and marching bands with drums, whistles and cowbells take to the streets of Tarpum Bay in the early dawn.

Practicalities

If you are looking for **accommodation** in Tarpum Bay, **Cartwright's Oceanfront Cottages** (☎334-4215; ④) has three two- and three-bedroom cottages on the waterfront at the western edge of town, with a homely and eclectic decor of crocheted doilies, china cats and a great view of the sea. **Ethel's Cottages** (☎334-4030 or 4233; ②) on the waterfront in the centre of the village rents six clean and spacious one and two-bedroom apartments with full kitchens. Rental cars are also available. On the beach on the north edge of town, the frequently deserted **Ingraham's Beach Inn** (☎334-4066;

❸) caters mainly to local business travellers with spacious and well-maintained doubles and one-bedroom apartments. The accommodations are fine, but the atmosphere is quite dead and not really holiday-oriented. A couple of miles north of Tarpum Bay, **Seaview Cottage** (☎334-4356, 🌐www.seaviewcottage. com; ❹) has two lovely secluded weekly rental cottages on a 63 acre forested citrus estate that runs down to a fine beach on the Atlantic side. The aptly named **Seaview Cottage** is a studio efficiency with a view of the water, while **Valleyview House** is a two-bedroom lodge nestled among the trees a short walk from a private stretch of beach.

Eating is a bit of an afterthought in Tarpum Bay. Filling deep-fried and Bahamian fare ($7–10) can be procured at **Barbie's** (Mon–Sat 9am–10pm; closed Sun), which has a few booths in its tidy dining room; much the same is served at friendly **Sheila's New Royal Restaurant** (☎334-4463) on the southern end of town. The adventurous might seek a drink at the rough-and-tumble **Pink Elephant** on the west side of town.

Rock Sound

Eight miles south of Tarpum Bay, **ROCK SOUND** is a green and tidy little waterfront village of well-kept cottages with fenced gardens and several candy-coloured buildings, including the medical clinic, a colonial-style government administration building and a BaTelCo office. Vast quantities of pineapples were shipped from Rock Sound in the nineteenth century, but there really is not much doing in the laidback hamlet these days; many inhabitants are retired or work in the civil service, and there's little to do save for a peaceful stroll with a constant view of the blue-green sea as your companion.

The rainbow-coloured clapboard cottage on the main street houses the delightful **Luna Sea Gift Shop**. Run by the charming Janice Gibson, inside is an imaginatively displayed collection of original Bahamian artwork and crafts. Across the street is the real commercial centre of the village, the **Dingle Motors** petrol station (daily 7am-9pm), offering car and bicycle rentals, laundry service and Internet access. Other sights include the **Ocean Hole** off Fish Street, a rock crater about 50yd across and 50yd deep filled with rather murky saltwater and a population of fish that rise up to eat bread tossed in by bystanders. Further towards the Atlantic coast on Fish Street, the **Nor'Side Beach** (see box, p.216) is a dramatic stretch of sand with a nice spot for a drink or a meal.

Practicalities

There are two **places to stay** in Rock Sound. In the village, **Sammy's Place Restaurant and Bar** has four simple double rooms with a/c and TV (❷), along with a pair of two two-bedroom cottages with full kitchens (❸). About two miles outside of town, ⚔ **The Nor'Side Resort** (☎334-2573; ❸) has a spectacular setting perched on a bluff overlooking a long and lonesome stretch of beach on the Atlantic side of Rock Sound. To get there from the centre of Rock Sound, follow Fish Street for about a mile to a T-junction, then turn left and continue on for about 500yd. A cluster of four hexagonal cottages house eight studio apartments, each beautifully decorated in soothing neutral shades accented with floral fabrics. The rooms are bright and airy and feature deep tubs, TVs, kitchens and a dining nook.

There is good snorkelling from the beach, and a cosy sand-floored bar and a **restaurant** serving the best home-cooked Bahamian meals on the island, including grouper fingers, cracked conch, barbecue chicken and generous helpings of traditional side-dishes (open daily from noon–9pm; reservations appreciated, but not required).

The other **eating** options in Rock Sound include the **Haven Bakery** (☏334-2155; Tues–Sat 10.30am–6pm, closed Sun and Mon) in the middle of the village, where Julian Haven turns out yummy pastries, pies and sweet Bahamian bread and cooks up a lunch special most days or on request ($8). **Sammy's Place** (☏334-2121; daily 8am–10pm) serves tasty and filling deep-fried fare, pizza and fresh seafood done Bahamian-style in a casual diner on a back street near the primary school (mains $10–13). The **Rock Sound Marketplace** on the north edge of town has the biggest grocery store on Eleuthera, a pharmacy, liquor store, petrol station and a branch of the Bank of Nova Scotia.

For friendly and reliable **car rentals**, call Wilfred Major (☏334-2158); rates start at $350 a week. **Taxi** drivers meet every flight at Rock Sound Airport, or call Friendly Bob (☏334-8112 or 334-8184).

South from Rock Sound

South from Rock Sound the Queen's Highway hugs the ocean to the west for a short while before cutting inland through low undulating bush. The island broadens into a wide inverted triangle at its southern end, encompassing several small inland settlements and stretches of mangrove swash. There are a few points of interest down this way, safe for Cotton Bay for golfers, Lighthouse Beach for beach aficionados, and the Island School for young aspiring marine biologists.

Just over seven miles south of Rock Sound is the turn-off to the defunct **Cotton Bay Club** on your left, currently being redeveloped as a luxury resort (ⓦwww.cottonbayeleuthera.com) Nine of the eighteen holes on the golf course (☏334-6156) are still open, and the pretty curved beach can be accessed by a short path about 20yd south of the guardhouse, where you can rent clubs and pay the greens fees ($70 for nine holes, $100 for eighteen holes; $15 to rent clubs).

If you don't make the turn-off to Cotton Bay, but continue a mile further south on the Queen's Highway, the road divides at **Greencastle**, with the Queen's Highway heading southeast to Eleuthera Point and a paved road veering southwest out of town. The latter reaches a T-junction, where, if you continue right a few miles you reach **Deep Creek**, a smattering of houses and several churches strung along the road facing an expanse of waterlogged mangrove swash. The highlight here is the **bonefishing**, for which Alfred McKinney (☏334-8097 or 8184) serves as the local guide.

A couple of miles past Deep Creek is the **Island School** (PO Box 6008, Lawrenceville, NJ 08648; ☏609/620-6700, ⓦislandschool.org), a private school offering a semester abroad for high school students interested in environmental conservation and community service projects. The school's dive shop is located nearby at the Cape Eleuthera Marina (☏334-6327), and equipment can be rented when not in use by students. Costs are $175 for full scuba gear including a two-tank dive, $7 to fill an air tank and $7 to rent snorkelling gear for the day. Guides, boat charters and sea kayak rental can all be arranged through the school. The tiny **Sandpiper Cays**, visible to the northwest, are a good destination for a picnic on the beach if you have a boat. Cape Eleuthera was briefly the site of a resort and a new resort and marina is in the works. The Marina (☎334 6327 or 6326) currently has boat slips, fuel and electrical hookups. A narrow gravel beach here offers rich pickings for shell collectors on a good day, with the ruins of a stone foundation in the bush nearby dating from the American Civil War.

Lighthouse Beach

A right turn at the T-junction in Waterford (one mile south of Greencastle) leads to Cape Eleuthera. If instead you turn left, the road eventually reaches **Lighthouse Beach** at Eleuthera Point, 24 miles south of Rock Sound. En route it passes the Hobo Marina at Davis Harbour (☎334-6303), with boat slips and a laundry. A bit further on, the settlement of **Wemyss Bight** features a handful of ramshackle houses and several well kept churches. To reach Lighthouse Beach stay on the Queen's Highway until you come to a sharp right-angle turn leading to **Bannerman Town**. Instead of making the turn, take the dirt road straight ahead. It's a three-mile drive on an extremely rocky track, but the beach at the end is simply stunning. While passable in a regular car, a 4wd is recommended for the thirty-minute trip. Your reward is six miles of pristine pink and white sandy beach and turquoise surf with the dark shadows of coral reef visible beneath the surface. On a clear day, you can see Cat Island on the horizon. The jutting headland at the beach's south end is topped by a derelict but picturesque lighthouse; park below the lighthouse and follow the path up over the dunes and onto the beach.

Practicalities

There is nowhere to **stay** south of Rock Sound, but the area is easily visited on day-trips from elsewhere on the island. **Eating** options are likewise limited down this way – it's best to pack a lunch when coming for the day. **DJ's Pizza** (sporadic hours; ☎334-9401) in Waterford does takeaway, and you can grab a basic fish dinner at **Sharil's Inn** (☎334-8111; open for lunch and dinner, closed Sun) in Deep Creek, which serves your basic fish dinners; it's best to call ahead, however, as hours can vary.

The Exumas

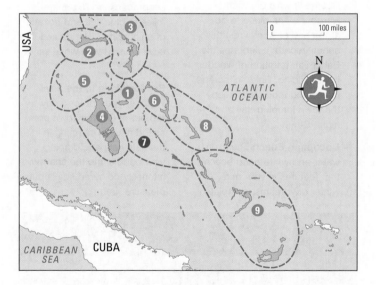

CHAPTER 7

Highlights

* **Stocking Island** A mile off George Town, this island's an idyllic place to while away the day, with a long wind-swept beach that runs almost the length of its Atlantic side and crescents of soft sand along the protected shore. See p.258

* **The Out Island Regatta** George Town's Elizabeth Harbour is the place to be at the end of April when this annual regatta celebrates the Bahamian tradition of wooden boat building. Rake 'n' scrape music and food stalls keep the town jumping day and night. See p.259

* **Cocoplum Beach** The azure water and white-sand beach that features in your mid-winter daydreams, complete with a gourmet beach bar and grill. See p.263

* **Thunderball Grotto** Snorkel-ling heaven, Thunderball Grotto is a limestone vault arching over a pool filled with brilliant corals and fish. See p.271

* **The Exuma Land and Sea Park** Serenely beautiful and splendidly remote, the park encompasses 176 square miles of blue sea and dozens of uninhabited islands and cays rimmed with white sand. See p.272

* **Sea kayaking in the cays** Whether you opt for a day trip out of George Town or spend a week camping in the national park, dipping your paddle into the shallow, intensely-coloured sea is pure pleasure. See p.274

△ Kayaking in the cays

7

The Exumas

With a name like a contented sigh, the laid-back **EXUMAS** bear a fitting label. Some 365 islands, cays and rock outcroppings of various sizes make up the island chain, which lies in a narrow band stretched over one hundred miles along the eastern edge of the Great Bahama Bank. The islands are bound on one side by the shallow, clear waters of the bank, and on the other by the deep heavy waves of Exuma Sound. It's not surprising that human life here is very much oriented towards the sea, and those Exumians not engaged in fishing, farming or government services cater to a small yet growing tourist trade here.

The shallow protected waters and deserted beaches make the Exumas ideal for **sea kayaking**, and several outfitters run expeditions through the cays and in the pristine **Exuma Land and Sea Park**. Great and Little Exuma and the islands south of the park boundaries are flanked by prime bonefishing and deep-sea **fishing grounds**, and throughout the region the seas teem with brilliant underwater life that ensures memorable **diving** and **snorkelling**.

On the bigger, settled islands of **Great and Little Exuma** at the south end of the chain, land has been cleared and planted over generations, giving them a more pastoral air. Blessed with a fine natural harbour, the capital **George Town**, located in the centre of Great Exuma, is a popular destination for boaters and contains most of the chain's hotels, restaurants and outdoor outfitters. To the north and south of the capital, several small fishing and farming settlements, such as **Williamstown** and **Rolle Town**, offer a picturesque glimpse of Out Island life, and make a pleasant day-trip from George Town by car or bicycle.

North of Great Exuma, the **Exuma Cays** stretch out for forty miles. The showstopper here is the remote Exuma Land and Sea Park, an area of extraordinary beauty. There are, though, several other worthwhile stops, including the small fishing settlements on sleepy **Little Farmer's Cay** and pretty **Staniel Cay**, which draws a yachting crowd and hosts a good-time New Year's Day Regatta that lasts for three days.

Some history

Although no archeological evidence has been unearthed, it is quite likely that there were Lucayan settlements here before the **British** laid claim to the Exumas in the seventeenth century. Sometime around 1700, the whole of Great Exuma was granted to Englishman **Henry Palmer**, who never lived on the island chain but sent his ships to gather salt and braziletto, a valuable hardwood used in cabinetry and to make a red or purple dye. While others soon came to hunt whales and rockfish off the islands, the most frequent

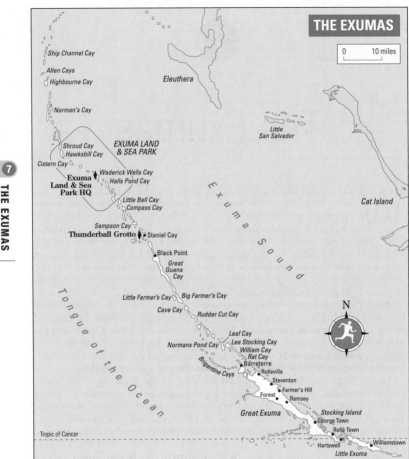

visitors were pirates and privateers, who plied the waters of the Bahamas in their dozens. Records from 1706 show that the total population of the Bahamas at that time was five hundred permanent residents, of whom maybe less than thirty had settled in the Exumas.

As elsewhere in the Bahamas, the population jumped drastically with the arrival of **Loyalist** exiles from the southern United States at the end of the American Revolution. Among them was wealthy English aristocrat **Denys Rolle**, who years earlier developed a grandiose vision for a model town in the New World. He gathered three hundred unfortunates from the slums of London and shipped them to Florida, where he built a mansion for himself and laid out a tidy little settlement that he first called Charlotia, after the queen, then modestly renamed Rolleton. When most of the English settlers fled the arduous daily grind of the humid settlement, Rolle replaced them with African slaves.

When the peace accord of 1783 returned Florida to Spain and the Bahamas to England, Rolle loaded his 140 slaves, dismantled houses, livestock and other possessions aboard the *Peace and Plenty* and set sail for Great Exuma. The British government granted Rolle two large tracts of land in the north and south of the island, equalling 2000 acres, which he proclaimed **Rolleville** and **Rolle Town,** respectively. Rolle was by far the biggest landowner in the Exumas and the biggest slave-owner in the Bahamas, and by 1789, the population of the Exumas had exploded to 704 (66 European and 638 African). When his cotton farms failed due to soil exhaustion and the damage caused by the chenille bug, Rolle packed up and went back to England, leaving his properties in the hands of overseers.

In 1828, his son Lord John Rolle tried to move his Exumian slaves to more productive enterprises on Trinidad, but the slaves in question were adamantly opposed to being uprooted. Their basic needs largely neglected by an absentee landowner, they had out of necessity made a home for themselves on Exuma, raising crops and livestock and starting families. Under the leadership of a man named **Pompey**, a group of slaves took to the woods for a month to avoid being transported. Then they commandeered Rolle's boat and defiantly set sail for Nassau, where they were captured, flogged and sent to the workhouse. When they returned home to Exuma, they were greeted with cheers from their fellow slaves, who immediately staged a strike. Fearing an open revolt, the Governor sent fifty soldiers out from Nassau to quell the unrest. The soldiers locked up all the slaves at Steventon, and then set off to Rolleville, a short distance away. Pompey, who had eluded capture at Steventon, ran up the beach to warn the residents of Rolleville, who hid in the bush until the soldiers left. Pompey was eventually caught and cruelly whipped, and the sobered slaves returned to work. Nevertheless, they henceforth refused to labour more than half of each day for their masters, insisting on reserving the rest of their time for their own business. Troops were called out three more times before **Emancipation** was proclaimed in 1834.

The Loyalist planters generally drifted away from Exuma after the failure of cotton and the abolition of slavery. Africans seized from illegal slave trading vessels augmented the population over the next few years. Small settlements of freed captives were established at Williamstown and in the tiny, desolate and remote Ragged Islands. Well into the mid-twentieth century, Exumians got along on a combination of sponging, fishing, subsistence agriculture and wrecking. Following World War II, the Exumas were discovered by the international yachting set. Cruising through the cays became the thing to do for the in-crowd, and a handful of swanky resorts opened to cater to them. Although the relatively modest tourist trade here is a far cry from the wall-to-wall carnival of Paradise Island or Freeport/Lucaya, it provides a vital source of income for many Exumians.

In the 1970s, a less welcome form of economic growth emerged as **drug smuggling** boomed throughout the Bahamas, and George Town was the scene of what was, at the time, the largest seizure ever of pure cocaine – 247 pounds worth over two billion dollars. The Bahamian government subsequently launched an intensive campaign to rid the islands of drug runners, and things have calmed down considerably since then. Today, the islands continue to maintain a simple, sleepy way of life.

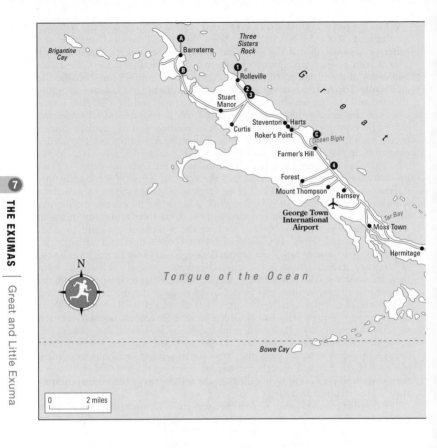

Great and Little Exuma

The two biggest islands in the Exumas, **GREAT EXUMA** and **LITTLE EXUMA**, lie head to toe only 200 yards apart at the southern end of the chain, joined by a narrow bridge. All but a few hundred of the Exumas three thousand residents live on these two isles, most in the capital **George Town**, located in the centre of 35-mile-long Great Exuma. With plenty of accommodation, restaurant and evening entertainment options, George Town makes a good base for exploring the surrounding area, but its most appealing features are the emerald depths of **Elizabeth Harbour** and the cays that lie offshore. A perfect destination for a picnic outing is **Stocking Island**, with a long dune-backed beach on its Atlantic side, walking paths and a couple of casual beach bars. Heading north from George Town, you have your pick of inviting beaches at **Hooper's Bay**, **Jolly Hall** and **Tar Bay**. Further north, the beach at

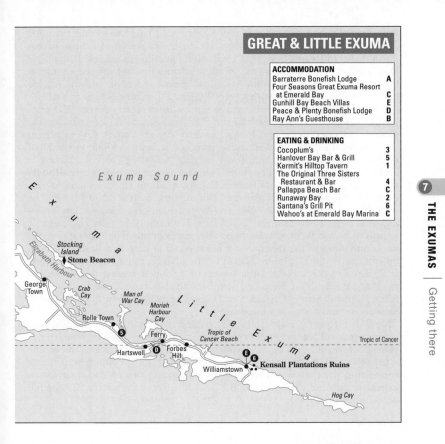

GREAT & LITTLE EXUMA

ACCOMMODATION
Barraterre Bonefish Lodge	A
Four Seasons Great Exuma Resort at Emerald Bay	C
Gunhill Bay Beach Villas	E
Peace & Plenty Bonefish Lodge	D
Ray Ann's Guesthouse	B

EATING & DRINKING
Cocoplum's	3
Hanlover Bay Bar & Grill	5
Kermit's Hilltop Tavern	1
The Original Three Sisters Restaurant & Bar	4
Pallappa Beach Bar	C
Runaway Bay	2
Santana's Grill Pit	6
Wahoo's at Emerald Bay Marina	C

Steventon offers a pleasant pit stop en route to the most spectacular strand of all, **Cocoplum Beach** near **Rolleville**. The work-a-day settlement of **Barreterre** at the very northern tip of Great Exuma is the jump-off point for trips into the southern Exuma Cays.

Six miles long and two miles wide, Little Exuma to the south is hilly and green. Here you'll find a handful of quiet rural hamlets and a few pretty strands of powdery white beach that make for worthwhile day-trip destinations from George Town. Highlights include the seaside settlement of **Rolle Town**, the beach and hilltop ruins on **Man of War Cay**, long and sandy **Tropic of Cancer Beach** and the **Hermitage**, a Loyalist plantation ruin in peaceful **Williamstown**, at the south end of Little Exuma.

Getting there

Exuma is well served by flights into **Exuma International Airport**, located eight miles north of George Town. American Eagle (☎345-0124 or 1-800/433-7300, ⓦww.aa.com) makes two direct runs daily from Miami, and Continental Connection operated by Gulfstream (☎1-800/523-3273,

@www.continental.com) flies in twice a day from Fort Lauderdale. Lynx Air (☎345-0108, 954/772-9808 or 1-888/596-9247, @www.lynxair.com) also has direct flights to Exuma from Fort Lauderdale several times a week. Bahamasair (☎377-5505 or 1-800/222-4262, @www.bahamasair.com) offers daily flights from Nassau, plus options from Miami and Fort Lauderdale, and the reliable Sky Unlimited (☎337-8993) has several flights a day from Nassau as well.

A twelve-hour **ferry** from Nassau is run by *Bahamas Fast Ferries* ($50 one-way; ☎323-2166, @ww.bahamasferries.com), pulling into the centrally located government dock in George Town. The ferry departs Potter's Cay in Nassau on Monday, Tuesday and Wednesday evenings at 5pm, 7.30pm and 9.30pm respectively, arriving in George Town early the following morning, leaving at 6am on Tues, 8am Wed, and noon on Thurs for the return trip. Two **mailboats** also service the Exumas from Potter's Cay, though both schedules tend to vary so call the dockmaster in Nassau ahead of time to confirm (☎393-1064). The well-maintained *Grand Master* ($45 one-way) departs on Tuesday at 2pm, arriving in George Town fourteen hours later. Depending on tides and cargo, it returns to Nassau Wednesday night or Thursday morning. The *Captain C* serves the communities of the Exuma Cays, but also calls at Barreterre at the northern tip of Great Exuma. It leaves Nassau on Tuesday afternoons at 2pm, stopping at Staniel Cay, Black Point, Little Farmer's Cay and Barreterre on Wednesday; the Ragged Islands on Thursday; then back to Barreterre, Little Farmer's Cay, Black Point and Staniel Cay again on Friday. The mailboat returns to Nassau on Saturday around noon ($45 one-way).

Note that if your primary interest is visiting the Exuma Land and Sea Park, you're better off landing at Staniel Cay, just outside its southern boundary. If you plan to explore all of the Exumas, it's difficult – though not impossible – to get from George Town to Staniel Cay. There are no commercial flights connecting the two, and it requires a combination of cars and boats or an expensive airplane charter (around $700 for a five-seater); see p.270 for full details on Staniel Cay.

Information

Located in the centre of George Town, the Ministry of Tourism's **visitor centre** (Mon–Fri 9am–5pm; ☎336-2440) has a selection of maps, brochures and glossy magazines for the taking, plus friendly staff to answer your questions. Sandpiper Gifts, across from *Club Peace and Plenty*, stocks a good selection of books about the Bahamas. A community newspaper, *The Exuma Sentinel*, is published monthly out of Nassau by the *Nassau Guardian* and is available for free at shops and hotels. Bahamas Broadcasting Corporation transmits on Radio frequency 1540 AM, though more entertaining information can often be garnered by tuning a VHF ship to shore radio onto the locally monitored Channel 16.

Getting around

George Town's restaurants, entertainment and shops are all within easy walking distance, but should you want to explore Great and Little Exuma you will more than likely want to **rent a car** for at least a day or hit the highlights on a guided **bus tour**. **Taxis** are accessible, but unless you prefer to have a chauffeur it's more economical to hire a car or take the **public bus**, which covers the stretch between George Town and Rolleville to the north. Keep in mind that most hotels and restaurants on the outskirts of George Town offer **complimentary transportation** between their establishments and George Town for their guests. **Ferries** and **water taxis** operate between George Town and Stocking Island, while perhaps the most exciting way to see Exuma would be to rent a **boat** to explore the coastline and the numerous nearby cays. **Hitchhiking** is easy on the islands, and plenty of people rely on it to get to work and around.

Buses and taxis

Run by Lawrence Saunders, the Exuma Bus Service (cell ☎554-3227) makes three runs a day Mon–Sat up the Queen's Highway between George Town and Rolleville. **Buses** leave George Town at 7.15am, 11am and 4pm with returns from Rolleville at 8.15am, 11.50am and 5.05pm. The afternoon trip makes detours to Moss Town, the Forest and Stuart Manor. Fares cost $2–5 per trip, depending on distance.

Taxi drivers meet every flight, and the trip into George Town costs $25 for two passengers. If you arrive on the *Captain C* mailboat at Barreterre, a taxi to George Town will cost around $75. Two reliable and courteous operators in the George Town area are Leslie Dames (☎357-0015 or 336-2911) and Willie Rolle Jr. (☎345-5106) or call the taxi association at ☎345-0232. In Barreterre, call A.A. McKenzie (☎355-5024).

Rental cars, bicycles and scooters

None of the major **car rental** companies operates in the Exumas, and the island's fleet of available rentals range from perfectly fine to downright dodgy. Three reputable rental companies are the aptly named Airport Rent-a-Car (☎345-0090 or 358-8049); Don's Car Rental (☎345-0112), also at the airport; and Thompson's Rentals (☎336-2442, ✉thompsonsrental@batelnet.bs) on the Queen's Highway in the centre of George Town. All charge $60–70 a day for a regular car with 4wd drive available for extra.

Heavy truck traffic and narrow roads make **cycling** in the area immediately surrounding George Town a bit of a hair-raising experience. However, the roads south of town or north past the airport turn-off are quiet and offer scenic vistas to savour. If you plan to do some cycling, you will have to bring your own bike. Prestige Cycle Rentals (☎357-0066) opposite Regatta Park rents motor **scooters** for $12/$50 per hour/day.

Boats

Boats are the Exumas' most common mode of transportation, and renting your own craft is an exciting and convenient way of getting around George Town and environs. In town, Minn's Water Sports on Victoria Pond (Mon–Fri 8am–5pm, Sat 8am–noon, Sun 8am–11am; ☎336-3483, ⊕www.mwsboats .com) rents 15–22ft boats for $85–195 a day, with discounts for longer rentals. Minn's also offers boat service, fuel, dock rental and snorkel gear sales and rental. They restrict use of their boats to Elizabeth Harbour – a ten-mile stretch of coastline sheltered by a string of offshore cays. To travel further afield, you must make special arrangements. **Starfish Adventure Center** (☎336-3033 or 1-800/451-9972, ⊕www.kayakbahamas.com) rents a variety of well-maintained kayaks (including doubles) and sailboats; kayaks range $30–65 per day, with sailboats for $100 a day, and good weekly rates are available as well.

Organized tours around George Town

George Town and the rest of Great and Little Exuma are made for meandering by rental car, bicycle or powerboat. However, if you want a local view of the island, you can take a **guided tour** by boat or bus. The outfits listed below are all based in George Town, offering half and full-day-trips ranging from a sedate sunset cruise along the coastline with a cocktail in hand, to an introduction to Bahamian bush medicine to a full-day nature and snorkelling expeditions.

The Arabella George Town marina (☎357-0934). This catamaran heads out for three-hour day or sunset sails along the coastline and offshore cays, with soft drinks, rum punch and snorkel gear on-board. $75 per person.

Christine Rolle's Island Tours (☎358-4014). Provided there's enough demand, two daily bus tours of the island are offered at 10am and 2pm. One heads southeast from George Town to Little Exuma, the other northwest of George Town along the coast to the northern tip of the island. Both include visits to rural settlements, local history and discussions on bush medicine, along with lunch at a local restaurant. $15 per person.

Off Island Adventures Bahama Houseboat Dock, (☎345-0074 or 554-2768, @st.cole@batelnet.bs). Captain Steven Cole leads stimulating chartered boat tours of the cays around Great and Little Exuma, stopping off to visit with dolphins, turtles and giant iguanas and to jump in the water for some snorkelling. Rates to charter the boat are $350 for four hours, $600 for eight hours, with room for eight passengers. If on your own, you may be able to join an already scheduled tour.

Starfish Adventure Center ☎336-3033, @www.kayakbahamas.com. Along with their kayak trips and boat rentals (see p.253), this outfitter runs half-day guided boat tours of Elizabeth Harbour and the surrounding cays. $55/$44 adult/child, including a snack.

The S/V Emerald Lady George Town marina (☎357-0441 or 336-2128). Tours on this 63ft catamaran, equipped with a water slide, sail around Elizabeth Harbour with snacks and time for snorkelling. A half-day sail costs $85, with a shorter sunset sail $75; kids under twelve half price.

Watersports and outdoor activities

Though typical tourist sights are thin on the ground on Big and Little Exuma, the wealth of outdoor adventures available easily picks up the slack. Located in a bright-blue two-storey building on the main drag overlooking Kidd Cove, **Starfish Adventure Center** (☎336-3033 or 1-800/451-9972, @www.kayakbahamas.com) is George Town's top multipurpose outfitter. Activities range from guided kayaking half-day trips of the cays around Elizabeth Harbour ($55/$44 adult/child) and Moriah Cay National Park ($70/$56 adult/child), to a four night camping/kayak expedition through the uninhabited southern cays, packaged with three day-trips out of George Town including hotel accommodation and meals ($1700). They also rent a variety of sailboats and kayaks.

Diving and snorkelling

With scores of pristine coral reefs and sea gardens, underwater valleys and caverns, wrecks and blue holes to explore, the Exumas are one of the best places in the Bahamas to **dive** or **snorkel**.

Dive Exuma *Peace and Plenty Beach Inn*, north of George Town, ☎336-2893, ⓦwww.divexuma .com. Dive Exuma is the only local dive operator. Rates range from $75/125 for one-tank/two-tank dives; PADI certification $525 and open water referral completion $350. Equipment rental is $30; introductory pool sessions are free.

Snorkelling trips by reef boat cost from $65 for a two-hour outing.
Starfish Adventure Center see opposite. Starfish offers a half-day "Marine Adventure" snorkelling boat trip, zipping from blue hole to coral reef to sea caves to see giant turtles, starfish and schools of tropical fish ($55/$44 adult/child).

Fishing

The Exumas are well known to serious fisherman for superb **deep-sea and bonefishing grounds**, and a number of fishing guides are based in and around George Town. Rates are in the range of $240 for a half-day to $450 for a full-day of fishing, equipment included. Guides will generally pick you up from your hotel anywhere on the island, and the Ministry of Tourism can supply interested anglers with a list of independent guides.

Bandit's Bonefishing Mt Thompson ☎358-8062 or 358-7011, ⓦwww.banditsbonefishing.com.
Cely's Fly Fishing Stuart Manor ☎345-2341 or cell 357-0139. Cely's runs bonefishing, deep-sea fishing and reef fishing charters, and will also take you snorkelling or sightseeing by boat.

Fish Rowe Charters George Town ☎345-0074, ⓦww.fishrowecharters.com. Reef, bottom and deep-sea sportfishing charters for $800/$1600 a half/full-day for up to six people.

Accommodation

You won't find the polished, mints-on-your-pillow resort experience in George Town, where most of the **accommodation** within Great and Little Exuma is concentrated. There's still an ample range of comfortable accommodation available, but you can expect to pay a bit more than the average price in the Bahamas. Most of the larger hotels add a mandatory tax and service charges of between ten and seventeen percent which can add up to $35 to your nightly bill – ask before you book. If travelling in a group, the most economical as well as the most pleasant option is to rent a **cottage**. In addition to those listed below, see p.32 for a list of companies handling such rentals. If visiting during the Out Island Regatta in late April, you'll have to book months in advance.

The advantage to staying in the centre of George Town is the proximity to services and entertainment in the evening. There is no beach, although there is a regular ferry service to the gorgeous beaches on Stocking Island. Within the immediate area surrounding George Town are several beachfront hotels that offer a quieter, more private retreat, and most of these offer free transportation to and from George Town. Further beyond George Town are several other worthwhile ones from the simple to the luxurious, but staying outside the capital means you will likely need to rent a car unless content with sun-soaking on the beach or angling for bonefishing in the nearby flats.

George Town

Bahamas Houseboats ☎336-2628, ⓦwww .bahamashouseboats.com. These bright, airy floating apartments are an appealing and economical option for families, a romantic retreat for couples, or simply a fun way to explore Elizabeth Harbour. The 35ft houseboats claim to

sleep "two in luxury, four in comfort, and six at a squeeze". Each has big windows to let in the view, a/c, a fully equipped galley, and an outdoor barbecue. Most boats have a waterslide off the top deck and they all have a motorized dinghy to get to shore. Weekly rate around $2000, daily rate (three-day minimum) $300. Longer 43ft boats and a deluxe 46ft boat are also available. ⑨

Club Peace and Plenty ☎ 336-2551 or 1-800/525-2210, ⓦ www.peaceandplenty.com. The town's most historic hotel overlooking Elizabeth Harbour with 35 stylishly renovated rooms with balconies, done up in fresh, bright colours. Each room has s/c, fridge, coffee-maker and satellite TV. ⑥

Regatta Point ☎ 336-2206 or 1/800-688-0309, ⓦ www.regattapointbahamas.com. An appealing choice for those who like to have the option of cooking, *Regatta Point* is centrally located, but still feels secluded thanks to its location dock in a stand of coconut palms on a tiny point of land at the end of Kidd Cove. Each of the six spacious and bright apartments, tastefully detailed in weathered wood, has a kitchen and private balcony. Rental boats and fishing trips can be arranged. ⑦

Two Turtles Inn ☎ 336-2545, ⓕ 336-2528. Overpriced, the carpeted rooms at this inn are dark, dingy and devoid of aesthetic appeal. The establishment's only advantage is its central location, if all you want is a place to lay your head. Note that noise from the patio bar filters up to the rooms. ④

George Town's outskirts

Coral Gardens Bed and Breakfast Hooper's Bay, ☎ f336-2880, ⓦ www.coralgardensbahamas.com. This pleasant and fairly-priced B&B is run by a knowledgeable English couple and sits only a five-minute walk from the beach. On a breezy hilltop at Hooper's Bay with views of both coasts, there are three airy rooms (king, queen and twin), each with a private bath. Also available are two spacious, modern apartments with private decks. Rental cars can be arranged from $55 a day, and there is a discount for stays over fifteen days. Rooms ③ (min stay three nights); studio apartment ④, one-bedroom ⑤ (min stay 5 nights).

Higgins Landing Stocking Island ☎ 336-2460, ⓦ www.higginslanding.com. Located on Stocking Island, this hotel is a luxurious secluded retreat with five quaint whitewashed timber guest cottages furnished with antiques, each with a private ocean view and a kitchenette. Guests have use of a private expanse of beach on Turtle Cove, kayaks, and snorkel gear, hiking maps, a library and honour bar. The resort is solar-powered and smoke-free. Open mid-Nov to Aug, and rates include dinner. One-bedroom cottages $400 per night, two-bedrooms $600. ⑨

Minns Cottages ☎ 336-2033, ⓦ www.bahamas-exuma.com/minnscottage.htm. A delightful respite from the bustle of George Town, these cottages are set in a shady grove on the northern outskirts of town but still within walking distance (10min). Each of the three rainbow-coloured clapboard units has a screened-in porch looking out over the ocean. The interiors are cool white tiles with full kitchens, satellite TV and a/c. Minimum four night stay. One-bedroom cottage ④; two-bedroom ⑥

Mount Pleasant Suites Hooper's Bay ☎ 336-2960, ⓕ 336-2964. The rooms here are set back from the highway in a modern two-storey building on a wide expanse of lawn at Hooper's Bay, across the road from a nice beach. There are 23 comfortably furnished one-bedroom suites and a two-bedroom townhouse, each with a fully equipped kitchen, satellite TV, a/c and a patio or balcony. ③

Palm Bay Beach Club ☎ 336-2787 or 1-888/396-0606, ⓦ www.palmbaybeachclub.com. A somewhat crammed holiday home development with cheerily painted studio to two-bedroom cottage units located by the beach. Some have ocean views, and each is tastefully decorated in warm neutral tones with handsome dark wicker furniture. The cottages have a/c, ceiling fans, satellite TV and full kitchens, while on-site perks include a laundry, swimming pool, tennis courts, spa, restaurant and a beach bar. Studio ⑥, one-bedroom ⑧, two-bedroom ⑨

Peace and Plenty Beach Inn ☎ 336-2250 or 1-800/525-2210, ⓦ www.peaceandplenty.com. A quiet retreat located a mile and a half north of town, featuring sixteen very nicely appointed rooms, each with a private balcony and an ocean view. Amenities include a pool, a small swath of white-sand beach and an outdoor bar. A shuttle service is available to transport guests to and from George Town. ⑦

South of George Town

Club Peace and Plenty Bonefish Lodge Hartswell ☎ 345-5555 or 1-800/525-2210, ⓦ www.ppbonefishlodge.com. This handsome timber and stone lodge, complete with wraparound verandah overlooking Little Exuma, is Great Exuma's most luxurious hotel. The eight spacious rooms have tile floors, a/c, deep balconies and windows looking out onto the turquoise waters of the shallow bonefishing flats nearby. A broad wooden deck extends out over the water with covered areas for dining or relaxing, plus hammocks are strung in the shade of trees all around. Rates include meals, a bonefishing guide, taxes and gratuities, along with use of kayaks, bicycles and snorkelling equipment. Three nights and four days fishing runs $780 /$1113 per person double/single occupancy. Non-fishers also welcome at $150/$250 per person a night double/single occupancy covering all taxes and breakfast.

Gun Hill Bay Beach Villas Williams Town ☎ 336-2964, ⦿ www.gunhillbaybeachvillas.com. Originally built to house crew for the *Pirates of the Caribbean* movies filmed on nearby Sandy Cay, these half dozen candy-coloured one-bedroom cottages sit side by side on the edge of a quiet village with their own tiny patch of beach. Nicely done up in natural wood and ceramic tile, with TV, a/c and full kitchens. Quite isolated, but with plenty of peace and quiet. One-bedroom cottage $1500 a week.

Master Harbour Villas Master Harbour ☎ 345-5076, ⦿ www.exumabahamas.com/masterharbour.html. Three miles south of George Town sit these three white clapboard cottages, set in a green grove of coconut palms and blooming trees on a rocky shore looking out on Crab and Redshank cays. The high-ceiling villas are nicely furnished and equipped with both a/c and ceiling fans and kitchens. Weekly rates available. One bedroom ❺, two-bedroom ❼, four-bedroom ❾

North of George Town

Barreterre Bonefish Lodge Barraterre ☎ 355-5052. Comfortable doubles in a tidy yellow lodge sitting on the water's edge, close to good bonefishing flats. Each room has private bath, satellite TV, a/c and a view of the southern cays. The dining room serves three meals a day. Guided fishing available from $350/$600 a half/full-day. ❼

Four Seasons Resort Great Exuma at Emerald Bay Farmer's Hill ☎ 336-6990, ⦿ www.fourseasons.com/greatexuma. A huge, upscale resort on a secluded cove fifteen miles north of George Town, with a great beach, an eighteen-hole golf course designed by Greg Norman, formal and informal dining, a spa, gym, three swimming pools, and all the luxurious furnishings and manicured lawns you'd expect from a Four Seasons. The pampering comes at great cost, with rooms starting at $700 a night. ❾

Ray Ann's Guesthouse Queen's Highway south of Barreterre ☎ 357-0786. Don't be put off by the isolation and lack of landscaping – this is a clean and comfortable place to crash if you arrive late on the mailboat. Large doubles with patios face a mangrove lagoon. Heading south from Barreterre, it's the last house on the right before you cross the first bridge. ❷

George Town and around

With a population of around a thousand, **GEORGE TOWN** is a bustling little hub of commercial activity with a constant stream of cars buzzing along the circular main road around Victoria Pond in the centre of town. Happily, though, it's not such a rat race that you can't still do your banking in bare feet with a cocktail in hand, if you so choose. And just as refreshingly, it's a town with a sense of humour – note the sign on the small bridge over the channel connecting Victoria Pond to Elizabeth Harbour that reads "This bridge freezes before the road".

Settled in the late eighteenth century and formally incorporated in 1793, George Town's location was selected for its excellent natural harbour. A pleasant if slightly ramshackle settlement with few landmarks, the town is made up of mainly modern cinderblock buildings of various sizes, colours and states of repair that line the main road. The residential areas lie on the flat land east of the town centre and climb the hill behind Victoria Pond. Views of the brilliant turquoise sea and Stocking Island greet you at every turn and you can walk from one end of the village to the other in about fifteen minutes. Alternatively, from a seat at the *Two Turtles Inn* (see p.264) patio bar in the centre of town, you can survey almost all of its primary attractions.

On the northern edge of town on a rise of land overlooking the sea is **Saint Andrew's Anglican Church**, which was consecrated in 1802 but has burned to the ground twice since then. Across the street and towards the centre of town stands the peach and white **Club Peace and Plenty**, looking like a Cotswold country cottage with its steep-pitched roof, dormers and picket fence. The residence of a prominent local family, it was converted to an inn in the 1940s and has hosted celebrities and royalty (including the King of Greece and Duke

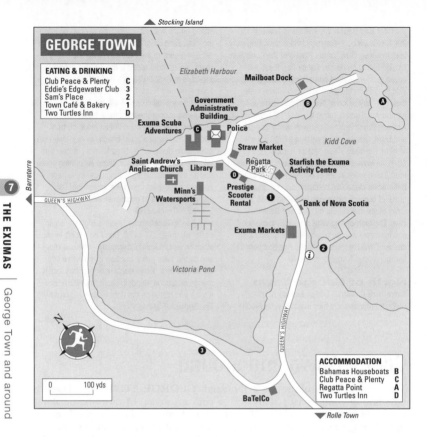

of Edinburgh) over the years. The hotel bar, now a popular watering hole with yachties, is thought by local historians to be on the site of **Bowe's Tavern**, where slaves from West Africa were auctioned off two hundred years ago.

Walking east from the inn, you'll pass the **Government Administration Building**, which houses the Commissioner's office, the police station and the post office. The building overlooks the government dock on **Kidd Cove**, named for the pirate captain who may or may not have ever visited it. It is here that the mailboat calls. Directly in front of the *Two Turtles Inn*, looking out towards the dock, lies **Regatta Park**. This forlorn patch of grass and dirt comes into its own during the Out Island Regatta and the George Town Cruising Regatta, when it is filled with food stalls, musicians and revellers (see box, opposite). At the north end of the park is the open-air **Straw Market** (daily 9am–6pm), where local women sell handmade straw hats, bags, and baskets as well as mass-produced jewellery and tropical-print beachwear.

Stocking Island

A string of small cays along the windward coast of Great Exuma encloses fifteen-mile-long Elizabeth Harbour. The largest of these – though still only three miles end to end and just a few hundred yards across – is **STOCKING ISLAND**, a mile off George Town, its high white-sand dunes shimmering in

The Out Island and George Town regattas

Usually sleepy, Elizabeth Harbour in George Town fills with upwards of four hundred boats during the **Out Island Regatta**, which lasts for several days at the end of April. The regatta has been held every year since 1954 as a celebration of the long tradition of wooden-boat building in the Bahamas – indeed, the race only involves Bahamian-designed, -built, -owned and -sailed vessels – and draws racing

△ Band at the Out Island Regatta

crews from all over the Out Islands. It's one of the premier social events of the year, and government mailboats are diverted from their regular routes to carry the racing sloops to George Town. On land, the festivities continue day and night, with rake 'n' scrape music, food stalls, games and dancing. Foreign yachts get in on the action during the **George Town Cruising Regatta** (ⓦwww.georgetowncruisingregatta.com), held in early March. This weeklong regatta features races, a beach volleyball tournament, sandcastle-building contest, live music as well as copious amounts of eating and drinking. Contact the Ministry of Tourism (☏336-2440) for details.

the sunlight. It's an idyllic place to while away the day, with a long windswept beach that runs almost the length of its Atlantic side and crescents of soft sand along the protected shore facing George Town. Covered picnic tables and benches are connected by a walking path that runs along the top of the high ridge overlooking the Atlantic beach, making a spectacular setting for a picnic. Keep an eye out for giant red starfish a foot or more in diameter that can be found in large numbers in the shallows. There are no roads on the island and just a handful of luxurious winter homes tucked into sheltered coves.

The *Club Peace and Plenty* operates a twice-daily **ferry service** (free for guests, $10 round trip for others; departing at 10am and 1pm from the hotel, returning at 12.45pm and 3.45pm) to **Hamburger Beach**, on the northern end of the island. This area of the island is undeveloped (for the moment – the ocean front lots are for sale) and crisscrossed by hiking paths ending at private vistas. The most prominent feature of the island is the **beacon** that tops its highest hill, erected in the nineteenth century to guide ships into the dock. Heading toward it from the snack bar (open 10am–3pm) at Hamburger Beach, look out for a sandy track up to the peak, a ten-minute hike that rewards with an amazing view of Elizabeth Harbour. A network of hiking paths lead down the steep slope to the Atlantic beach as well.

The southern end of Stocking Island is marginally more developed, with a couple of small hotels and beach bars. The popular *Chat 'n Chill* bar and grill (see p.264) sits on Volleyball Beach. During the Out Island Regatta and the George Town Cruising Regatta, this is the scene of a beach volleyball tournament, and the nets stay up year-round. For the less energetic, there are hammocks strung in the palms and cool drinks and snacks close at hand. The party atmosphere ratchets up a notch when the boat tours pull in for lunch and during the weekly Sunday pig roast. If heading over by ferry, note that it's not possible to walk overland from the north end of the island to the south end (i.e. from Hamburger Beach to the *Chat 'n Chill*). The way is obstructed by private homes and dense brush. However, if you rent a boat, you can easily zip from one end to the other in about two minutes. The *Chat 'n Chill* runs a water taxi from George Town on demand ($5; see p.264 for details).

South to Williamstown

Heading **south from George Town**, the Queen's Highway weaves in and out from the shore until it reaches **Williamstown**, on the southern tip of Little Exuma seventeen miles away. Along the way are the scenic hilltop settlements of **Rolle Town**, **Forbes Hill** and **Ferry**, as well as several inviting deserted beaches. Williamstown, with its ruins of a Loyalist plantation, salt ponds, and a couple of cheery spots for refreshment, makes a good destination for a leisurely day-trip.

Rolle Town and around

From George Town, the road south climbs a steep hill that curves around and down to follow the water's edge, passing the posh resort community at February Point on Flamingo Bay. Beyond here, the Queen's Highway runs along the rocky shore edged with mangroves and dotted with small cays, then cuts inland. On this stretch of road, two concrete pillars stand on either side of the highway, marking the western boundary of Lord Rolle's former estate, now the commonage of Rolle Town, although the village itself is several miles further south.

Seven miles from the capital sits the pretty hilltop settlement of **ROLLE TOWN**, where all visitors should turn off the main highway to enjoy one of the most spectacular views in the Exumas. From the top of the hill, you can look out over **Man of War Cay**, where the shallow waters surrounding it create a beautiful multi-hued panorama of turquoise and bright white. From the junction at the top of the hill facing the water, turn right onto the road leading

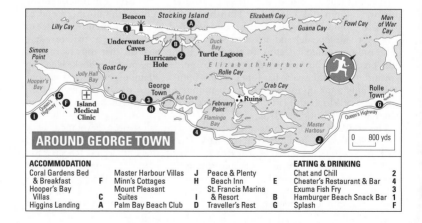

Strewn in a long wisp off the southern tip of Little Exuma, the stony **Jumento Cays** and **Ragged Islands** mark the southeast edge of the Great Bahama Bank. Remote and undeveloped, they get few visitors apart from migratory birds, part of their appeal for the rare passing boat cruiser. The only way to visit is on your own plane or yacht, or on the mailboat, the *Captain C*, which sails from Nassau on Tuesdays and calls at the sun-baked outpost of **Duncan Town** at the southern end of the chain. Home to all the archipelago's fewer than one hundred residents, most of whom make a hardscrabble living from the sea, the settlement is named for Duncan Taylor, a Loyalist exile who, with his brother Archibald, established a briefly thriving salt-harvesting operation here in the mid-nineteenth century. In those days, it was a lively village of several hundred workers, many of them Africans freed from illegal slave-trading vessels captured on the high seas after Emancipation. Rather than being repatriated, they were deposited at Duncan Town and left to start over. Given the isolation, the barren landscape of the islands and the backbreaking exertion of salt raking, it must have seemed a dubious deliverance to some, and when the demand for Bahamian salt declined, most left Ragged Island.

The peaceful rhythm of daily life was violently shattered in May 1980, when Cuban fighter jets attacked and sank a Bahamian naval vessel while it was in the process of arresting two Cuban boats fishing illegally in Bahamian waters. Four Bahamian marines were killed, and under a hail of bullets, the rest escaped in rubber dinghies, coming ashore at Duncan Town. Cuba eventually issued an official apology and offered a financial settlement to replace the ship, and for the families of the killed marines. The intervening years have passed in a calm interrupted only by the weekly arrival of the mailboat. There are no places to stay, so before you disembark from the mailboat, reiterate to the captain that you'd like to catch a lift back to Nassau or the Exuma Cays. The mailboat will stay in port long enough to unload its cargo and load up – maybe a couple of hours or overnight. You have to ascertain the plan with the captain before the trip as the precise schedule changes slightly week to week.

down to the shore. A short distance along this road, a grassy path on the left leads to a **grave** enclosed by a high rock wall. Interred here is the 26-year-old Loyalist settler Ann McKay and her infant son, who died in 1792; their graves are one of the few physical reminders of the Loyalists who came to make a new life on the island. At the bottom of the hill, an overgrown cemetery at the edge of the sea is the final resting place of several generations of Rolles. When the tide is low, you can walk out onto Man of War Cay to explore its tantalizing stretches of white sandy beach and the fortifications on the bluff.

Williamstown and around

Past Rolle Town, the highway drops down to the water's edge, passing through the eastern gates of the Rolle estate at Hartswell and over the short, narrow bridge, built in 1966, that connects Great Exuma to Little Exuma. The appropriately named hamlet of **Ferry**, where the ferryman lived before the bridge was built, holds St Christopher's Church, perhaps the smallest church in the Bahamas – its about the size of a garden shed – and built in 1946 for the devoutly Anglican Fitzgerald family. Further on, **Forbes Hill** is a shady, hilly little settlement named for a Loyalist planter. Note the unexplained cannon hidden in the bushes next to the Variety Store on your left as you enter the community. South of Forbes Hill, a road on the left leads to a beautiful stretch of beach that straddles the Tropic of Cancer, known appropriately enough as

Tropic of Cancer Beach. To reach it from Forbes Hill, head south exactly 2.6 miles, then make a left-hand turn off the highway, following a dirt road for a quarter of a mile to Ocean Drive, and turn right for the final 500 yards. Park next to the small beach cabana, where the latitude markings on the floor provide a good photo opportunity. The beach itself is a long, beautiful strip of white sand, but there is no shade or facilities, so pack drinks, snacks, sunscreen and all other beach necessities.

At the southern tip of Little Exuma is **Williamstown**, a peaceful settlement of 300 residents set between the intensely turquoise sea and two large saline ponds, whose edges are rimmed with salt glinting in the sunlight. There is no accommodation in the town, and goats, chicken and sheep roam freely, some taking up residence on the steps of the abandoned BaTelCo building. At the southern end of the settlement, **The Hermitage** – the ruins of the Kelsall Plantation house – stands overgrown in tall grass at the top of a steep knoll overlooking the salt ponds and the sea, too dilapidated to enter, but picturesque in its decay. A modest one-storey affair built in traditional Bahamian style with a steep-pitched roof and deep veranda, the house is a testament to the very limited success of the Loyalist plantation owners during their short stay in the Bahamas – a far cry from the opulent lifestyles many left behind in the southern US states. A row of tiny mud and limestone rooms that were slave quarters still stands downhill from the main house.

North to Barreterre

North of George Town, the Queen's Highway runs close to the shore, though views of the sea are obscured by houses much of the way. Unless you're bedding down at the deluxe *Four Seasons* resort in Farmer's Hill, most visitors will want to head north to explore a string of secluded sandy strands – including stunning **Cocoplum**, south of Rolleville – or to visit **Barreville**, a jumping off point for boat trips to the Exuma Cays.

North to Farmer's Hill

Leaving George Town, the Queen's Highway north passes three beaches along the eastern shore of the island in quick succession over a five-mile stretch. First up is **Jolly Hall Bay**, an attractive, lightly used crescent of white sand with a picnic table and casuarinas for shade (public access to beach 500 yards north of *Palm Bay Beach Club*, with a small marked parking area and stone steps up to a path). About a mile further on, there is a cluster of shops and another appealing beach at **Hooper's Bay** (heading north just past *Mount Pleasant Suites*, look for a two-storey pink house on the waterside. There is a public path down to the beach on the left side of this property). Finally, there is an exquisite pearly white beach lining **Tar Bay**. Edged with vacation homes, the beach is accessible by walking over the dunes from the highway.

Further north, **Ramsey** and **Mt Thompson** are farming communities where onions, bananas and other vegetables are grown and readied for market at the Government Packing House, while the main attraction at the next settlement north on the Queen's Highway, **Farmer's Hill**, is the sprawling *Four Seasons Great Exuma at Emerald Bay*. Located on a lovely cove called Ocean Bight, the resort is one of the island's major employers. If not a guest at the resort, you can still make use of its golf and tennis facilities. Eighteen holes cost $175 (call the pro shop at ☎336-2600; open 7am–6pm), while the tennis courts run $25 per

Bowe Cay

Lying off the southwest side of Great Exuma opposite George Town, at the end of a row of small islands extended like an arm towards Cuba, is **Bowe Cay**, a flat 200-acre area covered in low, dense bush and mangrove swamp. Bowe Cay achieved brief notoriety in the mid-1990s when two writers for *Condé Nast Traveller* magazine were marooned on the island for a week to fend for themselves *Robinson Crusoe*, or maybe *Lord of the Flies*, style. It was a grand publicity stunt staged by a New York company that hoped to market the island as the ultimate getaway destination, and the island was subsequently featured in several magazines – indeed, soon after *Men's Journal* named Bowe Cay one of the top ten great island escapes. Unfortunately for the company, they hadn't asked permission of the island's owner, Glenville Clark, who soon put a stop to their plans.

Mr. Clark's family has owned the island since 1843 when it was acquired by his great-great-grandfather, a freed slave named John Rolle. Though never inhabited by the Clarks, it has been used intermittently for farming and grazing. The original deed to the cay was discovered in the 1970s among the papers passed down to Mr Clark's grandmother, who could not read. Also among them was a Certificate of Indenture dated 1839 binding John Rolle to a man from New Providence for a debt incurred, the full repayment of which was to be symbolized by a final payment of one peppercorn.

The western side of the cay has a small pretty curve of white sandy beach and a mangrove creek that beckons exploring by dinghy or kayak. A coral outcropping just off the beach offers good snorkelling on a calm day, but the plywood cabana inhabited by the Condé Nast castaways was destroyed in a hurricane. Perhaps encouraged by the media attention, Glenville Clark (☎345-0054) is asking a **rental fee** of $1500 a week for the island, but you might be able to negotiate a more reasonable rate. He hopes to eventually develop a resort on the beach, but for now be prepared to camp and to bring all of your food and water. If roughing it on a deserted island appeals to you, note that there are a dozen in the Exuma Land and Sea Park (see p.272) where you can camp for a slightly more affordable $5 a night.

---

hour (☎336-6989). In addition, there are a couple of appealing places to eat in this area (listed on p.264), as well as a marina (☎336-6100).

Rolleville and Barreterre

A couple of miles further on, the rambling roadside settlement of **Steventon** is notable as the site of a slave revolt in the nineteenth century, led by Pompey (see p.249). A couple of miles past this tiny hamlet, the highway splits. Heading right leads to **Rolleville**, the largest slave settlement on the island in Lord Rolle's time and the site of several slave uprisings in the 1820s and 1830s. The local residents, many of whom are descendants of those slaves, now hold a **regatta** on Emancipation Day, the first Monday in August. The village's collection of ramshackle buildings have an attractive setting, running over a hill down to a stretch of sandy beach. En route to Rolleville, a turn-off to the right leads to the breathtaking **Cocoplum Beach**. One of the most beautiful in the Bahamas, the beach is a gentle curve of soft white sand protected by a string of offshore cays, enhanced by an outstanding beach bar and grill (see p.264).

Back at the highway junction, the road forking off to the left leads to **Barreterre**, about eight miles away. The village itself is a forlorn collection of buildings spread along a rocky shore, but it's also the jumping-off point for excursions to the southern cays for those travelling by mailboat or aboard their own watercraft. From Barreterre, Captain Martin (☎358-4057 or 345-6013) offers snorkelling, fishing and sightseeing outings in the cays north of Great Exuma, including a visit to the giant iguanas on Leaf Cay (see p.269). En route to Barreterre, the highway weaves through **Stuart Manor**, a pleasant farming community that's home to the *Stuart Manor Bakery* (7am–4pm; ☎345-2313), selling sweet Bahamian bread and banana loaves.

Eating

As might be expected, seafood dominates **restaurant** menus on Great and Little Exuma, be it conch, lobster, or fish just hours or even minutes out of the ocean. In the settlements up and down the islands, you will find a few simple roadside diners as well as some waterside cafes with spectacular views and tasty food to match, with prices on a par with similar establishments in the United States.

George Town

Club Peace and Plenty Restaurant *Club Peace and Plenty*, Queen's Highway ☎336-2551. Set in a glassed-in alcove off the hotel's lobby with a nice view of Stocking Island, the menu features fish, lobster, steak and a few pasta dishes ranging $15–40. The dining experience is marred by poor service. Open daily for breakfast 7am–10.30am and dinner by reservation 6.30–7.30pm.

Eddie's Edgewater Club On Victoria Pond ☎336-2050. A local institution overlooking Victoria Pond. Come here to sample native dishes such as steamed turtle or to play a game of pool. Live rake 'n scrape music Mondays and Saturdays.

Mom's Bakery Several mornings a week around 10am, Doris "Mom" Rahming parks her van across from the Exuma Markets grocery to sell her delicious coconut bread, banana cakes and other home-baked goodies. If you happen to miss her, you can go to the source in Williamstown.

Sam's Place On the waterfront, town centre ☎336-2579. Located upstairs in a grey timber two-storey building overlooking the marina, *Sam's* is the best place in town for a morning meal, specializing in Bahamian boiled breakfasts and American-style platters including pancakes, bacon and eggs ($5–9), provided you can overlook the lackadaisical service. At lunchtime, the inexpensive seafood plates and burgers are pretty good too. Dinners, when mains average $15–25, include blackened crawfish, grouper and conch served with traditional Bahamian sides.

The Town Café and Bakery Queen's Highway, town centre ☎336-2194. Beside the Shell petrol station, this inexpensive café doles out Bahamian and American standards including crab and conch patties, sandwiches, ice cream and pastries. There are a couple of daily lunch specials, with dishes

like shrimp fettuccine in the rotation. The view of the car park is not a big draw, but the bright interior, friendly service and hearty meals make it a local favourite. Mon–Sat 7.30am–3pm.

Two Turtles Inn Queen's Highway, town centre ☎336-2545. The outdoor patio bar overlooking the main drag and the wharf is a great place to watch the world go by while sampling tasty fare such as conch done everyway, along with burgers and salads. Open for lunch and dinner, depending on the traffic. On Friday nights there is an outdoor barbecue with live entertainment.

George Town's outskirt

The Chat 'n Chill Stocking Island ☎357-0926 or 336-2800, ⊛www.chatnchill.com, VHF Ch 16. This breezy, open-air beach bar fronting Stocking Island's Volleyball Beach makes for a relaxing place for a burger, fresh seafood or just a cool drink and a swing in a hammock. Locally famed for the delicious and garlicky coleslaw, perhaps best sampled at the popular Sunday Pig Roast ($17). Daily 11am–7pm; hourly ferry service Sundays on the hour from noon–6pm and by request other days, departing from the Bahamas Houseboats dock ($5).

Exuma Fish Fry Queen's Highway, a half mile north of George Town. This collection of brightly-coloured shacks on the waterfront is a popular choice for Bahamian cooking and fresh seafood. *Charlie's* (Wed–Sun from 5pm) serves up grouper, conch, lobster and chicken wings; jerk chicken is the house speciality at the *Big 12 Sports Bar* (Thurs–Sun from 5pm); and steamed grouper is the star at the *Honey Dew Café* (Mon–Fri 8am–5pm). *Tino's Deck* (daily 8am–midnight) is another popular spot for seafood and sides.

Hamburger Beach Bar and Grill Hamburger Beach, Stocking Island. A simple snack bar catering to beachgoers alighting from the *Club Peace and Plenty* ferry, selling burgers and hot dogs, chips and pop. Daily 10am–3.00pm.

Splash *Palm Bay Beach Club*, Queen's Highway north of George Town ☎ 336-2787. A pleasant and reliable place for a casual bite, this cheerful eatery overlooks Stocking Island, with a menu featuring seafood snacks like conch fritters, grouper and lobster with flavourful side dishes as well as salads, sandwiches and pizza. Dinner entrees range $13–28. Daily 7am–10.30pm.

South of George Town

Cheater's Restaurant and Bar Queen's Highway ☎ 336-2535. A no-frills roadhouse two miles south of George Town serving delicious home-style Bahamian meals like fresh fish and fried chicken with sides of coleslaw, peas and rice and macaroni and cheese. Tuesday nights feature a fish fry with rake 'n' scrape music. Open 7.30am until late; closed Sundays.

Club Peace and Plenty Bonefish Lodge Hartswell ☎ 345-5555. Appealing restaurant with a decor of terracotta tiled floors, cosy wooden booths, and windows looking out over the bright blue-green water. The menu lists (not surprisingly) local seafood, and traditional American cuisine like steak, chicken and pasta. Open for dinner only to outside guests Wed–Sun from 6.30pm; reservations required. Free transportation available from George Town.

Santana's Grill Pit Williamstown ☎ 345-4102. This open-air grill on the waterfront is the perfect destination for a meander south from George Town. The welcoming proprietor prepares copious platters of Bahamian home-cooking daily, including cracked conch and lobster, grouper, shrimp and lip-smacking ribs. Lunch runs $12–18. Open noon–3pm and sometimes for dinner 6pm–8pm if you call ahead. Closed Sun and Mon.

North of George Town

Barreterre Bonefish Lodge Barreterre ☎ 355-5052. Catering primarily to fishermen, the friendly folks at the lodge serve meals designed to fuel a full-day on the water. Mains $16–18. Open for breakfast, lunch and dinner; reservations advised but not required.

Big D's Conch Spot Steventon ☎ 358-0059. This popular spot has outdoor seating on a wooden deck facing a ribbon of beach. The conch salad ($9) is

what gave *Big D's* it's good reputation, though burgers, fried chicken, lobster, fish and shrimp are also served ($7–13) along with several choices of grilled fish ($12–16), with cool drinks to wash it all down. Tues–Sat noon–midnight, Sun 2pm–midnight.

🏃 **Cocoplum's Beach Club** Cocoplum Beach, south of Rolleville ☎ 554-3358. One of the finest beach bars in the Bahamas, with a gorgeous beach to match. The snacks and lunches are served on a shady wooden patio, and include the likes of lobster fritters with chili mayo ($12) or Tandoori shrimp skewers ($10), followed by jerk chicken with red beans and rice ($15) or blackened grouper with pineapple salsa and sweet potato fries ($22). Burger options include a mouthwatering portobello mushroom topped with smoked tomato, onions and melted mozzarella and served fries or salad ($12). Great desserts, too. Mon–Sat 11.30am–7pm, closed Sun.

Kermit's Hilltop Tavern Rolleville ☎ 345-6006. Located in a hot-pink building with a commanding view of the sea, *Kermit's* doesn't get enough business to keep the fryer on all day, but the friendly staff will whip you up a hearty Bahamian meal if you call ahead.

Pallappa Beach Bar Grand Isles, Emerald Bay ☎ 358-5000. A chic, open-air café situated on high ground overlooking a pool and the Emerald Bay beach at the *Four Seasons*. Serving light meals like salads, sandwiches, wraps, a spicy spinach quesadilla and tropical cocktails. Meals $9–14. Daily 11am–4pm.

Runaway Bay Beach Club south of Rolleville ☎ 345-6279. A rustic snack bar serving hearty lunches on a quiet stretch of beach. Menu items include fresh cut fries, beef and conch burgers, grilled fish and chicken with plantains. From noon until business cools down (call first); closed Thurs.

Wahoo's Grand Isles Marina, Emerald Bay ☎ 336-6516. An elegant restaurant overlooking the partially completed marina and some very fancy boats. Despite its address, it is not outrageously expensive. Lunch options ($8–15) include a coconut, kalik (local beer) and wild mushroom soup or conch chowder laced with sherry as well as sandwiches and burgers. Equally imaginative dinner dishes features seafood and standbys like steak and lamb ($22–32). Open for lunch and dinner 11am–9.30pm, last seating at 8.30pm.

Drinking and nightlife

Although sizeable quantities of rum and other tropical libations are consumed on foredecks and poolside in the Exumas (mainly by visitors), **nightlife** is pretty low-key and non-existent outside of George Town. Any night of the week in George Town, though, you can usually find an interesting conversation, a game of pool and/or some rake 'n' scrape music at one or another of a handful of local watering holes. At regatta time, the place is a 24–hour party every day.

The tiny, cosy country pub at *Club Peace and Plenty* (see p.264) is a gathering point for the boating crowd in the evenings. Its outdoor pool bar overlooking Stocking Island is a pleasant place for a sunset drink, presided over by charismatic bartender Doc Lermon, one of George Town's bright lights. On Saturdays, there's a live band and dancing under the stars at the *Peace and Plenty*, with karaoke at *Splash* at the *Palm Bay Beach Club* (☎336-2787) from 8pm. On Fridays, the action shifts to the outdoor patio bar at the *Two Turtles Inn* (see p.264), with live music and a barbecue 7pm–1am; the *Two Turtles* also hosts karaoke Tuesday nights (from 9pm). *Eddie's Edgewater Club* (see p.264) is a popular local hangout for a game of pool and live rake 'n scrape music on Mondays and Saturdays (from 7pm), and feel free to bring a washtub, saw and screwdriver, bongos or cow bells if you want to join in.

Listings

Airlines American Airlines (☎345-0124), Bahamasair (☎345-0035), Continental (☎345-0279), Lynx Air (☎345-0108), Sky Unlimited (☎345-0172).

Bank There is a Bank of Nova Scotia (Mon–Thurs 9.30am–3pm, Fri 9.30am–4.30pm) located in the centre of George Town by the bridge, and at the Four Seasons resort to the north. Royal Bank of Canada also has a branch in George Town. All have ATMs.

Groceries Exuma Markets (Mon–Wed 8am–6pm, Thurs–Sat 8am–7pm, Sun 8–11am), across from the Bank of Nova Scotia, has well-stocked shelves, a paperback-book exchange and fax service.

Health clinic The government clinic is located on the northern edge of town (Mon–Fri 9am–1pm; ☎336-2088, after-hours emergencies ☎336-2606). There are also clinics at Hooper's Bay, Steventon and Forbes Hill.

Internet Access is available at *Eddie's Edgewater Club* and the *Two Turtles Inn*. Most hotels offer access for guests.

Laundry There's a laundromat at the marina next to the Esso station; dry-cleaning and laundry service is available from Exuma Cleaners on the main street in George Town.

Library Run by volunteers out of a small wooden building sandwiched between the primary school and the *Two Turtles Inn*. There is a book exchange. Open Mon–Sat 10am–noon.

Petrol There is a *Shell* station (Mon–Sat 6am–8pm, Sun 7–11am and 2–5pm) in the centre of town and an *Esso* station (8am–7pm) on the waterfront behind Thompson's Car Rental. There is no petrol

available south of George Town; north of town, you can fill up at Farmer's Hill and Barreterre.

Pharmacy *Smitty's Convenience Store*, Hooper's Bay (Mon–Sat 8.30am–5.30pm, Sun 8am–10am; ☎336-2144).

Police Located in the pink Government Administrative Building on the waterfront (☎336-2666, ☎919 in emergencies, VHF Ch 16 "Boys in Blue").

Post office Housed in Government Administrative Building (Mon–Fri 9am–4pm).

Shopping George Town's Sandpiper Arts and Crafts (Mon–Sat 8.30am–5pm), across from *Club Peace and Plenty*, has a tasteful selection of jewellery, Caribbean-made crafts, original artwork, postcards and a good selection of books. The Peace and Plenty Boutique next door also sells fabrics, souvenirs and gifts. Local artisans sell handmade straw work, souvenir trinkets and textiles at the Straw Market in the centre of town. Starfish Activity Center and Minns Watersports both sell watersports gear.

Telephone BaTelCo (Mon–Fri 9am–5.30pm) is located at the south end of town, and you can send and receive faxes here. There are pay phones at *Club Peace and Plenty* and in front of *Two Turtles Inn*. Prepaid phonecards are on sale at the Exuma Markets. You can rent a cellphone from *Thompson's Car Rental* (☎336-2442/6) for $25 a week with a $100 cash deposit or a credit card imprint.

Travel agency H.L. Young Travel (Mon–Fri 9am–5pm; ☎336-2703) is located above the Bank of Nova Scotia in George Town.

The Exuma Cays

From the tip of Barreterre on the northern tip of Great Exuma, the **EXUMA CAYS** stretch along a northwest trajectory for approximately forty miles. Uninhabited for the most part, this string of a couple of hundred islands and cays of various shapes and sizes shares a similar topography of white sand, honeycombed black coral rock and hardy vegetation, surrounded by a rich marine environment.

The southernmost cluster of cays includes the **Brigantines**, frequented mainly by kayak day-trippers and fishermen, and tiny **Leaf Cay**, home to a colony of giant iguanas and situated about five miles from Barreterre. The only permanent settlements in the Exuma Cays are found north of here on sleepy **Little Farmer's Cay**, **Great Guana Cay** – in the scruffy village of Black Point – and on pretty **Staniel Cay**. The latter is also the easiest access point to the magical **Thunderball Grotto**, a top snorkelling destination. There are dozens more islands sporting sandy beaches hereabouts, notably **Big Major's Spot**, with its sociable population of feral pigs, and **Compass Cay**, where you can explore a network of scenic walking trails.

In the centre of the Exuma Cays chain lies the impressive **Exuma Land and Sea Park**, a marine conservation area encompassing 176 square miles of serene and pristine natural beauty. Within its boundaries are fifteen sizeable cays – and a seemingly infinite number of smaller ones – home to empty, powdery white beaches and hiking trails, and around which splashes fabulous sea kayaking terrain as well as an astounding variety of marine life to delight snorkellers and divers.

Beyond the park's boundary, the northern end of the Exuma Cays lies closer to Nassau than George Town and is easily accessible on day-trips from Paradise Island. Most excursions take in the beaches and hiking trails of **Ship Channel Cay** and a visit to the iguanas on **Allan's Cay**. Also worth a visit are **Highbourne Cay** and **Norman's Cay**, both home to more spectacular beaches, nature trails and marinas.

The Southern Cays

The **SOUTHERN CAYS**, extending from just off Great Exuma's Barreterre northwards to Staniel Cay near the southern boundary of the Exuma Land and Sea Park, are the most settled part of the cay chain. About five hundred people in all live in the three settlements of Farmer's Cay, Black Point and Staniel Cay, while several of the surrounding small cays are privately owned, capped with vacation villas occupied by seasonal residents. Directly off the leeward side of Great Exuma near Barreterre lies a short strand of little cays known as **The Brigantines**. George Town's Starfish Adventure Center (see p.254) offers guided camping and kayaking expeditions in the islands departing from George Town, travelling by van to Barreterre and putting the boats in there.

Arrival and getting around

The main transport hub in the Exuma Cays is Staniel Cay, which is most easily and economically reached from Nassau on Flamingo Air (☎377-0354;

@www.flamingoairbah.com; $90 one-way) or from Fort Lauderdale with Watermaker's Air (☎954/467-8920, @www.watermakersair.com; $250 one-way). A more costly option, but viable if you are doing some island hopping with a party of four to six, is to charter a plane; see p.24 for details.

A more leisurely transport option from Nassau is the *Captain C* **mailboat** ($120 round-trip). Though the schedule can vary greatly, the boat typically leaves from Nassau on Tuesday afternoons, calling at Staniel Cay, Black Point, Little Farmer's Cay and Barreterre the next day. After heading down to the Ragged Islands on Thursday, the mailboat calls in again at Barreterre, Little Farmer's Cay, Black Point and Staniel Cay Friday, and is back in Nassau on Saturday around noon. Call the dockmaster at Potter's Cay (☎393-1064) for the latest.

Once on Staniel Cay, you can rent or charter a **boat** to explore the nearby cays, Thunderball Grotto and the Exuma Land and Sea Park. Berkie Rolle at *Isle General Store* (Mon–Sat 8am–noon and 1.30–5.30pm; ☎355-2007) rents 13ft and 17ft motor boats for $100/$200 a day plus fuel; rates include lifejackets and a VHF radio. The Staniel Cay Yacht Club rents boats the same size for $110 and $235 per day respectively, including fuel. If exploring by motorboat, always take the latest nautical charts, available at the Yacht Club and Isle General Store in Staniel Cay. Though you are always within sight of land in the cays, it's easy to confuse one rocky point with another and get turned around. Non experienced boaters should instead hire a guide; Wayde Nixon (☎355-2049) offers sightseeing **boat tours** of local sights within a ten mile radius of Staniel Cay for $350/$550 a half/full-day for up to four passengers. Nixon will also run up to four people to Warderick Wells for $450, and is a recommended bonefish and deep-sea fishing guide.

Staniel Cay itself is small enough to get around on foot, but to explore its nooks and crannies, you can rent a **golf cart** from *TC Rentals* behind the Staniel Cay Yacht Club (daily 8am–5pm; ☎355-2147;) for $20/$35/$65 an hour/half-day/day. Transport to the airport is $5 a head.

Lee Stocking Island

Six miles north of Barreterre sits the densely forested **LEE STOCKING ISLAND**, owned by American philanthropist John H. Perry Jr., who in 1984 funded the establishment of the nonprofit Caribbean Marine Research Center (☎561/741-0192, @www.perryinstitute.org, VHF Ch 16 "Research Center"). Every year, scientists from all over the world come here to study various aspects of tropical marine ecology, ranging from animal population trends and the effects of coral bleaching to the nutrient value of sea grass for turtles. Pristine waters as deep as 6000ft in nearby Exuma Sound make it an ideal environment for marine research.

As there are sensitive ongoing experiments on the island and in the waters surrounding it, the CMRC asks that you respect a half-mile no-wake zone around the island and call ahead for permission to come ashore. There are no public facilities on the island, and access to most areas is restricted, but there is an impressive view down the Exuma chain from **Perry's Peak**, the highest point in the Exumas at 123ft. A well-defined trail begins at the south end of Coconut Beach in the middle of the island, and it takes only ten minutes to reach the lookout. If you are a student or amateur with a serious interest in marine biology, the CMRC runs a six-week internship programme – see their website for details.

Leaf Cay

Just south of Lee Stocking Island, tiny, sandy **LEAF CAY** is home to a colony of giant iguanas, one of the few places in the Bahamas this endangered species can still be found. The hefty yard-long lizards sun themselves on a small, pretty curve of beach on the leeward side of the cay. Beyond the low ridge behind the beach is a freshwater pond encircled by dense leafy trees that allows the iguana population to thrive here. The beach is a spectacular venue for a picnic, with views of both the deep dark waters of the sound and the bright blues and greens of the shallow banks. Just remember to take a good last look around before you leave, removing any rubbish that may be hazardous to the health of the dwindling giant iguana population.

Musha Cay

If your latest movie is doing well at the box office but life in the public eye is getting you down, a week or two on sumptuous and remote **MUSHA CAY** (☎203/602-0300 or 1-877/889-1100, ⊛www.mushacay.com), north of Lee Stocking Island, could be just the right pick-me-up. This fantasy island, with its palm-shaded beach, mosaic-tiled pool, exercise studio, tennis courts, TV station and a staff of 35 – including a masseuse and a pastry cook – is available for parties of up to fifteen for just under $350,000 per week. While remnants of old stone walls suggest the cay may have once been the site of a Loyalist plantation, these days, sun-kissed celebrities gather in the evening for cocktails and dinner in the wood-panelled dining room overlooking the dock. The four guest cottages are furnished with polished marble floors and antiques, and each has a hot tub and a fireplace or two. However, some well-heeled guests prefer to bunk down in the relative austerity of the one-room beach cabana with its outdoor toilet and shower. You can park your jet on nearby **Rudder Cut Cay**.

Little Farmer's Cay

Immediately north of Musha Cay, **LITTLE FARMER'S CAY** is a pretty, peaceful fishing village of less than a hundred residents built on a low green hill-side around a small horseshoe-shaped harbour. Many of the gaily painted houses are built in the traditional Bahamian style with steep-pitched roofs and deep verandas. The first weekend in February the community bursts with partygoers who come for the **Farmer's Cay Festival and Regatta**.

A short walk up the hill overlooking the wharf, the spotless and informal *Ocean Cabin Restaurant* (☎355-4006) serves breakfast, lunch and dinner. It has tables inside and out, a cosy bar and a book exchange. On Tuesday night, owners Terry and Ernestine Bain host a potluck dinner (bring anything but pork), and on Wednesdays during the tourist season cookouts and crab races are held. You can rent two cottages (from $120) on top of Dabba Hill, the highest point on the island; contact the *Ocean Cabin* for details.

About a mile from the wharf (you have to drive down the landing strip to reach it) is the Farmer's Cay Yacht Club and Marina (☎355-4017, ℗355-4017). The *Captain C* mailboat calls here every week, the main harbour being too shallow. A rustic **restaurant** and bar is located directly on the water, serving traditional Bahamian dishes. There are four cramped but adequate twin rooms in the back equipped with satellite TV and air conditioning (❸). For guided **snorkelling trips** or a **water taxi**, call "Little Jeff" over on the wharf (☎355-4003).

Great Guana Cay

Continuing northwards, twelve-mile-long **GREAT GUANA CAY** is the largest cay in the chain, and **Black Point** at its north end is the largest settlement with a population of 300. It is named for the long finger of dark rock that juts towards Staniel Cay, visible across the water. The village, strung out along a strip of pavement that follows the shore, has the dissipated and depressed atmosphere of a forgotten outpost, and fishing provides a meagre living. *Lorraine's Café* (☎355-2201) is a cheerful oasis, serving traditional Bahamian **meals**, such as grouper fingers, conch fritters and home-baked goods like banana bread, and is a favourite with passing boat cruisers. *De Shamon's* (☎355-3009) also serves native dishes in its small, neat dining room. The mailboat *Captain C* calls every week, and if for some reason you want to linger in Black Point, there are four spacious double rooms over *De Shamon's*, each equipped with a fridge (❸).

Staniel Cay and around

The contrast between Black Point and the tidy, green settlement on **Staniel Cay** is striking. Though also a sleepy fishing village, the latter has a more prosperous air and a holiday atmosphere due to its popularity with yacht cruisers and a well-heeled expatriate presence, the latter making up about half of the island's 160 residents through winter. Staniel Cay is also the most logical gateway to the Exuma Land and Sea Park, with an airstrip and regularly scheduled flights from Nassau and Florida.

The action is centred on the **Staniel Cay Yacht Club** (☎355-2024, ⓦ www .stanielcay), sitting at one end of a flat paved road lined with small stucco cottages that runs past the public beach and over a gentle rise to connect with a few residential lanes. What little traffic exists on the island is of the golf-cart variety, and if looking for a place to stretch your legs the long beach running along the Atlantic side of the island is a logical choice. An especially fun time to visit is over New Year, when Staniel Cay hosts a well-attended **regatta**. Warm-up events include a cookout on the public beach, a children's boat race, fireworks and a Junkanoo rush-out early New Year's morning. Another great time to visit is in August during the bonefishing tournament, held in conjunction with the Staniel Cay Homecoming. If you want to vary the regular lounging at the bar and on the beach with other activities, the yacht club rents **snorkel** gear ($15 a day) and ocean **kayaks** (singles $20, doubles $35 per day). Your first destination should be **Thunderball Grotto**, a few hundred yards offshore (see box opposite).

Around Staniel Cay

Visible from a bar stool at the yacht club and a five-minute motorboat ride northwest of Staniel Cay is **Big Major's Spot**, an island a few hundred yards long. The southernmost beach on the west side of the island is populated by feral pigs, which will swim out to your boat for treats. Separated from Big Major's Spot by a narrow channel, **Fowl Cay** is home to an ultra-exclusive cottage resort, while **Sampson Cay** three miles north of Staniel Cay holds a resort, marina and restaurant open to passing boaters (see opposite for details on accommodation at both cays). Rounding the northwest point of Sampson Cay, you enter **Pipe Creek**, a shallow corridor of clear blue water and sand bars with cays lining both sides that's heaven for bonefish anglers.

Another good bonefishing spot located immediately west of Staniel Cay is **Harvey Cay**, a boomerang-shaped island and scattering of small cays enclosing

Thunderball Grotto

Just offshore from Staniel Cay is the spectacular **Thunderball Grotto**, one of the Bahamas' most enchanting places: a hollowed-out island with a limestone vault arching over pools filled with colourful corals and fish, with shafts of sunlight pouring in through openings in the roof. It boggles the mind that a whole film crew got down here to film scenes from the James Bond movie that gave the grotto its name – and then did it again to film *Never Say Never Again*. You have to dive or snorkel into the undersea cavern through a current, and unless you are an expert go with a guide – or just rent the movie. In Staniel Cay, you can **rent or charter a boat** to take you to the Thunderball Grotto, into the national park or to nearby cays (see p.268). You might also ask on the dock for a local fisherman who could run you wherever you want to go.

a triangle of shallow water (inches deep at low tide) frequented by elegant rays. A strip of fine sand in the crux of Harvey Cay makes for a secluded spot for a swim and a picnic.

Practicalities

When it comes time to **eat** on Staniel Cay, the relaxed *Staniel Cay Yacht Club Restaurant and Bar* (☎355-2024; breakfast 8am–10am, lunch 11.30am–3pm, dinner at 7.30pm, reservations required by 5pm; snacks at the bar all day) has one of the most pleasing and inviting interiors in the Exumas, dressed up with a nautical theme. Lunch is tasty burgers, sandwiches and salads ($6–12). Dinner is pricey but pretty middle-of-the-road, typically featuring a four-course meal ($38) with an entrée of meat, poultry or fish with a baked potato and vegetable. On a bluff north of the settlement overlooking Thunderball Grotto and Big Major's Spot, *Club Thunderball* (daily 11am–9pm; ☎355-2012) serves Bahamian standbys, burgers and salads. There is a pool table, dancing on weekends and a very popular Friday night barbeque ($15, reservations required; call for free transportation). If you are self-catering or picnicking, there is a food store at *Sampson Cay Marina* and two grocery stores in Staniel Cay: the *Pink Pearl* and the *Blue Palm*, located beside one another and painted pink and blue respectively. You can order delicious fresh bread and banana cake at both.

As for **accommodation**, there are a couple of nice options in the village. Alternatively, for the privacy and perks that only money can buy, you can bed down on one of the private islands nearby.

Chamberlain's Cottages Staniel Cay ☎355-2043 or cell 357-0986, ⓦwww .stanielcaycottages.com. Five cosy, colourful cottages on stilts atop a little knoll just across the road from the public beach, each with excellent sunset views from the front porch, as well as kitchens, TV, and a/c. Minimum three-night stay, with weekly rates and golf cart rentals available. No credit cards. One-bedroom cottages ❹, two-bedroom ❻

Fowl Cay Fowl Cay ☎804/288-1081 or 1-866/369-5229, ⓦwww.fowlcay.com. Five attractive and luxurious rental cottages on a secluded fifty-acre private cay. Rates include transfers from Staniel Cay a mile away, all meals, use of a

powerboat, pool, tennis, snorkel gear, kayaks and sailboats and a golf cart to putt around the island. There are two beaches on the island as well as a walking trail. One-bedroom cottages from $8000 a week; three-bed/three-bath from $13,300. ❾

Sampson Cay Club and Marina Sampson Cay ☎242/355-2034, ⓦwww.sampsoncayclub.com. A bit busier than Fowl Cay, with its own lovely beaches and charming cottage rentals, 31-acre Sampson Cay is located three miles north of Staniel Cay. There is a marina (usually chock-a-block with big yachts), grocery store and restaurant and bar open to outside guests. The marina has sailboats and snorkelling gear for guest use, or you could rent a 13ft Boston Whaler to explore the area for

$80 per day. The kitchen-equipped cottages sleep two, four or six; one-bedroom unit ❼, including transport from Staniel Cay Airport.
Staniel Cay Yacht Club and Marina Staniel Cay ☎ 355-2024, ⓦ www.stanielcay.com. Nine cute wooden cottages and suites, each with

its own verandah overlooking the water and equipped with a coffee-maker and a small refrigerator, grouped around a small swimming pool. Meal plans and weekly rates available. One-bedroom cottage ❺; two and three-bedrooms also available.

Compass Cay

At the northern end of Pipe Creek and eight miles from Staniel Cay lies **COMPASS CAY**, just outside the southern boundary of the Exuma Land and Sea Park. Tooting along in a 13ft motorboat, you can reach Compass Cay from Staniel Cay in about an hour and a half, with more than enough petrol for the return trip. The island is privately owned and undeveloped save for a small **marina** (☎ 355-2137, ⓦ www.compasscay.com) at its southern end. It costs $5 to come ashore, payable at the marina where you can buy cool drinks, hamburgers, hotdogs and snacks; look out for the resident nurse sharks cruising the dock for stray tidbits. There is beautiful, long white-sand beach, several miles of well-marked and very scenic hiking paths and a tidal creek that bisects the island lengthwise, beckoning both bonefishers and kayakers, which can be rented at the marina for $40 a day.

Should you want to stay, the marina rents a homely three-bedroom **cottage** here sleeping up to six people, with a full kitchen, satellite TV, one bathroom, and a spectacular view; expect to pay $2200 a week for two people and $3000 for six. There is also an attractive two-bedroom apartment in the owner's hilltop house ($1800/$2200 for two/four people). Rates for both the cottage and the apartment include use of a 13ft motorboat and return transfers from the airport at Staniel Cay.

The Exuma Land and Sea Park

Beginning eight miles north of Staniel Cay, the **Exuma Land and Sea Park** encompasses fifteen substantial cays – including **Warderick Wells Cay**, the park's headquarters – and numerous smaller islands and outcroppings stretched over 22 miles of the Exuma chain. The park covers an area of 176 square miles, bound to the east by the deep cobalt waters of Exuma Sound, and in the west by the endless jade and sapphire shallows, reefs and sandbars of the Great Bahama Bank, both sides brimming with tropical marine life. The low rocky islands are rimmed by stretches of brilliant white sandy beach, some windswept and backed by rolling dunes, others sheltered by tall stands of coconut palms. As there is no commercial development of any sort within park boundaries, visitors should bring their own food and shelter, and be able to entertain themselves – not particularly hard with the spectacular sunrises and sunsets, and at night an opulent canopy of stars that appears close enough to pluck one.

Arrival and getting around

Unless you are piloting your own watercraft, getting to the park takes some money and effort. The park is most easily accessed from Staniel Cay (see details on p.270), from where you can **rent or charter a boat** to take you into the park (the trip to the park's southern boundary takes about an hour and a half). A costly though undoubtedly memorable option is a week-long **sailing**

Underwater Bahamas

As lovely as its beaches are, the Bahamas' most spectacular scenery is found underwater. Viewed from dry land, the sea is a pleasing palette of vibrant blues and greens. Dip your snorkel or dive mask below the surface, and an explosion of colour and dramatic topography envelops you. Here you can witness orange- and white-striped clownfish outlined in black, flashes of cobalt blue tangs mingling with schools of banana-yellow grunts and graceful spotted eagle rays gliding over the sandy bottom. Elsewhere, divers float over lush clumps of brain coral and underwater forests or meander through marine canyons inhabited by glow-in-the-dark creatures.

The reef world

One of the most tragic developments in the Bahamas has been the demise of large patches of **coral reefs**. The warm waters brought by El Niño in 1998 are held responsible for considerable damage, but the primary culprit is human activity. A coral reef is a colony of tiny **polyps**, creatures that secrete a limestone exoskeleton that combine to form stone-like structures. They survive through a symbiotic relationship with the algae **zooxanthellae**, which lives in the polyps and gives the corals their glorious colours. Some of the reefs in the Bahamas are several thousand years old, and all harbour a huge diversity of species that have led them be to called "the tropical rainforests of the ocean". In times of stress – like violent storms or a sustained increase in water temperature – the polyps expel the zooxanthellae, and the coral begins to die. The sight of the barren, white skeleton emptied of algae has led this process to be called **coral bleaching**, and scientists estimate that in the Caribbean, the area of the seafloor covered by living coral has decreased by an astounding eighty percent over the past thirty years.

There are a few things you can do when visiting to avoid placing further strain on the reef systems. Never touch or stand on living corals, and use boat moorings where possible to avoid dropping anchor on a reef. Don't pocket or buy coral as a souvenir, but do pick up any plastic

Reef residents

The reefs surrounding the Bahamas are home to hundreds of astounding creatures. Certain ones, like Atlantic bottle-nosed dolphins, can often be seen from the deck of a boat. Others, like the reef residents listed below, must be visited in their underwater universe to appreciate.

French Grunts Elegant yellow and white pin-striped fish that meander about the reef in small, close-packed schools, often in the same neighbourhood as their yellow and sky-blue striped relatives, the blue-striped grunt.

Fairy Basslets Tiny spots of brilliant colour found along shallow reefs. About two inches long, the front end of this fish looks as if it has been dipped in violet ink and the tail end in a rich yellow or gold.

▼ Queen Angelfish

Queen Angelfish One of the showier reef all-stars, painted a psychedelic palette of rainbow colours.

Sergeant Majors One of the most populous residents, their pale silvery bodies are daubed with a faint spot of yellow on the back and five black bars on the body. The male turns dark blue or purple during mating season, when he guards the eggs.

Trumpetfish Long, slender creatures with flared blue mouths, used to disguise themselves as branches of coral to escape predators.

or other garbage floating in the water or on the beach. If interested in learning more about reef ecology and efforts to protect it, contact the Earthwatch Institute (Ⓦwww.earthwatch.org), the supporter of several marine research projects in the Bahamas as well as learning vacations for amateur marine biologists, or the Bahamas National Trust (Ⓦwww.thebahamasnationaltrust. org), the non-profit organization which manages the marine conservation areas in the islands.

Taking the plunge

▲ Sugar Wreck, Grand Bahama

The waters surrounding the Bahamas offer a variety of world-class diving opportunities, from snorkelling just offshore and diving excursions by boat followed by a fine meal back at a cozy lodge, to overnight scuba trips on a sailboat threading its way through the islands. The **Tongue of the Ocean**, a cavernous channel that passes between Andros, the Exumas and New Providence, is abutted by walls, or cliffs, down which experienced divers can enjoy an exhilarating slide into the abyss. Andros is further celebrated for its majestic **coral reef** as well as its collection of **blue holes**, underwater entrances to large circular limestone pits that range from thirty to several hundred feet deep. The islands' history as a pirate haven and wrecking centre have left a legacy of numerous **wrecks**, particularly in the waters off Grand Bahama. Among the most memorable experiences of any visit, though, is diving among **dolphins** and **sharks** – indeed, the Bahamas are one of the few countries that allows forays among the latter – which can be arranged in New Providence, Long Island or Grand Bahama. On some tours, you can even watch sharks being fed by a diver in a protective coat of chain mail.

For the uninitiated, there can be no more idyllic classroom in which to learn to dive than the shallow, clear and warm waters surrounding the Bahamas. Most dive operators offer full SCUBA **certification courses** for around $500, as well as a beginner taster session that lasts a few hours for $80–100.

Top dive spots

➡ **Andros** The biggest island in the Bahamas has it all – the world's third longest barrier reef, blue holes and sea gardens, and top-notch diving facilities.
➡ **Grand Bahama** Wrecks, reefs and diving with dolphins, coupled with fine dining, gambling and duty-free shopping.
➡ **Long Island** Home of the world's deepest blue hole along with trips to the waters around Conception Island, offering wall diving and shallow water meadows of staghorn and elkhorn corals.

▲ Lookdown fish

When sharks attack... and when they don't

▲ Hammerhead shark

A nagging worry in the minds of many would-be divers and snorkellers – especially those who watched *Jaws* at a formative age – is "Am I going to be eaten by a shark?" While no great white sharks live in Bahamian waters, nine other species do, including tiger sharks (which can grow up to thirty feet long), bull sharks, hammerheads, lemon sharks and harmless bottom-feeding nurse sharks. Sharks may be fierce predators, but humans are not their snack of choice and they are typically as eager to get away from you as you are from them.

Shark attacks are generally the result of mistaken identity in murky waters or occur when spearfishers accidentally attract a shark with blood and bait fish, and the odds of being attacked while swimming, diving or surfing are very low. Globally, more people die from altercations with deer or honeybees each year than from shark bites, and in 2005 there was only one reported unprovoked attack in the Bahamas. Dive shops and field guides typically supply long lists of ways to minimize the already miniscule risk for provoking an attack. Some of the most useful **tips** include:

* Keep out of the water during twilight or night hours, when sharks are most active.
* Avoid murky water, as it's difficult for sharks to distinguish between a human and their preferred prey.
* Stay in a group when diving or swimming, as sharks are more likely to attack a solitary individual.
* Avoid waters used by fishermen as sharks often hang around the area scrounging for leftover bait.
* Should a shark appear, move steadily but cautiously to safety, avoiding jerky, splashing movements.

The southern stingray

A frequently observed inhabitant of Bahamian waters is the graceful **southern stingray**. Sporting a flat diamond-shape three- to five-feet across, the ray has a dark brown top and creamy underbelly along with a long, barbed tail. They spend most of their day hidden in the sand, and you may not see one until a big piece of the ocean floor seems to rise in a cloud of sand and glide away. Their sting is painful, but rarely fatal. Most injuries are minor wounds to legs and feet incurred when waders accidentally step on a dozing ray. Very rarely – as in the case of the "Crocodile Hunter" Steve Irwin in 2006 – an unfortunate fatal accident can occur when the barb lands near the victim's heart. A simple precaution against being stung is to shuffle your feet in the sand when wading, and avoid provoking the animal into attack by cornering it or otherwise getting too close.

▼ Southern stingray

△ Exuma Land and Sea Park

cruise aboard the catamaran *Cat Ppalu* (Davie, Florida; ☎954/734-7111 or 1-800/327-9600, ⓦwww.catppalu.com). You can charter the boat with crew and dive master for $12,000 a week including meals, with room for 12 people in six cabins. Alternatively, you can make up the numbers on other tours for $1450 per person. From Nassau, the boat heads out on excursions through the park several times a year carrying kayaks, and diving and snorkel gear with plenty of time made for exploring the cays topside. Alternatively, George Town's Starfish Adventure Center (see p.253) offers an eight-day guided sailing expedition that wends its way up the full length of the island chain from Barreterre to Allen's Cay and back to Staniel Cay, from where you will be flown back to George Town ($2000).

From Nassau, Captain Paul Harding of Safari Seaplanes (☎393-2522 or 1-866/272-5728, ⓦwww.safariseaplanes.com) can fly you directly to Warderick Wells or anywhere else in his **floatplane**; you'll need to call direct and negotiate the rates.

Accommodation

Most visitors to the Exuma Land and Sea Park arrive on their own sailboats or with organized kayaking and camping expeditions. There are 22 moorings at the north anchorage of Warderick Wells by the park headquarters (see p.274), and four more at the south anchorage off Hog Cay. The **mooring fee** is $15 a night, and the park asks that you call (VHF Ch 16 "Exuma Park") the morning before you intend to arrive. There are no hotels within the park boundaries, but there are dozens of soft sandy beaches on which to pitch your tent. **Camping** fees are $5 a night, and the park relies on campers to drop their payment at the park headquarters or mail it in after they leave. Camping is allowed on any beach, provided you clean up fully after yourself and cook only with camping fuel. There are also accommodations available just outside the park boundaries on Staniel Cay, Compass Cay, Sampson Cay and Fowl Cay to the south (see p.271); and on Norman's Cay to the north (see p.278).

Sea kayaking in the Exumas

One of the best and increasingly popular ways of exploring the Exumas is by **sea kayak**, and happily there are a couple of reliable outfitters offering guided expeditions through the cays and in the Exuma Land and Sea Park. If you want to explore the Exuma Land and Sea Park **on your own**, your easiest option is to rent sea kayaks and camping equipment from George Town's Starfish Adventure Center outfitter (see p.253) or bring your own inflatable boats and gear into Staniel Cay. Though the sunny skies and generally placid turquoise sea can make one forget, this is a remote wilderness area and you'll need to be experienced, fit and well equipped. There are few visitors, even fewer places to replenish drinking water, and in high winds the sometimes wide cuts between the cays become extremely dangerous. It is essential to carry the following **safety equipment** if travelling independently: a first aid kit; nautical charts and a compass; a VHF radio with a range of at least five miles and extra AA batteries. You also need a GPS (Global Positioning System); an EPIRB (Emergency Position Indicating Radio Beacon) signalling device for extreme emergencies; and flares, smoke signals and a horn for attracting the attention of passing boats. Only a few cays at the southern end of the chain outside the park boundaries are permanently inhabited and within the Land and Sea Park, one park ranger is responsible for patrolling its entire 176 square miles. It could be a long time in an emergency before being spotted by a passerby. You will also need to bring sufficient food and drinking water for the duration of your trip – at least a gallon of water a day per person. Only small cooking fires are permitted, and the use of camp stoves is encouraged.

Another point to keep in mind is that several of the islands in the chain are **privately owned**. The owners have paid millions of dollars for their privacy, and do not appreciate uninvited campers on their beaches. This means that you have to plan your route carefully. When you come into the national park, call "Exuma Park" on VHF Ch 16 and let the warden know where you are camping and your intended route through the park. If you are travelling outside the park boundaries, it is a good idea to check in with the police detachment in George Town or Staniel Cay beforehand. On a more

Warderick Wells Cay

In the middle of the park sits **Warderick Wells Cay**, home to the park's **headquarters** (Mon–Sat 9am–noon & 3–5pm, Sun 9am–1pm; c/o Bahamas National Trust, PO Box N-4105, Nassau, Bahamas; ☎393-1317, ⓦwww .bahamasnationaltrust.org, VHF 16 "Exuma Park"). The visitors' centre, housed in a wooden building at the cay's northern end, holds an interesting display on the natural history of the Exumas, along with maps, information sheets and reference books to guide your explorations. The office also has a book exchange and sells postcards and T-shirts, but does not stock food of any kind. On Saturdays through the winter, the park hosts a happy hour for visitors on the verandah.

Warderick Wells is well worth the considerable effort it takes to reach it. The island's undulating ridges and valleys offer relief to eyes accustomed to the generally flat topography of the Bahamas, and seven miles of hiking **trails** crisscross the island, leading through groves of thatch palm and silver buttonwood, past limestone sink holes and along a broad tidal creek bed to impressive lookout points and Loyalist plantation ruins. A dozen soft white-sand beaches dot the windswept Atlantic coast and secluded palm-fringed coves of the leeward side of the island, while the coral reefs and sea gardens surrounding the island teem with life.

positive note, don't forget your snorkelling gear and sturdy closed-toe shoes so you can explore the islands and reefs.

Kayakers and sailors alike should equip themselves with Stephen Pavlidis's *Cruising Guide to The Exuma Cays*. Nautical charts for the area can be found in the *Explorer Chartbook: Exumas and the Ragged Islands* by Monty and Sara Lewis and *The Yachtsman's Guide to The Bahamas*.

Guided tours and programmes

Several outfitters run **guided expeditions** through the cays. Starfish (see p.39) offers kayaking day-trips from George Town on Great Exuma that involve a leisurely paddle followed by a picnic lunch on one of the several small islands that enclose Elizabeth Harbour. Starfish's knowledgeable guides also overnight camping trips of varying length into **southern cays**.

For those who have never sea-kayaked before, North Carolina Outward Bound (☏828/299-3366, ⓦwww.ncobs.org) offers an eight-day sea-kayaking course **in the waters off Great Exuma**. The expeditions, which cost $1900 excluding airfare to George Town, are run several times December through April. Days are spent practising strokes and rescue techniques, learning chart navigation, snorkelling and paddling from island to island. Contrary to popular Outward Bound myth, you won't be stranded alone on a deserted island with only a safety pin and a magnifying glass to save you, though the course does include a "solo" period for reflecting on the beauty of the surroundings.

Also available are eight-day guided expeditions ($1800) run by well-respected Ibis Tours (PO Box 208, Pelham, NY 10803; ☏914/409-5961; ⓦww.ibistours.com), which head through the Exuma Land and Sea Park in March, April and May. Paddlers put in at Staniel Cay and leisurely wend their way up towards Norman's Cay at the southern end of the park, with plenty of time made for snorkelling, swimming, fine dining and lolling on the many beaches which beckon along the way. The kayaks are equipped with sails to lessen the level of exertion required.

In the days of pirates and privateers, the cay was a source of freshwater for passing sailors. At the southern end of the island, opposite Hog Cay, a conch-shell-lined path marks the way to **The Pirate's Lair**, a secluded stand of tall cabbage palms with a floor of soft sand used as a rest stop by Blackbeard and his ilk. Some of the grasses growing here are not indigenous to the Exumas and are found only on the coast of Louisiana, leading historians to believe that their seeds were brought in the sleeping mats of the pirates who gathered here to plan raids and collect water from the nearby spring. Sometime in the late eighteenth century, unknown Loyalist exiles settled on the island. **Anita's Trail** leads to the ruins of a stone house discovered in 1995, about two miles south of the headquarters (trail maps are available from the latter). Just south of the ruins, a waist-high stone wall runs across the width of the whole island, from the windward to leeward shores. It is likely that the settlers built it to confine their cattle to the southern part of the island. Follow the wall to its western end, and you arrive at **Beryl's Beach** in a lovely, sheltered cove.

A fifteen-minute hike from the park headquarters, **Boo Boo Hill** marks the highest point on a limestone ridge at the north end of Warderick Wells and has a commanding view down the length of the island and of both coastlines. A path at the east end of **Powerful Beach** near the park office leads to the rocky summit where it is believed a cairn was erected in the nineteenth century by survivors of a shipwreck, missionaries en route to save wayward souls. For years,

Marine conservation in the Exuma Land and Sea Park

The Exuma Land and Sea Park was established in 1958 by the Bahamas National Trust (BNT) as a **marine conservation area**. The nonprofit BNT, alarmed at the destruction of the historically abundant diversity of plant and animal life in the islands, successfully lobbied to have this part of the Exumas set aside to protect and replenish species of fish and wildlife. Local fishermen were allowed a limited catch in park waters until 1986, when it became a no-take zone for fish, lobster, coral and even seashells. Ten years after the ban took force, grouper and lobster were around fifty percent larger and fifty percent more plentiful than those found outside park boundaries.

Nevertheless, the no-take policy is resented by some local fisherman, and **poaching** is a continuing problem. After the park's sole warden began strictly enforcing the no-take policy, poachers brought death threats against him and Bahamian Defence Force officers were stationed on Warderick Wells Cay to both protect him and his family and arrest violators.

As you travel through the park, you may see "For Sale" signs on various lonely humps of land. Some of the cays in the park were owned by wealthy foreigners before it was established and remained in private hands, in some cases jeopardizing conservation efforts as the park's authority does not extend beyond the high-water mark on privately owned cays. In the mid-1990s, for example, a developer bought **Hall's Pond Cay**, planning to establish a resort community on the island. In cutting roads and digging foundations, vast quantities of loose earth were washed into the sea, and the coral reef located 400yd offshore began to die. Eventually, the Bahamian government repossessed Hall's Pond Cay, but considerable damage had already been done.

Volunteer programmes

For those interested in helping out, the Land and Sea Park runs a **volunteer programme**. With limited support from the government – the park currently relies completely on private donations for its day-to-day operations – the park depends heavily on volunteers to staff the office on Warderick Wells and maintain the park facilities. Each year, passing boaters, school groups and a small cadre of long-term resident volunteers put in some 27,000 hours of unpaid labour. The tasks are often far from glamorous. Projects include cutting hiking trails, beach clean-up, machinery maintenance and sorting nails and screws, even babysitting the warden's children. Facilities at Warderick Wells are limited, so you must be prepared to sleep on your boat or bring a tent (mooring and camping fees are waived). There is drinking water, showers and a kitchen for use by volunteers, but you will need to bring your food. Periodically, a boat goes to Staniel Cay or Nassau for supplies. Contact the warden at least a month in advance outlining your skills and availability (see park headquarters details, p.274 for contact information). If just passing through the park, the headquarters has a long "To Do" list of jobs requiring a few hours or a few days; any help is appreciated.

passing boaters have made a pilgrimage up Boo Boo Hill to leave a marker of their voyage, some of them quite elaborate, and they make for interesting reading. Just below the steps to the park office, at the south end of Powerful Beach, rests the mounted skeleton of a huge sperm whale, 52ft long and over 6ft high. The whale, which suffocated after swallowing a plastic bag, washed up on Shroud Cay in 1995.

In another conservation effort, 25 **hutias**, small hedgehog-like creatures, were introduced on Warderick Wells in 1985. They were, and are still considered to be, an endangered species, though there are now an estimated 2500 on the island. You are unlikely to see the hutias as they are nocturnal, but you might smell them – they have a scent akin to decaying leaves. The cay is also home to all kinds of birds, lizards and a wide variety of plant life, not to mention lemon sharks that have taken up residence in the shallow waters near the park headquarters. They have acquired a taste for food scraps, and may often be seen drifting motionless between the docks on hot afternoons. By all accounts quite timid, they disappear when anyone else is in the water but are fascinating to observe – though more than a bit unnerving if you fancy a swim or snorkel around the reef.

The rest of the park

Just to the north of Warderick Wells is **Alligator Cay**, where the resident giant iguanas can be found sunning themselves on the beach. Further north, the long and narrow **Hawksbill Cay** boasts inviting stretches of beach on both sides. Besides sun-worshipping, you can also explore the ruins of a Loyalist settlement set in a grove of tamarind trees; a marked trail begins from the beach midway along the west side of the island. Historically a watering place for pirates, spongers and fisherman, **Shroud Cay**, north of Hawksbill Cay, is traversed by several tidal creeks and mangrove swamps that are breeding grounds for various species of fish and birdlife. These may be explored carefully by kayak or dinghy. On the northern end of the cay, overlooking Exuma Sound, is Camp Driftwood, a structure constructed incrementally by passing boaters out of flotsam and jetsam. In the 1980s, it was used by US drug agents to spy on Carlos Lehder's smuggling operations close by on Norman's Cay (see below).

At the southern end of the park, **Little Bell Island**, also known as **Cambridge Cay**, is a popular stop-off for boat cruisers. It is privately owned, but visitors are welcomed ashore. Towards the north end of the cay, a trail from a beach on the leeward side takes you to a lookout where you can make out the length of the island and a chain of cays extending north and south. Immediately south of Cambridge Cay are the **Rocky Dundas**, two tall rocky piles that house grottoes dripping with stalactites and stalagmites that visitors claim rival the more famous Thunderball Grotto. The Rocky Dundas stand exposed to Exuma Sound in Conch Cut, which can be rough in windy weather, and as there is a strong northward current on the incoming tide, it is recommended that you visit in calm weather at low tide.

The Northern Exumas

Although the northern boundary of the Land and Sea Park was placed arbitrarily at the Wax Cay Cut, the Exuma chain continues on a northwest trajectory for another ten miles. From the relatively sizeable islands of **Norman's Cay** and **Highbourne Cay** just outside the park boundary, the string of cays gradually peters out to a series of rock outcroppings forty miles southeast of Nassau. In between, numerous inviting beaches, cays and rocks of various shapes and sizes, plus great opportunities for diving, snorkelling and bird-watching, are all yours to explore. Note, however, that many of these cays are privately owned, as marked on nautical charts for the area.

Just north of the Land and Sea Park, remote Norman's Cay was the focus of international attention in the early 1980s when it was revealed that the Colombian drug lord Carlos Lehder was using it as a base of operations for running cocaine. After terrorizing the other wealthy residents of the cay into abandoning their properties, he smuggled billions of dollars of contraband into the United States from here before being caught and jailed. These days, with its long beach, gracefully swaying palm trees and a pleasant casual restaurant and rental cottages, the cay is once again a popular stop-off for yachters cruising the Exumas. A few miles to the north, Highbourne Cay is the only other permanently inhabited cay in the chain. It's privately owned, but boaters are permitted ashore at the **Highbourne Cay Marina** (☎355-1008, ℱ355-1003, VHF Ch 16), which has a grocery store, pay phone and berths for boats up to 130ft.

Practicalities

The Northern Exumas are most easily reached from Nassau, which lies forty miles to the west. Powerboat Adventures (☎393-7116, ⓦwww .powerboatadventures.com) leads an action-packed full-day outing ($190) that includes a visit to the resident Bahamian dragon iguanas on Allan's Cay, snorkelling, a nature hike and a barbecue lunch on the powdery white beach on Ship Channel Cay. Apart from organized excursions, visiting the northern cays is logistically difficult and expensive unless you have your own yacht or aeroplane. You will have to charter a water taxi or aeroplane from Nassau or Staniel Cay. There is an airstrip on Norman's Cay.

Accommodation options in the Northern Exumas are extremely limited. On Norman's Cay, *MacDuff's* (☎357-8846 or 1-877/790-1199, ⓦwww .macduffs.com, VHF Ch 16) rents four cute and colourful one-bedroom beachfront cottages, each of which can sleep up to four (❼). You can cook your own meals or buy a meal plan at the casual *MacDuff's Bar and Grille*, patronized by passing boaters (open daily from noon, serving lunch until 3pm and dinner 5–8pm; reservations required for dinner).

Cat Island and
San Salvador

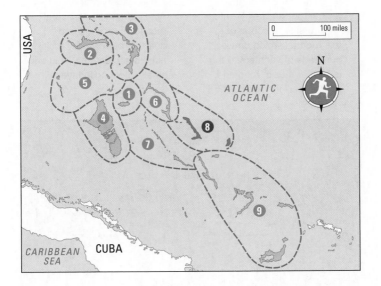

CHAPTER 8

Highlights

✳ **Diving Cat Island** The south shore of Cat Island boasts some great diving spots, including the Black Coral Wall, Vlady's Reef and the Anchor, which feature massive sheets of coral and sea fans as well as plentiful tiger fish and parrotfish. See p.285

✳ **Annual Cat Island Regatta** If you are here in August, pick a spot on New Bight's harbourside to scope out this regatta, which draws hundreds of yachters to the island for music, food and, of course, sailing. See p.288

✳ **The Hermitage on Mount Alvernia** On top of the highest "mountain" (206ft) in the Bahamas, The Hermitage is a religious retreat with terrific views of the Atlantic coast. See p.288

✳ **Diving San Salvador** San Salvador's walls and reefs are legendary among divers. Acres of underwater coral meadows drop off into oblivion, patrolled by multi-hued sea creatures – big and small – floating in layers. See p.296

△ Snorkelling at San Salvador

Cat Island and
San Salvador

A world away from the cruise ship crowds, casinos and duty-free shops of Nassau and Freeport, **CAT ISLAND** and **SAN SALVADOR** offer peace to go with a glimpse of rural life in the Bahamas. Unfortunately the islands' younger generations haven't had much of a chance to stick around and enjoy it in recent years as the economy hereabouts, based on the traditional pursuits of farming and fishing, has been in steady decline. So while the population's youth leave in droves for service jobs in New Providence and Grand Bahama, the considerable charms of both islands – splendid powdery white and blush-coloured **beaches**, superb **snorkelling** and **diving**, and a handful of exquisite waterside lodges – attract visitors from afar.

On the extreme eastern edge of the Great Bahama Bank, 130 miles southeast of Nassau, Cat Island lies within sight of Eleuthera on a fine day. San Salvador rests another seventy miles to the east, sitting alone in the deep Atlantic Ocean and marking the most easterly point in the Bahamas. The two islands are forever linked not only by their relative proximity but

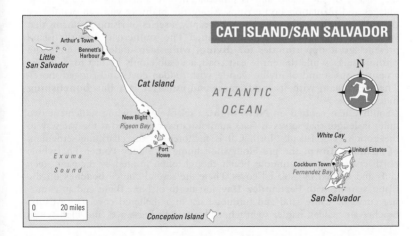

281

by the enduring controversy surrounding Columbus's first landing in the New World. Both have long claimed this historic yet unproven distinction as well as the name "San Salvador", which the explorer gave to his original landfall in his journals. Until the twentieth century, Cat Island was widely accepted as the island where Columbus first set foot and was consequently known as San Salvador, while modern San Salvador was known as Watling's Island. However, after detailed studies of the sixteenth-century Spanish missionary Bartolomé de Las Casas's version of the Columbus journals, the consensus shifted. On May 6, 1926, the Bahamian legislature formally renamed the islands to their current status. Of course, to this day some Cat Islanders still claim their parcel of land the original New World stop for Columbus.

Cat Island

Cat Island is a slender 48-mile-long boot-shaped slice, no more than four miles wide at any one point until it reaches the sole in the far south, where its width triples. Lush and hilly by Bahamian standards, Cat has some of the best soil for farming in the Bahamas, and consequently boasts more vegetation and animal life than other islands. These days, small-scale farming is far more important than fishing as a source of livelihood for its roughly 2000 permanent residents, and the island has a deserted feel that can be comforting for those seeking a refuge from fast-paced modern life. Life remains quiet here most days, though things can heat up during the **Cat Island Regatta** in August, which attracts hundreds of yachters, and the boisterous **Cat Island Music Festival** in June, which celebrates home-grown rake 'n scrape folk music.

North to south, a single smooth and well-paved **Queen's Highway** runs the length of the island and is punctuated here and there by ramshackle villages and plantation house ruins. Along the highway, you can plainly see the ridgeland that dominates the topography, a series of rising platforms that were once dunes, but have now solidified. The southern end of the island presents great opportunities for **diving**, with steep underwater cliffs and offshore reefs, while the entire east coast, accessible only by dirt roads, offers a continuous strand of idyllic seaside, with hidden coves and rugged shores. The west coast, with its mud creeks and estuaries, is a fine **bonefishing** hideout.

South Cat is centred on **New Bight**, a relatively sprawling settlement two miles in length that serves as Cat's administrative centre and is the gateway to the boot of Cat Island. North Cat is anchored by the charming settlement of **Arthur's Town**, the pre-Hollywood home of Sidney Poitier. The whole north coast is one continuous beach, though often fronted by dramatic steep cliffs and broken by isolated coves. There are several choice **beaches** on the island, starting with **Fernandez Bay**, just north of New Bight and an exquisite curve of white sand and turquoise sea in a sheltered cove. The Atlantic beaches are wilder, harder to reach, and home to big waves and high winds

CAT ISLAND

0   5 miles

N

ATLANTIC

OCEAN

Exuma

Sound

Man O'War Point
Blue Hole
Orange Creek
North East Point
Arthur's Town
Zion Hill
Bennett's Harbour
Thurston Hill
Alligator Point
Pigeon Creek Beach
Roker's Bluff
Tea Bay
Queen's Highway
Smith Bay
Blue Lake
Fernandez Bay
Freetown
Mt. Alvernia
Armbrister Plantation Ruins
New Bight
Pigeon Bay
Armbrister Creek
Old Bight
Gambier Lake
Deveaux Mansion
McQueens
Port Howe
Bailey Town
Hawk's Nest
Red Pond
Cutlass Bay
Bain Town
Columbus Point
Hawk's Nest Creek
French Bay
Springfield Bay (Morgan's Bay)

EATING & DRINKING

Bluebird Restaurant & Bar	2
Fernandez Bay Village	E
Hawk's Nest Resort & Marina	I
Hazel's Seaside Bar	1

ACCOMMODATION

Bridge Inn	F
Fernandez Bay Village	D
Gilbert's Inn	E
Greenwood Beach Resort	G
Hawk's Nest Resort and Marina	H
Orange Creek Inn	A
Pigeon Cay Beach Club	C
Sammy T's Resort	B

– a tempting challenge for windsurfers and swimmers. At the southern end of the island, **Greenwood Beach** is eight miles of gorgeous blush-coloured sand washed by crashing surf. Towering over the island terrain near New Bight, **Mount Alvernia** stands 206ft above sea level – the highest point in the Bahamas – and offers a sweeping view of the island's rolling terrain and coastline.

Wildlife thrives in this untrammelled interior and may well be unrivalled in the Bahamas. Burrowing owls, numerous non-poisonous snakes and a number of amphibians are observable in the inland scrub and near ponds, while giant land crabs emerge in the evenings on sandy paths near the ocean. However,

Obeah

In addition to the Out Island bush medicine (see p.254), which resembles the indigenous medicine of other cultures that have had little experience with modern physicians, some Cat Islanders still practice **obeah**. This form of witchery concentrates on the application of "cures" and "spells" to guard against evil eyes or thefts. Empty bottles are a particular fetish of obeah, and you can see them dangling from the occasional tree, or littered about graveyards, all in homage to the spirits of the dead, who are said to enjoy a libation in preference to more destructive behaviour. Farmers fill their bottles with hair, dirt or fingernails, and place them at strategic spots in their fields to protect crops. Another manifestation of obeah is the placing of lightning rods on some Cat Island houses, particularly in New Bight, to protect against ghosts and spirits.

the once-ubiquitous freshwater turtle (*Chrysemys felis*), once abundant on not only Cat Island, but also Eleuthera and Andros, is now in serious decline. On Cat Island, these turtles are found in only a few hectares of lakes. Cat Islanders enjoyed hunting "peter" as they called it, both for food and as adornments for freshwater reflecting pools.

Some history

While the Spanish established a number of settlements on the island, it is widely accepted that the island is named for **Arthur Catt**, a seventeenth-century pirate who was based on Cat Island. Locals often say that the name of the island is derived from the large numbers of feral cats abandoned on the island when the Spanish left, but most historians are skeptical of this claim. In any event, the first significant influx on Cat was made up of **American Loyalists** fleeing the American Revolution in 1783, and the number of Hepburns, Deveauxs, McDonalds, Campbells and Sutherlands on Cat Island today attests to those early families. They set up cotton plantations and cattle farms; at the height of plantation agriculture, there were perhaps forty slave-labour farms on the island, the remains of which can still be found scattered about the bush.

The land was soon depleted, however, and the slave-plantation culture pretty much ended in 1831 with widespread slave revolt. When Britain abolished slavery in 1834, many slave owners fled the island, and the newly emancipated settlements were taken over by the former slaves. (New Bight, for instance, began its life as Freetown, where freed slaves settled after the British banned the trade.) Soon, a new form of colonial agriculture began to dominate Cat Island with the establishment of huge pineapple and sisal farms on the interior. In the mid-1850s, the population of Cat hit five thousand, a railroad was built to carry produce to shipping points and the production of ethereally sweet pink pineapples rivalled that of Eleuthera.

Only fifty years later, however, with the emergence of world markets, Cat's relative isolation and constant competition from American and British conglomerates drove both the pineapple and the sisal business into bankruptcy. Since then, Cat Islanders have lived a traditional and quiet life, farming small pothole plots in the deep interior of the island, fertilized with guano gathered from bat caves. The most successful of these plots grow tomatoes, onions and pineapples, though only for local consumption. For most of the island, electricity only came about the late 1980s, and the effects of tourism are still minimal.

Arrival

There are two **airports** on Cat Island: the small Arthur's Town Airport (☏354-2049) in the north and the more heavily used New Bight Airport (☏342-2017) servicing the south. As most accommodations are clustered towards the island's southern end, most visitors will want to land at the latter. Bahamasair (☏377-5505, ⓦwww.bahamasair.com; $82 one-way) flies into both airports several times a week from Nassau. *Cat Island Air* (☏377-3318) has daily flights between Nassau and New Bight ($75 one-way), while both *Pineapple* (☏377-0140) and *Southern Air* (reservations ☏323-6833, ⓦwww .southernaircharter.com) fly between Arthur's Town and Nassau several times a week for around $85 one-way. If travelling from Florida, both Continental (☏1-800/231-0856) and Lynx Air (☏954/772 9808, ⓦwww.lynxair.com) fly directly to New Bight from Fort Lauderdale; expect to pay $350 for a round trip ticket. At the south end of the island, *Hawk's Nest Resort* (☏342-7050 or 1-800/688-4752, ⓦwww.hawks-nest.com) has a **private airstrip**, along with an eleven-slip **marina**, although pilots have to clear customs in New Bight. Given the limited marina facilities on Cat, most yachters simply anchor in shallow Fernandez Bay and spend a few days in idleness, taking dinghies ashore during the day and spending evenings on board their vessels.

If looking to arrive via the slow boat, the MV *Lady Emerald* **mailboat** departs Nassau on Tuesday afternoon, calling at Smith Bay north of New Bight about twelve hours later ($50). The *Lady Rosalind* serves North Cat Island, departing Nassau on Thursday evening, calling at Arthur's Town, Dumfries, Orange Creek and Bennett's Harbour ($50). As with all mailboats, the schedule is subject to change; call the Dockmaster (☏393-1064) at Potter's Cay in Nassau for up-to-the-minute information.

Information and getting around

There are no formal **information** services on Cat Island, but material is available through Nassau's Ministry of Tourism (☏1-800/224-2627, ⓦwww.bahamas.com), or the Out Island Tourist Board (☏305/931-6612 or 1-800/688-4752, ⓦwww .bahama-out-islands.com). It's important to note that there are **no banks** on Cat Island. While the resorts are set up to accept credit cards and traveller's cheques, you'll have to pay with cash elsewhere so plan accordingly.

As for getting around, **taxis** meet all flights and can be arranged through your hotel; a trip from New Bight to Fernandez Bay Village will cost about $20. If you want to do some exploring, **renting a car** will more than likely be the more economical option. Gilbert's Inn and Car Rental in New Bight (☏342-3011) offers well-maintained cars for $80 a day, while at the island's north end the *Orange Creek Inn* (☏354-4110) rent a few cars at the same rate. Some of the resorts keep **bicycles** for guest use as well, so check before booking if interested.

Diving and watersports

While the Atlantic or "north coast" is storm-tossed, Cat Island's south coast, from Columbus Point in the east to Devil's Point in the west, is one of the most spectacular **diving sites** in a region filled with impressive choices. Here along the coast, the reef wall begins at only around 50ft and drops off steeply into a variety of gulleys, chimneys, canyons and troughs. The best dive sites along the south shore include **Black Coral Wall**, **The Maze**, **Vlady's Reef**, **The Anchor**, **The Cut** and **The Cave**. While only The Cut is reachable from shore, the others are regular stops on the itinerary of Cat Island's two dive shops. Most feature massive sheets of coral, along with plentiful tiger fish, snapper, grunt, parrotfish and flamingo tongue shells, among hundreds of other species of flora and fauna. Elsewhere the seagrass beds are alive with wrasse, hermit crabs and sand gobies, and it's possible to sometimes spot skittish reef shark at The Cave. One must-see for experienced divers is the **Tartar Bank**, an offshore pinnacle that doesn't so much feature coral as huge schools of pelagic triggerfish, many sharks, spadefish, barracuda, jacks and eagle rays. It lies sixteen miles southeast of Cat, a boat ride of at least 45 minutes, and the best time to dive it is November to January, though the weather can be wild.

All of the major resorts in the south can assist with arranging **snorkelling** trips as well as diving. For the most part, snorkellers are welcome to go out on dive boats, and in most places in-shore snorkelling in grass beds and shallow reefs presents the opportunity to see starfish, rays and small fish.

Dive operators

Cat Island Dive Centre *Greenwood Beach Resort* ℡ 342-3053, Ⓦ www.greenwoodbeachresort.com. The *Greenwood Beach Resort* caters primarily to divers, though outside guests are also welcome to use the dive shop and its two dive boats to explore the wide range of spectacular sites minutes from shore. Courses are conducted in both English and German, and the dives offered include a complete array of south shore dives. Costs run $65/$60 for one/two-tank dives and $540 for PADI open water certification. Snorkelling trips are $35. Equipment rental is available.

Hawk's Nest Resort and Marina Hawk's Nest Point ℡ 342-7050 or 1-800/688-4752, Ⓦ www .hawks-nest.com. *Hawk's Nest* specializes in dives on the offshore reef – a spot that is also good for snorkellers –and sites around Devil's Point, where massive stands of elkhorn and staghorn coral punctuate the reef. One and two tank dives are $60 and $80 respectively, with four-day PADI open water certification courses for $500. Equipment rental is available and outside guests welcome.

Fishing

With its mud creeks, shallow sandbanks and mangroves, the entire west coast is best suited to **bonefishing**; count on paying around $350 a day for two people per boat. Near Fernandez Bay, **Joe's Creek Sound** and **Pigeon Creek** are great bonefishing sites, and the best place to find guides is at *Fernandez Bay Village Resort* (℡ 342-3043). Bonefishing in North Cat is just as good and you can contact Wilson or Lincoln Cleare in Orange Creek (℡ 354-4042) for both bonefishing and sightseeing. Additional information on sightseeing, bonefishing and trips to Little San Salvador (see box, p.293) can be had by contacting personnel in Arthur's Town at the tiny Commissioner's Office at the harbour. Likewise, the *Cookie House Bakery* (℡ 354-2027) in Arthur's Town can be a good place to line up a guide.

    Sport fishing has had a slow start on Cat Island, though it is quite spectacular. The hot spot is the south shore, which can be great for wahoo, white marlin and yellowfin tuna. *Fernandez Bay Village Resort* (℡ 342-3043 or 1-800/940-1905, Ⓦ www.fernandezbayvillage.com) and the *Hawk's Nest Resort* (℡ 342-7050 or 1-800/688-47520, Ⓦ www.hawks-nest.com) are the most experienced with sport-fishing trips.

△ Palm Trees on Cat Island

South Cat Island

Two-thirds of the way down Cat Island, the rambling roadside settlement of **New Bight** serves as the island's tourism and administrative centre, home to the police station and a BaTelCo office in the Government Administrative Complex. Settled a couple of hundred years ago, New Bight is also home to the hermit priest Father Jerome's celebrated **Mount Alvernia Hermitage**, and has quick access to several beaches, most notably **Fernandez Bay**. Three miles south, **Old Bight** is the jumping off point for trips to **Greenwood Beach** as well as several blue holes. The waters off the broad south end of the island hold some of the island's best **diving** and **snorkelling** in the stretch between Columbus Point and Hawk's Nest Point.

Accommodation

Accommodation in the southern part of Cat Island is comprised of a clutch of small and secluded beachfront resorts and a few bare bones budget options nearby. The resorts are quite self-contained, offering a full range of activities and pristine expanses of private beach. *Fernandez Bay Village*, located on a secluded cove three miles north of New Bight, is one of the Bahamas' loveliest and most relaxing small resorts. However, if you have a rental car or plan to spend most of your time diving, *Greenwood Beach Resort* or *Hawk's Nest* are also good options as they have the island's only dive shops.

Bridge Inn New Bight ☎ 342-3013, ⓦ www .catislandbridgeinn.com. A basic but still restful motel-style option for budget travellers, located a five-minute walk from the beach, with a simple restaurant on site serving filling Bahamian fare. Along with fifteen standard double rooms, six two-bedroom units with kitchenettes are available. ➍

Fernandez Bay Village New Bight ☎ 342-3043 or 1-800/940-1905, ⓦ www .fernandezbayvillage.com. On an exquisite and secluded curve of white sand backed by casuarinas and palm trees, this casually elegant beach lodge is a Bahamian gem. Featuring a dozen romantic stone and timber guest rooms and cottages tucked along the shore, each with a private terrace, ceiling fans, a/c and outdoor showers so you can bathe by starlight. Wonderful buffet meals are served in the open and airy main lodge and on the terrace with a sunset view. Sea kayaks, bikes and snorkels are all freely available for guest use, while those looking for a more relaxed time can pick from a collection of board games, well-stocked bookshelves, hammocks and beach lounge chairs shaded by umbrellas. A local musician entertains guests a few nights a week, and there is a nightly bonfire on the beach. ❽

Gilbert's Inn New Bight ☎342-3011. Clean, modern motel rooms roadside opposite the New Bight Food Store, each equipped with a/c and TV. Car rentals are also available.

Greenwood Beach Resort 3.5 miles north of Port Howe, then 2 miles east on a coral road ☎342-3053 or 1-800/688-4752, ⓦwww .greenwoodbeachresort.com. In an isolated spot on the Atlantic coast, this relaxed family-run resort is popular with divers, offering twenty cheerful and simple rooms located only steps from a gorgeous eight-mile strand of blush-coloured sand. There is a small swimming pool and hot tub, as well as a dive shop offering dives and certification courses. Guests eat together at one long table in the main lodge's airy restaurant and bar; a meal plan available for $55 a day for three meals. ❸ with ceiling fan; ❹ with a/c.

Hawk's Nest Resort and Marina Devil's Point ☎242/342-7050 or 1-800/688-4752, ⓦwww .hawks-nest.com. Set on four hundred acres of beachfront at the isolated southeast tip of the island, this small, laid-back hotel caters to fishermen, boaters and private pilots with ten nicely decorated ocean-view rooms done up in wicker and ceramic tile. There is also a large house for rent with two bedrooms ($455 per night). Meals are served in a small simple dining room with a view of the pool, located a few hundred yards from the beach. There is a 28-slip marina, an air strip and three dive instructors on staff. ❻

New Bight and around

Most visitors land at the airport by the scattered settlement of **NEW BIGHT**, gateway to a clutch of small beach resorts on the southern half of Cat Island. The village itself is functional rather than picturesque, comprised of a petrol station, grocery store, the government services complex and a couple of small restaurants and motels. The annual **Cat Island Regatta** draws hundreds of sailors from around the Bahamas and the world to New Bight every August for four days of racing, eating, music and visiting with old friends and family. The event is scheduled to coincide with Emancipation Day (the first Monday in August), celebrating the end of slavery. For details on the regatta schedule, contact the Regatta Desk in Nassau at (☎502-0600).

Just south of the sprawling Government Administrative Complex on the Queen's Highway stand the ruins of the **Armbrister Plantation.** All that remains are some crumbling stone fences and the shell of Henry Hawkins Armbrister's house, built in the pre-Loyalist 1760s. Much of the land hereabouts is owned by the Armbrister family, which holds family deeds to properties that go back to the 1780s. In the 1950s, Hollywood film producer Cyril Armbrister and his wife Frances returned to the abandoned family estate on Cat Island after Frances convinced her husband to "do something with all that worthless land in the Bahamas". One of the results was the magical *Fernandez Bay Village*, three miles north of town and still owned by the Armbrister family.

The Mount Alvernia Hermitage

The highlight of any visit to New Bight is the 206-foot climb to the **Mount Alvernia Hermitage**, perched atop Como Hill, the highest point in the entire Bahaman archipelago. The miniature stone monastery was built by one Father Jerome, and is accessible by a steep climb up a dirt track that begins immediately south of the government complex. Born John Hawes to an English middle-class family in 1876, Father Jerome was an ordained Anglican minister who first came to the Bahamas in 1908 on a mission to rebuild churches destroyed by a recent hurricane, and his St Paul's Anglican Church in Clarence Town on Long Island still stands as a testament to his zeal. Though his staunch belief in racial equality did him little good with the entrenched aristocracy near Marsh Harbour on Abaco, he still spent several years on his mission in the Bahamas before leaving for Rome in 1911, where he converted to Catholicism. After two decades preaching in Australia, he returned to the Bahamas in 1939 and spent the last seventeen years of his life on Cat Island, living as a hermit and ministering to the needs of the desperately poor. Throughout this time, he also worked on building the Hermitage, which served as a medieval-style sanctuary and retreat.

The laborious climb – best done to coincide with either sunrise or sunset – rewards the effort with a panoramic view of the undulating, densely vegetated interior and the seacoast. The rock staircase leading up was carved by hand into the hillside by Father Jerome himself, and includes hand statuettes representing the fourteen Stations of the Cross. The tiny hermitage itself comprises only three Spartan rooms, including a cloister and chapel, sparsely furnished, with a cone-shaped bell-tower fashioned from stone. To one side of the tiny chapel, Jerome's **tomb** is a simple stone sarcophagus kept free of weeds by a loving caretaker.

North of New Bight: Fernandez Bay and around
Three miles north of New Bight on Cat Island's western shore is **Fernandez Bay**, a tranquil cove filled with turquoise water and lined with fine white sand backed by casuarinas, cacti and palms. There is good snorkelling around the edges of the bay, and the lovely *Fernandez Bay Resort* with an inviting beach bar open to outside visitors for lunch and drinks.

Five miles north of **Smith Bay** just off the east side of the Queen's Highway, the twin **Tea Bay Ponds** are home to many herons and moorhens, and are especially noted for their populations of ducks, grebes, paired white-cheeked pintails and some sandpipers. Tea Bay is also one of the few places left on Cat Island where you might catch a glimpse of the endangered Cat Island turtle.

Old Bight and Cat Island's boot
Essentially a flat, hot, palmetto scrub riddled with lakes and salty depressions, Cat Island's "boot" isn't very hospitable country. However, off the south coast, or **sole of the boot**, you will find most of Cat Island's dive sites and two appealing resorts fronting long, empty beaches. Four miles south of New Bight, the boot of Cat Island begins at **OLD BIGHT**, a slightly seedy settlement, and encompasses an area that is ten miles long and five miles wide. The town is home to two small churches – **St Francis of Assisi Catholic Church**, one of Father Jerome's Gothic stone fabrications, which is decorated by oddly camp frescoes, and **St Mary's Church**, a monument to Emancipation, which was given to the Cat Islanders by the family of Blaney Balfour, a British governor during late slave days.

The Queen's highway continues south for another ten miles through mainly featureless bush, arriving at the rather grand Deep South Roundabout, a roundabout in the wilderness that controls the sporadic trickle of traffic in the area. The road east leads to **Bain Town**, **Port Howe** and the *Greenwood Beach Resort*. The road west takes you to **Morgan's Bay** and *Hawk's Nest*.

East of the Deep South Roundabout
Heading east from the roundabout, the highway leads five miles, past the few tidy cottages and small grocery store that make up **Bain Town**, to the pictur-esque village of **Port Howe**. Not much more than a collection of village

limestone homes these days, Port Howe is believed by some to have been a Spanish settlement for the transhipment of Lucayan Indian slaves to Hispaniola in the sixteenth century. During the 1700s, English wreckers established a village that was regularly attacked by Spaniards and pirates, and by 1783 English Loyalists had arrived and established several important plantations. It came to be called Port Howe after the British naval commander of the same name during the American Revolutionary War.

On the western edge of the settlement sit the ruins of the **Deveaux Mansion**. A large, stark stone building, it looms like an apparition out of the lush foliage that entangles it. The main house of a cotton plantation owned by Captain Andrew Deveaux of the British Navy who recaptured Nassau from Spain in 1783, the mansion copied the contemporary style of American plantation houses in the Deep South, and its interior was created by French craftsmen in the late 1780s. Its wood galleries overlook the sea, and it has a surviving grandeur despite the fact that what remains is mostly the roof and heavy wood floors. Near the still-standing kitchen – marked by a chimney, fireplace and an ablution block – are the slave quarters.

Continuing past the Deveaux Mansion on the paved road for 3.5 miles north of Port Howe, then 2 miles east on a coral road brings you to *Greenwood Beach Resort* (signposted from the main road) built alongside the spectacular eight-mile long **Greenwood Beach** on the Atlantic side. The beach is a great destination for a long walk and a picnic.

West of the Deep South Roundabout

West from the Deep South Roundabout, the landscape is sparse and lightly populated. The big draw is the excellent fishing and pristine snorkelling and diving sites found offshore. There is only one road traversing the generally empty landscape, running alongside the south coast before making a sharp turn northward to the sun-baked hamlet of McQueen's. The snorkelling is especially good in the neighbourhood of **Morgan's Bay** on the south coast because the reef is so close. Where the paved road makes its turn northward, a rough potholed road straight ahead leads to **Devil's Point**, a slumberous but pretty fishing village named in the local belief that "cork did sink and iron did float" in its adjacent waters.

Continuing north instead on the main paved road leads you to the scruffy settlement of **McQueen's**, about three miles further on. At MacQueen's, a dirt road striking out westward leads to **Hawk's Nest Point**, at the southwest tip of the island and fifteen miles west of the Deep South Roundabout. The creek and estuary that cut hard into the point are brimming with prime bonefish, and the relaxed *Hawk's Nest Resort* located here is perfectly situated to take advantage of this bounty. Along with guides and boats available for rent, the resort also has a dive shop, restaurant and a fine strip of beach.

Eating

All of the resorts within the southern half of Cat Island welcome guests at their **restaurants**, while most of the settlements each have small bar/restaurants serving basic Bahamian specialities like fried chicken, grouper and snapper. The finest dining experience is the buffet-style dinner at *Fernandez Bay Village* (☎342-3043; open for three meals a day; reservations required for dinner), with its torch-lit patio and brilliant sunsets augmenting the likes of barbecue ribs cooked on an open fire, great crab legs and a justly famed conch chowder that sets the standard in the islands. The nightly dinner buffet is $45 per person;

the breakfast buffet of hot and cold dishes (included fresh baked rolls) is $15; and you can order a variety of tasty sandwiches, burgers and salads from the a la carte lunch menu for $8–10. In New Bight, the restaurant at the *Bridge Inn* (☎342-3013) is decent for such Bahamian standards as fish stew, lobster, johnnycake and the ubiquitous Bahamian grouper, peas and rice; Fridays are barbecue night. The down-home ✻ *Bluebird Restaurant and Bar* (☎342-3095;) on the water opposite the government complex is recommended for tasty fried chicken, seafood and local delicacies including pig's feet and sheep's tongue souse (mains $8–12).

On the island's southern end, the *Greenwood Beach Resort* (☎342-3053) offers call-ahead seating for non-guests at their evening outdoor buffets, usually consisting of soup and salad followed by grilled seafood specialities, barbecue chicken and one pasta dish each night, with typical Bahamian side dishes ($30). On the opposite coast, the restaurant at the *Hawk's Nest Resort* (☎342-7050) is smaller, but the food is a good mix of European and Bahamian entrees, with the speciality being lobster/shrimp-stuffed muttonfish, a gargantuan meal serving at least four. Dinner runs at about $30 per person.

Drinking and nightlife

Most after dark activity is centred on New Bight. Both the *First and Last Chance Bar*, located between the airport and town, and the central *Blue Bird* are good spots for a beer and a game of pool with a local crowd. The *Bridge Inn* (☎342-3013) has live rake 'n' scrape music some Saturday nights. North of New Bight in Smith Bay, *Hazel's Seaside Bar* is a simple bar with a relaxed atmosphere for a cold beer, while to the south in Old Bight dominoes and cold beer are the main attraction within the *Pass Me Not Bar* in Old Bight (☎342-4016).

North Cat Island

Arthur's Town and nearby **Orange Creek** are the main settlements in lightly populated North Cat, which is studded here and there by ruins, many thought to predate even Loyalist hamlets. Smaller villages, such as **Bennett's Harbour**, are isolated settlements with no services or amenities, but it is pleasant to pass by these traditional villages on a bright, windy day. A couple of attractive small **beach resorts** are tucked into sandy coves around Bennett's Harbour.

Arthur's Town and around

Thirty miles north of New Bight, **ARTHUR'S TOWN**, near the northern terminus of the Queen's Highway, is the administrative headquarters for northern Cat, housing little more than a BaTelCo telephone station, a medical clinic, a police station and a coral-coloured Commissioner's Office. A small village of only a few hundred people, it was the boyhood home of **Sidney Poitier**, yet there is surprisingly no museum or monument to him, and the home where he grew up is now decrepit and abandoned. The family presence, however, is still strong and his daughter Pamela is the guiding force behind the annual **Cat Island Music festival**, held here in June to celebrate traditional Bahamian rake 'n scrape folk music.

Right in the centre of the village, Sir Roland Symonette, a local historian, politician, and major landowner on the island, has a decent little park named for him. Besides the park, the only real building of note, on the main road to the airport, is **St Andrews Anglican Church**, built of stone in the 1870s. Continuing along the airport road leads to **Camperdown Beach** on the Atlantic coast, favoured by locals and lined by sea grape and coconut palms.

Just up the road three miles is the tiny two-part village of **ORANGE CREEK**; the older section, north of the actual creek, is a bit more interesting, composed of attractive limestone and pastel-painted clapboard houses. There isn't much to see or do on either side, and those who come do so mainly to snorkel in the nearby reefs or go bonefishing, at much cheaper rates than elsewhere in the Bahamas.

North of Orange Creek, the land peters out into a series of creek beds, muddy mangroves and palmetto bush. Several paths out of Orange Creek are good for hiking. One, just north of town, forks west for about half a mile to **Port Royal Beach**, an isolated stretch running to Man O' War Point that is good for snorkelling and swimming. A second easily followed track heads north a mile to **Oyster Lake** and then branches off north for half a mile to **Glass Hill**, which overlooks a nice blue hole. East of Oyster Lake lies **Griffin Bat Cave,** home to a sizable population of leaf-nosed bats in the dark. It is very tough going, hot and buggy; the Cleare brothers in Orange Creek (☎354-4042) can act as guides.

Practicalities

Most people opt to stay in Orange Creek at the *Orange Creek Inn* (☎354-4110, ⓕ354-4042; 2), the most appealing option in the area, with sixteen rooms with fans. There is no restaurant or bar, but there is a grocery, laundry and car rentals are available. Near Symonette Square in the centre of Arthur's Town, Pat Rolle's *Cookie House Bakery* (☎354-2027) is a great **place to eat** for lunch or dinner if you're in the mood for basic fried-fish dishes or burgers. There are a couple of other takeaways in town.

Bennett's Harbour and around

Some fifteen miles south of Arthur's Town along the Queen's highway, **BENNETT'S HARBOUR** lies hard against a wonderful half-mile sweep of picturesque bay. Initially a pirate hiding place, the actual settlement was founded by slaves freed by British naval vessels, and Bennett's earned its income by exporting hundreds of tons of salt from evaporating ponds nearby. These days, Bennett's looks weather-beaten and rough, with clapboard houses that have seen better days, but the bay is beautiful, and the area does have a few rooms to let. Bennett's Harbour is also a departure point for birding or bonefishing trips to Little San Salvador (see box opposite).

Just south of Bennett's Harbour is Roker's Bluff, often called simply **the Bluff**, once reputed to be one of the wealthiest settlements on the island. It is the site of former cotton plantations that took advantage of its high ground and thus of its good soil and excellent drainage. Many of its original inhabitants were Scottish Loyalists who migrated from Virginia following the American Revolution. On the north side of the Bluff is a sign about a quarter-mile out of town indicating "Pigeon Cay". A dirt road leads to the lovely **Pigeon Creek Beach**, a curved mile of white sand on the south-facing side of Pigeon Cay. The beach is backed by palms and casuarinas and affords visitors ultimate solitude.

Practicalities

In the Bluff/Pigeon Cay area the **place to stay** is the intimate *Pigeon Cay Beach Club* (☎354-5084 or 1-800/688-4752, ⓦwww.pigeoncaybahamas.com; ⑤).

Small, uninhabited, privately owned **Little San Salvador** lies about fifteen miles due west of Bennett's Harbour. Nine miles long, the tiny island is wrapped around a large inner lagoon, which serves as a comfortable anchorage to yachters and fishermen in bad weather. In 1996 it was sold to Holland America Lines and is now used as a landing spot for some of its cruises through Bahamian and Caribbean islands. The elliptical lagoon is a favourite with **birders**, who can often spot white-tailed tropicbirds and four species of terns. Resident land birds include burrowing owls, ospreys, vireos, bananaquits and black-faced grassquits. The **bonefishing** in its mangroves is also widely celebrated.

Those with a yen for adventure can try to arrange transport to Little San Salvador by visiting the Commissioner's Office in Arthur's Town in person, or by boldly approaching a fishing captain on the docks of Arthur's Town or Bennett's Harbour. The Cleare brothers in Orange Creek (☎354-4042) can arrange trips there as well, even though the island is privately owned. The average birdwatching expedition is around $200 per day, while bonefishing, given the distance and permissions required, is slightly more expensive than on the main island of Cat.

There are five rooms and eight thatched villas of stone and stucco with Mexican tile floors, a beach bar, as well as canoes, bikes, snorkelling and fishing trips on offer. Closer to Bennett's Harbour, *Sammy T's Resort* (☎354-6009, ⓦwww .sammytbahamas.com; ⑤) earns rave reviews from visitors for its relaxed, welcoming atmosphere and aesthetic appeal. This small, secluded seaside resort has a handful of tastefully appointed wood and stone cabins built steps from a long and lovely white-sand beach. Each one or two-bedroom cabin is equipped with a kitchenette, a/c, TV, DVD player with a library of movies and a sitting room. Other amenities include a games room, fitness centre, kayaks, bicycles and a restaurant in the main house serving imaginatively prepared local seafood. For **food**, stop at Len's Grocery in Bennett's Harbour.

San Salvador

Only twelve miles long and five miles wide, **SAN SALVADOR** is low and hot, with a swampy interior dominated by large saline lakes and brine ponds surrounded by scrub palmetto bush. The island's northern and western shores are liberally dotted with long sweeps of sandy **beach** backed by tall grass. However, by far the biggest draw for visitors is spectacular **wall diving**, supplemented by a variety of wrecks, underwater canyons and undisturbed reefs. In fact, unless you are here to enjoy a packaged beach holiday at the Club Med compound or are otherwise content to wile away your time reading a few good books, there isn't a whole lot to do or see topside. You can take a small boat through Pigeon Creek to do some **bird-watching**, go **deep-sea fishing** out over the abyss, or go for a **hike** in the bush (with a guide), but these activities are probably better viewed as a way to spend time getting your nitrogen levels back to normal than as reasons to visit on their own.

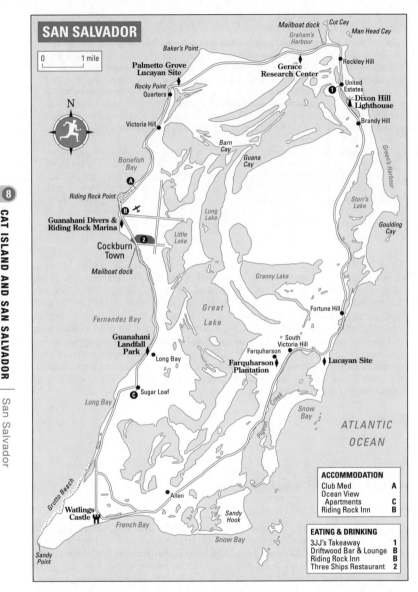

San Salvador's population hovers around a thousand, most of whom are involved in either tourism or small-scale farming and live in the capital of **Cockburn Town**, in **Victoria Hill** in the northeast or in **United Estates** in the northwest. The Queen's Highway circles the island, touching **Sandy Point Beach**, home to the former plantation **Watling's Castle**, on the southwest tip, and **Graham's Harbour** on the northeast point.

In the interior of San Salvador, **Great Lake** covers several square miles, stretching almost the full length and breadth of the island; at one point, the lake was the main thoroughfare for islanders. **Little Lake**, closer to Cockburn Town, is accessible by dirt road, and is worth a visit for its bird-watching opportunities. Offshore, several cays offer excellent naturalist encounters, including the rock iguanas of **Green Cay**. In the southeast quadrant of the island, Pigeon Creek wends its way through mangrove bush to the ocean, where a fine view of uninhabited **High Cay** and **Low Cay** awaits. Further afield, the unspoiled beaches of **Rum Cay** should appeal to all, while **Conception Island National Park**, encompassing the whole of the island a 20-mile boat ride to the southwest (and also reachable by charter from equidistant Long Island), is home to thousands of birds and is a nesting site for sea turtles.

Some history

San Salvador was originally home to **Lucayan Indians**, whose refuse piles and cave dwellings are still dotted across the island. They fished for tuna from canoes, hunted large squadrons of turtle in the lagoon sea-grasses, gathered conch and even snared or trapped birds including heron, grebe and osprey. They also had the grave misfortune to be the first inhabitants of the New World to meet with Christopher Columbus on his voyage of European discovery in October of 1492. In his journal, Columbus identified his landfall by the Indian name **Guanahani**, and while scholars have debated its exact location, most have settled on present-day San Salvador – though some still plump for either Cat Island or uninhabited Conception Island some thirty miles southwest. In any event, within fifty years of his arrival, the Lucayans of San Salvador had disappeared, victims of disease and shipment for slavery on Hispaniola.

After the pirate George Watling claimed the island during the late sixteenth century, San Salvador was dubbed **Watling Island**, yet until the Loyalist influx in the late 1700s there was almost nothing on it. Thereafter, a few cotton plantations were established but failed to thrive. During the middle 1800s, there were attempts to grow sisal, but these were failures as well, and were completely wiped out with the advent of synthetic fibre, and the island was largely uninhabited when it was renamed San Salvador in 1926. The island remained a backwater until the 1970s' discovery of wall diving and international tourism. A retired diver named Bill McGehee plunged into the water off the west and south coasts of the island and was astonished by the reef's beauty and complexity, the inspiration for a more-than-modest industry and the odd modern resort.

Arrival

The only **airport** on the island, San Salvador Airport is one mile north of Cockburn Town. *Bahamasair* (☏377-5505 in Nassau, 300-8359 in the Out Islands, 1-800/222-4262 in the US and Canada, ⓦwww.bahamasair.com) has two flights a week from Nassau to Cockburn Town ($180 one-way). *Spirit Air* (☏586/791-7300 or 1-800/772-7117, ⓦwww.spiritair.com) flies direct from Fort Lauderdale on Saturdays ($500 round-trip), while *Club Med* provides direct charter service for its own guests from Miami, New York and Paris.

The **mailboat** from Nassau's Potter's Cay dock makes a rather uncomfortable weekly eighteen-hour-plus crossing ($50) on the MV *Lady Francis* to the government dock in Cockburn Town, calling at Rum Cay en route. It departs Nassau Tuesday evening at 4pm. Contact the Potter's Cay dockmaster (☎393-1064) for exact sailing times. The eleven-slip, full-service **marina** at the *Riding Rock Inn* (☎331-2631, ⓦwww.ridingrock.com, VHF Ch 16) is the only one on the island, charging $1 a foot plus utilities. There is also a full-service marina on Rum Cay.

Getting around

A few **taxis** are always on hand to meet arriving passengers at San Salvador Airport ($12). **Car rental** is also available at the airport from C and S Car Rentals (☎331-2714); expect to pay $85 per day, and cars can be delivered to your hotel. The *Riding Rock Inn* rents **bicycles** for $10 a day, and the entire island can be circled on bike in five or six hours – provided you can stand the heat. If touring, be prepared with plenty of water and snacks as the road cuts through empty bush or runs along the undeveloped shore for much of the way. Alternatively, K's Scooter Rental (☎331-2125 or 331-2651) rents motor **scooters** for around $40 a day.

There are no government-run **information** centres on the island. With the increase in tourism, the resorts have stepped up, however, and both the *Riding Rock Inn* and *Club Med* offer **island tours** for their guests. Privately operated by a local entrepreneur who is a seasoned and enthusiastic tour guide, *Lagoon Tours* (☎359-4520) offers a selection of outings around the island, including a scenic motorized canoe cruise through Pigeon Creek ($70). Depending on your interests, these small group tours can focus on flora and fauna, bush medicine and historical sights.

Diving and watersports

Famous for its calm, clear water, San Salvador has become the top wall-**diving** destination in the Bahamian chain. Dive spots number in the hundreds from the northwest coast to Sandy Point in the south, and operators have spotted close to fifty mooring buoys around the island, with another twenty placed in sheltered sand holes clear of reefs used primarily for snorkelling. The most famous dive is the **Frascate** wreck north of the airport. This huge steel-hulled vessel (262ft long) broke up on New Year's Day in 1902, and its wreck is strewn over half an acre of reef. It's now home to parrotfish, wrasse and surgeonfish. Other quality dive spots include **Riding Rock Wall, Telephone Pole, Vicky's Reef, Snapshot, Double Caves** and **Great Cut**. All the sites are located at or near the drop-off into deeper water, and the majority are close by Cockburn Town in a two-mile stretch on Fernandez Bay. Double Caves is at Sandy Point, while Great Cut is located at the southwest tip of the island near Hinchinbroke Rocks.

Midway down Fernandez Bay is a shallow spot known as **Snapshot**, a particular favourite of **snorkellers** and photographers, where a series of coral patches on a white-sand bottom is home to yellowhead jawfish and squirrelfish. The many gulleys, vertical walls, canyons and shallow reefs are home to a seemingly infinite variety of sea life including eels, barracuda, starfish, lugworms, golden stingrays, peacock flounder, shrimps, reef sharks, surgeonfish, turtles and damselfish, among others.

While the possibilities for **sport fishing** off San Salvador have barely been tapped, the northern hump of the island is a major winter collection point for flying fish, which are food for both tuna and wahoo. During the winter season – September through April – there are regular catches of large marlin as well. Both *Club Med* and *Riding Rock Inn* offer sport-fishing charters in the neighbourhood of $500 for a half-day, $800 for a full-day.

Dive operators

Columbus Isle Dive Centre *Club Med* ☎331-2000 or 1-800/258-2633, ⓕ331-2222, ⓦwww.clubmed .com. Catering exclusively to *Club Med* guests, the centre includes all costs in the *Club Med* price. They have four dive boats with a capacity of 170 divers and fifty snorkellers. With that many people, the operation is rather impersonal, but it does have the latest equipment along with a tiny retail shop. Riding Rock Inn Dive Shop ☎331-2631 or 1-800/272-1492, ⓦwww.ridingrock.com. Both

guests and not-guests of the *Riding Rock Inn* use this operation based at the marina, which has three dive boats and offers a varied range of dives and instructional courses. The basic one- and two-tank dives are $50 and $70, with full PADI certification at $450. A variety of speciality courses, including underwater naturalist and search and salvage, are also offered for $150 each. If planning on diving daily, look into their package deals including dives, meals and accommodation. Equipment rental available.

Island practicalities

Within Cockburn Town, you'll find a bank (no ATM), grocery, petrol station, Internet café and laundry. **Accommodation** on the island is limited to a resort and a hotel, both near Cockburn Town, and a simple guesthouse further south with no amenities near by. There are also a few vacation cottages for rent; see p.31 for websites with vacation rentals in the Bahamas.

Club Med Columbus Isle ☎331-2000 or 1-800/932-2582, ⓦwww.clubmed.com. One of the best dive resorts in the world, this Club Med sprawls across eighty acres and boast a gorgeous beach. A huge swimming pool anchors the resort, around which are entwined over two hundred rooms, three restaurants, two bars, a dance club, a fitness centre, twelve tennis courts and just about every other recreation imaginable, with the emphasis on taking advantage of the fantastic diving and snorkelling opportunities. Children are welcome at the resort, but there are no special facilities or activities for them. Rates include all meals and alcoholic beverages, along with airport transfers, use of sports equipment (from sailboats and kayaks to tennis and gym gear) along with activities like beach volleyball, island tours and nightly entertainment. From $1500 per person, per week, all-inclusive; diving, fishing, and spa packages extra).

Ocean View Apartments ☎331-2348. Located roadside in the quiet settlement of Sugar Loaf, these three one-bedroom apartments with small kitchenettes and a/c are a good choice for longer

stays. A car is a must if you stay here, as it stands alone quite a distance from shops, restaurants, or major attractions. There is a small, not particularly inviting swathe of beach about 500 yards away, across the road. Units are available for $1000 a month. ❸

Riding Rock Inn Resort and Marina ☎331-2631 or 1-800/272-1492, ⓦwww.ridingrock. com. Situated one mile from the airport on a small patch of land between the main road and the water, this ocean-front accommodation has 42 large, attractively furnished rooms with a/c, TV, and small balconies or patios. There is a small pool and tennis court, but the *Riding Rock* caters almost exclusively to dive groups, who gather at the atmospheric bar in the evening to talk about the big hammerhead they saw that day. A large, old-fashioned dining room serves hot and filling but otherwise unexciting (and rather expensive) meals. The rooms have all the creature comforts you might require and a big ocean view, but unless you spend most of your day underwater, you might find the 'resort' aspect a bit lacking, and the beach is a twenty minute walk or short drive away. ❺

Eating and drinking

Eating establishments on San Salvador generally ascribe to a "food is fuel" philosophy of cooking and dining room decor. To sample the local grub, try the clean and cheerful *Three Ships Restaurant* (Mon–Sat 7am–9pm; ☎331-2787, dinner reservations required) in Cockburn Town, serving the likes of fish and grits for breakfast along with fried chicken, lamb chops or grouper with sides of plantain and peas 'n rice for lunch and dinner. Another option is the restaurant at the *Riding Rock Inn* (open for three meals a day), which serves expensive, unimaginative Bahamian dishes like conch, smothered grouper and broiled snapper for around $25. The breakfasts are better, with heaping piles of pancakes, johnnycake and delicious omelettes for $10. If you have wheels, *3JJ's Take Away* (Mon–Sat noon–8pm; ☎331-2544) in United Estates dishes up fried fish and chips and chicken to go. Come nightfall, the main local hot spot in Cockburn Town is the rough-looking but friendly *Sunrise Lounge* on the highway at the south edge of town. The *Driftwood Bar* at the *Riding Rock Inn* is a cosy seaside nook for a nightcap, decked out with diving memorabilia.

Cockburn Town

Though not the largest settlement on San Salvador – that prize goes to United Estates on the northeast coast – **COCKBURN TOWN** is nonetheless its centre of island activity. With the island's two resorts located just north of town, as well as having the airport, government complex and medical clinic, Cockburn Town is as close as it gets to urban convenience on San Salvador.

The town itself is three blocks square and contains an odd mixture of old stone houses, tumbledown clapboard homes and modern structures. The centre of life is the **government dock**, where the weekly mailboat delivers island supplies and mail, and its arrival creates a stirring of expectation and excitement. Near the dock, across from the BaTelCo building, you can stroll on the **fossil coral reef**, where you can see old brain coral and various staghorn corals, as well as molluscs embedded in the reef.

Just north of First Avenue, which holds most of the local administrative offices, is the **San Salvador Museum**. In the neighbourhood of Victoria Hill, this musty museum is free to the public, but you'll have to ask at the bank next door for someone to come and unlock the doors. Located in a nineteenth-century jailhouse, the mouldy collection of artefacts includes Lucayan archeological finds and is worth a brief look for the strange folk-art mural adorning the outside wall.

Cockburn Town is near two lakes of great interest to bird-watchers. Follow First Avenue to the east: it ends only half a mile away at **Little Lake**, where there is a pier from which one can see numerous cormorants, herons, ducks and grebes. Going north from town you'll encounter a dirt road running east toward the end of the airport runway near the *Riding Rock Inn*. With a right turn inland on an old dirt road, you pass the city dump, a construction vehicle parking area, then the north shore of Little Lake, finally ending up at a rather flimsy observation platform on **Great Lake**. Birders come for glimpses of cormorants, reddish egrets and herons. Beware of the observation platform. It is not well maintained, and you should test it carefully before climbing.

The southwest coast: towards Sandy Point

The **southwest coast** of San Salvador was once home to cotton and citrus plantations, whose place was taken by a number of small villages. These too have largely been abandoned, with only ghostly remnants of stone houses standing vacant along beautiful sweeps of beach. **Long Bay**, just two miles south of Cockburn Town on the Queen's Highway, is the alleged site of Columbus's original landfall. The grandly named **Guanahani Landfall Park** here is really a modest stretch of scrub and beach punctuated by four monuments, none of which is particularly inspiring. One commemorates the spot where the Olympic flame arrived in the New World on its journey from Greece to the 1968 Olympic games in Mexico. Another much photographed local attraction is the concrete cross near a plaque presented by Spain on the occasion of a visit by three caravel replicas to the island on February 10, 1992, marking Columbus's historical passage through the Bahamas in 1492.

Travelling further south, the coastal road passes through the small, scattered settlement of **Sugar Loaf** en route to **Grotto Beach.** Accessed via Sandcliff Avenue off the Queen's Highway, it's an extremely pretty stretch of white sand along the southwest shore, good for swimming and snorkelling. Beyond the beach is the island's southwestern tip, called **Sandy Point**. The only sign of life in the area is **Columbus Estates**, a tiny subdivision where a few wealthy Americans have built vacation homes interspersed with large expanses of bush. On a hill in the estates is **Watling's Castle**, the crumbling remains of a plantation established by Loyalist settler Cade Matthews, who named it for San Salvador's famous pirate. While the plantation, operated until 1925, is now defunct, a watchtower and some slave quarters provide a good and breezy view of the sweep of Sandy Point.

The east coast

A couple of miles south of Sugar Loaf, the Queen's Highway rounds the southern tip of the island (bypassing the detour to Sandy Point) and swings eastward towards the **High Cay Land and Sea Park**. The park is most easily accessed by boat via **Pigeon Creek**, which is visible from the highway where the road begins its trek northwards through the uninhabited eastern side of the island. The park is a nature conservation area designated to protect nesting sites for ospreys, terns and boobies along with a handful of endangered iguanas. The birds nest on High Cay, Porus Cay and Low Cay, all a fifteen-minute boat ride offshore. Because the cays are nesting sites, you are asked not to land, but the trip through Pigeon Creek out to the cays makes for a fun day-trip anyway. *Lagoon Tours* (☎359-4520) in Cockburn Town offer a close-up look at the rich marine life inhabiting the creek and the cays on their flat-bottom canoe tours ($75). Pigeon Creek is also good bonefishing territory, and baby sharks can sometimes be seen swimming about here.

The rest of the east coast is even more lonely, though punctuated here and there by excellent empty beaches suitable for swimming and sunning, especially five-mile-long **East Beach**, a stretch of exposed white sand that lies four miles north of Pigeon Creek.

The northeast coast: United Estates and around

Continue up the east coast on the Queen's Highway and three miles before coming to **UNITED ESTATES** you'll reach Crab Cay. Follow signs for Storr's Lake and East Beach, and then head down a path to the beach to the **Chicago Herald monument**. Placed here in 1891, it was the newspaper's contribution to the 1892 World's Fair held in Chicago to celebrate the 400th Anniversary of the "discovery" of the New World. The plinth is a rugged affair made up of a stone marker topped by a weather-pitted globe supporting a plaque commemorating the supposed first landfall of the explorer. The lack of any historical confirmation that this is indeed the spot makes it a rather bogus monument.

A few miles north and far more impressive, the **Dixon Hill Lighthouse** (daily 9am–noon & 2–5pm; free) is a towering structure that dominates the immediate landscape. A genuine delight, this smooth, white-stone tower slopes gently to a capped top where visitors can roam the first balcony for views. Virtually alone on a bluff overlooking the Atlantic Ocean, the lofty structure stands 163ft above sea level, rising 67ft from its base. The ragtag collection of hovels, homes and shacks called United Estates due north is the most populated settlement on San Salvador. Apart from a handy takeaway, it is a mainly residential area and not likely to detain sightseers.

Graham's Harbour and around

From United Estates, the Queen's Highway sweeps along to **GRAHAM'S HARBOUR** on the northeast tip of San Salvador, where, it is widely believed, Columbus anchored his ships and surveyed his discovery, sometime after first making contact with the Bahamas on San Salvador. At the end of North Point lies the large wreck of the *Columbia*, which ran aground in 1980. The highlight of the year, the Columbus Day Regatta, is held in Graham's Harbour on October 12.

Rounding the top of the island and continuing along the west coast, the **Gerace Research Center** (☎331-2520, ⓦwww.geraceresearchcenter.com) is a research and educational facility on the site of a former US Navy base. The marine biologists stationed here conduct research in the waters around San Salvador, while archeologists use the centre as a base to explore Lucayan sites on the island. Those with an interest in marine biology can take an extended field course through the centre, or join an Earthwatch expedition to help scientists studying coral reefs (☎1-800/776-0188 or 978/461-0081, ⓦwww.earthwatch.org). South of the station grounds, there's a series of **trails** of particular interest to birders, who can see many species of ducks like pintails, along with Zenaida doves, woodstars, warblers, grassquits, and, on the ponds, osprey and cormorants.

Rum Cay and Conception Island

A small island 25 miles southwest of San Salvador, **Rum Cay** is reputedly named after the wreck of a freighter loaded with the eponymous drink, which foundered on the coral reefs offshore. Ten miles long and five miles wide, the cay hosts the village of **PORT NELSON**, home to a couple of restaurants and bars and a hundred hardy souls hanging on amid coconut palm groves and salt ponds. The cay is also fringed all around with a reef tailor-made for snorkelling, and while its beaches are delightful, you will need a boat to access most of them as there are no roads in the wild interior.

This undeveloped wild shore and overall isolation are a large part of Rum Cay's attraction. It's a relatively popular stop-off for yacht cruisers, with regular air and mailboat service and a few rental cottages for other adventurous travellers. Self-sufficient divers will particularly enjoy the wreck of the 101-gun man-of-war HMS *Conqueror*, built in 1855 and which sank nearby in 1861. Sport fishing is also bountiful, and can be arranged through the Sumner Point Marina in Port Nelson (☎331-2823, ⓦwww.rumcaymarina.com). The eighteen-slip **marina** rents four cute one-bedroom cottage rentals with kitchenettes (6), and is also home to the *Out of the Blue Restaurant*, which serves breakfast, lunch and dinner. Dockage rates are $1.45 a foot with electricity, water and fuel available at additional cost. The marina is a port of call for the MV *Lady Francis* **mailboat** once a week from Nassau, while Cat Island Air (☎377-3318) runs three **flights** in from Nassau each week as well.

Ten miles north of Rum Cay and twenty-five miles southwest of San Salvador and visible in prime weather conditions, **Conception Island** is a national land and sea park. Three miles long and one mile wide, the island is uninhabited but for green turtles, boobies and migratory seabirds, and sits on its own shallow bank surrounded by a fringing reef and circled on all sides by fabulous beach. Visitors to the island must make their own arrangements with local owners of ocean-going yachts on Rum Cay (ask around at the marina) and get permission to land from the Bahamas National Trust (The Retreat, PO Box N4105, Nassau; ☎393-1317, ⓦwww.bahamasnationaltrust.org). Alternatively, the *Stella Maris Resort* on Long Island (14 miles to the northeast; see p.309) can take groups up to ten to Conception Island for the day from Long Island for $875.

The south islands

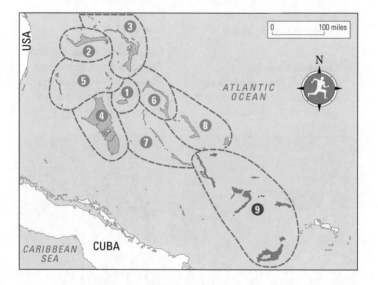

CHAPTER 9

Highlights

✳ **Chez Pierre** A unique and secluded idyll, where a handful of rustic beach cabanas and an excellent gourmet bistro front a ribbon of white sand. See p.311

✳ **Cape Santa Maria Beach** Five miles north of Stella Maris, the long powdery white sand and turquoise water of Cape Santa Maria Beach is the most gorgeous and unspoiled in Long Island. See p.312

✳ **The view from the Columbus Monument** Stand by this Long Island monument – at the spot the explorer himself was believed to have done over 500 years ago – and survey the cliffs leading down to the Atlantic and to Exuma Sound. See p.313

✳ **Inagua National Park** This 287-square-mile conservation area on the shores of Lake Windsor in Great Inagua is home to the largest breeding colony of West Indian Flamingoes in the world. See p.323

✳ **Bonefishing in Mayaguana** The north coast of isolated Mayaguana features some of the best bonefishing in the Bahamas. See p.326

△ Flamingoes in Inagua National Park

9

The south islands

T he most remote islands in the Bahamian archipelago, the SOUTH ISLANDS begin 250 miles southeast of Nassau. Consisting of Long Island, Crooked Island, Acklins Island, Great Inagua and Mayaguana, the south islands are comparatively free of tourist development and offer a taste of the slowly vanishing traditional Out Island life.

Of the five main islands, **Long Island**, a narrow sliver of land dividing the Great Bahama Bank from the deep Atlantic Ocean, is both the most populated and visited. It has the double virtue of unspoiled natural beauty and a few lovely, small resorts offering appealing accommodation, fine dining and a full range of activities, including excellent **diving** and **snorkelling** options. Owing to its fortuitous position along the North Equatorial current, Long Island also boasts superb **fishing** all year round.

Further south, the less developed **Crooked and Acklins islands** are known for their matchless tarpon and bonefishing, while at the southern extremity of the archipelago – actually closer to Cuba than to Nassau – the islands of **Mayaguana** and **Great Inagua** are largely untouched by human hand. Home to a large diversity of flora and fauna, including nesting sea turtles and the largest colony of West Indian flamingos in the world, Mayaguana and Great Inagua offer long stretches of virgin beach, trackless interiors and coral reefs.

As isolated as the southern islands may be, they each have regular air service from Nassau along with weekly passenger service from Nassau on the government mailboats. A large percentage of visitors to islands, however, arrive by private plane or yacht, and there are also marinas on each island.

Some history

During his two-week cruise through the Bahamas in October of 1492, Christopher Columbus paused long enough to admire the scenery of Long Island – which he named "Fernandina" in honour of the king of Spain – and to catch a whiff of the sweet cascarilla growing on Acklins and Crooked islands, which he duly dubbed "the fragrant islands". As with the rest of the Bahamas, if he spent any actual time on the south islands, it was probably only to size up the Lucayan natives as potential slaves.

Following the American Revolution, Long, Crooked and Acklins islands were carved up into **Loyalist** estates. The exiles that washed up on their shores were of a more modest economic status than those who settled elsewhere in the Bahamas and they farmed cotton, pineapples and livestock on small acreages. A majority of the settlements on Long Island are named for these Loyalist settlers, who for the most part had abandoned their plantations by 1803, having exhausted the thin soil.

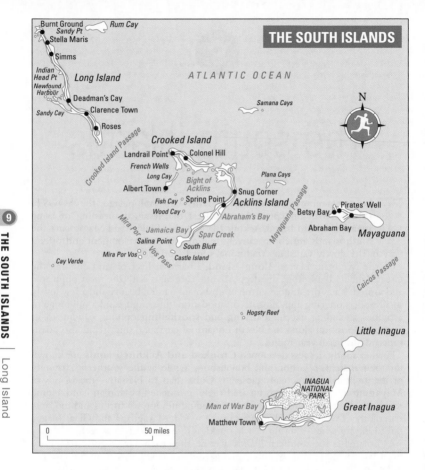

As elsewhere in the Out Islands, for most of the past two hundred-odd years, Long Islanders have scraped a modest living from fishing, subsistence farming, salt production and boat making. At the height of the thriving **sponge trade** in 1921 (see box, p.315), Long Island had a population of 4600. However, with the collapse of traditional local industries, including sponging, salt raking and wooden boat building, the island's population has since been in steady decline. **Tourist** development began on a small scale in the 1960s with the opening of the *Stella Maris Resort* at the north end of the island. The intervening years have seen further development, but the island's communities have remained relatively stable in size and industry, and the whole island has preserved its rural character.

Long Island

Despite a wealth of lovely beaches, fine diving and snorkelling, and some of the prettiest scenery in the Bahamas, **LONG ISLAND**, some thirty miles south of

Cat Island, remains well off the beaten track. The roughly 3200 residents who call the island home earn their living from the sea and live in a dozen or so small fishing settlements dotting the seventy-mile-long coastline. From Seymour's on the north tip to Gordon's in the south, the **Queen's Highway** runs the length of the island, directly along the seashore for much of the way. Whether based at one of the three resorts in the north, or at one of the smaller lodges or guesthouses to the south, it is possible to explore the whole of the island on day-trips by car, or a good portion of it by bicycle.

Long Island has a long tradition of boat building, and the **Long Island Sailing Regatta**, held mid-May in the relatively bustling commercial centre of **Salt Pond** towards, the island's centre for the past 35 years is one of the Out Island's premier social events. The rest of the year, life in the tidy little villages is pretty quiet, with many of the young people off seeking their fortunes in Nassau or elsewhere. Long Islanders are a devout lot and on Sunday mornings, the numerous **picturesque whitewashed churches** up and down the island fling open their doors and the air is filled with hymns and birdsong.

Most visitors congregate at the north end of the island, where nearly all accommodation and tourist services are located. The real estate development of **Stella Maris** is the site of the island's oldest – and one of its finest – resorts, with its affiliated airport, marina, dive outfit, a few shops and a bank. In the immediate vicinity are several inviting beaches, most notably the spectacular, three-mile-long **Cape Santa Maria Beach**. Another worthwhile expedition by car or bicycle is to the **Columbus Monument**, which tops a rocky bluff at the northern tip of the island, with a fantastic panoramic view of sapphire and jade bonefish flats and the white-sand rimmed clots of land that Columbus surveyed on his tour through the Bahamas in 1492.

South of Stella Maris, the island's landscape begins to change from rocky cliffs and cactus-covered flats to pastoral seaside villages interspersed with stretches of dense bush. Around **Salt Pond**, an unpretentious village in the island's centre, are more enticing beaches, including **Guana Cay**, where good snorkelling is found. A break from the beaches is afforded by nearby **Hamilton's Cave**, where several underground chambers are filled with stalactites and stalagmites and within which Lucayan artefacts have been found. Nearby in the roadside settlement of Petty's, the **Long Island Historical Museum** is well worth a stop for its succinct survey of local history and culture. While the sparsely populated southern end of Long Island is mainly given over to farming and fishing, the area boasts an exquisite beach on **Lochabar Bay**. The main settlement in the area is **Clarence Town**, featuring two photogenic historic churches and the secluded **Lowes Beach**.

Getting there

There are two **airports** on Long Island, and at the time of writing both were planning extensive updates. The strip at Stella Maris (☎338-2015) serves the north end of the island, while Deadman's Cay Airport (☎337-0877) serves the island's central and southern portions. The airports are close to an hour's drive, so book flights to the one closest to your final destination, provided the airport is up and running. As of early 2007, Stella Maris Airport had closed for runway refurbishment, while plans were in the works to expand the landing strip at Deadman's Cay to allow direct flights from Florida. Until that time, a time-consuming transit through Nassau is necessary to reach Long Island.

Several airlines fly to Long Island from Nassau, including Bahamasair (☎377-5505 Nassau, 300-8359 Out Islands or 1-800/222-4262 US and Canada,

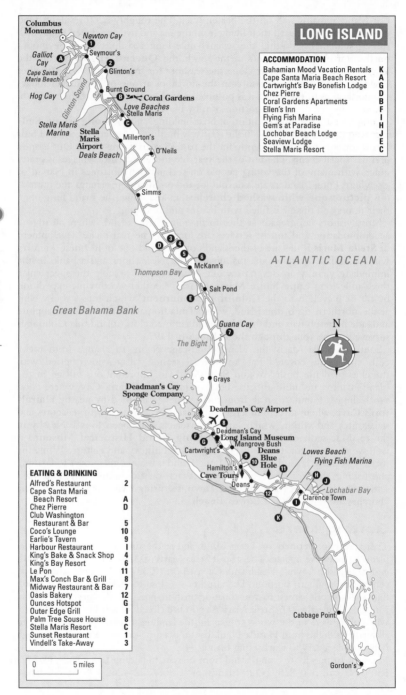

LONG ISLAND

ACCOMMODATION

Bahamian Mood Vacation Rentals	K
Cape Santa Maria Beach Resort	A
Cartwright's Bay Bonefish Lodge	G
Chez Pierre	D
Coral Gardens Apartments	B
Ellen's Inn	F
Flying Fish Marina	I
Gem's at Paradise	H
Lochabar Beach Lodge	J
Seaview Lodge	E
Stella Maris Resort	C

Columbus Monument
Newton Cay ①
Galliot Cay Ⓐ Seymour's
Cape Santa Maria Beach ②
Hog Cay Glinton's
Burnt Ground
Ⓑ Coral Gardens
Love Beaches
Stella Maris
Stella Maris Marina Ⓒ
Stella Maris Airport Millerton's
Deals Beach O'Neils

Glinton Sound

Simms

Ⓓ ③ ④
⑤ ⑥
McKann's

ATLANTIC OCEAN

Thompson Bay

Salt Pond

Ⓔ

Great Bahama Bank

Guana Cay ⑦

The Bight

N

Grays

Deadman's Cay Sponge Company

Deadman's Cay Airport

⑧ Deadman's Cay
Ⓕ Ⓖ Long Island Museum
Cartwright's Mangrove Bush
Deans Blue Hole
⑨ Lowes Beach
Hamilton's ⑩ ⑪ Flying Fish Marina
Cave Tours Ⓙ
Deans ⑫ Lochabar Bay
Ⓘ Clarence Town
Ⓚ

Cabbage Point

EATING & DRINKING

Alfred's Restaurant	2
Cape Santa Maria Beach Resort	A
Chez Pierre	D
Club Washington Restaurant & Bar	5
Coco's Lounge	10
Earlie's Tavern	9
Harbour Restaurant	I
King's Bake & Snack Shop	4
King's Bay Resort	6
Le Pon	11
Max's Conch Bar & Grill	8
Midway Restaurant & Bar	7
Oasis Bakery	12
Ounces Hotspot	G
Outer Edge Grill	I
Palm Tree Souse House	8
Stella Maris Resort	C
Sunset Restaurant	1
Vindell's Take-Away	3

Gordon's

0   5 miles

@www.bahamasair.com) who operate one daily flight ($90), stopping first at Stella Maris and then on to Deadman's Cay. Southern Air (☎323-6833, @www.southernaircharter.com) flies to Deadman's Cay twice daily save for Tuesday ($95), while Pineapple Air (☎377-0140, ℱ377-0351) has four flights per week to Deadman's Cay at similar rates. Other options include the *Stella Maris Resort* (☎338-2050), which operates a plane for guests flying to Nassau as well as George Town on Great Exuma, and *Island Wings Charter* (☎338-2022, @www.islandwingscharter.com) with private flights between Stella Maris Airport and any of the other Bahamian islands in a five-seater plane; as an example, up to five passengers can fly to Long Island from George Town (where direct flights from the US land) for a total of $360.

Two government **mailboats** serve Long Island. The *Mia Dean* ($60 one-way) departs Potter's Cay in Nassau (☎393-1064 for the dockmaster) on Tuesday at noon, reaching Clarence Town at the southern end of Long Island twelve to eighteen hours later and departing for Nassau early Thursday morning. The *Captain Emmett* ($50 one-way) departs Nassau Tuesday at 2pm, calling at Deadman's Cay, Salt Pond and Seymour's in north Long Island after an eight to fifteen-hour crossing; it heads back for Nassau on Thursday at about 11am.

If arriving by private yacht, there are two full-service **marinas** on the island. The Stella Maris Marina (☎338-2055, VHF Ch 16), located near the *Stella Maris Resort*, features fifteen boat slips and offers access to the resort's amenities. The Flying Fish Marina (☎337-3430, @flyingfishmarina.net, VHF Ch 16) in Clarence Town also has fifteen slips, along with electric hook-ups, showers, laundry, store and a restaurant; nightly rates are $1 a foot.

Getting around

There is no public bus service in Long Island, but **taxis** meet every flight and are a dependable means of transport. A taxi ride from Stella Maris to Deadman's Cay will cost about $80, while going from one end of the island to the other is close to double that. For reliable service in northern Long Island call Shervin Smith (☎338-6009 or 357-1408). In Deadman's Cay, Olivia Turnquest, the proprietor of *Ellen's Inn*, runs an efficient taxi service (☎337-0888) and is very knowledgeable on the island's natural and cultural history. To travel long distances or take a tour, however, it certainly makes more economic sense to **rent a car**. At the northern end of Long Island in Glinton's, Alfred Knowles (☎338-5009, ℱ338-5091) rents cars for $65 a day. In Salt Pond, Rent-a-Ride Car Rental (☎338-0041) charges about the same; delivery to the Stella Maris Airport or your hotel can also be arranged. Inell Ditez (☎338-7049) in Burnt Ground rents **scooters** for $40 a day, while the *Stella Maris Resort* (☎338-2052) rents them out to guests at a similar rate; the resort also rents cars to guests for $75 a day, including petrol but charging 35¢ a mile. In the Deadman's Cay, both Olivia Turnquest (☎337-0888) and *Ophelia's Rental Cars* (☎337-1042) rent cars for $70 a day.

With varied scenery and little traffic, Long Island is a wonderful place for **cycling**. A few gentle inclines in the generally flat roads offer the reward of beautiful views up and down the coastline. The two biggest resorts on the island have serviceable touring bikes for guest use – *Cape Santa Maria Beach Resort* (☎338-5273) charges $10 per hour, while *Stella Maris Resort* (☎338-2052) lends them out for free.

Diving and watersports

The pristine waters surrounding Long Island hold some of the best and most varied **diving** sites in the Bahamas, including the **world's deepest blue hole**, nineteenth-century wrecks, lush reefs and coral gardens. There are also gorgeous **snorkelling** grounds accessible from shore surrounding the island, notably from the beach overlooking **Guana Cay**; the **Coral Gardens** on the Atlantic coast at Stella Maris; the southern end of **Cape Santa Maria**; and over a sea fan garden at the south end of **Deal's Beach**.

Diving and snorkelling outfitters

Cape Santa Maria Beach Resort Northern tip of Long Island ☎ 338-5273 or 1-800/663-7090, ⓦ www.capesantamaria.com. The resort offers both visitors and guests reef, wreck and wall dives, as well as a short taster course for novices and as snorkel gear rentals and trips. One and two-tank dives both cost $85, shark dives $60, and snorkel trips $100 for up to six people. SCUBA certification is not offered, but you can take a four-hour introductory session for $85. Closed Sept & Oct.

Stella Maris Resort Stella Maris Marina ☎ 338-2050 or 1-800/426 0466, ⓦ www.stellamarisresort .com. One of the longest-established dive operations in the Bahamas, *Stella Maris* offers a variety of dives to guests and non-guests alike exploring coral reefs, blue holes, a shipwrecked 1848 British Navy vessel and the San Salvador and Conception Island walls. They also offer night and shark dives, as well as a full three-day PADI certification course

for $405, with a deep saltwater training tank at the marina. A full-day of diving (two to three dives) costs $75, including equipment rental; a six-day package is $405. Diving packages can be organized around where you want to go, travelling as far as Crooked and Acklins islands, the Ragged Islands, Rum Cay, or the nearby Exumas. The dive-shop also offers daily snorkelling trips ($30 per person), with free all-day guided excursions for guests twice a week, and use of the equipment any time ($6 a day for guests, $12 for others).

Reel Divers Salt Pond ☎ 338-0011, ⓦ www .reeldivers.com. A couple of dive masters from California seeking a quiet life opened this operation in sleepy Salt Pond, and now offer dives at a variety of underwater hotspots around the island and a full range of certification courses. They also lead snorkelling and kayaking excursions and do boat charters. Two-tank dives cost $125, three-hour snorkelling trips $50, and a half-day kayaking excursion with snorkelling along the way $65.

Fishing

Long Island can brag about its good **fishing** options all year round. Many dedicated anglers choose to book through their resorts or stay at a bonefishing lodge (see "Accommodation" for some good picks), but you can also make arrangements with an independent guide. Costs vary with the fame and experience of the guide, but for bonefishing the average daily rate hovers around $350 for two people. The *Cape Santa Maria Beach Resort* (☎ 338-5273, ⓦ www.capesantamaria.com) offers a variety of fishing options and welcomes outside guests; a day of bonefishing costs $350, reef-fishing (mainly barracuda, grouper, snapper, jacks and dorado) runs $450 for a half-day for a boatload of up to six, and deep-sea fishing costs $850 a day for six. A short distance south, the *Stella Maris Resort* (☎ 338-2050, ⓦ www.stellamarisresort .com) has similar packages for guests, with bonefishing expeditions led by the well-regarded James 'Docky' Smith and his equally competent colleagues. A day of fishing the flats costs $400 for two anglers. Smith can also be booked independently at the same rates through the *Bonefide Bonefishing and Tackle Shop* in Stella Maris (☎ 338-2035, cell 357-1417, ⓦ www .bonefidebonefishing.com). Operating out of Miller's, Presley Pinder (☎ 338-8987 or cell 464-2972, ⓔ tjsboatrental@hotmail.com) charges $150/$250 a half/full-day of bonefishing for two or for a **boat tour** of the surrounding waters with some snorkelling time. In the south, Colin Cartwright has a good reputation for finding the bones on the flats off Deadman's Cay (☎ 337-0215 or cell 357-1067, ⓔ colin@batelnet.bs) and charges $275 a day for his expertise. Another good guide working the area is Dwayne Knowles (☎ 337-0187, ⓔ bonefishdwayne@msn.com).

Accommodation

Accommodation in Long Island ranges from the small-sized resorts at the north end of the island to a couple of secluded self-catering beach cottages south of Clarence Town, with a handful of less expensive local guesthouses situated in the settlements in between. For diving, snorkelling and other organized activities as well as fine dining, the resorts are your best bet. While you can save by staying at one of the other guesthouses listed below – especially if you are staying for a week or more – you may have to sacrifice the ocean view and will probably need to rent a car to get around.

Northern Long Island

Cape Santa Maria Beach Resort Long Island's northern tip ☎338-5273 or 1-800/663-7090 US and Canada, ⊛www.capesantamaria.com. Situated on a pristine strand of powdery white beach on a flat, sandy peninsula, this luxury resort features twenty attractive double rooms spread across ten beachside cottages. Each room is decked out with colourful tropical fabrics, clay-tile floors and rattan furniture, along with a screened porch steps from the water's edge. There is an appealing dining room and bar, a fitness centre, bicycle rentals, and full range of watersports on offer including fishing trips. The one possible draw back is its isolation, as the resort sits alone five miles from the nearest settlement, so you will need to rent a car or bike to do some sightseeing. Including tax, doubles start at around $350 with an additional adjoining bedroom available for $175. Closed Sept & Oct. ❾

Chez Pierre Miller's ☎338-8809 or 418-210-3605 (Montréal), ⊛www .chezpierrebahamas.com. This idyllic retreat is located on a secluded sweep of soft white sand. Rustic but still stylish, the six elevated timber guest cabanas have a beautiful simplicity, wide open to the ocean view in front, but protected by a screened-in porch. The feeling is akin to sleeping under the stars, with the added luxuries of fine sheets and a gourmet restaurant a few steps away. Kayaks and snorkel gear are available for guest use, while guided bonefishing trips as well as diving can be arranged. One of the finest deals in the entire country, rates include superb breakfasts and dinners, with $20 nightly discounts for stays over five nights. Cheaper singles also available. ❺

Coral Gardens Apartments Stella Maris ☎338-5009, ⊛www.bahamas-li.net/coralgar.html. Located on an inland road a quarter of a mile from the ocean and the *Stella Maris Resort*, the *Coral Gardens* offer simple but well-maintained two-bedroom apartments that sleep four and have full kitchens. ❹

Stella Maris Resort Stella Maris ☎338-2052 or 1-800/426-0466, ⊛www.stellamarisresort.com. Sitting on a green hilltop with views of both coasts, this friendly, unpretentious resort offers two dozen bright double and one-bedroom guestrooms – each with a private balcony – housed in a couple of one- and two-storey buildings set in a lush ocean-front garden. The resort has one of the island's longest established diving operations (package deals available), as well as an excellent restaurant and cosy bar, three small swimming pools, a hot tub, tennis courts (with a pro on staff), fitness centre and children's play area, and the scenic ocean-front drive leads to several secluded beaches within walking distance with daily transportation to others. There are bicycles, kayaks and snorkelling gear available for guest use at no charge and a free all-day boat trip twice a week. One, two, three and four bedroom ocean-front villas are also rented out. ❻

Salt Pond to Deadman's Cay

Cartwright's Bay Bonefish Lodge Cartwright's ☎337-0215/0443 or cell ☎357-1067, ⓔsacrifice2000@gmail.com. Respected bonefishing guide Colin Cartwright has built lodgings for his clients overlooking the flats. He has room for four in a spotlessly clean two-bedroom cottage with a big kitchen and sitting room, TV and a/c, with meals available at *Ounces Hotspot* a short walk away. $2300 for six days including fishing, based on double occupancy.

Ellen's Inn Deadman's Cay ☎337-0888, ⓔellensinn@batelnet.bs. This roadside guesthouse in the settlement of Deadman's Cay has sparkling clean, homely rooms with private baths, TV, telephone and a shared kitchen and sitting room, set on a tree-shaded lawn. Weekly rentals run $500, with rental cars available for $60 a day. ❷

Greenwich Creek Lodge Cartwright's ☎337-6278, ⊛www.greenwichcreek.com. Situated on a mangrove-edged shore, the lodge caters to serious bonefishermen. Its well-maintained two-storey timber lodge with wraparound verandas houses eight nicely furnished doubles (containing two beds) and four king rooms, some with TV. There is a small dipping pool and a common room where meals are served. Based on double occupancy, a week of bonefishing including accommodation, meals and a guide costs around $2100.

Seaview Lodge Southern edge of Salt Pond ☎ 337-7517. A cosy budget option located within sight of the mailboat dock. Three airy, spacious and tastefully appointed one- and two-bedroom cottages with fully equipped modern kitchens and satellite TV sit on a tree-shaded expanse of lawn between the Queen's Highway and the water's edge. Guests get a choice view of the sailing races during the Long Island Sailing Regatta in mid-May. ❷

Clarence Town and around

Bahamian Mood Vacation Rentals Galloway Landing ☎ 357-1150, ⓦ www.bahamianmood .com. A handful of fresh and airy beachfront studio apartments, done in natural wood with bold colour accents. Each has a full kitchen, a/c, one queen and two twin beds. There is an outdoor hot tub, a barbeque, kayak rentals and a long stretch of beach to explore. The secluded location means you will need to rent a car or stay put. There's a minimum two-night stay, with weekly ($700) and monthly ($2000) rates available. ❹

Gem's at Paradise Lochabar Bay ☎ 337-3019, wwww.gemsatparadise.com. High on a bluff overlooking a string of cays just south of Clarence Town, this large three-storey gabled house has six beautifully furnished en-suite double and twin rooms sharing a small kitchen, as well as three self-contained one-bedroom apartments. Half of the rooms have private balconies with a view of the sea, and all of them have TV and phone. There is a small beach with kayaks and a bar. ❺

Lochabar Beach Lodge Lochabar Bay ☎ 337-1555 or cell ☎ 357-1340, ⓔ jknowles @bahamasreality.bs. On an exquisite curve of white-sand beach with a blue hole a few metres offshore, this lodge is a secluded idyll for those who really want to get away from civilization. The two-storey timber and stucco structure, housing two studio apartments and a one-bedroom apartment sleeping up to five, sits directly on the beach. The rooms feature clay-tile floors and whitewashed walls or rustic wood panelling and floors, and French doors that open onto a balcony or patio. Neither the owners nor the manager live on site, so rooms must be reserved ahead of time through local real estate agent Judy Knowles. ❹

Northern Long Island: Stella Maris and around

STELLA MARIS encompasses the *Stella Maris Resort*, the airport and marina, and a smattering of vacation homes built along the rocky shore overlooking the Atlantic. The resort lies on the site of English settler William Adderley's nineteenth-century cotton plantation; the stone ruins are still visible along the shore just north of the airport. After Adderley's demise, the cotton fields returned to bush until a large chunk of the area was purchased in the 1960s by the German families who continue to own and run the *Stella Maris Resort* – the pilot who flew you in last night may be your waiter at lunch today.

For those who crave a crashing surf and solitude, Ocean View Drive, which follows the Atlantic for three miles in front of the resort, offers cliff-top views, several rock pools and secluded beaches. The **Love Beaches**, three small rocky coves backed by high dunes at the southern end of the drive (signposted from the road) are a great destination for a picnic and a dip in calm weather. At the north end of the road are the **Coral Gardens** snorkelling grounds (the path is signposted from the road). The surf along the Atlantic coast can be treacherous in breezy or inclement weather, so take all necessary precautions.

North of Stella Maris

The lightly populated region of Long Island north of Stella Maris contains several of the island's highlights. For swimming and general beach bumming, the gorgeous long, powdery white-sand beach and turquoise water at **Cape Santa Maria**, five miles north of Stella Maris, can't be beat. A great destination for a bike excursion, Cape Santa Maria runs the length of the western side of Galliot

△ Cape Santa Maria

Cay, a flat, sandy and treeless peninsula set in the calmer waters of the island's leeward coast. To hit the beach, head north from Stella Maris on the Queen's Highway, passing through **Burnt Ground** and **Glinton's**, two rather down-at-heel roadside settlements where you can stock up on provisions. The turn-off to the beach is on the left side of the highway (signposted) after you cross a short causeway built over a salt pond at **Snow Hill**, a small collection of cottages topping a low knoll.

Retrace your steps to the Queen's Highway and head north for a pit stop in the quaint hilltop hamlet of **Seymour's**, a small cluster of cottages with goats and fruit trees in their yards that boasts a lovely panoramic view from the steps of its tiny whitewashed **church**. A rough dirt road on the left just before you reach the church leads to the **Columbus Monument** two miles away. The track is steep in places and alternatively sandy or very rocky, passable by four-wheel-drive, but otherwise best traversed on foot or bicycle. About halfway, you pass a turn-off on the left, which leads to a **lighthouse** overlooking Galliot Cay, about a mile away. Continue straight on the main path to reach the monument, a concrete and iron obelisk perched atop a steep rocky headland. It is believed that Columbus stood here over 500 years ago, taking in the same breathtaking cliffs and small rocky cays rimmed by white sand and blue-green water. The north side of the bluff on which the monument sits is an abrupt drop off into the deep Atlantic – take care, it is often windy up here – but the view to the south takes in a shallow, sheltered emerald-green bay edged with white sand. Known as Columbus Cove, it's an ideal spot for swimming and bonefishing.

Back on the Queen's Highway at Seymour's, the road continues north over a hill and down to the water's edge overlooking **Newton's Cay**, a small unin-habited island joined to the mainland by a short bridge across the narrow tidal creek. A three-minute walk across the bridge and up the path on the other side leads you to a small bush-backed beach on the far side of the cay, rather ho hum in comparison with other Long Island beaches but still a decent spot for a swim and usually deserted.

South of Stella Maris

From Stella Maris, the Queen's Highway hugs the western shoreline on the way south to **Millerton's** 3.5 miles away, where there is a school and a beautiful old whitewashed church set behind a stone wall. One mile south of Millerton's, **Deal's Beach**, fringed by casuarina trees, runs for a mile alongside the road, then sweeps out to a more secluded point of land. It is a pleasant place for a swim and picnic, with good snorkelling over a sea fan garden off the point at the beach's south end. Continuing south, a dirt road on the right leads to **O'Neil's** on the Atlantic coast, just a couple of houses and another secluded beach on a double bay.

Back along the Queen's Highway, the pretty hamlet of **Simms**, where a few tidy cottages are shaded by tall fruit trees, features a tiny stone prison (no longer in use) and a pink-painted post office dating from the early nineteenth century. From Simms, the highway heads inland over gently undulating terrain, passing a few scattered houses along the way. Opposite *Vindell's Takeaway* in the community of **Miller's** is the sign-posted turn-off to the secluded seaside resort *Chez Pierre*, a highly recommended stopover for a midday lunch or a cool drink on the beach.

At the settlement of **McKann's** – really just a few houses along the road – a sign marks the turn-off to the *King's Bay Resort*, with a casual restaurant and bar on a scenic piece of Atlantic beach. South of McKann's, the road climbs a steep hill topped with another pretty little church boasting a spectacular view of **Thompson Bay**, and moves inland again, travelling through flat scrubby bush until it reaches the settlement of Salt Pond, three miles further on.

Salt Pond and around

Named for the saline ponds that lie behind the settlement, **SALT POND** is a small hub of low-key commercial activity stretched out along the highway, with a large general store, a few dozen modern bungalows, a fish processing plant and a busy dock. In mid-May, the village hosts the **Long Island Sailing Regatta**, one of the most popular events in the Out Islands for the past 35 years. Long Island boat makers work all year to craft the perfect sailing vessel and on the weekend of the regatta, crews from all over the Bahamas descend on Salt Pond to race, cheered on by crowds from shore. Long Islanders always have a good showing, and winning trophies are on display in various bars up and down the island. It's a chance for Long Islanders working off-island to come home for a visit, but tourists are welcome to enjoy the live music and delicious food as well.

Salt Pond itself is very much workday the rest of the year, but there are a couple of lovely beaches on the Atlantic shore behind the settlement. If pointing south on the Queen's Highway, the road on the left (the Atlantic side) just past the H.C.S. store (where you can pick up picnic supplies) leads to a picturesque double bay suitable for swimming and beachcombing. Four miles south of Salt Pond, a wide dirt road on your left (follow the power lines) leads to a cove edged by a soft golden-sand beach overlooking tiny **Guana Cay**, about 500 yards offshore. There is good snorkelling in the shallow protected bay between the beach and the hilly cay, on which there is another sandy beach, a grove of tall coconut palms, an abandoned hut perched on the hilltop and a colony of curly-tailed iguanas. The adventurous can swim out to the cay, the only way to get there unless you are hauling kayaks.

South to Clarence Town

The 25 miles between Salt Pond and Clarence Town to the south makes up the most heavily-populated area on Long Island. A string of roadside settlements,

The sponge trade

The harvesting of **sea sponges** provided an important source of income for many Bahamians since the 1840s and was one of the islands' primary exports until the double whammy of fungal blight and the invention of artificial sponges wiped out the local industry in the late 1930s. At its height around 1905, sponging employed up to one third of the Bahamian work force, although few got actually rich in the business. During the harvesting heydays, bales of Long Island sponges were sold at auction in Nassau to Greek merchants, and a sponge sold in a London shop might fetch up to twelve times what the fisherman was paid for harvesting it.

Anchored over the sponge beds, where the water ranged between 8ft and 24ft deep, crews would hook the sponges from their moorings, sometimes using a water glass or oil spread on the surface of the water as a lens through which to find a lush clump for harvesting. They would then skin-dive to collect the clumps where necessary, and the sponges were left in saltwater "kraals" on nearby cays to be washed clean before being trimmed and strung in the boat rigging to dry on the voyage home.

With the gradual recovery of the sponge population and a growing international market for natural health products, there has been a modest revival in Bahamian sponge harvesting in recent years. In Long Island, Roland McHardy runs the **Deadman's Cay Sponge Company**, Lower Deadman's Cay (t337-0013), harvesting the sponges himself and exporting them around the world. He welcomes visitors to stop by and have a look around and a chat. You can buy natural sponges of several types from the drying sheds.

none with more than a few dozen residents, merge one into another along the rocky leeward shore, interspersed with a few stretches of dense bush. The highest concentration of activity is in **Deadman's Cay**, where there are several shops, schools, service stations and a bank, but little to see or do besides grabbing a bite to eat. A few miles further south in **Buckley's** is the **Long Island Museum** (Mon–Fri 9.30am–4.30pm, Sat 9am–1pm; ☎337 0500; $3), housed in a pink colonial style home. The excellent bite-sized exhibits on Long Island history and culture inside include items relating to sponging and spearfishing, junkanoo, straw plaiting, Lucayan artefacts and a corner devoted to recreating part of a nineteenth-century homestead. Along with postcards, the gift shop sells beautiful, locally made straw baskets and home-made jam made from tropical fruits.

Further south, the small settlement of Hamilton's is notable as the site of **Hamilton's Cave**, an extensive cave system where Lucayan artefacts were discovered in 1935. The cave is on private land, but Leonard Cartwright (☎337-0235) offers guided tours through the underground chambers filled for $10 per person. Cartwright can also bring along examples of the Lucayan pottery found inside if requested. Also in Hamilton's is an attractive whitewashed Catholic church – Our Lady of Mount Carmel – built in 1938, which is bare inside but has a lovely tiled floor and compelling rounded architecture. In sharp contrast right next door, a huge modern **Jehovah's Witness Temple** attests to the rapid growth of evangelical churches in Long Island in recent times.

At Deans, a few minutes south on the Atlantic side, there is a nice long stretch of beach with a picnic shelter and a barbecue pit. The primary attraction, however, is the **world's deepest blue hole**, surrounded on three sides by a sweep of white sand and rocky ledges, and plunging 663ft to the ocean floor just a few yards from shore. Check with local dive-shops should you want to tour the depths.

South again on the Queen's Highway, a rough dirt road on your left before you pass the *Oasis Bakery* leads to **Lowes Beach**, marked by a sign for the now closed *Compass Rose Guesthouse*. The view south along the narrow, scoured sand beach reveals white rollers pounding the shore all the way to Clarence Town in the distance. The beach itself makes for a good walk, but if instead you take the sandy path on the left facing the water, it leads to a hidden treasure 200yd away – a perfect oval **pool** almost enclosed by a low wall of coral rock and rimmed by a powdery white-sand beach. The water drains from the pool at low tide, but otherwise forms a completely private, calm, sandy-bottomed pool, with a view of the crashing surf through a narrow gap in the rock barrier.

Clarence Town and around

Forty-five miles from Stella Maris, hilly and green **CLARENCE TOWN** is built around a small natural harbour on the Atlantic coast, sustained by fishing, farming and its role as the seat of government for the island. It is notable primarily for two picturesque whitewashed stucco **churches** built by Father Jerome, the hermit of Cat Island. Originally ordained as an Anglican minister, he built the red-trimmed, traditional Gothic St Paul's Anglican Church first and the blue-trimmed, Spanish-looking St Peter's Catholic Church after his conversion to Catholicism in 1911.

South of Clarence Town, the Queen's Highway travels inland through flat, scraggly bush until it reaches the minute settlement of Gordon's – just a couple of buildings – at the southern tip of Long Island, nearly nineteen miles away. Few people live in the region, and the only points of scenic interest are **Lochabar Bay**, a unspoiled curve of white sand surrounding a deep blue hole two miles south of Clarence Town, and the long lonely beaches at **Cabbage Point** and **Gordon's**, both promising destinations for shell collectors. This area was, for a short period in the 1970s, a hub of salt production until several seasons of heavy rains and falling world prices wiped out the market. You can see the abandoned saltpans along the highway, now used seasonally to farm shrimp and fish.

Eating and drinking

If fine **dining** is what you are after, head for the northern resorts, each home to relaxed but elegant dining rooms and gourmet menus. Otherwise, your options are generally limited to deep-fried fast food and simple but tasty Bahamian fare in one of several roadside diners and cafés up and down the island. There is very little **nightlife** to speak of on the island. The bar at the *Stella Maris Resort* has a decent buzz most evenings, and the resort also organizes happy hours, barbecues and a cave party every week, with live music some evenings. Each community has a roadside bar where a predominately male crowd gathers to play pool or dominoes. The island hotspots are the *Midway Restaurant and Bar* in The Bight, *Earlie's Tavern* at Petty's, *The Swamp Thing Sports Bar* in Scrub Hill and the *Forest Satellite Bar and Restaurant* south of Clarence Town, a popular hangout for the younger set.

Northern Long Island

Alfred's Restaurant, Bar and Ice Cream Parlour Glinton's ☎ 338-5009. A clean and simple chrome and tile eatery serving deep-fried food, liquid refreshment and, of course, a variety of ice cream.

Cape Santa Maria Beach Resort Northern tip of Long Island ☎ 338-5273. The resort has a beautifully atmospheric dining room set in a glass-walled two-storey timber beach house facing the white-sand beach. The expensive menu features gourmet seafood dishes and imaginative American cuisine.

Breakfast is the usual American and Bahamian hot and cold dishes ($12). Lunch runs $9 for conch fritters with calypso sauce, while dinner mains include curried coconut chicken, jerk chicken and a shrimp and crawfish pasta for $21–24. Reservations required for dinner.

🏃 **Chez Pierre** Miller's ☎ 338-8809. If you dine out only one night on Long Island, make this the spot. Featuring exceptional Italian cuisine, the setting is supremely romantic or simply relaxing, depending on your frame of mind, with the glow of firelight, soft music and the gentle lapping of the waves a few steps away. The menu features home-made pasta and fresh seafood accompanied by fine wine, gorgeous salads and oven-warm bread rolls. Chef Pierre's entrees ($12–18) includes mahi mahi with mustard and white wine sauce, fresh pasta filled with lobster and served in a spicy white sauce, and Italian sausages slowly cooked in red wine and onions. During the day, the breezy beach bar serves a less elaborate lunch menu. Open daily for dinner by reservation.

Club Washington Restaurant and Bar McKann's ☎ 338-0021. A roadhouse serving tasty and filling local fare for $10–15 a plate. Try the steamed chicken with sides of coleslaw, peas and rice and plantain or the souse with Johnnycake served on Saturday.

King's Bake and Snack Shop Miller's ☎ 338-8916. Divine smells emanate from this tiny bakery which turns out racks of soft sweet bread and pastries. Breakfast is ham and egg on a bun ($3), and on Friday and Saturday nights they do a booming trade in takeaway pizzas ($12; call ahead to order). Closed Sun & Mon.

King's Bay Resort Near McKann's ☎ 338-8945. *King's* serves traditional Bahamian dishes and fresh seafood in a simple, casual dining room or on the deck with a spectacular ocean-front setting. The food is pretty good, but the real draw is the view. Go in the daylight hours.

Stella Maris Resort Stella Maris ☎ 338-2050. An airy hilltop dining room that's sophisticated but not stuffy, with sunny decor featuring huge windows on three sides looking out to flowering trees and the ocean beyond. Non-guests are welcome. The breakfast buffet ($12) is a fine start to the day, with fresh fruit, pastries, hot eggs and meat dishes. The lunch menu features soups, sandwiches, salads, seafood specials and a spinach tortilla ($10–15). Dinner is a candlelit affair where the constantly changing menu might feature the likes of chicken fricassee with green asparagus and poached filet of grouper with Chablis sauce, with apple fritters or a caramel

flan for dessert ($15–25). Come early for a cocktail at the hilltop bar. Reservations recommended for dinner.

Vindell's Takeaway Miller's ☎ 338-8954. Uncomplicated Bahamian dishes and cool drinks served on a shady verandah or packaged for takeaway. Daily 7am–9pm.

Salt Pond to Deadman's Cay

Coco's Lounge Hamilton's ☎ 337-6242. A basic restaurant serving cold drinks and local dishes; both the cracked conch and shrimp are recommended.

Earlie's Tavern Petty's ☎ 337-1628. A popular local watering hole with a small, cheerful restaurant attached serving traditional Bahamian and deep-fried fare like curried chicken with sides of peas and rice, coleslaw and macaroni. In the evenings, it's a popular spot for a game of pool, cards or sports on TV. Daily from 9am until everyone goes home.

Max's Conch Bar and Grill Deadman's Cay ☎ 337-0056. Specializing in conch cracked, frittered and marinated, this colourful local favourite also offers jerk chicken, pumpkin soup and fish, beef and conch burgers made from scratch ($5) at an outdoor kiosk ringed with bar stools. 9am until late. Closed Sun.

Midway Restaurant and Bar The Bight ☎ 337-7345. The area's most hopping spot, this well-scrubbed diner with a pool table and satellite TV specializes in both chicken and conch. Sits roadside in the middle of a long stretch of unbroken bush between Salt Pond and Deadman's Cay, and best visited during the Friday afternoon happy hour. Closed Sun.

🏃 **Ounces Hotspot** Deadman's Cay ☎ 337-0215. The top place to go on the island for tasty plates of Bahamian food. The menu includes baked chicken, pork chops and meatloaf, served with scrumptious potato salad, peas and rice, coleslaw, fried plantains and green salads. Located a short distance down a side road on the waterside of the highway just south of the Royal Bank, food can be eaten either in the spotless tiny dining room or on the covered deck with picnic tables. The sign above the bar says "no politics and gossip talking allowed and absolutely no hustling and swearing allowed", with hustling in these parts meaning trying to cadge drinks off other patrons. Open daily.

Palm Tree Souse House Deadman's Cay ☎ 337-0023. Right across from *Ellen's Inn*, this unadorned wooden shack lets you do like the locals do, serving sheep's tongue souse and other traditional Bahamian specialities. Open daily.

Clarence Town and around

Harbour Restaurant Clarence Town ☎337-3247. Right near the government dock, this clean and pleasant lunch room has windows overlooking the harbour and a menu listing tasty versions of basic seafood, deep-fried grub and sandwiches.

Le Pon Clarence Town ☎337-3766. Located roadside on the northern edge of town, this casual family place where you can eat well for $10 has a rustic feel, with seating on a screened-in hexagonal verandah overlooking a small pond. The delicious home-style meals of fried chicken, conch and souse come with the expected sides of coleslaw, plantain and mac and cheese. Sunday is game day, when the board games, dominos and darts are brought out. Open daily.

Oasis Bakery and Restaurant A mile north of Clarence Town ☎337-3003. A lovely spot for a snack with tables set on a deep wooden veranda overlooking a small pond. The *Oasis* offers freshly-baked bread, pastries and cookies to eat in or take home as well as a limited menu of inexpensive sandwiches, hot patties ($2.50), fish and chips ($6) and conch done several ways for lunch ($6). Souse and Johnnycake is the Saturday special. Open daily.

Outer Edge Grill Flying Fish Marina, Clarence Town ☎337-3445. A bright spot with a few tables on a covered wooden deck hanging out over the water. The grill turns out burgers, conch fritters and fish fingers with sides of plantain, macaroni and coleslaw topped off with lots of cool liquid refreshment. Expect to pay $10–15 for a filling meal. Closed Tues.

Listings

Banking There are branches of the Bank of Nova Scotia at the Stella Maris Airport (☎338-2057) and at Buckley's (☎337-1029); and of the Royal Bank of Canada at Gray's (☎337-1044) and Cartwright's (☎337-0001). All have ATMs and are open Mon–Thurs 9.30am–3pm and Friday 9.30am–4.30pm. Note that outside the larger resorts, credit cards are generally not accepted.

Petrol You can buy petrol in Simms, Salt Pond, Deadman's Cay, Hamilton's and Clarence Town; on Sundays, the Esso in Salt Pond is open 8.00–10.30am and the Shell in Deadman's Cay is open 8.30am–8.30pm.

Groceries There are general stores selling groceries in Burnt Ground, Stella Maris, Simms, Salt Pond, Deadman's Cay, Hamilton's and Clarence Town. On Sundays, shop from 8.00–10am before the stores close for church.

Laundry There are laundries in Stella Maris and in Deadman's Cay.

Medical services Government clinics are located in Clarence Town (☎337-3333), Deadman's Cay (☎337-1222) and Simms (☎338-8488). In emergencies, a doctor can be reached at home in Deadman's Cay at (☎337-0555) or in Stella Maris (☎338-2026).

Police Emergency ☎919. There are police detachments in Clarence Town (☎337-3919), Deadman's Cay (☎337-0999), Simms (☎338-8555) and at the Stella Maris Airport (☎338-2222).

Post office Located in Clarence Town, Deadman's Cay, Simms and at the Stella Maris Airport.

Telephone BaTelCo offices and call boxes are found in Clarence Town (☎337-3000), Deadman's Cay (☎337-1337) and Simms (☎338-0841), while there are phone booths in Salt Pond at the *Stella Maris Resort*. Be prepared for patchy service. Internet service is available at the larger resorts.

Crooked and Acklins islands

Dots in the ocean sought out by hardcore anglers and few others, **CROOKED** and **ACKLINS ISLANDS** lie close together, about sixty miles east of Long Island, and are connected to each other by a daily ferry service. While there were around fifty Loyalist cotton plantations on the islands two hundred years ago, today they are sparsely populated and barely developed. One of the few industries left on both islands is the harvesting of cascarilla bark, exported to Italy to make the bright-red aperitif Campari. Roughly four hundred people live on each of the two islands in a

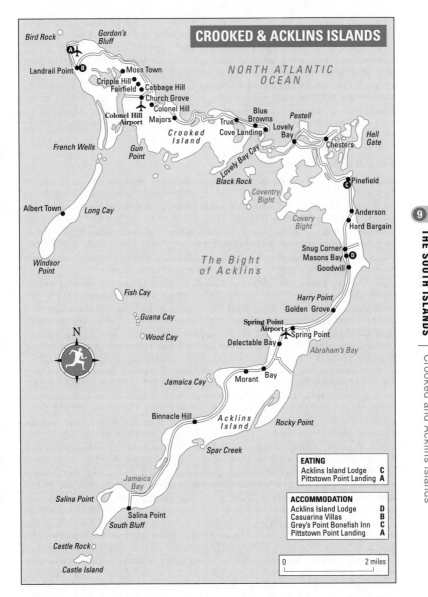

smattering of small coastal villages, many still without electricity or running water. While they lack traditional sights or even the typical beaches you might expect to find in the Bahamian chain, they are home to some of the finest **tarpon** and **bonefishing** around and committed anglers should seriously consider visiting the islands. Guides can be readily booked through area lodge or guesthouses for an average of $300 per day.

For non-fishermen, there are several nice long stretches of **beach** to explore on Crooked Island, which stretches 23 miles from end to end. Larger Acklins is 45 miles long, and a single road runs the length of each island. A day of sightseeing is all that's needed to fully explore one or the other. **Snorkelling and diving** in the near virgin waters surrounding the islands can be arranged through *Pittstown Point Landing Resort* on Crooked Island (☎561/799-1673 or 1-800/752-2322, 🅦www.pittstownpoint.com); on Acklins, you'll have to be self-sufficient. Note that most residents are devout Seventh Day Adventists, so no pork or alcohol is sold on the islands (except at the self-contained fishing resorts), and things shut up tight on Saturdays.

Practicalities

Bahamasair (☎377-5505, 🅦www.bahamasair.com) **flies** to Crooked Island's Colonel Hill twice a week from Nassau, with onward service to Spring Point on Acklins. The *K.C.T./United Star* **mailboat** sails to the Crooked and Acklins islands once a week from Nassau calling at Colonel Hill and Long Cay on Crooked Island and Spring Point on Acklins Island ($70 one-way; ☎393-1064). A government-operated **passenger ferry** ($5) runs twice-daily from Cove Point on Crooked Island to Lovely Bay on Acklins. Rental cars and sightseeing tours are most easily arranged through your guesthouse host.

The nicest **place to stay** on either island is *Pittstown Point Landings* (☎561/799-1673 or 1-800/752-2322, 🅦www.pittstownpoint.com; ❹), located on a white-sand beach four miles north of Landrail Point on Crooked Island. Here you'll find a dozen bright rooms with a/c. The dining room is situated in what was once the local post office – the first in the western hemisphere – built in the eighteenth century. The resort offers guided fishing expeditions and will arrange diving and snorkelling outings. Alternative accommodation on Crooked Island includes *Casuarina Villas* (☎344-2036; ❹) single/double/two-bedroom cottage $110/$135/$220; no credit cards), on the beach near Landrail Point village with a half-dozen cottages with kitchens, a/c and TVs. Close by, the *Frank and Ruth Guesthouse* (☎344-2676 or ☎361-4807 (Nassau); ❷ with a full meal plan for $60 a day) has six en-suite guestrooms with a shared kitchen and sitting room handy to the beach. A good choice for a group is *Scavella's Guesthouse* (☎344-2343 or cell ☎357-9472; ❷). Situated in Landrail Point, the house has two bathrooms and two bedrooms furnished with two double beds each, a kitchen, sitting room and a/c; $2000 gets you an all-inclusive week of fishing with the owner and bonefish guide Kenny Scavella. As for **eating out**, most options are concentrated around Landrail Point. The *Sunset Bar and Grill* (☎344-2507) at *Pittstown Point Landing* serves three meals a day, with cocktails served in the beachfront *Tiki Bar*. In Landrail Point village, filling Bahamian cooking can be had at *Gibson's Restaurant* (☎359-0238) and the *Seaside Café* (☎344-2417).

The few guesthouses on Acklins Island cater mainly to fishermen. The highest end option is the *Acklins Island Lodge* in Mason's Bay (🅦www.acklinsislandlodge.com; $3000 all-inclusive for a week of fishing, based on double occupancy), with six rooms fitted out with a/c, private bath and twin or king beds. As comfortable are *Grey's Point Bonefish Lodge* (☎344-3210 or 326-2686; 🅦www.greyspointbonefishinn.com; $2700 all-inclusive for a week of fishing, $2000 for non-anglers) in Pine Fields with the addition of Bahamian home-cooking on offer, and *Top Choice Lodge* in Mason's Bay (☎344-3628; 🅦www.topchoicelodge.com; $2000 per person, including meals and guides with reduced rates for those who might not be equally devoted to fishing). For

9

simpler digs minus the fishing package, try *Nai's Guesthouse* (☎ 344-3089; ❷) in Spring Point, which has an in-house restaurant.

There are **no banks** on either islands; traveller's cheques are accepted at most lodgings and cash is required elsewhere. A few small shops sell groceries and non-prescription drugs in Landrail Point, Cabbage Hill and Spring Point, and there are medical clinics in Landrail Point and Spring Point; the post office and BaTelCo office is in Colonel Hill.

Great Inagua

A few thatch palms dotted some distant ridges and stood out starkly against the sky… Yet they were not devoid of flowers, for even on the cacti pads bloomed scarlet and yellow blossoms. A subtly pleasing scene, tropical, yet not gaudy, the sort of thing that does not tire one too quickly.
Gilbert Klingel, *Inagua, Which is the Name of a Lonely and Nearly Forgotten Island*

Anchoring the southern tip of the Bahamian archipelago, **GREAT INAGUA** is the third largest island in the Bahamas, after Andros and the Abacos. Forty miles long and twenty miles across at its widest point, a quarter of the island's interior is covered by the shallow waters of **Lake Windsor** and much of the remaining area is low, flat bush or swamp. While for some the landscape seems stark and forbidding, it's not without its virtues, and when the young American Gilbert Klingel shipwrecked on the island in 1930 he found it to

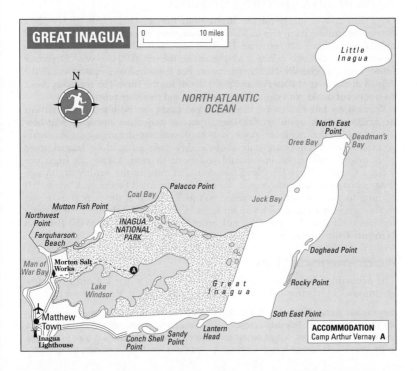

GREAT INAGUA

0   10 miles

N

Little Inagua

NORTH ATLANTIC OCEAN

North East Point

Oree Bay

Deadman's Bay

Palacco Point

Coal Bay

Jock Bay

Mutton Fish Point

Northwest Point

Farquharson Beach

INAGUA NATIONAL PARK

Man of War Bay

Morton Salt Works

Ⓐ

Doghead Point

Lake Windsor

Great Inagua

Rocky Point

Matthew Town

Soth East Point

Inagua Lighthouse

Conch Shell Point

Sandy Point

Lantern Head

ACCOMMODATION
Camp Arthur Vernay A

be a magical world bursting with life. Klingel stayed on for months to study the unique flora and fauna, and returned several times, eventually penning the well-written *Inagua, Which is the Name of a Lonely and Nearly Forgotten Island* (see p.351) describing the vegetation of the island in detail.

Great Inagua's interior has changed very little since Klingel washed ashore, and therein lies its main charm. The bulk of the island – 287 square miles – has been set aside as **Inagua National Park**, a protected conservation area that's home to a massive colony of West Indian flamingos. Flamingos aren't the only birds to call Inagua home, however, and nature lovers can hope to spot the likes of the endangered Bahamian parrot, the roseate spoonbill, pelicans, herons and egrets, Bahama pintail ducks, burrowing owls, the glossy ibis, kestrels and ospreys. There are also herds of wild donkeys roaming the island along with wild boars and several species of iguanas.

All that said, the island is far from a deserted Eden for animals. Great Inagua sits squarely in the path of the relentless trade winds, which combined with the relentless sun provides ideal conditions for solar salt production. That has made the sole settlement, **Matthew Town**, quite the anomaly in the Out Islands. Built on the southwest corner of the island, it's a prosperous company town comprised of a neat grid of tree lined streets and freshly painted houses that are home to employees of the **Morton Salt works**.

Five miles to the north of Great Inagua, **Little Inagua** is thirty square miles of wilderness, uninhabited except for herds of feral goats and wild donkeys, nesting sea turtles, and varied birdlife. Its seclusion is ensured by a vast barrier reef that encircles the island, making it difficult for boats to come ashore.

Arrival and getting around

Great Inagua is a ninety-minute **flight** from Nassau. Bahamasair (T377-5505, Wwww.bahamasair.com) flies to Matthew Town three times a week, with a stop-off on Mayaguana (see p.326) en route. The *Lady Mathilda* **mailboat** pulls into Matthew Town once a week, also calling at Mayaguana on the way ($90 one-way). Departure from Nassau is generally Tuesday afternoon, but the schedule is spotty so call the Nassau dockmaster at Potter's Cay (T393-1064) for the latest. The trip takes about 48 hours, but bunks with clean sheets, a shower, and meals are provided.

There is no bus service on the island, but **taxis** can be hired at the airport or mailboat dock upon arrival. The airport is two miles north of Matthew Town, while the mailboat dock is within walking distance of the town's accommodation. There are only about eighty miles of road on Inagua, most of it rough bush tracks, but should you want to **rent a car** call Ingraham Rent a Car (T339-1677). Note, however, that most of the roads run through Inagua National Park, where you must be accompanied by the park warden. If coming to visit the park, the warden will pick you up at the airport, take you to your guesthouse, and pick you up again in his truck for the tour. All of these services are included in the daily park entry fee you have to pay to the Bahamas National Trust in Nassau in advance of your visit.

Accommodation

The **accommodation** on Inagua is about a simple as it gets, consisting of a few guesthouses in Matthew Town and a rustic bunkhouse in the national park.

Camp Arthur Vernay T339-1616, F339-1850, VHF Ch 16 "Inagua Park". This simple camp, booked via the park warden, is in an isolated spot on the shore of Lake Windsor in Inagua National Park. The cement-block bunkhouse sleeps nine, with a shared shower and outdoor kitchen with a wood stove (a better idea is to bring a gas camping stove). Sheets and mattresses are provided but you must bring your own food and drinking water. $25 per person, and reservations are essential. ❶

Cartwright's Bonefish Lodge Taylor Street on the waterfront, Matthew Town ☎ 339-1362. In a yellow bungalow shaded by tall trees, the pair of two-bedroom units with full kitchens here have an attractive sunset view of the waterfront. Built as basic accommodations for Mr Cartwright's fishing clients, non-anglers are welcome as well. ❹

Gaga's Nest East Street at Maud, Matthew Town ☎ 339-2140. On the inland edge of town, Gaga's has five modern rooms with TV and a/c. There is one two-bedroom unit with a full kitchen and four double or twin rooms equipped with a microwave and fridge. While there's no view to speak of, there is a shady verandah with lounging chairs. ❷

Morton Salt Company Main House Kort-wright Street, Matthew Town ☎ 339-1267, ℱ 339-1265. A scrupulously well-maintained guesthouse with six spacious and comfortable double rooms in the centre of town. Each has a modern private bathroom, a/c, TV and a mini fridge. Breakfast and lunch are served daily on request and coffee and tea are available all day. Guests share a common sitting room equipped with a phone and there is a pleasant patio overlooking a small grassy yard. The power plant is located across the street, but the noise is minimal. ❷

Walkine's Guest House Gregory Street at Alice, Matthew Town ☎ 339-1612. Across the road from the tiny public beach, this modest guesthouse offers five dark but air-conditioned double and twin bed rooms with TV and mini fridge; three with private bath. Meals available on request. ❷

Matthew Town and around

Part of the appeal of **MATTHEW TOWN** is that it's one of the few communities in the Bahamas where tourism is not the major preoccupation. A hefty portion of the 1200 souls living here are employed at the **Morton Salt Works** just north of town, and their friendliness is genuine, not a prelude to trying to sell you something. The settlement itself is about ten blocks long and four wide, containing the island's administrative centre, medical clinic, a US Coast Guard station, bank and grocery store. It's a friendly and tidy settlement of quiet lanes lined with freshly painted bungalows and neat gardens shaded by mature leafy trees.

The nearby **saltpans** cover 12,000 acres and produce a million pounds of salt a year to be exported around the world. Stored in a small mountain range of towering white piles of salt five miles from town, you can arrange a free tour of the works by calling ☎ 339-1300. The pans lie within the boundaries of Inagua National Park, and a tour of the park will take you through them. In town, the **Erickson Museum** on Gregory Street (open on request; ☎ 339-1638; free) is devoted to the history of the salt works.

While nature is the main attraction on Inagua, the nineteenth-century **Great Inagua Light House** (☎ 339-1370), built in 1870 and still operational on a point of land a mile south of Matthew Town, makes a great destination for a short hike. Climb the 114 steps to the top for a wonderful panoramic view of the coastline and the lush blue sea beyond.

Inagua National Park

A 287-square-mile protected conservation area for **West Indian flamingos** founded by in 1962, **INAGUA NATIONAL PARK** encompasses Lake Windsor and a somber patchwork of shallow salt pans that's home to the world's largest breeding colony of the birds.

The park lies northeast of Matthew Town, and the inland vegetation thins as you approach its salt pans, vast squares of shallow, brackish water stitched together by miles of narrow causeways sitting just a few inches above the water. In the early morning light (the best hour for bird-watching), the landscape makes for an eerie scene; a stark, flat vista devoid of vegetation but still very much alive, teeming with birds feeding on fish within the pans. Flocks of cormorants often block the road, and when spooked by visitors they fill the air with the whispers of their beating wings.

The star of the show is the West Indian Flamingo, wading in the brine or looking prehistoric in flight, their pink bodies startling against a subdued backdrop. Upwards of 50,000 flamingos call the park home, nesting and hatching their fluffy white chicks on the shores of Lake Windsor throughout March and April. Traditionally, both flamingo meat and eggs were considered Bahamian delicacies, and they were hunted nearly to extinction on the island in the 1930s and 1940s. The colony did not recover for several decades, and its resurgence was due in large measure to the establishment of the national park.

The park and island on the whole is also home to the endangered **Bahamian Parrot**. Once prolific in the archipelago, today there are an estimated 3000 left in the country and are found only on Great Inagua and Great Abaco. They are surprisingly easy to catch sight of in the park, and in late June, they flock into Matthew Town to feed on the ripe fruits of the trees lining its quiet streets. Within the national park is also the **Union Creek Turtle Reserve**, a protected habitat and research station devoted to giant sea turtles. The warden can take you here if you want to visit.

Park practicalities

To **visit the park**, you must first make arrangements with the *Bahamas National Trust* office in Nassau (T393-1317, Wwww.thebahamasnationaltrust.org) and pay a daily park fee of $25. The amiable park warden Henry Nixon (T339-1616, F339-1850, VHF Ch 16 "Inagua Park") will meet you at the airport and give you a guided tour of the park in his own car. There is no additional fee for the tour, but a tip is customary.

Eating and drinking

Eating on Inagua can be an adventure for the health-conscious. Fresh vegetables and fruit are often scarce, and what's on offer in local restaurants depends heavily on what the mailboat delivered. There are a handful of simple local diners around Matthew Town serving a similar menu of deep-fried fare and traditional Bahamian dishes like boiled fish and pig's feet souse. Most appealing is the *Cozy Corner Restaurant and Bar* (T339-1440; Mon–Sat 10am–9.30pm) on North Street where you can get fried chicken or conch with salad and fries for about $5. There's also a pool table and beer is served. *Geneva's Café* (T339-1638; 8am until close, depending on business; closed Sun) on East Street at Mortimer is a bright lunch room overlooking a pond and serving meals of chicken, fish, crab or conch with peas and rice for about $8. It is best to make arrangements in advance for a meal here as Geneva doesn't bother turning on the stove unless she knows someone is coming for a meal. For home-cooked takeaway dinners, call *Norrie's Takeaway* (T339-1612), located at *Walkine's Guesthouse* on Gregory Street at Alice. A final option is the deli counter at the *Inagua General Store* (Mon, Tues, Thurs, Fri 7am–6.30pm, Wed and Sat 7am–1.30pm), which sells hotdogs, donuts and coffee along with a decent selection of groceries.

Outdoor activities

For a picnic and a swim, there is **Farquharson Beach** north of town past the salt works. In addition to the official tours given in Inagua National Park, *Great Inagua Tours* run by Colin Ingraham (T339-1336 or cell 464-7050) offers **snorkelling** excursions as well as **bird-watching** and **nature tours** of the island.

Land tours average $30 for a half-day, $70 full-day. Inagua is surrounded by rich, teeming coral reefs that are largely undisturbed and unexplored. Unfortunately, there is no **dive** operator on Inagua, meaning you'll have to charter a dive boat from elsewhere to explore the watering depths. Ezzard Cartwright (☎339-1362) is Inagua's only **fishing** guide; day-trips in search of bonefish, tarpon, permit or snook cost $300 a day for two people.

Listings

Banking Bank of the Bahamas (No ATM; Mon, Tues, Thurs 9.30am–2pm; Fri 10am–4.30pm; closed Wed; ☎339-1264).

Internet Access Available at the BaTelCo office (see below) for $5 an hour.

Medical clinic ☎339-1249; doctor's residence ☎339-1226 after hours.

Police Gregory Street on the north side of Matthew Town (☎339-1444; ☎919 in an emergency).

Post office In the Government Administrative Building on Gregory Street in the middle of Matthew Town.

Telephone The BaTelCo office (Mon–Fri 9am–4pm; ☎339-1000) is located north of the mailboat dock, a half-mile from the centre of Mathew Town.

Mayaguana

About as far off the beaten track as you can get in the Bahamas, **MAYAGUANA** sits alone in the ocean roughly fifty miles from Acklins Island to the west, and slightly further from the Turks and Caicos to the east. The island is almost completely undeveloped, having only had electricity and telephone service since 1997, and visitors mainly consists of fisherman, the occasional passing yachters and scientists who come to study the distinct bird and lizard life on the island. The varied and large population of birds includes flamingos, booby birds and osprey, while sea turtles also swim ashore to nest. On **Booby Cay**, located a few hundred yards off the island's eastern shore, lives a colony of Bartschi's rock iguana, an endangered species found nowhere else in the world.

The island's 320 or so residents live in three small settlements tucked in along the shore on its western half. The village of **Abraham's Bay** is the administrative capital, located slightly inland from the waterlogged south shore, with a

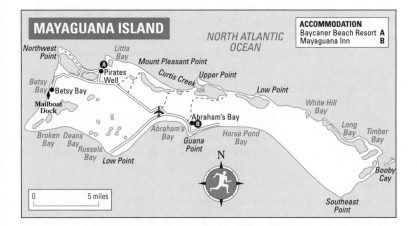

couple of small shops and simple guesthouses, a post office and BaTelCo office. **Betsy Bay** is where the mailboat docks each week, and **Pirate's Well** on the north coast is a pretty little settlement of a few houses in a clump of palm trees fronting a long white-sand beach. **Curtis Creek**, almost directly due north of Abraham's Bay on the north coast and accessible by road, is an inviting vista of white sand and turquoise water threading its way among a handful of small cays in a shallow bay. It's an ideal venue for a picnic, some snorkelling and a paddle by kayak or dinghy (you will have to bring your own collapsible kayak and snorkel gear).

The main reason visitors come to Mayaguana is to **bonefish** off the island's north coast. A week's package, including accommodation and meals at the *Baycaner Beach Resort* (see below) and equipment, runs around $2000, excluding airfare. The *Baycaner* can also arrange diving and snorkelling trips; a one-tank dive is $40 and a snorkelling day-trip is $60. Tanks and weights are available, but you must bring the rest of your equipment. If heading to Mayaguana, don't forget insect repellent, as the mosquitoes can be fierce in the evenings.

Practicalities

Mayaguana is a 24-hour voyage by the **mailboat** *Lady Mathilda* from Nassau, with departures once a week, continuing on to Great Inagua ($90 one-way). The schedule changes weekly, so call the dockmaster at Potter's Cay, Nassau (☎393-1064) for times. Bahamasair (☎377-5505 or 1-800/222-4262, ⓦwww .bahamasair.com) has three scheduled **flights** a week, with continuing service to Great Inagua.

The *Baycaner Beach Resort* in Pirate's Well (☎339-3605 or 377-2356, ⓦwww . baycanerbeach.com; ❸, or $1330 a week including meals for two people) is the most appealing **accommodation** on the island. The sixteen rooms are housed in a one-storey yellow stucco Spanish-style house situated directly on a white-sand beach running for several miles in both directions. The resort can arrange island tours as well as scooter and **car rentals** for $40 and $80 respectively. A second lodging option, located in Abraham's Bay, is the *Mayaguana Inn Guest House* (☎339-3116; ❷), with five no-frills rooms in which to lay your head. It has the advantage of being within walking distance of the mailboat dock and a couple of small grocery stores.

Contexts

Contexts

History

For three centuries after Columbus arrived in the Bahamas in 1492, the islands became an outpost of the great imperial struggles that consumed England, France and Spain. Because of its strategic position astride the Gulf Stream passage leading toward Europe, Nassau, the deepwater port on the northern side of New Providence, became first a rendezvous for English privateers preying on Spanish galleons and then a rambunctious haven for pirates from many nations. When England finally won control of the islands in 1783, the focus of Bahamian history shifted from Europe to North America, with the American Revolution being only the first wave in a series of influences and distortions that both dovetailed with and determined Bahamian lives. After World War II, the Bahamas achieved its independence and set about defining itself as a free and democratic country with an authentic culture.

Pre-Columbian Bahamas

Many anthropologists believe that the first temporary inhabitants of the Bahamian chain were ancient Siboney Meso-Indians, who migrated from the Greater Antilles for a short period well before the time of Christ. The first permanent settlers were, however, a tribe of Venezuelan Indians who spoke Arawak, and were related to larger groups of **Arawak–speaking peoples**, who had fled their more warlike neighbours, the Caribs. Around 500 AD, hustled along by population pressure and contests for land, a pulse of Arawak migration brought the first true settlers to the Bahamas. They called themselves the *lukki-caire*, a term that evolved into **Lucayan**, meaning simply "island people". Firmly established in Hispaniola and Cuba, these Lucayans practised a basic Neolithic Taino culture, living simply by fishing and basic agriculture. By 900, they had had firmly established themselves throughout the Bahamas in large numbers.

According to Columbus's diaries, the Lucayans were light brown in skin colour, with jet-black hair and broad, flat foreheads. They were indubitably peace-loving, played a ball game called *arieto*, smoked tobacco for ritual pleasure, tattooed their bodies and adored body ornaments and jewellery, though they wore few clothes. Although the Lucayans did have weapons like bows and arrows, they had not developed armour.

Their settlements throughout the islands were composed of rectangular or circular huts. Though essentially egalitarian, each community was headed by a chief, or *cacique*, who personified the ideal of wisdom. Despite having neither a written language nor the use of the wheel, the Lucayans managed to evolve a culture that made pottery, carved elaborate wooden articles, wove cotton and built watertight boats.

Little trace of Lucayan society remains in the Bahamas today. Anthropologists have unearthed numerous "sites", but most artefacts are limited to shards of pottery. **Petroglyphs** remain etched into rocks around the islands, but most are badly weathered. Scientific estimates of the Lucayan population on the Bahamas at the end of the fifteenth century put the figure at 40,000–50,000.

The first encounter

It was the Lucayans who greeted **Columbus** on or about October 12, 1492, the explorer having left Spain under the commission of Queen Isabella and King Ferdinand to search for a route to the East Indies. After a 33-day crossing of the Atlantic powered by the trade winds, he landed on what was probably modern-day San Salvador, an island the Indians called *Guanahani*. The one hundred or so Spaniards found the Lucayans very welcoming, so much so, in fact, that Columbus observed that "they should be good servants".

Taking several Lucayans with him as guides, Columbus sailed south and east, discovering other Bahamian islands like Rum Cay, Long Island, Crooked Island and finally the Ragged Islands, bestowing Spanish names on each as he went. There was little there to bring prosperity, however, and he moved on to Cuba and then Hispaniola. Subsequent waves of Spanish explorers came, and between 1500 and 1520, the Spanish deported most Lucayans as **slaves** to work the mines and plantations of the New World. Many Lucayans succumbed to illness and disease, while others committed suicide in despair. Legend has it that when Juan Ponce de León visited the island of Andros looking for the fountain of youth in 1513, he found but a single native. Within 25 years of their first encounter with European society, the Lucayans had been exterminated.

Imperial struggles

For nearly a century after the initial encounter between Columbus and the Lucayans, the Bahamas came under the nominal **control of Spain**. Despite the Treaty of Tordesillas in 1494, which had divided the western world between Spain and Portugal, the Spanish had little use for their possessions in the Bahamas. Consequently, English freebooters and privateers, such as Sir Walter Raleigh and Sir Francis Drake, were able to use Bahamian waters to hide after plundering Spanish galleons; explorers like Sir John Hawkins and John Cabot also briefly visited the Bahamas during the 1500s. However, dangerous reefs, tricky tides and frequent hurricanes made actual settlement on the islands unfeasible.

In 1629, Charles I of England ignored the Spanish claim on the islands and granted the Bahamas to one of his favourites, Sir Robert Heath, as part of the English effort to colonize the northern and middle Atlantic. At the same time, France's King Louis XIII granted the islands to a member of his court. And while neither Charles I nor Louis XIII sent actual colonists to the Bahamas to cement their claims, the tone of imperial struggle was set, dictating the course of Bahamian history for the next two centuries.

The Adventurers

The first European settlers of any consequence here were **Puritans**. The English Civil War (1642–48) visited great persecution on the country's Puritans, who fled for the American colonies. One, William Sayle, became the first governor of Bermuda, yet after his tenure there he grew dissatisfied with the religious freedom on the island. With the approval of the Crown, he left Bermuda in 1648 with his **Company of Eleutheran Adventurers** and set sail for the uninhabited Bahamas. Sayle's group arrived on the island of Cigatoo, now known as Eleuthera, where it had hopes of establishing large-scale plantations. However, the colonists were quickly disappointed by the thin soil and unreliable rainfall, and also cursed by political faction, ultimately splitting up, with some departing for Virginia and others returning to Bermuda. After more than ten years of struggle, most of the colonists were gone, and those who remained lived at near-starvation levels. Sayle himself returned to Bermuda and was later made governor of South Carolina in 1663. As governor, he advocated for Bahamian colonists, enlisting support from Puritan communities as far away as New England.

At the same time that Sayle and the Adventurers were colonizing parts of the Bahamas, **Oliver Cromwell** dethroned King Charles I. Shortly thereafter, Cromwell initiated his "Grand Western Design", an imperial enterprise designed to challenge Spanish supremacy in the Caribbean. He planned to entice settlers with promises of land and to secure the services of privateers against Spanish shipping interests. Government-sponsored Puritan settlers began arriving, as did freed black slaves and even, in 1659, a number of American colonists from New Providence, Rhode Island, who gave their name to an island of major importance in the chain.

Piracy and war

Although the Adventurers had committed a constitution to paper, the colonists lived for decades without any formal government. In 1670, Charles II, newly restored to the throne, parcelled out the islands to six **Lords Proprietors of the Carolinas**. The Proprietors were led by Lord Ashley of South Carolina, who promptly dispatched three hundred new settlers to New Providence's Charles Town (renamed **Nassau** in 1695 in honour of King William III of England, prince of Orange-Nassau). The Proprietors were absentee landlords who didn't find much profit in their lands, and when the first governor died en route to the islands, the unruly islanders on New Providence elected their own. The Proprietors soon dispatched other governors, but throughout the 48-year period of Proprietary Government, Nassau was a tumultuous place to say the least, and most of the dispatched governors were easily corrupted, exiled by local residents or even murdered. Perhaps the government's greatest achievement was the first formal census of Bahamian residents in 1671, which revealed a population of 1097, of whom 443 were slaves working plantations of cotton, tobacco, sugar cane and sisal.

By the late seventeenth century, a hundred years of constant warfare between England, France and Spain allowed Nassau to become a haven for **pirates** and **wreckers**. Its many reefs, cays, rocks, shoals and inlets, along with unforgiving tides and bad weather, forced many a ship aground only to be plundered, and allowed the shallow-draught vessels that pirates preferred to hide effectively from imperial navies. Perhaps the most famous privateer of the time was Henry Jennings, who, in 1715, attacked a Spanish galleon and captured five million pieces of eight, returning to Nassau a hero. Pirates like Edward "Blackbeard" Teach and Calico Jack Rackham became infamous for their cruelty, but were also prominent as de facto island leaders. After thirty years of raiding and wrecking ships, Nassau's outlaws grew even bolder and were beginning to prey on ships of all nations, even going as far as raiding towns in the south Caribbean and the Carolinas. Something had to be done.

Royal government

In an effort to bring order to his disorganized subjects in the Bahamas, King George II took control from the Proprietors in 1718, made the Bahamas a **Royal Colony** and sent out a former privateer and explorer named Woodes Rogers as Royal Governor, with a mandate to clean up Nassau. Rogers sailed into Nassau Harbour in late 1718, advising the pirates they could accept either death or a pardon. Backed by three warships and a cadre of Royal Marines, Rogers executed a few outlaws, chased others away and co-opted still others into royal service. However, just as calm returned to Nassau, a new war between England and Spain broke out in 1720, leaving many residents of the crown colony fearful of attack. Rogers organized militias for defence and fortified Nassau, repelling a Spanish attempt to sack the city. When an epidemic seared through Nassau, many of his supporters died, stripping him of badly needed political support, and he returned to England a poverty-stricken man in 1721. Rogers, though, returned in 1729, again on a mission to root out piracy and corruption that had made a comeback in his absence.

It was during his second period as Royal Governor that Rogers created a **General Assembly** made up of 24 elected land-owning members, which first convened on September 29, 1729. In form, it remained virtually unchanged throughout the succeeding two and a half centuries, until Bahamian independence in 1973. The Assembly of 1729 was notably oligarchic, governed by an elite class of landowners that served its own interests and those of its friends in England. Quite often, though, the interests of the Nassau elite conflicted with the Crown, setting the stage for a series of political battles between royal governors and wealthy landowning whites. This tension was only compounded by the tide of imperial wars between England, France and Spain, which flared anew in 1738, 1748 and 1756, and saw England once again legalizing privateering.

The Bahamas remained a poor outpost in an increasingly wealthy Empire. Its thin calcite soil could not support mass slave-labour plantations as in the southern Caribbean, and tobacco, cotton and sisal failed in turn. Once the islanders had cut down great stands of hardwoods, the trade in forest products dwindled, leaving most Bahamians to scrape a living from subsistence agriculture and fishing, salt farming, turtle hunting and wrecking; indeed, by 1750 more than three hundred salvage ships were employed in Bahamian waters.

The American Revolution

Because of its location amid shipping lanes to and from Europe and North America, the Bahamas has always been affected by the tides of North American immigration and colonization. Moreover, many residents of the Bahamas had family and religious ties to American colonists. When the **War for American Independence** broke out in 1776, the Crown responded by blockading trade with its American colony. Bahamians were torn, with many remaining loyal to the Crown while a significant minority supported the American rebels. Almost immediately the American Navy attacked Nassau, capturing Fort Nassau in hopes of spiriting away its huge cache of gunpowder, which had, however, been taken away beforehand. Again in 1778, the American Navy attacked Nassau, and a joint French–Spanish fleet opportunistically captured New Providence for Spain in 1782, just as the Revolutionary War was winding down. With the Spanish in formal control of Nassau at the end of 1783, a pro-British group of 200 mercenaries and British Loyalists sailed into Nassau Harbour led by Andrew Deveaux, a Loyalist American colonel. Deveaux had his men sail to and from their landing vessels repeatedly, inducing a Spanish retreat under the illusion of an onslaught by so many troops. When the Treaty of Versailles formalized the end of the American Revolutionary War, England was granted sole possession of the Bahamas.

The Loyalists and Emancipation

Many American colonists – mostly merchants from New England or planters from the Old South – remained loyal to England during the Revolutionary War and fled the newly independent country for Canada, England or the Bahamas. Between 1783 and 1785, more than 8000 **Loyalists** and their slaves arrived in the islands, tripling the colony's population. While some of the Loyalists soon moved on to more southerly English colonies like Barbados, others stayed, purchased land and set up plantations devoted to cotton and worked by slaves. George III, seizing an opportunity to oversee a more closely-knit colonial government, guaranteed Loyalist settlers free land and sent out an autocratic Scottish earl named **Lord Dunmore** to be the new governor. Corrupt and dissolute, Dunmore had been a former governor of New York and was widely despised in America for having destroyed the port of Norfolk before fleeing George Washington's troops. In the Bahamas, he spent lavishly on himself, building two huge forts, Fincastle and Charlotte, and came close to bankrupting the colony by doing so. Ultimately replaced in 1796, Dunmore left behind an economy that was only marginally successful as well as a political and cultural decadence based on slaveholding, oligarchy and corruption in public works.

At the beginning of the 1800s, the Bahamian population hovered around 12,000, 75 percent of whom were **slaves**. The rest were whites and black freemen, who themselves sometimes owned slaves. Although some Loyalists were devoted to plantation-style agriculture, the islands could never adequately supported such a system, and the industry quickly went downhill, disappearing entirely shortly after 1800. As no large sugar culture emerged on the islands as elsewhere in Caribbean, many blacks were freed to become farmers, mariners, fishermen, labourers and the like, and slavery never flourished on the islands. Freed slaves were often joined by thousands of slaves liberated from slave ships on the high seas by the Royal Navy, leading to the establishment of towns like Adelaide and Carmichael on New Providence.

The Loyalist era extended until 1834, when the British parliament abolished slavery in the colonies and granted limited freedom to ex-slaves. While parliament hoped a period of adjustment would precede **Emancipation** and that slaves would work as apprentices to their former masters for wages, most slave owners were simply too poor to uphold the system. Bahamian blacks almost immediately became free men, though some remained as indentured servants and domestics, and those Loyalists opposed to abolition soon fled the islands. The resultant social fabric consisted of a large majority of blacks barely subsisting, a few wealthy white landowners controlling the General Assembly and commerce in general and an economy surviving on barter and very little trade. A few immigrant Greeks, Jews, Syrians and Chinese joined their fellow islanders in looking for ways to make a living, though they likewise faced difficulties.

In fact, for much of the nineteenth century, the entire West Indies was mired in poverty and disillusionment. In the Bahamas, wreckers still worked their salvage boats, spongers continued to hunt for dwindling supplies of sponges around Andros and other Out Islands, and some enterprising farmers grew citrus and pineapple on Eleuthera and the Exumas. But latter on when huge American conglomerate interests like the United Fruit Company persuaded the US Congress to slap high tariffs on fruit imports, the Bahamian fruit industry collapsed. And as the British mapped the islands and erected lighthouses, wrecking as a cash cow dwindled as well.

The American Civil War

The **American Civil War** (1861–65) had an immense impact on the struggling Bahamian economy. When, at the outset of the war, President Abraham Lincoln imposed a blockade along the Atlantic that decimated Southern shipping, it drastically curtailed the vital export of cotton from Charleston and Wilmington to Britain. Almost overnight, the Bahamas – and Nassau in particular – became an important cog in the Confederacy's survival, as the South sought to circumvent the blockade by rerouting shipping through the Bahamas. Bahamians of all stripes and sizes became involved in **blockade running**, an adventurous industry that would become the lifeblood of the Bahamas during several episodes in its later history. Shipbuilding received a boost as well, with Bahamian smugglers building specially outfitted vessels designed to outrun Northern gunboats. In return, Bahamians smuggled manufactured goods to the Confederacy, engaging in a lucrative two-way trade.

Between 1859 and 1866, Nassau boomed, the *Royal Victoria Hotel* was built on Bay Street, and the bars, cafés and nightclubs along Bay were jammed with Southerners, Bahamian blockade runners and English entrepreneurs. But with the end of the war, the Bahamian economy slipped into reverse, and depression conditions returned.

Prohibition and the World Wars

While the end of the Civil War halted Nassau's brief reign as a smuggler's paradise, it brought budding prosperity to the United States, helping create a middle class that had enough disposable income to travel. By the turn of the century, American transportation magnate Henry Flagler had almost single-handedly created Florida as a tourist destination, building roads, railroads and hotels, luring thousands to Florida's warm winter climate. Nassau was beginning to get a spillover of tourists, which only increased when Flagler inaugurated steamship service connecting Miami with Nassau.

World War I saw some Bahamians entering the British army and serving on the Western Front, and patriotic Bahamians from all walks of life contributed funds to the war effort. Save for supplying fruits, vegetables, medical supplies and clothing, the tiny Bahamian economy, had little impact on the war effort; sadly, the reverse was not true. The devastation of English export ability further depressed an already struggling Bahamian economy, and by the war's end the Bahamas was again in decline, a steady downward trend that was only halted by the passage of the 1920 Volstead Act by the US Congress. This law made the production and sale of alcoholic beverages illegal on the territory of the United States, ushering in the era of **Prohibition**.

Rum-running days

Almost immediately Bahamian smugglers entered the illegal alcohol trade. With their skills at boat building and navigation, and the close proximity to the Miami haunts of American gangsters, Nassau's rum-runners sped across the Gulf Stream to meet larger boats accepting cargoes of liquor. Between 1920 and 1933, when Prohibition was finally repealed in the United States, Nassau boomed again, with construction projects fuelling a labour short-age, hotels jammed with tourists and gangsters, and many of the Out Islands profiting from shipbuilding and smuggling alike. Riding a crest of profits from whiskey, rum, beer and gin, the British parliament was not eager to clamp down on the trade. For thirteen years, Bahamians got to ride the high end of their boom-and-bust cycle – until the end of Prohibition and the beginning of the Great Depression.

It was an expansive Canadian multi-millionaire who set the course for the Bahamas to escape the Depression. **Sir Harry Oakes**, who made his fortune from mining, came to New Providence in the 1930s looking for a place to invest his money without enduring high Canadian and British taxes. He bought huge chunks of New Providence and Out Islands land, built Oakes Airfield on New Providence, and initiated a round of construction that provided jobs when none were to be found. Though mysteriously murdered in his palatial home outside Nassau in 1943, Oakes managed to plant a fertile seed, being one of the first to envision the Bahamas as a tax haven and winter get-away for wealthy expats.

World War II

What truly helped shock the Bahamas out of its Depression doldrums, though, was the beginning of **World War II**. The conflict brought the Allies to the Bahamas in force, and in the early 1940s five US/UK naval bases were estab-lished on the Out Islands, from where ships swept the South Atlantic on anti-submarine duty. Two new airports were built as well, one of which was later to become Nassau's International Airport.

At the outbreak of war, the British government sent out the **Duke of Windsor**, the former Edward VII who had abdicated his throne to marry an American divorcee, to become Royal Governor. While he arrived with a tarnished image, including accusations that he was soft on Fascism, his appeal lay in his celebrity. The duke soon gained a popular following for his work in establishing the Out Island Economic Committee, Windsor Camp at Clifton on New Providence (a camp for kids) and an infant welfare clinic on Blue Hill Road in Nassau. Even so, his most vocal critics saw the duke as yet another prop for the white oligarchy – basically the merchants, lawyers, landowners and politicians commonly known as the "Bay Street Boys" – that controlled the General Assembly and business in Nassau since virtually 1729.

At the same time, a formal apartheid existed in public facilities in the Bahamas, and black labourers were paid lower wages than their white counterparts. Eventually, on June 1, 1942, thousands of labourers working on an airport construction project met in Nassau's Over-the-Hill and marched down Burma Road to Bay Street in protest of their poor treatment. The march escalated into a riot, and five people were killed by a company of Cameron Highlander troops and police. With hundreds of injured workers on their hands, the builders granted the labourers an increase in pay. Afterwards, their consciousness raised, it was unlikely that black Bahamians were going to return to the days of apartheid without a fight.

Tourism and independence

Save for a small spurt in the early 1900s when wealthy Americans flocked to Henry Flagler's *New Hotel Colonial*, **tourism** in the Bahamas remained the preserve of a few fishermen and wealthy businessmen. All that, though, began to change around 1960 with the advent of the Cuban Revolution and the activities of Sir Stafford Sands.

Before Fulgencio Batista's corrupt dictatorship was replaced by Fidel Castro's Communist regime in 1959, Americans from the East Coast considered Cuba a gambling, swimming and nightclub paradise. **Sir Stafford Sands**, a prominent Nassau businessman and landowner, saw the closing of Cuba as a prime opportunity for the Bahamas and organized the Bahamas Development Board, composed of prominent citizens. Sands's goal was to see the total of 32,000 visitors of 1960 raised to one million by 1970. Aided by government laws modelled on those of Switzerland, Sands oversaw the development of European-style banking secrecy, favourable tax laws and lucrative government subsidy for private business. Soon, capital from highly taxed English sources flowed into Nassau banks, providing a fund from which hotels, roads, airports and infrastructure of all kinds could be financed. The US air base on New Providence was expanded and open as the **Nassau International Airport**, Prince George Wharf was dredged to allow cruise ships and high-end resorts open for business. Finally, Hog Island was transformed into Paradise Island, and gambling as an attraction began to take hold. Elsewhere on Grand Bahama, the new city of Freeport sprang up on land that had been palmetto scrub, and resorts began to appear on a lesser scale on the Out Islands.

The battle for power

Not all, though, revolved around sun and fun during the middle half of the twentieth century. It was inevitable that the anti-colonial struggles of Africa and Asia, as well as the Civil Rights movement in the US, would have a profound effect on racial politics in the Bahamas, and by the early 1950s a small black middle class had developed, fuelling calls for representative government and a more even distribution of economic profits. In 1953, a political organizer from Andros named **Lynden Pindling** formed the Progressive Liberal Party (PLP) on a platform of social, economic and political equality leading to independence. The Bay Street Boys formed the United Bahamian Party (UBP), and a country that had seen no political parties in its history all at once had a fight on its hands.

Through the 1950s and early 1960s, the PLP and UBP jockeyed for power and influence. In 1963, a huge national strike brought matters to a head in the British parliament, which drew up a new constitution for the Bahamas with the aim of creating a more representative form of government. When the new **1964 Constitution** was adopted, it replaced the old colonial-style government with a two-chamber House of Assembly elected by Bahamians themselves and headed by a prime minister whose cabinet members would be drawn from the party with the most votes. In national elections in 1964, the leader of the UBP, Roland Symonette, won by a narrow majority. However, discontent was rampant and the election was seen as illegitimate because of restrictive voting laws (only landowners could vote) that diluted black power. Pindling and his PLP adopted a strategy of non-cooperation, resulting in a new election in 1967, which Pindling won.

Independence at last

By 1969, further changes to the Bahamian constitution gave the country control over most of the economy. Now, only defence, foreign policy and internal security were vested in the British parliament. The drive for independence was not without its detractors, however. Joining with the UBP, a number of minority parties formed a new Free National Movement (FNM), which opposed complete independence from Britain. On the Abacos and in Eleuthera, home to the original Loyalists, a wave of anti-independence sentiment developed which led to a proto-secessionist movement. Despite such pressures, the independence movement could not be stopped. At elections held in September of 1972, Pindling's party won overwhelmingly. As a result, on July 10, 1973, Bahamas was granted **independence**. At midnight, the Union Jack was lowered over Fort Charlotte in Nassau, and the Bahamian flag with a black triangle and stripes of aquamarine and gold was raised. Thousands celebrated joyfully in the streets.

Modern-day Bahamas

The **Pindling years** were a mixed bag. At first, there was a great deal of enthusiasm, yet with the Oil Embargo and the high inflation of the late 1970s, too much foreign capital was flowing into the Bahamas for purely speculative purposes. Land was being purchased for resale instead of development, and Pindling's efforts to redress abusive labour practices led to a backlash from developers who refused to negotiate government deals. In addition, the banking system and construction industry were awash in foreign cash, and many government officials succumbed to the lures of bribe-taking and kickbacks.

As the new nation slid into recession, **drug smuggling** from Colombia blossomed, with the Bahamas becoming a major stopover for shipments to Miami. With its many hiding spots, the Bahamas had always been a magnet for outlaws, and the drug trade was no different. Operating out of hidden airstrips, or with heavily laden seaplanes, Bahamians, even those in government, became ensnared in the lure of the drug business. It got so bad that Colombian drug lords managed to bribe the government at its highest levels. The US Drug Enforcement Administration led a massive crackdown in the mid-1980s, by which time the stench of rotting political flesh was pervasive in the islands.

Pindling's time came to an end on August 19, 1992, when the Free National Movement led by **Hubert Ingraham** swept into power by winning 31 of 49 Assembly seats. The new government was conservative, pro-business and anti-corruption, and among its first acts was to sell off inefficient government-run properties and adopt a programme of fiscal restraint. In 1997, the FNM was returned to power with an increased majority, winning 35 of 40 seats in the Assembly.

Ingraham's conservative FNM government adopted a business-friendly National Investment Policy, bringing together attractive elements of the banking laws, tax advantages and fiscal restraint, all designed to reduce the national debt, which was $1.1 billion by the end of the Pindling years. By 1996, the debt had been reduced to $358 million, inflation was down to 0.5 percent, and unemployment had been reduced to ten percent.

The current outlook

Despite the achievements of Ingraham's government, Bahamian voters booted the FNM in the general election of May 2002, handing power back to the PLP under Prime Minister **Perry Christie**. Christie had resigned from Pindling's PLP government in 1984, disgusted by allegations that government officials had accepted bribes from drug traffickers. To boost the Bahamian economy, the PLP government has focused on expansion of the tourism industry, which currently accounts for sixty percent of the GDP and directly or indirectly employs half the country's labour force. The tourism industry and the country more generally suffered millions of dollars of damage under the assaults of Hurricanes Jeanne and Frances in 2004 and Wilma in 2005, but most areas are now rebuilt and refurbished. With government encouragement, several new resorts are under construction in Nassau and the Out Islands. Occasionally, this dependence on foreign disposable income has placed the Bahamas in a precarious position – particularly in the immediate aftermath of the September 11 attacks, when worldwide tourism ebbed – yet the islands still appear to be in better economic shape than most of their Caribbean neighbours.

Society and culture

The Bahamas are a somewhat strange amalgamation of Caribbean island life, American influence, Anglo leanings and African heritage. It hasn't necessarily served to make for the most distinctive culture, though a few arts do flourish, among them music. More interesting probably are the people themselves: their ethnic heritage, religious rituals and the like.

People and customs

Almost 85 percent of Bahamians are the descendants of **slaves** imported to the New World from West Africa, often via mainland North America. Some of the slaves who moved here from the United States came along with their owners, typically Loyalists who ran plantations in the South and fled during the American Revolution. Similarly, white Bahamians often trace their ancestry back to these **Loyalist migrations**, or even further back to the Eleutheran Adventurers who fled England or Bermuda on account of religious persecution.

The largest minority in the Bahamas are **Haitians** – some twelve percent of the population – many having left Haiti to escape poverty and political repression. Chinese, Hispanics, Greeks and Jews constitute about three percent of the population, and each group tends to remain separate from the others and from Bahamians in general.

Despite the fact that there is somewhat of a divide between black and white here, and more narrowly defined ethnicities too, Bahamians are a largely tolerant people, and have seen quite a bit of racial intermingling over the years.

Daily life and rituals

Above all, Bahamian society is generally **laid-back**, which means that enjoying life is more important than any formalities. Punctuality, for example, is not a primary value: events are sometimes seemingly delayed for no real reason; concerts, theatre openings or mailboat sailings are assigned approximate times; only cricket games in Nassau, scheduled to begin at 1pm on Sunday, often get started an hour later, after the teams exchange pleasantries. That doesn't necessarily translate into a persistent lack of efficiency – buses and taxis in the main cities, for instance, can be quite well run – but you may have to exercise a good deal of patience while on the islands, or getting from one island to another.

On the Out Islands, where most people pursue rural lives on a seasonal schedule, rising with the sun and retiring at dark, life proceeds in a fairly consistent manner. Rural Bahamians tend to live on roads without addresses, in houses haphazardly built and disdain town living in general. They fish, they tend a small field, gather some fruits, pay attention to their families, have fun on Saturday night and go to church on Sunday.

Religion

The overwhelming majority of Bahamians are **Christian**, many of them Baptists or Methodists, though a growing number have adhered to evangelical sects that have been heavily proselytized in recent years. The Anglican Church, because of its British origin, holds sway with the majority of white Bahamians. Going to church on Sunday is extremely important, quite clearly indicated by the profusion of churches throughout the islands: Roman Catholic cathedrals, stone Anglican churches, small single-room buildings thrown up by a congregation using clapboard. Ministers, always in short supply, often island-hop to serve their flocks, and services take on a form not unlike Southern Baptist proceedings, with music and "testimonial" services in which members of the congregation loudly confess their sins. As well, religious processions are common, and the major Christian holidays like Christmas and Easter, are celebrated with fervour.

Despite the widespread acceptance of Christianity in the islands, older **folk superstitions**, part of the African cultural heritage, have a place in Bahamian life. Many superstitions centre on supernatural spirits who put evil spells on people. Bahamians may whisper secret incantations to ward off these evil spells, or may sprinkle guinea grain around a home to keep away illness or death. Love potions derived from *santeria* practices can be found in some markets, particularly cuckoo soup, a dark broth thought to have tremendous power. More pernicious forms of superstition survive as **Obeah**, a variant of Voodoo, which sees some practitioners advertising spiritual powers or psychic ability for the purpose of casting spells or curses. Some Bahamians practise both Christianity and Obeah, particularly those who believe in white magic and keep a dream book in the belief that good spirits that come in dreams will help them be happy, successful and rich.

Language

Although the official language of the Bahamas is **English**, most Bahamians on the street speak a combination of King's English and a dialect that draws heavily on African logisms, Caribbean slang and Creole. The present tense is often used, even when indicating that something happened in the past, plurals are often dropped and repetition is used for emphasis. Bahamian slang uses cockney English, American forms and made-up words to form a unique and often obscure but spirited form of talk. Most people are addicted to proverbs, and can speak quite animatedly when excited.

Words are spoken in a type of patois not dissimilar from the type associated with Jamaican speakers. For example, "thought" becomes "tot", and "child" becomes "chile", and the pronounced words are spoken with a definite island lilt.

Music

Bahamians share a West African oral tradition, as well as a cultural heritage of myth and folktale, which has easily translated into a strong **musical tradition**. The underpinning of all West African oral tradition is the chant, which appears in African music as an all-encompassing storytelling dynamic usually accomplished by a main singer backed by a chorus that provides a dynamic accompaniment. In the Bahamas, this chanting aesthetic, filtered through the slave experience and Caribbean influences from other islands, reappears as rigging or chatting, both of which are forms of musical improvisation. Though neither of the major Bahamian musical expressions has had the worldwide influence of, say, soca or Cuban *son*, each gives a spirited sense of the people. For an introduction to island music, check out either Folkways Records compilation *The Bahamas: Islands of Song*, with its shanty tunes and local renditions of popular songs, or *The Real Bahamas*, notable especially for the wondrous guitar sounds of **Joseph Spence**.

Goombay and Junkanoo

Almost everybody in the Bahamas gets involved with the exuberant New Year's festival called **Junkanoo**, whose roots lie in an improvised slave music called **goombay**. Using all manner of instruments for its various flourishes, goombay features a regular, unsyncopated beat that forms the heart of the fast-paced sustained melodies, often hypnotic in their regularity. At the heart of the beat is the **goatskin drum**, which takes the place of the huge drums used to convey messages across the vast forests of West Africa, and was developed by slaves as a replacement in the New World. Other instruments contributing to the unique sound include bongos, conch-shell horns, maracas, homemade rattles of all types, click sticks, flutes, bugles, whistles and cowbells, all of which were available wherever slaves gathered.

Rigging, chatting and rake 'n' scrape

Rigging and **chatting** are part of the gospel tradition in Bahamian churches, a form of call-and-answer singing that somewhat mirrors what you might find in a Southern Baptist church in the US. Homemade instruments, impromptu lyrics and storytelling, are the foundation of another kind of music called **rake 'n' scrape**, which is popular in nightclubs and on street corners. Starting with a rhythm section composed of seed-pod shakers, musical saws and other household implements, then laying on instruments like accordions and cheap guitars, rake 'n' scrape has emerged as an authentic popular Bahamian musical form. On almost every Out Island, bands perform the music in small clubs, at regattas and festivals, or simply at get-togethers.

Popular imported forms of music like reggae from Jamaica, soca from the southern Caribbean, American rhythm and blues and hip-hop are popular as well, sometimes integrated into the musical customs though no notable new hybrids have arisen.

Flora and fauna

By any standard Bahamian forests are spare. Only species adapted to the stresses of salt, thin soils, wind and harsh sunlight can survive. Today, 1371 species, varieties and hybrids of **trees** and **flowering plants** grow in the Bahamas, a small number by subtropical standards. Much of the original hardwood forests of mahogany, strangler fig, lignum vitae and gumbo limbo were felled to clear land and build ships, and even the secondary pine forests on the larger islands have been logged heavily. Salt-tolerant species like the red, black and white mangrove still survive, but their range is diminishing due to development and pollution.

The Bahamas have only thirteen native land **mammals**, most being bats. But for the elusive hutia, a small rodent-like creature that was hunted nearly to extinction over the years, the rest of the land mammals are semi-domesticated sorts of animals like pigs and donkeys, or scavengers like raccoons. The islands host a number of **reptile** species like iguanas and snakes, and there are many land crabs crawling about; **birdlife** is also abundant. It is in the sea, however, that the numbers of species explode. **Marine life** here consists of thousands of types of sea mammals, echinoderms, crustaceans, reef fish, pelagic fish, algae and more, all occupying unique ecological niches in order to survive through adaptation.

Terrestrial habitats

The original **forests** (in Bahamian lingo, the "coppice") that greeted conquistadores were magnificent stands of mahogany, horseflesh, mastic, cedar and poisonwood, among many others. In the remotest areas of islands like Little Inagua, some vestiges of this can still be seen. To better comprehend what you're encountering, it's useful to know a bit about the various categories of forest.

The blackland coppice

The **blackland coppice** makes up the interior of most Bahamian islands, save for the most southerly ones. In this coppice, the understorey is starved of light, making the ground below relatively sterile. Apart from the types of trees listed above, both the gum elemi with its reddish-brown bark and aromatic resins once used as a coagulant for wounds, and the short-leaf fig, which grows to heights of 50ft and more, dominate. Nearly as abundant is the strangler fig, whose wind-borne seeds lodge in the branches of other trees and begin life as an epiphyte, sending roots down to the earth below. Also part of the canopy is the marvelous Bahama **strongbark**, whose brilliant-white flowers in late summer attract swarms of fast-flying ringlet butterflies – the reason it's also called the butterfly tree. Included in the overstorey of the blackland coppice are easily recognizable trees like the common **poisonwood**, a member of the sumac family along with poison ivy, mango, cashew and pistachios, and the unmistakable silk cotton tree, remarkable for its flying-buttress-style flanking roots.

The understorey of the blackland coppice contains a number of interesting plant species. Most beautiful is the silvery **satinleaf**, which quakes like aspen in a strong breeze, the leaves undercoated with a soft brown down, the tops a dark, shiny silver. Particularly after abundant rain, or in the spring, the understorey can come alive with pigeon plums, a relative of the sea grape, the blolly, which produces a fleshy red fruit and the willow bustic, another plant that produces a fruit attractive to birds.

With its humidity and stillness, the coppice provides ideal conditions for **orchids** and **bromeliads**, which cling to the barks of trees. These epiphytes derive their nourishment from wind-blown dust and debris, and unlike the strangler fig remain airborne all their lives. Orchids are represented worldwide by more than 20,000 species, and perhaps 800 are known on the Bahamas, ranging from the genus *Epidendrum* with nine species in the northern Bahamas, to the tiny yellow *E. inaguensis*, with its linear leaves. Three native species of vanilla are climbing orchids found in central and southern portions of the islands. Bromeliads are best represented by wild pineapple, Spanish moss and wild pines. Most are epiphytic, and all resemble pineapple in some way; the wild pines, for example, have a rosette of long, green leaves.

Hikers in the blackland coppice should be alert for signs of the **crab spider**, which spins a massive web that often hangs across trails between the trunks of large trees. A much larger spider, the orange and black Santa Claus spider, also builds a radially symmetrical web in the arching vaults higher up. During the dry summer months green **anolis lizards** can be seen skittering around the dry leaves on the ground, while cicadas chorus wildly and the air fills with mosquitoes, flying beetles and sandflies.

Along with the chattering of cicadas and the buzzing of insects, the silence might be shattered by the call of the **smooth-billed anis**, an aggressive blackbird with a broad high-crowned bill with which it snares insects and lizards. Because they are intensely social birds, they can easily be spotted in flocks of twenty or more where one bird stands sentinel while others feed. The anis even builds its nests socially, constructing huge communal nests in the topmost folds of the canopy where females in a troop lay their eggs in clutches. Less common in the coppice is the **great lizard cuckoo**, a large flightless bird which can be found on Andros, New Providence and Eleuthera. Preying on lizards, frogs and large insects, the lizard cuckoo can sometimes be approached to within touching distance as it perches in low-hanging branches. Every dense blackland coppice has a fair abundance of **pigeons**, the most elusive of which is the Key West quail dove, a very lovely small bird with green and purple colouring which allows it to forage almost unseen in the leaves of the floor.

Where some sun does reach the forest floor, or in the low branches of the understorey, one can sometimes see the Bahamian **fowl snake**, a member of the boa constrictor family. The fowl snake has speciated into many varieties and subspecies, distributed on all the islands save for Grand Bahama and San Salvador. A few grandaddies that survive to old age can reach lengths of up to 6ft.

The whiteland coppice

On lower terrains and usually nearer to coasts, with soils composed of more rock and lime than in the blackland coppice, the somewhat impoverished forests are known as **whiteland coppice**, and are relatively more common in southern islands than in northern ones.

While here and there large shading trees like the mahogany, sea grape and manchineel do grow, most of the whiteland coppice can best be classified as woody **shrubland**, home to animals like goats and pigs. Hikers in the whiteland coppice will find themselves wandering about in stands of **Braziletto**, which resembles the palmetto of Florida, as well as growths of several species of acacias, small trees or large shrubs with large, bipinnate leaves. Some members of the whiteland coppice like the **haulback**, come armed with spines shaped like a cat's claw. Also common to the whiteland coppice is the **common tea**, widely used in the West Indies as an antidote to fish poisoning.

The depredations of goats, the vagaries of rainfall, salty winds and violent hurricanes all make life difficult in the whiteland coppice. Perhaps no plant is better suited to this terrain than the **cactus**; there are dozens of species and subspecies in the Bahamas, some of which produce incredibly beautiful flowers. The largest is the dildo cactus, a columnar candelabra-branched variety that can grow over 20ft in height and incorporates huge amounts of calcium carbonate in its tissues. Cut into one and it seems dry as dust. Another cactus is the Turk's Cap, a non-branching columnar type, which produces a cap of red flowers, a must-see for visitors to the southern islands. The most spectacular cactus, though, is undoubtedly the queen-of-the-night, which grows like a vine on trees and rock walls; it develops a huge bud which soon bursts into an even larger white flower that smells of vanilla and attracts swarms of sphinx moths. Huge **bat moths** can also be seen in the whiteland coppice clinging to the trunks of the acacia or other larger trees. These massive dark-brown moths have geometrical patterns on their wings and tend to favour the balsam tree for their habitats.

Four species of **crab** inhabit the Bahamas, and the density of their populations can be monumental. Some biologists estimate that upwards of 7500 white crabs utilize every acre of whiteland habitat. The species of Bahamian land crab include the commonly eaten **giant white crab**, which can be as much as 2ft from claw to claw in breadth, and the smaller, perhaps tastier, **black crab**. It is hard to tell these species apart when they're immature because both are blackish-blue; when mature, however, white crabs are larger and turn a dirty yellowish colour. The **hermit crab** has no shell of its own, but adopts places to live, like the abandoned shells of marine animals. Its muscular blue claw is used to open fruits and seeds, as well as for defence.

The windward shore

The **windward shore** comprises a few different ecological zones, moving from the white-, rose- or pink-coloured sand back to an algae-filled quagmire, home to many shrimp, crab and shore flies, which gives way to the dunes, a harder place still for wildlife to flourish.

Perhaps the most noticeable animals around the shore are **birds**, exemplified by the graceful white-tailed tropic bird that flies in pairs or floats on the sea parallel to the shore searching for squid and fish. The tropic bird is startlingly white, with black patches over its eyes, and long central tail feathers. Almost as common are the Bahamian swallows, which dart and course looking for insects.

Harder to spot, inhabiting as it does more lonely coastal areas of the windward shore, is the impressive **fish hawk**, more commonly known as osprey. Fish hawks have long, sleek bodies and distinctive black bands behind their eyes. They build massive nests in colonies on isolated cliffs that are often inhabited by generation after generation of birds for forty years or more.

The dunes are **high-stress zones** for plants and animals. Without fresh water, subject to harsh sunlight and driven by winds, only hardy species survive in this niche. Both the sea grape and the cocoplum are rambling shrubs that help to anchor dunes against the wind. The sea grape is a vine, and its purple fruit is made into tarts, jellies and jams by many Bahamians. The large white fruits of the cocoplum are too sour to be edible for humans, but birds and iguanas love them. Perhaps the earliest colonizer of the dune environment is the sea oat, which produces a panicle full of seed, and the beautiful white lily, beloved by beachcombers because of its white blossom that erupts into bloom after a rainfall. White lilies grow so thickly that some dunes are completely covered in them. Few animals are able to survive for long in the dune zone, although the wing nighthawk, a member of the swift family that feeds on shore insects, lays its eggs in the sand.

Shade is hard to come by on the windward shore. The **geiger** tree graces some Bahamian beaches, as does the common **manchineel**, which has poisonous green fruit and a toxic latex-like sap. The geiger is recognizable by its bushy orange flowers on which numerous nectar-sipping birds perch. Many Bahamian beaches have been planted with stands of Australian **casuarina**, a tall wind-resistant tree with thin needle-like leaves. It does produce some shade, but grows sometimes at the expense of native species, and also drops its needles onto the beaches, ruining the smooth sand texture underfoot.

Just behind the dune zone is the **palm niche**. Here, shimmering silver palms, buccaneer palms, and the more utilitarian **thatch palm**, all stand; the last of these has been put to use for generations, its leaves woven into baskets, rope, shoes, hats, mats and thatched roofs. Sheltered well enough from wind and storm, the thatch palm can grow to over 40ft in height.

Among all the clutter of palms, downed palm fronds, grasses and dunes, are smaller shrubs like the love-vine and passionflower, where many types of **butterfly** roam, picking off loads of nectar. Zebra butterflies with their striped black wings often feed on the berries of the guana berry plant, which has clusters of bright red and white flowers, or the pale pink flowers of the common ernoda. One of the great pleasures of the dunes, especially early in the morning or at dusk, or after rain, is to wander under the palms spotting butterflies and blooming shrubs, and even the tiny **worm snake**, its two varieties only a few inches long.

Unfortunately for humans, the windward shore is home to the ubiquitous **sandfly**, an insect no larger than a grain of pepper but which can produce a healthy welt on the skin. There are two species of sandfly: the so-called ferocious sandfly is active during evening and night, while the Becquaert's sandfly operates from dawn to dusk. Only the female sandfly bites, using blood as nourishment to manufacture huge batches of eggs. The males, meek and mild, seldom stray far from their hatching sites, and spend their time sipping nectar from flowers. Researchers have concluded that female sandflies can produce three thousand bites per hour on unprotected flesh. Fortunately for beachgoers, wind provides considerable relief from sandfly activity, and it's a rare day indeed when relief doesn't come in some form.

Tidal pools, cliffsides and rockbound coasts are less hospitable to life than most other niches on the windward shore. Called the **ironshore**, this rocky saline zone is almost lunar in appearance, with a few ground-hugging shrubs dotting the landscape.

The Carribean pine

The pine forests of the Bahamas are found on only four islands: Grand Bahama, Andros, Abaco and New Providence. The lovely **Caribbean pine** (*Pinus caribaea*) is a light-demanding relative of Florida's slash pine, and like its Florida cousin thrives on a system of fire and regeneration. Its adaptation to fire includes an ability to release seeds from cones almost immediately after a fire, the seeds colonizing ashy soils in a matter of days, as well as a fire-retardant resiny sap that allows most pines to survive all but the hottest blazes. As in Florida, bush fires in the forest are not uncommon during the dry season or in droughts, but almost immediately after a fire the forest floor is covered with new pine seedlings, orchids and fresh grasses.

Despite its great height, the Caribbean pine allows enough light to the forest floor for a vigorous understorey to develop, which can include beautiful flowering shrubs like the **wild guava**, with its prominently veined leaves, and **five finger**, which produces leaves with five fingers and flowers that range in colour from white to red to purple. Birdwatchers come from all over the world to catch a glimpse of the rare **Kirkland warbler**, attracted to the flowering plants, or the **Bahamian parrot**, a colourful remnant species found in southern Abaco; of the many other bird species, note the giant **turkey vulture**, which can often be seen wheeling in the sky above the massive forests of Andros or the Abacos. The understorey is also home to many species of **butterfly** such as the one-inch-long atala hairstreak, known to occur on Grand Bahama, Abaco and New Providence. You can recognize it by its metallic blue colour, brown wings and an orange spot on the bottom of its thorax.

Meandering through the understorey of a typical Bahamian pine forest provides a chance to observe **sago palms**, which are not palms at all, but descendants of non-flowering cycads, prehistoric plants dating to the Jurassic Age. The caterpillar of the atala hairstreak butterfly feeds on sagos, as do large echo moths.

Ocean habitats

Divers and snorkellers from around the world come to Bahamian resorts to witness the panorama of colourful tropical fish, sharks and rays that inhabit deeper waters, going so far as to wall-dive to depths of 100ft and more. Many visitors overlook the biological drama of the shallow beds of turtle and manatee grasses, which may be only a fifty-foot swim away from the door of their resorts. Spending an afternoon floating in a shallow bed of turtle grass, with its compliment of tiny lettuce coral, limestone rock and sand bottom, can reward a patient observer with many astounding discoveries.

Turtle grass

Turtle grass provides a habitat that harbours many species that have adapted by mimicking the appearance of sea grass itself. Several types of sea horses can be seen floating in the grass, tail down, while pipefish also mimic the look of a piece of grass. Large numbers of shrimp, small crabs and juvenile cowfish also tend to imitate the colours around them. Equally prevalent are echinoderms like starfish, sand dollars, crinoids and sea cucumbers. On the beds of sea grass often lurk urchins and sea potatoes, both of which are oval in shape and covered by spines.

The most famous denizens of the shallow grass beds are **sea turtles** and **sponges**. Once mainstays of the Bahamian economy, turtles have been hunted with wild abandon and their numbers are vastly reduced from the multitudinous herds that greeted Columbus. The common green turtle haunts the shallow waters of the grass savannas, feeding on grass, while the larger loggerhead and hawksbill inhabit deep-sea and reef environments respectively, chomping into conchs and other prey with their huge beaks.

Unlike green turtles, sponges are ubiquitous in Bahamian water. Coming in many sizes and shapes, sponges are no more than a gelatinous mass with a soft, crunchy skeleton that filters seawater for tiny organisms on which it feeds. They can be coloured anything from pure white to a bright hallucinatory red.

Creeks and mangroves

Almost every Bahamian island has its domain of **creek** and **mangrove** country, mostly on the leeward side, away from the windswept beaches and dunes. Particularly representative of this bio-regime are the western flats of Andros and the northern Abacos, where shallow basins, circular lagoons, wide creeks and mangrove swamps exist in an environment of mud flats and algal plains.

There are no freshwater rivers or creeks in the Bahamas. Instead, thousands of saline tidal creeks drain rainwater from interiors, while other smaller creeks simply rise and fall with the tide. Almost all tidal basins are fringed with either red, white or black mangroves which, while biologically separate, serve to anchor limey soils while at the same time providing a phenomenally productive habitat for wildlife. Only the red mangrove is a true mangrove, dropping roots into salty water, the only flowering plant that can perform this feat. The mangrove forest not only provides shelter and shade for hundreds of juvenile fish, crustaceans and shark, but provides food in the form of decaying plant matter, fungi and algae.

To penetrate this habitat, you'll often need a kayak or shallow-bottom boat, and the ability to withstand swarms of mosquitoes. Inhabitants include encrusting sponges, mangrove crabs, shells and tunicates, as well as a wide variety of crustaceans. Even larger predators like barracuda and snapper prowl the shallow creek beds and the mangrove fringes. In particular, the lemon shark uses the shallow red mangrove habitat to breed and calve its young, sending the juveniles off among the mangroves to feed on a variety of small bony fish, crustaceans and other juvenile fish like snapper. Lemon sharks are the colour of dirty mustard, which distinguishes them from other mangrove juveniles like the nurse shark, typically metallic grey, though sometimes mottled as well.

At dusk, creeks and mangroves burst into action. Young lemons, nurses, bonnetheads and blacktips – all sharks – begin to feed in earnest. The juveniles of many common reef fish are present in the evenings as well, including schoolmaster snapper and the mangrove snapper which turns red as an adult, but that is bluish-green in the mangrove. For many, though, the mangrove and creek are the special realm of the bonefish, which spends its early years in the ocean as a tiny eel-like larval form feeding on plankton, but heads to the shelter of the creeks as a juvenile where it grows to 2–4lb and eats anything that moves.

Large areas of the creek and mangrove regime are composed of **shallow muds**. While generally unpleasant because of heat and insects, the muds play host to an amazing variety of life, including the *Cassiopeia xamanchana*, or upside-down jellyfish, which swarms in the hundreds turning their tentacles down into the mud where they drift and sift for tiny organic debris. Puffer fish, with their boxy body and dark-banded sides, and green morays can be seen in the shallow muds beside black mangrove growths, and the creek bottoms are filled with variegated urchins, young crawfish and juvenile land crabs.

Lagoons and patch reefs

The **tidal foreshore** is much overlooked by visitors to the Bahamas, a place where the water is only a few feet deep in most spots, sometimes dropping off to four or five feet, where coastlines turn into inlets and lagoons, and small waves ripple shoreward. Where the water is a little deeper, sandy bottoms give way to patches of sea grass that provide some stability, and the bottom is littered with debris like rock, coral fragments and what is known as patch reef.

Much of the foreshore is the domain of the calcareous alga, a tiny plant that looks like a cross between a lichen and a coral, and secretes coloured calcium that often tints Bahamian beaches pink. Even the sands of shallow seawater are teeming with life – hundreds of varieties of tiny bivalve shelled animals, crustaceans and various marine worms. In slightly deeper water, or in **shore lagoons**, the rose coral attaches itself to the bottom by a short pointed stalk, while the clubbed finger coral grows in a clump of stout branches that may form extensive beds. A snorkeller floating in 3ft of water on a clear day can see a host of life, including small filter-feeding shrimp, sea horses, urchins, sea cucumbers, sponges, gorgonians, bryozoans and even a bizarrely big-mouthed yellowheaded jawfish or two.

Perhaps the most fun of all in shallow water comes from spotting **sea stars**. Probably the most prominent of all species in the shallows is the *Oreatus reticulatus,* or orange sea star, a huge specimen, which, when fully grown, can be as much as 2ft across. With five stumpy arms radiating outwards, it propels itself slowly through this habitat with spines located on the underside of its body. Less obvious is the slender-limbed brittle star. Half a dozen sub-species make their homes in shallow grasses or amid gorgonians, where they take on a lavender colour and are characterized by long slender arms with a stripe of purple or red along each.

Above sandy bottoms inhabited by sand dollars, sand biscuits and heart urchins, evening feeders like primitive bonefish, pompanos, pompano jacks and permits often cruise looking for marine invertebrates and small fish. The jacks and permits have narrow oval bodies and long dorsal and ventral fins, with deeply forked tails. They travel in small groups close to shore, or in the warm-water inlets of lagoons. Once ubiquitous in shallow water, the famous Bahamian **conch** emblematic of the islands. The most recognized is the queen conch (*Strombus gigas*), a huge coral-coloured specimen with the famous curved shell which is used to make jewellery, tools and other ornaments. The overfishing and overexploitation of conch in the Bahamas has led to progressively smaller and smaller conch being taken for food, and a deterioration in the species in general.

In slightly deeper water begins the **patch reef**, composed of small areas of dome coral, elkhorn, star and brain coral, as well as patches of staghorn, which stand like stone trees. Wave action and occasional hurricanes reduce the patch reef to a flat-topped and highly buttressed form with valleys of pillar coral, finger coral and lettuce coral, forming an underpinning for the patchy beds. Marine life here includes numerous species of fish, anemones, sponges, crustaceans and worms, such as the slightly poisonous bristleworm, a bright-orange worm that crawls over brain coral and can burn and sting human skin. The predators of the patch reef include bright schools of French and blue-striped grunts, blue tang and snapper, all of which hunt invertebrates. Every patch reef in shallow water seems to have its resident barracuda, a long (up to 2ft), slender silver fish with a mouthful of sharp teeth and a forked tail. Genetically designed as a speedy killer, the barracuda isn't particularly dangerous to snorkellers or divers, though eating one can subject you to ciguatera poisoning.

Another visually upsetting member of the patch reef community is the **moray eel**, which ranges in type from the plain green moray, which is quite common and reaches a length of up to 6ft, to the smaller spotted moray and goldentail.

Not uncommon in the shallow water of the foreshore, or in the patch reef, is the **stingray**. Lying partly buried in sand, eagle rays have pointed wings, a spotted back and long graceful tail, while southern rays have grey bodies and rounded wings. The smaller yellow stingray is usually only about 1ft in diameter, with bright blue spots on yellow skin. Stingrays aren't particularly aggressive, but they do have a poisonous spike at the end of their tail, to be avoided at all costs.

Feeding mostly at night, two cephalopods, the **octopus** and the **squid**, can sometimes be seen at dusk by intrepid snorkellers, or by night divers. The reef octopus is a feeder on molluscs and crustaceans, which it crushes with strong jaws and teeth, while its smaller cousin the Joubin's octopus feeds on bivalves.

As every snorkeller knows, the patch reef is teeming with **reef fish**, varieties that often show up in home aquariums. Starting with the damselfish, which comes in dozens of varieties from the ubiquitous sergeant major to the blue-bodied, yellow-tailed damselfish, these quick swimmers are a constant source of delight.

The deep reef

Beyond a buttress zone of rock and rubble at about 15ft, the **deep reef** begins, in water some 20–35ft in depth. The framework of the buttress zone is the same as that of the patch reef, with stars and dome corals supported by pillars and valleys of smaller corals like the lace or lettuce coral. As the water deepens, everything becomes larger and more developed; systems grow in fantastic shapes, encrusting corals of huge dimensions, sponges and swarms of reef fish, along with pelagic species.

At almost all depths, there is some kind of fish, from the common parrotfish, giant rainbow parrotfish, which can weigh up to 5lb and comes in many hues (but all with green throats) the parrot and rainbow and queen triggerfish, to wrasse, gobies, and angelfish. The deep reef is also the realm of the **spiny lobster**, a favourite with diners in Nassau. Also roaming the deep reef are numerous kinds of grouper (some of which can be well over 6ft in length and attain a weight of 135lb) and the lovely fairy basslet, with its distinctive blue head and yellow tail.

At a depth of 50ft, the cliff walls become jagged, corals begin to disappear, and you enter the world of the **sponge**. Even hunters like shark, jack, tuna and rays treat these depths with caution. At the heads of cliffs, one often sees huge grouper, while cardinalfish, squirrelfish and barracuda hug the cliff wall. Still, many divers go over the edge in search of sharks, which can include hammerheads, tigers, white-tips, silkys and the occasional great white. As light diminishes, ahermatypic corals have the upper hand, fragile branch-like corals that do not shelter algae. Sponges at this depth come in many shapes and sizes, mostly huge; and colour at depth is important, with fragile glass sponges sometimes turning bright red and the Venus fly-basket a pale yellow or white. At the bottom, where no diver goes, is the abyssal plain, its muddy bottom inhabited only by deep-water invertebrates such as crustaceans, worms and burrowing anemones.

Books

A substantial amount of printed matter, scientific as well as popular, is available to those interested in the Bahamas – though some of it can be hard to find. One of the best sources for books on the Bahamas is Macmillan Caribbean Publishers (ⓦwww.macmillan-caribbean .com), who produce a solid list of books on history, natural studies, geography cooking and more, many of which are available at bookstores in both the UK and Nassau. They will send a catalogue on request, and you can order from them direct as well. Highly recommended reads are marked with the 🏃 symbol.

History

Paul Albury *The Story of the Bahamas*. Written by a member of the old school of Bahamian society, this slightly dated book remains, despite its stilted style, a rather charming introduction to the history of the islands.

David Allen *The Cocaine Crisis*. Written during the 1980s when the Bahamas were undergoing a crisis of mismanagement, corruption and smuggling, this is one reporter's take on the cocaine problems that so staggered Bahamian society.

Wayne Alleyne *Caribbean Pirates*. With contemporary and historical illustrations in black and white, and a faithful rendering of the historical circumstances of the Spanish Main, this relatively short book on pirates is a good introduction to the tactics, politics and reality of pirating. Though mainly focusing on Hispaniola and Cuba, the book sheds light on the Bahamian connections as well.

P.J.H Barratt *Grand Bahama*. A comprehensive account of the history and economic development of Grand Bahama, written by a former town planner in charge of creating Freeport. Dense, with plenty of photos and maps.

Philip Cash *Sources of Bahamian History*. An analysis of many social and political trends in Bahamian history that continue to have an

impact. Not overly technical, the book hits all the high points and draws some fearless conclusions as well.

David Cordingly *Under the Black Flag: The Romance and the Reality of Life Among the Pirates*. A vivid account of the rise and demise of the pirates of the Caribbean, with detailed reportage on the notoriously bloodthirsty set that held sway over the Bahamas for years.

🏃 **Michael Craton and Gail Saunders** *Islanders in the Stream, A History of the Bahamian Peoples: Vol I* and *Vol II*. This definitive study of Bahamian history by two respected scholars comes in two volumes, the first running from aboriginal times to slavery, the second completing the story through the twentieth century. Both scholarly and accessible, it is the most detailed and exhaustive history of the Bahamas to date.

William F. Keegan *The People who Discovered Columbus: The Prehistory of the Bahamas*. This volume in a monograph series is both technical and expensive, but it is one of the few complete paleo-historical analyses of the Lucayan Indians and their cultural and social practices.

Gail Saunders *Bahamian Loyalists and their Slaves*. A slim volume written by one of the Bahamas' pre-eminent historians, detailing the sudden influx of American Loyalists and their African slaves in the dying days of the American Revolution. Enlivened by lots of interesting and evocative historical photographs and by descriptions of the lives and fortunes of particular Loyalist families and estates.

Everild Young *Eleuthera, the Island Called Freedom.* Although the style is rather florid in places, this island history contains some interesting glimpses of Bahamian and expatriate lifestyles on the Eleuthera in the 1950s and 1960s.

Culture and society

Harry G. Dahl *Literature in the Bahamas 1724-1992: The March Towards National Identity.* Best for serious students, this somewhat dry dissertation-like tome is the only exhaustive study of Bahamian literature for those seeking an in-depth disquisition.

Patricia Glinton-Meicholas *How to be a True True Bahamian* and *More Talkin' Bahamian.* Humorous pocket guides to Bahamian culture and language, reviewing such topics as the art of "liming" and why dogs are called "potcakes" (because they were traditionally fed the leftover

peas 'n' rice congealed at the bottom of the pot).

Leslie Higgs *Bush Medicine in the Bahamas.* Descriptions of native plants and their traditional uses accompanied by illustrations.

Karen Knowles *Straw! A Short Account of the Straw Industry in the Bahamas.* Plaited straw baskets, hats and bags are big business in the Bahamas and this little book, aimed primarily at schoolchildren, provides the low-down on the craft and the development of the industry for export and sale to visiting tourists.

Travellers' tales

Evans Cottman *Out Island Doctor.* A dated but mildly engaging memoir of a retired American school teacher who set up shop as a self-taught physician on Crooked and Acklins islands in the 1940s.

Gilbert Klingel *Inagua, Which is the Name of a Very Lonely and Nearly Forgotten Island.* As a young man on his first scientific expedition in 1930, Klingel was shipwrecked on Great Inagua, and this magical and often poetic book is his account of the voyage and the months that followed. The human inhabitants of Inagua are not as sympathetically treated in his recounting of events as the myriad other creatures he meets. However, you may never look at the ocean surf in the same way again after reading his dramatic description of the battles for survival fought

daily at the water's edge. Reprinted by Lyons and Burford (US) as part of the *Wilder Places* series, with an introduction by naturalist Stephen J. Bodio.

L.D. Powles *The Land of the Pink Pearl: Recollections of Life in the Bahamas.* A colourful memoir of an English magistrate's two tours of duty through the Out Islands as a Circuit Court judge in 1887, after which he was recalled to London for sentencing a white man to one month hard labour for assaulting his African maid. Particularly interesting are Powles' disillusioned impressions of Nassau society and of the colonial government.

Aileen Vincent-Barwood *This Sweet Place: Island Living and Other Adventures.* A slightly self-satisfied but readable account of a retired couple's relocation from the northern US to Great Exuma, filled with local characters, local history and lore, and descriptions of many of the island's settlements and landmarks.

Fiction

Marion Bethel *Guanahane, My Love.* Probably the best-known poet in the Bahamas, Bethel's work has appeared in many American journals. She won the Casas de las Americas Prize in 1994 for this volume.

Jimmy Buffett *Tales from Margaritaville: Fictional Facts and Factual Fictions.* Better known for a string of mellow hits in the 1970s, Buffett also spins a fine rollicking tale with a cast of cowboys, sailors and no-nonsense women in roadside diners, cosy beach bars and boats. The Bahamas is a favourite locale of his, and this collection of sunny, whimsical short stories evokes an image of laid-back island living.

College of the Bahamas *Bahamian Anthology.* Home-grown fiction is still in a nascent stage in the Bahamas, but this collection of short stories, poetry and drama by contemporary writers offers a glimpse of what is on the minds of emerging authors. Recurring themes include the legacy of slavery and colonialism and the authors' relationship with the landscape and the sea that surround them.

Barry Estabrook *Bahama Heat.* An amusing drug-deal-gone-wrong thriller that is tailor-made for lazy beach reading.

Amos Ferguson and Elaine Greenfield *Under the Sunday Tree.* Along with a pleasing story by Greenfield, the book features beautiful illustrations by the visual artist Ferguson; this is a children's book for everybody.

Ernest Hemingway *Islands in the Stream.* Hemingway's novel, published posthumously, concerns the adventures of an artist-fisherman, which, as usual, are a metaphor for the author's own internal contradictions and boasts. Though it isn't a particularly good novel, it nevertheless accurately reflects Bimini and Gulf Stream life.

Gregor Robinson *Hotel Paradiso.* Almost to the exclusion of all other subject matter, the Bahamas are the chosen setting for a plethora of novels about drug smuggling and rum-soaked expatriates on the run from something or other, most of it dross. This book is about the best of the lot, with rough-drawn vignettes of a dissipated life in an island outpost in the Abacos peopled by wealthy American retirees, Haitian refugees and drifters in limbo, as seen through the eyes of a burnt-out banker from Montréal.

Herman Wouk *Don't Stop the Carnival.* First published in the 1960s, this entertaining cautionary tale concerns a dyed-in-the-wool New Yorker who buys a resort hotel on an idyllic Caribbean island. He spends the next three hundred-odd pages of the novel fixing burst water mains, wrestling with the local bureaucracy and ferrying disgruntled guests to and from the airport, while pursuing a torrid affair with a faded movie star, downing copious quantities of rum and disposing of corpses. Still popular and widely available throughout the Bahamas, it was also made into a musical by Jimmy Buffett in the 1990s.

Nature and the environment

David G. Campbell *The Ephemeral Islands: A Natural History of the Bahamas.* One of the best overall studies of Bahamian natural history, complete with a generous scattering of colour plates and detailed line drawings of various plants and sea creatures. Chapters tell the tale of paleo-Bahamian structure, and progress through clear-eyed descriptions of every Bahamian habitat. It is thorough in its treatment of marine life as well, though it focuses on terrestrial habitats.

Osha Gray Davidson *Fire in the Turtle House.* A naturalist, Davidson reports on the habitat of the green turtle, and in particular on the neoplasms (growths) that have been attacking and killing large numbers of green turtles around the world. It's a compelling story that ought to act as a wake-up call to environmentalists and citizens everywhere. Along the way, he delineates everything you might want to know about turtles and their astonishing lives.

Paul Humann and Ned DeLoach *Reef Fish, Reef Coral, Reef Creatures* and *Snorkelling Guide to Marine Life: Florida, Caribbean, Bahamas.* The first three are beautiful full-colour books that will help you identify every living thing in the waters of the Bahamas, Florida and the Caribbean; available separately or in a boxed set. *Reef Fish in a Pocket* and *Reef Creatures in a Pocket* are drastically abridged waterproof editions for divers and snorkellers. The snorkelling guide contains plentiful locale descriptions along with colour photos of 260 species.

Erika Moultrie *Natives of the Bahamas: A Guide to Vegetation and Birds of Grand Bahama.* A pocket-size spiral-bound booklet that provides an overview of the six different terrestrial ecosystems found on Grand Bahama, colour photographs of native plants and detailed illustrations of the varied birdlife on the island.

Rob Palmer *Baha Mar: The Shallow Seas.* A complete analysis of the structure and dynamics of every underwater habitat found in the Bahamas. Filled with good photographs and scientific descriptions, this book is a must for serious divers and naturalists alike. Moreover, it contains an excellent bibliography for anyone who wishes to pursue studies of sharks, invertebrates and other marine life in Bahamian waters.

Peterson Field Guides *Coral Reefs: Caribbean and Florida.* Standard high-quality and comprehensive Peterson field guide. Loaded with clear colour and black and white photographs and line drawings, as well as extensive listings and factual information, including descriptions of 33 different species of sea stars, the nine kinds of sharks that are found in the Bahamas and a section on the sex life of coral.

Herbert Raffaele, editor *Princeton Field Guides: Birds of the West Indies.* A user-friendly and comprehensive guide to birds found in the Bahamas. Less detailed than the ABA guide listed below, but including excellent colour drawings and notes outlining identifying characteristics.

Neil E. Sealey *Bahamian Landscapes: An Introduction to the Geography of the Bahamas.* A textbook chock-full of charts, graphs and illustrations, it is great for beginning students of geography and climate, but also good for anyone who wants to discover the hows and whys of Bahamian geology, geography and natural resources.

Anthony White *A Birder's
Guide to the Bahama Islands
(including Turks and Caicos)*. This
volume, published by the American
Birding Association (ⓦwww
.americanbirding.org), is the
ultimate bird book. It contains a
wealth of information on behaviour,
habitat and seasonal variation, and
has detailed maps and practical
advice, as well as travel and weather
information. The book comes
with a complete bibliography on
technical birding information,
articles and serious scientific studies,
along with a glossary and bird
checklist.

Stephen Vletas and Kim Vletas
The Bahamas Fly-Fishing Guide.
A detailed handbook for fishing
fanatics, complete with maps and
descriptions of prime fishing rounds
for bonefish and various other
species, recommended tackle and
listings for fishing guides and lodges.

Lawson Wood *The Dive Sites of
the Bahamas.* An expensive book
for committed divers, *Dive Sites* is
worth it for the exquisite colour
photography alone. It provides
advice on diving sites, equipment,
lodging and prices, safety and
underwater photography.

Nautical guides

Monty and Sara Lewis *Explorer
Chartbooks* for *Exuma and the Exuma
Cays*; *Far Bahamas* (from Eleuthera
south to Inagua); *Near Bahamas*
(the northern islands). Each spiral-
bound 12 x 18-inch book contains
seventy detailed nautical charts of
Bahamian waters accompanied by
photographs, text and tide tables.
Available from ⓦwww
.explorercharts.com.

Maptech *Chart Kit: The Bahamas.*
The only full set of nautical
charts for the Bahamas, in a larger

22 x 18-inch format, spiral-bound
in a vinyl case. See ⓦwww.maptech
.com for more information.

Stephen J. Pavlidis *The Exuma
Guide: A Cruising Guide to the
Exuma Cays.* A comprehensive guide
aimed primarily at boaters, but also
recommended for sea kayakers and
others planning a visit to the Exuma
Land and Sea Park. With detailed
information on approaches, routes,
anchorages, dive sites, flora and
fauna and the history and lore of the
Exuma Cays.

Small print and

Index

A Rough Guide to Rough Guides

Published in 1982, the first Rough Guide – to Greece – was a student scheme that became a publishing phenomenon. Mark Ellingham, a recent graduate of English from Bristol University, had been traveling in Greece the previous summer and couldn't find the right guidebook. With a small group of friends he wrote his own guide, combining a highly contemporary, journalistic style with a thoroughly practical approach to travellers' needs.

The immediate success of the book spawned a series that rapidly covered dozens of destinations. And, in addition to impecunious backpackers, Rough Guides soon acquired a much broader and older readership that relished the guides' wit and inquisitiveness as much as their enthusiastic, critical approach and value-for-money ethos.

These days, Rough Guides include recommendations from shoestring to luxury and cover more than 200 destinations around the globe, including almost every country in the Americas and Europe, more than half of Africa and most of Asia and Australasia. Our ever-growing team of authors and photographers is spread all over the world, particularly in Europe, the USA and Australia.

In the early 1990s, Rough Guides branched out of travel, with the publication of Rough Guides to World Music, Classical Music and the Internet. All three have become benchmark titles in their fields, spearheading the publication of a wide range of books under the Rough Guide name.

Including the travel series, Rough Guides now number more than 350 titles, covering: phrasebooks, waterproof maps, music guides from Opera to Heavy Metal, reference works as diverse as Conspiracy Theories and Shakespeare, and popular culture books from iPods to Poker. Rough Guides also produce a series of more than 120 World Music CDs in partnership with World Music Network.

Visit www.roughguides.com to see our latest publications.

Many Rough Guide travel images are available for commercial licensing at www.roughguidespictures.com

SMALL PRINT

Rough Guide credits

Text editor: Stephen Timblin
Layout: Anita Singh
Cartography: Animesh Pathak, Katie Lloyd-Jones
Picture editor: Nicole Newman
Production: Aimee Hampson
Proofreader: Camilla Cooke
Cover design: Chloë Roberts
Editorial: **London** Kate Berens, Claire
Saunders, Ruth Blackmore, Polly Thomas,
Richard Lim, Alison Murchie, Karoline Densley,
Andy Turner, Keith Drew, Edward Aves, Nikki
Birrell, Alice Park, Sarah Eno, Lucy White, Jo
Kirby, Samantha Cook, James Smart, Natasha
Foges, Roisin Cameron, Joe Staines, Duncan
Clark, Peter Buckley, Matthew Milton, Tracy
Hopkins, Ruth Tidball; **New York** Andrew
Rosenberg, Steven Horak, AnneLise Sorensen,
Amy Hegarty, April Isaacs, Ella Steim, Anna
Owens, Joseph Petta, Sean Mahoney
Design & Pictures: **London** Scott Stickland,
Dan May, Diana Jarvis, Mark Thomas, Jj Luck,
Harriet Mills; **Delhi** Umesh Aggarwal, Ajay
Verma, Jessica Subramanian, Ankur Guha,
Pradeep Thapliyal, Sachin Tanwar, Madhavi
Singh, Karen D'Souza

Production: Katherine Owers
Cartography: **London** Maxine Repath, Ed
Wright; **Delhi** Jai Prakash Mishra, Rajesh
Chhibber, Ashutosh Bharti, Rajesh Mishra,
Jasbir Sandhu, Karobi Gogoi, Amod Singh,
Alakananda Bhattacharya, Athokpam
Jotinkumar
Online: **New York** Jennifer Gold, Kristin
Mingrone; **Delhi** Manik Chauhan, Narender
Kumar, Rakesh Kumar, Amit Kumar, Amit Verma,
Rahul Kumar, Ganesh Sharma, Debojit Borah
Marketing & Publicity: **London** Liz Statham,
Niki Hanmer, Louise Maher, Jess Carter, Vanessa
Godden, Anna Paynton, Rachel Sprackett; **New
York** Geoff Colquitt, Megan Kennedy, Katy Ball;
Delhi Reem Khokhar
Special Projects Editor: Philippa Hopkins
Manager India: Punita Singh
Series Editor: Mark Ellingham
Reference Director: Andrew Lockett
Publishing Coordinator: Megan McIntyre
Publishing Director: Martin Dunford
Commercial Manager: Gino Magnotta
Managing Director: John Duhigg

Publishing information

This second edition published April 2007 by
Rough Guides Ltd,
80 Strand, London WC2R 0RL
345 Hudson St, 4th Floor,
New York, NY 10014, USA
14 Local Shopping Centre, Panchsheel Park,
New Delhi 110017, India
Distributed by the Penguin Group
Penguin Books Ltd,
80 Strand, London WC2R 0RL
Penguin Group (USA)
375 Hudson Street, NY 10014, USA
Penguin Group (Australia)
250 Camberwell Road, Camberwell,
Victoria 3124, Australia
Penguin Books Canada Ltd,
10 Alcorn Avenue, Toronto, Ontario,
Canada M4V 1E4
Penguin Group (NZ)
67 Apollo Drive, Mairangi Bay, Auckland 1310,
New Zealand
Cover concept by Peter Dyer.

Typeset in Bembo and Helvetica to an original
design by Henry Iles.
Printed and bound in Singapore by SNP Security
Printing Pte Ltd
© Rough Guides Ltd, April 2007

368pp includes index
A catalogue record for this book is available from
the British Library
ISBN: 9-78184-353-776-2

The publishers and authors have done their
best to ensure the accuracy and currency
of all the information in **The Rough Guide
to The Bahamas**, however, they can accept
no responsibility for any loss, injury, or
inconvenience sustained by any traveller as a
result of information or advice contained in the
guide.

3   5   7   9   8   6   4

Help us update

We've gone to a lot of effort to ensure that the
second edition of **The Rough Guide to The
Bahamas** is accurate and up to date. However,
things change – places get "discovered", opening
hours are notoriously fickle, restaurants and
rooms raise prices or lower standards. If you
feel we've got it wrong or left something out,
we'd like to know, and if you can remember the
address, the price, the time, the phone number,
so much the better.
We'll credit all contributions, and send a copy of
the next edition (or any other Rough Guide if you

prefer) for the best letters. Everyone who writes
to us and isn't already a subscriber will receive
a copy of our full-colour thrice-yearly newsletter.
Please mark letters: "**Rough Guide The
Bahamas Update**" and send to: Rough Guides,
80 Strand, London WC2R 0RL, or Rough Guides,
345 Hudson St, 4th Floor, New York, NY 10014.
Or send an email to **mail@roughguides.com**
Have your questions answered and tell others
about your trip at
www.roughguides.atinfopop.com

SMALL PRINT

Acknowledgements

Natalie Folster would like to thank Carmeta Miller at the Grand Bahama Tourism Office, Marie Rolle at the Exuma Tourist Office, and the Bahamas National Trust in Nassau and Inagua for vital information; Tom Muir of Nassau and Peter and Betty Oxley of Great Exuma for their great generosity in taking the time to share their expert knowledge of the islands; North Carolina Outward Bound for the opportunity to participate in a sea kayak course in the Exuma Cays; Steven Horak, April Isaacs and Anne-Marie Shaw for shepherding the guide through its early stages; and especially book editor Stephen Timblin for his professionalism, patience and skill.

Readers' letters

Thanks to all the readers who have taken the time to write in with comments and suggestions (and apologies if we've inadvertently omitted or misspelt anyone's name):

Susan Bell, Lynn June, Maggie Kemper, Ryan Rogers

SMALL PRINT

Photo credits

SMALL PRINT

SMALL PRINT

Index

Map entries are in colour.

Map symbols

maps are listed in the full index using coloured text

`------`	Chapter division boundary		⚲	Gardens
`======`	Paved road (regional maps)		🅿	Petrol station
`_____`	Unpaved road (regional maps)		✈	Airport
`======`	Road (town maps)		✈	Airfield
`-------`	Footpath		★	Public transport stop
`— — —`	Ferry route		▪	Point of interest
`======`	Waterway		♀	Museum
▲	Mountain peak		◉	Accommodation
	Reef		ⓘ	Information office
◠	Cave		✉	Post office
∴	Ruins		⊞	Hospital
♜	Castle		▪	Building
�	Spring		✚	Church
⚲	Lighthouse			Park
⊙	Statue			Beach
✄	Diving site			Christian cemetery
⛳	Golf course